Young Offenders and Youth Justice

A Century After the Fact

Third Edition

Sandra J. Bell

St. Mary's University

THOMSON

NELSON

Australia   Canada   Mexico   Singapore   Spain   United Kingdom   United States

THOMSON

NELSON

Young Offenders and Youth Justice
A Century After the Fact
Third Edition
by Sandra J. Bell

Associate Vice President,
Editorial Director:
Evelyn Veitch

Editor-in-Chief,
Higher Education:
Anne Williams

Executive Editor:
Ann Millar

Executive Marketing Manager:
Lenore Taylor

Senior Developmental Editor:
Rebecca Rea

Permissions Coordinator:
Paulee Kestin

Content Production Manager:
Lara Caplan

Production Service:
Sachin Sharma/Interactive
Composition Corporation

Copy Editor:
June Trusty

Proofreader:
Dianne Fowlie

Indexer:
Patti Schiendelman

Manufacturing Coordinator:
Ferial Suleman

Design Director:
Ken Phipps

Interior Design:
Katherine Strain

Cover Design:
Johanna Liburd

Cover Image:
Rachel Simon/Shutterstock

Compositor:
Interactive Composition
Corporation

Printer:
Edwards Brothers, Inc.

Library and Archives Canada
Cataloguing in Publication

Bell, Sandra Jean, 1943–

Young offenders and youth justice: a century after the fact / Sandra J. Bell.—3rd ed.

Previous eds. published under title: Young offenders and juvenile justice.
Includes bibliographical references and index.
ISBN 0-17-625270-3

1. Juvenile delinquency—Canada—Textbooks. 2. Juvenile justice, Administration of—Canada—Textbooks. I. Bell, Sandra Jean, 1943–Young offenders and juvenile justice. II. Title.

HV9108.B44 2006   364.36'0971
C2006-902996-2

CONTENTS

CHAPTER 3:   THE "FACTS" OF YOUTH CRIME   64

CHAPTER 4:   THE SOCIAL FACE OF YOUTH CRIME   98

CHAPTER 5:   EXPLAINING CRIME AND DELINQUENCY:
IN THE BEGINNING . . .   126

CHAPTER 6: DIFFERENT DIRECTIONS IN THEORIZING ABOUT YOUTH CRIME AND DELINQUENCY   152

CHAPTER 7: FAMILY, SCHOOL, PEERS AND THE YOUTH CRIME PROBLEM   180

CHAPTER 8: FIRST CONTACT: POLICE AND DIVERSIONARY MEASURES   214

CHAPTER 9:   GOING TO COURT   244

CHAPTER 12: A CENTURY AFTER THE FACT: WHAT DO WE KNOW? WHERE ARE WE GOING?   342

| PREFACE

My concern for young offenders began in 1980. I was employed in a residential facility for juvenile delinquents, and at the time, the justice system for them was framed by the Juvenile Delinquents Act. The young people with whom I worked had all been transferred from training schools, a euphemism for "children's prisons" under that act. I wanted to work at the facility because I liked young people and believed that I could effect a positive change in their lives. Unfortunately, for the most part, I was wrong. I found myself hopelessly enmeshed in a justice system that could not meet even the basic needs of these young people. Worse, I discovered it was a system that inflicted even more damage on their already shattered lives.

I was unable to prevent the suicide of a gentle 15-year-old poet who could not bear the continual rejection of his parents. Nor could I prevent the pregnancies of 15-year-old girls, so desperate for loving families that they believed they could create them by becoming child mothers. I could not prevent the sexual exploitation of these imprisoned girls by an unscrupulous male employee. Management refused to act on or even hear my complaints because, in their words, this individual had a "calming" influence on the girls. And I was unable to convince a 15-year-old that a police officer, who arrested her when she was 13 and subsequently had an ongoing sexual relationship with her, was not likely to leave his wife and children to marry her, as she believed.

In spite of my efforts and good intentions, I could not shield these children from the devastating social and psychological effects of arbitrary and often cruel administrative policies and staff indifference. Nor could I prevent them from committing more crimes while on the run from the institution: cold, hungry, frightened, and exhausted. A few committed particularly violent offences during these escapes, not because they were somehow inherently violent, as some might suggest, but rather because they were desperate not to be caught and sent back to prison.

My knowledge of young offenders and juvenile justice continued while I researched the youth court after the Young Offenders Act was implemented in 1984. Here, I interviewed parents and came to understand better why their children behaved as they did. Some parents were caring and doing their best with meagre resources, but were unable to provide a decent lifestyle for themselves or their children. Others were struggling to cope with family tragedies—a spouse lost through desertion, divorce, or death; a missing or dead child; a demeaning and debilitating life of poverty, drugs, alcohol, or abuse. Most of the parents I talked to were tired and worn beyond their years. Far too many, it seemed, quite simply did not like or want their children.

This book is dedicated to these children—to Paul, Michelle, Geoff, Tammy, Fred, Jane, and Kenny—and to all the children in Canadian society whom we have failed to protect, guide, provide for, and teach; to all the children who have been failed by our schools, our social services, our justice system; and to all the children who have been maligned as young criminals in public discourse. It has always been my hope that this book might in some way contribute to an awareness of what needs to be done to address the inequities and injustices that bring these children into the justice system. Royalties from the sales of this book will be shared with these young people through Phoenix House, a safe haven for homeless youth, and with the Community Justice Society, an organization working toward restorative means of getting and keeping young people out of the justice system.

ABOUT THE TEXT

Nearly a century has passed since the Canadian government created a justice system for youth separate from the adult criminal justice system. When I began writing the first edition of this book in 1996, youth crime and juvenile justice were major public issues: many thought that the juvenile justice system was not working to control youth crime and the federal government was announcing a Strategy for Reform to address these issues. The first edition of the book, *Young Offenders and Juvenile Justice: A Century After the Fact*, was organized around the concerns expressed about youth crime and justice in public forums that were part of the Minister of Justice's attempts to reform the justice system. The concerns at that time were whether youth crime was on the increase, whether young offenders received merely "a slap on the wrist" for their offences under the Young Offenders Act, and whether youth were more violent than in the past. By the time I was writing the second edition in the summer of 2002, these concerns had not changed and Canadians were also now wondering if the Youth Criminal Justice Act would change anything. Now, as this book goes to press for the third time, three years after the YCJA came into effect, Canadians are still asking these questions. Some seem convinced that the situation is worse under the new legislation, and this book is still addressing these issues.

Beyond these public concerns is a more fundamental question, one not addressed in public forums: How far have we come in 100 years of juvenile justice? What did we know about youth crime and justice in the past, and how does that compare to what we know today? More important, have we changed our thinking about youth crime and our responses to it? To address these broader questions, the book takes a historical comparative approach and locates contemporary youth justice issues in a historical context. Where appropriate, chapters begin with a discussion of either contemporary and/or historical issues and proceed to a discussion of contemporary knowledge, practice, policy, and issues.

This book is also about law reform, and putting it into a historical context allows an understanding of how the justice system has changed over the last hundred years and also how it has not. Many of the issues have changed over the years, while others have been dragging along for a century, with the same groups taking the same positions in relation to reform. For this reason, the Young Offenders Act is still discussed in this book, as is the Juvenile Delinquents Act. Where it is relevant, the chapters offer comparisons of the new Youth Criminal Justice Act with the Young Offenders Act, both in legislation and in practice.

This new edition is still about juvenile justice, but the title has changed to reflect the new legislation and the new way that juvenile justice is now talked about—youth justice. The terms "juvenile justice" and "youth justice" are used interchangeably throughout the book, reflecting the time period of the discussion and the usage of the works being cited. Generally, when the justice system is being talked about in theoretical, conceptual or historical terms, the term "juvenile justice" is used. When the discussion is about the contemporary system in practice, I refer to the system as the "youth justice" system.

Young Offenders and Youth Justice differs from other texts in its approach to youth crime and justice in that it is not just a collection of "facts" and "theories" about crime and delinquency, nor is it a book *about* delinquents or young offenders. Rather, it is about how we think about youth and their behaviour, and about how these views are reflected in public discourse, scholarly theorizing, public policy, and institutional responses to "troublesome" youth behaviour. As such, the book is also not one that decontextualizes, depersonalizes, or objectifies young people or their behaviour. The voices of youth, past and present, together with the voices of people who work in the justice system, are brought into the discussion of the issues in the form of boxed features that appear throughout the text. This material is intended to give students an opportunity to reflect on the realities of other lives and views.

This book also differs from other texts on the subject in that it moves away from a presentation of youth as "perpetrators" of crime and emphasizes in various ways that they are also victims and survivors. As Schissel (1997) succinctly points out, young offenders are "victims first and offenders second . . . survivors who are punished by law for offences viewed out of context" (p. 108). I believe that discussions of youth crime and justice devoid of this context will never result in appropriate or effective responses. Each chapter is organized into topics and issues relevant to that chapter that are revisited in various places throughout the book. Issues such as violence, homelessness, victimization and marginalization are multifaceted issues and need to be addressed from a number of angles.

Of course, since this is a textbook, I have presented an accumulation of facts, theories, and knowledge about youth crime and justice, but I have not been exhaustive. With the exception of the chapters on theory, I have focused on Canadian literature and research, particularly in the chapters on juvenile justice. Other sources have been used when they are central to an understanding of an issue or when Canadian literature is lacking. I do not intend that this book be used as a source of "objective fact" but rather as a tool for college and undergraduate university students in developing their own understanding of public issues about youth crime and justice. This is particularly important as we begin a new era of youth justice under the Youth Criminal Justice Act and likely one of intensified public debate. In addition, there is sufficient knowledge and information in the book to provide students with a solid foundation to pursue professional careers or more advanced academic studies in the field.

In the second edition of this book, my challenge was how to present and discuss the justice system during the time of transition from the last days of the YOA to the start of the YCJA. To some extent, the same challenge existed for this third edition. Even though we have now had the new legislation for three years, official data are available for only one or two years and are not yet sufficient to establish trends. Similarly, it is too early for research-based analyses. We do have the beginnings of case law, and this is used when it was available. Many questions are now being addressed with data on child and youth behaviour from two of Statistics Canada's national surveys: the *General Social Survey* (GSS) and the *National Longitudinal Survey of Children and Youth* (NLSCY). These data are presented throughout the book where relevant.

This book divides easily into two parts. The first half focuses on youth crime and how we explain it, while the second half addresses the justice system. Chapter 1 sets the stage for the remainder of the book by raising contemporary questions about youth crime and justice by examining those questions in a historical context and by attempting to provide answers. Chapter 2 continues this historical framework with a discussion of the creation of the juvenile justice system and Canada's ongoing reform process, from the Juvenile Delinquents Act, to the Young Offenders Act, to the Youth Criminal Justice Act. Comparative discussions of the content of these acts and the public issues associated with them are presented. A central theme in this chapter, linking it to the first chapter, comes from a discussion of public opposition to each act and the similarities in the debates between each historical era.

Chapter 3 revisits the central questions raised in Chapter 1. Here, we examine crime statistics and their sources and demonstrate that statistics can be misleading without a thorough understanding of their origin. This chapter exposes students to a variety of statistics so that comparisons of varying statistical interpretations are possible. Chapter 4 discusses youth crime statistics in a social context by focusing on race, class, gender, and victimization, and the issues associated with these concepts in making sense of statistics. Chapters 5 and 6 examine attempts at scholarly explanations of youth crime. Chapter 5 presents "the beginnings" of scholarly attempts to explain youth crime, while Chapter 6 discusses different directions in thinking—those based on labelling, critical and feminist directions, and recent efforts at integrating classic versions of control, conflict, and learning theories, as well as contributions from newer perspectives in criminology—peacemaking and the postmodern approach.

A wealth of research and critique is associated with most theories of youth crime and delinquency, and it is beyond the scope of this book to review it all. Instead, Chapter 7 focuses on the factors most consistently identified theoretically as the keys to explaining and understanding youth crime—family, school, and peers. This chapter reviews the most recent empirical evidence pertaining to these factors and summarizes "what we know" about the relationships between youth crime and family, friends, and school, as well as current issues such as school violence and zero-tolerance policies.

The focus of the book then shifts to the justice system. Since Chapters 8 through 10 present thorough descriptions of the structure of the justice system and of how youth are processed through the system, students may want to review parts of Chapter 2 before moving on. The role of the police and extrajudicial measures programs are discussed in Chapter 8, the courts and sentencing issues in Chapter 9, and youth correctional programs and institutions in Chapter 10. Attempts are made throughout to present examples from various parts of Canada and to discuss variations across the country.

Chapter 11 addresses the issue of minority youth in the justice system. To some extent in this chapter and in Chapters 3 and 4, race is missing. This is due to a lack of research and therefore data on minority youth in the justice system. Hence, the focus in this chapter is on girls and Aboriginal youth, but issues are raised in relation to injustice in a more general sense. Specific issues relevant to girls and Aboriginal youth are discussed and examples of alternative programming are presented.

The final chapter, Chapter 12, returns to the fundamental questions about youth crime and juvenile justice and answers them through a summary of the main points of the text. The chapter then moves on to a discussion of new developments in our thinking about youth crime and justice. Then, law reform is discussed and new and old reform issues are reviewed to determine whether they offer "more of the same" or fundamental shifts in how we think about and respond to youth crime.

NEW IN THIS THIRD EDITION

The major impetus for this edition is the new Youth Criminal Justice Act in action, and every chapter in this third edition of *Young Offenders and Youth Justice: A Century After the Fact* has been substantially revised. While the content of Chapters 1, 5, 6, 7, 11, and 12 are not directly affected by the introduction of the YCJA, the context of the issues has changed because of the new legislation and this is reflected particularly in changes to Chapters 1, 11, and 12. Chapters 3, 4, 8, 9 and 10 have been revised to include the latest statistics; the latest Canadian research, publications, and case law; relevant sections of the Youth Criminal Justice Act; and, where appropriate, comparisons to the YOA in legislation and practice.

Chapters 1 and 2 have been revised to reflect YCJA issues. Chapter 1 introduces a public inquiry regarding a case subject to an adult sentence that has also resulted in an attempt to have car theft and joyriding classified as violent offences. The situation leading up to the inquiry is outlined and the case is followed throughout the text in each relevant chapter. Chapter 2 now contains a full discussion of the development of the *UN Convention on the Rights of the Child* and the ability of the justice system under the YCJA to meet international standards.

Chapters 3 and 4 discuss new sources of data, including new classifications for official statistics, data from the *General Social Survey* and the *National Longitudinal Survey of Children and Youth*. These chapters contain the most recent research, *Juristat* reports, and youth court, police, and victimization statistics.

Chapters 5 through 7 have been expanded to include a critique of positivism and a discussion of contributions from cultural studies, feminist criminology, peacemaking criminology, and the postmodernist perspective to an understanding of youth crime and justice. Chapter 7 has been developed considerably not only to include recent research and results from the GSS and NLSCY, but also to raise important issues around child and parent blaming, school violence, and zero-tolerance policies. The issue of girl violence is revisited to develop an understanding of the racialization of youth crime issues.

Chapter 8 introduces students to the YCJA concepts of extrajudicial measures and sanctions, and presents a discussion of the variety of ways in which diversion has been practised in Canada; these range from informal police practices under the JDA to alternative measures under the YOA to the new structure and practices of the YCJA. This chapter offers a detailed discussion of YCJA provisions and principles, examples of diversion programs in different parts of the country, and a discussion of new and ongoing issues associated with diversion, including the continuing problem of inequality of access. Police use of extrajudicial measures is discussed, their role in family conferencing is outlined, and a critique of conferencing is provided. The issue of racial profiling is also raised.

Chapter 9 provides specific details on YCJA sentencing principles; custodial requirements and limitations; and the extensive range of sentencing options, including the entirely new "intensive support and supervision" option, the "intensive rehabilitative custody and supervision" option, and the "custody and conditional supervision" option. The new offence categories "presumptive offence" and "serious offence" and their effect on eliminating the issues associated with transfer hearings are discussed in detail. The implications for youth justice of automatic liability to adult sentences are discussed, and case law resulting from the YCJA is used to raise new issues with sentencing and the balancing of YCJA principles. All sentencing statistics are updated with the most recent YCJA court statistics.

Chapter 10 offers updated YCJA custody statistics and a discussion of new program philosophies, along with examples of new program models.

Chapter 11 includes recent statistics, research, and discussions of recent publications on girls and Aboriginal youth. A full discussion is offered of the issues associated with each in the justice system, as well as new directions in programming.

Chapter 12 is a completely new chapter. It offers a summary of the most important points in the other chapters and raises new questions about where we are going in current thinking about youth crime and justice. This chapter also discusses how current issues compare to the "facts" of youth crime and justice as discussed throughout the text. In addition, it assesses current reform proposals along with alternative models of justice and discusses the issues still missing from public discourse: youth marginalization, child poverty, victimization, and homelessness.

IN-TEXT LEARNING AIDS

Chapter Objectives and Introductions

Chapter objectives and an introduction are presented at the beginning of each chapter to give students an overview of major topics and act as an aid for reviewing the central points of each chapter.

Key Terms, Running Glossary, and Glossary

Key terms are presented at the beginning of each chapter to alert students to important concepts and also to provide a review. These terms are highlighted in bold print in the text, with the definitions appearing in the margin beside them (new to the third edition). All of these key terms and their definitions also appear in the glossary section at the back of the book.

Chapter Summary

Each chapter ends with a concise summary of key points, "facts," people, issues, and theoretical perspectives. The summary is designed as a review for students, not as a replacement for reading the chapter.

Web Links

Each chapter ends with a Web Links section that provides links to Internet sites for further research and consideration specific to the topic studied in the chapter.

TEXT SUPPLEMENTS

Instructor's Manual/Test Bank

The Instructor's Manual provides chapter outlines, chapter summaries, chapter objectives, student learning objectives, key terms and people, issues for discussion, and additional ideas (suggestions for guest speakers, student projects, etc.). A revised Test Bank is available, with over 2,000 review, multiple-choice, short-answer, and essay questions. Questions are designed to test conceptual understanding, concept application, or factual knowledge, and a text page reference is provided for each answer.

    The Instructor's Manual/Test Bank was written by the author of the text.

Companion Website: www.bellyoungoffenders3e.nelson.com

The website for this book is designed for both students and instructors, and features chapter links and quizzes, degree and career information, study resources, and much more.

InfoTrac® College Edition

InfoTrac® College Edition is automatically bundled FREE with every new copy of this text! InfoTrac® College Edition is a world-class, online university library that offers the full text of articles from over 5,000 scholarly and popular publications—updated daily and going back as far as 20 years. Both adopters and their students receive unlimited access for four months.

ACKNOWLEDGMENTS

A few special people made it possible for me to write this book. Above all, I wish to thank my parents, Jeanne and John Best, and grandmothers, Florence Roy and Louise Best, whose love, guidance, support, teaching, and example saved me from the juvenile justice system. The book is also due, in large part, to my gentle and generous partner in life, Rick Edwards, who kept me going throughout this project, and to Ollie and Lucy, my constant companions. Others have supported and assisted me along the way, through various stages. I am grateful to Marianne Parsons, Angela Dinaut, and Tena Boutilier, and to my research assistants, Cindy Bayers, Nancy Slipp, and Wendy Stephens. I am especially grateful to Nicole Landry, a graduate student and research assistant extraordinaire.

I am also indebted to the reviewers who took the time to offer constructive comments on the text. These include Anne Morris, Memorial University of Newfoundland; Marilyn Belle-McQuillan, University of Western Ontario; Barbara Ruttenberg, Concordia University; and Scott Brandon, University of Guelph. The book is greatly improved because of their efforts and because they helped push my analysis in important directions.

Finally, I wish to thank the publisher, Evelyn Veitch, for supporting this project, and Charlotte Forbes who, as acquisitions editor at Nelson, initially convinced me to take on this project. My gratitude also extends to June Trusty for her skilled final touches and to Rebecca Rea, senior developmental editor, and Lara Caplan, production editor, for their patience and assistance in keeping the project moving on schedule.

Sandra J. Bell
Saint Mary's University
Halifax

Young Offenders and Youth Justice

A Century After the Fact

Third Edition

CHAPTER ONE

The Rise and Fall of Delinquency

CHAPTER OBJECTIVES

1. To situate contemporary public issues about youth crime in a historical context.
2. To demonstrate that concerns about youth crime are created as much by particular sociohistorical circumstances as by actual levels of youth crime.
3. To provide a sociological perspective on youth crime and public issues.
4. To examine the nature and level of youth involvement in crime throughout Canada's history.
5. To understand what is new about contemporary youth crime and public issues.

KEY TERMS

Public issues

Discourse

Politics of youth crime

Juvenile justice system

Problematize

Penitentiary

Primary data

Secondary data

Rehabilitative philosophy

Juvenile delinquent

Reformatories

Official crime

Structural

Demographic

Denied adulthood

Marginalized

Moral panic

Decontextualize

INTRODUCTION

This chapter examines youth crime issues from a historical perspective. Through an examination of historical documents and sociohistorical analyses, public concerns about youth crime in the 18th and 19th centuries are compared with contemporary **public issues** about youth crime. This approach provides a framework and background for a presentation of a sociological perspective on the subject and a broader understanding of public issues regarding youth crime.

The chapter begins with a discussion of the issues as we understand them today and then proceeds to compare these views to perceptions of youth crime, crime statistics, and public issues from the past. Three distinct periods in Canadian history are discussed: the pre-Confederation period, in which children and youth were treated the same as adults; the Victorian period, in which the behaviour and well-being of children and youth became a subject of concern; and the post-Victorian period, in which youthful offenders were separated from adults in an attempt to prevent them from developing a criminal lifestyle that could last a lifetime.

By putting the current issue of youth crime in a historical context, we will see that youth crime has always been a part of Canadian society, but not always a public issue. The last 150 years of Canada's history have witnessed the rise and fall of youth crime as a public issue, as well as the rise and fall of delinquency itself.

public issues
Matters of public concern that are debated in a variety of forums and usually involve demands for action.

THE PUBLIC ISSUE

Over the last two decades, youth crime has been the subject of considerable public concern and **discourse.** Across Canada, newspaper headlines warned of a serious crime problem if appropriate steps were not taken to curb youth crime. Headlines in the *Calgary Herald* warned of imminent danger: "Youth violence soaring" (Oct. 15, 1992, p. B15); "No end seen to spiral in teenage crime" (May 14, 1992, p. A1); "Toll keeps mounting as violent youth spawn an epidemic of violence" (June 27, 1992, p. G4). While on the other side of the country, *The Chronicle Herald* in Halifax reported, "Youth crime puts the squeeze on business" (July 1993, p. A4) and "The YOA a slap on the wrist for violent offenders" (May 1992). Beyond the headlines, newspaper articles painted horrific accounts of the criminal deeds of young Canadians. In one summer month in 1995, we were informed that five teens in Prince Rupert, British Columbia, were charged with second-degree murder for the fatal beating of a fisherman (Fisherman murdered, 1995); a 7-year-old boy in La Ronge, Saskatchewan, was responsible (along with a 14-year-old) for the murder of another 7-year-old child (Riley, 1995); a 15-year-old in Winnipeg was charged with first-degree murder in the fatal drive-by shooting of a 13-year-old Aboriginal youth (Oosterom, 1995); and four Halifax teenagers were charged with aggravated assault for trying to kill a man who was a total stranger to them (MacKinlay, 1995).

By the end of the 1990s, newspaper and magazine headlines and stories were fuelling public concerns about violent events involving girls. Headlines in *The Globe and Mail* such as "Teen's torture again reveals girls' brutality" (January 20, 1998, A1) and "Police arrest members of girl gang" (January 22, 1998, p. A12) reinforced images of out-of-control teenaged girls created by journalists' coverage of the death of Reena Virk in Victoria, British Columbia, in 1997. A 16-year-old boy and 15-year-old girl were convicted in adult court of second-degree murder in Reena's death and six teenaged girls, aged 14 to 16, were also convicted of aggravated assault in youth court for their part in Reena's final ordeal (Chisholm, 1997; Joyce, 2000; Purvis, 1997). In the same year, two

discourse
How things are talked about and understood, both orally and in written form, including formal talk such as theory; professional talk such as reports, books, and media; and conversations.

15-year-old girls were charged with first-degree murder for stabbing Helen Montgomery to death in her North Battleford, Saskatchewan, home. The girls had been living in her home under an open-custody arrangement at the time of her murder (Cross, 1998).

School violence was also added to the list of horrors presented about youth behaviour. The *National Post* informed readers that "Teen felt good after killing girl . . ." (May 30, 2001, p. A8) and *The Chronicle Herald* that "High schools [are] simmering with angry, verbally abusive teens" (November 18, 2000, p. A6), "Teen charged in Taber school shooting . . . listens calmly . . . in court" (August 29, 2000, p. C10), and "Teen in beating case not rehabilitated or reformed" (December 14, 2000, p. A5). All were stories about beatings and killings in Canadian schools by seemingly unconcerned youth.

It is often said that "crime is news" and so we should not be surprised that the news media devotes as much time as it does to reporting crime events. What is of significance to those who study the **politics of youth crime** is the amount of coverage devoted to youth crime, particularly when, as we will see in later chapters, adult crimes far surpass youth crimes, both in quantity and severity. In addition, the amount of emphasis on youth violence is disproportionate to the amount of youth crime that actually involves violence of a serious nature. According to the most recent police statistics, the rate of violent youth crime has remained relatively stable since 1992 and actually decreased by 2 percent in 2004 (Sauve, 2005, p. 13). Yet, a study of *The Globe and Mail*, the *Toronto Star*, and the *Toronto Sun* over a two-month period in 1995 showed that 94 percent of the youth crime articles were about violent crimes (Sprott, 1996, pp. 271, 276). Furthermore, criminal activity is the primary focus of stories about youth. Reid-MacNevin (1996) found in her analysis of the *Toronto Star*, *Toronto Sun*, *Guelph Mercury*, and *Kitchener-Waterloo Record* from May to August in 1966 that almost two-thirds (56.7 percent) of the articles about youth were crime-related and 52 percent were about violent crime. At the same time, violent crime accounted for only 18 percent of all youth crime and property crime accounted for about half (Reid-MacNevin, 1996; Reid-MacNevin, 2005, p. 146). Reid-MacNevin also examined news stories about youth that were available on the Internet for June, July, and August in 2002 and found that while there were fewer stories about youth crime than found in newspapers (30 percent), the emphasis on youth violence was staggering—64 percent of the articles were about violent crime (Reid-MacNevin, 2003; Reid-MacNevin, 2005, p. 147).

Not surprisingly, newspaper headlines and stories, along with personal experience in some cases, prompted many Canadians to voice their concerns about "today's youth" and about the effectiveness of our youth justice system in curbing youth crime. The general consensus seemed to be that youth justice under the Young Offenders Act (YOA) was a "slap on the wrist." Politicians responded to these concerns by presenting youth crime and the YOA as a major election issue in the 1993 federal election campaign (see Table 1.1). Legislators, for their part, revised the YOA three times before finally proposing legislation to replace it. In 1995, while deliberating reforms for the third time, then-Justice Minister Allan Rock requested that the House of Commons Standing Committee on Justice and Legal Affairs undertake a comprehensive review of the **juvenile justice system** and that a Federal–Provincial–Territorial Task Force review the YOA and its application. The recommendations contained in these reports provided a foundation for further modifications to the justice system and the first drafts of new legislation. In the spring of 1998, then-Justice Minister Anne McLellan announced plans to introduce the new legislation (McIlroy, 1998a, 1998b). By the fall of 2001, the Youth Criminal Justice Act (YCJA), Bill C-3, was poised to replace the YOA, and after a lengthy consultative process and parliamentary discussion, the YCJA came into effect April 2003.

politics of youth crime
The ways in which youth crime is understood and talked about, both formally and informally, and the actions, laws, and policies that derive from this discourse.

juvenile justice system
A system of laws, policies, and practices designed under the guiding philosophy that children and youth, because of their age and maturity, should not be subject to criminal law in the same manner as adults.

TABLE 1.1

Federal Party Platforms on Young Offenders and Juvenile Justice, 1993

Liberal	Recommends that the Young Offenders Act be amended to increase sentences for violent crimes.
Progressive Conservative	Recommends increasing the severity of punishment under the Young Offenders Act.
NDP	Advocates a review of the Young Offenders Act.
Reform	Advocates an overhaul of the Young Offenders Act.
National	Expresses general concern about handguns and repeat violent offenders.
Bloc Québécois	No set policy in this area, but expresses concerns about law-and-order rhetoric.

Source: Adapted from Voter's Guide to the Issues. (1993, October 1). *The Globe and Mail*, p. A5.

Federal Party Platforms on Young Offenders and Juvenile Justice, 2006

Liberal	No set policy regarding youth justice, but proposes fines, not jail, for simple marijuana possession, the raising of mandatory minimum sentences for gun crimes, and the toughening of penalties for gang violence; promises $325 million for RCMP anti-gang squad.
Conservative	Advocates amending the Youth Criminal Justice Act, proposing that 14-year-olds should be tried as adults for serious or repeat crimes, the elimination of house arrest for serious crimes, the maintaining of marijuana laws, and mandatory prison sentences for serious drug trafficking and for weapons and violent offences.
NDP	Advocates that young offenders 16 and older should be tried as adults for gun crimes, promises $400 million for youth at risk, recommends funding community and education programs to keep youth from joining gangs and increased funding for anti-addiction programs.
Bloc Québécois	No policy in this area.
Green Party	Advocates for restorative justice, no jail time for first offenders, and the legalization of marijuana.

Source: Adapted from Policy Primer. (2006. January 21). *The Chronicle Herald* [Halifax], p. A6.

Unfortunately, this lengthy process and new legislation did little to curb the flow of the media's litany of horrors about youth and their criminal activities, nor the rhetoric of political parties. The party positions on youth justice did not change in the 2006 federal election, and we are still being told that youth violence is out of control. As we enter the 21st century, the news media reports, that "kids" are "roaming wild," "terrorizing our town," "holding us hostage in our own town" (Howe, 2003; MacDonald, 2002; Medel, 2005; Two girls . . . , 2003), that youth are carrying and using weapons (Lethal driver's mother . . . , 2005; Toronto mom . . . , 2006), that school bullying is getting worse (*CBC News*, March 26, 2002; Conrad, 2005), that girls are behaving in more criminal and more violent ways and that parents are being viciously attacked and murdered by their children (Girl, 12, charged in triple slaying, 2006; Baseball bat boy . . . , 2003; Boy charged with mother's murder, 2001; Girls drowned alcoholic mom, 2005; Newfoundland girl . . . , 2001; Student gets life . . . , 2005), and that toddlers are being murdered by young teens and adolescents, including girls (Berlin teen . . . , 2005; 11-year-olds arrested . . . , 2005; Girl charged . . . , 2005).

New to the list of teen horrors this time around are stories of "swarmings." We are told, for example, of a Vancouver incident in March 2005 that "Swarmers could be future killers . . ." (2005) and by the Toronto police chief in December 2004 that "there's an element of young people that are . . . out of control and accountable to no one . . . there's this pack mentality" (Gray & Tchir, 2004). "Joyriding" is also being reframed in the media discourse as a major threat to public safety, causing property damage, serious injuries, and death. An example of this is the McEvoy case, where the accused youth was described in newspaper headlines as a "significant threat," an "unrepentant teen killer," and a "lethal driver" (Jeffrey, December 17, 2005; Stewart, December 15, 16, 2005).

A final new, but also old, ingredient is that the legislation is under attack in the media. In spite of the federal government's efforts at reform, if one were to draw a conclusion about the YCJA from the newspaper stories and headlines that began even before it was implemented, it would surely be that nothing has changed, that youth justice is still "a slap on the wrist." Headlines and stories tell us that: "Act expected to staunch flow of public information on youth crime" (MacDonald, 2003); ". . . more non-jail sentences . . . so much for getting tougher on the violent punks . . ." (Howe, 2003); "Teen arrested six times for weapons . . . every time they let him go . . ." (Arsenault, December 30, 2005); "Our whole justice system has to be taken apart and put back together" (Medel, 2005); "Teenage killer gets maximum sentence: 3 years" (VonKintzel, 2005). Even the *Reader's Digest* jumped into the fray with its headline in February 2002 that the YCJA is an "Easier Time for Youth Crime." After explaining to its readership that "There are a lot of things wrong with the new Act . . .", the article concluded that the act is "Pretty scary. At a time when Canadians are demanding tougher sentences for violent crime, the federal government is *shortening* sentences for young offenders" (pp. 113–114). [Italics in the original.]

Two Opposing Sides

Part of the Liberal federal government's 1995 YOA reforms involved a *Strategy for Reform* of the entire youth justice system, an important part of which involved consultations with the public and special-interest groups. As a result, public forums were held in various communities across the country to discuss youth crime and propose solutions or make recommendations to the House of Commons Standing Committee on Justice and Legal Affairs. At the heart of the public issue were questions about whether the YOA effectively controlled youth crime: the public was clearly divided into two camps on the youth crime issue as demonstrated, for example, at a public forum held in Halifax in the summer of 1995.

Youth advocates in this forum, often including social workers, lawyers, and others who work directly with young offenders, saw children and youth as victims in need of protection and believed that neither youth nor the YOA was a problem. The important issues, as they saw it, were those related to the difficulties that youth encounter in an increasingly complex society. From this perspective, current economic, social, and political realities are a source of tremendous hardship for some young people and their families. Often, economic or social problems exacerbate other problems within families, and young people are forced to leave home as a matter of survival (see Box 1.1). One lawyer who works with youth poignantly reflected, "I look at these kids and their horrible family lives, and I think, 'There but for the grace of God go I.'"

VOICES BOX 1.1

Street Kids' Perspectives

Ocean, 18, female:

I'm a ward. Social services took me out. They took me out of the home because I was sexually abused . . . It was my stepfather that abused me. It went on from the age of seven until I was fourteen . . . My Dad left when I was three. It was really hard because we had no money at all. Nothing. He took everything. I was in grade three when the abuse started. My mother knew about it a year later. She did something in a way but she didn't go to anybody. She said, "If he ever does anything again, come tell me." That night he came into my room and it started all over again . . . I was in grade seven and I told Mum again and she still didn't do anything. It was at this time that I was put into my first foster home. For me if they had put me in with a family that wanted me I think I would have been okay. Jane was okay but she and everyone turned against my mother for kicking me out of the house and staying with him . . . Me and my Mum never got along. We fought and fought. I guess it was from all the abuse and all the tension. I guess I took it out on my Mum and my brother. I used to abuse my brother. I used to beat him . . . I'm real sorry for that. The day my Dad went to jail my Dad's second-youngest brother came up to me in a car and stopped and said, "Thanks a lot. You just put your Dad in jail for five years." . . . From there I went to live with my aunt in B.C. Things were no better there, and I left there and came home to Nova Scotia . . . Things were real bad here. I even tried to kill myself at one point and was put into the N.S. Hospital for five months . . . Things were no better when I got out. Nobody wanted me, so they put me into Phoenix House. I have been there ever since.

Clarissa, 17, female:

When did we move there . . . I think I was eleven . . . but once I was twelve I decided I wanted out . . . so I ran. When I got off the bus, the police were waiting for me. So I was, well, quickly returned home and I was put into a foster home . . . It was only a temporary agreement, voluntary, for three months. My parents had to sign a thing so after three months were up I was supposed to be returned to them . . . I did go home for Christmas and I got a big bawling out from my stepmother about how I wasn't there and they weren't going to get their tax deductions at the end of the year . . . It didn't make me feel very good, like, well jeez, is that all you want me for, the money . . . My Dad is a pervert, put it that way . . . oh yeah, I lived with that for years . . . I was five and a half when it started, that's as far back as I can remember . . . My stepmother knows but she denies that she knows, she denies that it is true . . . I lived in many different group homes. I got kicked out because I wasn't following the rules . . . I was fourteen when I started doing it [prostitution] but now it is just when I need the money . . . I gotta chill out because I'm doing the dope again . . . The system sucks . . . They don't do anything for us . . . they take us and stick us in a group home and that's all they do . . . they stick you there . . . I don't have a place I would call home. I have been basically without a roof over my head and you bunk where you can find a spot . . . I have had to stay out on the streets and all I do is get so stoned out of my tree I don't know whether I am comin' or goin' and the night passes like that.

Source: *Homeless Youth in Perspective* (1994, pp. 12–21).

Youth advocates were primarily concerned with the problems experienced by young people rather than youth crime. It was their view that youth crime had been exaggerated and misrepresented in most public accounts, particularly by the media. At the Halifax public forum, youth advocates presented statistics from the Department of Justice showing that crime in Nova Scotia had dropped in all categories since 1986 and that recent increases in violent crime had "flattened out." Other statistics indicated that youth were being treated far more harshly under the YOA than they ever were under the former legislation, the Juvenile Delinquents Act (Leschied & Jaffe, 1991). Further, with the exception of the most serious offences of murder and manslaughter, youth were treated at least as harshly as adults who had committed the same offences (Bell & Smith, 1994; Doob, Marinos, & Varma, 1995). Among other things, youth advocates preferred policies that would address poverty and high youth unemployment rather than focus on punitive justice reforms.

The other perspective presented at the Halifax public forum was the one most often seen in the media. This "law-and-order" group viewed children and youth accused of crimes as an enemy from whom adults needed protection (Sherr, 1996). Proponents of this view saw youth as "out of control" and favoured a law-and-order approach to youth crime. Included in this group were what one police officer described as the "old buffalo police officers," store security personnel, small-business owners, and homeowners associations. From their perspectives, both youth and the YOA were problems. Youth were a problem because they were said to (1) lack respect for anyone or anything, as was often reflected in foul language and "no fear of using it"; (2) lack a sense of responsibility for their criminal behaviour; and (3) be increasingly involved in violent criminal behaviour. The YOA was viewed as a problem because it was believed that (1) youth could not be identified; (2) youth were not punished for their crimes; (3) youth had more rights than their victims; and (4) youth were too protected by the YOA.

Law-and-order proponents at the Halifax forum cited a Statistics Canada release reporting an 8 percent increase in youth involvement in violent crime. They were further armed with information about incidences of particularly violent youth crime, readily supplied from news media. These stories usually portrayed the young offender in such cases as remorseless and lacking feeling—the "superpredator" (Sherr, 1996). The law-and-order view advocates a "get-tough" approach to young offenders.

Ten years later, we find that people are again gathering in Halifax to discuss the youth justice system. Once again the issue is the apparent inability of the justice system to control young offenders, only this time it is the Youth Criminal Justice Act that is under scrutiny and the forum is a public inquiry into the circumstances leading up to the death of Theresa McEvoy on October 14, 2004, as a result of her car being broad-sided by a 16-year-old youth. The youth was driving a stolen car and was reportedly in a high-speed chase with the police when the accident occurred. What complicated the case was that the youth had been released from court custody just two days prior, pending sentencing, after pleading guilty to an earlier theft and car chase incident. Furthermore, at the same time that he was released from custody, an arrest warrant already existed in relation to a number of charges laid against him for similar offences three months earlier (Hayes, February 15, 2006). The specific question asked by all professionals involved in this case and by the public and the McEvoy family is why the youth was released when there was sufficient evidence that he was at risk of reoffending and when there was also an outstanding warrant for his arrest. The answers to this question are sufficiently complex that the Nova Scotia Justice minister, Michael Baker, called for a public inquiry (the Nunn Commission of Inquiry) at the request of the McEvoy family (see Box 1.2). The larger questions to be addressed concern the

CASE STUDY BOX 1.2

The McEvoy Inquiry

On October 12, 2004, Theresa McEvoy was killed when her car was struck by a 16-year-old youth driving a stolen car. The case against the youth in McEvoy's death took 15 months to process, even though the youth entered a guilty plea. He received a $5\frac{1}{2}$-year adult sentence for criminal negligence causing death and dangerous driving causing death. His sentence was reduced by one year because of the time he had already served over the course of his trial and sentencing.

On November 4, 2004, McEvoy's family asked for a public inquiry into her death and on November 10, then-Nova Scotia Justice Minister Michael Baker announced that he would hold a "full, independent and public inquiry" into McEvoy's death (Hayes, January 12, 2006). In June 2005, retired Supreme Court Justice Merlin Nunn was appointed to head the inquiry, which began on January 16, 2006, and recessed its first session in March 2006. The second stage began in May 2006 and involved a public forum where, as well as hearing continued testimony from professionals, members of the public were invited to speak to their experiences with the youth justice system and to make recommendations for changes.

Eight parties were granted standing at the inquiry: the RCMP, the Halifax Regional Police, the Attorney General's Department, two prosecutors representing the Crown Prosecution Service, the Canadian Bar Association, the convicted youth, and the McEvoy family. Some 40 to 50 witnesses testified at the inquiry (Jeffrey, January 14, 2006). Details on the Inquiry can be found at www.nunncommission.ca.

The case and the inquiry are expected to have broad-reaching effects, both within the province and across the country. In December 2005, the Justice minister for Nova Scotia met with then-Federal Justice Minister Irwin Cotler to discuss toughening the YCJA with regard to car theft. The argument is that car theft and joyriding should be considered violent crimes because they both pose a potential threat to public safety. The Director of Prosecutions in Nova Scotia has also changed the procedures for cases where youth plead guilty. The Crown will now be required to request an immediate bail hearing to decide on detaining the youth before sentencing (Hayes, January 22, 26, 2006).

Details on the youth in the McEvoy case and his processing through the youth justice system will be outlined in feature boxes at the beginning of relevant chapters throughout this textbook. Because he was sentenced as an adult, his identity is no longer protected. Nonetheless, in respect of his rights under the UN *Convention on the Rights of the Child* (to be discussed in the next chapter), he will be referred to as "Johnny" in these feature boxes.

YCJA itself and the administration of the law in Nova Scotia, and the McEvoy family is interested in three things: (1) the systemic and individual failures leading to the release of the youth two days prior to Theresa McEvoy's death; (2) the extent to which YCJA provisions contributed to the release of the youth; and (3) the role of service providers in responding to at-risk youth both before and after a youth's criminal activity (Jeffrey, January 14, 2006).

Beginning January 14, 2006, local newspapers and television and radio stations began relaying the details of the Nunn inquiry to the public. During the seven weeks of the first stage of inquiry testimony, no fewer than 26 articles appeared in one newspaper alone, with mostly front-page coverage. Of particular interest to us is that even though the participants in this public forum have all changed from the one 10 years ago, the focus of attention is the same—the youth justice system. Furthermore, even though the public discussion is now about the justice system under the YCJA rather than the YOA, the views presented so far in the public discourse still fall into the law-and-order and youth advocate camps. In this case, as opposed to 10 years earlier, from a law-and-order perspective, youth involvement in car theft and joyriding is **problematized** and the youth himself was described as a "serial car thief," "a frequent flyer," someone who was on a "car theft rampage." One local newspaper article during the hearing reported statistics from a Joint Halifax Regional Police–RCMP auto-theft unit indicating that there were more than 1,800 stolen vehicle reports in the Halifax Regional Municipality in 2004. The police report claimed that joyriding is the major reason for car theft and that the "thieves are young people in 60–70 percent of the cases." Furthermore, the article cited from the police report that ". . . joyriders take pride in their crimes, believe they have little chance of being caught and aren't worried there will be serious consequences if they do get caught." (Bradley, 2006). In contrast is the youth advocacy view—a group home supervisor described the youth in the McEvoy case as "a very lost boy."

> **problematize**
> A process whereby something, someone, or some group is defined as a problem.

As for the act itself, law-and-order views were that the YCJA "goes overboard in reducing custody," that "there is too much reliance on community punishment," that "kids are getting too many chances," that "judges can't jail youth who need it," that there are "no threats to motivate youth," and that some kids are "spiralling out of control" and judges "need the ability to lock up kids." Perhaps this perspective is best reflected in the words of a Crown prosecutor who is quoted as saying that the YCJA might as well stand for "You Can't Jail Anybody" (*CTV Evening News*, January 18, 2006). On the other hand are the views that there is "nothing wrong with the act," that "at-risk kids need more social supports," that the problem is "not enough resources from the province to do the job," and that the problems lie "in communities and schools." At the time this book was being written, the McEvoy inquiry was in recess and was to resume hearing from witnesses and the public in May 2006, when a public forum designed to address the public's experiences with the justice system will also be held. By far, in this first stage of the inquiry, the law-and-order view had outweighed the youth advocate perspective in public discourse.

"THE GOOD OLD DAYS"

Perhaps the most basic assumption underlying many public views about youth crime, particularly the law-and-order perspective, is the notion that today's youth are worse than they were in "the good old days." Interestingly, every generation of adults seems to remember a time when things were "better" and not what they are "today." Yet, available crime statistics do not indicate any such period in Canadian history. Canadian crime statistics, as far back as 1885 (see Table 1.2), indicate that young people have always been involved in criminal activity, some of it serious violent crime.

Moreover, young people have always been responsible for a considerably smaller amount of criminal activity than adults, and most of their offences have involved petty property crime. According to Carrigan (1991, p. 216), this pattern of criminal activity was established in early pioneer days and has continued to the present. In 1909–1910, for example, documents in the annual reports for the City of Halifax indicated that youth under 18 were responsible for 18 percent of all criminal charges (City Marshal, 1909–1910). The Nova Scotia Department of Justice reported that in 1993–1994,

TABLE 1.2

Juvenile Convictions for Indictable Offences, 1885–1899

	Under Age 16		16–20	
Type of Offence	Male	Female	Male	Female
Offences against the person	371	16	1,593	62
Offences against property with violence	805	4	1,456	3
Offences against property without violence	7,750	398	7,328	704
Malicious offences against property	161	10	106	5
Forgery and offences against the currency	24	1	106	5
Other offences not included in the above classes	125	40	336	169
Totals	**9,236**	**469**	**10,963**	**948**

Source: Adapted from *Statistical Yearbook of Canada, 1899*.

youth accounted for the same proportion of all criminal activity—18 percent (Bell, 1995). For Canada as a whole, youth under 18 accounted for 19 percent of all Criminal Code charges and 16 percent of all violent crime in 1998 (Statistics Canada, 1999a, pp. 18–19).

Some youth crimes are particularly horrendous, such as the 1993 abduction and brutal murder of 2-year-old James Bulger by two 10-year-old boys in Liverpool, England. Some view this crime as "evidence" that children are far more criminal now than ever before. However, most people have no way of knowing what crimes occurred decades ago. Few of us would recall that an 11-year-old girl in England murdered two children in her care in 1968; fewer still would know that in 1861, two 8-year-old boys murdered a 2-year-old in a case very similar to the James Bulger murder. Similarly, Carrigan (1991, p. 204) tells of a 10-year-old boy who, on a hunting party in March 1802, took a loaded gun to a tent and shot a man dead. The lawyer representing one of the young Liverpool defendants argued to the judge hearing their case that "there is no evidence of an increase during this century of crimes of murder by young children" (Reduced sentences . . . , 1996).

Unfortunately, historical data on youth crime and public responses are not readily available since youth crime statistics were not always kept in the manner that they are today. In the early years of European settlement, crime information was recorded in the reports of colonial administrators. Some statistics are available for Upper and Lower Canada (Ontario and Quebec) after Confederation, and slightly more detailed information is available in general reports from city administrators. Prison records provide a source of information on youth crime, but the ages of prisoners were not always recorded. There are no consistent prison records until 1835, the year in which Kingston **Penitentiary,** the first Canadian prison, opened. Beyond these **primary data** sources, there are a few academic analyses of youth crime that provide **secondary data.** These analyses are scant since contemporary Canadian scholars and researchers seem to have been far more interested in the justice system than in the actual behaviour of children and youth in Canada's history. Most Canadian criminologists now studying in this area have relied more on the work of historians than criminologists (Smandych, 1995, p. 13).

penitentiary
A 19th-century term for prisons based on a philosophy of penitence and punishment to atone for wrongs.

primary data
Research information gathered directly from the original source.

secondary data
Research information or data that was originally collected for another purpose.

Lawless and Disobedient Youth: The 17th and 18th Centuries

Information on youth involvement in crime in Canada during the 17th and 18th centuries is sketchy. Although we cannot ever know the actual incidence of lawbreaking among youth during this period, what information is available indicates that concerns were expressed about youth as a problem in the North American colonies as early as the late 17th century. In his analysis of youth in New France, Moogk (1982) documents the concerns expressed by colonial administrators regarding the children of the colonies:

> The great liberty of long standing which the parents and Governors have given to the youth, permitting them to dally in the woods under the pretext of hunting or trading . . . has reached such an excess that from the time children are able to carry a gun, fathers are not able to restrain them and dare not anger them. (Governor Brisay de Denonville, 1685, cited in Moogk, 1982, p. 17)

Other reports described boys in New France as "lawless" and "disobedient," and girls as "vain" and "lazy." Similarly, in 1707, an intendant of the colony described the children of New France as "hard and ferocious" (Moogk, 1982, p. 18).

Carrigan (1991, pp. 203, 205) examined the historical records of crime and punishment from the earliest European records and reported that the majority of documented cases were of a petty nature. They involved vandalism, petty theft, brawling, swearing, immorality, violations of local ordinances, and the abandonment of indentured service contracts. Young people were involved in serious crimes and murders, but their ages are often not recorded. One recorded example is the case of a 10-year-old indentured servant who set fire to his master's house in Annapolis, Nova Scotia, on April 19, 1737; the house and contents were totally destroyed.

Throughout recorded history, children in European society have had a different legal status than adults. Mostly, this meant they had no rights and were at the mercy of their parents and the state. Infanticide, child slavery, and child labour were common. The idea that children had rights as individuals independent of their parents, or that they had a right to protection from adults, did not gain popularity until the 19th century (Bala & Clarke, 1981, pp. 1–6). With regard to crime, from about the 11th century, English common law recognized that a child's capacity to understand the wrongfulness of crime was limited. Hence, children under seven were considered to lack the "capacity to commit a crime" (*doli incapax*) (Bala & Clarke, 1981, p. 163). Evidence of capacity was required to convict children 7 to 13 of a crime. Nonetheless, 7-year-old children were charged with crimes, tried in court with adults, and faced with the same punishments upon conviction (Bala & Clarke, 1981, p. 163).

Colonial administrators brought these legal codes and traditions to the New World. The first European settler executed in the territories of Canada was a 16-year-old girl who had been found guilty of theft in 1640. Her execution was ordered by Champlain (Carrigan, 1991), and she was hanged by a male offender who escaped execution by agreeing to act as her hangman (Adelberg & Currie, 1988). Smandych (1995) cautions that we should not conclude that children were always or usually treated exactly like adults in the colonial justice system; rather, they "were usually shown an even greater degree of mercy than adults" (p. 15). Thus, we find that in 1672, a 13-year-old girl who had helped her parents murder her husband escaped execution because of her age; instead, she was required to attend the execution of her parents (Carrigan, 1991, p. 203).

The Colonial Public Issue
The issue for colonial administrators in the territories of Canada was the freedom and independence that young people had relative to their counterparts in the Old World.

In Europe, children were subservient to adults and dependent on parents. As Moogk (1982) notes:

> The official culture of France glorified submission to authority . . . The family, the church, and the state were organized as hierarchies in which authority descended from the top. An orderly society was one in which people accepted their hereditary social rank and obeyed their superiors. (p. 42)

However, the largely rural nature of the population in New France meant that parents were dependent on their children's labour for economic success. Hence, rural and working-class children in the New World had considerable independence from their parents. In the view of colonial administrators, parental authority was significantly undermined by this arrangement, and this lack of authority was evident in young people's behaviour. According to administrators' reports:

> Rural children stole produce from their parents in order to buy trifles . . . [and] among "the common people" . . . "boys of ten or twelve years of age . . . run about with a pipe in their mouth" . . . Young *Canadiens* drank brandy, refused to doff their hats in the presence of ladies while indoors, and rode about on their own horses . . . The fact that in New France young peasants rode horses and country girls dressed in the finery of gentlewomen did not accord with the outsider sense of propriety. (Moogk, 1982, pp. 41–42)

The freedom and independence displayed by young people in New France likely posed a significant threat to the authority of the administrators themselves, since 42 percent of the population was composed of children under 15 (Moogk, 1982, pp. 42–43).

"Causes" and Solutions: An Era of Control and Punishment

From historical documents of the colonial period, two factors emerge as perceived "causes" of youth crime—parents and the fur trade. Overindulgent parents were often cited by administrators as a reason for youth problems:

> The residents of this country have never had a proper education because of the overindulgence (*la foiblesse*) resulting from a foolish tenderness shown to them by their mothers and fathers during their infancy. In this they imitate the Amerindians. It prevents them from disciplining the children and forming their character. (Intendant Jacques Raudot, 1707, cited in Moogk, 1982, p. 18)

Some officials complained about the children of "gentlemen," accusing them of "debauchery" and "abusing the daughters and wives of the natives" (Denonville, 1685, cited in Carrigan, 1991, p. 204). Another identified problem was the fur trade, one of the most lucrative businesses of the times. Since the seigneurial system of inheritance in New France dictated that only eldest sons inherited family farms, other children had to look elsewhere for a livelihood. The fur trade promised freedom, adventure, and a lucrative career. Merchants and military officers also saw business opportunities for their sons in the fur trade and apprenticed them to experienced voyageurs. According to Carrigan (1991), the fur trade was "rife with fraud, immorality, theft, assault, and murder," and teenagers "probably contributed their fair share to the lawlessness" (p. 204). Apparently, many carried these habits back to their homes after they left the fur-trading business, for they were accused of having contracted "an habitual libertinism" (cited in Carrigan, 1991, p. 204).

Beyond this, a very real source of problems came from the active promotion of immigration to the New World. Impoverished Europeans had been lured to the New

World with promises of a prosperous life, but once there, many found only unemployment, sickness, destitution, or death. Countless numbers of children found themselves in desperate circumstances because of the hardships faced by their parents in the New World. Some parents died as a result of these hardships, while others simply abandoned their children once they reached the New World.

> Between 1752 and 1760 the Orphan House in Halifax admitted a total of 275 children. Of that number 114 were orphans while the remainder were either neglected or abandoned . . . One ship that arrived in Halifax in 1752 landed eight orphans whose parents had died during the voyage. More deaths shortly afterwards increased the number of parentless children to fourteen. (Carrigan, 1991, p. 206)

In the 18th century, a variety of disciplinary measures were proposed as solutions to youth crime. Some were remarkably similar to modern proposals. While such solutions as more schools, more priests, and confinement to settled parts of the colony were, as informal forms of legal governance (Hogeveen, 2001, pp. 45–47), uniquely suited to the political, social, and economic structures of this period, other proposals, such as fines and punishment for parents of offenders, military justice, and an increase in garrison troops [police] should sound very familiar to a modern reader (Moogk, 1982, p. 18).

A Question of Immorality: The 19th Century

Urban problems associated with immigration and poverty continued and worsened throughout the 19th century. Carrigan (1991) reported that one relief agency in York cared for 535 orphans over a two-year period in the early 1800s. Some fathers were deserting their families "in despair of bettering their situation," and York was "overwhelmed with Widows or Orphans" (Archdeacon John Strachan, 1831, cited in Carrigan, p. 206). The Irish famine exacerbated the orphan problem in Canada by increasing the number of people emigrating to the New World. The effect of these increased numbers was to worsen the quality of life on the ships and to make passengers more susceptible to typhus fever.

> In 1847 an estimated 20,000 immigrants died from sickness. Some 5,000 died at Grose Isle, the quarantine station in Quebec, the rest in places like Quebec City, Montreal, Kingston, and Toronto. One estimate suggested that 500–600 orphans were left in Montreal from this epidemic. (Carrigan, 1991, p. 206)

By the mid 1800s, British and Canadian authorities had developed policies to send Britain's orphaned, poor, and destitute children to Canada as indentured servants. Between 1873 and 1903, more than 95,000 children came to Canada under the sponsorship of child immigration agencies (Carrigan, 1991, p. 208). While the migration scheme was seen as a means of providing a better life for the children of Britain's poor and destitute families, many of these children found only a life of misery and harsh working conditions in Canada. In the words of one young female immigrant, "'doption, sir, is when folks gets a girl to work without wages" (cited in Sutherland, 1976, p. 10). Some children abandoned their contracts (even though to do so was a punishable offence), which left them dependent on their own resources for survival.

Life for the poor was very difficult in Victorian Canada. Fingard (1989) contrasts the lifestyle of the "respectable middle class" with that of the people who lived in the poorer sections of Halifax and vividly documents the difficulties faced by urban young people in 19th-century Canada. Many did not have work, and those who were lucky enough to secure employment were often at the mercy of unscrupulous employers. Girls were particularly vulnerable. Those working as domestics and servants for shop-keepers were often forced to "service" male customers in order to keep their jobs. They were not free to leave these places of employment because to do so would require them to forfeit a letter of reference without which they would be unable to secure other employment (Fingard, 1989, pp. 101–102).

This situation was only too common in most North American cities. Stansell's analysis of sex and class relations in New York City (1986) documents the grim lives of girls who sought self-reliance.

> Juvenile prostitution stemmed not just from class encounters but from the everyday relations of men and girls in working-class neighborhoods. Rape trials . . . show that sex with girl children was woven into the fabric of life in the tenements and the streets . . . Poor girls learned early about their vulnerability to sexual harm from grown men, but they also learned some ways to turn men's interest to their own purposes. Casual prostitution was one . . .
>
> Laboring girls ran across male invitations in the course of their daily rounds—street selling, scavenging, running errands for mothers or mistresses, in walking home from work, in their workplaces and neighborhoods . . . Opportunities proliferated as New York's expanding industry and commerce provided a range of customers extending well beyond the traditional clientele of wealthy rakes and sailors. Country storekeepers in town on business, gentlemen travellers, lonely clerks and working men were among those who propositioned girls on the street. (pp. 182–183)

Most of our information on youth crime from the Victorian period comes from city police records and prison reports. Juvenile institutions were not built until after 1857, so when young offenders were imprisoned they were sent to adult jails. This included the penitentiary in Kingston, which opened in 1835. In 1846, 16 children were imprisoned at Kingston Penitentiary (Bowker, 1986). Carrigan (1991) reported that in 1849–1850, 36 of the prisoners released from Kingston Penitentiary were between the ages of 10 and 17. One of these prisoners had been convicted of murder at age 15, and another of manslaughter at age 10. The 1848–1849 report from a government inquiry on the Kingston prison, the Brown Commission report, tells of children 8, 11, and 12 being housed with adult criminals. Six percent of the convicted population in other jails scattered throughout Upper and Lower Canada were under 16. Compared to today's institutionalized populations, a much higher percentage of imprisoned youth were girls. In 1859, 29 percent of youth detained in the jails of Upper and Lower Canada were girls under 16 (Carrigan, 1991, pp. 209–215). This may be because arrest rates for female offenders were higher in the 19th century than they are today (Boritch, 1997, pp. 46–47).

Many incarcerated youth had been convicted of relatively minor offences and many were as young as seven. Throughout the 19th century, it was not uncommon to find children not yet in their teens in city jails as well. In 1881, for example, the annual prison report for the City of Halifax indicated that 7.9 percent of the prison population that year was between 8 and 14 (Prison Report, 1881, p. 113). Many youth were imprisoned because they were "habitual" offenders. Houston (1982, p. 134) tells of a 10-year-old break-and-enter artist in Toronto who was outdone in his crimes by three 7-year-olds who, when convicted of felony in 1890, already had three previous convictions for break and enter.

After Confederation in 1867, the proportion of youth in jails declined somewhat, especially in regard to girls and young women.

> In 1869 approximately 6.6 per cent of all people put in Ontario jails were juveniles. The percentage dropped to 4.2 in 1879 and to 3.9 in 1889. The percentage fluctuated over the years but there was never any significant increase . . . In 1869 girls accounted for 21.8 percent of juvenile incarcerations, dropping to 11.3 per cent in 1879 and to 9.2 per cent in 1889. (Carrigan, 1991, p. 210)

Rates for boys continued to fluctuate. In Ontario, Houston (1982) notes:

> Males under sixteen years old fluctuated as a proportion of total male committals to provincial gaols within a relatively short span from Confederation to 1890. At its highest (7.8 per cent) in the late 1860s, the figure dropped in the 1870s, rising briefly in 1882 to its decade high of 6.7 per cent, falling again to its lowest percentage for the total period (3.8 per cent) in 1886. (p. 133)

Houston cautions that fluctuations in the use of institutions should not be seen as indicative of changes in criminal behaviour. Committals to prisons tended to reflect "governmental and judicial faith" in the institutions rather than any actual change in youth behaviour. "There is little to suggest that the behaviour of youngsters altered. Larceny dominated the list of offences committed; only the addition in 1880 of "incorrigibility" as a grounds for committal significantly altered the picture" (Houston, 1982, p. 133). In addition, some of the decline and fluctuation in youth incarceration was likely due to changing attitudes about young offenders, the development of separate institutions for children, and the ability of boards of directors of these institutions to affect court commitments to their facilities (Rains & Teram, 1992, pp. 27–31).

Passed in 1857, An Act for Establishing Prisons for Young Offenders provided for separate institutions for youth (Hagan & Leon, 1977). Two facilities were opened shortly thereafter, one in an unused military barracks in Penetanguishene on Georgian Bay in Upper Canada and one at Isle-aux-Noix on the Richelieu River in Lower Canada. When the institution at Penetanguishene opened, it housed 40 boys; by 1872, there were 193 inmates. The institutionalized population at Penetanguishene reached a record high of 263 boys in 1882 (Jones, 1988, p. 279). Many of these boys were very young; according to Carrigan (1991, p. 212), 55 percent of the boys admitted to Penetanguishene in 1889 were under 14.

The Victorian Public Issue

By the mid-1800s, the urban middle class in North America began to express concerns about the morality of those who were poor and destitute. Various urban relief agencies sprang up in cities across the continent to address such problems as illiteracy, prostitution, alcohol abuse, juvenile delinquency, and "family squalor" (Fingard, 1989, p. 119). The discourse surrounding those agencies and their activities served to define problems, their "causes," and seemingly appropriate solutions.

In Halifax, one agency instrumental in bringing social issues to public attention was the Halifax City Mission. Established in 1852, the mission identified three problems—prostitution, the liquor trade, and infanticide—and lobbied the city and provincial governments to take action (Fingard, 1989, p. 122). The criminal activity of young people was also of some concern to the agency. In 1862, an annual report for the City of Halifax reported that "juvenile offenders of both sexes are constantly brought before the Police Court, charged with thefts and other similar offences . . . The numbers of these youthful criminals are far greater than would be imagined" (Mayor's

Report, 1862, p. 14). The 1898–1899 report of the Chief of Police for the City of Halifax indicates that 10.8 percent of the convicted offenders whose ages were known were under 16, while 18.9 percent were between 16 and 20 (*Annual Report, 1898–99*, p. 76). In other words, almost 30 percent of the convicted offenders in Halifax a century ago were under 21.

Throughout the latter half of the 1800s, the issue of youth crime seemed to be a moral one. Because of poverty and destitution brought on by a lack of employment and severe working conditions, countless numbers of children and young people were spending a good portion of their lives on city streets, which they worked by begging, stealing, and selling whatever they could to make a living. In Toronto, these children were referred to as "waifs," "strays," and "street arabs" in public discussions (Houston, 1982). The public issue was not poverty and destitution, however. Rather, it was the morality of this impoverished working class. The parents of these children were perceived as immoral and unable or unwilling to control their children. Attitudes toward the poor were very unsympathetic. One of the brothers at St. Patrick's Home for Boys in Halifax made the following observation:

> I find that boys sent to us for theft have absolutely no realization of its gravity. I had two lads committed here not long ago for stealing clothing. I questioned them, and they replied with perfect directness, that they stole the clothes because they needed them. ("Suspended sentences . . . ," 1908)

Much of the morality discourse about youth problems revolved around discussions about "children on the streets." As cited in Doob, Marinos, and Varma (1995), the 1890 annual report of the Chief Constable of Toronto stated that "vagrant bands parading the streets at night have given the police a good deal of trouble, composed as they are, of rowdy youths." The report goes on to indicate that the police had received numerous complaints "from all parts of the City respecting the conduct of boys in the streets. Concern was expressed that the police were fighting a losing battle because "boys are ubiquitous" and the constables are "not omnipresent." The report of the following year continues to express police frustration with youth crime. "Juveniles are responsible for depredations of all kinds, and, as a class, are more difficult to deal with than the professional thief . . ."

City administrators in other parts of the country reported similar concerns. The people of Halifax debated the merits of a curfew to solve the problem of youth on the streets at night. It would seem that boys were the curse of authorities everywhere at the turn of the century. As the Halifax *Morning Chronicle* reported on May 11, 1909:

> The problem of the nation is the problem of the City, and the problem of the City is the "Boy Problem" . . . The problem of the boy is largely one of providing him with a proper environment during his "off hours" . . . The boy, if neglected during the character forming period of his life, has in him the power of making the future as black as night. (Y.M.C.A., 1909)

Young women on the streets were also a concern, not for their safety, as we might assume, but for perceived danger to their morality. This view is evident in an article that appeared in the Halifax *Evening Mail* on January 11, 1908. The author of "Danger of the street: Where lieth responsibility?" had this to say about the perils of the street for young women:

> Perhaps there is merely a rendezvous of young friends, but in no case can these boys and girls be improving their minds, characters or their manners. The whole effect upon them is insidious and degrading. The young girl must hear conversation unfit

for her ears, she must attain worldly knowledge that she never should attain, she must grow careless, 'flip', and used to the 'license of touch'. **She will lose the essential qualities of womanliness that command every man's respect. In some cases, the girl will go down and out, and the end will be ruin, sorrow and misery.** [Boldface in original]

"Causes" and Solutions: An Era of Social Reform

According to Rothman (1980), a reform movement swept North America in the latter half of the 19th century. The essential tenets of this movement were a focus on the individual, a widespread belief in the goodness of humanitarian sentiment, and, above all, a belief in the ability of the state and professionals to reform individuals. The emergence of the progressive reform movement marked the birth of **rehabilitative philosophy.** Reformers maintained that it made no sense to return "evil with evil" by imprisoning and punishing criminal offenders. They argued that it was far more effective in the long run to return "evil with good" by trying to rehabilitate individuals who had committed crimes.

This reform philosophy applied most readily to children and young people. For the "child savers" it was easy to believe that, if young enough, a child could be "saved" from a life of crime through interventions designed to correct the factors believed to influence children in the development of criminal ways (Platt, 1969a). Consistent with this idea, the practice of confining children in prison with adults also fell into public disfavour. Prisons were seen by many as "schools of crime" where children would associate with, and learn the habits of, "hardened" adult criminals.

One of the recommendations of the 1848–1849 Brown Commission report on Kingston Penitentiary was that a separate justice system be created for juveniles. The opening of juvenile institutions at Penetanguishene and Isle-aux-Noix was the first of a series of reforms that culminated in the establishment of a separate law governing the misdeeds of children and youth. Implemented in 1908, the Juvenile Delinquents Act (JDA) made **juvenile delinquent** a legal status (Hagan & Leon, 1977, p. 591). This does not imply that there was unanimous agreement as to the problem of youth crime or the most appropriate solution. Few seemed to object to separating children from adults, but there was disagreement over how this should be done. Some reformers believed that lengthy sentences in **reformatories** were necessary to rehabilitate young people, while others were opposed to institutionalizing young people, whether in youth or adult prison (Leon, 1977).

W.L. Scott, one of the people instrumental in drafting the first juvenile legislation, posed the question, "What wise parent would place a naughty child with other naughty children in order to make him better?" (cited in Leon, 1977, p. 591). J.J. Kelso, another important player in the Canadian reform movement, elaborated on this sentiment:

> Gradually we are coming to see that youthful offenders against criminal law cannot be reclaimed by force but must be won over to a better life by kindness, sympathy and friendly helpfulness; that we should substitute education for punishment and secure the hearty co-operation of the boy or girl in his or her own reclamation by awakening in them the dormant ambition to excel and to show themselves capable of responding to good influence . . . To save the lad through humane agencies, to awaken in him true repentance, promise of restitution and determination to retrieve the past, is far nobler work, and decidedly more in the public interest than to send him to a felon's cell, with revenge in his heart, and continuance in crime his only ambition. (1907a, p. 106)

rehabilitative philosophy
A belief that the right treatment can change a person's attitudes, values, and/or behaviour.

juvenile delinquent
A concept popularized in the Victorian era, referring to children and youth who were considered problematic for a variety of reasons.

reformatories
A 19th-century term for juvenile prisons that were based on a belief in the ability of prisons to reform or change an individual.

Others worried that anything less than a term in an institution would serve to "cheapen" the offence in the mind of the offender. An apparent rash of thefts in the city of Halifax in 1908 was attributed to a growing tendency toward "lenient" sentencing.

> The boys know perfectly well that their youth is sure to plead eloquently and with probable success for 'release on suspended sentence'. There was a time when a boy suffered death for stealing a shilling . . . The pendulum has now swung to the extreme point in the opposite direction . . . the present tendency is directly responsible for an increase in the very serious crime of dishonesty. (E.H. Blois, Superintendent of the Protestant Industrial School, cited in "Suspended sentences . . . ," 1908)

A century earlier, it had been argued in public debates that improper parenting was the cause of youth problems. By the end of the 19th century, improper parenting was once again emerging in the public discourse as the primary "cause" of youth crime. This time around, the claims took on a new dimension. Now, youth problems were attributed not to a lack of parental discipline or a loss of authority, but to neglectful or immoral parents. Poor working-class parents were viewed as inadequate or as bad role models for their children (see Box 1.3). The public issue in the latter decades of the 19th century was the moral state of youth and children, in particular those from working-class backgrounds. As West (1991) notes:

> Juvenile crime and misbehaviour were seen as not only evils linked to working-class and immigrant parents' drunkenness, sexual immorality, laboural sloth, and resultant poverty, but also as a challenge to a moral crusade for the construction of a New Jerusalem on this "virgin" continent. (p. 6)

By the end of the 19th century, the juvenile delinquent had been born, and "growing up on the street became the subject of public condemnation and regulation . . . a life style—a street culture—had become the most common definition of juvenile delinquency" (Houston, 1982, p. 131).

VOICES BOX 1.3

Early 20th-Century Analysis of Case Files from an Orphanage

CASE A:
Samuel, age 7, entered the institution January 12, 1917.

The Problem

1. Delinquency

   (a) Petty pilfering.
   (b) Sexual precocity.
   (c) Uses obscene language.
   (d) Tells lies.

2. School

   Expelled after a few months in kindergarten class, because of attack on little girls.

(continued)

Box 1.3 continued

3. Home

   (a) Disobedient and impertinent.
   (b) Unmanageable.
   (c) Attempted sex act on mother.

4. Society

   (a) Lured little girls in hallways and lavatories.
   (b) In a number of boarding homes, foster-mothers complained that he was troublesome and constantly annoying little girls.
   (c) Friendly and good-tempered.
   (d) Rifled pockets, purses, drawers, any place where he knew money was kept or suspected that it was hidden.
   (e) Offered his stolen gains to little girls for the privilege of taking liberties with them.
   (f) Juvenile Court Record (at age of seven): Sexual precocity. Stealing and lying. Minor without proper care . . .

The Analysis

1. Mental

   (a) Examination—Psychiatrist's Report:
   Intelligence: Apparently normal.
   Character: Poor basis and poor organization.
   Health: Normal.
   Impression: Definite sexual pervert.
   (b) Personality Traits:
   Sweet, winning manners. Ready smiles. In appearance, an overgrown, innocent, and lovely baby.
   Hearty eater. Excessively fond of ice-cream, soda-water, and candy.
   Plays with dolls and picture-books. No desire for any boy's toys.
   Sleeps like a baby, and sucks his thumb . . .

3. Social

   (a) Heredity: . . . Boy believed to be illegitimate . . .
Mother: slovenly, brazen, and of questionable character . . . Blond. Extremely attractive in appearance . . .

Had been cared for till three years of age by a very young colored girl, paid by the mother . . .

After that age, he was left to himself in the streets . . .

At the age of four, he was taken by the mother to the Psychiatric Clinic and examined upon her complaint that, when sleeping with her, he had attempted to assault her.

The mother also said that she had noticed he had marked sexual tendencies since babyhood, and was always trying to entice little girls into her home, for the purpose of attacking them.

She further complained that he stole money, used vile language, and was very unreliable and troublesome.

At the age of five, the neighbors reported him as a menace to their children and an incorrigible.

He was then taken from his home and sent to a boarding home . . .

Samuel's Story:

. . . In spite of the fact that he was only seven years old, he spoke with the knowledge of a man of the world. His mother had been a prostitute, and had entertained men in his presence ever since he could remember anything. She had never done any cooking, but had fed him on delicatessen stuff and beer since babyhood. He had been made to join his mother and her "friends" at their cardgames, and told how he had seen his mother and the men at times steal money from one another, "in a cute way." "Nobody was ever caught," he said, "and I asked the smartest one, Mr. Hinky, to learn me how, and he learned me."

There were even worse things that the poor little lad learned. Sometimes some men would give him money for candy and send him out of the room for a while; but others did not even heed the presence of the child. The mother seemed entirely indifferent to his presence or absence; and the boy in describing the immorality of which his mother had accused him, said, as if he were narrating some very usual incident, "Honest, I didn't mean to do any wrong. I seen the men do it and I wanted to do it too."

He also described, in full revolting detail, the acts of sex-perversion his mother's visitors had taught him; and added that they all laughed when he did it and said he was "a smart kid."

It was easy to understand how the spirit of imitation had prompted the child to wrongdoing, of the serious consequence of which he was utterly unconscious; and how, in his many foster homes, he had easily succumbed to the temptations excited by the propinquity of little girls (pp. 329–334).

CASE C:

Mary, age 15, entered the institution July 20, 1916.

The Problem

1. Delinquency

   (a) Attempted suicide by drinking carbolic acid.
   (b) Morbid; melancholic; obsessed by thoughts of suicide and death.
   (c) Exceedingly difficult case—first in child-caring institution, and then in girls' home, working girls' club, and in different private homes—by reason of extreme untidiness, disobedience, and impertinence.
   (d) Very quarrelsome and unwilling to do any work.
   (e) Indolent; defiant and anti-social.
   (f) Undesirable associations.

2. The School

   (a) Very poor scholarship. Had not gone beyond the Fourth Grade.
   (b) Antagonized teachers by attitude of indifference and general carelessness.
   (c) Frequent truancy.

(continued)

Box 1.3 continued

3. Home

    (a) Unmanageable and very troublesome in institutions, and defiant and quarrelsome in own and private homes.

    (b) Obstinate, sullen, and bitter.

    (c) Discontented and very miserable, brooding over possibilities of revenge, and encouraging sentiments of hatred, resentment, and rebellion, to one and all alike.

4. Society

    (a) Intolerant of reproof; bitterly incensed against any criticism.

    (b) Disobedient and disrespectful to elders, and very quarrelsome with girls of the same age.

    (c) Freely expressing hate and scorn for her superiors.

    (d) Disliked; ostracized by young people of both sexes . . .

The Analysis

1. (a) Examination—Psychiatrist's Report:
    . . . Health: Poor. Congenital syphilis. Should be under anti-syphilitic treatment.
    Impression: Peculiar circumstances affecting the case render institutional adjustment impossible. Superior private home should prove beneficial. Wholesome, sympathetic environment, and essential for improvement.

    (b) Personality Traits:
    Untidy in habits. Careless about person.
    Deep wrinkles marked by an habitual frown strongly outlined on the young face.
    Sullen, unfriendly attitude to strangers, very retiring, and very anxious to avoid the least attempt at social intercourse.
    Pessimistic, bitter, biting words ready to flow from her lips at the smallest provocation.
    Hasty, furtive glance, as if both ashamed and afraid.
    Hands never still: either fingers interlacing, or pulling at the knuckles, or the nails being bitten.
    Sad, unyouthful drooping of the head.

3. Social

    (a) Heredity:
Father: . . . The first impression usually formed of him is that of an illiterate, ignorant, and besotted wretch . . .

He found his near-sightedness a very convenient explanation for many of his delinquencies, even offering his defective vision in exculpation of the brutal beating he had administered to his wife . . . His gross sensualism and corrupt morals stamped him a moral degenerate. He was afflicted with syphilis in an infectious state . . .

The four children had been sent to institutions, when their mother's insanity deprived them of her care. In April 1911, the man suddenly appeared in the institution where his daughter and two younger sons were living, and demanded that the children be returned to him . . .

In February 1915, his daughter, then a girl of fourteen, attempted to commit suicide by poison. In the hospital, she gave as the reason for her act seduction by her father.

The man was arrested and in March 1915, was sentenced to three years in the penitentiary, on the charge of incest.

Mother: . . . In addition to her four living children, she had a number of miscarriages and abortions. Steeped in direst poverty, ill-treated and constantly deserted by her husband, the poor woman, whatever her reasons may have been for clinging to the creature she married, at no time manifested any independence of thought or action, but submissively accepted her ruined life without complaint. When her neighbors, outraged at the treatment accorded her, had the man brought to court, she always intervened in his favor and had him pardoned.

She was infected with syphilis by her husband, first became paralyzed, then insane, and was sent to the State Hospital for the Insane, where she remained till her death, in 1916.

Mary's Story:

. . . "It's no use," she ended bitterly, "wherever I'll be, wherever I'll go, they'll soon know all about it. Why didn't they let me die at the hospital? I can't live, and they won't let me die. What do they want me to do?" . . .

She was sent to a trade school and carefully watched for any preference that might manifest itself in an individual line of work. Ultimately she evinced great enthusiasm for the milliner's art, and while she was learning to become "a hat artist," as she quaintly expressed it, efforts were made to give her the benefits of well-regulated and wholesome home life. The sympathies and interest of her boarding-home mother had been enlisted, by informing the woman only of such facts as were necessary to awaken her pity, with the happy result that she was very gentle and patient with the girl's faults.

After six months' apprenticeship, she became the "hat artist" she yearned to be, and shortly earned a salary sufficient to support herself. "It's not such a bad thing to be alive," she confided, as with the joy of achievement shining in her eyes, she told of the "creations" which had brought her a substantial raise; "that is," she hastily caught herself, "if they let you live."

Source: Drucker & Hexter (1923, pp. 352–365).

The Era of the Juvenile Delinquent: The 20th Century

The turn of the 20th century saw continued increases in population and a rapid growth of cities that was accompanied by a variety of social issues, including increases in youth crime. As cities grew and commercial activities expanded, there were more opportunities for criminal activities and for different types of crime. The expansion of the railway brought breaches of the Railway Act, the introduction of the automobile brought car theft, and the growth of the banking industry brought increases in bank robberies—all offences engaged in by teenagers as well as adults (Carrigan, 1991, pp. 218–219).

Statistics for all of Canada show dramatic increases in youth crime rates throughout the 20th century. Convictions of children under 16 increased by over 124 percent between 1911 and 1921, and by over 67 percent between 1921 and 1931 (Carrigan 1991, p. 219). During the 1920s, drug use and drug dealing surfaced as a social issue and led to a number of arrests and convictions of young people in Canadian cities.

> Authorities in Vancouver claimed that drugs were in common use among boys and girls fifteen to eighteen years of age, and children were brought before the courts on drug charges in a number of cities . . . Newspapers carried stories claiming that young boys were selling in the streets. Dope dealers, it was claimed, were offering free drugs to young people to get them addicted. (Carrigan, 1991, p. 221)

One city particularly troubled by high rates of delinquency and an apparent rise in serious offences during this period was Winnipeg. According to Kaminski's 1994 analysis of delinquency rates in Manitoba, from 1926 to 1935, rates of youth crime in Winnipeg surpassed any other Canadian city, including Toronto. "In the 1920s and early 1930s, the years just before and just after the stock market crash of October 1929 and into the decade of the Great Depression, youth crime trends were regarded with alarm" (Kaminski, 1994, p. 1). Public concern in Manitoba about youth crime was such that in 1934, the province's attorney general asked the Welfare Supervision Board to conduct a study of juvenile delinquency (Kaminski, 1993, p. 1). The commissioning of this study and the final reports of the board are notable for the fact that by the time the study began, youth crime rates were on the decline. Nonetheless, the board continued to speak of "the crime problem," arguing that immigrants and their children were responsible (Kaminski, 1994).

While crime rates in Manitoba during the 1930s declined to levels lower than they had been in the early 1920s, statistics from other provinces show a continued escalation in juvenile convictions through to 1945. The statistics for the country as a whole (see Table 1.3) show a similar growth, with minor fluctuations from year to year (Statistics Canada, 1947). From 1963 to 1983, youth crime continued to increase, with some fluctuations. Table 1.4 shows a decline in the theft category from 1971 to 1976 and declines in all categories except theft, offensive weapons, and municipal bylaws from 1980 to 1983. Overall, the figures suggest there was more youth crime in 1983 than 20 years earlier and that youth crime levels were higher in both these periods than they were in 1945.

Increases in the numbers of youth involved in criminal activity do not necessarily mean that young people were or are behaving in a more criminal manner. As the total number of people in a population increases, the amount of crime will also increase simply because there are more people to engage in criminal activity. Another way of looking at youth crime is to compare standardized rates, which account for differences in overall population size and composition. These statistics also show increases in youth crime throughout the 20th century. In 1911, the conviction rate for youth 10–15 years of age was 172 per 100,000 population. In 1921, the rate was 300 per 100,000 and by 1931, it had climbed to 423 per 100,000. From 1940 to 1954, it dropped to slightly under 300 per 100,000, but rose to a high of 459 per 100,000 in 1966 (Carrigan, 1991). In 1989, the rate of youth crime was 2,568 per 100,000 (Winterdyk, 1996, p. 15). Of course, as we will see in Chapter 2, the 1989 rate is not directly comparable to earlier rates because it is indicative of criminal activity, while the earlier rates refer only to convicted young people.

Another comparative technique is to examine what proportion of all crime is accounted for by young people. In 1972, juveniles accounted for 19.5 percent of all

TABLE 1.3

Convictions of Juveniles for Major Offences, by Province, Years Ended September 30, 1922–1945

Year	P.E.I.	N.S.	N.B.	Que.	Ont.	Man.	Sask.	Alta.	B.C.	Canada
1922	5	167	45	655	1,852	627	196	240	278	4,065
1923	10	253	60	864	1,633	581	249	246	268	4,165
1924	31	251	59	782	1,977	750	362	192	251	4,655
1925	18	263	77	971	2,064	915	280	215	277	5,080
1926	6	187	55	870	2,081	1,002	246	326	317	5,090
1927	21	174	169	888	2,033	989	253	267	362	5,156
1928	11	225	145	880	1,800	970	273	340	419	5,063
1929	7	158	130	882	1,962	976	318	349	374	5,106
1930	10	203	131	1,033	2,155	869	381	443	428	5,653
1931	14	155	166	1,260	1,758	885	297	430	346	5,311
1932	4	184	186	1,293	1,772	820	229	306	302	5,096
1933	9	209	262	1,426	1,686	786	149	261	356	5,144
1934	9	300	155	1,444	1,814	635	185	409	401	5,353
1935	33	240	247	1,633	2,059	428	239	318	317	5,514
1936	20	321	204	1,324	2,021	275	228	315	262	4,970
1937	46	344	276	1,392	2,016	196	311	344	299	5,224
1938	21	283	224	1,357	2,162	222	225	298	263	5,055
1939	45	228	244	1,245	2,164	293	201	321	277	5,018
1940	41	195	251	1,461	2,229	286	208	364	262	5,298
1941	58	244	344	1,637	2,588	315	263	378	377	6,204
1942	60	220	279	1,617	3,071	503	397	472	301	6,920
1943	53	373	337	1,455	2,804	363	359	349	401	6,494
1944	82	362	363	1,212	2,901	345	356	431	477	6,529
1945	55	390	221	1,239	2,394	277	282	384	516	5,758

Source: *Canada Yearbook 1947*, Cat. No. 11–402, p. 253.

TABLE 1.4

Juvenile Crime: Selected Offences, 1963–1983

Offences	1963	1971	1976	1980	1983
Assaults	652	1,390	1,926	7,792	6,439
Robbery	345	790	1,339	2,641	1,354
Breaking and entering	8,052	14,989	23,212	42,175	34,524
Theft–motor vehicle	3,736	5,178	7,680	10,064	5,651
Theft over $50	1,849	4,663	2,263*	6,120*	6,329*
Offensive weapons	202	340	700	1,601	2,104
Provincial statutes	3,974	8,860	12,062	21,666	20,116
Municipal by-laws	1,571	1,345	1,023	2,420	2,959

*Theft over $200.

Sources: Adapted from Statistics Canada, Cat. Nos. 85–201, 85–202, 85–205.

persons charged with Criminal Code offences; by 1980, they accounted for 32.2 percent (Carrigan, 1991, p. 238). In 1989, young people under 18 years of age were responsible for 22 percent of all Criminal Code charges and by 1999, 19 percent (Statistics Canada, 1999a, p. 19). In 2003, Statistics Canada reported that youth accounted for 17 percent of all Criminal Code charges (Wallace, 2004, p. 25). Thus, while there may be higher numbers of youth involved in crime, since youth charges relative to adults are slightly lower than they were 35 years ago, it is reasonable to assume that youth today may account for the same proportion of overall crime as youth in even earlier periods. This is certainly the case for Nova Scotia where, as we reported at the start of the chapter, youth under 18 accounted for 18 percent of all Criminal Code charges in both 1909–1910 and 1993–1994, and that for Canada as a whole in 1998, youth under 18 accounted for 19 percent of all Criminal Code charges and 16 percent of all violent crime.

MYTHS AND FACTS ABOUT YOUTH CRIME

It is tempting to conclude from the foregoing discussion of the history of youth crime in Canada that nothing has changed for at least 200 years. To some extent this is true. Bernard (1992), from an analysis of 200 years of youth crime in the United States, draws the same conclusion. Some things about youth crime in Canada have not changed; for example, over the last century in Canada, the sheer volume of **official crime** has increased, but the overall pattern of youth crime has not. Most youth crime has consisted of minor property crime, with a small proportion involving serious personal injury or death to others. Young males have always been responsible for the largest share of criminal activity engaged in by young people.

official crime
Offender and offence data based on information collected for administrative purposes by justice agencies such as the police, courts, and correctional institutions.

Another thing that has not changed is that most people always seem to think pessimistically about youth crime (and justice)—that youth crime is worse than it actually is, that there is a "crime wave" among the youth population. Bernard argued that this is the "myth that nothing changes" (1992, p. 12). It is a belief typically shared by some youth advocates. While it is true that youth crime has always existed, we have seen that how it is perceived and understood does change over time, as do the kinds of activities in which young people are involved. With the growth of industrialization and urbanization came increases in property crime and the specific nature of these crimes, just as our current "technological age" is opening up opportunities for cyber crimes such as "chat room bullying" and "hacking." Furthermore, as West (1991) observes, a century ago, Canadian streets were also filled with "errant youths: but, now, in addition to the traditional mainstay of [begging, brawling] and petty property crime, instead of selling newspapers and pencils, they offer 'speed,' 'crack,' 'ecstasy,' and they still offer their bodies if not their very souls and lives" (p. 9).

On the other hand, there is the widespread "myth of the good old days" that is characteristic of the law-and-order group. More people seem to believe that youth crime is worse today than ever before and that youth no longer respect authority, rather than that "nothing has changed." Bernard argued that this myth is "true some of the time and false some of the time." The problem is that people "believe it without any particular concern about whether it is true. People always like to believe in the 'good old days,' whether delinquency was actually better or worse back then" (1992, p. 13). The important assumption to investigate in this view is that "youth crime is more serious now than in the past" and the answer depends on one's interpretation of the historical data. Statistics do not speak for themselves; their meaning is a matter of interpretation, and interpretations can differ dramatically depending on the statistics and information being viewed.

Is Youth Crime More Serious Now?

According to Carrigan (1991), a non-critical social historian, youth crime in the 1990s was out of control:

> The post-World War Two era witnessed some dramatic changes in juvenile delinquency. Offences increased significantly and the trend was toward more major crimes and more violence. Manifestations of the new direction were found in all parts of the country as young people turned to alcohol and drugs, and captured media attention by the commission of major and sometimes brutal crimes. The violent turn taken by many delinquents in the form of assaults, weapons offences, and destruction of property had continued; indeed, this trend seems to have worsened by the early 1990s. The most publicized examples are the gangs of teenagers who now terrorize many communities across the country . . . The nature of these gangs, in contrast to those of an earlier day, offers a vivid illustration of the changed direction that modern delinquency has taken. In 1965 the Department of Justice Committee on Juvenile Delinquency reported that "gang delinquency is generally not a problem in the large urban areas of Canada." Obviously things have changed. (p. 242)

A more sociological and critical reading and interpretation of youth crime statistics would point to a number of factors that could account for increases that have little or nothing to do with changes in actual delinquent or criminal behaviour among youth. As we will see in the next chapter, the 20th century was the period in Canadian history when the juvenile court was created, and it was also a period of rapid population growth. Hence, we should expect increases in criminal activity over time for at least two reasons. The Canadian population increased and a new organization was created specifically to work with children who were involved in criminal and delinquent activity. Schissel's examination of Criminal Code charges for youth from 1973 to 1995 (1997) clearly indicates that the Young Offenders Act created increased crime rates, because more youth were arrested and brought to court than under the Juvenile Delinquents Act (pp. 80–81).

Furthermore, as we will see in Chapter 8, changes in policing, juvenile legislation, and administrative practices affect official crime rates, as do public pressures to "crack down on crime." Therefore, even though official crime statistics show increases in youth crime over the last century, we cannot assume that youth behaviour is any worse now than in past decades. Contrary to Carrigan's view, Tanner (1996), a sociologist, argued that youth crime and even gang activity are no more or less serious today than they were in the past. He reminds us that, in the 1940s, the Toronto *Globe and Mail* was given to such proclamations as "Another outbreak of street gang fighting has reawakened citizens to the extent of the problems these young people present" (1996, p. 1). This particular story concerned Halloween riots in 1945 that ended with some 7,000 people besieging a police station in Toronto's west end because 13 young men had been arrested for setting fires and vandalism (Campbell, 1998; Tanner, 1996, p. 3). Similarly, Bernard (1992, p. 24) points out that street gang violence drives the action in Shakespeare's *Romeo and Juliet*, a play that takes place in 15th-century Italy.

"Outbreaks" of crime and gang activity are also a matter of interpretation. Zatz's classic research on gangs in Phoenix, Arizona (1987), cautions us that gang activity is often over-reported and exaggerated by both the news media and the police. According to her study, notwithstanding news and police reports of increasing gang activities in Phoenix, police files and records showed no difference between gang members and non-gang delinquency in terms of level or type of offences. It is important to remember when interpreting official statistics that both the police and the media have a vested interest in crime—it ensures their jobs. For journalists, crime is "news"; for the police, "crime waves" usually mean increased funding for policing activities.

Further complicating our attempts at interpretation is that the information available to us is limited and not always comparable from one period to another. Comparing crime statistics from different periods and drawing anything other than tentative conclusions is extremely difficult. Throughout this chapter, the terms "youth crime" and "delinquency" have been variously used, depending on which term was used in the original reports. However, the terms are not necessarily measuring the same behaviours. Legally speaking, "delinquency" and the "delinquent" young person ceased to exist with the passage of the Young Offenders Act; they were replaced with the terms "youth crime" and "young offenders." "Youth crime" statistics tend to measure Criminal Code offences, while "delinquency" statistics also include non-criminal "offences" such as incorrigibility. (Chapters 2 and 3 will discuss the differences between these terms in more detail.) Hence, with regard to the "myth of the good old days," sometimes it is true and sometimes it is not, depending on the data one is consulting, the perspective that is brought to that interpretation, and the frame of reference. If we are looking for "gang" activity or violent youth crime that existed and was a cause of public concern in the past, we can always find it if we go back far enough. However, if we pick a particular period or place (urban vs. rural) for our search, it may not be there. This period then is the "good old days" (Bernard, 1992, p. 13). This is why perhaps, when a particularly horrific crime occurs in a small town or a "nice" neighbourhood, we hear people expressing their shock that something like this could have occurred. For them, in their space and in their memory (history), it probably never has. For them, there were "good old days."

The final myth discussed by Bernard (1992, p. 13) is not common at all—the "myth of progress." This myth is based on the notion that youth crime is not as bad now as it was in the past, and very few people share this belief. Hence, for most, it is considered a myth that there has been progress in levels or seriousness of youth crime—progress is a myth. Yet, as we will see in Chapter 3, for some types of crime, such as murder, we do see progress, so it is a myth that there has been no progress. Far fewer young people are responsible for homicides in Canada today than 30 years ago, so the myth of progress is true, although few believe this.

A SOCIOLOGICAL PERSPECTIVE ON YOUTH CRIME

The argument from the foregoing discussion is that to a great extent, youth crime is about what people believe it to be, perceive it to be, and this takes us to a discussion of the sociological perspective on youth crime and its use as an organizing component in this book. A sociological perspective is different from other perspectives, such as a psychological one, because the sociologist tries to put the individual into a larger context to understand behaviour; the individual's history, family, school, or neighbourhood become important, but that then leads to questions about the family, school, and neighbourhood that also need to be understood in a context—the history of the family and the structure of government and how that regulates family, or the culture, economy, polity, and philosophy of Canadian or Western society, and the impact of all of these factors on family structure and dynamics. This too also needs a broader context for a fuller understanding, one more global that locates Canada in Western society and Western society in the international community. Hence, sociological questions about crime in general and youth crime in particular range from looking at why individuals behave as they do, by examining the family, school, or peers, to questions about crime in a global context.

Questions about crime also include questions about the meaning of crime, how we talk about it and define it, how we respond to it and regulate it, and how we think about both. In other words, a sociological perspective on youth crime goes beyond the question of whether crime levels are increasing or decreasing because the sociologist asks questions about why crime levels change. Hence, from a sociological perspective, our discussion on the history of youth crime takes us far beyond the question of interest in public forums about whether youth crime is increasing, or is more violent, or whether the justice system is able to control youth crime. The history of youth crime tells us that youth crime and how it is regulated, from era to era, is periodically defined as problematic and, as a result, becomes a public issue. What is important from a sociological perspective revolves around the nature and dynamics of public issues because their dynamics serve to frame what is problematic. The main questions here concern why youth crime is a public issue and how it is problematized.

Youth Crime as a Public Issue

Public issues, in particular, youth crime issues, are influenced more by **structural,** social, **demographic,** and political factors than by actual criminal behaviour. As discussed earlier in this chapter, children made up a significant portion of the population of Upper and Lower Canada. Before industrialization, life expectancy was considerably lower than it is today. As a result, more than half of the population was usually under 25 years of age, and there were twice as many school-aged children as middle-aged people (Gottlieb, 1993). By the 19th century, these population proportions began to change and today they are roughly equal. Smandych (1995, p. 15) argued that these demographic shifts partially explain why the "deviant" behaviour of children began to be viewed differently by adults. These shifts stimulated structural changes (such as legislation restricting child labour and enforced compulsory schooling), which in turn had consequences for the social status of children and youth.

As children were moved out of factories as a result of child labour laws in the 19th century, they became a sedentary population and, at the same time, a surplus population. Children were no longer useful as labourers and producers. As a result, their social status and position within their communities and families changed from one of economic asset to one of economic liability (Smandych, 2001a, p. 18) and consequently to one of dependence on adults for their survival. West (1991, p. 12) describes the status of youth in the 20th century as that of **denied adulthood.** Children and youth in the 20th century are subordinate to adult authority and are not permitted such adult rights as holding decision-making positions, working for a wage, obtaining credit, getting married, or engaging in adult pleasures. As a result, youth and children are not only dependent but are also marginal to adult society and exist on the periphery; their status is a **marginalized** one. They are the "Other," the stranger in the midst of adult society, and the stranger is always suspect. Adults not only control youth through their dependent and marginalized status, it is the adult who defines the meaning of youth— who they are, their place, and their purpose. In this regard, for the adult, they become a "mirror of society" (Rush, 1992) or "projection screens" (Davis, 1990), reflecting both what adults wish for and what they fear. They are made to "represent . . . the hopes and fears of a nation" (Brown, 2005, p. 210). As Rush puts it, increases in youth crime are indicative of "impending social doom" (1992, p. 24).

structural
Refers to how something is ordered and organized, how its parts relate and connect to each other and to the whole.

demographics
The basic or vital statistics of a group, usually factors such as age, gender, ethnicity, marital status.

denied adulthood
Refers to the notion that youth, because of their legal dependency in Western society, are prevented from attaining the things that many adults take for granted, such as the right to make decisions about their own lives and the right to express their views.

marginalized
A condition in which people are excluded from mainstream society. This exclusion can be economic, social, cultural, political, or all four.

As we have seen, the media play a crucial role in defining youth as "a dangerous class," largely because of the pervasiveness of media news coverage in today's society and because people with only a little information about a particular crime are more fearful and punitive than those with more information (Covell & Howe, 1996, pp. 347, 352). Hence, the media play a crucial role in ". . . constructing youth crime into a social issue" (Hartnagel & Baron, 1995, p. 56). Since youth, as the Other, are threatening to adult society and are perceived as continually "troubled" or "troubling" (Tanner, 1996, p. 17), sensationalistic media coverage of youth crime easily arouses public fear and moral indignation. Stanley Cohen (1972) refers to this phenomenon as "**moral panic.**" Furthermore, Critcher (2003) maintains that as the Other, youth are subject to the extremism of moral panics. The media generate a panic about youth crime through continual and sensationalized crime reporting. It then reinforces this panic through selective reporting of public outrage toward "out of control" youth—an outrage that usually implicated the YOA as a "cause" and now blames the YCJA.

moral panic
Refers to situations where people, groups, circumstances, or events are defined and perceived to be a threat to security and public order.

Schissel (1997) argues that media crime reporting does more than sensationalize. In his view, it presents "hateful, stereotypical views of youth misconduct" (p. 49) and identifies the poor and marginalized as dangerous people from whom law-abiding citizens need police protection. In these media accounts, race and class become "code words for gang criminality," and class and gender are code words for factors that "cause" youth crime—poor mothers lacking in parenting skills. Because of this, Schissel argues that media crime reporting borders on hate literature (p. 51). He states:

> Hatred and fear are political emotions that people in positions of political and economic power use to garner public opinion. Fear and hatred are staples of popular culture and populist politics . . . [T]hey exist as an unquestioned part of our ideology and discourse. Hatred is fundamental to news accounts [about crime], and fear is what sells them . . . [T]he groups who dominate the media—white, male, professional, capitalist classes—hold hateful, stereotypical views of youth misconduct. Further, when they present these views, they obliterate other, more favourable images of youth. (1997, pp. 31, 49–50)

Criminologists have identified a variety of ways in which printed news media promote panic, hatred, and fear about youth. As we saw in examples of headlines at the beginning of this chapter, headlines frame the discussion to follow in a "predetermined ideological context" (Schissel, 1997, p. 41)—teens are violent and out of control. The stories that follow take the form of morality plays that prey on adults' fear of crime and an immoral world by presenting atypical, unusual youth crimes as typical and representative of youth behaviour (Reid, 2005; Schissel, 1997, p. 33). Most importantly, the media **decontextualizes** criminal events and the lives of those accused of the crimes. Crimes are always, by the limiting nature of newspapers, discussed out of the context within which they occur. Context is provided by the journalist, usually in a manner that generates a number of emotions: fear, moral outrage, despair, panic, and hatred. These emotions are easily displaced to the vulnerable in society, the marginalized youth, by the details provided about the crime event—such as "teen shows no remorse" (Schissel, 1997, p. 37). The message in these stories is also decontextualized by what is missing (Reid, 2005). Stories of youth crime seldom present the views of youth advocates, rather it is the voices of police officers and Crown prosecutors, victims, and irate individuals that are heard. In this way, media discourse is extremely powerful in promoting the law-and-order agenda and reinforcing a sense that nothing can be done about youth crime but to implement ever more punitive repressive measures of control (Kappeler, Blumberg, & Potter, 1996; Schissel, 1997, p. 37).

decontextualize
Remove something from its context.

For some, moral panics are what we should be concerned about and the problem that needs to be addressed. Schissel, for example, argues that the moral panic about youth is a far greater problem than youth crime.

> I contend that we are on the verge of an acute "moral panic" in this country that, if allowed to continue, will result in the continuing scapegoating of youth for political purposes and, as is the irony of punishment, the alienation of a more uncompromising, more disaffiliated youth population . . . Despite the hollow political rhetoric to the contrary, Canadians scarcely consider children a valuable resource. In fact, we consider them to be one of our most dangerous threats. (1997; 2001, p. 84)

While questions about youth crime and whether it is changing are debatable, what has clearly changed over the last century is how Canadians have perceived, defined, responded to, and regulated the misdeeds and criminal acts of children and youth. At the turn of the 19th century, the public view of youth crime was of delinquents engaged in juvenile delinquency. One hundred years later, the view was of young offenders engaged in youth crime (Smandych, 1995, pp. 14, 20). Now, as we begin the 21st century, the legislative terminology—beginning with its title: the Youth *Criminal* Justice Act—is poised to frame the public issue as one of "youth criminals" (Hogeveen & Smandych, 2001, p. 166). Certainly, as we saw from the discussion of newspaper headlines and story content, this new frame is already developing.

The next chapter discusses the other set of questions in the public discourse about youth crime and the other focus of moral panics: how we respond to and regulate youth crime. Its focus is on changes in Canadian laws and public perceptions regarding children and crime in the 20th century. In brief, we no longer think of young people as children in need of care and guidance. Over the last 20 years, Canadians have come to believe that young people need to be held "responsible" for their criminal behaviour. The basic elements of this way of thinking are not new; this view brings us closer to treating child and youth offenders in the same manner as adult offenders, and thus to the response of authorities in the colonial era to children and youth involved in criminal behaviour.

SUMMARY

The argument presented in this chapter is that the problem of youth crime, defined as "out of control" youth and an ineffectual justice system, is not new and that equally important issues to address are the myths about youth crime and justice as well as the moral panic that surrounds both. While the history of youth crime suggests that we are not facing a "youth crime wave," what has changed is the discourse of youth crime and how it is problematized. Now, instead of saving the children from their corrupt and immoral environments, we are concerned about a depraved class of youth criminals preying on the good people of society.

A common view of youth crime, the one most often reflected in the media, is the law-and-order perspective. This view sees youth crime as out of control and far more serious than it was in the past. An opposing perspective, that of youth advocates, argues that youth crime is probably no better or worse than in other periods in history. From this perspective, the most important issues are youth marginalization and the social problems affecting youth, not youth crime.

In the colonial era, from the earliest time of European settlement in North America to the early 1800s, anyone over the age of 7 who committed a crime could be treated the same as an adult. Some convicted children were imprisoned with adults, while others were executed. English common law allowed leniency for children 7 to 14, and many were indeed treated more leniently than adults. Colonial administrators worried that children and youth had too much freedom and lacked respect for authority.

The mid-1800s to the turn of the century, the Victorian period, witnessed increasing numbers of poor, abandoned, orphaned, and neglected children in North American cities. This period also witnessed perceptions of a rise in criminal activity by children and young people. Concerns were expressed about children's well-being as well as their behaviour. Reformers wanted to "save" the children of the poor from corrupting and criminalizing influences.

The post-Victorian era, the modern period, was characterized by a rise in official criminal and delinquent behaviour by children and young people. Much of this increase can be attributed to demographic changes, changes in the administration of juvenile justice, and changes in police practices.

Despite the limitations of historical records pertaining to youth crime, it appears that we have always had youth crime, that young men are responsible for most of this crime, and that most youth crime is of a petty nature, with only a small proportion involving serious violent crime. Young girls have always been sexually exploited in the prostitution trade by men, and children and youth have always stolen what they needed to ensure their material survival. Only the specifics of the crimes and the availability of different goods to sell (e.g., crack, speed, and ecstasy) are different today.

Public concerns about youth crime today are similar in many ways to those expressed in the past. People worry today as they did in the colonial era that children have no respect for authority, that they have too much freedom, and that we need more policing of youth. Similarly, in the Victorian era, people worried about bad parenting and lack of appropriate guidance for youth. What is different is the gradual criminalizing of youth issues. Over the last 100 years, we have gone from talking about youth as "delinquent" to "young offenders" to "youth criminals."

The media are major and powerful players in public discourse. They frame the discourse in such a way as to define and reproduce views of youth and youth crime in a manner that promotes hatred and fear. A result is moral panic. Some maintain that moral panics are a greater problem than is youth crime.

DISCUSSION/CRITICAL THINKING QUESTIONS

1. Can we answer questions about the severity of youth crime today compared to the past? Explain your answer.
2. Should the media be prevented from the reproduction of materials that reinforce and perpetuate harmful views of marginalized groups and individuals? Explain your answer.
3. Who has the most realistic view of youth crime and justice: the law-and-order group or youth advocates? Explain your answer.

WEB LINKS

What's the matter with kids today?
www.uoguelph.ca/news/alumnus/backissues/Fall01/9.html

Youth Crime Is Not Out of Control
www.expressnews.ualberta.ca/article.cfm?id=3529

PBS: Little Criminals
www.pbs.org/wgbh/pages/frontline/shows/little

Problem Youth
www.track16.com/exhibitions/site/youth.html

For chapter quizzes and more links, visit this book's accompanying website at
www.bellyoungoffenders3e.nelson.com

CHAPTER TWO

Creating a Juvenile Justice System: Then and Now

CHAPTER OBJECTIVES

1. To trace the history of the Canadian juvenile justice system from its origins in the 19th century to the present.
2. To situate opposition to the Young Offenders Act (YOA) and the Youth Criminal Justice Act (YCJA) in a historical context.
3. To discuss details and interpretations of the principles underlying the Juvenile Delinquents Act (JDA), the YOA, and the YCJA.
4. To discuss the juvenile justice law reform process from the JDA to the YCJA.
5. To identify concerns about the YCJA.

KEY TERMS

Child savers
Welfare-based juvenile justice system
Parens patriae
Indictable
Probation
Status offences
Limited accountability
Justice

Modified justice
Crime control
Restorative justice
Reparation
Reintegration
Bifurcated
Cycle of juvenile justice

INTRODUCTION

Although today we tend to associate the juvenile justice system with notions of crime prevention and crime control, the creators of the system had other objectives in mind. According to some scholars, the juvenile justice system was created as a response to problems generated by an emerging system of capitalism that served to undermine traditional family supports. Two resulting problems were growing numbers of poor children on the streets and higher levels of street crime committed by young people. This street crime generated fear and a sense among middle-class Victorians that the children of the poor and working class (the "dangerous class") needed to be controlled (Alvi, 1986; Platt, 1969b; West, 1984).

According to other scholars, the juvenile justice system was the creation of Victorian reformers, or **child savers** (Platt, 1969a), who believed that delinquency was the product of bad environments and that the state should act like a parent to "save" children from these environments, even if that meant removing them from their parents' homes and placing them in an institution. These reformers were motivated primarily by humanitarian concerns and a desire to save children from harmful family influences and protect them from the full force of criminal law and the negative influences of adult criminal offenders.

child savers
A term used to refer to 19th-century North American middle-class reformers who were instrumental in the creation of a separate system of justice for juveniles.

The Canadian juvenile justice system was officially created in 1908 through the passage of the Juvenile Delinquents Act. This legislation did not occur in isolation but rather was the culmination of a number of pieces of legislation and welfare reform efforts that began 100 years earlier (see Box 2.1). These legislative initiatives developed from initial welfare/protection provisions, moved to provisions for child and

---

BOX 2.1

Some Precursors to the Juvenile Delinquents Act

1799—An Act to Provide for the Education and Support of Orphaned Children

1813—An Act to Provide for the Maintenance of Persons Disabled and the Widows and Children of Such Persons as May Be Killed in His Majesty's Services

1827—An Act Respecting the Appointment of Guardians

1837—An Act to Make the Remedy in Cases of Seduction More Effectual, and to Render the Fathers of Illegitimate Children Liable for Their Support

1847—An Act for Compensating Families of Persons Killed by Accident, and for Other Purposes Therein Mentioned

1851—An Act to Amend the Law Relating to Apprentices and Minors

1857—(Ontario) An Act for Establishing Prisons for Young Offenders

1857—An Act for the More Speedy Trial and Punishment of Young Offenders

1862—An Act to Incorporate the Boy's Industrial School of the Gore of Toronto

1869—An Act Respecting Juvenile Offenders within the Province of Quebec

(continued)

Box 2.1 *continued*

1870—An Act to Empower the Police Court in the City of Halifax to Sentence Juvenile Offenders to Be Detained in the Halifax Industrial School

1874—(Ontario) An Act Respecting Industrial Schools

1877—(Ontario) An Act Respecting the Reformatory Prisons

1880—An Act Respecting the Reformatory for Juvenile Offenders in Prince Edward Island

1884—An Act Respecting a Reformatory for Certain Juvenile Offenders in the County of Halifax in the Province of Nova Scotia

1886—An Act Respecting Public and Reformatory Prisons

1888—(Ontario) An Act for the Protection and Reformation of Neglected Children

1890—(Ontario) An Act Respecting the Custody of Juvenile Offenders; An Act Respecting the Commitment of Persons of Tender Years

1891—An Act Respecting Certain Female Offenders in the Province of Nova Scotia

1893—An Act Relating to the Custody of Juvenile Offenders in the Province of New Brunswick

1894—An Act Respecting Arrest, Trial and Imprisonment of Youthful Offenders

1903—An Act Respecting the Good Shepherd Reformatory in the City of Saint John, New Brunswick

Source: Leon (1977, pp. 75–79, 82–83, 88).

youth institutions by mid-century as a result of the Brown Commission report in 1849 on Kingston Penitentiary and recommendations regarding the unsuitability of locking up children with adults, and culminated at the end of the century with the development of a system of probation and a separate court system for children and youth (Hogeveen, 2005, pp. 32–34).

This chapter discusses the development, philosophy, and structure of the juvenile justice system under the JDA, how the system was modified by the introduction of the YOA and YCJA, and the reform process for each modification to the system. Interestingly, while there have been significant legal, philosophical, and structural changes to the system over the last century, much of the public opposition surrounding it has remained the same.

THE SOCIAL AND LEGAL UNDERPINNINGS OF THE JUVENILE JUSTICE SYSTEM

The 19th century was a period of industrialization, urbanization, and rapid population growth, much of it from immigration. It was also a period of social reform and increasing concerns among urban middle-class Canadians about the welfare of children and the family. As Sutherland (1976) notes in his analysis of Canadian children in the late 19th and early 20th centuries, this was a period when English Canada "intensified a century-long effort to impose higher standards of order on itself" (p. 95). Governments at all levels were enacting laws designed to curb immorality and encourage moral behaviour. Drinking and spitting in public were prohibited, as was child labour in factories. Campaigns were waged against alcohol and cigarettes, regular school attendance was required, and vaccinations and child welfare programs were encouraged (Sutherland, 1976, p. 95).

Neglected and Delinquent Children

The Victorian child savers were primarily concerned with the welfare of children and families. Thus, their activities and reforms did not focus solely on crime. Of particular concern to reformers were neglected, dependent, and delinquent children (Sutherland, 1976, pp. 97–98). Notions of delinquency came from English common law and applied to children between the ages of 7 and 14 who broke any municipal, provincial, or federal law. This encompassed a broad range of children. Among those considered delinquent were "waifs, arabs, strays, newsboys, hawkers, beggars, habitual truants, and other children of the streets, and children whose parents instructed them in intemperance, vice, and crime" (Sutherland, 1976, p. 97). If it was determined that an accused child aged 7–14 was capable of discerning right from wrong and good from evil, then that child could be convicted and suffer the same penalty as an adult, including execution. Youth over 14 were subject to the same law as adults, while children under 7 were considered unable to distinguish right from wrong. Dependants were children who were considered to be without families, either because they were deemed illegitimate or because they had been abandoned to orphanages (Sutherland, 1976, p. 98). Neglected children were those deemed to be not properly cared for by their parents (see Box 2.2).

BOX 2.2

Legal Definitions of Neglect

Ontario's Act for the Prevention of Cruelty to and Better Protection of Children, passed in 1893, provided for this period the most wide-ranging and widely used descriptions of what, in law, was a neglected child. The Act empowered various officers to apprehend without warrant and bring before a judge as "neglected" any child "apparently under the age of 14" who fitted into one of five general groups. A neglected child, the Act stated, was any child

(1) who was found "begging or receiving alms or thieving . . . or sleeping at nights in the open air";
(2) who was found "wandering about at late hours and not having any home or settled place of abode, or proper guardianship";
(3) who was found "associating or dwelling with a thief, drunkard or vagrant," or who "by reason of the neglect or drunkenness or vices of the parents was 'growing up without salutary parental control and education' or in circumstances which were exposing him 'to an idle or dissolute life'";
(4) who was found "in any house of ill fame, or in the company of a reputed prostitute"; and, finally,
(5) who was found "destitute, being an orphan or having a surviving parent" who was "undergoing imprisonment for a crime."

Source: Sutherland (1976, p. 97).

Public concern about neglected children was part of a larger anti-cruelty movement that began with the creation of Humane Societies mandated to address animal cruelty. While Canadian historians generally credit Toronto and Ontario with developing the first child-protection laws, Fingard (1989, p. 171) maintains that Nova Scotia was the first province to establish a Humane Society. In 1876, the Nova Scotia Society for the Prevention of Cruelty was founded. Initially mandated to address animal protection, by 1880 its activities had been extended through legislation to include neglected women and children. Montreal followed Halifax's lead in 1882 (Fingard, 1989, pp. 171–172). The Toronto Humane Society was established five years later. In 1893, Ontario passed its first child-protection legislation, an Act for the Prevention of Cruelty to and Better Protection of Children, also known as the Children's Charter (Sutherland, 1976, p. 97). Although legislation addressing neglect and cruelty did not begin in Ontario, most of the impetus for the juvenile justice system came from social reformers in Ontario, largely due to the superior financial resources available to Ontario reformers (Fingard, 1989; Sutherland, 1976).

Reformers may have identified different types of "problem" children, but they made no distinctions when responding to these children. For the child savers, only the end result mattered, and the desired result was for children to be "saved" from a life of crime. For Victorian reformers, the only difference between a neglected child and a delinquent child was the difference between a "potential" criminal and an "actual" one (Houston, 1972, p. 263). Leon (1977) elaborates:

> Because of [reformers'] focus on control, or the lack thereof, in the family context, distinctions between behaviour attributed to parental absence or neglect, and behaviour characterized as criminal or delinquent, were not seen to be relevant. The rationale for the control of juvenile misbehaviour, and hence for the prevention of future criminal behaviour, mixed the perceived need for the protection of others from children with the perceived need for the protection of children from themselves and others. The question was not whether a child would be held accountable for his or her behaviour—criminal or otherwise—but rather how best to treat the child in order to effect adequate socialization before the child became a "convicted criminal." If the family was not capable, then the state would intervene to reform the child. (p. 76)

Canadian Child Savers

While many women were involved in the activities of the child-saving movement, two men are credited by historians with creating the juvenile justice system—J.J. Kelso and W.L. Scott. Kelso (1907a, 1907b) was a Toronto newspaper reporter who, through his concern about the plight of poor children in the city, became a driving force behind the establishment of the Toronto Humane Society and the Children's Fresh Air Fund. Following passage of the Ontario Children's Charter in 1893, Kelso was appointed Provincial Superintendent of Neglected and Dependent Children (Sutherland, 1976, p. 112). In this capacity, he began campaigns aimed at getting children, including delinquents, out of institutions and into foster homes.

Kelso's reform activities were complemented by the children's court movement. In 1892, the federal Criminal Code was amended to allow separate non-public trials and custody for those under 16 (Leon, 1977; Sutherland, 1976, p. 115). For its part, the Ontario Children's Charter provided for separate magistrates to hear cases involving youth under 16. It also provided, for youth under 21, separate trials and commitment to places other than prisons (Leon, 1977, p. 83).

Meanwhile children's courts were being established in American cities. In 1906, W.L. Scott, a lawyer and president of the Ottawa Children's Aid Society, went to Philadelphia to examine that city's system of separate children's courts, judges, and probation officers. Before the end of the year, he had persuaded Ottawa to appoint two probation officers for the supervision of child offenders. Scott went on to draft the juvenile delinquents bill, which was accepted in the House of Commons and became law on July 8, 1908 (Sutherland, 1976, pp. 119, 121). This legislation created a justice system for children and youth separate from the adult system.

THE CANADIAN JUVENILE JUSTICE SYSTEM

JDA: Philosophy and Definitions

Section 31 of the Juvenile Delinquents Act (JDA) stated:

> This Act shall be liberally construed to the end that its purpose may be carried out to wit: That the care and custody and discipline of a juvenile delinquent shall approximate as nearly as may be that which should be given by its parent, and that as far as practicable every juvenile delinquent shall be treated, not as a criminal, but as a misdirected and misguided child, and one needing aid, encouragement, help and assistance.

The JDA created a **welfare-based juvenile justice system** (see Table 2.1). The main philosophy underlying the legislation, the justice system it created, and the decision making of justice personnel who implemented the act, came from the doctrine of ***parens patriae,*** meaning "parent of the country" (Reitsma-Street, 1989–1990, p. 512). The doctrine originated in medieval England, where it began as the king's right to control the property of orphaned heirs for the purpose of protection. By the 18th century, *parens patriae* had been expanded to include a "best interest" principle as a means of actively promoting the well-being of a child or young person. By the 19th century, the doctrine had extended beyond the monarch to the state and to children without property who were orphaned or neglected by parents or guardians. The numerous acts of legislation passed in the 19th century to protect young people in need (see, for example, Box 2.1 on pages 35–36) were supported and reinforced by the principle of *parens patriae*. Thus, a doctrine that began as "the King's prerogative" had by the 19th century become "legitimized in common and statutory law in various English-speaking countries" (Reitsma-Street, 1989–1990, pp. 512–513).

Whereas in the United States delinquency was considered a state of being or a condition, under the original JDA, a youth had to break a law, not necessarily criminal, to be adjudicated delinquent by the court. The JDA defined delinquency as the violation by persons under 16 (this age varied by province) of any federal, provincial, or municipal law for which a fine or imprisonment was the penalty, or the commission of any other act that would make the young person liable to be committed to an industrial school or reformatory. In 1924, the act was revised to include a much broader range of behaviour. Following the addition of this omnibus clause, a delinquent was defined in s. 2(1) of the act as

> "any child who violates any provision of the Criminal Code or of any Dominion or provincial statute, or of any bylaw or ordinance of any municipality, or who is guilty of sexual immorality or any similar form of vice, or who is liable by reason of any other act to be committed to an industrial school or juvenile reformatory under the provisions of any Dominion or provincial statute" (cited in West, 1991, p. 33).

welfare-based juvenile justice system
A model of juvenile justice based on a rehabilitative philosophy.

parens patriae
A doctrine based on English common law that gives the state the power to take on a guardian or parenting role for children.

TABLE 2.1

Different Models of Juvenile Justice

	Welfare	Justice	Crime Control	Restorative
Focus	The individual offender's needs	Individual rights	Protection of society	Harm caused by crime Repair harm done to victims Reduce future harm by crime prevention
Philosophy	Best interests of the child and family *Parens patriae*	Minimal interference with freedoms Right to due process	Law and order in society are paramount State responsibility for maintaining order	Peacemaking Reparation of past harms Reconciliation between victims, offenders, and communities
System Features	Informality Indeterminate sentencing Focus on unacceptable behaviour	Focus on criminal offences Determinate sentences	Crime/status offences Punishment Determinate sentences	Full and equal participation of victims, offenders, and communities in the justice process Mediation, conferencing, circles
Key Professionals	Child care and social workers	Lawyers	Lawyers Criminal justice professionals	Community agencies, volunteers, non-profit organizations, criminal justice professionals play a minor role
View of Crime/ Delinquency	Determined by social, psychological, and environmental factors	Free will Individual responsibility	Responsibility Accountability Determinate	A violation of people and relationships
Purpose of Intervention	Treatment	Appropriate sanction	Protection of society Retribution Deterrence	For parties to a crime to work out satisfactory solutions
Purpose of System	Individual rehabilitation	Ensure justice is done Maintain individual rights	Maintenance of social order	Redress for victims Recompense for offenders Community reintegration of victims and offenders

Sources: Adapted from Corrado (1992, p. 4); Reid & Reitsma-Street (1984); Reid-MacNevin (1991, p. 28).

JDA: The System

The JDA gave the courts extensive powers. Cases were to be handled summarily. If an offence was **indictable**, it was up to the court to decide if the youth would be tried in an adult court. More like hearings than trials, juvenile cases were conducted privately and notices of delinquency hearings were sent to parents or guardians. Separate detention and jail facilities were mandated for delinquents. In addition, the JDA provided for a wide range of sentences or dispositions. Within the broad requirement to act in "the child's own good and the best interests of the community," the court could adjourn the hearing, impose a fine for as much as $10, place the child in a foster home or in the care of a Children's Aid Society, impose a probationary sentence, or send the child to an industrial school or reformatory.

indictable
In the Canadian Criminal Code, refers to offences that are of a serious nature; the maximum sentence is never less than two years.

Probation was a central element of the juvenile court, with the probation officer playing a key role. The court could place a child in the custody of a probation officer as a form of sentence. The JDA required probation officers to conduct investigations for the court, to assist and direct the court, and to represent the interests of the child in the court (Leon, 1977, p. 100; Sutherland, 1976, p. 122). The probation officer was also responsible for supervising children sentenced to a period of probation, and W.L. Scott, the "author" of the JDA, envisioned this as probation's most important function (see Box 2.3). Scott argued that the probation officer's object was to work to reform the child and "the whole family" and that this could be achieved only through working with the child in the home, school, and workplace. Interestingly, he envisioned women as more appropriate for probation work because the tasks required were suited to a woman's "nature" and also because, in his view, the labour of even "better-class" women could be obtained more cheaply than that of men.

probation
A sentence of the court that involves supervision in the community and set conditions that must be adhered to if the person is to remain in the community.

VOICES BOX 2.3

W.L. Scott on the Role of the Probation Officer

By far the most important element in the system is probation. It is the keystone of the arch. Without it the Juvenile Court would be almost powerless for good. With it, and nothing else, a vast amount can be done. You cannot deal with children as a class. You must deal with them as individuals. You must win the confidence, the respect, even the love of each individual child, would you make of it what you desire it to be. It is the personal touch that counts, and that touch is supplied by the Probation Officer.

The duties of the Probation Officer are threefold: before trial, at trial, and after trial.

As soon as the child is arrested, or informed against, a Probation Officer is at once notified. Her first duty is to see the child as a friend, to get its confidence, and to hear its story. She then visits its home, school, or place of employment and any other place where information about its habits and its history may be obtained . . .

In the Court, the Probation Officer appears to represent the child, as friend, though not as excuser. She represents to the Judge the course which the result of her inquiries has led the Juvenile Court Committee to consider would be for the best interest of the child. In most cases the issue will be the release of the child on probation in charge of the officer. The Judge takes advantage of the occasion to make as strong an impression as possible on the mind of the child, and the Probation Officer

(continued)

seizes on this precious psychological moment, immediately after the trial, to deepen and supplement the impression already made by a serious talk and words of advice.

After the trial comes her most important range of duty. She must see the child frequently, at first it should be every day, and by her personal influence endeavour to form it into what it should be. She comes into touch with the home, and occasionally reforms the whole family as well as the child. She visits the school, or place of employment, and enlists the teacher, or the employer, in the work of helping the child. While the keynote of all this is kindness, yet there is behind her the firm hand of the law. The child and its parents both know that on her report he may be sent to the reform school, and the knowledge adds greatly to her influence, and to the respect in which she is held. If all care fails, she brings the child before the Judge, for commitment to an institution. If the home is so bad that reform there is hopeless, she recommends that the child be placed in a foster home.

The question of the sex of the Probation Officer is an open one. The feminine gender is here used because experience has shown hitherto that women, intended by nature for motherhood, are better fitted for the work than men. Moreover, it is important that Probation Officers should be chosen from the best class—should represent the highest order of men and women—and the better class of women than of men can frequently be got for the money available . . .

Source: Scott (1908, pp. 895–896).

It is worth noting here that some scholars have long maintained that probation never lived up to its promise as the ultimate tool for reforming the individual because it quickly reverted to a policing role (see Rothman, 1980). It is also worth remembering this early vision, because as we will see in Chapter 8, it sounds remarkably similar to family intervention models currently being promoted as the most effective way of reducing recidivism among young offenders.

Once adjudicated as delinquent, children remained wards of the court until the court released them or until they reached the age of 21 (Sutherland, 1976, p. 122). Under the JDA, the provinces were allowed to set the maximum age under which a youth could be adjudicated as delinquent. By the late 1970s, the maximum age of delinquency was 16 in Saskatchewan, Ontario, New Brunswick, Nova Scotia, and Prince Edward Island; 17 in British Columbia and Newfoundland; and 18 in Manitoba and Quebec. Alberta had a separate age for boys and girls—16 for boys, 18 for girls—until 1978, when the age for both sexes was set at 16.

Because the juvenile justice system required probation officers, separate courts, separate judges, and separate detention facilities, its implementation was costly. In order to allow provinces to put in place these necessities, the JDA did not require immediate implementation; as a result, its implementation across the country was sporadic.

In February 1909, the first juvenile court under the JDA was set up in Winnipeg in the dining room of a house on Simco Street. The judge of this court was the Honourable T. Mayne Daly (Sutherland, 1976, p. 125). Within five years, courts had been set up in Halifax, Charlottetown, Montreal, Ottawa, Toronto, Vancouver, and Victoria. Within a decade, Alberta and Saskatchewan also had juvenile courts (Sutherland, 1976, p. 125). The JDA was not implemented in Prince Edward Island until 1974, in the Yukon until 1978, and in the Northwest Territories until 1979. Newfoundland never did implement the JDA, but rather established juvenile courts through provincial legislation (Wilson, 1982, p. 17). While men were the main actors in creating the justice system, once the JDA was passed, and as Scott envisioned, women played a major role in the system as probation officers and also as judges. Helen Gregory-MacGill was a youth court judge in British Columbia, and Emily Murphy was one of the first judges in Alberta (Leon, 1977, p. 82).

Opposition to the JDA

The JDA was not passed without opposition. Those who opposed the bill did so either on the grounds that it was not punitive enough or out of concern about potential abuses to children's and parents' rights. Two police officials (Inspectors William Stark and David Archibald) and two police court magistrates (George Dennison and R.E. Kingsford) were the most outspoken in the opposition to a juvenile justice system and the proposed legislation (Leon, 1977). Kingsford was concerned that since the new juvenile court would replace existing children's courts—which were run by police magistrates—the employees connected with those courts would also be replaced. "It would be a great pity," he stated, "if the notion got abroad that the police were so harsh in their dealings with juveniles that it was necessary to take from them that portion of work." Archibald, on the other hand, saw reform proposals as too lenient ("coddling") and was more concerned about the effect that these policies would have on "a class of perverts and delinquents":

> [The reformers] work upon the sympathies of philanthropic men and women for the purpose of introducing a jelly-fish and abortive system of law enforcement, whereby the judge or magistrate is expected to come down to the level of the incorrigible street arab and assume an attitude absolutely repulsive to British Subjects. The idea seems to be that by profuse use of slang phraseology he should place himself in a position to kiss and coddle a class of perverts and delinquents who require the most rigid disciplinary and corrective methods to ensure the possibility of their reformation. I would go further to affirm from extensive and practical experience that this kissing and coddling, if indiscriminately applied, even to the best class of children, would have a disastrous effect, both physically, mentally, morally and spiritually. (Cited in Leon, 1977, p. 96)

On reading some of the reformer J.J. Kelso's arguments (see Box 2.4) on the need for the court to act more like a loving parent than a police officer, Kingsford's and Archibald's reactions are not surprising.

There was some minor opposition to the proposed legislation from Children's Aid Societies in Toronto, in particular the Saint Vincent de Paul Society. According to Leon (1977), this opposition was based on concern over the ability of probation officers to "properly" supervise delinquent children. The bill was supported by members of the Senate, with the exception of Senator Wilson, who echoed the concerns of the Children's Aid Societies:

> We are all desirous of making every child as it grows up a useful member of society, but we may differ as to the means of accomplishing that. Here we pass an act to permit a child being taken away from its parents and put in other charge, and who is as solicitous for the welfare of the child as the parent? We put young children in the hands of an officer and that officer has absolute power and control over them. He may do anything under the Act and he is protected. I say that it is an unreasonable proposition to make, and I am fearful that instead of lessening the criminal juvenile class it will increase them. (Cited in Leon, 1977, p. 98)

Among members of Parliament, only Mr. Lancaster, a lawyer from Ontario, opposed the bill. Lancaster, who was clearly 60 years ahead of his time, worried that children's rights would not be protected by the new law or the new justice system. In particular, he feared that children would not be represented by lawyers, that their fate would rest entirely in the hands of probation officers, and, most important, that they would be denied the right to a trial (see Box 2.5).

VOICES BOX 2.4

Parens Patriae *as Expressed by J.J. Kelso*

[T]here are so many problems of a social and domestic character involved in the child's delinquency that to expect the ordinary magistrate and police authorities in a large city to deal with it is simply to invite failure. Anyone can decide in five minutes whether or not a youth is guilty of theft or some other offence, and liberate or banish him to a reformatory, but either decision may be equally unjust, and the problem still remain[s] unsolved. The court should be parental in the truest sense and should be so constituted in all its branches as to make the child intuitively realize that love and not hostility is the atmosphere into which he has entered. When one has had the experience of years in dealing with wayward youth, has studied the moral conditions, visited the wretched homes, comprehended the utter absence of real affection, the heart hunger, the longing for appreciation and sympathy, then [one] begin[s] to recognize that what is needed is not severity, not flogging, not jail or reformatory, but a true friend and an opportunity under clean auspices to develop worthy character. It is an intense realization of the erring boy's need, gained in many a sad interview with the children themselves, that entails the writing of these lines.

Source: Kelso (1907b, pp. 164–165).

VOICES BOX 2.5

The Right of Trial by Jury

The following exchange between Lancaster and Leighton McCartney (also an Ontario lawyer) took place in the House of Commons.

Mr. M.: If the child is allowed the inherent right of trial by jury, which he undoubtedly has under the British Constitution, it is put in the hands of the child to do away with the entire benefit of the Act. We are passing extraordinary legislation for the protection of the child, and to amend that as my Hon. friend suggests would be to do away with the benefits of the Act.

Mr. L.: You are providing that the parents shall be notified. On being notified, if the case is a serious one, the parent will employ counsel, and the child will have the advice of both the parents and the counsel, and the decision can be safely left to them. But you are leaving the decision entirely in the hands of someone [probation officer] who has no direct interest in the child's welfare.

Mr. M.: It is the converse of the case which the Hon. gentleman puts. We are passing an enactment for the benefit of the juvenile delinquent.

Mr. L.: How do you know it is?

Source: Cited in Leon (1977, p. 99).

Victorian reformers shrugged off the opposition. Most were not the least concerned about children's rights because they were convinced that what they were doing was protecting children. Since this was their motive, they believed that decisions and actions of those working in the justice system would similarly always be in the "best interest" of children. The system itself was focused on meeting children's needs, on "helping" rather than punishing and the objective was to treat and rehabilitate. The belief that this welfare-based justice system would act to ensure the best interest and welfare of the child was not significantly challenged until 1967, when a Supreme Court justice in the United States concluded, in connection with the Gault case, that *parens patriae*—the basis of the juvenile justice system—accords very different rights to children and adults: more specifically, adults have autonomous legal rights; children do not.

> The right of the State, as *Parens Patriae* to deny the child procedural rights available to his elders was elaborated by the assertion that a child, unlike an adult, has a right "not to liberty but to custody . . . If his parents default in effectively performing their custodial functions—that is, if the child is "delinquent"—the State may intervene. In doing so, it does not deprive the child of any rights, because he has none. It merely provides the "custody" to which the child is entitled. (Justice Abe Fortas, cited in Wilson, 1982, p. 5)

MODIFYING THE JUVENILE JUSTICE SYSTEM

Serious challenges to the Juvenile Delinquents Act began to surface in the 1960s as a result of a growing international and national rights discourse (Hogeveen, 2005, pp. 36–37). In 1959, the United Nations, through its *Declaration of the Rights of the Child*, gave legitimacy to notions that children should have rights and 1979 was designated as the year of the child (Denov, 2005, p. 68). Meanwhile, the 1960s also marked an era in which the United States witnessed its civil-rights movement and Canadians created their first Bill of Rights. It was in this environment that challenges to the principle of *parens patriae* as a foundation for juvenile justice became more frequent, as did concerns regarding the inability of the JDA to ensure due process for young people. These rights and legal concerns were buttressed against the welfare focus and practices of the JDA.

A major source of criticisms was directed at the JDA with regard to **status offences.** These were acts not considered criminal if engaged in by an adult, behaviours such as sexual behaviour, truancy, or incorrigibility. Critics argued that lumping together all child and youth offences, be they status offences or criminal offences, undermined the seriousness of some criminal offences and thereby inhibited any deterrent effect of punishment on criminal behaviour. And the opposite effect was considered by some to be equally problematic. Young people who were not breaking criminal laws were being punished in the same manner as those who did and, furthermore, were seen as negatively affected by close association with chronic offenders in institutions. There was also no set term for sentences—incarceration terms lasted as long as it took for a young person to be "reformed" or rehabilitated. While this served welfare interests, it flew in the face of those concerned about matters of due process.

Related issues revolved around inconsistencies in the application of the law. Sentence lengths varied according to individuals' characteristics and circumstances rather than by the nature of their behaviour, maximum ages for delinquency varied across the country, and treatment provisions were not consistent from one jurisdiction to another. In addition, concerns were also raised about the role of social workers in the system and the amount of discretionary power that they were able to exercise.

status offences
Behaviours considered to be illegal only because of the age status of the individual (e.g., truancy).

Since social workers were not part of the juvenile justice system, they were not accountable to the courts for their decisions. Other critics charged that the JDA failed to provide adequate public protection from the criminal behaviour of children and youth (Hogeveen, 2005, pp. 36–37; Hylton, 1994, pp. 232–233). Furthermore, according to Hylton (1994), a major factor contributing to the demise of the JDA was changing public and political attitudes about youth crime. In addition, as we will see in Chapter 10, critics were also skeptical about the efficacy of treatment.

Reform attempts began in 1965 with the release of a federal report from the Committee on Juvenile Delinquency in Canada. A number of legislative proposals followed this report and the YOA was the end product of nearly two decades of fine-tuning. Most of the opposition during this period came from provincial governments that, concerned about what changes would cost them, looked for federal funds to support implementation. Important points of contention in these debates included the maximum age at which youth would be brought into the juvenile system from the adult system, and the cost of providing for additional numbers of youth being supervised in the community.

The first drafted legislation, the Children and Young Persons Act of 1967, was rejected because of provincial objections to changes in jurisdiction and federal cost sharing. The first Young Offenders Act, introduced in 1970 and supported by the Canadian Bar Association, met with considerable opposition from welfare professionals and other interest groups because it was seen as too legalistic and too punitive—a "Criminal Code for children." In 1975, legislation entitled the Young Persons in Conflict with the Law also met with provincial concerns over costs and jurisdiction. By 1977, a new Young Offenders Act had been drafted. It contained aspects of the earlier Young Persons in Conflict with the Law bill—that is, accountability, responsibility, and legal rights—but it added as a central guiding principle the protection of society (Corrado & Markwart, 1992, pp. 148–150; Hylton, 1994, p. 232).

As described by Corrado and Markwart (1992), there was extensive discussion of these draft legislative proposals and the eventual 1977 YOA submission. Presentations on the proposed YOA were made to a parliamentary subcommittee by more than 40 interest groups. There was a general acceptance of the bill's philosophy and legal rights orientation; debate centred on more narrow issues, such as the meaning of legal rights for young people (Corrado & Markwart, 1992, p. 151). Finally, in April 1984, the Young Offenders Act came into effect, replacing the Juvenile Delinquents Act.

The actual passage of the YOA was fairly straightforward. The act was generally seen as a progressive piece of legislation, as reflected in the comments of Justice Omar Archambault (1986), who played a significant role in drafting the legislation:

> [The YOA] is based on a new set of fundamental assumptions reflecting [cultural] evolutions and inspired, as well, by extensive research and a more sophisticated knowledge of human behaviour generally, and the moral and psychological development of children in particular. (p. 45)

Principles of Juvenile Justice under the YOA

The Young Offenders Act created a juvenile justice system very different from that which had prevailed under the JDA. Whereas the JDA referred to delinquents as "misdirected and misguided" children in need of "aid, encouragement, help and assistance," the YOA referred to young persons as in a "state of dependency" who have "special needs and require guidance and assistance" as well as "supervision, discipline and control" (see Box 2.6). More specifically, the YOA introduced new principles to the

BOX 2.6

General Principles of the YOA

3 (1) It is hereby recognized and declared that:

(a) crime prevention is essential to the long-term protection of society and requires addressing the underlying causes of crime by young persons and developing multi-disciplinary approaches to identifying and effectively responding to children and young persons at risk of committing offending behaviour in the future (December 1, 1995);

(a.1) while young persons should not in all instances be held accountable in the same manner or suffer the same consequences for their behaviour as adults, young persons who commit offences should nonetheless bear responsibility for their contraventions;

(b) society must, although it has the responsibility to take reasonable measures to prevent criminal conduct by young persons, be afforded the necessary protection from illegal behaviour;

(c) young persons who commit offences require supervision, discipline and control, but, because of their state of dependency and level of development and maturity, they also have special needs and require guidance and assistance;

(c.1) the protection of society which is a primary objective of the criminal law applicable to youth, is best served by rehabilitation, wherever possible, of young persons who commit offences, and rehabilitation is best achieved by addressing the need and circumstances of a young person that are relevant to the young person's offending behaviour (December 1, 1995);

(d) where it is not inconsistent with the protection of society, taking no measures or taking measures other than judicial proceedings under this Act should be considered for dealing with young persons who have committed offences;

(e) young persons have rights and freedoms in their own right, including those stated in the Canadian Charter of Rights and Freedoms or in the Canadian Bill of Rights, and in particular the right to be heard in the course of, and to participate in, the processes that lead to decisions that affect them, and young persons should have special guarantees of their rights and freedoms;

(f) in the application of this Act, the rights and freedoms of young persons include a right to the least possible interference with freedom that is consistent with the protection of society, having regard to the needs of young persons and the interests of their families;

(g) young persons have the right, in every instance where they have rights or freedoms that may be affected by this Act, to be informed as to what those rights and freedoms are; parents have responsibility for the care and supervision of their children, and, for that reason, young persons should be removed from parental supervision either partly or entirely only when measures that provide for continuing parental supervision are inappropriate.

juvenile justice system that gave emphasis to youth responsibility, protection of society, special needs, alternative measures, and legal rights and freedoms.

Accountability

For the first time since its creation, a principle of juvenile justice was established [s. 3(l)(a.1)] that young people who commit criminal offences would have to assume responsibility for their behaviour. However, the YOA also recognized, in the same section, that young people have **limited accountability**: children and youth are held accountable by the justice system, but in a limited manner compared to adults. This was and is an important principle, for without it there would be no need for a separate system for youthful offenders. If we were to hold youth as accountable for their offences as adults, we could simply process all young people through the adult system.

This subsection of the YOA also underscored the significance of provisions relating to the transfer of youth to the adult system. In the absence of these special provisions, a youth's accountability for his or her offence following transfer would be the same as that of an adult. Thus, we find in other sections of the YOA provisions for shorter maximum sentences for youth. Initially, the maximum sentence for young offenders was three years; this was changed to five years in 1991. By December 1, 1995, the maximum sentence for teens was ten years for first-degree murder and seven years for second-degree murder. This issue of limited accountability continued as a major source of contention for opponents of the YOA (as we see below) and transfer rules were significantly altered by the YCJA.

Protection of Society

The protection of society, a principle expressed in s. 3(1)(b) of the YOA, was revisited in the 1995 amendment, subsection (c)(c.1), which underscored its importance as a guiding principle for juvenile justice by stating that it is a *primary objective of the criminal law*. This principle has an even more prominent position in the YCJA.

Special Needs

Section 3(1)(c)(c.1) outlined more specifically the rationale for a youth justice system. Because of their immaturity and dependency relative to adults, young people are said to have "special needs." According to Reid and Reitsma-Street (1984) and Reid-MacNevin (1991), the welfare principles expressed in the JDA lived on in this section of the YOA. Other scholars and Canadian judges interpreted this section to mean that any intervention with regard to special needs should be commensurate with the youth's offence (Bala, 1992; Bala & Kirvan, 1991). This latter interpretation was supported by the 1995 amendment, subsection (c.1), which requires that the needs of young persons be addressed in a manner that is relevant to their "offending behaviour." This too, as we will see below, is made a cornerstone of youth justice by the YCJA. The term "special needs" is not defined in the legislation and, based on case law, seems to be interpreted as social and psychological needs of a child—a safe and secure home environment, parents or guardians who are willing and able to provide for the child's psychological and physiological needs (Reid & Zuker, 2005, pp. 107–108).

Alternative Measures

Section 3(1)(d) expresses the principle of diversion: that where the protection of society is not compromised, measures other than formal court processing, with its potentially negative effects, should be considered. In most provinces, only first offenders and young persons guilty of relatively minor offences were to be processed

limited accountability Children and youth are held accountable by the justice system, but in a limited manner compared to adults.

through alternative measures. Once again, the "protection of society" principle is expected to balance the use of alternative measures. As we will see below, this is still an important principle under the YCJA, so important that "societal protection," as a principle, is expanded to the point where it may have a significant impact on the very structure of the juvenile justice system. Diversion principles and practices are further entrenched and expanded with the YCJA.

Rights of Young Persons

It is in s. 3(1)(e) and (g) that one finds the major difference between the YOA and the JDA and the historical significance of the YOA. In addition to rights and freedoms guaranteed through the Canadian Charter of Rights and Freedoms and the Canadian Bill of Rights, the YOA established that young people would have special guarantees, including the right to legal representation and the right to be informed as to their rights and freedoms under the act. Some of these pertained to statements made to "persons in authority." These rules most clearly applied to questioning by police officers and other officials such as teachers or school principals. Section 56 of the YOA outlined a complex set of procedures governing the questioning of young people. Interestingly, parents were not usually considered "persons in authority," so that things said to them by their children, in confidence, would be admissible regardless of cautions regarding legal rights (Bala, 1992, p. 41). Other parts of the YOA made it clear that youth had fewer justice rights than adults with respect to preliminary hearings, jury trials, and issues of privacy and search. Many of these have been changed with the YCJA.

Minimal Interference with Freedom

Section 3(1)(f) applied to every aspect of youth justice and affected every young offender, except in cases where there were concerns having to do with the protection of society. This principle of "least possible interference" encouraged the use of alternative measures, but it also encouraged police officers to divert youth from the system altogether. This principle also influenced bail proceedings and sentencing: it encouraged the court to apply sentences more lenient than custody, and discouraged the court from effecting transfers to the adult system. This principle has been maintained by the YCJA but is no longer stated as a principle in its own right.

Parental Responsibility

Section 3(1)(h) marked another major difference between the YOA and the JDA systems. Under the JDA, parents or guardians whom the court considered to be providing inappropriate parental care could be held responsible for their children's offences; they could be made to pay fines or provide financial support for their children. In contrast, the YOA did not consider parental responsibility. Rather, it addressed parental involvement with youth and the justice proceedings. Parents or guardians were required to be notified of their child's arrest (s.8) or of youth court proceedings (s.9), and they could be ordered to attend court (s.10). Other sections of the YOA allowed parents to make statements to the court regarding dispositions and transfers.

At the same time, s. 3(1)(h) indicated that parents were to be judged along with their children. If they were not considered "responsible" parents, the court could remove children from the parents' guardianship. In this regard, Bala (1992) cautions that

> It is important . . . not to "romanticize" the role of parents in the lives of their children . . . Some young offenders have been victims of physical, emotional or sexual abuse at the hands of their parents, and some youths have ceased to have meaningful

relationships with their parents before they are involved in the youth court system. The fact that a youth is charged with a criminal offence often strains the relationship with parents, and those involved with dealing with young offenders need to be realistic about the role that parents are likely to play in their children's lives. (p. 32)

From another perspective, LaPrairie (1988) argued that the parental responsibility principle expressed in the YOA had a negative impact on Aboriginal youth, precisely because of the impoverished state of many First Nations communities, particularly those in remote regions of the country. In one case, an Aboriginal youth was sentenced to two years' custody for a second break-and-enter offence because of his family's impoverished circumstances (Bala 1992, pp. 28–29). Some of these issues were addressed by the YCJA and in some ways, to be discussed below, parents now have more responsibility for their children's offences.

Because of the predominance of justice principles over welfare principles in the YOA, some argued that it was based on a **justice model** (see Table 2.1 on page 40), others described the system as a **modified justice model** because it maintained some of the welfare principles that underpinned the JDA (Corrado, 1992). Most of the revisions to the YOA moved it in the direction of a **crime control model**. That is one where a central premise is that criminal behaviour is motivated by free will and, as such, needs to be punished in order to deter further crime. The belief is that the fundamental purpose of the justice system is to protect the public through laws and practices that are considered "tough enough" to deter crime.

Modifications to the YOA

Most resistance to the YOA came after its enactment. Much of this controversy originated from the different ways in which its principles were interpreted. A good deal of opposition also came from conservative interest groups who advocated a crime control approach to juvenile justice (see Table 2.1 on page 40). Their efforts were bolstered and reinforced by provincial governments that remained concerned about the cost of correctional programs (Corrado & Markwart, 1992, pp. 160–162) and the actual introduction of "get tough" policies and programs by Ontario and Manitoba (Hogeveen & Smandych, 2001, p. 148). In addition, media coverage of youth crime helped both to create and to fuel a sustained opposition to the YOA. By engaging in sensationalism and over-reporting of the most violent cases of youth crime, the media created, maintained, and reinforced public perceptions that violent youth crime was on the rise and that the YOA was too lenient to be of any consequence in preventing or controlling it (Corrado & Markwart, 1992, p. 161; Sprott, 1996).

The debate over the YOA was reminiscent of the debates provoked by the creation of the juvenile justice system 100 years ago. Not unlike police then, police groups in the YOA debates expressed concerns about children under 12 committing criminal offences, about restrictions on record-keeping, and about restrictions on obtaining confessions (Sapers & Leonard, 1996, p. 86). A survey of professional groups in the juvenile justice system conducted by the Ministry of the Solicitor General in 1982 found that attitudes toward the YOA varied by role in the system. Police and Crown prosecutors were the most negative, while defence counsel and probation officers were the most positive. Judges, who were somewhere in the middle, expressed concerns about setting the maximum age at 18, as well as about the destruction of records, reviews of custodial dispositions, and the three-year maximum on sentences for offences for which adults would receive a life sentence (Moyer & Carrington, 1985). Among politicians, Reform (now Conservative) Party MPs were the most vocal proponents of crime

justice model
Refers in this text to a philosophy and orientation to criminal justice that posits the rule of law as the primary means of achieving a "just" justice system.

modified justice model
A particular model of criminal or juvenile justice that is not in strict adherence to a pure justice philosophy.

crime control model
A theoretical model representing a retributive set of beliefs and philosophies about crime and justice.

control principles. They continually raised concerns, both in the House and the media, that

- horrible crimes committed by youth were going unpunished;
- the YOA was incapable of controlling youth violence;
- youth rights were protected at the expense of their victims;
- the YOA was far too problematic to ever be "fixed"; and
- youths' legal rights were a major obstacle to the protection of society (Hogeveen & Smandych, 2001).

After the YOA was implemented, there were three sets of major revisions, all of which moved the justice system closer to a crime control model (see Table 2.1 on page 40) (Corrado & Markwart, 1992; Hylton, 1994; Sapers & Leonard, 1996). The first set of YOA amendments came in 1986 (Bill C-106) in response to concerns from the police and provincial governments about problems in implementing the legislation and a need to "toughen" the legislation. These changes primarily addressed technical and procedural changes (Bala, 2005; Sapers & Leonard, 1996, p. 95), more specifically, provisions to facilitate breach of probation charges and to allow publication of information about the identity of young offenders in the community who were considered dangerous (Bala, 2005, p. 43). Nonetheless, opposition to the YOA continued (Bala, 1989, 2005) and public criticism was raised with regard to sentences for serious youth crime. Judges could choose only between the extremes of a three-year sentence in youth court or a life sentence in adult court and there were concerns about the discrepancy between these extremes. Following a number of consultative meetings, a second set of amendments was made (Bill C-12) by the then-Progressive Conservative government and was passed by Parliament in December 1991. These changes included raising maximum sentences for first- and second-degree murder to five years less a day and changing parole eligibility for youth transferred to adult court to five and ten years in adult custody (Bala, 2005 p. 44; Hylton, 1994, p. 237; Sapers & Leonard, 1996, pp. 90–91).

In spite of the 1986 and 1991 revisions, some interest groups were still not satisfied with the YOA. Following the 1991 amendments, public concerns continued to be expressed regarding the so-called leniency of the YOA and its perceived inability to control youth crime. In addition, those analyzing the youth courts were beginning to notice a trend toward an increased use of custody. Arguments were made that this trend was dangerous in that, in the long run, it thwarted the goals of societal protection.

In June 1994, the then-Liberal federal government responded to these concerns with a two-part strategy of reform for the juvenile justice system. Part 1 of the strategy involved more amendments to the YOA (Bill C-37). Part 2 mandated a parliamentary subcommittee, with the assistance of a Federal–Provincial–Territorial Task Force, to assess public opinion with respect to the act, and to provide a public consultative process and make recommendations for reform. Bill C-37 was approved by the Senate in June 1995 and came into force on December 1, 1995. Once again, the YOA had been amended in the direction of crime control, but the extensive use of custody was also addressed and feeble attempts were made to emphasize rehabilitation principles and increase the use of community-based sentences (Bala, 2005, p. 44). The major change to the YOA this time included:

- sentences of ten years for youth convicted of first-degree murder and seven years for second-degree murder;
- automatic transfer to adult court for 16- and 17-year-olds charged with serious "personal injury" offences unless able to satisfy a judge that the two

objectives—public protection and rehabilitation—could be achieved better through the youth court; and

- an emphasis that rehabilitation for youth charged with minor offences is best achieved in the community.

Still, law-and-order groups were not satisfied. At the time, Sapers and Leonard (1996) observed that "the level of public involvement in the current debate will likely spur politicians to get more tough rather than to look at issues already identified as important . . . [C]rime control policy will [likely] continue to reflect muddled, reactionary tinkering" (p. 97). Unfortunately, their prediction came true as reform efforts continued through the turn of the century.

A Strategy for Reform

Bill C-37 had been the first phase of the federal government's plan for reform. For the second phase, the House of Commons Standing Committee on Justice and Legal Affairs was given a mandate to undertake a comprehensive review of the youth justice system, youth crime, and the operation of the YOA. They were to accomplish this review by surveying a broad cross-section of the Canadian public, as well as those who worked in the system.

On the basis of their meetings with individuals and groups, their visits to youth facilities, the information presented at local and national forums, and the recommendations of the Federal–Provincial–Territorial Task Force, the standing committee made 14 recommendations. These recommendations included changing the declaration of principle to a statement of purpose, with the primary purpose being the protection of society; supporting crime prevention and rehabilitation as "reinforcing strategies" for this crime control principle; increasing federal funding for community-based crime-prevention initiatives and public education on youth crime and justice issues; more use of alternative measures; mandatory parental/guardian attendance in court; and lowering the minimum age to 10 (Cohen, 1997, pp. 73–76). These recommendations reflected an emphasis on protection of society that ran counter to the emphasis on rehabilitation and prevention in Quebec's Youth Protection Act. It was an emphasis that led to the Bloc Québécois's dissenting position on the standing committee's recommendations and the party's continued rejection of government reform proposals, including the YCJA (Cohen, 1997, pp. 115–117; Hogeveen & Smandych, 2001).

Interestingly, the Federal–Provincial–Territorial Task Force's recommendations, which were based on a review of research and literature rather than public consultation, were as oriented to crime control as those of the standing committee—with two notable exceptions. The task force recommended no change to the minimum age and presented a very different view of the conflicting principles issue. Rather than proposing a statement of purpose (protection of society), the task force recommended a review of the YOA's principles for the purpose of distinguishing between "fundamental principles" and "other principles." It also recommended that "other principles" should include:

1. the circumstances of Aboriginal youth;
2. the involvement of families in the justice process;
3. the interests of victims;
4. the need for coordination between youth justice and other youth services; and
5. sentencing principles (Report, 1996, p. 629).

As with the recommendations of the standing committee, the task force's recommendations did not meet with unanimous provincial approval, and recommendations for tougher policies continued. Nonetheless, in May 1998, then-Justice Minister Anne McLellan responded to these recommendations with a Youth Criminal Justice Act proposal to replace the YOA and, as Box 2.7 indicates, all of the task force recommendations, with the exception of item 4 above, were adopted in the YCJA.

BOX 2.7

The Youth Criminal Justice Act

The general principles of the Youth Criminal Justice Act are found in its Declaration of Principle.

3 (1) The following principles apply in this Act:

(a) the youth criminal justice system is intended to
  (i)   prevent crime by addressing the circumstances underlying a young person's offending behaviour,
  (ii) rehabilitate young persons who commit offences and reintegrate them into society, and
  (iii) ensure that a young person is subject to meaningful consequences for his or her offence in order to promote the long-term protection of the public;

(b) the criminal justice system for young persons must be separate from that of adults and emphasize the following:
  (i)   rehabilitation and reintegration,
  (ii) fair and proportionate accountability that is consistent with the greater dependency of young persons and their reduced level of maturity,
  (iii) timely intervention that reinforces the link between the offending behaviour and its consequences, and
  (iv) the promptness and speed with which persons responsible for enforcing this Act must act, given young persons' perception of time;

(c) within the limits of fair and proportionate accountability, the measures taken against young persons who commit offences should
  (i)   reinforce respect for societal values,
  (ii) encourage the repair of harm done to victims and the community,
  (iii) be meaningful for the individual young person given his or her needs and level of development and, where appropriate, involve the parents, the extended family, the community and social or other agencies in the young person's rehabilitation and reintegration, and
  (iv) respect gender, ethnic, cultural and linguistic differences and respond to the needs of aboriginal young persons and of young persons with special requirements; and

(d) special considerations apply in respect of proceedings against young persons and, in particular,
  (i)   young persons have rights and freedoms in their own right, such as a right to be heard in the course of and to participate in the processes, other than the decision to prosecute, that lead to

(continued)

> *Box 2.7 continued*
>
> decisions that affect them, and young persons have special guarantees of their rights and freedoms,
>
> (ii) victims should be treated with courtesy, compassion and respect for their dignity and privacy and should suffer the minimum degree of inconvenience as a result of their involvement with the youth criminal justice system,
>
> (iii) victims should be provided with information about the proceedings and given an opportunity to participate and be heard, and
>
> (iv) parents should be informed of measures or proceedings involving their children and encouraged to support them in addressing their offending behaviour.
>
> (2) This Act shall be liberally construed so as to ensure that young persons are dealt with in accordance with the principles set out in subsection (1).

Responses to this proposed legislation were predictable. The Reform (now Conservative) Party justice critic endorsed the punitive crime control aspects of the proposal. Progressive Conservative and New Democrat critics charged that the minister was merely "tinkering" with the system. And provincial governments worried that the changes would increase their costs (McIlroy, 1998b). Newspaper articles and editorials ran the gamut, from "YOA changes 'right approach'" (Borden, 1998) to "More dressing than meat" (1998).

The YCJA was eventually introduced in the House of Commons on March 11, 1999, as Bill C-68. It was debated in the House and reintroduced October 14, 1999, as Bill C-3. Following this debate, it was referred to the Standing Committee on Justice and Human Rights, and hearings were conducted through to the spring of 2000. As a result of the federal election of 2000, the act had to be reintroduced to the House of Commons in May 2001, now as Bill C-7, and went to the House of Senate in June 2001. It was reintroduced to the House of Commons for final reading in fall 2001 and finally came into effect in April 2003. It took seven years, three drafts, and more than 160 amendments to accomplish.

Throughout this process, Reform (now Conservative) Party MPs and conservative interest groups such as victims' rights groups continued to argue that the YCJA had not gone far enough. The Bloc Québécois continued its opposition and maintained that the YCJA constituted a step backward for youth justice in Quebec and constituted a substantial problem for any real attempts to rehabilitate and reintegrate youth. Quebec maintained that the YCJA was an attempt to impose a "criminal" justice model that would undermine its juvenile justice system that had been built on principles of rehabilitation and *l'approche educative* (loosely translated as "educative") (Trepanier, 2004, p. 273). Quebec's basic position was that youth problems could be resolved with the existing YOA (Hogeveen & Smandych, 2001, pp. 163–165). In the end, Quebec won the right to "opt out" of the YCJA and continue operating juvenile justice through its Youth Protection Act.

Principles of Juvenile Justice under the YCJA

As we saw in Box 2.7, the Youth Criminal Justice Act has maintained the principles introduced by the YOA, but the way in which it has done so creates a very different justice system, both in terms of its structure and its focus. First, the crime control thrust introduced to the system by YOA amendments is maintained, but there are a number of important differences in how this has been accomplished. Unlike the JDA and YOA, the YCJA is explicit about the purpose and objectives of the juvenile justice system. The YCJA specifies clearly that the purpose of a *youth* (no longer defined as *juvenile*) justice system is protection of the public through crime prevention, rehabilitation, and meaningful consequences [s. 3(1)(a)(i–iii)]. So, while maintaining the JDA principle of rehabilitation, this is to be undertaken for the sole purpose of protection of the public in the context of "meaningful consequences" rather than as an end in itself. Further, it is no longer sufficient to establish, as the YOA did, that youth will be held responsible; now the system will emphasize "fair and proportional accountability" [s. 3(1)(b)(ii)]. We will also see in Chapter 9 that there have been other changes, such as the introduction of sentencing principles, that will have a crime control impact on the system and on youth charged with "serious" and violent offences.

Interestingly, at the same time that the YCJA moves juvenile justice more in the direction of crime control, s. 3(1)(c)(ii) and (iii), it also opens the door for **restorative justice** principles (see Table 2.1 on page 40) to be realized through encouraging **reparation** and the involvement of parents, victims, families and communities in the justice process (also discussed in Chapters 8 and 9). Section 3(1)(b)(i) introduces **reintegration** as a goal of the justice system. Further, in keeping with the Federal–Provincial–Territorial Task Force recommendations, the YCJA justice system is progressive in that s. 3(1)(c)(iv) recognizes that the legislation and system has differential impacts on youth depending on their status in society, thereby at least paving the way for a more equitable justice system in practice.

Justice principles are preserved through s. 3(1)(b) and (d). While s. 3(1)(d)(i) preserves the rights and freedoms of youth, including special rights because of their social status and age (s. 3(1)(c) (iv), to be discussed further in Chapters 8 and 9), justice principles are enhanced through s. 3(1)(b) (iii) and (iv). These subsections emphasize the need for timely intervention and prompt and speedy processing of cases, all of which are recognized as of particular importance for young offenders. Sections 3(1)(d)(ii) and (iii) further extend justice and restorative principles by addressing the role, rights, and significance of victims in the justice process—a first in the juvenile justice system.

Finally, the YCJA has revived the JDA principle of rehabilitation as an objective, one that was lost in the YOA system, with its justice and crime control orientation. While rehabilitation and reintegration is established as a goal, s. 3(1)(c)(iii) specifies that these processes should involve the parents and extended family, and that parents should be encouraged to support their children in these efforts. This is a more positive, welfare-oriented statement than that contained in the YOA [3(1)(f)], which merely established the powers of the justice system, relative to parents, with regard to removing children from parental custody.

The YCJA also maintains the welfare system orientation toward the "special needs" of young people through s. 3(1)(b)(ii) and (d)(i) and by maintaining the YOA focus on the "greater dependency of young persons and their reduced level of maturity." As before, this principle serves as the justification for a separate system of justice for youth. It is significant though that this is stated as a given in s. 3(1)(b) and is therefore no longer a matter of interpretation. This principle, as we will see in later chapters, also now serves as a fundamental guideline for every other aspect of the act's implementation, from police contact, court proceedings and sentencing to correctional and interventionist provisions.

One of the most significant changes to the system comes through the omission of alternative measures as a stated principle. Nonetheless, diversionary aspects of the youth justice system remain, but they have been redefined as "extrajudicial measures"

restorative justice
A justice model that focuses on the harm caused by crime and seeks to repair the damage done to offenders, victims, and communities.

reparation
In restorative justice models, this involves offenders making amends in any of a variety of ways to their victims for the harm done by the offence.

reintegration
A correctional concept referring to policies and programs designed to introduce offenders back into their communities as productive, participating, law-abiding members.

and now occupy a separate section in the new act. Part 1 of the YCJA begins with the principles and objectives of diversion (referred to as "extrajudicial measures"), and proceeds to lay out appropriate responses, conditions, restrictions, and the role of police, parents, and victims in the diversionary process. Hence, the familiar practices of YOA alternative measures are far more formalized in the YCJA. Depending on how these practices are implemented by individual provinces and jurisdictions, the end result may be a mini youth justice system in its own right but one with far greater discretionary powers afforded to professionals working in the system, something reminiscent of the system under the JDA. The specifics of these new sections (s. 4 through s. 12) are discussed in greater detail in Chapter 8.

Minimal interference is no longer a stated principle of youth justice under the YCJA. Rather, this principle is implied through changes to other sections of the act. So, for example, police are advised in s. 6(1) to consider that no action beyond a warning or referral to a community program might be sufficient action toward a young offender to satisfy the principles laid out in s. 3 of the YCJA.

A New/Old Justice System

The youth justice system under the YCJA is substantially and structurally different from that under the YOA and the JDA. It has retained the welfare focus on rehabilitation and individual needs; the justice focus on individual rights, due process, and individual responsibility, as well as the crime control focus on protection of society and accountability. While these principles have been retained, they have also been revised in ways that give a new focus and structure to the system. So, for example, instead of vague references to "special needs," the YCJA speaks specifically of the need to separate youth from adults and that a young person's perception of time requires "promptness and speed."

The act also addresses the necessity of responding to individual needs, in combination with the level of maturity of a child, and to involve families and communities in the processes of rehabilitation and reintegration. Furthermore, the new act goes so far as to imply differential needs on the basis of gender, ethnicity, culture, and language, and then identify special-needs groups as Aboriginal youth and those with "special" requirements. Similarly, welfare principles are reconceptualized so that rehabilitation is consistently paired with reintegration and as such, implies something other than earlier notions of treatment for the individual.

Gone as fundamental overriding principles are alternative measures, least possible interference, parental responsibility, and the right to be informed of rights and freedoms. These principles have been revised and restated elsewhere as principles applying to specific sections of the act, such as the new "extrajudicial measures." New concepts and principles have been added that are, at least on the surface, restorative: reintegration; parental, family, and community involvement; victim rights; and reparation. New concepts more in a crime control and justice tradition are: meaningful consequences and timely intervention. As we will see in later chapters, many aspects of the YCJA are regressive revisions of old principles and practices, while many are indicative of new ways of thinking—restoratively rather than punitively—and as such offer a potential for progressive changes. Either way, new problems and issues continue to arise as the system in action unfolds to public purview.

Living Up to Its Promises

Already we wonder: Is it working? Is the YCJA doing what was intended? The latter half of this book is designed to answer these questions through an examination of the system in action: the police, the court, and the correctional system. Preliminary statistics from the police and courts suggest that one goal has been accomplished: diversion. The police are arresting fewer youth and are processing more through extrajudicial measures. Fewer youth are going to court and fewer are receiving custodial sentences: institutions are closing down.

Nonetheless, some old issues remain or are being revived in new terms, and new issues are being identified. An important case in point concerns children's rights. While this was never a public issue under the YOA, there were a number of court challenges to some of its rights provisions and the matter has begun to receive more critical attention. While the YCJA has provided more specific provisions to protect the rights of children and youth, partially as a result of these challenges (see Chapter 8 for a full discussion), it still falls short of its promise.

According to Denov (2005), the idea of children's rights is not a new one but how the concept is understood has changed over time. Covell and Howe (2001) identify three distinct stages in Canadians' perceptions of children. In the first stage, from the colonial era to the 19th century, children were viewed as possessions and subject to parental authority. Children were entitled to the necessities of life but only by default, in that parents were required by common law to provide for their children. As we have seen in this and the last chapter, from the time of Confederation through to the turn of the century, views of children and childhood changed dramatically. Children were no longer seen as the property of parents but as individuals in their own right who were vulnerable and requiring of state protection (*parens patriae*); nonetheless, they were still viewed as objects in need of care, rather than as individuals with a right to care and protection.

Not until the mid-20th century, however, did children begin to be viewed as subjects with entitlements, rights of their own. In 1959, the United Nations afforded official recognition to the human rights of children through its *Declaration of the Rights of the Child*. Its fundamental thrust is that children, defined as people up to age 18, are entitled to special protections and that the *best interests of the child* are paramount with regard to protection and rights. After nearly 20 years of discussions and attempts at drafting an agreement that would be a legally binding one, on November 20, 1989, the *Convention on the Rights of the Child* was unanimously adopted by the UN. Canada became a signatory to the convention in 1991.

While children's rights now have international recognition, the convention has no legal standing; it is merely a set of guidelines for nation–states. Canadians are guaranteed protections under the Charter of Rights and Freedoms and so too are children, but only as Canadians, not as children. Canadians are also afforded particular rights through specific legislation, such as the YCJA for youth and children. Yet, even though people generally recognize the value of our rights in a general sense, specific rights are often at issue and are pitted against each other. So, for example, with regard to youth and the YCJA, even though youth are guaranteed legal representation, what happens when parents don't want to pay for the lawyer or feel that their child is best served by a custody sentence and don't want a lawyer for fear that legal representation might help their child "get off" from legal sanctioning? These are some of the specific rights issues addressed in the YCJA and we will discuss them in greater detail in later sections of this book. At this point, we want to recognize that there are international standards regarding the rights of children and consider the extent to which these standards are realized in the YCJA.

The most glaring issue regarding children's rights in the YCJA comes from its blatant disregard for article 37 of the UN *Convention on the Rights of the Child* (see the appendix at the end of this chapter). Section (c) of article 37 clearly states that "... every child deprived of liberty shall be separated from adults unless it is considered in the child's best interest not to do so ..." Canada is clearly in violation of this article through provisions in the YCJA for adult sentences for youth that include imprisonment in adult institutions. Not only do we allow for youth to be imprisoned with adults, the YCJA has made this easier to do than it was under the YOA, and it expands the net to include more offences and younger ages. In short, because of the YCJA, we can now put more youth in adult prisons, for more offences, and at younger ages, and it is easier to do so (see full discussion in Chapter 9). Furthermore, the YCJA allows youth who are awaiting their day in court to be held in detention with adults, and these are the young people and children who have not yet been found guilty of an offence.

Not surprisingly, when Canada joined the convention it expressed its reservations regarding article 37 and is continually chastised by the UN Committee on the Rights of the Child, the monitoring body of the UN convention, for its failure to protect children (Denov, 2005, p. 72). Canada is in dubious company in this regard, as the United States and Somalia have refused to ratify the convention because of article 37. For them, the objection is to section (a). They wish to retain and exercise the right to execute children. The Human Rights Watch, an independent body that oversees human rights violations, indicates in its *Children's Rights* report that in the decade following the UN convention, 10 juvenile offenders were executed in the United States; the youngest, Sean Sellers, was 16. As of July 1, 1999, there were 75 juvenile offenders on death row in the United States (Human Rights Watch, 1999, p. 8).

The YCJA also blatantly disregards article 16 of the convention, which speaks of a child's right to privacy, by permitting the publication of names as well as dissemination of information about young offenders who have received an adult sentence. Furthermore, it permits disclosure of names and information about youth to victims and "other individuals deemed acceptable to the court." The YCJA circumvents UN committee censure in that, while article 16 insists that children have the "... right to protection of the law against ... interference or attacks" against honour, reputation, and privacy, it indirectly provides for lawful "interference" and "attacks" by maintaining that children should not be subjected to "unlawful interference [or] ... attacks."

The YCJA has also brought censure upon Canada through its omissions. As we will see in later chapters, there are a number of issues related to the administration of youth justice left over from the YOA that have not been addressed by the YCJA. The first concerns issues that arise from the insistence by the UN convention that "the best interests of the child" should be the fundamental principle of rights and protections legislation. Nowhere does the YCJA mention "best interests" in its provisions, nor is this even stated as a declaration of principle in Section 3. "Best interests" receives mention only in the Preamble of the YCJA (Denov, 2005, pp. 80–81). The importance of this omission is highlighted by the UN committee report in 1995, in which Canada was reminded that

> ... principles relating to the best interests of the child and prohibition of discrimination in relation to children should be incorporated into domestic law and it should be possible to invoke them before the courts. (UNICEF, 1998, p. 43, as cited in Denov, 2005, p. 81)

Such matters are particularly pertinent to sentencing, and nowhere do YCJA provisions allow for these matters to be addressed in youth court. Furthermore, Denov (2005) maintains that this failure to provide for "best interests" is a significant contributing factor in the erosion of the "boundaries between the youth and adult criminal justice systems" (p. 81).

One final area of concern regards regional disparities. We will see in later chapters that youth justice is administered unevenly and inconsistently on a regional basis and even within jurisdictions. This too is a holdover from the YOA that has not been addressed in the YCJA, and the issue is ensured to continue because the YCJA permits provinces not only to determine how they will administrate and administer the law but also to determine the minimum age for an adult sentence. So far, only Quebec and Newfoundland and Labrador have set the minimum at 16 years of age. Youth in all other parts of the country are subject to adult sentences at 14 years of age. Again, we find ourselves admonished by the UN committee for these disparities (UNICEF, 1998, p. 27, as cited in Denov, 2005, p. 81).

And so we have it. As Sapers and Leonard (1996) predicted toward the end of the YOA era and impending law reform, politicians got tougher, public concern over the juvenile justice system continued, and involved parties—lawyers, judges, police officers, and social workers—took positions adopted by their predecessors a century ago. Have we come full circle? First we were punitive and made few distinctions between youth and adult offenders. Then we were concerned about the welfare of children and separated youth offenders from adult offenders. Now we are moving in the direction of putting more youth into the adult justice system while at the same time trying to keep minor offenders out of the justice system altogether.

As will become more apparent in later chapters, we have essentially created a **bifurcated** system. The youth justice system has been bifurcated by the YCJA's formalization of diversion for more youth while at the same time requiring prison terms and adult sentences for more youth. The end result is one set of rules, rights and protections for minor offenders and another for those charged with more serious offences; the system will be a very different experience for youth depending on which "half" she or he falls into. Are we returning to the point at which we started? Bernard (1992) maintains that in the Western world, juvenile justice is an ever-revolving cycle. He describes this **cycle of juvenile justice** from his analysis of two centuries of criminal justice in the United States:

> This cycle arises from the fact that, at any given time, many people are convinced that the problem of high juvenile crime rates is recent and did not exist in the "good old days." These people conclude that the problem lies in the policies for handling juvenile offenders, whether those are harsh punishments or lenient treatments. The result is a cycle of reform in which harsh punishments are blamed for high juvenile crime rates [for Canada, pre JDA] and are replaced by lenient treatments [JDA], and then lenient treatments are blamed for high juvenile crime rates and are replaced by harsh punishments [YOA and its revisions]. (p. 22)

At this point in time, we can only speculate as to whether the YCJA will be able to break the cycle. As we saw in Box 1.2 on page 9, reform efforts are already underway to harshen the legislation by having motor vehicle theft and joyriding offences reclassified as violent offences.

bifurcated
Divided into two parts.

cycle of juvenile justice
Refers to the tendency toward a never-ending cycle of juvenile justice reform common in Western society.

SUMMARY

A century ago, middle-class Victorians in Canadian cities were concerned about the welfare of neglected and delinquent children and believed that housing them in penal institutions and adult prisons was too punitive. As a result of their reform efforts, a juvenile justice system was created with the passage of the Juvenile Delinquents Act in 1908. Some critics argued that the system was not punitive enough, others that children would be deprived of their legal rights. Now, nearly a century later, the juvenile justice system has been significantly modified to incorporate due process rights and legal responsibility for criminal behaviour. Still, law-and-order groups worried that the system was not punitive enough. Politicians responded with punitive recommendations and the Youth Criminal Justice Act. The cycle of juvenile justice reform continues with the YCJA.

Prior to the creation of the juvenile justice system in Canada, English common law dictated that anyone over 14 was subject to the same law as adults. Those under 7 were considered unable to distinguish right from wrong. Children between the ages of 7 and 14 could suffer the same consequence as adults if it was determined that they had the ability to distinguish right from wrong.

J.J. Kelso and W.L. Scott are credited with creating the Canadian juvenile justice system, which began with the passage of the Juvenile Delinquents Act in 1908. The justice system under the JDA was based on the doctrine *parens patriae*, which required the court and justice system to act in "the best interests of the child." Under this welfare-based system of justice, delinquents were viewed as "misdirected and misguided" children in need of "aid, encouragement, help and assistance."

Serious challenges to the JDA began to surface in the 1960s, largely as a result of the human-rights movement in North America and rising public concerns about youth crime and public protection. After a 20-year debate, the Young Offenders Act was enacted in 1984. The system it created was described as a modified justice system because it maintained some welfare principles, incorporated justice principles, and used crime control principles to modify both. This combination of conflicting principles fuelled a 15-year debate over the purpose and effectiveness of the juvenile justice system under the YOA.

The principles of juvenile justice under the YOA were accountability, protection of society, special needs of youth, alternative measures, due process rights of young persons, minimal interference with freedom, and parental responsibility.

The YOA was amended three times after it was implemented. All revisions moved the justice system further from welfare principles and closer to a crime control model. The Youth Criminal Justice Act continues this trend toward crime control principles by allowing more youth to be placed into the adult justice system and at younger ages, while at the same time keeping more youth out of the juvenile justice system by means of extrajudicial measures. In so doing, the new justice system is a bifurcated one.

Under the YCJA, the new aspects of youth justice as reflected in its principles are reintegration; meaningful consequences; timely intervention; parental, family, and community involvement in rehabilitation and reintegration processes; victim rights; reparation; and a recognition of special-needs groups. Many of these principles are supportive of a restorative model of justice.

The notion of children as independent people with their own needs, including the need for special protection, began developing in the latter part of the 19th century and culminated in the recognition of legal rights and protections in the mid-20th century. Children's rights were formalized in the UN *Convention on the Rights of the Child* in 1989. While rights and protections for youth based on their needs as children are an important part of the YCJA, it has fallen short of its promise with regard to protecting them from confinement with adults, protecting privacy rights, and ensuring that the best interests of the child are a central part of the administration of justice, as well as in ensuring that the act is enforced with consistency across the country.

DISCUSSION/CRITICAL THINKING QUESTIONS

1. Should children's rights be a part of the Canadian Charter of Rights and Freedoms? Does this omission explain why children's rights, as viewed by international agreements, are not fully protected in the YCJA? Explain your answers.
2. How have the principles and philosophy of juvenile justice changed over time, and do you consider this to be progressive?
3. Does it make sense to have a bifurcated youth justice system? Explain your answer.
4. Considering the past 100 years of juvenile justice reform, which changes are most significant and why?

WEB LINKS

What's new in youth justice?
www.cleo.on.ca/english/pub/onpub/PDF/youth/newact.pdf

The Great Youth Criminal Justice Act Debate
www.lawyers.ca/ycja/subindexbottom.htm

The United Nations Convention on the Rights of the Child
www.crin.org/docs/resources/treaties/uncrc.htm

International Bureau for Children's Rights: Canada's Juvenile Justice Law & Children's Rights
www.ibcr.org/PAGE_EN/2004%20Conference%20documents/Bala%20_ENG.pdf

For chapter quizzes and more links, visit this book's accompanying website at
www.bellyoungoffenders3e.nelson.com

APPENDIX

The United Nations *Convention on the Rights of the Child*

In 1992, over 100 countries, including Canada, ratified the United Nations *Convention on the Rights of the Child*, and 191 states are now parties to the convention. The United States and Somalia refused to ratify the convention because of article 37(a). Children are defined as those under the age of 18. Among other things, UN document A/44/736 (1989) addresses the special needs of children, the concept of "best interests," children's rights, and juvenile justice systems. The following are excerpts from the convention that are relevant to juvenile justice matters.

Recalling that, in the Universal Declaration of Human Rights, the United Nations has proclaimed that childhood is entitled to special care and assistance, *convinced* that the family, as the fundamental group of society and the natural environment for the growth and well-being of all its members and particularly children, should be afforded the necessary protection and assistance so that it can fully assume its responsibilities within the community,

Recognizing that the child, for the full and harmonious development of his or her personality, should grow up in a family environment, in an atmosphere of happiness, love and understanding, . . .

Bearing in mind that, as indicated in the Declaration of Rights of the Child, "the child, by reason of his or her physical and mental immaturity, needs special safeguards and care, including appropriate legal protection . . ."

Article 3
1. In all actions concerning children, whether undertaken by public or private social welfare institutions, courts of law, administrative authorities or legislative bodies, the best interests of the child shall be a primary consideration.

Article 12
1. States Parties shall assure to the child who is capable of forming his or her own views the right to express those views freely in all matters affecting the child, the views of the child being given due weight in accordance with the age and maturity of the child.
2. For this purpose, the child shall in particular be provided the opportunity to be heard in any judicial and administrative proceedings affecting the child, either directly, or through a representative or an appropriate body, in a manner consistent with the procedural rules of national law.

Article 16
1. No child shall be subject to arbitrary or unlawful interference with his or her privacy, family, home or correspondence, nor to unlawful attacks on his or her honour or reputation. The child has the right to protection of the law against such interference or attacks.

Article 37
States parties shall ensure that:

(a) No child shall be subjected to torture or other cruel, inhuman or degrading treatment or punishment. Neither capital punishment nor life imprisonment without possibility of release shall be imposed for offences committed by persons below 18 years of age;

(b) No child shall be deprived of his or her liberty unlawfully or arbitrarily. The arrest, detention or imprisonment of a child shall be in conformity with the law and shall be used only as a measure of last resort and for the shortest appropriate period of time;

(c) Every child deprived of liberty shall be treated with humanity and respect for the inherent dignity of the human person, and in a manner which takes into account the needs of persons of his or her age. In particular, every child deprived of liberty shall be separated from adults unless it is considered in the child's best interest not to do so and shall have the right to maintain contact with his or her family through correspondence and visits, save in exceptional circumstances;

(d) Every child deprived of his or her liberty shall have the right to prompt access to legal and other appropriate assistance, as well as the right to challenge the legality of the deprivation of his or her liberty before a court or other competent, independent and impartial authority, and to a prompt decision on any such action.

Article 40
1. States Parties recognize the right of every child alleged as, accused of, or recognized as having infringed the penal law to be treated in a manner consistent with the promotion of the child's sense of dignity and worth, which reinforces the child's

respect for the human rights and fundamental freedoms of others and which takes into account the child's age and the desirability of promoting the child's reintegration and the child's assuming a constructive role in society . . .

3. States Parties shall seek to promote the establishment of laws, procedures, authorities and institutions specifically applicable to children alleged, accused of, or recognized as having infringed the penal law, and, in particular:

   (a) the establishment of a minimum age below which children shall be presumed not to have the capacity to infringe the penal law;

   (b) whenever appropriate and desirable, measures for dealing with such children without resorting to judicial proceedings, providing that human rights and legal safeguards are fully respected.

4. A variety of dispositions, such as care, guidance and supervision orders; counselling; probation; foster care; education and vocational training programmes and other alternatives to institutional care shall be available to ensure that children are dealt with in a manner appropriate to their well-being and proportionate both to their circumstances and the offence.

CHAPTER THREE

The "Facts" of Youth Crime

CHAPTER OBJECTIVES

1. To discuss the meaning of crime statistics through an examination of the strengths and limitations of various sources as measures of criminal activity—media, official, self-report, and victimization surveys—including issues of reliability and validity.
2. To compare crime patterns under the Juvenile Delinquents Act (JDA), Young Offenders Act (YOA), and Youth Criminal Justice Act (YCJA).
3. To profile youth crime patterns and trends and provide a focus on selected offences.
4. To discuss the violent-crime debate and contradictions in statistics and interpretations.
5. To revisit questions raised in Chapter 1 about youth crime by considering what is measured by the various sources, by comparing statistics from the three legislative periods (under the JDA, YOA, and YCJA), and by comparing rates of adult and youth crime.

KEY TERMS

Concept
Social control agencies
Field research
Aggregated
Crime index
Administrative charges
Self-report survey
Victimization survey
Clearance rates

Administrative offences
Empirical
Zero-tolerance policies
Reliability
Validity
Unfounded offences
Telescoping
Self-fulfilling prophecy

INTRODUCTION

This chapter is about the interrelated activities of defining and measuring youth crime. Before youth crime can be understood or explained, it must be measured or counted. Prior to this measuring or counting, the meaning of the term "youth crime" must be formalized—it cannot be accurately measured or counted without an exact definition of the term. For example, we measure a person's height in metres and centimetres or feet and inches. This implicitly sets the definition of the **concept** "height" in terms centimetres or inches. All concepts must be defined before they can be measured with any accuracy or reliability. Youth crime, as a concept, has been defined and measured in different ways over the last 150 years. This knowledge has important implications for our efforts to make sense of youth crime statistics.

As mentioned in the last chapter, under the Juvenile Delinquents Act, youth misbehaviour was defined, measured, and recorded as delinquency. Hence, statistics predating the Young Offenders Act include behaviours other than criminal acts as defined by the Criminal Code of Canada. As we saw in Chapter 2, delinquents were often children or youth who were deemed to be unmanageable by their parents and a Family Court judge. Since 1984 and the implementation of the Young Offenders Act, statistics have included only behaviours that are charged under the Criminal Code or various special provisions of the YOA and now the YCJA, such as failure to comply with a court order, which would mean that a youth might have not complied with the conditions attached to her or his probation. As well, delinquency law applied to a different age group than the YOA and YCJA, and this varied by province and over time. For example, the Juvenile Delinquents Act applied to those aged 7–17 in Quebec and 7–15 in Ontario and Nova Scotia.

Even the concept "young offender" has not been defined in a consistent manner. When the YOA was implemented in 1984—some sections did not become effective until 1985—it did not apply to 16- and 17-year-olds. This changed in 1986. So, for the first two years, 1984 and 1985, youth crime statistics for Ontario and Nova Scotia included only youth aged 12 to 15. Thus, statistics gathered prior to 1985 are not directly comparable to those gathered in later years.

Beyond the question of definition, we also need to know something about crime measurement. This chapter begins with a discussion of the sources of statistics on youth crime and what they are measuring. It moves on to develop a profile of youth crime by discussing types of youth crime and what we know about crime from different sources. The chapter ends with a discussion of measurement issues and a revisiting of key questions about youth crime that were raised in Chapter 1.

concept
A general or abstract term that refers to a class or group of more specific terms (e.g., "crime" refers to any number of specific behaviours).

MEASURING YOUTH CRIME

Measuring youth crime, or delinquency, is not an easy task, because what gets counted depends on the source of the information. The most common source of information on youth crime for many people is the media. The other major source, less accessible to the average person, is statistics provided by **social control agencies**. These agencies include police, courts, and various correctional institutions. Only some of this information is available to the public through Statistics Canada. Other information on youth crime comes from researchers who, over the years, have developed various techniques for measuring youth and adult crime through population surveys and **field research.** The two most common types of surveys are victimization surveys, which ask people if they have been victimized, and self-report surveys, which ask about a

social control agencies
Usually government agencies mandated to perform various functions in the justice system, such as police courts and correctional institutions.

field research
A method in which research is conducted outside of a laboratory, in the setting where the behaviour of interest is occurring.

TABLE 3.1

Relationship between Criminal Activity and Criminal Statistics

Criminal Activity	Source of Information
Actual crime	None
Voluntary admission of crime	Self-report survey
Detected crime	Victimization survey
Known about and Cleared Crime	
Reported, recorded, arrested	Police statistics
Convicted crime	Court records
Offenders serving terms of probation, prison, parole	Corrections agencies

person's involvement in criminal and delinquent activities. Most field research has been done with "street kids" and institutionalized populations. Each source is useful, but each has shortcomings as a measure of youth crime. Unless we understand the strengths and weaknesses of each of these sources, youth crime can easily be misunderstood or misrepresented in some very significant ways. Further, and most important, what we think we know about youth crime will depend on which source has been used.

Sources of information on crime and delinquency vary considerably as measures of actual criminal activity. Table 3.1 illustrates that surveys and field research are more representative of actual criminal activity than is the information we get from control agencies such as the police, courts, and prisons. Among agencies, a steadily diminishing amount of criminal activity is measured depending on whether the source is police records, court records, or correctional records. For example, not all crimes known to police result in charges, as charges may be dropped or reduced before going to court, and not all convictions result in probation or prison sentences. Further, agency statistics tell us as much (or more) about the activities of the agencies themselves as they do about youth crime. In fact, the statistics that we get from these agencies have not been designed to measure youth crime. Rather, they have been designed by agencies to be used for their own purposes. Courts, for example, need to know how long it takes to process a case for scheduling purposes. Survey and field information on youth crime provides a more valid measure of what we would consider to be the actual amount and character of youth crime, primarily because these measuring tools and techniques have been designed by researchers solely for the purpose of measuring criminal activity.

SOURCES AND WHAT THEY TELL US ABOUT YOUTH CRIME

The Media

Most people obtain information about youth crime exclusively from newspapers and television news reports. Sometimes journalists write books about youth crime. An example is Kevin Marron's *Apprenticed in Crime*, in which he tells his readers that

> the rate of violent offenses . . . has been increasing steadily in recent years, and such crimes now account for about 18 percent of the charges before youth courts.

Between 1987 and 1989, violent offenses by youths rose by about 10 percent, while property crimes decreased by 8 percent. Ontario, which accounts for 40 percent of all convictions under the Young Offenders Act in Canada also has the highest rate of violent offenses, which appear to be endemic in large urban centres. (1993, p. 49)

While this information is correct, when it is presented without a historical context or discussion of the limitations and shortcomings of the sources, it becomes misleading and contributes to public fears of a youth crime wave.

Bortner (1988) argues that all too often what appear to be crime waves may be more accurately described as "media waves." To make her point, she discusses Mark Fishman's analysis of how New York City's three daily newspapers and local television stations reported a surge of violent crime against elderly people. A public outcry for greater protection followed the news coverage. Politicians responded with get-tough measures and additional resources to increase policing activities. Fishman compared the media reports to police arrest statistics and found that youth violence had not increased. In fact, there had been a 19 percent decrease in violent criminal activity in the areas of the city that had been reported in the news as being particularly violent (Fishman, 1978, pp. 531–543).

Closer to home, we find that Canadians seem increasingly concerned about crime, and violent crime in particular. This concern becomes centred on youth when a few high-profile cases involving teenaged killers fuel public fears about youth crime. Surveys indicate that 4 in 10 Canadians rate juvenile delinquency as a "very serious problem" (Bibby, 1995, p. 101). Diane Ablonczy, as justice critic for the Reform Party (now the Conservative Party), stated that more young people were accused of homicide in 1994 than in 1993 and that violent crime by youths had increased at a faster pace than adult violent crime. Many Canadians and politicians, notably former Reform Party Leader Preston Manning, have been calling for the public to rule on reinstating the death penalty. An opinion poll conducted in June 1995 reported that 69 percent of those surveyed strongly or moderately supported capital punishment. Yet, figures released by Statistics Canada in July 1998 showed that the crime rate for young offenders charged with Criminal Code offences dropped for the sixth year in a row, and that the violent crime rate for youths had been on the decline since 1995 (Kong, 1998, p. 20).

Criminologists tend to have a very different view of youth crime than do politicians and the general public. Criminologists' interpretations of the statistics would suggest that Canadians are experiencing a media wave rather than a crime wave. According to Neil Boyd, a criminologist at Simon Fraser University, "all of the evidence is contrary to the majority of public perception, that crime is something that we are losing control of. In fact, the best evidence is something to the contrary" (quoted in Cox, 1995). Elliott Leyton, a professor of anthropology at Memorial University of Newfoundland, argues that Canadians are in a "violence panic . . . and are unaware that the threat of real crime 'in Canada is low by world standards'" (quoted in Bailey, 1995). Schissel (1997) concludes from an analysis of street youth and police statistics that

> . . . the logic and rhetoric of politics and news is so flawed and poorly struck that malicious intentions cannot be dismissed . . . the reality of youth crime shows that there is no substance to the contention that youths are progressively becoming more criminal and more dangerous. (p. 99)

Police Statistics

Crimes "known to police" refer to crimes for which the police have been provided information through complainants or from their own observations. Crimes "cleared by

TABLE 3.2

Percentage of Apprehended Youth Charged by Police (Selected Offences): Ontario, 1992; Canada 2004

| | Apprehended Youth | | Percentage of Apprehended Youth Who Are Charged | |
| | 1992 | 2004 | 1992 | 2004 |
Offence Type	(Ont.)	(Can.)	(Ont.)	(Can.)
Assault	16,723	2,512	63.1%	40.6%
Assault II	1,917	6,769	83.3%	69.7%
Assault III	147	447	98.6%	93.1%
Robbery	1,335	3,687	91.6%	82.8%
Theft over $1,000	821	332	73.7%	50.9%
Theft $1,000 & under	24,483	41,088	52.5%	24.2%

Sources: Statistics Canada, Canadian Crime Statistics, 1992, adapted from Doob, Marinos, & Varma (1995, p. 7); adapted from Statistics Canada, *Juristat*, Cat. No. 85-002, 25(5).

the police" refer to crimes for which police are satisfied they have a suspect and are prepared to process the case. Cases are processed either through laying charges or some other action, such as deciding to take a youth home to her or his parents, or referring the youth to a community agency or program. Whether police clear a charge varies considerably by type of offence.

Prior to 2003, standardized statistics on both police apprehensions and charges were not publicly available; these became available when the YCJA was implemented. In Table 3.2, which provides Ontario police statistics for 1992 under the YOA and new police statistics for the entire country under the YCJA, we see in both cases that the police have considerable discretion in deciding whether or not to charge a youth. Under both the YOA in 1992 and under the YCJA in 2004, we see that the more serious the offence, the more likely it was that police would lay a charge and take a youth to court. As Table 3.2 shows, the proportion of youth charged increased with the severity of assault. In 1992, charge rates, which are shown as 63.1 percent for first-level assault, increased to 98.6 percent for third-level assault. Similarly, the charge rate for theft over $1,000 is almost 74 percent, but only 52.5 percent for theft under $1,000. We see the same pattern for 2004 in that the percentage of apprehended youth who were charged by police increased from almost 41 percent for minor assault to 93 percent for serious assault. The percentage of youth charged for property charges ranged from 83 percent for robbery to 24 percent for theft under $1,000.

Individual police departments produce the majority of statistics on criminal activity in Canada. Record-keeping is limited to 132 Criminal Code offence categories and several drug and traffic offences (Creechan, 1995, p. 99). Police data in Canada were standardized by the *Uniform Crime Reporting* (UCR) system in the early 1960s. These standardized reports are sent to the Canadian Centre for Justice Statistics in Ottawa where they are **aggregated** and made available to the public. Police statistics are often reported as general indexes—the violent **crime index,** the property crime index, and the "other" crime index (Creechan, 1995, p. 100). UCR statistics include all police departments across the country. Since 1988, a revised UCR survey has collected,

aggregated
Statistics on crime and other social behaviour are deemed aggregated when they are grouped into categories that make it impossible to match individuals on other characteristics.

crime index
A Statistics Canada categorization scheme for classifying police crime statistics as property, violent, and "other" index crimes.

from a sample of police departments, detailed information concerning individual incidents. After the YCJA was implemented, UCR statistics for youth crime are reported for "youth charged" as well as "youth cleared otherwise." This latter category includes youth processed through formal extrajudicial measures programs, a caution by the Crown, and more informal police actions, such as a warning or referral to a community agency or program.

What Police Statistics Tell Us About Youth Crime

UCR statistics comparing offences from 1986 to 2004 indicate that the number of youth charged with Criminal Code offences has both increased and decreased on a year-to-year basis over this time period and, with the exception of increases in 2000–2001, has been on the decline since 1992. Hence, Tables 3.3A and 3.3B show that the total number of youth charges rose steadily from 107,698 in 1987 to a high of 142,316 in 1991, dropped to a low of 99,322 in 1999, then increased to 102,690 in 2001. While the years 1992 to 1999 showed a consistent decline, the most dramatic decline over the entire eighteen-year period took place over the last three years, which culminated with a record low number of 78,100 charges for 2004. While the decline over the 2003–2004 period is likely due to the 2003 formalization of extrajudicial measures in the YCJA, it is important to note that 2002, one year prior to the YCJA, had the lowest number of charges since 1986, when the YOA was fully implemented.

Furthermore, Figure 3.1 shows that the rate of youth cleared otherwise remained fairly consistent throughout the period of the YOA and actually began its decline in 2000. However, in the face of these declines, the number of youth charged with violent offences consistently increased until 1995 before showing declines, and then increased again until 2001. Since then, youth charges for violent offences have been on the decline, with the most dramatic rate decline (15.9 percent) in the first year of the YCJA. Figure 3.2 shows that of the 78,100 youth charged with Criminal Code offences in 2004, 21 percent were charged with violent crimes, 41 percent with property crimes, and 37 percent with other Criminal Code offences (Kong, 1998, p. 20; Sauve, 2005, pp. 12–13).

While these figures could be used to support public concerns, particularly regarding violent crime, viewing the statistics in a more detailed or comparative context presents a less dramatic view of youth crime. First, as Tables 3.3A and 3.3B show, except for a slight increase in 2000 and 2001, the youth violent crime rate has remained relatively stable for the last 10 years, and both the rate of youth charged and cleared otherwise declined in 2004. Second, about three-quarters of young people charged or cleared for violent crimes have been involved in minor assault incidents, such behaviours as pushing and shoving, incidents not resulting in physical injury (Sauve, 2005, p. 13). Third, the most serious offence, homicide, is consistently low for youth, with a rate that has fluctuated from 2 to 3 per 100,000 youth since the introduction of the YOA and actually declined by 27 percent between 1994 and 2004.

Furthermore, as we will see later in this chapter, adults are responsible for considerably more crime, including crimes of violence, than are young people. Compared to youth violence at 22 percent, violent crimes accounted for 31 percent of all adult Criminal Code offences in 2000 (Logan, 2000, p. 12). Finally, an examination of the ratio of youth to adult charges compared to total incidents from 1973 to 1995 shows a dramatic increase in youth charges for violent offences after the YOA was

TABLE 3.3A

Youth Charged in Criminal Code Incidents, Canada, 1986–1994*

	1986	1987	1988	1989	1990	1991	1992	1993	1994r
Population (aged 12–17)	2,272,400	2,260,900	2,249,500	2,245,700	2,260,100	2,284,800	2,315,800	2,341,200	2,360,400
Violent crime:									
Number	9,275	10,165	11,437	13,780	15,690	18,919	20,028	21,477	21,629
Rate	408	450	508	614	694	828	865	917	916
% change in rate from previous year	...	10.2	13.1	20.7	13.1	19.3	4.4	6.1	−0.1
Property crime:									
Number	78,862	74,769	74,316	76,317	83,741	91,656	83,603	74,981	68,907
Rate	3,470	3,307	3,304	3,398	3,705	4,012	3,610	3,203	2,919
% change in rate from previous year	...	−4.7	−0.1	2.9	9.0	8.3	−10.0	−11.3	−8.8
Other Criminal Code:									
Number	20,869	22,764	24,136	25,865	27,118	31,741	31,651	30,429	29,089
Rate	918	1,007	1,073	1,152	1,200	1,389	1,367	1,300	1,232
% change in rate from previous year	...	9.6	6.6	7.3	4.2	15.8	−1.6	−4.9	−5.2
Total Criminal Code:									
Number	109,006	107,698	109,889	115,962	126,549	142,316	135,282	126,887	119,625
Rate	4,797	4,764	4,885	5,164	5,599	6,229	5,842	5,420	5,068
% change in rate from previous year	...	−0.7	2.6	5.7	8.4	11.2	−6.2	−7.2	−6.5

*Rates are calculated on the basis of 100,000 youths. Population estimates from Statistics Canada Census and Demographic Statistics, Demography Division.

Populations as of July 1st: Revised intercensal estimates from 1985 to 1990 and final intercensal estimates for 1991 to 1994.

r Revised

... Figures not appropriate

Sources: Adapted from Statistics Canada, *Juristat*, Cat. No. 85-002, 15(12); Cat. No. 85-002, 21(8).

TABLE 3.3B
Youth Charged in Criminal Code Incidents, Canada, 1995–2004*

	1995	1996	1997	1998	1999	2000	2001r	2002	2003r	2004
Population (aged 12–17)	2,348,600	2,417,500	2,445,400	2,449,696	2,449,097	2,451,701	2,471,230	2,502,828	2,535,053	2,547,801
Violent crime:										
Number	22,375	22,521	22,252	22,195	21,102	22,635	23,617	23,364	20,434	20,082
Rate	938	932	910	906	862	923	956	934	806	788
% change in rate from previous year	2.4	−0.9	−2.3	−0.3	−4.9	7.2	3.5	−2.3	−15.9	−2.3
Property crime:										
Number	68,138	66,702	59,532	54,104	48,009	46,248	45,175	43,349	34,190	30,317
Rate	2,857	2,759	2,434	2,209	1,960	1,886	1,828	1,732	1,349	1,190
% change in rate from previous year	−2.1	−3.3	−11.8	−7.6	−11.2	−3.8	−3.2	−5.3	−28.4	−13.4
Other Criminal Code:										
Number	30,119	30,187	29,952	31,153	30,211	31,978	33,898	32,287	28,439	27,701
Rate	1,263	1,249	1,225	1,272	1,234	1,304	1,372	1,290	1,122	1,087
% change in rate from previous year	2.5	−1.0	−1.9	2.3	−3.0	5.7	5.0	−6.0	−15.0	−3.2
Total Criminal Code:										
Number	120,632	119,410	111,736	107,452	99,322	100,861	102,690	99,000	83,063	78,100
Rate	5,059	4,939	4,569	4,386	4,055	4,114	4,155	3,956	3,277	3,065
% change in rate from previous year	−0.2	−2.3	−7.5	−3.5	−7.5	1.4	1.0	−4.8	−20.7	−6.9

*Rates are calculated on the basis of 100,000 youths. Population estimates from Statistics Canada Census and Demographic Statistics, Demography Division. Caution must be used in interpreting rates for 2003 because of changes in police reporting of apprehended youth.

Populations as of July 1st: Final intercensal estimates for 1995; final postcensal estimates for 1996 and 1997; updated postcensal estimates for 1998, 1999, and 2001; and preliminary postcensal estimates for 2000, 2002, and 2004.

r Revised

Sources: Adapted from Statistics Canada, *Juristat*, Cat. No. 85-002, 15(12); Cat. No. 85-002, 21(8); Cat. No. 85-002, 23(5); Cat. No. 85-002, 25(5).

FIGURE 3.1

Youth Crime Rates: 1984–2004

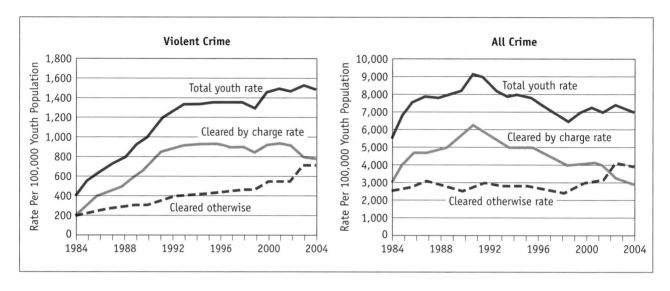

Sources: *Uniform Crime Reporting Survey*, CCJS; Statistics Canada, *Juristat*, Cat. No. 85-002, 25(5), p. 13.

FIGURE 3.2

Young Offender
Index Crime

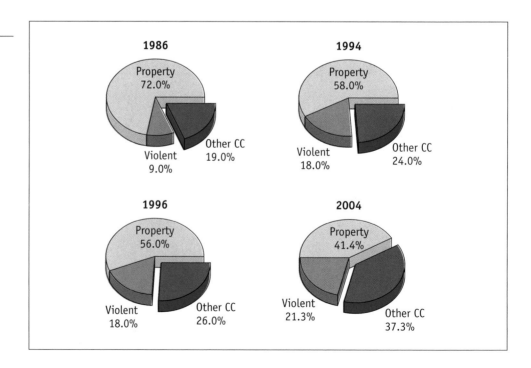

Sources: Statistics Canada. (1990b, 1995, 1997, 2001), *Juristat*, Cat. No. 85-002, 25(5).

implemented, which suggests that youth are processed through the justice system for violent offences in greater numbers than adults (Schissel, 1997, pp. 80–81). Hence, official adult rates for violent crime are also likely underestimated compared to youth rates, and the gap is greater than official statistics suggest.

Nonetheless, despite decreasing rates of reported youth crime since 1986, the violent crime rate for 2004 was still higher than it was for 1990 (788 vs. 694 per 100,000). This fact, along with support from media stories about violent youth crime, continues to fuel public concern. In 1986, as we saw in Figure 3.2, 9 percent of all police charges against young people were for violent crimes; by 1996, this proportion had doubled to 18 percent and then rose to 21 percent in 2004 (although this was a decline when compared with the 22 percent rate reported in 2000) (Logan, 2000, p. 12; Sauve, 2005, p. 13).

Court Statistics

Court statistics are kept by individual courts and yield smaller numbers than police statistics. Not all people who are known to the police end up arrested, and not all arrested people end up in court. The value of court records is that they can provide information about offenders and their offences. Court files can provide detailed information, for example, on whether other people were involved in the offence or who the victims might be. If a report on a young offender has been prepared, information is also available on the young person's family, school records, prior criminal activity, and various other information of a social nature that is not ever available from police records. In addition, court records provide information about sentences.

Youth court records are not accessible to the public in every province, but basic data are sent to Ottawa and compiled for public distribution by the Canadian Centre for Justice Statistics. These public statistics are similar to police statistics in that the information is aggregated. An advantage of police and court statistics is that they are usually available for the entire country. Part of the negotiations for acceptance of the YOA by provincial governments involved a commitment on the part of the federal government to provide record-keeping for young offender courts. To this end, the federal government set up a special branch of the Centre for Justice Statistics to compile youth court data. This information is published on a yearly basis (*Youth Court Survey*) for the entire country and for individual provinces.

What Court Statistics Tell Us About Youth Crime

Figure 3.3 shows court statistics comparing 1986–1987 with 1996–1997, 1999–2000, and 2003–2004. We see the same patterns that are evident in police statistics. In 1986, 67 percent of all cases heard in youth court were property offences, 13 percent were violent offences, and 19 percent were all other offences. By 2004, property offence cases going to court had decreased to 36 percent and, with the exception of other Criminal Code offences, all other types of offences showed continual increases over this period. Court cases involving violent offences increased to 29 percent, drugs to 6 percent, and other federal offences to 1 percent. The most dramatic increases occurred for YOA/YCJA offences. These have increased consistently from 3 percent of court cases in 1986–1987 to 21 percent in 2004. While it appears the YCJA is accomplishing its goal to keep less serious offences out of the courts, increasing rates of administrative offences are continuing with the YCJA. These will be discussed later in the chapter.

Despite the same general pattern that exists between court statistics and index crimes, a word of caution is in order regarding comparisons of anything other than

FIGURE 3.3

Youth Court Cases by Offence Category, Canada: 1986–1987, 1996–1997, 1999–2000, 2003–2004

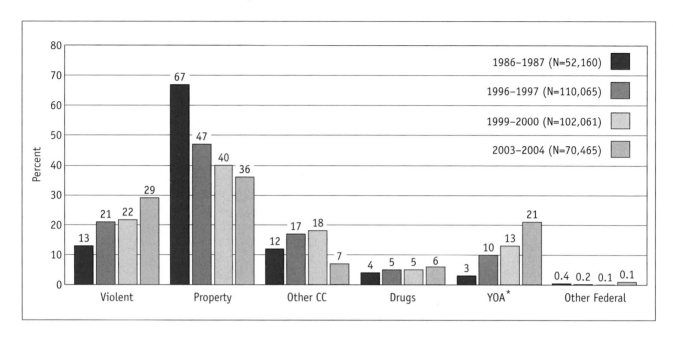

Note: Data exclude Ontario and the Northwest Territories in the 1986–1987 period.

*Includes YOA and administration of justice offences.

Sources: Adapted from deSouza (1995); Statistics Canada (1998, p. xiii), *Juristat*, Cat. No. 85-002, 21(3); *Juristat*, Cat. No. 85-002, 25(4); Sudworth & deSouza (2001, pp. 4, 14).

administrative charges
Charges laid for behaviours that are not generally considered to be criminal (e.g., failure to appear in court).

broad patterns. First of all, with index crime categories, "other" offences include only Criminal Code charges, whereas in court statistics the "other" category also includes some **administrative charges** under the Young Offenders Act. A major weakness with youth court statistics—particularly problematic when we try to compare across years—is that, in 1986, Ontario and the Northwest Territories were not included in the statistics. Ontario is not included in youth court statistics until after 1992 and, even then, only partially. Nonetheless, this exclusion is not likely to affect proportions or rates by category of offence but only the figures for numbers of cases appearing before the courts. Finally, youth court statistics measure only cases going to court and are therefore not a valid measure of youth criminal activity. As such, they are more useful as a measure or indicator of youth justice than of youth crime.

Self-Report Surveys

self-report survey
A criminology questionnaire survey, in which individuals are asked to report on their involvement in criminal or delinquent activities.

An interesting way of measuring crime and delinquency is to use a **self-report survey.** Under this approach, people are simply asked about their involvement in criminal or delinquent behaviour. Typically, surveys are administered to school population samples. Some recent Canadian research has surveyed people in natural settings. Such field research is often conducted on the streets. McCarthy, for example, surveyed young people who hung around the Eaton Centre on Toronto's Yonge Street (McCarthy & Hagan, 1992). In some ways, as we will see in Chapter 5, nothing changed the face of criminological theory more than the discovery of self-reported measures of delinquent behaviour.

According to Creechan (1995, p. 97), the use of self-report studies originated with a sociologist named Austin Porterfield, who experimented with them at Texas Christian University in the 1940s (Porterfield, 1946). The first self-report study of delinquent behaviour to have a significant impact on criminologists' thinking about delinquency was that done by Nye and Short (1957, p. 328). Prior to this research, the only statistics available on the criminal and delinquent behaviour of young people came from official sources (i.e., courts, police, or institutions). When the self-report questionnaire was introduced, it immediately became apparent that the actual amount of criminal and delinquent behaviour by young people was much higher than had ever been reported through official statistics. In addition, self-report studies revealed a profile of people involved in crime and delinquency that was very different from that gleaned from official records. Official records tend to under-represent the offences of middle-class youth, presenting instead a profile of delinquents and young offenders as poor, working class, and members of visible minorities.

In the mid-1990s, Statistics Canada and Human Resources Development Canada began a joint project to collect longitudinal data on children and youth—*the National Longitudinal Survey of Children and Youth* (NLSCY). Beginning in 1994–1995, the project began collecting information on a sample of 22,000 children up to age 11. These children will be interviewed every two years until they reach age 25. Prior to age 10, teachers and/or parents or guardians are interviewed. Self-report information is now available on delinquency, since included in the survey are a few questions about child and youth involvement in stealing, vandalism, and aggressive behaviours directed toward others (Dauvergne & Johnson, 2001, p. 2; Sprott, Doob, & Jenkins, 2001, pp. 2–3).

What Self-Report Surveys Tell Us About Youth Crime

Typically, results from self-report studies indicate that delinquent and criminal behaviour is far more widespread than one would ever think from looking at official statistics. According to Bortner (1988, p. 144), self-report measures of delinquency report estimates that range from four to ten times the amount reported by official statistics. In one American study that Bortner cited, 88 percent of the 13- to 16-year-old youth surveyed admitted to participating in at least one delinquent act during the three years prior to the study; less than 3 percent of these offences had been detected by police, while only 22 percent of the juveniles had ever had contact with police and less than 2 percent had ever gone to court (Bortner, 1988, p. 145).

One of the first Canadian self-report studies was done by Marc Le Blanc. Seven surveys were carried out by Le Blanc and his colleagues in Montreal schools between 1967 and 1976. A relatively stable proportion of adolescents (approximately 90 percent in each of the seven surveys) admitted to having committed a delinquent act (Le Blanc, 1983, pp. 33–35). Things have not changed much since then; a comparative study of self-reported delinquency in Montreal in 1974 and in 1985 showed no change in the level or nature of self-reported delinquency (Le Blanc & Tremblay, 1988).

Data from the NLSCY indicates that for the 1994/95 and 1996/97 survey, at age 12–13, approximately 30 percent of the girls surveyed reported involvement in delinquency of a property or aggressive nature, while 40 percent of the boys reported involvement in property-related delinquency and 66 percent in aggressive behaviours

(Sprott, Doob, & Jenkins, 2001, p. 3). These rates may be lower than those reported by Le Blanc and other studies because the NLSCY is limited at this point to 11- to 13-year-olds. On the other hand, a 1999 survey of Grades 7 to 12 students in Alberta that asked about specific delinquencies over a 12-month period found delinquency rates higher than reported in the NLSCY and lower than reported in the Montreal studies. Slightly more than half (55.7 percent) of the Albertan youth reported engaging in at least one act of delinquency in the previous year (Gomes, Bertrand, Paetsch, & Hornick, 2003, p. 81).

Using a different approach, something more like field research and with a focus on criminal rather than delinquent behaviour, Stephen Baron surveyed 200 male street youth, all under the age of 24, about their illegal behaviour over a 12-month period. Most of the boys and young men that he surveyed had not had a fixed address or had lived in a shelter during the last year. Among those who were homeless, most had spent almost five months living exclusively on the street during the survey period, and 19 percent had been without shelter for at least six months. Baron's survey yielded the following results:

> These 200 youth reported committing some 334,636 crimes during the twelve months prior to the interview—an average of 1,673 per respondent. Although this figure seems astronomical, analysis by type indicates that drug offenses are responsible for 72 percent of the reported crime. Thus, most of the crime takes place between willing participants on the street . . . [T]he bulk of the non-related offenses . . . appears to be directed against others leading similar 'risky lifestyles'. The group fights, the robberies and the assaults are all a result of interactions in the risky areas frequented by the respondents. (1995, p. 145)

Baron's self-report survey of criminal activity among male street youth provides a very different picture of criminal activity from that provided by official statistics or the earlier Montreal studies. While the most frequent offence reported by the youth in Baron's sample was drug-related (72 percent), violent offences accounted for only 5 percent of all the reported offences. Aggravated assault and common assault most often stemmed from disputes, horseplay, or drunkenness, or from a situation that "called for revenge," such as somebody getting "ripped off" in a drug deal (Baron, 1995, pp. 143–144).

Property crime accounted for only 20 percent of the offences reported by the male youth in Baron's sample. Usually, a small number of male offenders are responsible for the majority of property offences. This result is consistent with findings in other studies. Nonetheless, twenty-four of the 200 youth that Baron surveyed "insisted that they had been involved in a combined total of over 500 property offences" (1995, p. 141). McCarthy and Hagan (1992), who used self-report measures in their survey of 475 homeless youth in Toronto during 1987 and 1988, argued that the crimes of homeless youth are directly related to the adversity of living on the streets: "Consistently, hunger causes theft of food, problems of hunger and shelter lead to serious theft, and problems of shelter and unemployment produce prostitution" (p. 623).

victimization survey
A survey questionnaire that asks individuals whether they have been victimized over a particular time period, and in what ways.

Victimization Surveys

A more recently developed method of acquiring information about criminal behaviour is the **victimization survey.** This approach involves asking people if they have ever been victimized by the criminal behaviour of others. Although victimization data do not provide a direct measure of the nature or prevalence of youth crime, they do provide considerable information that is useful in combination with other sources.

The U.S. government collects victimization data on an annual basis from a sample of the population. The first national survey in the United States was conducted in 1966. Since that time, victimization surveys have become the principal method of gaining information about the volume of specific types of crime and delinquency. The U.S. government also conducts victimization surveys of high-school students to determine how crime affects the daily lives of teenagers (Creechan, 1995, p. 98).

The first Canadian victimization survey was conducted by the Ministry of the Solicitor General and Statistics Canada in the early 1980s. Known as the *Canadian Urban Victimization Survey* (CUVS), it gathered data from some 61,000 Canadians aged 16 and over. The respondents, who consisted of residents of seven cities (Greater Vancouver, Edmonton, Winnipeg, Toronto, Montreal, Halifax/Dartmouth, and St. John's) were interviewed about their experiences with certain crimes during the 1981 calendar year (Johnson & Lazarus, 1989, p. 311). Since then, information collected by Statistics Canada about crime victimization has been incorporated into the federal government's *General Social Survey* (GSS). In this survey, which began in 1988 and is undertaken every five years, a sample of more than 10,000 Canadians over the age of 15 are asked questions about assault, robbery, sexual assault, personal theft, break and enters to their homes, theft of household property or cars, and vandalism. In 1999, questions on spousal violence were added to the GSS (Besserer & Trainor, 2000, p. 2). In addition, in 1993, Statistics Canada conducted a survey of women (*Violence Against Women Survey*) regarding their experiences of sexual and physical assault, and some victimization data is available for children and youth from the NLSCY.

What Victimization Surveys Tell Us About Youth Crime

Victimization surveys focus on crimes against individuals and households and thus do not measure other common offences, such as shoplifting. Nonetheless, victimization surveys do tell us something about crime trends. Comparisons between the four GSS survey periods (1988, 1993, 1999, 2004) show a relatively flat trend with respect to the victimization rate. Victimization rates were 24 percent for the first two periods (Gartner & Doob, 1994) and increased slightly to 26 percent in 1999 and to 28 percent by 2004. These increases are primarily due to increases in household-related property crimes (Gannon & Mihorean, 2005, pp. 4, 5). Interestingly, the 2004 GSS also indicates that more people feel safe from crime and satisfied with their personal safety than they did in 1999 (Gannon& Mihorean, 2005, p. 4).

As with other victimization surveys, the 2004 GSS confirms that official crime rates are under-reported and that this varies by offence. About 34 percent of the 2004 GSS respondents reported their victimization to police. Among violent victimizations, more robberies and physical assaults were reported (46 and 39 percent, respectively) than sexual assaults (8 percent). Approximately half of the reported break and enters and motor vehicle/parts thefts (54 and 49 percent, respectively) were reported to police, while 31 percent of vandalism incidents and 29 percent of household property thefts were reported to the police (Gannon & Mihorean, 2005, pp. 12, 16). Young people between the ages of 15 and 24 are less likely to report victimization than older people (Gannon & Mihorean, 2005, pp. 13, 25).

clearance rates
Refers to statistics that indicate the rate at which police process criminal incidents as charged offences.

What is particularly useful about victimization surveys, then, is that they allow us to know something about police **clearance rates** for specific offences and about which offences will be underestimated in police statistics. Comparison of the victimization survey results with police clearance rates generally shows that reporting and clearance rates for crimes against persons are very different from property crimes. We have seen that reporting rates for crimes against persons tend to be lower than household property crimes, but clearance rates for these offences are considerably higher than for property offences. According to the 1999 GSS, about half of the vandalism cases were not reported to the police, and only 15 percent of those reported were cleared. For household break and enters, 17 percent of the cases reported to the police were cleared. Of the 10 percent of sexual assault cases that were reported to police, a suspect was named in about two-thirds of the cases. Most homicides are reported, and police are able to name a suspect in 75 percent of the cases (Doob & Cesaroni, 2004, p. 82).

With regard to measuring the offences that young people commit, victimization surveys are not able to give us information about an offender's age if there has not been any contact between the victim and the offender. Even if the victim saw the offender in a particular case, age is not always easily discernible. Hindelang and McDermott (1981) reported that gender is the easiest characteristic for victims to recall, race is somewhat difficult, and age is the most difficult. Nonetheless, they did find that victims' accuracy rates for estimating the age of an offender was not less than 89 percent for any age group.

On the other hand, Doob, Marinos, and Varma (1995) point out that if an offender is a stranger and around the age of 18, victims are not likely to be able to judge whether the offender is an adult or a youth. Age is known when a victimization is reported to the police and someone is charged. In this case, the GSS indicates that in 2004 only 15 percent of the accused in reported victimizations were young offenders (Gannon & Mihorean, 2005, p. 24). Furthermore, Doob and Cesaroni (2004) compare the age of accused and the age of victims from the 1999 GSS and find that young people are more likely to victimize other young people and older people to victimize people their own age rather than youth (p. 81).

Victimization surveys are also limited in that they cannot measure victimless crimes such as drug offences. Nor can they measure crimes against people who are not aware that they have been victimized. For example, jewellery may be stolen and not missed by the owner until months or even years after the theft; at that point, the owner may simply assume that the item is lost. Offences committed against businesses or corporations are also not counted in victimization surveys.

Some critics have raised concerns about victimization surveys because of the possibility that victim reports may be influenced by popular stereotypes of criminals. Media crime images are such that minorities and young people may be more likely reported as offenders. Hindelang and McDermott's findings from victimization surveys in the United States (1981) indicate that actual crimes committed by juveniles contradict media portrayals of juvenile crime. Their comparisons of juvenile offenders (under 18 years), youthful offenders (18 to 20 years), and adult offenders (over 21 years) show that juvenile crime is "demonstrably less serious than youthful offender and adult crime in three major areas." There is less weapon use by juveniles, juveniles are less successful than adults in committing theft-motivated offences, and there are lower rates of victim injury for juvenile offences (p. 72). As we saw in Chapter 1, these facts are contradicted by many media images of youth crime.

PROFILING YOUTH CRIME

Property Crime

As we have seen, according to police statistics, property crime is the most common of all youth offences, but its frequency declined between 1990 and 2004 relative to other types of offences. The rate of youth property crime is now the lowest it has been in 25 years. Index crime figures for property offences in 2004 indicated that most property crime charges were for theft (60 percent), followed by break and enter (22 percent). Both have been declining such that the rate of youth charged for these offences was one-half in 2002 what it was in 1990. Motor vehicle theft rates, on the other hand, have shown more fluctuation, with a rate, on average, of one-half to one-third that of break and enter (Logan, 2000, p. 20; Sauve, 2005, p. 21; Wallace, 2003, p. 23). The peak age of youth charged with property crimes is 16 (Kong, 1998, p. 11) and most youth property crime is of a petty nature; the majority involves shoplifting (Creechan, 1995, pp. 102–103).

Baron's study of male street youth (1995) also found that most property crime is of a petty nature. He reports that stolen items tended to be things easily concealed and distributed, such as clothes, game cartridges, and cassette players. Cash, jewellery, guns, TVs, VCRs, and stereos were the kinds of items most often taken during a break and enter. Baron further notes that respondents usually received only 10 to 15 percent of the value of their stolen property. Not surprisingly, the primary motivation for property crime among Baron's respondents was purely utilitarian: they needed the money. Sometimes their thefts were directly related to their homelessness in that they would often break into houses or buildings in order to sleep or steal food. Cars were sometimes stolen so that goods from burglaries could be moved, but most of the motor vehicle thefts involved joyriding (Baron, 1995, p. 142).

Violent Offences

In 2004, 78 percent of all youth violent crime offences were assault, 10 percent were robbery, 7 percent were sexual assault, and 0.2 percent were homicide (Sauve, 2005, p. 21). As with property crime, the majority of violent crimes that young people commit are minor (in particular, minor assault). This is particularly true for girls. In 1998, more than two-thirds (67.3 percent) of violent crime charges for girls were for common assault, the corresponding proportion for boys was 46 percent. However, girls are charged at younger ages than boys. Violent offence charges peak for male youth at ages 16 and 17, but at 14 and 15 for girls.

The next most frequent violent offence charges for both male and female youth are assault causing bodily harm (20 percent and 16 percent, respectively) and robbery (19 percent and 9 percent). These proportions have changed little over the past 10 years (Savoie, 1999, pp. 5, 6, 9). What has changed, and dramatically, is robbery. The rate of youth charged with robbery doubled from 1988–1998, from 7 to 15 per 10,000, and then levelled at 14 per 10,000 since that time (Logan, 2000, p. 23; Sauve, 2005, p. 23; Savoie, 1999, p. 23). These increases in youth violent crime rates are largely attributed to increases in charges for common assault and robbery (Savoie, 1999, p. 6). Later in this chapter, we will discuss the extent to which increases in violent offence charges can be accounted for by changes in police charging practices.

Contrary to media impressions, the elderly, the very young, and strangers are not the primary targets of youth violence. Figure 3.4, which presents the most recent

FIGURE 3.4

Age and Gender of
Victims of Violent
Crimes Committed
by Youth, 1998

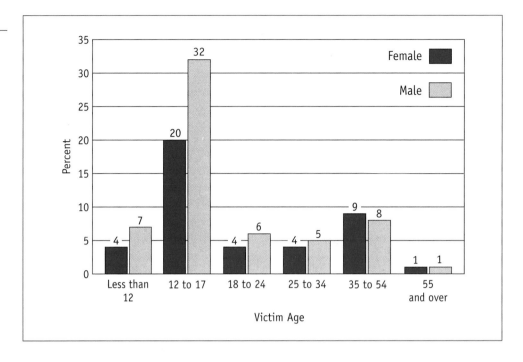

Note: Percentage may not add to 100% due to rounding.

Source: Statistics Canada, Cat. No. 85-00219(13).

available data on the age and gender of the victims of youth violence, shows that, in 1998, only 2 percent of the victims of youth violence were aged 55 or older, 11 percent were younger, and the majority (52 percent), were their own age. Furthermore, two-thirds (60 percent) of the victims of youth violence were acquaintances of the youth, and boys' offences more often involved strangers (22 percent) than did girls' offences (12 percent).

Youth are also no more likely than adults to use weapons. Fourteen percent of youth violence charges involved a weapon, compared to 13 percent of adult charges. Nonetheless, boys and girls used knives with the same frequency, which was more than adult males (48 percent vs. 38 percent) and about the same frequency as women (45 percent). Boys (15 percent), similar to men (18 percent), used firearms more than did girls and women (3 percent) (Savoie, 1999, p. 12).

Location of the offence is one area where youth violence differs from that of adults. Whereas most adult violence occurs in the home (60 percent), youth violence most often occurs in public places (35 percent), 24 percent occurs at school, and 24 percent occurs at home. Of all youth violence charges in 1998, only 10 percent occurred on school property, but charge rates are lower for school-related violence than for other types, suggesting that this is an underestimate (Savoie, 1999, pp. 9–12). School self-report surveys indicate that more minor assaults occur on school property than is suggested by police statistics. A 1995 survey of Calgary middle and high schools reported that 31 percent of boys and 41 percent of girls reported having slapped, punched, or kicked someone in the previous year, and 24 percent of the girls and 33 percent of the boys reported having threatened to hurt someone (Smith et al.,

1995). Another Canadian survey, focusing on more serious acts of violence, found that half of the boys surveyed (52 percent) and one-fifth of the girls (21 percent) reported that "they had beaten up another kid once or twice" (Artz, 1998, p. 27). As we saw earlier, similar findings on adolescent aggressive behaviour have been reported in the NLSCY (Sprott, Doob, & Jenkins, 2001, p. 3).

Sexual Assault

Sexual assault is an area of youth violence about which we know relatively little. The most recent report from Statistics Canada on sexual assault (Kong, Johnson, Beattie, & Cardillo, 2003) provides only limited aggregate information on sex offenders by age and considerably more detailed information on persons victimized by sexual assault. The latest GSS victimization report is also unable to provide information on young offenders. Here, Gannon and Mihorean (2005) report that specific offence information for youth accused of violent incidents is "too unreliable to be published" with regard to sexual offences and to be used "with caution" regarding other violent offences (fn 24).

Police statistics indicate that youth sexual offences appeared to increase after the YOA was implemented. From 1986 to 1988, sexual assault charges increased from 0.94 percent of all police youth charges to 1.10 percent, and Corrado and Markwart (1994, p. 352) report a 103 percent increase in the rate of sexual assault charges against youth from 1986 to 1992. However, with the exception of an increase in 2000 (from 58 to 69 per 10,000, or 1.7 percent of all police youth charges) (Logan, 2000, pp. 12, 14, 20), the rate of youth sexual assault has been on the decline since 1992 (Wallace, 2003, p. 23). Sexual assault now accounts for 1.8% of all police youth charges and 6.8% of all youth violent crime charges (Sauve, 2005, p. 21), a rate that is almost one-third less in 2004 than it was in 1992. While overall rates of sexual offending are low for youth and the majority of sexual offenders are adult males, with a mean age of 33, comparisons of age-specific offence rates show that in 2001, the highest rates of sexual offending were for youth aged 13–17. Among this group, the highest rate of sexual offences was found among 13- and 14-year-olds, who were mostly involved in minor offences (behaviours such as "unwanted sexual touching") with victims their own age (Kong, Johnson, Beattie, & Cardillo, 2003, p. 7).

On the other hand, children and youth are far more likely to be victims of sexual assault. Police statistics also report that two-thirds (61 percent) of the victims of sexual assault in 2003 were under the age of 18 and 80% were girls. Three-quarters (75.4 percent) of the victims under age 14 were girls (AuCoin, 2005, pp. 7, 18–19). The highest sexual victimization rate was for girls aged 13 (78.1 per 10,000), while male sexual victimization rates were highest for boys aged 3 to 14; among these, the highest rate was for boys aged 4 (approximately 16 per 10,000). Half of the children under 12 had been victimized by a family member and only 9 percent by strangers (Kong, Johnson, Beattie, & Cardillo, 2003, pp. 7, 20). Girls are particularly at risk for violence in dating situations. While girls under 16 have the highest rates of sexual violence by a dating partner or close friend (35 per 100,000), young women aged 18 to 20 are at a greater risk of physical assault from their dates (308/100,000) (Kong, Johnson, Beattie, & Cardillo, 2003, p. 8). The next chapter discusses youth victimization in more detail.

Until recently, sexual assault by young people tended to be ignored or dismissed as minor or experimental in nature (Brayton, 1996). Increases in rates of sexual assault may thus be explained by changing attitudes. To the extent that the public is more sensitized to some behaviours as constituting sexual offences, people are likely reporting more behaviours as sexual offences and police are likely responding and charging these offences more often. Kong et al. (2003) suggest that the recent declines in overall rates of sexual offending are somewhat due to declines in the population aged 15–34, the group that historically is responsible for the highest rates of victimization and offending (p. 3).

While some sexual assault by youth and adolescents may be characterized as "experimental" or "minor," even these offences can have serious consequences for both victims and offenders. A sexual assault interpreted as "experimentation" may involve an older child taking advantage of a younger child. In these situations, the older child has often been placed in a position of trust. More specifically, babysitters (most often male) have sexually assaulted children (most often female) in their charge, and older children sometimes sexually assault younger siblings (see Box 3.1). According to the NLSCY, 3.3 percent of surveyed boys aged 12–15 reported they had "sexually touched someone who was unwilling" and 1.3 percent that they had "forced someone to have sex" (Kong, Johnson, Beattie, & Cardillo, 2003, p. 8). Hence, some youth sexual assault does involve rape, and the accused may be very young. In one case, an 11-year-old boy was accused of raping a 13-year-old girl; according to court testimony, four boys (aged 10, 11, and 13) "ripped off her jeans" and held her down "so that the eleven-year-old could rape her" (Wattie, 1996).

BOX 3.1

Professional Views: A Typology of Adolescent Sex Offenders

Naive Experimenter
- Offender: Young boys, 11–14 years of age
- Victim: Younger child, 2–6, usually female
- Usually involves one or a few acts that are sexually explorative (fondling)
- Offences not usually progressive
- No use of force or threat

Undersocialized Child Exploiter
- Offender: Older boys aged 12–17
- Victim: Younger child, aged 10–12, usually female, but not always
- Involves intercourse, masturbation, oral sex, exposure to pornography
- A high risk of reoffending
- Uses manipulation, rewards, and enticement

Pseudo-Socialized Child Exploiter
- Offender: Is similar to the undersocialized but has good social skills and acts self-confident—is himself a victim of ongoing abuse
- Gets sexual pleasure through exploitation of others

Sexual Aggressive
- Offender: Male, aged 13–18
- Victim: Generally female
- Offences violent, involve penetration with victim degradation—respond to resistance with aggression

- Desires power through domination and humiliation
- Offender often a victim of family violence and sexual assault

Sexual Compulsive
- Offender: Male, aged 14–18
- Victim: Either sex, any age
- Behaviour results from psychological disorder, substance abuse, severe family dysfunction
- Offence is impulsive

Peer-Group Influenced
- Offender: Male, young teen
- Victim: Females of own age
- Offence often involves gang rape
- Motivated by peer pressure and desire for approval

Source: O'Brien & Bera (1986).

Murder

While public fears have been fuelled by media reports of particularly violent murders, as mentioned earlier, there are not major gaps between murders known to and reported by police and cases that go to court. Of all crime statistics, those on homicide are the most reliable and they indicate that homicide rates, where young offenders are the accused, were much lower in 2004 than they were ten years ago (see Figure 3.5).

FIGURE 3.5

Youth Aged 12–17 Accused of a Homicide Offence

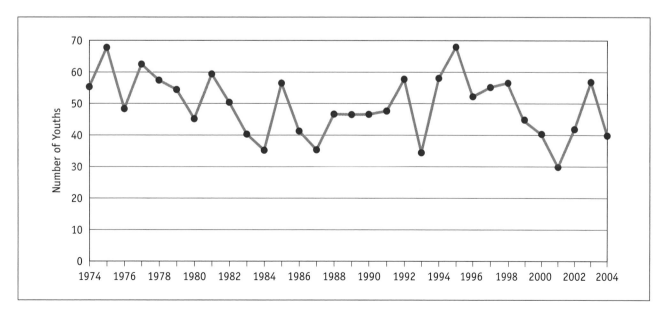

Sources: Dauvergne (2005); Doob, Marinos, & Varma (1995); Fedorowycz (1999); Logan (2000).

In fact, youth homicide rates were considerably higher 25 years ago than they were for all of the YOA years (1984–2002). Both Silverman (1990) and Silverman and Kennedy (1993) found no increase in the per capita rate of youth homicide in Canada between 1970 and 1990.

Homicide rates have remained fairly constant since 1986, 38 homicide cases accounted for 0.03 percent of all young persons charged by police. By 1988, the number of youth homicide cases had increased to 48, or 0.04 percent of total young persons charged by police. Even the addition of 16- and 17-year-olds to the youth justice system in 1985 did not impact significantly on the numbers of youth charged (Statistics Canada, 1996). Throughout the 1990s, young offenders accounted for, on average, 9 percent of all persons accused of homicide, and 14 percent of these were girls. Two-thirds of those accused of homicide were in the 16–34 age group, which accounts for only 27 percent of the total population in Canada (Fedorowycz, 1999, pp. 8, 12). In 2004, 40 young offenders, 3 of which were girls, were charged with murder or manslaughter, which amounted to 0.05 percent of all police youth charges for that year. This amounts to a rate of 1.57/100,000, the second-lowest youth homicide rate in more than 30 years (Dauvergne, 2005, p. 13).

Meloff and Silverman's (1992) examination of homicide rates for Canadian youth between the years 1962 and 1983 is the most detailed, and it provides us with the following information about youth homicide during this period:

1. Eighty percent of youth homicides in Canada involved one offender and one victim; only 3 percent involved more than three victims and offenders (p. 21). Statistics for 2004 show that one-half of all youth homicides involved two or more individuals in the commission of the offence (Dauvergne, 2005, p. 14). Whether this is a new pattern cannot be ascertained from current available data.
2. Thirty-five percent of youth homicide cases involved guns, 30 percent involved stabbing, and 22 percent involved beating. All other means of homicide (drowning, strangling, arson, etc.) accounted for 13 percent of the events (p. 22). No recent information is available for methods used in youth homicides cases.
3. Similar to homicide cases involving adults, homicides committed by youth most commonly involved parents, family, and acquaintances as the victims. Parents were victims in 14 percent of the cases, other family members in 19.5 percent of the cases, and acquaintances in 35 percent of the cases. Strangers accounted for 31.5 percent of the victims (p. 23). The most recent homicide statistics indicate a similar pattern of victim/offender relationship. In 2004, 21 percent of the victims of youth homicides were strangers, 16 percent were family members, 9 percent were intimate partners and the remainder (53 percent) were acquaintances (Dauvergne, 2005, p. 14).
4. Crime-based homicide is proportionately small, and when it does occur, it usually involves strangers. Of all crime-based homicides committed by youth in Canada during the 1962–1983 period, 70 percent were theft-related, 21 percent involved sex, and 9 percent involved some other crime (Meloff & Silverman, p. 24). No recent data is available on crime-related youth homicide.
5. Youth homicide rates in the United States are 10 times higher than those in Canada (p. 28).

One new piece of information on youth homicides indicates that youth criminal activity prior to their commission of homicide is similar to that of adults. Slightly more than one-half (54 percent) of the youth accused of murder in 2004, particularly male youth, already had a criminal history, and two-thirds (65 percent) of these had a prior conviction for a violent offence (Dauvergne, 2005, p. 13).

Administrative and YOA/YCJA Offences

Administrative offences, which occur after a person has been arrested, involve interference with the administration of justice. Some of these offences appear in police statistics, others in court data. This category includes failure to comply with a disposition, failure to appear (in court), escape from lawful custody, being unlawfully at large, failure to comply with a probation order, and less common offences such as breach of recognizance or contempt against the youth court.

Administrative offences occur at different stages of the judicial process. For example, failure to appear in court and failure to comply with an undertaking occur before a disposition is imposed. Offences that take place after the court disposition include escape from lawful custody, being unlawfully at large, and failure to comply with a probation order. Some administrative offences, such as failure to appear, or escape from lawful custody, are Criminal Code offences. Other offences involve charges under the Youth Criminal Justice Act. YCJA administrative charges, such as failure to comply, are connected with a disposition (usually probation or a community service order) that is ordered under the authority of the YCJA.

According to Statistics Canada figures, between 1987 and 1992, the number of cases involving offences against the administration of justice under the YOA and the Criminal Code almost doubled, rising from 9,440 to 17,007 (these figures exclude Ontario, British Columbia, and the Northwest Territories). In 1991–1992, one-quarter of the youth court caseload (26 percent) comprised offences against the administration of youth justice (Gagnon & Doherty, 1993, p. 3). In 1994–1995, when all provinces and territories were included in court statistics, there were 10,704 YOA charges, 10,633 of which involved failure to comply with a disposition; in addition, there were 10,041 Criminal Code charges for failure to appear. These two charges together accounted for most of the administrative charges against young offenders (Statistics Canada, 1996, pp. 9–12).

More recent figures are not directly comparable to pre-1992 statistics, but they do demonstrate that administrative offences continue to make up a considerable and steadily increasing portion of youth court cases. In 2003–2004, administration of justice offences and YCJA/YOA offences accounted for 31 percent of the charges heard in youth court (14.8 percent and 16.3 percent, respectively). Three-quarters (76 percent) of these administrative charges were for failure to comply with a court order (Thomas, 2005, p. 13). This is particularly significant, since these offences are more likely to result in a custody sentence, as compared to many other offence categories. More specifically, in 2003–2004, 37 percent of the failure-to-comply convictions and 27 percent of the YOA convictions resulted in custodial sentences (Thomas, 2005, p. 13). High rates of administrative charges are also significant because some portion of the increase in the overall youth crime rate may be due to these increases in administrative charges (Schissel, 1997, p. 82), a point we will return to later in the chapter. The characteristics of youth charged with these offences, in particular girls and Aboriginal youth, are discussed in the next chapter.

MEASUREMENT ISSUES

The Violent Crime Debate

While the public is concerned about violent crime and its concerns are fuelled by the reporting of specific cases in the news media, the academic community is divided on the question of whether or not violent crime is on the rise. The main concern for academics stems from an awareness that levels of reported or official crime are "a political as well as an **empirical** issue" (Doob, Marinos, & Varma, 1995, p. 16). As discussed earlier, determining how much crime we have in our society depends on which statistics we look at, on how police are behaving in relation to public pressures to clamp down on criminal activity, and on people's willingness to define or report activities as criminal. Concerns about violent crime have given rise to an interesting debate among Canadian criminologists.

According to a 1992 report prepared for Statistics Canada (Frank, 1992), the per capita rate of youth violence doubled after 1986. In 1986, the rate of crimes against the person was 41.5 per 10,000 youth. By 1992, the rate had more than doubled to 90 per 10,000 youth—an increase of 117 percent. Frank suggests that the overall increase in violent charges was largely owing to minor assaults. He adds, however, that some of this rate change may have been created by changes in public attitudes toward violence— changes that led to increases in the reporting of violent crime and/or changes in law-enforcement practices and the willingness of the Crown to prosecute cases.

By way of contrast, Corrado and Markwart (1994) argue that there has been a real increase in violent crime committed by Canadian youth. They present data for the same years as Frank, but calculate rate changes for specific offence categories. Their calculations show increased rates in all categories of violent offences. From 1986 to 1992, the rate of Assault Level I (minor assault) increased by 142 percent, assault causing harm by 90 percent, robbery involving firearms by 267 percent, and robberies involving other weapons by 121 percent. Contrary to Frank, Corrado and Markwart argue that these rate increases cannot be accounted for by changes in policing. *Uniform Crime Reporting* statistics indicate that, between 1986 and 1992, there was no change in the rate of police charging to not charging for assault causing harm or robbery. Although there was an increase (from 50 to 61 percent) in the proportion of youth charged (vs. not charged) with common assault, Corrado and Markwart argue that this change in charging practice "can only account for approximately 20 percent of the increase in that period" (1994, p. 351).

While it can be argued that a fear of further victimization would result in greater reporting of these incidents, Corrado and Markwart take the position that there are no survey data to support the hypothesis of a greater social sensitivity toward violence. Further, since half of the victims of minor and aggravated youth assaults are other youth (Frank, 1992), the authors suggest it is equally plausible "that the fear of retaliation, or peer group ostracization, might inhibit youth victims from reporting" (Corrado & Markwart, 1994, p. 353). And while Frank (1992) suggests that **zero-tolerance policies** toward youth violence in many Canadian school districts can also lead to more crimes being reported to police, Corrado and Markwart argue that it is equally plausible that increased reporting is a reflection of increasing levels of crime in schools. They point out that the Toronto-based Safer Schools Task Force reported an almost 40 percent increase in crimes on school grounds between 1987 and 1990. Similarly, a survey of 4,392 high-school students in Vancouver found that 40 percent of males had been involved in a fight in the previous year, while in the previous month,

empirical
An adjective describing knowledge that is based on observation, experience, or experiment rather than on theory or philosophy.

zero-tolerance policies
Policies related to the intolerance of behaviour that is considered undesirable.

VOICES BOX 3.2

Kids Who Kill

Jason Gamache . . . [was a] strapping six foot one inch handsome 15-year-old youth . . . Before October 24, 1992, there was nothing to suggest that this boy would lure an unsuspecting younger child into darkened woods, rape and . . . murder her . . . What the neighbours did not know was that the youth was already on probation for two previous minor sex offences . . . [A] B.C. supreme court jury in Victoria convicted him of murder. He is now serving a life sentence.

The 13-year-old boy left his house and walked down a short makeshift road, across the highway and through the woods to the comfortable cedar home where the Jarvis family lived. He rang the door bell and waited. When John Jarvis, 43, opened the door, the boy shouldered the pump-action shotgun and blew off the businessman's face from six feet away . . . Reta Jarvis, 41, was also shot and seriously injured on the same night by the boy that had shot her husband . . . [W]arning signs had been flashing. The youth allegedly came from a home marked by poverty and domestic violence. It was common knowledge that the youth also had a drinking problem, as well as an addiction to chewing tobacco . . . "It just happened, I was angry," he told the RCMP. The question of what sort of anger could make a 13-year-old commit that sort of atrocity still haunts all those touched by the crime. The boy, who turned 14 in February, pleaded guilty to second-degree murder and attempted murder, and received the maximum sentence allowed under the Young Offenders Act at that time—five years less a day.

The inside of Robert's quarters could be that of any teenager—an album of family photos even lies open on the desk . . . "When I got these pictures a few weeks ago," Robert says thoughtfully, "I could see the proof that they really did love me." But that simple realization, which so many sons and daughters take for granted, was far beyond Robert's grasp on Mother's Day of 1992. That is when he took a 12-gauge pump-action shotgun and killed his 17-year-old brother, 42-year-old mother and 49-year-old father at the home they shared. Robert had just turned 14 . . . [He] is now 16, faces three counts of first-degree murder and a possible life sentence . . . "He saw himself as helpless, worthless and completely dependent on his parents . . . yet he saw his parents as preventing him from living" . . . Robert has his own ideas about what would constitute an appropriate punishment. "I don't think it's possible," he says, "but if a judge wanted to give me the death penalty, I would accept that. I can't die three times, but I will never have a normal life."

Source: Excerpted from Kaihla (1994).

---

23 percent had carried a weapon, most notably knives and razors (McCreary Centre Society, 1993, as cited in Corrado & Markwart, 1994, p. 354).

Carrington's Challenge

Carrington (1995) disputes Corrado and Markwart's interpretation of UCR statistics and challenges their conclusion about the reality of violent crime increases. More specifically, he takes exception to the following two statements by Corrado and Markwart (1994):

> The per capita rate of young persons charged with Criminal Code offences increased by a relatively modest 25 percent between 1986 and 1992. (p. 350)

> There has been a real and substantial increase in youth violence in Canada in recent years. (p. 354)

With regard to the first statement, Carrington maintains that it is not useful to use police charges as a method of comparing changes in crime rates over time. He agrees with Frank that police charging practices are susceptible to changing public attitudes and zero-tolerance policies. For this reason, Carrington argues that rate comparisons should be based on crimes reported to police rather than on crimes charged by police. Making just such a comparison, he finds that between 1986 and 1992, violent crime increased by 19 percent, not the 25 percent reported by Corrado and Markwart. Since reported crime increases are lower than charge increases, police charging practices did change between 1986 and 1992.

Perhaps the most compelling evidence against Corrado and Markwart's position comes from a comparison of crime rates in 1992 to years prior to 1986. Compared to earlier years, 1986 was a year with one of the lowest rates of violent offence charges for young offenders, while the rate for 1992 was one of the highest. Carrington points out that comparisons based on these two years are meaningless. "Using 1986 as a baseline year for comparison of youth crime rates is like using the employment rate in the depths of a recession as a baseline for assessing annual employment rate: in comparison, any other year will seem high" (Carrington, 1995, p. 62).

In Carrington's view, a more appropriate approach is to compare the average level of reported crime for different periods. This type of comparison reveals increases in most violent offence categories and a decrease in robbery with firearms. Nonetheless, none of Carrington's comparisons show the kinds of increases reported by Corrado and Markwart. On the basis of these new figures, Carrington concludes:

> . . . [much] of the increase in police reported violent youth crime is actually in offenses against the person that are generally nonviolent; but there has been a substantial increase in the police reported rate of assaults causing harm. This indeed represents a substantial increase in police reported violent crime. (1995, p. 70)

While Carrington links this increase to a much wider trend toward increased police reporting of violent crime, another way of looking at the issue is through victimization surveys that tell us about incidents reported to the police. Looking at the years under debate by Carrington and Corrado and Markwart, the GSS supports the notion that increases during this period are due to changes in police reporting. Gartner and Doob report that neither rates of victimization nor reporting incidents to the police changed from 1988 to 1993. They state:

> . . . essentially the same proportion of the population (24 percent) experienced at least one incidence of criminal victimization in 1993 as compared to 1988. Any change in public attitudes, especially with regard to violent offenses, is likely to result in increases in crime rates known to police, specifically because such a small proportion of these offenses, in particular assaults and sexual assaults, are reported to police. In 1993 only 32 percent of assaults and 10 percent of sexual assaults of all levels were reported to police. (1994, p. 13)

Meanwhile, Gabor (1999) entered the debate and questioned Carrington's use of crime statistics aggregated for the whole country. He maintained that increases in violent charges for youth in specific Canadian cities were not likely attributable to increases in police charging. Gabor provided no evidence to support his claim, only the illogical suggestion that because motor vehicle thefts are consistently reported and had shown a doubling in charge rates from 1986 to 1996, this must also be true of violent youth crime in major Canadian cities (p. 387). As we will see later in the chapter, Carrington (1999) also examined provincial level data and provided strong evidence of major increases in police charging after the YOA was implemented.

Validity and Reliability

As suggested by the violent crime debate, another major issue for academics concerned with the measurement of criminal activity, be it youth or adult, is the **reliability** and **validity** of the measuring instrument. Reliability refers to whether or not we can repeat the results that we get; validity refers to whether we are measuring what we think we are measuring. We have come to accept that a ruler is a reliable and valid measure of length and height. Things are not as simple when it comes to measuring crime. Both reliability and validity can be compromised in official statistics. We have already seen how easy it is to find inconsistencies in police-based statistics that depend on what is compared and how the comparisons are made. In addition, the validity of police statistics is always an issue because crimes known to police and clearance rates are susceptible to public and political pressures, as well as changes in policy, police administration, training, and recruitment practices. Similarly, court statistics are susceptible to public, institutional, and political pressures, as well as police, Crown prosecutor, and judicial behaviour. In later chapters, we will also examine how race, class, and gender affect who is charged and who is taken to court.

reliability
In behavioural science, refers to the extent to which variable measurement and research findings can be or have been repeated.

validity
Refers to the extent to which research variables have been measured in a way that is consistent with the theoretical concept, or what was intended.

Lying About Crime

Self-report survey results are generally accepted as reliable in that researchers can obtain relatively comparable results from their surveys. Nonetheless, some are skeptical about self-report questionnaires because of an assumption that people will not be truthful in filling them out. This is particularly a concern with regard to young people because it is thought that they, more so than adults, may feel a sense of bravado about misdeeds and will want to elaborate and exaggerate their involvement. Adults, on the other hand, are thought to be more likely than young people to under-report their criminal activities because they fear the consequences of being caught.

A very interesting study was undertaken to address just this issue. Hindelang, Hirschi, and Weis (1981) conducted a large survey in Seattle, Washington, throughout the years 1978 and 1979 to test the reliability and validity of self-report questionnaires. Their research involved surveying a sample that included high-school students and young people not in school who had police records and/or court records. Responses to the self-report questions were then cross-checked with police records, court records, school records, and parents to determine the truthfulness of responses. They found that, in general, young people do not lie about their misdeeds.

What Are We Measuring?

Validity is considered to be particularly problematic in relation to self-report questionnaires. The issue concerns the types of questions that have been included in the survey, what they measure, and the usefulness of responses for making assessments about crime levels. As mentioned earlier, Nye and Short (1957) developed and conducted the first self-report questionnaire on delinquency. Their survey included such questions as: Have you ever skipped school? . . . disobeyed your parents? . . . defied openly the authority of your parents?

These questions are very different from the ones used by Tribble (1972) in one of the first Canadian self-reported delinquency studies. All of Tribble's questions (e.g., Have you ever seriously hurt an animal? . . . beat up another person? . . . damaged someone's property? . . . forged a cheque?) refer to behaviours that are controlled by the Criminal Code. Only some of Nye and Short's questions (e.g.: Have you ever hit children that haven't done anything to you? . . . hurt or inflicted injuries on someone just for kicks?) cite behaviours that could refer to Criminal Code items, but many of their questions, such as the ones referring to disobeying parents and skipping school, concern delinquencies, not crimes. The result, of course, was that Nye and Short's questionnaire yielded much higher rates of delinquent and criminal behaviour than did Tribble's.

The NLSCY is a case in point. Its first self-report survey (1994/1995) asked only very general questions about frequency of "stealing at home, stealing outside the home, destroying other people's things and vandalizing." Only two questions were asked about aggressive behaviour: "getting in fights and physically attacking people" (Sprott, Doob, & Jenkins, 2001, p. 3). The second survey (1996/1997) asked far more specific questions about property offences and aggressive behaviours (e.g., "stolen something from a store . . . from a school," "broken into a house," "threatened to beat someone up," "used knife for an attack," and "forced sex"). In all, eight questions were asked in this later survey about property-type offences and nine about aggressive behaviours (2001, p. 3). As a result of these changes in questions, not all responses are comparable across the two surveys and the authors of a report on the results of the two surveys caution about interpreting the findings of the surveys:

> Readers are cautioned that it is probably not meaningful to make simple comparisons across "types" of delinquency. The fact that, for example, delinquent acts involving property appear to be less prevalent than aggressive behaviour . . . may reflect more the nature and specificity of the two types of questions that were asked rather than any "real" underlying difference. (Sprott, Doob, & Jenkins, 2001, p. 3)

Similarly, since Nye and Short's questionnaire yielded higher rates than Tribble's, it would be wrong to interpret Nye and Short's survey results to mean that the young people were more criminal or delinquent in their behaviour than those in Tribble's survey. This is not to say that one questionnaire is right and the other is wrong. Rather, it is important to be knowledgeable about what is being measured when we interpret the results of self-report surveys. As we will see in Chapter 5, what is known about delinquent behaviour, and how it is explained and understood, depends a great deal on the kinds of questions that have been asked in self-report studies and on how the results of these studies have been interpreted.

Other validity problems stem from attempts to compare self-report or victimization surveys with police statistics or court statistics. It is often assumed that self-report questionnaires measure the true incidence or prevalence of crime and that police statistics do not. Strictly speaking, results from the two are not comparable because of the nature of police activity and the role of police in the criminal justice system. It is important to keep in mind when interpreting police statistics that they are as much a measure of police discretion to lay a charge as they are a measure of criminal activity (Doob & Cesaroni, 2004, p. 95). As we saw earlier, police have discretionary power with respect to the kinds of behaviours they will charge and also in their interpretation of the Criminal Code. A police officer must determine if someone's behaviour is a criminal offence in law.

Some potential offences known to the police are determined by them to be **unfounded.** Police may categorize an offence as "unfounded" after investigating a complaint and determining that either no crime took place or there wasn't enough evidence of a crime for a charge to be laid. Alternatively, police may use their discretionary power and determine that an offence is not serious enough to proceed with a charge (in lieu of a charge, the officer may give the person a warning). Yet, persons who have been involved in "unfounded" situations might report in a self-report questionnaire that they had committed a crime—or, in a victimization survey, that they had been victimized. In either case, it is a judgment call as to which source is valid as a "true" measure of whether a crime took place.

Recalling Crime

A related methodological problem stems from people's ability to recall with any accuracy the things they have done or experienced. For example, a teen may have broken into someone's house, but not recall when he did so. Nonetheless, the incident might stand out in his mind as a significant event. Assuming, then, that the incident occurred 15 months ago, the teen may report that it happened in the last 12 months. In this hypothetical example, the reporting of the incident, even if it had resulted in police charges and court appearances, would not appear in official statistics for the year in which it was reported in the victimization survey to have occurred.

Similarly, comparisons of self-report results with court statistics are problematic because of the way in which people are processed through the courts. What a person has done, what that person is charged with, and whether charges are dropped or modified through various plea negotiations can vary considerably. More important, as we will see in Chapters 8 and 9, these decisions vary by race, class, and gender. Hence, the resulting police and court statistics may not accurately reflect the actual offence that occurred.

In victimization surveys, people are even more likely to confuse or forget the time of occurrence because these events are usually always significant and sometimes frightening or traumatic. In addition, Bortner (1988, p. 149) suggests that victimization surveys give a less reliable picture of unreported crime than self-report surveys because victims are more likely to remember events that they reported to the police. In the 2004 GSS, questions on spousal violence asked how many times in the preceding 12 months the respondent had been assaulted, but asked only if respondents had *ever* reported any of these incidents to the police. Hence, it would be impossible to know how many offences reported in the survey were actually reported to the police (Gannon & Mihorean, 2005, p. 3).

Victimization surveys also suffer from the problem of **telescoping**—victims report an event correctly, but place it in the wrong time period. Finally, it is impossible to estimate the number of offenders involved in a particular offence because the unit of measurement in a victimization survey is the event, not the offender. Hence, unlike self-report surveys, victimization surveys do not allow us to determine if a small number of offenders account for a large portion of offences.

unfounded offences
Events investigated by the police as potentially criminal offences that are determined not to be offences.

telescoping
A problem faced by researchers conducting self-report or victimization surveys: people tend to lump offences that may have occurred several years ago into something that occurred "last year."

REVISITING QUESTIONS ABOUT YOUTH CRIME

Which Source of Information Is the "Best"?

As we have seen, all three major sources of information on young offenders—official statistics, self-report surveys, and victimization surveys—yield useful information if used appropriately. More to the point, all three sources provide answers to questions about how much and what type of crime young people commit. However, the answers they provide are different, and some seem contradictory. Thus, we are left with the question: Which source is the most accurate for the purpose of measuring youth crime? There are two very different answers to this question.

Hindelang, Hirschi, and Weis (1981) take issue with the question itself. Alleged discrepancies between official statistics, self-report surveys, and victimization surveys are an illusion, they argue. Because each source is measuring something very different, no one source is more accurate than the other. Official statistics, whether from police sources or court records, generally measure more serious criminal behaviour. Self-report surveys tend to measure more minor delinquent behaviours, such as mischief or vandalism.

self-fulfilling prophecy
A prediction or assumption that, in being made, actually causes itself to become true.

While there may be some truth in this argument, Bortner (1988) cautions against the belief that official statistics are representative of all youth involved in serious crime. Her argument suggests that there may be something of a **self-fulfilling prophecy** operating with regard to official statistics. To the extent that official statistics include minority and poor youth more than other youth, and to the extent that courts and police believe that these are the people most likely to be involved in serious criminal activities, police responses to minority and poor youth will be relatively severe. Similarly, a belief that middle-class, non-minority youth are less likely to be involved in serious criminal activity, or more likely to be involved in minor kinds of offences, decreases the likelihood that the official police response will be severe. The end result is that we may continue to respond severely to disadvantaged youth while ignoring the offences of more privileged youth (Bortner, 1988, pp. 150–152). These responses are then reflected in official statistics, which in turn reinforce stereotypical beliefs about who is involved in crime.

We can never say for certain that youth crime is increasing or decreasing, because none of the three major sources of information provides a direct measure of criminal activity. Nonetheless, there does seem to be some evidence that crime levels, overall, may be levelling off and in some cases even declining. And, in spite of various measurement problems, all three sources of information confirm that most criminal activity involving young people is property crime, and that only a small proportion of youth criminal activity involves violent crime, the largest portion of which is minor assault.

Crime under the YOA and YCJA versus Crime under the JDA

Many people were concerned and are convinced that the YOA was responsible for increasing youth crime and now many are convinced that the YCJA is responsible for increasing the levels of violent crime. According to a nationwide survey in the mid 1990s, 95 percent of Canadians maintained that the Young Offenders Act needed to be toughened (Bibby, 1995, p. 105), and a survey of a sample of Torontonians indicated that a majority believed that the youth court under the YOA was too lenient (Sprott,

1996). Today, news stories perpetuate the view that courts are too lenient and that the YCJA is to blame. As we have seen, a majority of academics disagree that the laws are responsible for raising levels of youth crime.

Schissel (1995, p. 122) takes the position that official rates of youth crime were more related to the changing political nature of crime control than to increases or changes in the criminal activity of youth from 1970 to 1990. His research examined the relationship between rates of Criminal Code offences for young offenders and the formal and informal processing of these cases in the years 1970 to 1990. "Formal processing" refers to cases handled through the courts, in which the accused enters a plea and has her or his case adjudicated by the judge. "Informal processing" refers to cases handled outside of courts, in which youth are not charged but are instead released to the custody of their parents or a social agency.

Schissel's work shows a dramatic increase in Criminal Code offences in 1984, the year in which the Young Offenders Act came into effect. Another increase followed in 1985, when 16- and 17-year-old youth were brought into the system. While these increases could be interpreted to mean that young people were more criminal, Schissel suggests otherwise. He points out that as the Young Offenders Act was being implemented, and as older youth were being brought into the system, the number of cases processed informally began to drop and there was a dramatic increase in the formal processing of young offenders. Hence, after the introduction of the YOA, there was more formal processing of teenagers through the courts than was evident under the Juvenile Delinquents Act (Schissel, 1995, pp. 123–125). Schissel argues that police were far more disposed to laying a charge under the YOA than they were under the JDA. Hence, any statistics based on police charges will reflect this change in police behaviour.

Carrington (1999) also addressed this issue by examining youth crime rates from 1977 to 1996 through a comparison of police reported crime to police charges for each province. His results confirm Schissel's findings. Carrington concludes that police charging practices did change such that, with the introduction of the YOA, police increased their charges for young offenders compared to their practices under the JDA. However, according to Carrington, this change "was especially pronounced" in Saskatchewan and Ontario, but also occurred in Nova Scotia, Prince Edward Island, and the Northwest Territories. New Brunswick and Manitoba maintained a fairly high apprehension and charge rate with both the JDA and YOA, whereas British Columbia and Newfoundland and Labrador began to decrease formal charging after a brief period of increases when the YOA was first implemented. Quebec's charge rate declined into the 1990s (hence, police use of discretion increased), and Alberta and the Yukon had consistently high charge ratios throughout the YOA period that are not clearly attributable to the YOA (pp. 24–25).

Of course, with the increased emphasis on diversion under the YCJA, we should expect to see reductions in charge rates. Table 3.3B (page 71) clearly shows this impact, with a 21 percent decrease in the charge rate for all Criminal Code offences. Since the YCJA emphasizes extrajudicial measures for non-violent offences, it is appropriate that reductions in charge rates for all offences other than violent ones should show dramatic decreases. And, considering that the majority of violent offences are minor, we should also expect some decrease in the rate of charging for violent offences. Nonetheless, it is important to note that these decreases began in the year prior to the YCJA and, with the exception of property rate decreases (which remain high), all other charge rate decreases for 2004 dropped to levels comparable to

2002. Furthermore, since both the rate of youth charged and the rate of youth cleared otherwise dropped, the drop in the overall youth crime rate cannot be attributed to increases in informal processing relative to charging. Hence, public concerns about increasing violent crime and a lack of consequences for violent youth under the YCJA seem unfounded when looking at police statistics. We will return to the question of consequences in Chapters 9 and 10.

Increases in youth charge rates under the YOA aside, comparisons with rates of delinquency under the JDA show the same pattern of offences that we had under the YOA and now see with the YCJA. Statistics Canada figures for juvenile courts in 1980 (excluding British Columbia) indicate that there were 97,264 charges of delinquency. The most frequent juvenile offences in 1980 were break and enter (accounting for 26 percent of all charges laid) and theft (21 percent). Violent crimes accounted for 4.2 percent of total charges (Statistics Canada, 1981, p. 2). Figures for 1982, which included British Columbia, indicate a total of 121,379 charges. The most common offences were break and enter (35 percent) and theft (29 percent). Overall, property offences accounted for 83 percent of total charges, and violent offences for 4.8 percent of the total (Statistics Canada, 1984, p. 3).

Youth Crime Waves

Another way of assessing the volume, severity, or magnitude of youth crime is to compare youth rates over time to crime rates for adults. While youth crime rates showed an increase from 1962 to 1990, so too did adult crime rates; hence, youth crime rates simply mirrored overall crime rates. Starting in 1962, property crime rates increased for about 20 years, began to level off in the early 1980s, increased slightly in the early 1990s, and then largely decreased every year through 2004. Violent crime rates showed a steady increase from 1962 to 1990 and then steady declined. On the other hand, other Criminal Code charges steadily increased from 1977 to 1990 (Statistics Canada, 1992a, pp. 4–5; Wallace, 2003, p. 3).

Parallels notwithstanding, there are some important differences between adult crime and youth crime. Table 3.4 indicates clearly that adults are responsible for far more criminal activity than youth. Eighty percent of all Criminal Code charges involve adults. For 2002, the last year when comparable police statistics are currently available for youth and adults, the only areas in which young people even began to approximate adult activity are robbery, break and enter, motor vehicle theft, arson, and mischief. Youth account for 30 to 40 percent of all police charges for these offences. Post-YCJA data indicate that the overall rate of accused youth in these areas has decreased. The next highest figures for youth (20 to 30 percent of all offences) are for petty theft and weapons offences. Only weapons offences showed an increase in charge rate post-YCJA (Sauve 2005, p. 21).

The proportionate figures for violent offences are even more striking. With the exception of robbery, every offence category is disproportionately represented by adults. Only 9 percent of homicide charges, 11 percent of attempted murder charges, and 15 percent of assault charges involved young offenders. In view of the larger crime picture, then, youth crime does not seem as alarming as is suggested by media reports. Young people are responsible for 16 percent of all violent crime and 26 percent of all property crime. While some would argue that this type of comparison is misleading because the youth age group is considerably smaller than other age groups, as we will see in the next chapter, even comparisons of more specific age groups show that adults far outnumber young people in criminal activity.

TABLE 3.4

Persons Charged[1] by Age Status, Selected Incidents, 2002

| | Age Group | |
| | Adult | Youth (12–17) |
	%	%
Homicide[2]	91	9
Attempted murder	89	11
Assaults	85	15
Sexual assaults	82	18
Other sexual offences	81	19
Abduction	96	4
Robbery	68	32
Violent crime—Total	84	16
Breaking and entering	63	37
Motor vehicle theft	60	40
Fraud	92	8
Theft over $5,000	87	13
Theft $5,000 and under	74	26
Property crime—Total	74	26
Mischief	67	33
Arson	60	40
Prostitution	99	1
Offensive weapons	80	20
Criminal Code—Total	80	20
Impaired driving[3]	99	1
Cocaine offences	95	5
Cannabis offences	82	18
Other drug offences	89	11

[1]Represents all persons charged in Canada. *Uniform Crime Reporting Survey*, Canadian Centre for Justice Statistics.

[2]*Homicide Survey*, CCJS.

[3]Includes impaired operation of a vehicle causing death, causing bodily harm, alcohol rate over 80 mg, failure/refusal to provide a breath/blood sample. Age of persons charged with impaired driving comes from the UCR *Incident-Based Survey* (UCR2).

Source: Adapted from Statistics Canada. (2003). *Juristat*, Cat. No. 85-002-XPE 23(5), p. 22.

SUMMARY

The major sources of information about youth crime are the media, official statistics, self-report surveys, and victimization surveys. Making sense of this information requires a knowledge of the source and what is being measured, as well as an understanding of the limitations of various crime measures. Making sense of public issues and conflicting discourses about the prevalence and severity of youth crime requires a consideration of all sources in a historical comparative context and a recognition of the political nature of information gathering.

Most people get their information about crime from the media. While statistics presented in the media may be correct, they can also be misleading in the absence of

(1) an understanding of the limitations of data sources and (2) a historical or social context.

Official statistics come from police and courts. These statistics are more a measure of the activities of the agencies themselves than they are of actual criminal or delinquent behaviour. As such, they are particularly susceptible to changing public attitudes and shifts in police surveillance, policy, charging, and sentencing practices. The exercise of discretion decreases with the severity of the offence. Police statistics indicate that youth crime is predominantly property-related and that a minority of this crime involves violence. Official statistics for homicide, which are the most reliable, indicate that youth homicide rates were higher 30 years ago than they are today. Youth crime rates increased after the YOA was implemented, then declined for eight years in a row beginning in 1992, showed slight increases in 2000 and 2001, and have declined since then, even after the YCJA was implemented.

Despite this general decline, official rates for some violent crimes increased in the 1992–2002 period; these include all levels of assault, robbery, and weapons offences. While there is agreement among criminologists that the majority of violent offences are minor, there is no agreement as to the reason for rate increases. Some argue that youth behaviour has changed and cite evidence that serious violent crime is on the increase. Others question the validity of this evidence and point out that there has been a change in police reporting and processing practices. Victimization survey data also suggest changes in police reporting rather than in the actual criminal behaviour of youth.

Self-report and victimization surveys give us a better indication than official statistics of the actual volume of crime. Self-report studies demonstrate that the volume of crime is considerably higher than that indicated in police statistics. Estimates range from four to ten times the amount reported in official statistics. A comparative study in Montreal showed no change in the level or nature of self-reported delinquency from 1974 to 1985. The NLSCY has reported data only for 11- to 13-year-olds and is not comparable to the Montreal study on rates of delinquency. An Alberta survey reports rates between these other two studies.

Although Canadian victimization surveys do not give us specific information about youth crime, these general surveys are useful in telling us something about general crime patterns and can be used with other sources to arrive at a more complete picture. Since overall rates of victimization are not significantly higher today than they were in the 1980s, and since police statistics show that youth crime rates parallel adult rates, it would appear that youth are not responsible for more criminal activity today than in the past.

Claims that the YOA is "soft on youth criminals" and led to a youth "crime wave" seem unfounded. Comparisons of youth charges under the JDA and YOA show that patterns of youth crime did not change with the YOA, and that more youth offences were charged and processed through the courts under the YOA than was the case under the JDA. Since the YCJA was implemented, charge rates for youth offences in all categories have declined, a trend that began in the latter years of the YOA.

Claims that youth crime is "out of control" also seem to be unfounded. Comparisons of official crime rates for young offenders and adults over the last 30 to 35 years show that youth crime rates have not increased as rapidly as adult rates, that adult crime far surpasses youth crime, and that adults are far more likely than youth to be involved in violent offences and drug offences.

DISCUSSION/CRITICAL THINKING QUESTIONS

1. In what ways might it be argued that people "lie" about the crimes they commit and/or that it is the statistics that "lie"?
2. How are reliability and validity concerns when measuring crime statistics?
3. What is the "best" measure of youth crime and why?

WEB LINKS

Centre for Research on Youth At Risk
www.stthomasu.ca/research/youth

All Stats Valid to Fight Crime
http://torontosun.canoe.ca/News/Columnists/Steward_Hartley/2005/07/31/1154110.html

Statistics, 2004. *Juristat* (section on Youth Crime, page 12)
http://dsp-psd.pwgsc.gc.ca/Collection-R/Statcan/85-002-XIE/85-002-XIE.html
Click on "Vol. 25, no. 5."

For chapter quizzes and more links, visit this book's accompanying website at
www.bellyoungoffenders3e.nelson.com

CHAPTER FOUR

The Social Face of Youth Crime

CHAPTER OBJECTIVES

1. To discuss who young offenders are with respect to race/ethnicity, gender, and age.
2. To emphasize the racialization and sociopolitical nature of youth crime.
3. To discuss age-specific crime rates and their significance in understanding trends in youth crime rates.
4. To clarify gender differences in youth crime rates by examining different sources of information.
5. To discuss the other side of youth crime: youth victimization and the links between youth crime, victimization, and the status of youth and children in Canadian society.

KEY TERMS

Racializes
Ethnographic method
Longitudinal studies
Race
Ethnicity
Socioeconomic status

First Nations
Gender
Status offences
Birth cohorts
Remedial solutions
Cycle of violence

INTRODUCTION

In the preceding chapter, we examined official, self-report, and victimization survey statistics on young offenders. The next step in understanding youth crime is to put these statistics into a social context and try to develop a more social profile of young people who have found themselves in conflict with the law. As we saw in Chapter 1, a number of public issues and questions about youth crime stem from assumptions about the social characteristics of youth who break the law. A central aspect of the public discourse on youth crime is that it identifies certain youth as more threatening than others. Age is a concern in the debates, in that some interest groups insist that youth criminals are younger now than ever before and that youth under 12 are committing crimes with impunity. Some of the discourse is gendered, in that young women and girls are said to be more criminal and more violent than in the past.

Perhaps the most destructive and vitriolic discourse is that which **racializes** youth crime. It seems that nothing fuels the fires of moral panic more than the image (a patently false one) of non-white youth gangs preying on the innocent. Depending on the region of the country, Aboriginal or black youth, or the children of Asian, West Indian, or South American immigrants, are consistently portrayed in the media as more criminal, more dangerous, more "out of control"—and hence more threatening—than Caucasian youth. Toward the end of the 19th century, middle-class Victorian Canadians living in cities felt threatened by "street arabs," their term for the children of the poor. Today, at the beginning of the 21st century, visible-minority youth have been defined in public discourse as a threat. In 1994, there were news stories about violence erupting at Toronto high-school basketball games. While this "hooliganism" was defined as a "black problem," violence is actually more frequent in hockey games and yet is not defined in terms of a "white problem" (Tanner, 1996, pp. 119–120).

For criminologists, the social face of youth crime has always been gendered and classed; the young offenders to be studied were impoverished and working-class males living in the urban core areas of large cities. As we saw in the last chapter, research findings from self-report surveys challenged this image. Only in the last 25 years have researchers begun to acknowledge the importance of class, race, and gender—as well as their interconnectedness—in the social construction of youth crime images. By the 1970s, it was apparent to some criminologists that the social face of youth crime was a sociopolitical construction that varied depending on the source of information, be it the media or police and court records. Furthermore, it is now also recognized that youth crime itself is a sociopolitical construction that is reinforced by media portrayals of crime.

Along with the self-report survey, two other methodological developments have altered the face of youth crime for criminologists. The **ethnographic method** of data collection, exemplified by Baron's (1995) research on "street kids" (discussed in the last chapter), is a type of field research in which the details of people's lives are documented through direct participation, observation, or comprehensive interviews. **Longitudinal studies** (data collected for the same group at different periods of time) have led to a greater emphasis on age and its relation to crime over the life of an individual. Research on intervention programs for disruptive schoolboys in Montreal by Tremblay et al. (1991) is an example of longitudinal research. In this case, the effect on the boys of the intervention program was tested for a number of years after the intervention program had been completed.

Only in the last decade have criminologists begun to address the other side of youth crime—youth and children as victims of crime. The growing body of ethnographic information concerning the lives of young offenders has directed attention to the fact

racializes
A concept that allows an understanding of racism that goes beyond overt expressions and discriminatory actions of individuals.

ethnographic method
A research method that involves richly detailed descriptions and classifications of a group of people or behaviours.

longitudinal studies
A research method in which data on a group of people are collected over a number of time periods, rather than at only one point in their lives.

CASE STUDY BOX 4.1

Johnny: The Crime

By the age of 16, Johnny had accumulated numerous criminal charges, mostly related to car theft and "joyriding" consisting of criminal negligence, fleeing police, possession of a stolen vehicle, and breaching a court order. On October 14, 2004, two days after being released from the court in Windsor, Nova Scotia, on charges related to a high-speed chase with police that lasted 55 kilometres, Johnny found himself in Sackville, Nova Scotia, stealing a car to go joyriding with several friends.

A Halifax police patrol spotted Johnny after he had driven through several stop signs, turned on their lights and sirens, and began following him. Johnny did not pull over, however, so the police pursued him down a residential street and through a red light at an intersection, where Johnny's vehicle collided with another car. The driver of the other car, Theresa McEvoy, was killed instantly. Johnny fled the scene but was quickly caught by the police. He later admitted to being high on marijuana at the time of the accident.

Source: Stewart, J. (December 15, 2005).
Researched and written by Nicole Landry.

that young people are not involved only in perpetrating crimes. In many instances, they are more likely than adults to be the victims of crime. The links between youth victimization and youth criminality are coming under increasing scrutiny as criminologists seek to understand the criminal behaviour of young people. More important, an understanding of the social face of youth crime is essential to the development of effective responses to youth crime. In this chapter, we will examine the social face of youth crime in terms of race/ethnicity, age, gender, and youth victimization.

RACE/ETHNICITY

race
A socially constructed category based on beliefs about biological differences between groups of people that have no basis in scientific evidence.

ethnicity
A person's group of origin, where origin is usually thought of in terms of ancestral location and/or elements of culture (e.g., language, style of dress, behavioural patterns, social customs).

socioeconomic status
Similar to social class, but specifically refers to a person's social standing or position in terms of education, occupation, income.

"Race" and "ethnicity" are commonly used terms, but their definitions are neither common nor objective. Generally, the term **race** refers to a group of people who share observable physical traits (most commonly, skin colour). **Ethnicity** refers more to identity—a means by which people distinguish themselves, as a group, from others. Language, cultural traditions, and place of ancestral origin are commonly used as distinguishing characteristics among members of an ethnic group (Li, 1990, pp. 4–5). As categories, both race and ethnicity are social constructions in that "physical and cultural traits are the basis for defining [racial or ethnic groups] only in so far as they are socially recognized as important" (p. 5). Unfortunately, racial and ethnic distinctions are most often produced and maintained by power differentials between a dominant "racial" or "ethnic" group and a subordinate one (p. 5). As a result, it is often difficult to distinguish empirically between race or ethnicity and class, as measured by **socioeconomic status.** LaPrairie (1994), for example, found in her study of Aboriginal peoples in the city core areas of Regina, Edmonton, Toronto, and Montreal that class may be more important than race in understanding the over-representation of Aboriginal youth in the justice system.

While race is clearly a factor of some consequence in the criminal justice system, little Canadian information is available on criminal activity by race or ethnicity, particularly with regard to official statistics. Some provinces and police departments record information on race, but this information is not widely available. Police departments do categorize racial and ethnic information in their occurrence reports (Doob, 1991). These categories range from multiple listings (e.g., white, Hispanic, Negro, Oriental, Arabic, Native Indian, East Indian) to simple "white/other" distinctions. In the latter case, "other" is used to distinguish "Canadians" from people with different cultural backgrounds (Ericson & Haggerty, 1997, pp. 283–284). Some police departments have created multicultural units and specialized intelligence units for the purpose of identifying and gathering information on perceived racial and ethnic crime problems. In this regard, "Asian organized crime," "Aboriginal organized crime," and "Asian gangs" have been identified as priorities for criminal intelligence activities (pp. 288–289). Over the last 10 years, Aboriginal "gangs" have become a focus of law-enforcement activities in Winnipeg. Ericson and Haggerty (1997, p. 290) tell of one minority family that was targeted for plainclothes-officer intelligence gathering simply because it was the only minority family in a particular community.

Federal statistics do not provide public information on race and crime, largely because human-rights organizations have objected to the collection of justice statistics by race. While this prevents exploitation of the data by white supremacists and other racist groups, it also means that much potentially useful information is not available for research or the development of justice policy. Our information on race as a factor in the Canadian justice system is sketchy. What is available comes from media reports, first-person police accounts, government reports, and academic research. Some police departments do report information on Aboriginal status to Statistics Canada for the homicide survey but others, such as the RCMP and Toronto Police, do not (Dauvergne, 2005, p. 13). Government reports on Aboriginal youth will be examined in Chapters 8 and 9 when we discuss the processing of youth through the justice system.

Immigrant Gangs

In the early 1990s, the Canadian media identified four groups of youth as problematic: Asian, Vietnamese, Latin, and black. Fasiolo and Leckie (1993) examined how gangs are presented in the media by analyzing gang stories that appeared in Canadian daily newspapers between the months of July and October 1992. Most of the gang stories (77 percent of which came from Vancouver, Montreal, Calgary, Ottawa, and Toronto) had not focused on a specific event, such as a gang-related crime. The gang most frequently cited was the Asian gang. The following example of Asian gang mythology appeared in *The Calgary Sun*:

> For only when *they* [Asian gangs] live in fear that *our* investigators will almost certainly uncover their nefarious deeds, *our* courts will certainly find *them* guilty and *our* prisons await *them*, will *they* stay away from *our* shores. *We* must let the purveyors of these obscenities know that *their* filth is not welcome in *our* city or in *our* province. (Fasiolo & Leckie, 1993, p. 25, cited in Tanner, 1996, p. 6) [Italics in original]

As Tanner (1996, p. 6) points out, the most horrifyingly racist aspect of Asian gang mythology is that Caucasian youth gang activities are never linked to the race of the perpetrators. The terms used in the media are broad, generic identifiers such as "Asian," which serve to brand all visible-minority individuals who are perceived to fit the category. As we entered the 21st century, "Aboriginal gangs" on the Prairies were being identified and problematized in the national media. In 2001, for example, *The Globe and Mail* featured an article entitled "Welcome to Harlem on the prairies" that reported on events occurring during a 12-hour police patrol "with the cowboy and the Indian" (November 4, 2001).

Gordon (1993, 1995), who researched gang members in British Columbian jails, reports that 68 percent of gang members serving prison sentences in British Columbia were Canadian-born (1995, p. 315). Vancouver's street gangs do draw members from particular ethnic groups (Latin American, Chinese, Iranian, or Vietnamese), but most gangs are multicultural. Asians are no more likely to be involved in street gangs than any other ethnocultural group or community. Gordon (1995) reported that while the Lotus Jung gang (also known as Jung Ching) "consisted of approximately 40 young males of Chinese and Vietnamese descent, there were two branch gangs (White Lotus and the Sparrows), which had a predominately European and mixed ethnic membership . . ." (p. 315).

Joe and Robinson (1980) studied youth gangs in Vancouver's Chinatown over a four-year period, from 1975 to 1979. What is interesting about this study is that of the four gangs that had been in existence in 1975, none was still active by 1979. The gangs had either ceased to exist or were no longer engaging in criminal activity (in some cases, members had graduated to adult gangs). Twenty years later, Gordon (1993, 1995) and Young (1993) reported the same finding: youth gangs are not long-lived. In spite of these findings, notions of immigrant gangs persist. As Schissel (1993) states,

> . . . in public policy research the conviction predominates that certain ethnic groups are especially prone to violent and anti-social behaviour. Carrigan (1991) and Fowler (1993) report, for example, that not only are youth gangs becoming increasingly common in Canada's major cities, but that they are drawn from Latin America or specific countries like China or Viet Nam. The underlying message in much of the social analysis is that with immigration comes violence prone youth. (p. 14)

Defining the children of immigrants as particularly troublesome is not a new phenomenon. You may recall from Chapter 1 that in the 1920s and 1930s, Winnipeg's youth crime problems were blamed on immigration.

Black Youth

Very little is known about the offences of black youth, but the media began to identify a "black crime problem" in such major cities as Toronto and Montreal in the early 1980s. Solomon (1992), who studied black male students (all recent immigrants from the West Indies) in a Toronto high school, argued that the subcultural practices of black students were in direct conflict with the all-white school authority structure. The "argot-patois" spoken among these students, their reggae music, their dreadlocks and tams are all seen as threats to authority. The hip-hop subculture, with its street-style fashion and (particularly) its "gangsta rap," is also perceived as threatening (Tanner, 1996, p. 89).

Current fears about young black men can be understood as a moral panic brought on by public apprehension about the profound social changes we have been experiencing in recent decades. Tanner (1996) applies Cohen's (1972) views on moral panics to Canadian society in arguing that

> . . . a growing inclination to link youth crime to race is symbolic of broader uncertainties about the impact of newcomers or cultural and racial outsiders on the fabric of Canadian society . . . For many citizens, and the police as well, the sight of what appears to be large numbers of black youth hanging out together, publicly playing music . . . and wearing strange clothes, is frightening and leads to exaggerated fears about "black crime." (p. 11)

Aboriginal Youth

Some research has examined offending among Aboriginal youth and found that the most common offences committed by Aboriginal youth are theft, break and enter, and willful damage (Shkilnyk, 1985, p. 30). Shkilnyk (1985) and York (1990) suggested that some criminal activity by Aboriginal youth stems from the boredom and despair of life on impoverished reserves. One youth counsellor in Winnipeg estimated that "30 percent of the reserve's teenagers are prepared to commit criminal offences to escape the reserve" (cited in York, 1990, p. 142). York (1990) reported that 75 percent of the young people in the Winnipeg Youth Detention Centre were Aboriginal. Aboriginal youth crime frequently occurs in the context of substance abuse and the violence that often accompanies it. This violence is often self-inflicted, as the tragic events at Davis Inlet, Newfoundland, testify.

> About 42 of 340 kids regularly sniff gas in this remote Innu island off the coast of Labrador, where six teens high on fumes tried to kill themselves last month. Youths have blown holes in their stomachs with shotguns. Some sniff gas until they're hallucinatory or brain-damaged. (Gorham, 1993)

York (1990, p. 97) reported that the suicide rate for Aboriginal peoples under 25 was six times higher than that for non-Aboriginal youth in the same age group.

While little can be said about actual criminal activity, we do know more about Aboriginal youth already in the justice system, most importantly, that Aboriginal youth are over-represented in court populations. Schissel (1993) found that 18 percent of young offenders processed through an Edmonton court were **First Nations** youth. Bell (1994a) examined a court in London, Ontario, and found that Aboriginal youth were the accused in 12 percent of the court cases. Schissel (1993, p. 11) suggests that much of this over-representation may be owing to a high concentration of policing in Native reserve areas. Police are also concentrated in urban core areas, which in some cities (particularly in the West) furthers the risk of apprehension for Aboriginal youth. Ratner (1996) reported that in the early 1990s, there were about 6,000 Native youth in Vancouver. Half were said to be "problematic," about 200 were "hard-core" street kids, and many were reserve runaways.

> Most of the reserve émigrés chose to flee the reserve and entertain dreamy expectations of the future—expectations that are quickly dashed, given that they lack work skills transferable to the urban area. Girls turn to prostitution and shoplifting; boys to car theft, stealing, and running drugs. Immersion in alcohol, sex, and drugs (often from the age of 12) ensures school failure, joblessness, and chronic welfare dependency. The predictable sequence for native youths caught in this spiral begins with entry into the child welfare system, advances to more serious delinquencies as the youths "rise" through the criminal justice system, and ends with a slow weaning off the latter, accompanied by burnout and apathy. Thus, the study of native youth delinquency epitomizes, with special poignancy, the obstacles to cultural regeneration faced by off-reserve Aboriginals. (Ratner, 1996, p. 188)

The National Indian Brotherhood, Assembly of First Nations, expressed concern for its youth in a discussion paper:

> A study entitled "Locking Up Indians in Saskatchewan" concluded that a treaty Indian boy turning 16 in 1976 had a 70% chance of at least one stay in prison by the age of 25. The corresponding figure for a non-Indian was 8%. Put into context, in

First Nations

Compared to the term "Aboriginal," "First Nations" has clear political connotations because it defines a group in historically specific terms. It means the first people who were a nation (i.e., a people with legal and political standing).

Saskatchewan, prison for young treaty Indians had become the equivalent to the promise of a just society which high school and college represented to the rest of Canada. (Canada, Department of Justice, 1991, p. 2)

Fisher and Janetti (1996, pp. 240–241) reported that the proportionate representation of Aboriginal youth in British Columbian correctional institutions increased from 19 percent in 1983–1984 to 25.5 percent in 1990–1991. Over the same period, Aboriginal representation in community correctional programs increased from 15 percent to 18 percent. The Aboriginal Justice Inquiry of Manitoba reported that Aboriginal youth in Manitoba had higher arrest rates than non-Aboriginal youth, were more likely to be denied bail, and were more likely to be held in detention prior to trial (cited in Hamilton & Sinclair, 1991). A two-year study of a northern Canadian community reported similar results; the same study found that Aboriginal youth become involved in the justice system at an earlier age than non-Aboriginal youth (LaPrairie, 1983). Similar results were found in Ontario (Jolly, 1983). Correctional statistics for 1998–1999 indicated that 23 percent of admissions to custodial institutions were Aboriginal youth; the highest proportion of Aboriginal admissions were still in Manitoba and Saskatchewan, and those in British Columbia were still about 25 percent (Statistics Canada, 2000b, pp. 25, 35).

Meloff and Silverman (1992) and Moyer (1992) examined Canadian youth charged and convicted of murder and manslaughter between 1961 and 1983. Meloff and Silverman found that Aboriginal youth were over-represented as offenders in homicide cases. Some 30 percent of young persons convicted of homicide during the 1961–1983 period were Aboriginal youth. At the same time Aboriginal peoples are also over-represented as victims of homicide (Dauvergne, 2005, p. 13). Meloff and Silverman reported that most Canadian juvenile homicide was intraracial: 68 percent of all the homicides committed by youth involved Caucasians killing Caucasians. When Aboriginal youth killed, the victim was an Aboriginal person 87 percent of the time. Aboriginal youth more than non-Aboriginal youth were found to have killed a member of their family (49 percent vs. 30 percent). Homicides by Aboriginal youth less often involved another crime (3 percent), and victims were more often friends and acquaintances than were the victims of non-Aboriginal offenders (in other words, non-Aboriginal youth had killed more people who were strangers to them).

AGE

Age is one of the most important factors to consider in attempting to understand youth crime patterns and changes in criminal activity over time. Three age-related issues in the public discourse surrounding youth crime are (1) increased criminal activity by youth under 12 years of age, (2) increases in overall youth crime (particularly after the Young Offenders Act was implemented), and (3) increases in violent crime.

Youth Under 12

In 1980, in all of Canada, 1,155 young people under the age of 12 appeared in juvenile court (Statistics Canada, 1981). This figure amounted to 3.5 percent of the entire juvenile court population. Bala and Mahoney (1994) reported that in the year before the Young Offenders Act (YOA) was implemented (1984), 7- to 11-year-olds accounted for "just under" 2 percent of the charges under the Juvenile Delinquents Act (JDA). In other words, children under 12 were not highly involved in criminal activity. This is likely one of the major reasons that youth under 12 were excluded from the jurisdiction of the YOA and the Youth Criminal Justice Act (YCJA), particularly since, even with these small proportions, not all would have been charged with an offence under the Criminal Code.

To learn about the behaviour of youth under age 12 since the YOA was implemented, Clark and O'Reilly-Fleming (1994) examined police files from 27 Canadian cities. Between 1988 and 1992, 4,757 of the 406,662 criminal incidents reported by police involved youth under the age of 12. Youth under 12 accounted for only 1.2 percent of the total offences, young offenders aged 12 to 17 for 21 percent of the total offences, and adults for the rest (pp. 307–308). Among young offenders, those under 12 accounted for approximately 5 percent of police apprehensions (DuWors, 1992, p. 3). Some 90 percent of the "under-12s" were males, and the majority (70 percent) were aged 10 or 11. Only 13 percent of those involved in criminal incidents were 7 or under.

Most of these children's offences were of a petty nature. For example, 41 percent had been involved in mischief and 23 percent in theft under $1,000. Only 2 percent had been involved in violent offences of a serious nature, such as sexual assault and Assault Level II. Three percent had been involved in arson. These violent crimes most often involved casual acquaintances (82 percent) or family and friends (6 percent). The great majority of under-12s (74 percent) did not use weapons; of those who did, 8 percent used knives, 7 percent a club or stick, and 1 percent a firearm.

Most under-12 offences (63 percent) were committed alone. According to Clark and O'Reilly-Fleming (1994), ". . . either organized or spontaneous peer involvement in crime, of a youth group or 'gang' nature, is negligible" (p. 311). Most important, public fears that older youth or adults are encouraging under-12s to be involved in criminal activity appear to be unfounded. When accomplices were involved in under-12 cases, they tended to be children 12 to 13 years of age (70 percent); only 6 percent of these cases involved accomplices over age 16 (Clark & O'Reilly-Fleming, 1994, pp. 309–311).

Doob and Cesaroni (2004) reported on an examination of under-12 offences that came to the attention of police in 1997, and the results were not different from earlier statistics. They too concluded that the problem behaviour of youth under 12 is mostly minor, with a very small number of serious offenders (p. 61). In spite of the view by some that crime by youth under 12 is a growing problem, a survey of police from across the country reported that most police officers did not see this area of criminal activity as something serious (Augimeri, Goldberg, & Koegl, 1999, p. 12). Using the *National Longitudinal Survey of Children and Youth* (NLSCY) data, Sprott and Doob (2000) found that the most aggressive among 10- to 11-year-olds were very unhappy children with a negative self-image and negative relationships with family and friends, who felt rejected by their parents and unfairly treated by teachers. They concluded that criminalizing children under 12 by processing them through the justice system would be more likely to exacerbate their problem behaviours than would other more welfare-oriented interventions (p. 131).

Youth Crime Trends

As we have seen, youth crime rates have steadily increased over the life span of the juvenile justice system in Canada, with periods of rapid increases and decreases. As mentioned in the last chapter, a considerable portion of the increase in youth crime rates when the YOA was implemented can be explained simply by the addition of 16- and 17-year-olds to the youth justice system in 1985. Prior to the implementation of the YOA, the youth justice upper-age limits were under 16 in New Brunswick, Nova

Scotia, Prince Edward Island, Ontario, Saskatchewan, Alberta, the Yukon, and the Northwest Territories; under 17 in Newfoundland and British Columbia; and under 18 in Quebec and Manitoba.

There are two reasons why age changes in the juvenile justice legislation account for increased crime rates. First, criminal activity increases with age and, secondly, as we saw in the last chapter, police charge older youth, particularly male youth, at a higher rate than younger youth. Carrington (1998a), for example, found that a large part of the increase in youth crime rates in Ontario and Saskatchewan was due to older youth coming into the system and police laying more charges.

Statistical comparisons can also be problematic when these factors are not taken into account in interpreting the statistics. A Statistics Canada (1992a) report, for example, stated that in 1991, 12- to 17-year-olds were charged with property crimes at a rate of 47 per 100,000, or "about four times the adult rate of 11 per 100,000 persons aged 18 or more" (p. 3). This is a very misleading comparison precisely because crime rates peak in the late 20s age group and decline thereafter.

More meaningful comparisons of age-specific rates between youth and adults would involve five-year age groups for adults as well as youth. By way of example, since similar data are not available for more recent periods, Table 4.1 presents crimes known to police by age groups as a percentage of the total population. This table shows that the 18–24 and 31–45 age groups, in that year, were responsible for far more crime than 12- to 17-year-old youth, and that 25- to 30-year-olds and 12- to 17-year-olds are responsible for about the same proportion of crime. Viewed in the context of their percentage of the total population, 18- to 30-year-olds comprised the group responsible for the greatest share (almost 50 percent) of police-recorded crime. Hence, we should expect that crime rates will continue to fluctuate as the proportion of 18- to 30-year-olds in the population changes.

Rates of violent crime also increase with age. Among adults, age-specific crime rates consistently show that the peak ages for persons charged with violent crime are the late 20s and early 30s. In particular, persons aged 15 to 28 account for the highest portion of violent incidents in Canada (Statistics Canada, 1995, p. 29) and persons aged 15–32 are the highest risk group for committing homicide. They accounted for three out of five of the accused in 1999 (Fedorowycz, 2000, p. 12). Similarly, Meloff and Silverman's homicide study (1992) showed that Canadian youth homicide rates

TABLE 4.1

Accused Status by Age, Canada, 1991

| Age | Total | Age Group as a % of | |
		Total Accused	Total Population
Under 12	1,611	0.8	16.8
12–17	33,781	18.4	8.2
18–24	54,207	29.9	9.9
25–30	33,140	18.1	10.6
31–45	45,527	24.7	24.6
46–64	13,106	7.2	18.4
65 and over	1,963	1.1	11.6
Total	183,115	100%	100%

Sources: CCJS, *UCR Survey*, Cat. No. 85-205, 1991; 1991 Census of Canada; adapted from Nova Scotia Youth Secretariat (1993).

from 1961–1983 ranged from 0.29 per 100,000 for those 13 years of age to 2.71 per 100,000 for those 17 years of age (p. 21).

While not directly comparable to police statistics, adult and youth court statistics show similar patterns in age-specific rates. Considering all cases going to both adult and youth courts in 2003–2004, 18- to 34-year-olds, who comprise about 22 percent of the population, accounted for about half of the cases overall and 42 percent of the cases for violent offences. In contrast, youth 12–17, comprising about 8 percent of the population, accounted for 14 percent of all of the cases and 23 percent of the violent cases (Sauve 2005, p. 21; Statistics Canada, 2005e, p.14; Thomas 2005, p. 13).

Overall then, young adults—not just youth—are responsible for far more crime, proportionate to their share of the overall population. Hence, it is reasonable to suggest that the amount of media attention paid to youth crime and justice issues compared to that paid to adult behaviour leads to undue public concern about youth behaviour. Furthermore, since earlier increases in youth crime rates and rates of violent crime resulted in large measure from the legislative inclusion of 16- and 17-year-olds in the justice system and changes in police charging practices, we should expect that the increased emphasis on extrajudicial measures in the YCJA will further impact on police charging practices, and that the declining rates of violent crime that began in 2003 will continue.

GENDER

One of the facts of crime and delinquency that is most consistent and least disputed is that boys are far more involved in crime and serious criminal activity than girls of any age (see Table 4.2). Nonetheless, girls' proportionate share of all police charges steadily increased throughout the YOA years. Reports on girls, based on police charges for 1990–1991 (Conway, 1992) and 1994 UCR statistics, indicated that 18 percent of all youth charged with Criminal Code offences in Canada were girls. In 2003, girls were responsible for 30 percent of all Criminal Code charges against youth, up from 23 percent in 2000 (Logan, 2000, p. 8; Wallace, 2004, p. 25). These increases were largely attributable to more charges being laid against girls, primarily for minor assaults and administrative offences (Carrington & Moyer, 1998, p. 38). Interestingly, girls' charge rates have always been higher than women's, particularly for violent offences, even before the YOA (Conway, 1992; Hatch & Faith, 1991, p. 77). In 2003, girls accounted for 26 percent of all youth violent crime, while women accounted for 16 percent of adult violent crime (Wallace, 2004, p. 25).

The consistency of these statistics notwithstanding, certain aspects of the "fact" of **gender** differences are debatable. At issue is the magnitude of the difference between boys and girls, whether the types of offences they are involved in differ, and whether girls are becoming more like boys in their behaviour. Answers to these questions are not straightforward and will depend on what type of statistics are used—official statistics or self-report or victimization survey results.

gender
The socially constructed aspects of a person's biological sex.

Official Statistics

Almost half of girls' offences (48 percent) involve petty theft, and most of these charges (86 percent) involve shoplifting. The next most common offences for girls are minor assault (9 percent), break and enter (7 percent), and bail violations (5 percent). Like that for girls, boys' most frequent charge is theft under $1,000 (22 percent). The second most frequent offence for boys is more serious: break and enter (21 percent), followed by mischief and damage (7 percent), and motor vehicle theft (7 percent).

TABLE 4.2

Youth Charged by Sex, Selected Incidents, 2003

	Sex	
	Male	Female
Homicide[1]	79	21
Attempted murder	94	6
Assaults	71	29
Sexual assaults	97	3
Other sexual offences	94	6
Abduction	100	0
Robbery	86	14
Violent crime–Total	**74**	**26**
Breaking and entering	91	9
Motor vehicle theft	84	16
Fraud	66	34
Theft over $5,000	84	16
Theft $5,000 and under	61	39
Property crime–Total	**75**	**25**
Mischief	90	10
Arson	91	9
Prostitution	23	77
Offensive weapons	92	8
Criminal Code–Total	**70**	**30**
Impaired driving[2]	84	16
Cocaine offences	85	15
Cannabis offences	79	21
Other drug offences	83	17

[1]Homicide survey, Canadian Centre for Justice Statistics.

[2]Includes impaired operation of a vehicle causing death, causing bodily harm, alcohol rate over 80 mg, failure/refusal to provide a breath/blood sample. Age of persons charged with impaired driving comes from the *Incident-Based Survey* (UCR2).

Source: Adapted from Statistics Canada, (2004), *Juristat,* Cat. No. 85-002, 24(6), p. 25.

Overall increases in Criminal Code charges are in large part due to increases in charges for minor assaults. Both boys and girls have shown an increase in minor assault charges, but the increase is greater for girls. Since 1986, the number of assault charges against girls has increased by 120 percent, compared with a 78 percent increase for boys. Nonetheless, their overall rate for assault is one-third of the male rate and compared to boys, more girls' violence involves common assaults (67 percent vs. 46 percent) (Conway, 1992, pp. 1–5; Savoie, 1999, p. 5; Wallace, 2004, p. 25). The other major area accounting for girls' increases in charge rates is administrative offences, more specifically bail violation. In the first five years after the YOA was implemented, this charge rate increased by 71 percent (Conway, 1992, pp. 1–5). Girls' rates for administrative charges rose from 6.1 percent in 1985–1986 to 27.3 percent in 1995–1996, while boys' rates rose from 3.9 percent to 21.6 percent (Reitsma-Street, 1999, pp. 338–339).

A typical scenario for violent and administrative charges occurred in Halifax. Two patrolling police officers noticed a 15-year-old girl on the street who they knew "was supposed to be at home." The officers chased the girl and a struggle ensued when they caught up with her. She was subsequently charged with assaulting a police officer, resisting arrest, and breaching an undertaking (Teen charged . . . , 2000).

Statistics from the youth courts show gender patterns similar to those reflected in police statistics. In 1999–2000, girls accounted for 21 percent of all charges appearing before youth court, 22 percent of all violent charges, and 16.5 percent of all property charges (Sudworth & deSouza, 2001, p. 6). Some of the most dramatic gender differences are more apparent in youth court statistics than in police statistics. More specifically, as we have seen, the only area in which girls' charges outnumber those of boys is in the area of administrative and YOA/YCJA offences. In 2003, 13 percent of all girls' charges were for YOA/YCJA offences and 11 percent of the charges were administrative. Boys' charges for these offences were 10 and 9 percent, respectively.

The gap between the overall rates has declined considerably but some important differences remain. As Figure 4.1 shows, as well as higher rates of YOA/YCJA charges, girls are more likely to be in court for failing to appear and for other administrative charges than are boys. Boys are more likely to be charged with being unlawfully at large. The majority of charges for both boys and girls are for breaching a court order. Girls accounted for 25 percent of all YOA/YCJA charges and 24 percent of all administrative charges. These proportions are the same as they were in 2000, three years prior to the YCJA (Sudworth & deSouza, 2001, p. 6).

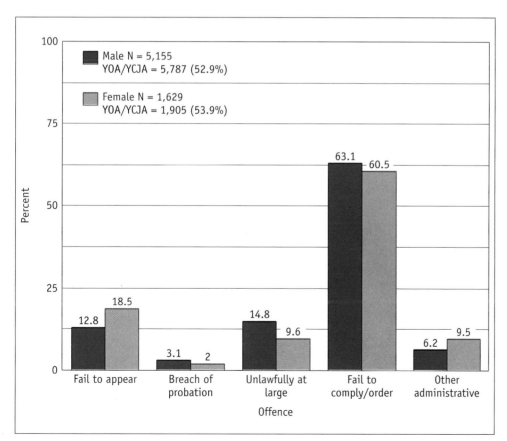

FIGURE 4.1

Distribution by Sex of Young Offender Cases Involving Administration of Justice and YOA/YCJA Offences, 2003–2004

Source: Adapted from Statistics Canada, Cat. No. 85-002, Vol. 19, No. 25(4).

FIGURE 4.2

Age and Sex
Distribution of Youth
in Violent Offence
Court Cases,
2003–2004

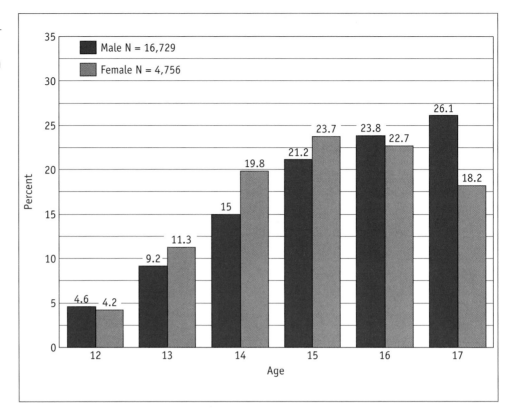

Source: Adapted from Statistics Canada, Table 252-0007; *Youth Court Survey*-3309.

The significance of these offences and differentials in rates is that, as discussed earlier, the chance of a custody sentence is higher for these than for any other offences, and custody sentences are more frequent for YOA/YCJA offences (27 percent) than for administrative offences in general, with the exception of unlawfully at large (79 percent) and other administrative offences (29 percent) (Thomas, 2005, p. 15).

Other striking sex differences in youth court statistics appear with comparisons of age-specific rates of charges. Figure 4.2, for example shows that violent offence charges going to court are more likely to involve younger girls—60 percent of the girls and 50 percent of the boys are under age 16. Girls' rates peak at age 15 and decline thereafter, while boys' rates continue to increase (Statistics Canada, Cat. 85-002, Vol. 24(2). *Youth Court Survey*, 2003–2004). This is the same age and sex pattern for all cases appearing in youth court for 2003–2004, and statistics from the Statistics Canada *Youth Court Survey* in the early years of the YOA show this same pattern (1990a). Age differences between boys' and girls' administrative charges were also apparent under the YOA and were even more dramatic. In 1991–1992, girls under 16 were far more likely than older girls and boys of the same age to be charged with these offences. Of all girls charged with administrative offences, 56 percent were under 16, almost twice the proportion for boys; only 36 percent of boys charged with administrative offences were under 16 (Gagnon & Doherty, 1993, p. 5).

More recent age-specific data are not available for administrative or YOA/YCJA data. Nonetheless, it does appear that subsequent changes in police charging practices during the YOA years have not yet affected sex differences in overall cases and in violent cases going to court. While there are reasons to be hopeful that the YCJA may reduce the criminalization of girls and young women for minor violent offences and "technical violations," some analysts caution that continued media depictions of "violent girls" and continued emphasis on "accountability" in the YCJA are just as likely to lead to increased levels of criminalization (Boyle, Fairbridge, Kinch, Cochran, Smyth, & Chunn, 2002, pp. 426–428; Reitsma-Street, 1999, p. 144). We will return to this issue in later chapters.

Self-Report Studies

Self-report studies corroborate official reports that there is more criminal behaviour among boys than girls, but suggest that the gap between them is much smaller than that indicated by official statistics. According to Le Blanc (1983), official statistics in the late 1970s showed a ratio of one girl to every eight or ten boys. His self-report study in Montreal during the same period indicated a delinquency rate of one girl to three boys (1983, p. 37). A more recent Canadian self-report study indicates little change in girls' behaviour—a 3:1 male–female ratio (Simourd & Andrews, 1996).

Most recently, the NLSCY of Canadian children reports that for the years 1994–1997, 30 percent of girls aged 12–13 reported involvement in property offences, compared to 40 percent of boys the same age, and 29 percent reported involvement in fighting with or attacking other people, compared to 56 percent of the boys. For both types of behaviour, only 7 percent of the girls reported a high frequency of involvement. The percentages for boys are almost double: thirteen percent of the boys reported a high involvement in property offences and 16 percent a high involvement in fighting and physical aggression (Sprott, Doob, & Jenkins, 2001, p. 3).

Reitsma-Street's discussions of Canadian self-report studies (1991a, 1999) suggests that while race, class, and gender do impact on girls' processing once they come into contact with the justice system, these things are not factors that differentiate involvement in delinquent behaviour (see Byles, 1969; Gomme, 1985; Le Blanc, 1983). Reitsma-Street argues that self-report studies in Canada and the United States "challenge the amount of real variation in delinquencies by background of the girls. They also question the numbers and rates of the official statistics" (1991a, p. 253). Most self-report studies suggest that girls and boys are involved in the same kind of criminal and delinquent behaviour. According to Reitsma-Street (1991a, pp. 253–254), the rate of official charges for girls is infrequent, but most girls report at least one or more delinquencies in any one-year period; only a small proportion of girls report an involvement in more than 10 acts of crime or delinquency.

Chesney-Lind and Shelden (1998), in their thorough review of self-report studies in the United States, report that female delinquency is more prevalent than official statistics indicate and that boys' and girls' behaviour is similar. The majority of girls' delinquency, like that of boys, is trivial. Contrary to what is indicated by official statistics and reports, boys report running away from home and being involved in prostitution as much as girls do. Later in this chapter, we will discuss how the consequences of these behaviours differ for boys and girls.

A major and important difference between boys and girls is that girls engage in delinquent behaviour far less frequently than do boys (Chesney-Lind & Shelden, 1992, p. 18, 1998; Conway, 1992, p. 9). Hindelang (1979) has argued that frequency rather than type of delinquent behaviour accounts for the greater number of boys in official police statistics. By contrast, Chesney-Lind and Shelden (1998) argue that while frequency may help to explain why there are disproportionate numbers of boys in violent offence categories, it does not account for the categories in which girls are

status offences
Behaviours considered to be illegal only because of the age status of the individual (e.g., truancy).

over-represented. More specifically, and with regard to youth in the United States youth, it does not account for the over-representation of girls charged with **status offences** (Chesney-Lind & Shelden, 1992, p. 18). In the Canadian context, Bell (1994) and Reitsma-Street (1999) have argued that the status offence of the JDA era was replaced under the YOA with administrative offences, and Hindelang's argument does not account for the high number of charges against girls for these offences. The questions of why girls are criminalized for some behaviours and not others will be addressed in later chapters.

Victimization Surveys

Results from victimization surveys confirm the aforementioned gender patterns, but only for face-to-face crimes and not in a manner that readily separates youth from adults. Johnson's report on the 1982 Canadian victimization survey (1986) and the more recent *General Social Survey* (GSS) reports from Statistics Canada (1999, 2004) found that:

- victimizations perpetrated by women and girls were increasing. Only 5 percent of all victimizations involved one or more female assailants in 1982, while the 1999 GSS reported that 18 percent of all assailants were female (Besserer & Trainor, 2000, p. 21);
- for all violent victimizations, 12 percent of the accused were women and girls and they were responsible for 14 percent of the reported physical assaults; for all other types of reported violence, the numbers of women and girls as assailants were too small to provide clear proportional figures (Gannon & Milhorean, 2005, p. 24);
- the age distribution of offenders was similar for males and females;
- females were the victims of female assailants more often than of male assailants (78 percent vs. 35 percent);
- female assailants were more likely to be acquaintances (50 percent) or relatives (15 percent) of their victims than were men (25 percent and 5 percent, respectively);
- males were more likely than females to use weapons (34 percent vs. 23 percent);
- females' victims were more likely to be injured (64 percent) than were males' victims (48 percent) or victims of both genders (59 percent);
- incidents involving males and females were more likely to be reported than were incidents involving only a man or only women; and
- incidents perpetrated by a female were more likely to be described as a "crime" than as a "threat" or an "attempt" (32 percent vs. 49 percent for male perpetrators).

It is sometimes suggested that female crime rates are low because men are too embarrassed to report having been victimized by a woman. Hatch and Faith (1991) argue that victimization survey results raise important questions about this assumption and about how similar acts may be interpreted differently, depending on whether they are perpetrated by a male or a female (p. 71). Victimization survey results also suggest a considerable amount of police discretion in charging, and support the argument that police and prosecutors are more inclined to charge and prosecute girls under 16 than they are older girls.

Delinquent Careers

birth cohorts
A group of people born in the same time period.

Other important differences between boys and girls have been revealed by longitudinal research on **birth cohorts**; for example, all children born in 1974 would constitute a birth cohort and could be used as a basis for longitudinal research. Chesney-Lind and Shelden (1992, 1998) reviewed this type of research and confirmed a considerable gender gap over time. Male offence rates were found to be four times greater than female rates. The ratio of male to female rates was 9:1 for all index offences and 14:1 for violent offences. One possible explanation for this difference is that boys' delinquent behaviour is more long-lasting than is girls'. Chesney-Lind and Shelden (1992) concluded from their review of in the United States research, as well as research in England, Wales, and Scotland, that boys' delinquent careers are longer, boys are more likely to begin their careers at an earlier age, and boys are more likely to extend their delinquent careers into their adult lives.

Girls' careers are not only shorter than are boys', but they involve less serious offences (Chesney-Lind & Shelden, 1992, pp. 19–20). Similarly, Biron's study of Montreal girls (1980, p. 7) found an overall decrease in delinquent behaviour after two years, especially with regard to violent crimes. More recently, a self-report questionnaire administered to the student bodies of four secondary schools in Metropolitan Toronto found that girls were more likely than boys to abandon delinquent behaviour after police contact (Keane, Gillis, & Hagan, 1989).

Girls and Violence

An emerging public issue with regard to gender differences and criminal activity is the so-called growth of "girl gangs" and their propensity for violent behaviour. A *Chronicle Herald* [Halifax] article in the mid-1990s entitled "Ruthless violence part of girl gang reality" exemplifies this concern:

> Girls used to be made of sugar and spice and everything nice, but today experts on youth violence see some of them as a dangerous threat to society—ruthless, volatile and brutal . . . [I]n its recently released *Women in Canada* report, Statistics Canada reported that, in 1993, females between the ages of 12 and 17 accounted for 24 percent of all young offenders charged with violent offences, compared with 21 percent charged with property crimes. (Vincent, 1995)

Research suggests that when viewed over time, girls' behaviour has not changed in any dramatic fashion. Reitsma-Street (1993b, 1999) compared court charges for girls before the Young Offenders Act with those after the YOA, from 1980 to 1995–1996. Table 4.3 presents these statistics, along with those for the first year of the YCJA (2003–2004), and indicates a number of interesting things about girls' court charges in general and over time. For example, the most violent offences, and the ones least susceptible to low or changing charge rates—namely, murder, attempted murder, manslaughter, robbery, and arson—are very low and show little change from the JDA to the latter years of the YOA (1980 to 1996). With the exception of robbery, all of these offences remained low in the first year of the YCJA.

Girls' involvement in robbery may be changing. Cases going to court with charges of robbery have steadily increased over this 23-year period, from 1.1 in 1980 to 2.4 in 2003–2004, when 350 cases involved girls charged with robbery. In contrast, only 7 girls were charged with robbery in 1980 and 66 in 1995–1996. While other charges "against the person" have seen a steady increase, from 9.9 percent in 1980 to 20.3 percent in 1995–1996 to 30.6 percent in 2003–2004, we know from police statistics that the majority of offences in this category are minor in nature. In 2003–2004, 58 percent of the cases in this category were classified as minor assaults; only 24 percent were considered to be major (Statistics Canada, 2004d).

TABLE 4.3

Criminal Code and Federal Statute Violations Charges Laid against Girls in Canadian Youth Courts, Pre- and Post-YOA (numbers in percentages)

Type of Charge	Pre-YOA (Includes Ont.)		Post-YOA (Excludes Ont.)		Post-YOA (Includes Ont.)	YCJA
	1980 (N = 7,919)	1983 (N = 9,876)	1986–1987 (N = 10,791)	1989–1990 (N = 13,361)	1995–1996 (N = 21,898)	2003–2004 (N = 14,915)
Murder or attempt	0.1	0.1	0.1	0.02	0.03	0.08
Robbery	1.1	1.3	1.5	0.7	1.7	2.4
Arson	0.5	0.2	0.4	0.4	0.2	0.0
Against person	9.9	9.5	13.0	12.5	20.3	30.6
Theft over/auto	5.4	5.3	3.7	3.1	2.4	24.6 (all theft)
Trafficking/possession	3.3	2.3	2.8	1.8	2.6	3.7
Break and enter	14.6	10.6	10.3	6.7	5.0	4.5
Fraud	5.8	6.9	7.2	7.2	2.6	2.6
Theft under/stolen goods	43.1	47.9	39.8	33.4	31.2	Included in "Theft over"
Mischief	5.6	4.5	4.5	4.6	3.0	3.1
Nuisance/disorderly	3.0	3.3	3.6	2.2	0.8	0.51
Immorality/vice/soliciting	1.2	0.6	(Decriminalized)		0.9	0.13
Other/unknown	0.6	0.6	0.9	5.9	2.1	4.1
Against administration of justice	5.7	6.9	12.2	21.5	27.3	23.7
TOTAL	100.0	100.0	100.0	100.0	100.0	100.0

Sources: Adapted from Reitsma-Street (1993b, p. 441; 1999, p. 343); Statistics Canada, Cat. No. 85-002, 25(4).

With regard to the most violent offence, murder, Meloff and Silverman (1992) reported that, between 1961 and 1983, 63 percent of youth homicides involved males killing males; girls accounted for 11 percent of the youth homicides during that period. Compared to boys, girls are more likely to kill family members (48 percent vs. 32 percent) than friends or strangers (p. 27). In the 1961–1983 period, 85 percent of the 65 people killed by girls were relatives (p. 28). According to Reitsma-Street (1993b), "street crime and stranger crime by female youth is definitely not a major source of public danger" (p. 444). In 1989, of the 563 people charged with homicide, 458 were men, 57 were women, 43 were boys, and only 5 were girls (Frank, 1991, pp. 6–7). In 2000, there were 542 homicides; less than 10 percent involved young offenders and five girls were charged, the same number of girls charged with homicide in 1989. In 2004, there was an increase in overall homicide to 622 cases and youth involvement decreased. Only 40 young offenders were charged with homicide and 3 of these were girls. This seems a far cry from "ruthless, volatile and brutal." We will return to this subject in later chapters.

Boritch's review of the literature and statistics on juvenile crime trends from 1965 to 1995 (1997)] concluded that female crime had increased. Nonetheless, while involvement in criminal activity (especially minor crimes) has escalated, there have also been changes in both victim-reporting behaviour and "law enforcement attitudes toward, and policies affecting, female offenders" (p. 46). Most interesting is the long-range historical view. Boritch reminds us that female crime rates were considerably higher in the early 19th century, declined from 1860 to the 1920s, and began to increase again in the 1930s (pp. 46–47). Recent increases are thus relative to the time frame under consideration.

YOUTH AS VICTIMS OF CRIME

While much public attention is focused on young people as offenders, until recently very little attention has been directed toward youth and children as victims of violence or the relationship between victimization as a child and later criminality. As a consequence, our thinking about the relationship between youth and crime is distorted, and social policies are directed more toward punitive measures than **remedial solutions.** Yet research in the United States has consistently shown evidence of a **cycle of violence,** most recently in a report from the United States Department of Justice, which indicates that victims of childhood abuse and neglect are more likely to be charged with criminal offences than other youth and that their offences are more likely of a violent nature (Widom & Maxfield, 2001). Some Canadian research also indicates that individuals who have been victimized have higher rates of delinquent behaviour (Fitzgerald, 2003).

Canada does not conduct child victimization surveys, but surveys conducted in the United States report that children are far more likely to be victimized than adults, girls are more likely to be sexually assaulted than boys, and boys are more likely than girls to be killed or physically assaulted (Finkelhor & Dziuba-Leatherman, 1994). These surveys also report that the risk of violent criminal victimization is greater for a 12-year-old than for anyone 24 or older, and that juveniles between 12 and 17 are more likely to be victims of violent crime than are persons past their mid-20s (Snyder & Sickmund, 1995, p. 14). While we usually hear that senior citizens are most afraid of violence, these victimization surveys indicate that senior citizens have much lower victimization rates than persons aged 18 to 24. In fact, 18- to 24-year-olds have the highest rate of victimization within the adult population. Among youth, victimization rates are so high for teenaged youth that "if not a single younger child were victimized, the level of teen victimization alone would make the rate for all children higher than the rate for all adults" (Finkelhor & Dziuba-Leatherman, 1993, p. 3).

remedial solutions
Programs designed to help overcome a weakness, as opposed to correct a problem.

cycle of violence
The theory that when children witness or experience violence, they are more likely to experience or initiate violence as they get older.

Canadian figures on child and youth victimization from police statistics and the *General Social Survey* show similar results: youth and young adults are victimized more than any other age groups. In 2003, slightly more than one-fifth (22 percent) of the victims of violent crimes reported to police were children and youth under age 18. Furthermore, 6 out of every 10 sexual assaults (61 percent) reported to police involved a child or youth under 18, as did 1 in every 5 physical assaults (AuCoin, 2005, p. 3). These rates become even more significant in light of the fact that the victimization surveys also indicate that youth are less likely to report victimization than adults, and that children must rely on adults to report offences against them. We also now know that while the majority of persons accused of violent crimes are adults, this is less often the case when victims are teens. In 1999, slightly more than half (52 percent) of those accused of violent crimes against teens between the ages of 12 and 17 were teens themselves (Besserer & Trainor, 2000, pp. 7, 9).

The GSS, which includes only people at least 15 years of age, reported that the victimization rate for youth aged 15–19 was more than double the national average in 1993 (217 per 1,000 vs. 92 per 1,000). In all three of these surveys, up to the most recent in 2004, the rate of violent victimization for youth aged 15–24 is higher than for any other age group. Compared to people over the age of 65, the rate of violent crime victimization for 15- to 24-year-olds is 21 times higher, and for theft victimization, 9 times higher. Twenty percent of all victims of violent crime reported to the police in 1994 were youth aged 12–19 (20 percent is double this group's proportion of the population) and in 2004, 35 percent of all self-reported victims of violence were 15 to 24 (Besserer & Trainor, 2000, pp. 7, 19, 21; Gannon & Mihorean, 2005, pp. 7, 23; Gartner & Doob, 1994; Johnson, 1995, p. 6).

Some of this higher rate of victimization is attributable to lifestyle, as rates of victimization are higher for students and those who spend time away from home in the evenings (Besserer & Trainor, 2000, p. 7). In 2004, people who reported leaving home for 30 or more evening activities in any month also reported rates of victimization that were four times those of people who reported leaving home for only 10 evening activities (Gannon & Mihorean, 2005, p. 7). Lifestyle, however, implies choice of activity and cannot explain that rates of violence are highest for Aboriginal peoples, the unemployed, and those with low incomes. In particular, it does not account for the most violent offences being perpetuated against young victims.

Among child victims of homicide during the 1974–2004 time period, the age group with the highest rate of victimization has been infants under one year of age (Dauvergne, 2005, p. 11). In some years, infant murder rates have been higher than rates for any other age group, as evidenced in Figure 4.3. In 1998, the murder rate for children under one year of age was 6.5 per 100,000; the next highest rate was for 23-year-olds, at 4.5 per 100,000 (Fedorowycz, 1999, p. 10). Between 1988 and 1998, an average of 12 infants under the age of one and 52 children under the age of twelve were murdered each year. Four out of five of these children were murdered by their parents (Fedorowycz, 2000, pp. 11–12). For the 30-year period from 1974 to 2004, a total of 1,164 children under 12 were murdered by their parents (Dauvergne, 2005, p. 24; Fedorowycz, 1999, p. 11). Wendy Regoeczi's research on all youth homicide victims from 1985 to 1995 (2000) showed that, on average, 29 youths aged 12–17 were killed each year, and one-third were killed by a family member (p. 497). Half (51.7 percent) were killed by a friend or acquaintance (p. 498). One-quarter of these homicides occurred because of a quarrel or argument, and the other quarter occurred during the course of a criminal offence not precipitated by the youth (p. 501).

FIGURE 4.3

Average Rates of Homicide by Age Group of Victims, 1991–1994

Source: Adapted from Statistics Canada, *Juristat*, Cat. No. 85-002, 15(15), p. 13.

Among the children and youth murdered between 1998 and 2003, older teens (14–17) were mostly stabbed, beaten, or shot (in that order of frequency); 11- to 13-year-olds were strangled, shot, or stabbed; 6- to 10-year-olds were shot, strangled, or stabbed and the youngest children, those under six, were strangled, shaken, or beaten. "Frustration" is most often cited as the reason for the deaths of small children, while for older youth, the reason is most often an argument between peers (AuCoin, 2005, pp. 11, 23).

Age and Sex

Just as age and sex are important indicators of youth involvement in criminal activity, they are also important ingredients in understanding who in our society are at the greatest risk of victimization. One of the earliest Canadian studies to provide information on young people as victims of crimes comes from Johnson and Lazarus (1989), who used data from 13 police departments in seven Canadian cities for the years 1981 to 1984. The risk of victimization, they found, is "not random"; rather, age and sex determine to a great extent who will be victimized and how. While young people aged 16 to 24 have higher victimization rates than any other group, male rates are generally higher than female rates. However, these gender differences vary by age, city, and type of offence. As women age, their chances of victimization increase. Women and girls experience higher rates of sexual assault and personal theft victimization, while men and boys experience higher rates of robbery and assault (Johnson & Lazarus, 1989, p. 312).

The 1993 GSS found that the total personal victimization rate for women over 15 was about 11 percent higher than that for men (151 per 1,000 vs. 136 per 1,000) and even higher in urban areas (Gartner & Doob, 1994; Kong, 1994). By 1999, the GSS reported very little difference in rates for women and men (189 per 1,000 vs. 183 per 1,000), but four times more sexual assaults were perpetrated against women (33 per 1,000 vs. 8 per 1,000), and men reported higher rates of assault and robbery (92 per 1,000 vs. 70 per 1,000 and 12 per 1,000 vs. 7 per 1,000, respectively). The most recent GSS survey (2004) shows very little difference between women and men over age 15 with regard to overall rates of violent victimization (102 per 1,000 vs. 111 per 1,000). Rates of assault and robbery were similar to those in 1993, but rates of sexual assault in 2004 were five times greater for women and girls (35 per 1,000 vs. 7 per 1,000) than for men and boys (Gannon & Milhorean, 2005, p. 23).

Based on information from crimes known to police, the chances of violent victimization were about equal for boys and girls in both 1994 and 2004. Nonetheless, there are important differences by age, type of offence, who the perpetrators are, and level of injury. More boys were the victims of homicide, attempted murder, assault, and robbery, while more girls were the victims of sexual offences. With the exception of relatively high rates of violent victimization for infants compared to children, the risk of violent victimization increases as children age: the highest rates of victimization are among youth aged 14–17. However, rates of victimization are higher for younger girls than for boys the same age. Similar to patterns of offending, victimization rates increase for girls until age 15 and then begin to decline, while boys' rates continue to increase to age 17 (Aucoin, 2005, p. 3).

Two-thirds of physical assaults against children are committed by parents, and mothers are more likely to physically assault daughters and fathers to assault their sons. Girls are more likely to be physically assaulted by family members, and boys by someone outside the family, most often peers. The younger the child is, the more likely that the assailant is a family member. The opposite is true for sexual assaults. Here, younger girls are more likely to be victimized. Girls younger than 12 are more likely to be sexually assaulted than to be victims of other types of violence, and the highest rates of sexual assault are for 13-year-old girls (Aucoin, 2005, pp. 4–5).

While 80 percent of the victims of sexual assault were girls, 86 percent of sexual assaults involved individuals known to the victim. Only 5 percent of the cases involved strangers and, the younger the victim, the more likely that the perpetrator was a family member. Only one-third of the charges against the accused in sexual offences resulted in a guilty finding, and 58 percent of the perpetrators received a prison sentence. Young children and teens are more likely to sustain major injuries from physical assaults, and girls sustain more injuries from sexual assaults than do boys (AuCoin, 2005, pp. 3, 5, 7, 8; Johnson, 1995).

According to the RCMP Missing Children's Registry, the number of missing children has been increasing over the last 10 years, and in 2003, more than 67,000 children were reported missing. Almost 80 percent of these cases involved "runaway" children (Dalley, 2004, as cited in AuCoin, 2005, p. 13). Other missing children have been kidnapped or abducted, and the RCMP also reported that only a very small number of reported cases of child abductions (only 0.1 percent in 1991) involved strangers. Given that the "stranger" category as defined by the police includes anyone other than a parent who does not have legal custody, "stranger abductors" can and do include grandparents and other relatives or friends of a child (Ericson & Haggerty, 1997, pp. 276–277). Hence, as is also the case with other types of violent victimizations of children and youth, media depictions of "stranger danger" present a highly misleading picture of the reality of child abductions and kidnappings.

When we look at official statistics, we find that while more than 1,200 children and youth were abducted in Canada over the 1994–2004 period, two-thirds of these (67 percent) were parental abductions. The non-parental abductions (33 percent) were mostly perpetrated by men (72 percent), were slightly more likely than parental abductions to result in a finding of guilt (30 percent vs. 27 percent), and were somewhat more likely to result in a prison sentence (40 percent vs. 31 percent) (AuCoin, 2005, p. 13).

Children under 12 are kidnapped or abducted in equal proportions regardless of sex, but girls over 12 are victimized in this manner far more than boys of the same age (Johnson, 1995, p. 5). More girls are abducted by friends and acquaintances, while

> **BOX 4.2**
>
> ## Teenaged Victims of Violent Crime: Facts to Consider
>
> - Twenty-two percent of all violent crime victims in 2004 were teenagers (between 12 and 17 years of age), double their representation in the Canadian population.
> - Both teenagers and children (under 12 years) constituted a larger proportion of victims of sexual assault than adults (18 and older). Of every ten reported sexual victims, four were teenagers and four were children.
> - Six out of ten physical assault victims and half of sexual assault victims under the age of six were assaulted by a family member.
> - For the years 1974–2004, children under one year of age were at greatest risk of homicide.
> - Between 1974 and 2004, 1,164 children under 12 years of age were killed by one or both of their parents.
> - Girls are more likely to sustain injuries from a sexual assault than are boys.
> - Girls at any age are more likely to be assaulted by a family member than are boys.
>
> Sources: Adapted from Statistics Canada (1992b, 2005a), *Juristat*, Cat. No. 85–002, 12(6); 25(1).

more boys are abducted by parents (Johnson, 1995, p. 8). Similarly, teenaged girls are more likely than all other age groups (including boys of the same age) (42 percent vs. 21 percent) to be kidnapped (forcible confinement), and the perpetrator is more likely to be a close friend, acquaintance, or person they know through a job-related relationship (54 percent vs. 46 percent for boys) (AuCoin, 2005, pp. 13–14).

Public information campaigns designed to educate parents about "streetproofing" children can create the impression that children are more likely to be victimized by strangers. However, as we have seen, victimization studies of children, both in the United States and Canada, clearly indicate that children and youth are more likely than adults to be victimized by family members, friends, or acquaintances (88 percent vs. 58 percent) (Snyder & Sickmund, 1995, p. 14). In a national family violence survey conducted in the United States, adults reported almost twice as much severe violence against a child in their household as against their adult partners (Strauss & Gelles, 1990). Importantly, all of this information involves underestimates because the younger the victim, the less likely the offence is to be reported to the police. This may be because children are more likely to report offences to other officials (adults other than police) and/or because complaints from children and youth are less likely than adult complaints to be taken seriously.

Location

While strangers are involved in only a very small proportion of violent victimization of youth and children, a new area of concern is child sexual exploitation on the Internet. As increasing numbers of young people access the Internet, they become prey to sexual offenders who are able to use this tool as a means to gain access to children and youth. One recent case in Halifax involved a 32-year-old man who tried to lure a 13-year-old girl with talk of masturbation and oral sex. He agreed to meet the girl in a Tim Hortons parking lot, but the 13-year-old was actually an undercover police officer. The man's defence in court was that he wanted to scare the girl. "I felt a 13-year-old girl should not be in that [chat] room". . . that he wanted to "tell her what she was doing was wrong'" (Jeffrey, February 7, 2006).

In response to increasing concern about Internet sexual predators, the Criminal Code has been amended so that "sexual interference" makes it illegal to communicate with a child on the Internet for the purpose of sexual exploitation. In January 2005, the federal government launched Cybertip.ca (www.cybertip.ca), a national program that provides an avenue for people to report online materials involving child sexual exploitation. This program was created and implemented by Child Find Manitoba in 2002. During its first two years of operation, more than 1,200 reports were received, of which 533 were reported to police agencies and resulted in 10 arrests and the shutdown of 320 websites; 48 cases are still under investigation. The majority of reported cases (87 percent) involved child pornography and the remaining cases involved luring children, mostly adolescent girls (10 percent), and child prostitution and sex tourism (3 percent). To address the latter, the Criminal Code is also being amended so that Canadians who participate in any form of sexual exploitation in another country will be prosecuted with a sentence range of 5 to 14 years' imprisonment (AuCoin, 2005, pp. 11–12).

Beyond the Internet, surveys from the United States report that more than half (56 percent) of child and youth victimization happens in school or on school property, and three-quarters of these incidents involve personal thefts. With regard to violent crimes, 23 percent occur at school (Snyder & Sickmund, 1995, pp. 14, 16).

Canadian data based on crimes known to the police indicate that the location of victimization varies depending on the age of the victim and the type of victimization. Two-thirds of sexual assaults occurred in homes, but for victims younger than 6 years of age, 82 percent of the assaults occurred in homes. Only 11 percent of sexual assaults occurred at school for 11- to 13-year-olds; older girls were more likely assaulted in public places. Similarly, younger children (under age 11) were more likely to be assaulted in a home; as age increases, so too does the likelihood of assaults outside the home. Girls, however, are more likely to be assaulted in the home at any age than are boys. Slightly more than one-third of boys aged 11–17 are likely to be assaulted in a public place. Twenty-eight percent of physical assaults for boys aged 11–13 occur at school, as do 22 percent of the assaults of 14- to 17-year-old boys (AuCoin, 2005, pp. 6, 8).

Physical assaults among children and youth are more commonly understood as "bullying." Since 1993, data have been available on bullying and on children's feelings of safety from the *Health Behaviour in School-Aged Children* (HBSC) study. According to results from the 2001–2002 HBSC study, about one-quarter of school-aged children report having been bullied. The most common forms reported by both boys and girls were teasing and the spreading of rumours. More boys who had been bullied reported physical assault (45 percent) than girls (21 percent), and this form of victimization decreased with age. Girls who were bullied were more likely to report sexual harassment, and this decreased with age (Craig, 2004). Girls were more likely than boys to be victimized by other girls, but both boys and girls were most likely to be victimized by boys (King, Boyce, & King, 1999).

Most schoolchildren feel safe at school. Only 6 percent of the girls and 10 percent of the boys reported feeling unsafe, and this feeling increased with age only for boys. An even smaller proportion reported that their friends carry weapons: nine percent of boys in Grades 8 and 9 and 3 percent of girls in Grade 8 reported that their friends carried weapons. This too decreased with age (King, Boyce, & King, 1999).

The risk of victimization in the home is greater for children and youth in households where adults, most likely the mother, have been victimized. A 1998 review of research on exposure to domestic violence found that between 45 and 70 percent of children exposed to family violence were themselves victims of physical abuse (Margolin, 1998). Girls are particularly vulnerable to this type of victimization (Mitchell & Finkelhor, 2001, p. 957). Many street youth describe their family lives as years of abuse that most commonly involved physical and sexual abuse by fathers (*Homeless Youth in Perspective*, 1994; Webber, 1991; see also Chapter 7).

My own analysis of young offender case files in a southwestern Ontario family court for the years 1986–1987 (Bell, 1993) revealed that a large number of young offenders in the court came from families where interpersonal relationships fell considerably short of an "ideal" family model. Fourteen percent of these families had a lengthy history of violence and abuse in the home, and another 14 percent were characterized by neglect and negative parent–child relationships. Six percent of the parents were very outspoken and insistent about wanting their child out of the family home. Fathers, stepfathers, and other male partners, as well as older brothers, were most often the source of violence and abuse.

Living on the streets also puts young people at great risk for violence (Baron, 1995; Gaetz, 2004; Miller, Donahue, Este, & Hofer, 2004). Whitbeck et al. (2001) reported that living on the street increases a youth's risk of physical victimization by five times and that the risk of sexual victimization is six times greater for girls on the street than for boys (p. 1200). Similarly, Gaetz (2004) reported from his survey of homeless youth in Toronto that compared to GSS results, which look only at "domiciled youth" (youth who have a home), rates of crime victimization are double overall: six times higher for physical assault, five times greater for theft, and ten times greater for sexual assault (pp. 434–436). The risk of sexual victimization for homeless girls is nine times greater than for girls who are domiciled.

Webber (1991) was one of the first to document the poignant and horrific details of street life for Canadian youth. Among other things, she described a problem that few people knew about—the growing street trade for young boys:

> If new girls on the stroll are hot sellers, fresh "male meat," called "chicken," is an even hotter commodity among "chicken hawks," usually middle-aged men who lust for boys, the younger the better. And since sexism translates on the street into self-employment, boys keep their earnings. Raised to control their own lives, most won't relinquish that power to pimps. Prepubescent boys, however, are vulnerable to being pimped, and some very young newcomers . . . do fall into the hands of "sugar daddies." Usually these chicken hawk pimps—some gay, some bisexual—will rape the child to initiate him into his new role on the home front and his night work on the stroll. Like street girls, boys are beaten by bad tricks, plus they risk incurring the rage of "fag bashers." However, most are spared pimp violence. (p. 123)

Tanner and Wortley (2002) reported from their victimization survey of Toronto youth, more than 10 years after Webber's work, that boys living on the street are far more likely to be victims of sexual assault than are both boys and girls who live at home. Gaetz found rates of sexual victimization for boys living on Toronto streets in the fall of 2001 to be almost 20 times higher than domiciled boys and 3 times greater than domiciled girls (2004, p. 435). As we have seen in other cases, under-reporting rates are high for these youth. However, the crime victimization experienced by youth living on the streets is even less likely to be reflected in police statistics than the victimization of domiciled youth. Only 12 percent of the youth in Gaetz's survey had reported crimes against them to police (2004, p. 440).

So, while youth are especially vulnerable to violence in their homes from parents and relatives, they are also vulnerable on the streets from each other and from predators who exploit their vulnerability. Many youth run from neglect and physical or sexual abuse in their homes, only to find themselves facing the same on the streets. They are ill-prepared to protect themselves or are vulnerable because of a lack of education or employment opportunities that would allow them to fend for themselves economically.

Hagan and McCarthy (1997) suggest that physical abuse at home is an important factor in youth running away, and the number of nights they spend away puts them at further risk for involvement in theft, drugs, violence, and prostitution. They and other Canadian researchers estimate that 18 to 32 percent of runaways are or have been involved in prostitution, a majority of whom are girls (Fisher, 1989; Hagan & McCarthy, 1997; Kufeldt & Nimmo, 1987; McCarthy, 1990).

Schissel and Fedec (2000) found that pregnancy is one significant consequence of prostitution for non-Aboriginal girls in Saskatoon and Regina. In addition, they are more likely to be coerced into unsafe sex by johns and so are more vulnerable to AIDS. Aboriginal youth are also twice as likely to have been physically assaulted than non-Aboriginal youth, and both are more likely to have been sexually assaulted than youth not engaged in prostitution, regardless of their race (Schissel & Fedec, 2000, pp. 49–50).

Far too many youth meet a tragic end on the streets. Hagan and McCarthy reported in a follow-up of their study of Vancouver and Toronto street youth that

> More than one worker told us of a youth who was later found dead—in an abandoned building or alley-way—the victim of a sex crime, a drug overdose or a violent attack. Other youth survived the day-to-day living of street life only to die later from other problems—most often AIDS or other diseases—some of which originated on the street and others which were exacerbated by it. (2000, p. 234)

Victimization and the State

Until recently, the extent of violence inflicted on male young offenders by their families has gone largely unexplored, as has violence and abuse in the childhood lives of adult males. One recent exception is Totten's work on male young offenders involved in violent offences, all of whom speak of the violence inflicted on them during their childhood by adult male relatives and their mothers' male partners (2000). Research on girl delinquents has also documented a high incidence of physical and sexual abuse stemming from their family lives. One U.S. study of an institutionalized female population found that 76 percent of the girls had suffered physical abuse with injury in their homes and 50 percent had experienced sexual assault (Phelps, 1982). Sandberg (1989) reported that 66 percent of the residents of a juvenile facility population had a history of child abuse, and for 38 percent of the girls, this involved sexual abuse (p. 129). Chesney-Lind (1988) argued that precisely because of this abuse, many girls have good reason to have "bad relationships" with their parents (and sometimes with their male siblings and other male relatives) and to be "unmanageable" and "out of control."

Closer to home, McCormack, Janus, and Burgess (1986) found family-related sexual abuse rates of 73 percent for girls and 38 percent for boys among youth in a Toronto shelter for runaways. Schissel (1997) also found high rates of abuse and neglect among street youth and young offenders in Saskatoon and Regina, particularly among those displaying physically aggressive behaviour and problems with anger (p. 94). Of 150 convicted women involved with a community helping agency in a Canadian city, one-third were victims of extensive physical and/or sexual abuse that dated back to their lives as children (Bell, 1994a). Artz (1997) reported from her analysis of Canadian girls with a history of violence that they are likely to have been subjected to or witnessed physical violence and sexual abuse. The NLSCY reports that children who have witnessed violence in their homes are more likely than other children to exhibit physical aggression, emotional disorders, and engage in property crime (Dauvergne & Johnson, 2001, p. 11).

Children of convicted women are particularly vulnerable to abuse and sexual assault. Often, when women come into conflict with the law, their children are placed in foster care or in the care of other relatives. In one particularly disturbing case, a teenaged girl placed in a foster home because of her mother's incarceration was subsequently murdered by her foster father; her younger sister remained in the same foster home, despite the mother's attempts to have her placed elsewhere. Another case involved a 14-year-old who bore her father's child. She was removed from her family home as a consequence, and her child was taken from her and placed in foster care. Sixteen years later, she finally was able to locate her child, only to discover that he had been physically and sexually abused while in foster care; he is currently serving time in a federal penitentiary for aggravated assault (Bell, 1994a). In a case in Nova Scotia, the grandparents of a five-year-old boy and his sister, who were given custody of the children by their mother, are facing first-degree murder charges for the starvation death of their grandson and charges for forcible confinement of his sister (Szklarski, 2006, p. A5).

The child protection system in British Columbia is now under investigation because of the recent beating death of a 19-month-old child at the hands of a relative. In this case, too, the mother had lost custody of her children and they had been placed in the care of an uncle. According to her testimony at a subsequent inquiry, the mother had reported to the children's agency responsible for the placement that her daughter was afraid of her uncle. "I knew she was afraid . . . she would never look [at him] . . . I just saw the fear in her eyes." The agency would not remove the child from the uncle's home because to do so would lead to the separation of her and her five-year-old brother. The uncle reported to the inquiry that "I should have never been allowed to care for anybody's children" and "Nobody should have been in my care." He pleaded guilty to manslaughter and admitted to "beating and kicking the child because she wouldn't stop crying" (Meissner, February 9, 10, 2006).

A significant number of children and youth in the justice system were formerly under state care. Bell (1993) reported that 85 percent of the families in one youth court had prior involvement with a social service agency, while Thompson (1988) noted that 47 percent of the first 2,539 individuals charged under the YOA in Alberta had previously been assigned child welfare status. Little is known about the welfare of children under state care or its relationship to criminal behaviour. Nonetheless, we know that institutional abuse exists because of court cases and investigations concerning abuse in residential schools and other specific youth institutions. Mount Cashel in Newfoundland, Kingsclear in New Brunswick, Shelburne in Nova Scotia, and Grandview in Ontario are but a few examples.

Judi Harris, one of the survivors of the Grandview Training School, "was in Grandview when she was 12 years old. She has memories of being locked up naked in solitary confinement; she also has memories of a guard who promised her a blanket for sex" (Edwards, 1992, cited in Reitsma-Street, 1993a, p. 1). In 1999, the Ontario government "apologized" to the women who suffered "physical and sexual abuse" as girls at Grandview but it appeared "as a few lines hidden away in the back pages of *The Globe and Mail*." As Sangster (2002) points out, this apology had already been preempted by articles that portrayed the women as "liars and criminals" and the guard who pleaded guilty to sexual assault as "probably innocent" (p. 8).

As Harris and others continue to speak out about their abuse, we are left with a picture of institutional sexual and physical abuse of children that is far more common than previously assumed. We also know from these individuals that many of their problems with the justice system are attributable to their institutional and legal experiences as well as to the failure of social agencies (Sandberg, 1989; Schissel, 1997; Totten, 2002). As the results of the investigations and inquiries unfold, it is becoming increasingly clear that Canadian politicians and institutional bureaucrats bear some responsibility for the acts of violence and abuse committed against children and youth under state care. It is also clear from the records of child advocacy agencies that institutional abuse is not a thing of the past. According to the chief advocate of the Office of Child and Family Services Advocacy program in Ontario, one-third of the agency's annual requests for advocacy come from youth facilities (Dorey, 1997). The implications of child and youth victimization for juvenile justice and law reform will be discussed further in Chapter 12.

SUMMARY

This chapter attempts to further deconstruct the public discourse on youth crime by addressing public issues that revolve around race, gender, and age. Once again, questions of the volume and seriousness of youth crime are addressed, but now in the context of social dimensions. The distorted view of youth as "perpetrators" of crime is balanced by an examination of statistics on youth as "victims" of crime.

Over the last 20 years, information on young offenders has been enhanced by the use of two new research tools. Ethnographic studies provide detailed information on the lives of youth and their families. Longitudinal studies of youth crime focus on age as an important factor in youth crime rates.

The public discourse on youth crime is highly racialized. Images of "out of control" visible minorities, "Asian" gangs, and "ruthless and violent" girl gangs fuel public fears of youth and their crimes. The crimes of Caucasian males are never presented as such in public discourse. The children of visible minorities are no more likely than Canadian-born or Caucasian youth to be "gang" members. Aboriginal youth crime is part of a larger pattern of violence directly related to their oppressed status in Canadian society. This pattern of violence includes suicide, substance abuse, and physical and sexual victimization.

Young adults (primarily males 18 to 30 years of age) are responsible for far more violent crime than youth. Notwithstanding changes in policing practices, a not insignificant portion of the increase in violent crime, as well as in all categories of youth crime, can be explained by the introduction of 16- and 17-year-old youth into the juvenile justice system. Crime rates for both adults and youth fluctuate with changes in the age composition of the overall population. Youth under 12 do not appear to be any more "criminal" than they were 25 years ago (less than 2 percent of all offences known to police). Nor are they being coerced into criminal activities by older youth or adults; only a small proportion of the under-12 cases in police files involved an accomplice over the age of 16.

Girls are far less involved in "official" crime than boys. Self-reported studies suggest that girls engage in the same behaviours as boys, but less frequently. Boys' criminal behaviour begins earlier than girls' and is more likely to extend into adulthood. There appears to be a gender gap with respect to charging practices. Proportionately more girls than boys are charged for minor crimes of violence (and at younger ages), and more girls are charged with administrative offences; however, the gap has narrowed over the last few years. As boys and girls age, violence charges increase for boys and decrease for girls.

The risk of violent victimization is greater for 12-year-olds than for anyone over 24, and 12- to 17-year-old youth are more likely to be victimized than anyone over 25. Twenty-two percent of all violent crime victims in Canada are youth aged 12–19, double this group's proportion of the Canadian population.

Men and boys are more likely than women and girls to be the perpetrators and the victims of violence. As women age, their chances of overall victimization increases relative to men. Women and girls experience higher rates of sexual assault and personal theft, while men and boys experience higher rates of robbery and assault. Girls are more likely than boys to have been assaulted, sexually or otherwise, by family members.

Almost half of those accused of crimes against teens are also teenagers. Adults are more violent with their children than with their adult partners. A majority of offences against children occur outside the home, but offences are as likely to occur at home as at school. In the home, adult males and older brothers are the most frequent perpetrators of violence against children and youth. For many young offenders, victimization at home leads to running away, which in turn puts them at risk for criminal activity and further victimization on the streets by each other and by predators who exploit their vulnerability. Recent investigations into violence and physical and sexual abuse in foster homes, correctional facilities, and other state institutions indicate that Canadian politicians and assorted institutional bureaucrats bear some responsibility for violence against children and youth under state care.

DISCUSSION/CRITICAL THINKING QUESTIONS

1. Does it make sense to respond to the offences of youth under 12 by processing them through the justice system? What are the alternatives?
2. How might we explain the gender gap in rates of criminal behaviour? Will the YCJA have an impact on this gap? If so, how?
3. Do you think that lifestyle is an adequate explanation for violent victimization? Explain your answer. How is this affected by race, gender, and class?

WEB LINKS

Why Do We Think Young Women Are Committing More Violent Offences?
www.creativeresistance.ca
Click on "British Columbia" at the top of the screen and then on "Crime" in the list that appears on the left-hand side of the screen. The name of this article appears in the list on this page.

Racism and Policing
www.amachi.biz/divers-files/en/pub/faSh/ePubFaShRacPol.pdf

Voices from the Margins: Experiences of Street-Involved Youth in Winnipeg
http://ius.uwinnipeg.ca/pdf/Street-kidsReportfinalSeptember903.pdf

Black Youth Violence Has a Bad Rap
www.oise.utoronto.ca/depts/sese/Mahiri%20&%20Coonor.pdf

For chapter quizzes and more links, visit this book's accompanying website at
www.bellyoungoffenders3e.nelson.com

CHAPTER FIVE

Explaining Crime and Delinquency: In the Beginning . . .

CHAPTER OBJECTIVES

1. To discuss scholarly and taken-for-granted understandings of events.
2. To understand theory and its relationship to research as well as the basics of empirical relationships, especially causal ones.
3. To outline the development of positivistic thinking about crime from the 19th century to the mid-20th century.
4. To understand the differences between biological, psychological, and sociological approaches to explaining youth crime and delinquency.
5. To introduce major perspectives and theories of youth crime and delinquency, along with general theoretical critiques of each.

KEY TERMS

Empirical
Postmodernists
Theory
Research
Fact
Positivist
Concepts
Classical school of criminology
Eugenics
Behaviourism
Conditioned

Cognitive
Development theory
Antisocial personality
Human ecology
Anomie
Strain theory
Delinquent subculture
Consensus theory
Control theory
Social bond

INTRODUCTION

Over the last 100 years, much has been written about the causes of crime and delinquency. Perspectives range from the biological and physiological to the psychological and sociological. Some views are academic or scientific, while others are what Anderson (1996) refers to as "taken for granted understandings." Taken-for-granted understandings are beliefs that are accepted as true simply because they are either felt to be true or are commonly shared as being true. They are based on "immediate experience" and are rarely examined (Anderson, 1996, p. 11). Taken-for-granted understandings differ from scientific beliefs that are accepted as true because these beliefs have been subjected to **empirical** testing. **Postmodernists,** those who reject or challenge all that has been considered to be modern—Western theory, art, philosophy, and knowledge developed in the 19th and 20th centuries—would take the position that even scientific knowledge, including academic theory, has no more claim to "truth" than taken-for-granted understandings. We will discuss these ideas more in the next chapter.

In this chapter, we will discuss the development of academic thinking and taken-for-granted understandings of crime and delinquency. We will trace the development of criminology theory, as it pertains to youth crime, from the 18th century to the 1960s. This will provide a framework for understanding the roots of current and popular theories, such as those in a biological tradition, and for tracing different directions in theorizing over the last 40 years that will be discussed in the next chapter. In order to appreciate science's claim to truth, we will begin with a discussion of the scientific method, its components—**theory,** explanation, and, **research**—as well as the relationships among them.

empirical
An adjective describing knowledge that is based on observation, experience, or experiment rather than on theory or philosophy.

postmodernists
Those who reject or challenge all that has been considered to be modern.

theory
Integrated sets of propositions that offer explanations for some phenomenon.

research
A systematic process of information gathering, analysis, and reporting of findings.

THEORY AND RESEARCH

Theory and Explanation

Broadly speaking, theories and explanations are the means by which we attempt to understand our world. When we observe events or hear about them and ask questions such as why or how they happened, we are searching for explanations. When we provide answers to these questions, we have essentially come to a theoretical understanding of the event. So, for example, crimes are sometimes understood or explained as "copycat" events. In one incident, a 12-year-old boy was struck and taped to a tree near a Halifax high school a short time after similar events had occurred elsewhere. The event was reported in *The Chronicle Herald* as a "copycat assault" (see Box 5.1). To the extent that this copycat explanation is an idea, it can be said to be a theory. In other words, unless we experienced the event or talked to the boys, we would not know if the copycat explanation was valid. Because the explanation makes intuitive sense to us, it seems plausible. It is an example of a common-sense or taken-for-granted understanding.

One way of understanding theory is to look at it as a set of interrelated propositions. An explanation can be derived by examining the relationships among these propositions. For example, if we look at the incident in Box 5.1, we see that there are at least five interrelated propositions from which can be drawn the conclusion that the Halifax incident was a copycat crime. The propositions might look something like this:

1. Some crimes occur because some people imitate or copy crimes that they see or read about in the news.
2. A Cape Breton boy is jumped, taped up, and strung upside down from a tree.

VOICES BOX 5.1

Copycat Assault

As we will see later in this chapter, acts or events are sometimes understood or explained as acts of imitation. The following excerpts from a newspaper article provide an example.

Copycat Assault Worries Parents

Duct tape and kids. It's a strange combination, but it's one that has police and parents fearful. Halifax Police confirmed . . . they're investigating the assault of a 12-year-old boy outside a north end school. The boy apparently was struck and possibly taped to a tree . . . [I]t was the second time in two weeks that a Nova Scotia junior high school student was attacked in that fashion . . . Last week, a 15-year-old Cape Breton boy was jumped, taped up and strung upside down from a tree . . . [The school] principal . . . is concerned that media attention to the Cape Breton bullies might have led to the assault in Halifax. [A] police . . . constable . . . said, "We have a major concern that kids were copycatting the Sydney incident."

Source: Hoare (1995).

3. The incident is reported in the news.
4. A Halifax boy is struck and taped to a tree.
5. The first incident is "like" the second incident.
6. Therefore, the Halifax incident is a copycat crime.

It is the connections or interrelationships among these propositions that provide a sense that the explanation is correct or plausible. The explanation seems to make "sense" because the idea takes the form of a logical argument and a conclusion can be deduced from the propositions.

Research and the Scientific Method

A scientific or empirical mind would be skeptical about the copycat explanation of the Halifax incident, however, and might contend that the propositions do not contain a logical argument, but are rhetorical, and that the argument in favour of a copycat theory is faulty. For example, if the copycat incident described in Box 5.1 is closely examined, it becomes apparent that there are several unconfirmed assumptions. It is assumed that the boys who carried out the act referred to in the fourth proposition learned via the news (the third proposition) about the Cape Breton incident in the second proposition, and that "taped up" and "taped to" constitute the same action (the second and fourth propositions). With so many assumptions involved, an empirical mind would question whether the first proposition is true, or simply a taken-for-granted belief because it sounds plausible.

Widespread acceptance of the scientific method makes us require empirically validated information—**facts**—as a basis for probable truth. The scientific method offers theories based on observation, rather than theories based solely on ideas. Figure 5.1 presents a diagram of the scientific method, showing the relationship between theory and research that is also the relationship between the conceptual world and the

fact
In everyday terms, a fact is usually something that is considered to be true. In a scientific sense, a fact is something that has been established through the research process.

FIGURE 5.1

The Scientific
Method

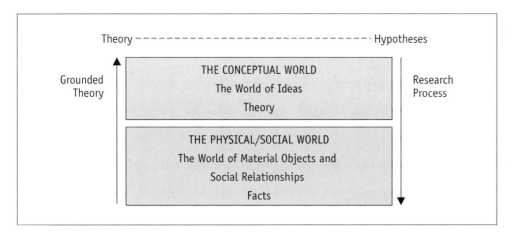

physical/social world. In the lower half of the diagram is the physical/social world or the world of material objects and social relationships. This is the world in which we make our observations by, for example, reading an article in the newspaper about copycat crime.

However, as we try to explain our observations, we have to move away from the physical/social world to the conceptual world, or the world of ideas. This is the upper half of the diagram, the realm of theory, and theory that is based on observations is "grounded theory." Once we have developed a theory and begin to examine it by asking questions about the truth value of our propositions or assumptions, we are adopting an empirical approach to the problem. For example, to say, "That is an empirical question" is to suggest that the question can be answered only by putting it to the test of systematic investigation. It cannot be answered through theoretical or logical reasoning. At this point of questioning, the research process becomes operative.

Research may begin in the conceptual world with ideas or grounded theory or questions such as: Did the boys who assaulted the Halifax boy actually know about the first incident in Cape Breton? If so, did they hear about it from the news? In order to answer these questions, we would have to move away from the realm of ideas to the physical/social world, the world of material objects and relationships. We would have to talk to the boys involved and find out if they had known about the first incident. Of course, the scientific method is not as simple as this example would suggest. It is more complicated simply because the skeptical mind would not be willing to accept that an observation of one incident would be sufficient to establish with certainty that new crimes occur because people imitate crimes reported in the news. We would need to examine many more incidents to satisfy the requirements of the scientific method.

Within the scientific method, research is the mechanism whereby we establish the truth value of our ideas, test our theories, and determine what will be accepted as factual. Strictly speaking, our facts are only as good as our research, and theories are never fact. Theory exists only as ideas and may be more or less supported by the information/ evidence that is gathered by research. We have not always looked to the scientific method to provide explanations. As Anderson (1996) notes, Copernicus, Galileo, and others laid the foundations for the scientific method in the 17th century, but it was not until the 1800s that their ideas gained widespread acceptance. Initially, science was applied exclusively to the physical world; only as late as the 19th century was its application extended to the study of the social world.

positivist
An 18th-century philosophical, theoretical, and methodological perspective positing that only that which is observable through the scientific method is knowable.

Auguste Comte (1798–1857), the founding father of sociology, was among the first to argue that society could best be understood by applying the scientific method to its study. Practitioners of this new scientific method shared with mathematicians and physical scientists the belief that science would allow them to discover laws of society and behaviour. In other words, they assumed that human behaviour is determined by natural laws, and they believed that their task, as scientists, was to discover these laws. What differentiates such **positivist** thinkers from other scientific thinkers is the assumption that behaviour is determined by some factor or factors beyond the control of the individual. Positivist criminologists, past and present, seek to discover the causes of crime by applying the scientific method.

Causal Relationships

Establishing a law or a cause is one way of explaining an event. While we may suggest or imply cause through our daily conversations, establishing cause by means of the scientific method is a complicated process. Three conditions have to be met before causality can be established. First, it has to be established that there is a relationship between **concepts** both within and among the propositions that constitute a theory. Second, a time priority has to be established between these concepts. In other words, the cause has to come before the effect. If we take as an example the proposition that seeing a criminal act on television caused that act to be repeated, we would have to establish (1) that there was a relationship between seeing a crime on television and committing a crime, and (2) that the "seeing" preceded the "committing." Most often, statistical tools such as chi square or correlation are used to establish a relationship.

concept
A general or abstract term that refers to a class or group of more specific terms (e.g., "crime" refers to any number of specific behaviours, such as assault or robbery).

While we may be able to establish on the basis of a statistical test that there is a significant relationship between watching crime shows and committing crimes, it is not likely that we would ever be able to establish time priority. Returning to the example of the copycat assaults in Nova Scotia, the boys involved may have learned of the Cape Breton incident through television, but it is also possible that they had a history of tying people to trees or had heard about others doing so (or had been tied to a tree themselves). Before we could say that seeing an incident on television or reading about it in a newspaper actually caused a similar incident to occur, we would have to establish that the people involved had never been exposed to such an incident before viewing it on television or reading about it.

A third criterion for determining causality concerns "spuriousness." In the copycat example, this would refer to whether we can be certain that there is no other "causal" factor related to both watching television and committing a crime. A possible third factor in that case might be boredom or having a lot of free time. People with a lot of free time often watch a lot of television. Moreover, when young people are bored, they are more likely to be involved in criminal or delinquent activities. Taking all of these considerations into account, it may very well be no more than coincidence that Halifax and Cape Breton boys tied someone to a tree. As for establishing the "cause" of crime, usually the best that we can do in the social sciences (and criminology in particular), in the positivist tradition, is to establish relationships between our concepts. Seldom if ever are we able to establish causal relationships.

News media reports of crime events are often rife with spurious statements about cause and effect, many of which have elements of "copycat" crimes to them. The school shootings in the late 1990s are a case in point. The 1999 movie *The Matrix* was said to have something to do with the Littleton shootings, yet we have never been able to establish that media and movie violence "causes" youth violence. The goth "culture," evidenced by black trench coats and Marilyn Manson, was posited as a "cause" of the Columbine shootings, yet neither Harris nor Klebold claimed to be goths, nor looked like goths, nor claimed to be fans of Marilyn Manson. First-person shooter games were presented as the cause of the shootings by a high-school student in West Paducah, Kentucky, that ended with three students dead and five wounded, yet millions of boys across North America play these video games and do not go on killing rampages in their schools (Wooden & Blazak, 2001, pp. 102–113). While all of the youth culture trappings of today's society—from heavy metal to gangsta rap, Quentin Tarantino movies, and video games—are posited as the causes of youth violence, postmodernists such as Donna Gaines (1993) and Tricia Rose (1994) reverse the cause–effect chain and maintain that these things are a reflection of the lived experiences of youth, rather than a cause of their behaviour.

Challenges to Positivism

A fundamental assumption of the positivist tradition is that the universe is "knowable" in an objective sense, that there is an objective truth that can be discovered through the scientific method. The logic of the method ensures that this objectivity can be attained largely through a myriad of rules and regulations required in the research process. This includes such things as quantification of methodological techniques, statistical analytic tools, and tests of significance, as well as sampling theory, to name but a few. All of these methods are designed to prevent the subjectivity of the researcher from creeping into and biasing the search for truth.

While positivism has been the dominant paradigm in North American youth criminology, it has not been without its critics. As we will see in the next chapter, some criminologists eventually began to move away from asking positivistic questions about what "causes" certain kinds of behaviours and asked questions about the nature and processes of crime. In this tradition, searching for "cause" made little sense. Rather, as we began to wonder about things such as how being processed through the justice system affects a person, it started to make more sense to simply ask people about their experiences—the subjective. It is now appreciated that situated and experiential knowledge is as much "truth" (and proponents would argue that it is closer to truth) as that gained through the search for objective knowledge. Hence, this paradigm uses different, more qualitative methods for research, things like ethnography, unstructured interviews with small groups of people, and first-hand experience.

A primary difference between the two traditions is that for the positivist, bias from the "subject" that is under observation is to be avoided, while those who espouse a more subjective approach would argue that "truth" can come only from the "subject." For example, the positivist would argue from our earlier example that you cannot ask boys who tape someone to a tree why they did it, because their answer will be biased toward their own perspective. The researcher will have to theorize and hypothesize why this occurred and then put the theory to the test. The other side of the argument would say that bias is not an issue. We are all biased by our social position and experience, so the only truth is that of the subject. Who better to know why they taped someone to a tree—and if hearing about it happening elsewhere prompted them to do it—than the boys who did it?

NINETEENTH-CENTURY THEORIZING ABOUT CRIME AND DELINQUENCY

Prior to the Enlightenment period in Western European history and the subsequent development of scientific methodologies, religion was the dominant force in society. Religious frameworks were used to understand and explain events and behaviours. When a person's behaviour was viewed as bad or evil, the devil or some type of devil possession would be blamed. Although such thinking declined in popularity with the rise of the scientific method, some people today claim that God or "voices in their head" made them commit their crimes. The scientific community is unable to confirm the existence of God and therefore whether God actually caused a person to commit a crime. Nonetheless, psychiatry has legitimized the notion of insanity and used it to explain some bizarre or criminal behaviours. Today, rather than saying "the devil made them do it," people are more likely to blame some criminal acts on things like membership in satanic cults.

Classical Criminology

classical school of criminology
The school of thought that assumes people are rational, intelligent beings who exercise free will in choosing criminal behaviour.

The earliest recorded scientific thinking about crime in Western thought dates back to the 18th century and is generally referred to as the **classical school of criminology.** A central tenet of the classical school is that people have free will—as opposed to being possessed by devils—and therefore must be held responsible for their misdeeds.

Cesare Beccaria (1819), an Italian philosopher, was one of the most influential writers of the classical school of criminology. Some of the ideas expressed in his famous essay "On Crimes and Punishments" (1764) sound remarkably similar to contemporary arguments. Among other things, Beccaria argued that offenders must be presumed innocent, that offences and punishments should be specified in a written code of criminal laws, that guilty people deserved to be punished because they had violated someone else's rights, that the punishment should fit the crime, and that offenders must be held responsible for their behaviour. In a similar vein, 18th-century English legal scholar Jeremy Bentham argued that repeat offenders should be punished more severely, that the punishment should fit the crime, and that people who commit similar offences should be punished in the same manner (Regoli & Hewitt, 1994, pp. 78–82).

BOX 5.2

Sherlock Holmes and the Scientific Method

The scientific method did not capture the public imagination, particularly with regard to the study of crime and criminals, until the late 1800s. One of the reasons that Arthur Conan Doyle's detective stories so fascinated the Victorian reader was their application of science—and the scientific method—to solving crime. If you think about the methods used by Sherlock Holmes in his investigations, you can see Figure 5.1 in operation. First of all, Holmes makes an observation. From initial observation, he develops a theory, which he puts to the test through further observation. If he is able to gather more evidence to confirm his theory, he is then convinced that he is on the right track to identifying the guilty party. The message of the Sherlock Holmes stories is that the scientific method is never wrong.

Biological Positivism

While the ideas of the classical school had a significant impact on restructuring criminal justice systems, little attention was addressed to the offender or to the "causes" of criminal behaviour. By the end of the 19th century, positivism was gaining a strong hold and scholars were beginning to pay more attention to the criminal person. The first positivistic criminologists focused on biological and physiological factors in their search for the causes of criminal behaviour. This biological positivism had a profound effect on public thinking about crime at the turn of the century.

The Born Criminal

Perhaps the most influential among biological positivists was the Italian physician and criminologist, Cesare Lombroso, who has been called "the father of scientific criminology." It is clear in his chief work, *L'uomo delinquente* (1876), that Lombroso was influenced by evolutionary ideas such as those of Darwin that were popular at that time. As a prison doctor, Lombroso had cause to examine hundreds of prisoners. On the basis of these examinations, he argued that criminals and non-criminals were at different stages of evolutionary development. The physical features of convicted criminals constituted the "evidence" for Lombroso's theory that some people were quite simply born criminals. He states that

> . . . at the site of that skull [of a notorious robber] I seem to see all of a sudden . . . the problem of the nature of the criminal—an atavistic being who reproduces in his person ferocious instincts of primitive humanity and the inferior animals. These were explained anatomically by the enormous jaws, high cheekbones . . . insensibility to pain, extremely acute sight, tattooing, excessive idleness, love of orgies, and the irresistible craving for evil for its own sake, the desire not only to extinguish life in the victim, but to mutilate the corpse, tear its flesh, and drink its blood. (Cited in Regoli & Hewitt, 1994, pp. 97–98)

Types of People

A variant of Lombroso's idea of the born criminal came from studies of entire families. One such study was conducted by Richard Dugdale, an investigator for the Prison Association of New York. Dugdale's study of 709 members of the Jukes family (1888) found that a considerable number of the Jukes had criminal records, worked at prostitution, or were on welfare. Dugdale concluded that the Jukes family suffered from "degeneracy and innate depravity," and he went on to argue that pauperism, crime, and prostitution were all inherited traits.

Similarly, in the early part of the 1900s, Henry Goddard attempted to establish a connection between heredity, crime, and "feeblemindedness." Goddard's study of the Kallikak family (1912) identified two distinct types of people. One branch of the family was the progeny of a "feebleminded barmaid," while the other branch was descended from a "respectable girl of good family." According to Goddard, the former branch was full of paupers, criminals, alcoholics, and "mentally deficient" family members. By the end of the 19th century, lack of intelligence, or "feeblemindedness," was viewed as a major causal factor in criminal behaviour. It was believed that low intelligence made people incapable of understanding the potential immorality of their behaviour and less able to control their emotions (Shoemaker, 1990, pp. 49–50).

By the late 1800s, "tainted life blood" was believed to be responsible for passing on such vices as drinking and prostitution, as well as the condition of feeblemindedness

---

VOICES BOX 5.3

Girls of This Class

At a Charities and Correction Conference in Buffalo, New York, in June 1909, Mrs. Orphelia L. Amigh, Superintendent of the State Training School for Girls, spoke at a special session on the "Education of Backward, Truant, and Delinquent Children":

> When girls of this class [somewhat deficient but not feebleminded] come before a judge for commitment to an institution, it never occurs to him that they are irresponsible and need constant care to keep them from going wrong. The judge as well as her parents call such a girl wayward and incorrigible and sometimes vicious, but never defective. These are the girls who are used in the traffic in the white slave trade, who become the mothers of illegitimate children, and sometimes if possessed of a pretty face become the wives of men who later regret the confidence with which they enter them into matrimonial bonds. They are usually fond of excitement, dress and display and with the faculty and energy they possess they are turned in this direction. The power of reasoning out things for their own benefit seems to be an unknown quantity so far as good is concerned and they are easily turned aside from the right path and into the wrong one.

Source: Defective Children . . . (1909, p. 5).

(Weinberg, Rubington, & Hammersmith, 1981, p. 17). People who engaged in these and other vices, as well as criminal behaviours, were generally classified into three broad categories: delinquent, dependant, and defective (Rubington & Weinberg, 1981). Delinquents were believed to be people who could change their ways if they received the right sort of guidance. Defectives were believed to have limited abilities, in some cases to be "feebleminded," and thus were not held responsible for what they did. Dependants were seen as people (not unlike children) whose well-being depended on the assistance of others.

Understanding crime in these terms meant there was little need to explain delinquent behaviour because the concept was an explanation in itself. A person who committed a crime was a delinquent, dependant, or defective for the simple reason that he or she was a delinquent, dependant, or defective (as illustrated in Box 5.3). The categories were not reserved for juveniles—adults could be delinquents also. Hence, at the time, it was necessary to differentiate "juvenile" delinquents from other delinquents.

"Types of people" views grew in popularity at the turn of the century and were bolstered by **eugenics** studies like those of Dugdale and Goddard. People who were considered to be defective, inferior, or feebleminded were sterilized to prevent them from having children. By the 1930s, 31 U.S. states had passed laws permitting the sterilization of people who were determined to be feebleminded, mentally ill, or epileptic (Regoli & Hewitt, 1994, p. 104). Involuntary sterilizations were carried out in Canada as late as the 1950s. There were also court cases in the 1980s that centred on the sterilization of young girls in Alberta who were considered to have low IQs.

eugenics
A branch of science based on a belief in genetic differences between groups that result in superior and inferior strains of people.

The "Dangerous Class"

Another public concern at the turn of the century was a "class of people" that consisted largely of the poor, who were struggling to survive in the face of rapid industrialization and urbanization in European and North American cities. Henry Mayhew, an investigative reporter at the turn of the century, expressed concern in his writings about the growth of "this dangerous class":

> There are thousands of neglected children loitering about the low neighbourhoods of the metropolis, and prowling about streets, begging and stealing for their daily bread . . . They have been surrounded by the most baneful and degrading influences, and have been set a bad example by their parents and others whom they came in contact with, and are shunned by the honest and industrious classes of society. (Cited in Sylvester, 1972, p. 48)

Often, then, it was not children but their parents who were seen as defectives, delinquents, or dependants. Another of Mayhew's observations was that children, from their earliest years, "are often carried to the beer shop or gin palace on the breast of worthless, drunken mothers" (cited in Sylvester, 1972, p. 51).

TWENTIETH-CENTURY THEORIES OF DELINQUENCY

Biological Positivism

Although very influential in their time, "types of people" theories may seem quaint or far-fetched to a modern reader who is more inclined to consider social or psychological factors as causes of criminal behaviour. Nonetheless, the influence of biological positivism has continued to this day. Some of the most intuitively convincing research on hereditary effects has come from the study of twins and adopted children.

Twins and Adopted Children

Twin studies, which began in the 1930s, have consistently shown that identical twins tend to have higher delinquency rates than fraternal twins. Studies of adopted children have shown that children are more like their biological parents than their adoptive parents. Most of these early studies are problematic because they involved very small samples. In one of the most recent studies, Mednick, Gabrielli, and Hutchings (1987) looked at the court records of 15,000 adopted children in Denmark and compared their criminal records to those of their biological and adoptive parents. They found that crime rates for adopted boys were higher when their biological parents had a criminal record, and that crime rates were higher for adopted boys than for adopted girls. Most important, however, they found that the rate of criminality among adopted sons was less than 25 percent, which is lower than the rate implied by earlier studies (Mednick, Gabrielli, & Hutchings, 1987, p. 86). Gottfredson and Hirschi (1990) re-examined these data, along with other adoption research, and concluded that "the magnitude of the 'genetic effect' as determined by adoption studies is near zero" (p. 60).

Studies of twins and adopted children provide very poor evidence in support of heredity as a causal factor in crime and delinquency because they merely compare rates of offending in the different groups. None of these studies isolates or identifies a specific genetic factor that is responsible for the behaviour in question (Shoemaker, 1990, pp. 28–29). Nonetheless, they remain highly influential in taken-for-granted explanations for youth crime because they provide a strong argument for the inheritability of criminal behaviour—something that seems to have an intuitive appeal for many people.

Body Type

Modern variations on Lombroso's work were under way in the United States by the mid-1900s. Most notable is Sheldon's work, *Varieties of Delinquent Youth* (1949). In the book, Sheldon argued that a young person's body type or "somatotype" affects his or her temperament and personality, which in turn can lead to delinquent behaviour. The basic body types or somatotypes are: endomorph, mesomorph, and ectomorph. Endomorphs tend to be soft and round; mesomorphs, muscular and athletic; and ectomorphs, thin and fragile. Not surprisingly, it was mesomorphic characteristics that were linked to delinquent behaviour. Sheldon found that both male and female offenders were more mesomorphic than non-offenders. Glueck and Glueck (1950) provided considerable support for Sheldon's research. They compared male delinquents with non-delinquents and "found them to have narrower faces, wider chests, larger and broader waists, and bigger forearms and upper arms than nondelinquents." In later works (1956, 1959), they reported that mesomorphs were "more prone to delinquency" (Regoli & Hewitt, 1994, p. 101).

Chromosomes

Some research has attempted to identify chromosomal abnormalities as causal agents. The average person has 46 chromosomes, two of which determine a person's sex. Males are typically XY and females are XX. Studies of sex chromosomes have found that some males (less than 1 percent) have an extra Y chromosome—the "super male." The extra Y chromosome has been used to explain violent criminal behaviour, the argument being that, proportionately, more males in prison populations have this chromosome than is found in the general population (Taylor, 1984). This evidence is not convincing for several reasons. First, the number of male prisoners with an extra Y chromosome is extremely small (1–3 percent). Second, the incidence of an extra X chromosome (Klinefelter syndrome) among male prisoners equals or exceeds that of the extra Y chromosome. Third, and most important, male prisoners with an extra Y chromosome are the least likely group within the prison population to have committed a violent offence (Akers, 1994, p. 76).

IQ, LD, and ADHD

While we no longer talk about feeblemindedness, some researchers have focused on IQ (intelligence quotient). Research in this area has consistently shown a relationship between IQ and delinquency. The lower the IQ, the higher the probability of delinquency (Gordon, 1987). The findings from this research are difficult to interpret because of the class and race bias inherent in the IQ test itself. Most problematic is the question of how much of the IQ is determined by biological factors and how much by environmental factors.

More attention has been devoted to learning disabilities and delinquent behaviour. The actual cause of learning disabilities is not known, although it is widely assumed that a learning disability has a biological origin. Learning disabilities are seen to be related to delinquent behaviour in a number of ways. Some view the existence of a learning disability as leading to poor performance in school, association with similarly performing peers, and subsequent delinquency. Others argue that learning disabilities create physical and personal problems that make children susceptible to delinquency. Still others have suggested that children with learning disabilities are unable to understand the relationship between behaviour and punishment (Shoemaker, 1990, pp. 31–33).

The most recent disorder seen to be related to delinquent behaviour is attention-deficit hyperactivity disorder (ADHD). ADHD children are said to have difficulty concentrating, which affects their ability to learn and behave in an otherwise normal manner. While approximately 10 percent of American children are reported to suffer from ADHD, research has shown that the disorder is nine times more likely to be found in delinquent children (Moffitt, McGee, & Silva, 1987).

Explaining the "Biological" Facts

In evaluating the strength of biological theories, past and present, we need to consider what facts people were trying to explain. While researchers like Lombroso were looking at a prison population, others were looking at boys who were delinquent. In most cases, researchers adopted a positivistic orientation to explanation, which meant they were trying to find the ways in which the people they were observing differed from non-criminals or non-delinquents.

In every case, however, cause–and–effect relationships are confused, and those who espoused biological explanations failed to consider the possible spuriousness of the relationships they thought they had discovered. Recall that one of the most important criteria to be satisfied in establishing a causal relationship is time priority. The argument that feeblemindedness causes criminal behaviour—and there is little doubt that an IQ develops before a criminal act—is likely based on a spurious relationship. Poverty is something that may affect both one's IQ and criminal behaviour. Living a life of extreme poverty and deprivation cannot help but "cause" a person to have a measurably lower intelligence quotient than a person who has lived an enriched lifestyle, and poverty puts one at greater risk for criminal justice processing.

The major problem with early biological explanations of criminal behaviour is that they failed to account for environmental impacts on behaviour and, in so doing, overestimated the biological impact on behaviour. Consider the following observations about Down's syndrome children:

> Children [born] with Down's Syndrome have a specific genetic inheritance . . . yet, even though the genotype remains the same for any such child, the behavioural outcomes associated with this genotype differ . . . Thirty years ago, Down's Syndrome children were expected to have life spans of no more than about 12 years. They were also expected to have . . . low IQ scores. They were typically classified into a group of people who . . . required custodial . . . care. Today, however, Down's Syndrome children often live well beyond adolescence. Additionally, they lead more self-reliant lives. Their IQs are now typically higher, often falling in the range allowing for education, training, and sometimes even employment. (Lerner, 1986, p. 84, cited in Regoli & Hewitt, 1994, p. 106)

The point Lerner was making is that the genotype responsible for creating Down's syndrome has not changed, but our responses to the condition have. As a result, the behavioural consequences of Down's syndrome are dramatically different today from those 30 years ago.

In their review of contemporary literature on genetics and criminal behaviour, Cloninger and Gottesman (1987) concluded, "there is no evidence that genetic factors are important in pre-pubertal delinquency as a class" (p. 106). The authors maintained that environment and heredity may interact to produce criminal or delinquent behaviour, but they insisted that, on the basis of the evidence, biological influences are limited or minimal. Not surprisingly, most modern biological theorists are a bit more positive about their work. They tend to take the position that "no specific criminal behaviour is inherited or physiologically preordained, nor is there any single gene that produces criminal acts." Rather, all behaviour is the result of biology interacting with the social and physical environment. Hence, modern biological theorists speak of behavioural "potentials," "susceptibilities," and "probabilities" rather than "causes" (Akers, 1994, pp. 76–77).

Psychological Positivism

Psychological theories did not develop until the 20th century. Essentially, these theories focus on the development of antisocial characteristics to explain criminal and delinquent behaviour. Unlike biological theories, some of the psychological theories stress environmental impacts on the formulation of antisocial characteristics. There are six groups of psychological theories on criminal and delinquent behaviour: psychoanalytic theories stemming from the work of Freud, behaviouristic explanations (B.F. Skinner), social learning theory (Albert Bandura), moral development theory (Jean Piaget), personality theory, and antisocial personality theory.

Psychoanalytic Theories

According to psychoanalytic theories, crime and delinquency are symptoms of an underlying emotional abnormality or disturbance that stems from childhood. The major theorists in this area are Sigmund Freud and Erik Erikson. Both assume that individual development occurs in stages and that personality abnormalities occur when individuals fail to resolve conflicts that arise in these various stages.

The Underdeveloped/Overdeveloped Superego   For Freud (1953), there are three parts to the personality: the id, ego, and superego. The id is present at birth and is the basic biological and psychological part of the individual. It is instinctual, biological desire and does not differentiate between fantasy and reality. Hence, a hungry child will suck her or his thumb. The ego is the part of the personality that is able to separate reality from fantasy. It is the rational part of the mind/self. The superego is the conscience. As the moralizing part of the self, it is responsible for generating such feelings as guilt, shame, and remorse.

In Freudian theory, there are five stages of personality (psychosexual) development. First is the "oral" stage (up to 1 year), second is the "anal" stage (ages 1–3), third is the "phallic" stage (ages 3–6), next is the "latency" stage (which lasts until puberty), and fifth is the "genital" stage. Conflicts arise between the id, ego, and superego in these stages. If unresolved, these conflicts will result in abnormal personality development. Crime and delinquency are seen as behavioural manifestations of abnormal personalities. The most crucial stage is the phallic stage (the Oedipus/Electra complex), in which the child loves the opposite-sex parent and hates the same-sex parent. Resolving conflict in this stage requires the child to identify with the same-sex parent. It is the resolution of these conflicts that leads to the development of the superego. Serious personality disorders are believed to develop from a fixation at this stage.

Crime and delinquency can be the result of either an undeveloped or overdeveloped superego. If underdeveloped, the superego is not strong enough to control or curb the id drives. People with an underdeveloped superego will do what they want, without concern for consequences or for the feelings of others. If overdeveloped, the ego will experience such intense anxiety and guilt that a person may engage in crime because she or he unconsciously wants to be punished (Akers, 1994; Friedlander, 1947; Shoemaker, 1990). Crime is sometimes attributable to a weak ego since such individuals have . . . "poorly developed social skills, poor reality testing, gullibility and excessive dependence" (Andrews & Bonta, 1994, p. 74, cited in Bohm, 1997, p. 55).

Some decades after Freud, Erik Erikson (1950, 1968) modified Freudian theory by identifying eight stages of personal and social development. In Erikson's theory, individuals face crises and conflicts at each stage of development throughout their lifetime. If conflicts are unresolved at the early stages, personality development will be affected at subsequent stages. In the first stage, infancy, the crisis to be resolved involves the struggle between trust and mistrust. If a child fails to learn to trust, this will carry through to later stages of life. The most important stage in terms of delinquency is the fifth stage, ages 12–18. Here the adolescent person is struggling to develop an identity as he or she grapples with such essential questions as: Who am I? What will I become?

According to Erikson, there are three possible outcomes when this struggle is not resolved: identity diffusion, identity foreclosure, or negative identity. "Identity diffusion" occurs when an individual has failed to develop a coherent sense of self. "Identity foreclosure" develops when individuals have a premature sense of self; such people will experience problems if they fail to meet their own expectations (e.g., "I will be a rock star"), since alternatives have not been considered. "Negative identities" are identities that are not accepted or approved by others, particularly parents. According to Erikson, negative identities usually occur only when important "others" have failed to respond positively to prior identities. In other words, for these youth, receiving attention for "bad" behaviour is better than receiving no attention at all (Regoli & Hewitt, 1994, p. 125).

A number of critiques of the psychoanalytic perspective have centred on the issue of causal connections. Psychoanalytic theories posit a causal connection between the mind—an internal entity that is not directly measurable—and some measurable delinquent behaviour. This causal connection is "virtually impossible to establish" (Regoli & Hewitt, 1994, p. 126).

Behaviourism

Behaviourism is one of the most widely used explanations of crime and delinquency. Quite simply, it suggests that people break the law because they can do so and not be punished. This idea is reminiscent of the classical school notion that punishment must fit the crime if crime is to be stopped. Behaviourists have attempted to explain how people learn to behave in particular ways. Whereas psychoanalytic and biological perspectives argue that behaviour is driven by forces within the individual, the behaviourist argues that a person's environment shapes or conditions her or his behaviour.

While this school of thought began with Pavlov's experiments with dogs at the turn of the century, B.F. Skinner (1938, 1953) is credited with developing behavioural principles of human behaviour. Simply put, any organism, human, animal, bird, or mammal, will repeat behaviour that is followed by pleasure (a reinforcement) and stop behaviour that creates pain (a punishment). Behaviour is **conditioned** by these rewards and punishments. Hence, reinforcement (a reward) increases the probability of a given behaviour and punishment decreases its probability.

Behaviourism is the cornerstone of the law-and-order approach to young offenders. Its proponents argue that the justice system, parents, and schools are "too

behaviourism
A branch of psychology based on a set of behavioural principles first developed by B.F. Skinner.

conditioned
In behaviourist theory, refers to behaviours that have been patterned to repeat or stop by a regime of rewards or punishments.

permissive," and that young people "get away with crime" (i.e., are not punished). If we toughen the justice system, then, young people will be punished and therefore conditioned to not commit crimes.

In spite of its massive influence, behavioural theory also has its share of critics. The most persistent critique is that it ignores the role of thought in learning. People do think about what they do, and mental processes cannot be ignored as a factor in all behaviour.

Social Learning Theory

Some psychologists responded to shortcomings in behaviourism by formulating explanations of learning that involve mental processes. Notable among these psychologists was Bandura (1977), who believed that the social environment was the most important aspect in learning, and that the learning process is **cognitive** rather than behavioural. This approach allows for one to learn through imitation and through watching others be rewarded or punished.

Social learning theory provided the impetus for concern about what children see on television and in movies. It also provides a theoretical basis for "copycat" explanations. There are also sociological and social psychological versions of social learning theory, which will be discussed in the next chapter.

The major criticism of social learning theory is its failure to account for differences in cognition. Why is it, for example, that only some of the children who watched *Power Rangers*, *Mutant Ninja Turtles*, or WWF events imitated what they saw in ways that were harmful or destructive?

Moral Development Theory

Part of the answer to the question regarding children and their exposure to violent movies and television programs comes from **development theory.** Jean Piaget (1932), who was one of the first to study cognitive and moral developmental processes in children, documented two stages of moral development: constraint and cooperation. Kohlberg (1964, 1969) expanded this two-stage model to six stages. In development theory, delinquents are said to be at a lower stage of moral development than non-delinquents. Hence, they are not concerned with the rights or feelings of others, focus on behavioural consequences (whether they will be caught or punished), and act to avoid punishment.

A major critique of this perspective comes from the fact that the research focused on boys to the exclusion of girls. Gilligan (1982) examined moral development in girls and found a very different orientation. For boys, moral development focuses on justice issues; for girls, it focuses on caring and responsibility issues.

Personality Theory

Like biological "types of people" theories, personality theory explains delinquent behaviour on the basis of "who" one is as a person. This perspective assumes that a particular trait or set of traits produces delinquent behaviour.

As early as the 1930s, personality traits were linked to delinquent behaviour. Healy and Bronner (1936), for example, reported that delinquents were unhappy, discontented, emotionally disturbed, jealous, and had feelings of inadequacy and guilt. Later research identified other personality traits of delinquents, including passivity, aggressiveness, emotional instability, egocentricity, immaturity, suggestibility, and lack of inhibition (Bromberg, 1953). Interestingly, many of these traits are contradictory

cognitive
Having to do with mental processes and how we develop knowledge about and understanding of ourselves and the world around us.

development theory
Focuses on states of development and posits inadequate development or failure to progress to higher states in explaining criminal and delinquent behaviour.

(e.g., passivity/aggressiveness), and they do not permit consistent differentiation between delinquents and non-delinquents.

The development and use of more objective personality testing methods in the 1950s and 1960s led to far more reliable test results. The most widely used of these tests is the Minnesota Multiphasic Personality Inventory (MMPI). Results from this test show that institutionalized delinquents score highly on the asocial, amoral, and psychopathic scales (Hathaway & Monachesi, 1953). This is not to say that the MMPI is able to predict delinquency. Nor does it mean that personality traits cause delinquent behaviour. Once again, time priority is important in that some of these traits may develop as a result of a history of criminal or delinquent behaviour and/or processing through the justice system.

Antisocial Personality Theory

People who are said to have an **antisocial personality** are sometimes referred to as "psychopaths" or "sociopaths." Hans J. Eysenck (1977) developed a theoretical scheme to explain the psychopathic personality. For Eysenck, personality is what causes certain behaviours to develop. Moreover, personality is determined physiologically and is possibly inherited. A psychopath is prone to criminal behaviour largely because of an inability to develop emotional attachments and to feel remorse or shame. The biological aspect of this theory comes from Eysenck's assumption that defects in the autonomic nervous system lead to the development of psychopathic emotional characteristics. Others have suggested that childbirth delivery complications, or birth trauma, may be responsible for the antisocial personality (Kandel & Mednick, 1991).

Clinical definitions of the terms "psychopath," "sociopath," and "antisocial personality" include the following traits: impulsiveness, an inability to relate to others or to learn from experience, insensitivity to pain (either one's own or that of others), and a lack of guilt or remorse. According to Shoemaker (1990), there is no agreement as to whether psychopathy or sociopathy applies to juveniles. While the MMPI measures psychopathology in delinquents, clinical definitions of sociopathy apply to adults. Children with these characteristics are generally referred to clinically as having an "impulse-ridden personality" or a "tension-discharge disorder" (Shoemaker, 1990, pp. 68–69).

One last "type of person" measure worthy of discussion because of its popularity in correctional settings is the Interpersonal Maturity Scale (I-Level). This scale developed from the work of Sullivan, Grant, and Grant (1957) and was applied in California as a focus for treatment plans in the 1970s (Palmer, 1974; Warren, 1970). It was also used along with the Conceptual Level Matching Model in Ontario youth correctional facilities in the 1980s (Leschied, Jaffe, & Stone, 1985; Leschied & Thomas, 1985). Similar to other developmental theories, the I-Level identifies a person's interpersonal development in stages. More specifically, it measures level of maturity in social and interpersonal skills through seven stages. Ninety percent of official delinquents are found in levels 2 to 4. Level 2 delinquents are asocial, aggressive, and power-oriented. Delinquents in level 3 are passive conformists and those in level 4 are neurotic. With this scale, delinquents may have combinations of traits, such as "passive-aggressive" or "neurotic-asocial."

According to Akers (1994, p. 89), personality theories are more testable than psychoanalytic theories, but, unfortunately, the results are inconsistent. Shoemaker's (1990) review of psychological theories and empirical research leads to the conclusion

antisocial personality
Psychological classification of people with traits of impulsivity, insensitivity to their own pain or the pain of others, and a lack of guilt or remorse.

that "the search for a unique set of personal, psychological antecedents of delinquency continues and remains unfulfilled" (p. 73).

Sociological Positivism

While biology and psychology offer some explanations for crime and delinquency, sociology is responsible for most of the theorizing and research in this area. Sociology did not develop as a discipline in its own right until the latter part of the 1800s. While 19th-century sociological theorists like Émile Durkheim (1933, 1951) addressed crime in their writings, most did not consider delinquency as something distinct from crime that needed to be explained.

In North America in the 1920s and 1930s, delinquency theory was developed by a group of sociologists at what became known as the Chicago School of Urban Sociology. With few exceptions, their work was positivistic in nature and focused on the study of social problems. Like the biological positivists, these early sociologists were trying to develop explanations by examining the differences between delinquents and non-delinquents. However, their main concern was to discover what it is about the environment that affects an individual's behaviour. In addition, sociologists were among the first to develop explanations of delinquency and not just criminal behaviour. Because of its focus on the environment, sociological theory has had a considerable influence on social policy, delinquency-prevention projects, and the manner in which young offenders are processed through the justice system. Psychology, with its focus on the individual, has had more impact on how we work with young people once they have been convicted or apprehended by the police.

Social Disorganization and Strain Theory

Social Disorganization Modern theories of delinquency began with the work of Clifford Shaw and Henry McKay at the Chicago School. Although some 19th-century thinkers had recognized that various social problems were associated with crime and poverty, Shaw and McKay (1931, 1942) were among the first to test this idea by looking at the distribution of delinquency by area—in their case, in the city of Chicago. This method of analyzing the spatial distribution of social problems and their relationship to the physical environment is known as **human ecology.**

human ecology
A branch of behavioural science that examines the relationship between people and their physical environment.

What Shaw and McKay found from their comparisons of three different periods—1900–1906, 1917–1923, and 1927–1933—was a consistent pattern of delinquency in the city. Rates of delinquency were always higher in the area surrounding the centre of the city (zone in transition) and decreased as the study moved out to the suburbs. The "zone in transition" was characterized by urban decay, poverty, high rates of adult crime, mental disorders, physical diseases, high dependency on social welfare, unemployment, and low rates of home ownership. For Shaw and McKay, who referred to this area as "socially disorganized," the social environment of delinquents—not their personality or physical characteristics—was the factor that distinguished them from non-delinquents.

As defined by Shaw and McKay, social disorganization describes a condition in which

- controls that would prevent delinquency are absent;
- parents and neighbours may actually approve of certain delinquent behaviours;
- opportunities for delinquency are numerous; and
- there is little opportunity for or encouragement toward employment (cited in Bohm, 1997, p. 74).

One of the major criticisms directed toward the social disorganization theory is that it fails to recognize that differences in social organization do not necessarily imply the negative; in other words, any form of organization other than that of the dominant group is viewed as disorganization. The Chicago School has also been criticized for failing to acknowledge the role that city planners and politicians play in the development of certain areas of cities at the expense of others (Bohm, 1997, pp. 76–77). Some have pointed to the reality of "defended neighborhoods" where stable, organized communities will encourage delinquency or gang activity, consciously or otherwise, to protect the community from external threat (Heitgerd & Bursik, 1987; Suttles, 1972).

In the early 1930s, Shaw and McKay established a delinquency prevention project known as the Chicago Area Project (CAP). The objective of CAP was to rebuild disorganized neighbourhoods through schools, churches, clubs, businesses, and educational programs designed to increase public awareness of delinquency, to provide crime-prevention activities, and to foster community involvement in dealing with neighbourhood problems. The program met with mixed results (Akers, 1994, p. 143; Lundman, 1993). A recent version of CAP is the Chicago Beethoven Project. Initiated in 1988, this program focuses on pregnant women and ways of breaking the cycle of welfare. Women receive prenatal care throughout their pregnancy, children receive health care, and mothers are taught how to care for their children (Regoli & Hewitt, 1994, pp. 147–148).

Anomie Closely related to social disorganization is **anomie,** a concept that was first formulated by Durkheim. Anomie refers to a state of normlessness in which rules and regulations are no longer sufficient to control social behaviour. Robert Merton (1938) used the concept of anomie to develop a theory of deviance that forms the core of a group of theories that have come to be known as **strain theory.** Strain theory assumes that children are basically good and engage in delinquent activity only when faced with undue pressure or stress. Thus, conformity is the normal state of affairs; what needs explaining is why people would deviate or why children would be delinquent.

According to Merton, all people in North American society are socialized to aspire to the same culturally mandated goals—a good job, marriage, home ownership, children, two cars in the driveway, a dog and a cat, etc. However, the legitimate means for achieving these goals are limited by the social structure. The educational system is an example of a legitimate institutionalized means of goal achievement. Nonetheless, because of the cost of postsecondary education, among other things, it is difficult for people with low incomes to avail themselves of this means of goal attainment. Merton argued that such contradictions or discrepancies between cultural goals and structural means—anomie—are created and reinforced by a class system of reward distribution. The anomic conditions create "strain" or pressures to find other means to success, some of which may be illegal. While this strain can affect people from all social classes, individuals from lower-class backgrounds are more likely to experience it.

While there is disagreement among contemporary scholars as to whether Merton's theory allows us to make predictions about individual crime and delinquency or whether it is instead a structural theory (Bernard, 1987), Merton did offer explanations of different types of deviance. He did so by viewing them as adaptive responses to strain. In response to strain, there are five "modes of adaptation": innovation, ritualism, retreatism, rebellion, and conformity.

anomie
A term coined by Émile Durkheim, referring to a state of "normlessness" or no rules.

strain theory
A group of theories that argue in a variety of ways that blocked opportunities are a cause of problem behaviours.

If people accept cultural goals but reject institutionalized means of goal achievement—that is, do not (or cannot) get a university education, or finish high school, or get a job in order to obtain the things that they want—then they are likely to innovate to achieve their goals. *Innovation* results in various kinds of white-collar crime, theft, and perhaps drug dealing or any other type of criminal behaviour that provides material gains. On the other hand, some people will accept institutionalized means of goal achievement but lose sight of or abandon their original goals. *Ritualism* occurs when people reject or alter cultural goals and focus instead on the means of goal achievement. People who reject both institutionalized means and cultural goals through lack of interest are engaged in *retreatism*, a mode of adaptation that may lead to drug addiction, alcoholism, or a life on the streets.

Rebellion occurs when people reject institutionalized means and cultural goals, but do so not for their own gain or for personal reasons. Rather than adopt a stance of passive rejection, these people will try to change the means and/or goals so that everyone can benefit. Merton maintained that this response was non-conformist and not in the same category as deviant behaviour for personal gain. Most people, however, will just simply conform to a state of anomie, meaning that they will try harder to achieve their goals by conventional means. Merton called this mode of adaptation *conformity*.

Merton's general theory of deviance provided a context for his discussion of the structural impediments to success experienced by those from lower-class backgrounds. Other theorists followed Shaw and McKay's lead and focused their attention exclusively on lower-class youth, particularly those living in poor areas of cities. While such a focus might seem unreasonable today, in the 1930s and 1940s, only official statistics provided "facts" on delinquency. That lower-class youth were over-represented in delinquency statistics from official sources was seen at the time as the most salient fact that needed to be explained. Theorists who focused on lower-class youth to develop explanations of delinquency included Cohen, Miller, and Cloward and Ohlin.

The Delinquent Subculture Albert Cohen's study of lower-class youth (1955) was chiefly concerned with gang delinquency. Cohen modified Merton's anomie theory, added a psychological dimension, and argued that delinquent behaviour is a "reaction formation" to the frustration of being a lower-class youth in a middle-class world. In this regard, delinquent behaviour is a group activity that offers a solution for lower-class youth. The **delinquent subculture** (gang) is a group solution to the frustration of being unable to achieve middle-class goals.

Like Merton, Cohen argued that lower-class youth aspire to the same goals as middle-class youth. However, lower-class youth and middle-class youth do not share the same social values, lifestyles, or skills. Hence, when lower-class youth find themselves in a middle-class education system, they are ill-equipped to achieve success. After experiencing repeated failures in school, lower-class youth are led to not only reject the school and the middle-class values that it espouses, but also to seek out others like themselves. This subculture affords a means of achieving success through the status it provides members who engage in delinquent activities. The delinquent subculture is hostile toward middle-class values and standards, and expresses this hostility by engaging in so-called senseless behaviour such as destroying school libraries. Not all lower-class boys, Cohen pointed out, resort to this kind of behaviour. Some will adopt a "college boy" response and continue to strive to achieve middle-class goals. Others become "corner boys" and resign themselves to life in the lower-class world.

delinquent subculture
A concept used in early criminology theory to explain youth crime.

Differential Opportunity Richard Cloward and Lloyd Ohlin also saw delinquency as a lower-class urban behaviour and developed differential opportunity theory to explain delinquent behaviour. Like Merton and Cohen, Cloward and Ohlin (1960) argued that pressures to achieve success combined with an inability to achieve success cause delinquent behaviour. However, while Merton focused on legitimate opportunities for achievement and success, Cloward and Ohlin recognized that some youth have access to "illegitimate" opportunity structures. If young people are denied access to legitimate opportunity structures or are unable to achieve success in legitimate ways, they will try to gain access to illegitimate opportunity structures. The extent to which illegitimate opportunity structures are available will depend on the neighbourhoods in which young people live.

According to Cloward and Ohlin, three types of delinquent subcultures are found in lower-class neighbourhoods: the criminal gang, the violent gang, and the retreatist gang. Some lower-class neighbourhoods are relatively stable in that they have organized adult criminal activities and young people have an opportunity to become involved in illegitimate opportunities that are provided through adult criminal activities. Stability is achieved because the community or neighbourhood provides adult role models for ways of making money, albeit criminal and/or illegitimate.

As was indicated by Shaw and McKay, however, some neighbourhoods are disorganized, and because of this there are no stable adult criminal activities. Any youthful criminality in this type of neighbourhood fosters conflict and violence between youth—hence the violent gang. Retreatist gang activities occur when youth are "double failures." As characterized by Cloward and Ohlin, retreatist gangs consist of young people who have not been able to achieve success in either legitimate or illegitimate ways. These are the youth who give up and retreat to a world of drugs and alcohol.

In the 1960s, an ambitious anti-poverty program was implemented in New York City. Following opportunity theory, the Mobilization for Youth Project was designed to improve living conditions and opportunities in high-delinquency neighbourhoods. This project was followed up in the United States by federal government policies that declared "war on poverty" and implemented community action programs, job corps programs, and Head Start programs. Despite the billions of dollars spent on those and other initiatives, the problem of poverty remains (Regoli & Hewitt, 1994, pp. 170–171).

Classical anomie and strain theories have been criticized for their focus on social class. Merton's theory primarily attempts to account for class differences in official crime rates, while Cloward and Ohlin focus on lower-class male subculture delinquency (Akers, 1994, pp. 54–55). Nonetheless, Merton maintains that strain can affect all classes. Some argue that this criticism is irrelevant because strain theories were never intended as an explanation for middle-class delinquency (Shoemaker, 1990, p. 141).

Strain theories are limited because of their focus on educational and occupational sources of strain. Agnew (1985b, 1992, 2001) developed a general strain theory that extended the strain concept to include other sources. These include (1) failure to achieve goals; (2) removal of positive stimuli, such as the death or loss of a family member; and (3) confrontation with negative stimuli (e.g., child abuse).

Culture and Learning Theory

Class Culture Walter Miller focused on cultural factors as he tried to identify characteristics of lower-class life that gave rise to delinquent behaviour. According to Miller

(1958), the problems experienced by lower-class youth begin with the family structure—primarily a female-headed household. This arrangement forces boys to join all-male peer groups, or "one-sex peer units" (p. 14). It is within these peer groups that boys learn the characteristics, or "focal concerns," of lower-class culture that generate delinquent behaviour.

The focal concerns of lower-class culture, Miller maintained, are trouble, toughness, smartness, excitement, fatalism, and autonomy, which lead lower-class boys to break the law. *Trouble* refers to the sense that getting into confrontational situations with police or people in authority is not something to be ashamed of and may even be encouraged and rewarded by the peer group. *Toughness* refers to a preoccupation with being physically strong or "macho." *Smartness* refers to an ability to outsmart or "con" other people, as opposed to being smart in an academic sense. *Excitement* refers to a desire for adventure, thrill, and risk-taking. *Fatalism* is believing that one has no control over the future, that things just "happen." *Autonomy* refers to a desire to be independent and in control, as opposed to bowing to authority. Adherence to focal concerns confers status on members of a peer group, but it is also likely to lead to delinquent behaviour. Hence, in Miller's view, delinquency was "normal" behaviour for lower-class boys rather than a reaction or adaptation to strain.

Miller's theory has two clear limitations: it cannot explain why many lower-class boys are not delinquent, nor can it explain female delinquency.

Differential Association Edwin Sutherland added a new dimension to the issue of delinquency through his theory of differential association. According to Sutherland (1939), delinquent behaviour is learned behaviour, or behaviour that is learned by interacting with others who are delinquent. What is learned are the techniques, motivations, attitudes, and definitions that permit people to break the law. Sutherland took issue with Shaw and McKay's notion of disorganized communities by pointing out that these communities are not necessarily disorganized, but rather are organized in a manner not evident in mainstream communities.

Sutherland presented his theory of differential association through a series of principles. Of the nine principles, two are of particular significance:

1. A person becomes delinquent because of an excess of definitions favourable to violation of law over definitions unfavourable to violation of law.
2. While criminal behavior is an expression of general needs and values, it is not explained by those general needs and values, since non-criminal behavior is an expression of the same needs and values. (Sutherland & Cressey, 1974, pp. 75–77)

Like Cohen and Merton, Sutherland suggests that what distinguishes people from one another is the means that they choose to acquire what they want. For Sutherland, people's behaviour patterns are created by "differential association." This proposition is the core of Sutherland's theory, and it is reflected in the first principle above. According to this principle, people become criminal because they have more contact with criminal patterns than with non-criminal patterns. In other words, people who have learned how to lie, cheat, or steal will act on this knowledge if they have not also learned how to be law-abiding citizens.

With regard to the second principle listed above, it is commonly assumed within the positivistic tradition that delinquents and non-delinquents have different value systems. Sutherland argued that delinquents and non-delinquents have the same needs and values. Delinquent behaviour cannot be explained by those needs and values because they are shared by people who do not engage in such behaviour.

Drift and Delinquency An extension of Sutherland's principle that criminal and non-criminal behaviours are expressions of the same needs and values is found in David Matza's theory of drift and delinquency. Like Sutherland, Matza (1964) argued that delinquents are not much different from non-delinquents in terms of their values; hence, they are not firmly committed to delinquent behaviour. Unlike Sutherland, Matza argued that delinquent behaviour is situational rather than learned; in other words, it is particular situations and circumstances that lead to delinquent behaviour.

Matza's ideas are also different from those of Cohen and Miller. According to Matza, groups might encourage delinquent behaviour in particular circumstances, but group membership per se is not sufficient to drive youth toward delinquent behaviour. Young people are not likely to develop a set of values totally opposed to that of adults because their status in society makes them far too dependent on adults. Rather, delinquency is something that juveniles drift in and out of as situations, circumstances, and opportunities present themselves. However, if delinquents are not any different from non-delinquents with regard to their values, why are some juveniles involved in delinquent behaviour while others are not? Borrowing from Freud's notion of defence mechanisms, Matza's answer is that delinquent behaviour occurs when young people are able to rationalize their delinquent behaviour (Bohm, 1997, p. 53).

Techniques of Neutralization Sykes and Matza (1957) suggest that there are five defence mechanisms, or "techniques of neutralization," that young people use to rationalize, justify, or excuse the negative aspects of their delinquent behaviour. *Denial of responsibility* occurs when young people refuse to accept any responsibility for their behaviour and blame others instead. *Denial of injury* occurs when a youth insists that no one was hurt in any way (e.g., "The storeowner is too rich to notice a loss of money"). *Denial of the victim* occurs when a young person argues that the victimization was deserved in some way (e.g., "He was a bully and I had to put him in his place"). *Condemnation of the condemners* refers to the argument that those in authority—for example, police, parents, and teachers—are hypocrites. *Appeal to higher loyalties* occurs when a young person argues that his or her motivations were essentially honourable (e.g., "I was protecting my friends").

In his book *Go-Boy!*, Roger Caron (1978), a Canadian who spent most of his adult years in federal prisons, uses this neutralization technique when he says that one of the robberies he committed was motivated by his father's inability to make a mortgage payment; in committing the crime, he was "helping" his father.

For Shoemaker (1990, pp. 157, 167), the most serious shortcoming of both differential association and drift theories relates to problems of measurement. In order to test the theories, it would be necessary to assess a person's motivations, intentions, and attitudes toward crime and delinquency prior to the commission of a criminal or delinquent act. Of course, such an assessment can realistically occur only after the act has been committed.

Control Theory

The majority of theories we have discussed to this point fit into a category sometimes referred to as **consensus theory**. An implicit or explicit assumption in these theories is that most people are essentially law-abiding. Given this assumption, what needs to be explained is why some people are involved in criminal or delinquent behaviour. The answer, of course, varies by theory: reaction formation, anomie, differential opportunity, and so forth.

consensus theory
Refers to a group of theories based on a fundamental assumption that people are essentially law-abiding.

control theory
Refers to a group of theories premised on an assumption that people will operate on the basis of self-interest unless constrained.

Other theories are driven by a different assumption about human nature. For some theorists, it is equally plausible to assume that unless people are constrained in some way, they will behave on the basis of self-interest; hence, the likelihood of delinquent or criminal behaviour will be fairly high. Given this assumption, what needs to be explained is why most people are not involved in criminal or delinquent behaviour. The answer is, quite simply, that they are constrained from doing so. Those who begin with this assumption produce theories that fit into a category referred to as **control theory,** because they seek to explain why some people's behaviours are controlled while others' are not. Two theorists who made major contributions to this perspective are Walter Reckless, who developed containment theory, and Travis Hirschi, who produced the theory of the social bond.

Containment Why don't all boys in high-crime neighbourhoods get into trouble? Reckless (1953) grappled with this question and concluded that "good boys" have a positive self-concept. According to Reckless, four factors influence delinquent behaviour. Pulling or pushing young people into delinquency are "outer pulls," or environmental factors such as poverty or unemployment, and "inner pushes," which are psychological or biological factors such as psychosis or hostility. Mitigating against push and pull factors are external and internal "containment" factors. External containments are outer controls (such as community ties) that protect young people from delinquent behaviour. Internal containments, the most important of which is a positive self-concept, also protect young people from pull and push factors. According to Reckless, a pro-social self-concept is the best defence against delinquent temptations.

social bond
The social ties that hold people together, cause people to care about each other.

The Social Bond The question "Why do they do it?" is simply not the question . . . The question is "Why don't we do it?" (Hirschi, 1969, p. 34). To answer this question, Hirschi (1969) began with the notion that most young people will engage in delinquent behaviour unless there is something to prevent them from doing so. Hirschi called this "something," which forms the basis of his theory, the **social bond.** The social bond consists of four elements that bind a person to a conventional lifestyle: attachment, commitment, involvement, and beliefs. Young people with *attachments* to parents, schools, and other agents of socialization are less likely than those without such attachments to become delinquent. Unlike Cohen and Miller, Hirschi argued that attachment to peers is a deterrent to delinquent behaviour; delinquents, he believed, tend to be socially isolated.

Commitment refers to successes, achievements, and ambitions and the extent to which one has invested in these things. The greater the investment, the more one has to lose by engaging in delinquency. So, for example, those who are achieving success in school or are highly motivated to achieve are less likely to be involved in delinquent behaviour. *Involvement* refers to activity and the extent to which young people are engaged in productive activities. Those who are bored and have too much time on their hands are more likely to be involved in non-productive activities, including delinquent behaviour. With regard to *beliefs*, Hirschi argued that a person who is committed to or believes in a conventional value system will be constrained from getting involved in criminal or delinquent activities. This is particularly the case when the person believes that rules and laws are morally correct and should be obeyed.

Hirschi later collaborated with Michael Gottfredson and developed a "general theory of crime" (Gottfredson & Hirschi, 1990), which refined Hirschi's original control theory by focusing on self-control. They argued that there are important elements of self-control: gratification, excitement and risk, long-term benefits, planning and skill, pain or discomfort to victims—an absence of which leads to a low level of self-control and a greater propensity toward "criminality." People with a low level of self-control tend toward impulsivity, lack of forethought, and insensitivity, accompanied by a lack of verbal skills and orientation toward physical risk-taking (pp. 89–91, 157–58). Based on this theory, crime prevention is a simple matter of improved child rearing, an idea to be pursued further in Chapter 7.

As we will see in the next chapter, social control theory is one of the most influential theories of youth crime. It is intuitively persuasive, readily lends itself to seemingly simple crime-prevention strategies, and has more empirical support than many other theories of crime and delinquency. Nonetheless, it has not escaped criticism. Bohm (1997, p. 106), for example, points out that control theory cannot account for "maturational reform"—the fact that most youth abandon criminal activities as they mature to adulthood.

SUMMARY

This chapter traces the development of academic thinking about delinquent and criminal behaviour from the 18th century to the 1960s. (For students interested in pursuing the theories discussed in this chapter, one of the most comprehensive books on delinquency theory, critiques, and research is Donald J. Shoemaker's *Theories of Delinquency: An Examination of Explanations of Delinquent Behaviour.*) In the next two chapters, we discuss how some of these theories have been revised or integrated to create more comprehensive explanations of delinquency and how they have been researched and applied to develop programs for youth.

Theories are ideas that are developed as explanations for events and behaviour. They are made up of interrelated propositions, which themselves are statements about the relationships between concepts. Research is a process whereby the empirical validity of theories or beliefs is tested. Statistical testing is a common method of establishing relationships between concepts. Causal relationships are the most difficult to establish because three criteria must be satisfied: a statistical relationship such as a correlation, time priority of the concepts in the "cause–effect" statement, and non-spuriousness. Not all are in agreement with assumptions of objectivity that are central to the positivist tradition. Subjectivity is also now valued as a source of knowledge in criminology.

The scientific approach to crime began in the 18th century and is known today as the "classical school of criminology." By the 19th century, positivism was gaining a strong hold, and scholars were trying to understand the differences between criminals and non-criminals. Early theorists focused on biological and physiological factors in their search for the causes of criminal behaviour. "Types of people" explanations of crime and delinquency included theories of the born criminal, feeblemindedness, tainted life blood, and the dangerous class.

More recently, biological positivism has focused on twins and adopted children, body type, chromosomes, intelligence quotient, learning disability, and, most recently, attention-deficit hyperactivity disorder in its attempts to explain crime and delinquency. Research suggests that environment and biology may interact to produce criminal or delinquent behaviour. As a result, modern biological theorists speak of behavioural "potentials," "susceptibilities," and "probabilities" rather than "causes."

Psychological theories fall into six groups: psychoanalytic theories, behaviouristic explanations, social learning theories, moral development theories, personality theories, and antisocial personality theories. Most of these theories posit a causal connection between the mind and behaviour. Since the workings of the mind are not directly observable, it is impossible to establish these relationships empirically.

Sociology is responsible for most of the theorizing and research on the subject of crime and delinquency. Delinquency theory began with the work of sociologists at the Chicago School of Urban Sociology in the 1920s and 1930s. Until the 1960s, sociological positivism offered three theoretical perspectives: social disorganization and strain theory, culture and learning theory, and control theory.

Social disorganization and strain theory includes the work of Shaw and McKay on social disorganization, Merton on anomie, Cohen on the delinquent subculture, and Cloward and Ohlin on differential opportunity. Social disorganization theory has been criticized for exhibiting a middle-class bias toward urban core areas of cities. Strain theories are limited because of their focus on lower-class youth and on only educational and occupational sources of strain.

Miller's culture theory identifies six focal concerns of lower-class culture that give rise to delinquent behaviour, but it cannot explain why many lower-class youth are not delinquent. Early learning theories included Sutherland's theory of differential association, Matza's drift theory, and Sykes and Matza's techniques of neutralization. These theories are impossible to measure, because to do so would require knowing what a person was thinking before he or she engaged in criminal or delinquent behaviour.

The most important and influential control theory is Hirschi's theory of the social bond. The social bond consists of four elements: attachment, commitment, involvement, and belief. Hirschi's theory has more empirical support than many other theories of crime and delinquency. Gottfredson and Hirschi (1990) developed a new version of control theory that focuses on the elements of self-control and its role in producing criminality.

DISCUSSION/CRITICAL THINKING QUESTIONS

1. Should we be concerned about bias in our search for knowledge about youth crime? Why or why not?
2. Are some of the early theories no longer relevant or useful for our thinking about youth crime? Explain your answer.
3. In what ways are the early theories reflected in common-sense or taken-for-granted understandings of youth crime?

WEB LINKS

Eugenics Resurrected: Is Crime in the Genes?
www.digitas.harvard.edu/~perspy/old/issues/1995/nov/crimegen.html

Moral Development and Developmental Theories of Crime
http://faculty.ncwc.edu/toconnor/301/301lect06a.htm

Robert K Merton's "Dream Machine"
www.crimetheory.com/Merton

Mapping Crime: Principle and Practice
www.ncjrs.org/html/nij/mapping/pdf.html

Control Theories of Crime
http://faculty.ncwc.edu/toconnor/301/301lect11.htm

For chapter quizzes and more links, visit this book's accompanying website at
www.bellyoungoffenders3e.nelson.com

CHAPTER SIX

Different Directions in Theorizing About Youth Crime and Delinquency

CHAPTER OBJECTIVES

1. To discuss labelling theory, the liberal and radical traditions of conflict theory, and the critical perspective in criminology.
2. To review types of integrative theory and discuss lifecourse developmental theory.
3. To examine the position of girls in classical and contemporary theory through the feminist critique.
4. To outline multidisciplinary theoretical developments and perspectives since the 1980s that are relevant to understanding youth crime and delinquency: cultural studies and postmodernism.
5. To discuss feminist theorizing about girls and delinquency.

KEY TERMS

Critical perspective on crime
Decarceration
Social order
Power
Criminalization
Social learning theory
Interactional theory
Oppression
Criminal event
Lifecourse developmental theory

Social capital theory
Role theory
Androgynous
Chivalry hypothesis
Liberation hypothesis
Power-control theory
Patriarchy
Care ethic
Semiotics
Deconstruction

INTRODUCTION

Prior to the 1960s, most explanations of crime and delinquency were positivistic in orientation and attempted to explain why an individual would behave in a criminal or delinquent manner. By the late 1950s and early 1960s, an entirely new perspective was taking root in criminology. This perspective, labelling theory, moved thinking away from a positivistic approach by asking questions about crime rather than about the person. Labelling theory eventually had a significant impact on social policy and our responses to criminal and deviant behaviour. This new way of thinking contributed to the emergence of a **critical perspective on crime.** In contrast to positivistic theories, which seek to discover the "cause" of deviant behaviour, the critical perspective focuses more on power relations and social control, tends to be less concerned with statistical testing of theories, and relies less on official data for analyses.

This chapter begins with a discussion of labelling theory and moves to a discussion of recent developments in the positivist tradition—namely, integration theories and lifecourse developmental theory. Some of the movement toward integration was stimulated by a feminist critique of criminology theory. We will examine this critique along with recent feminist theorizing about girls and delinquency, and the impact of cultural studies and postmodernism on youth criminology.

critical perspective on crime
Refers to the group of theories that begins with the assumption that structures of power and oppression are the source of crime (i.e., race, class, gender, and to some extent, age structures in society).

LABELLING THEORY

While it was through the work of Edwin Lemert and Howard Becker that the labelling perspective became a major force in sociology, the origin of this perspective can be traced to Frank Tannenbaum and, more specifically, his book *Crime and the Community*.

Play and Delinquency

Tannenbaum (1938) rejected the positivist supposition that delinquents are somehow different from non-delinquents and that in order to understand delinquent behaviour, it is necessary to determine what those differences are. Instead, he argued that children engage in delinquent behaviour without knowing that others view it as delinquent or bad. As Tannenbaum describes the process:

> . . . there is a gradual shift from the definition of the specific act as evil to a definition of the individual as evil, so that all his acts come to be looked upon with suspicion . . . [T]he young delinquent becomes bad because he is not believed if he is good. (pp. 17–18)

For Tannenbaum, the best adult response to delinquent behaviour is to do nothing. In his view, it is the conflict that develops between a child's play group and the community that turns play into delinquent or criminal behaviour. More specifically, adults in the community become annoyed or angered by what children are doing and respond by trying to control or stop the activity. If children begin to resent adult interference and start to act in a defiant manner, adults will define them as bad. Being so defined will isolate these children from the community and from other children. In their isolated state, they will come to accept themselves as different and be encouraged to engage in more delinquent behaviour. This process, in which "the person becomes the thing he is described as being" (Tannenbaum, 1938, p. 21), was later elaborated on by Edwin M. Lemert (1951, 1967) and Howard Becker (1963).

Secondary Deviance

Lemert (1951) argued that there are two types of deviance: primary and secondary. *Primary deviance* is the initial act. Anyone is potentially a "primary" deviant if he or she does things that would likely be considered deviant if they were known about by others. *Secondary deviance* refers to all of the behaviours that a person develops as a result of societal responses to her or his primary deviance. In other words, once discovered, a person may find it very difficult to behave or be seen as anything other than deviant precisely because his or her deviance is known to others. Hence, it becomes increasingly difficult for a secondary deviant to not be deviant in the eyes of the community. The person may begin to develop a self-concept as a deviant and act accordingly. The transition from primary to secondary deviance involves a lengthy interactive process between the person and societal reactions to both the person and her or his behaviour. According to Lemert (1951):

> . . . the sequence of interaction leading to secondary deviation is roughly as follows: (1) primary deviation; (2) social penalties; (3) further primary deviation; (4) stronger penalties and rejection; (5) further deviations, perhaps with hostilities and resentment beginning to focus upon those doing the penalizing; (6) crisis reached in the tolerance quotient, expressed in formal action in the community stigmatizing of the deviant; (7) strengthening of the deviant conduct as a reaction to the stigmatizing and penalties; (8) ultimate acceptance of deviant social status and . . . the associated role. (p. 76)

Like Tannenbaum, Lemert maintained that official responses to juvenile delinquency are more likely to increase delinquent behaviour than to prevent it from occurring again.

Societal Response

Becker (1963) began his work with the intriguing notion that acts are not deviant until they are so defined. According to Becker, deviance is not inherent in an act, but rather is created by our responses to the act. Consider the act of murder. We may define this act as "killing someone in cold blood," but there are circumstances in which killing someone in such a manner is not legally prohibited. Soldiers are trained to kill on command. Capital punishment also involves killing people in extremely cold-blooded circumstances. In both of these examples, killing someone does not constitute murder. Moreover, killing in the context of war or capital punishment is not even considered morally wrong by many people. This is the reasoning behind Becker's argument that there is nothing inherent in any act that makes it deviant, delinquent, or criminal.

Becker also considered the process whereby people become delinquent. Like Lemert, he maintained that this process begins with attaching a label to a person in response to his or her behaviour. Once attached, the label is generalized to attach to everything that the person does. In other words, deviance is a "master status," meaning that no matter what her or his other qualities, a person who has been labelled will be seen and responded to as a deviant. For example, before their crimes are discovered, serial killers are often described by their neighbours as "nice people." Subsequent to the discovery, the same neighbours will begin to view and respond to the person as a "serial killer." Edwin Schur (1973) called this aspect of the labelling process "retrospective interpretation." Once a person's deviance is discovered, we reinterpret all of his or her past actions in light of the new information.

By the early 1970s, labelling theory was influencing social policy. "Least possible interference" was the prevailing philosophy as **decarceration** policies were implemented,

decarceration
The practice of moving individuals from institutional settings into community facilities and programs.

for better or worse, across North America. People were released from psychiatric hospitals and left to fend for themselves. Halfway houses and group homes were opened to get adult and juvenile offenders out of institutions. (As we will see in Chapter 7, the principle of "least possible interference" was a major component in the Young Offenders Act.) In recent years, we have seen the emergence of an approach that runs counter to the one suggested by labelling theory. The idea behind "reintegrative shaming" is that public shaming of a person's behaviour, followed by community forgiveness and attempts at bringing the person back into the community, will decrease the likelihood of future criminality (Braithwaite, 1989).

CONFLICT THEORY

Like labelling theory, conflict theory focuses on questions concerning the creation and application of crime and deviance rules. In conflict theory, however, the emphasis is on law rather than on labels. In contrast to theories that assume **social order** is based on social consensus, conflict theories begin with the assumption that conflict is the natural state of affairs in society and order is possible only because one group has the **power** to impose its view, interests, values, or culture on another. According to conflict theory, power is an important component in society, and one that must be considered in any attempt to explain criminal or delinquent behaviour. This perspective leads to a focus on laws, law-making, the administration of law, and the impact of law on various groups of people. Some conflict theories have been influenced by Max Weber (liberal conflict theory), while others draw on the ideas of Karl Marx (radical conflict theory).

social order
Refers to assumptions about society as free of disorder.

power
The ability of a person or group to force others to do what they wish.

Liberal Conflict Theory

In keeping with a critical perspective, conflict theory has focused more on law, the application of law, and the administration of justice than on the etiology of criminal behaviour. Elements of conflict theory are apparent in some of the theories discussed in the last chapter. The theories of Shaw and McKay, Merton, and Sutherland focused on cultural and normative conflict and argued, albeit in different ways, that people behave according to what they have learned and what is considered normal in their own groups. Sometimes this behaviour is in conflict with learned behaviours that are considered normal in other groups.

Thorsten Sellin (1938) referred to the rules governing a cultural group as "conduct norms." He argued that since each culture has its own set of conduct norms, heterogeneous societies, which have more than one culture, will have more group conflict than homogeneous or single-culture societies. According to Sellin, heterogeneous communities, such as urban core areas of cities, will have higher rates of delinquency than will more homogeneous suburban communities.

The dominant cultural group in a homogeneous community will be the group with the most power and resources. When the normative behaviour of one group violates the normative behaviour of a group that has the power and resources to codify its conduct norms into law, the result is **criminalization** of the weaker group. Sometimes, groups of people such as black youth or street youth become criminalized through media coverage of crime issues and all individuals from these groups are perceived to be "criminal suspects."

criminalization
The process whereby a person comes to be officially and/or publicly known as a "criminal."

Two theories within the liberal conflict tradition more typical of a criminal perspective were developed by Austin Turk and George Vold. Turk (1969) argued that value conflicts perceived as threatening to those in authority will lead to less powerful groups being identified as criminal or delinquent. Hence, juvenile "gangs" who openly appear in conflict with police will have their behaviour defined as criminal or delinquent. In his book *Theoretical Criminology*, Vold argues that

> . . . groups come into conflict with one another as the interests and purposes they serve tend to overlap, encroach on one another and become competitive . . . [W]hichever group interests can marshal the greatest number of votes will determine whether or not there will be a new law to hamper and curb the interests of the opposing group. (Vold & Bernard, 1986, pp. 272–273)

Those groups least likely to be able to influence legislation, such as the poor, minorities, and young people, will find their behaviour viewed as threatening and thus more likely to be criminalized than the behaviour of more powerful groups.

Radical Conflict Theory

Although Marx and Engels wrote very little about crime, and even less about delinquency, their work forms the theoretical basis of radical conflict theory. According to radical conflict theory, capitalism is the root cause of crime. Capitalist society is composed of two major classes: the bourgeoisie, who control the means of production, and the proletariat, who sell their labour to the bourgeoisie. In capitalist society, conflict is inherent between the two major classes, and the criminal justice system is but one means used by the bourgeoisie to control the proletariat.

One of the first contemporary theorists to apply Marxist ideas to an explanation of delinquent behaviour was David Greenberg. Greenberg (1977) argues that young people are at greater risk of being involved in criminal activities because the age structure of capitalist society forces them into economic dependency. Particularly at risk are working-class youth who are excluded from all but the most degrading and low-paying jobs. As a result of their economic dependency, young people are particularly likely to commit property crime. As we will see in the next chapter, Greenberg linked these ideas to the school experiences of adolescents.

Herman and Julia Schwendinger (1979), who also see delinquency as a product of capitalist society, argue that delinquency is created by a drive for the profit on which capitalism depends. Profits are increased through technology or the introduction of machinery. Since young people are the least skilled or experienced workers, they are more likely than older workers to be displaced by new technology or machinery. Once out of the labour force, young people become increasingly dependent on school and family; they become *prototypic marginals*. Those young people who are not supported by their families, or who are unable to adapt to school life, are at particular risk of becoming involved in delinquent behaviour.

Radical conflict theory, with its focus on structures and relations of control served as a foundation for the development of a perspective sometimes referred to as "critical criminology." Critical perspectives grew out of a rejection of positivism's focus on individuals and the movement toward asking questions about crime and its definitions, as well as law, its creation and imposition. It tends to focus on the structures and relations of power and dominance in society and was perhaps partially inspired by the widespread political unrest and general social critique of the 1960s and 1970s.

Contrary to classical, neoclassical, and positivist theories, critical criminology does not assume either free will or determinism, but a combination of both. For the critical criminologist, people freely choose to create and reinforce institutional structures that eventually control and dominate them. The perspective also differs in assumptions about objectivity and tends to take the position that everything we do, even science, is value-laden. For the critical criminologist, the best we can do is be open and forthright about our value systems and beliefs (Bohm, 1997, pp. 109–111). As we will see throughout the rest of this chapter, a number of specific theories and other theoretical perspectives share these assumptions with critical criminology and can be considered part of "critical criminology."

INTEGRATIVE THEORY

You may have gathered from the last chapter that many theories are similar and/or complementary. Some criminologists came to the same conclusion. By the 1980s, one of the "new directions" in theorizing was to develop more general explanations of crime and delinquency through an integration of existing theories. Some scholars, such as Hirschi (1989), have questioned the feasibility of integrating theories. Others have argued that theories can be integrated by absorbing similar concepts, by integrating common concepts, or by integrating propositions in different theories (Akers, 1994, pp. 183–187).

SOCIAL LEARNING THEORY

Differential Association–Reinforcement Theory

In the late 1960s, Burgess and Akers (1966) reformulated Sutherland's theory of differential association by specifying the mechanisms whereby people learn criminal behaviour. Sutherland's eighth principle merely stated that criminal behaviour is learned. Burgess and Akers used learning principles from behaviourist psychology to explain *how* criminal behaviour is learned. They referred to their integrated theory as "differential association–reinforcement theory." This theory maintains that a person's voluntary actions, including criminal actions, are "conditioned or shaped by rewards and punishments" (Akers, 1994, p. 95). Akers revisited the 1966 theory in later works (1973, 1977, 1985) and referred to his modifications as **social learning theory.** This theory applied to delinquent and deviant behaviour as well as to criminal behaviour.

social learning theory
Attempts to explain crime and delinquency through notions of imitation and modelling.

Akers (1994, pp. 96–99) borrowed from neutralization theory and Bandura's (1977) work on imitation in developing his theory's key concepts: differential association, definitions, differential reinforcement, and imitation. *Differential association* refers to one's exposure to behaviour and norms for learning. *Definitions* refer to "attitudes or meanings that one attaches to given behavior" (Akers, 1994, p. 97). Hence, people might believe it is wrong to steal, but rationalize doing so by saying things like, "This person is so rich, he'll never miss the money." The actual commission of a crime depends on actual and anticipated rewards and punishments—*differential reinforcement. Imitation* helps to explain the initial or "novel" behaviour. Hence, according to Akers (1985):

> . . . principle behavior effects come from interaction in or under the influence of those groups with which one is in differential association and which control sources and patterns of reinforcement, provide normative definitions, and expose one to behavioral models . . . [D]eviant behavior can be expected to the extent that it has been differentially reinforced over alternative behavior (conforming or other deviant behavior) and is defined as desirable or justified when the individual is in a situation discriminative for the behavior. (pp. 57–58)

SOCIAL CONTROL AND SOCIAL LEARNING

Self-Derogation Theory

Howard Kaplan was one of the first to develop an integrated theory using a number of theories and perspectives. His self-derogation theory focuses on self-esteem and combines elements of social learning theory, control theory, strain theory, and labelling theory. Kaplan (1975) argued that we are all motivated to maximize our self-esteem and that our motivation to conform will be minimized by family, school, and peer interactions that devalue our sense of self. If these interactions are self-defacing, then the social control usually exercised in these groups will be ineffective. To the extent that a young person becomes aware of delinquent activities and feels that this behaviour will be self-enhancing, he or she will be attracted to delinquent groups. Involvement in delinquency will continue as long as the deviant group continues to meet the individual's need for positive self-evaluation.

Integrated Theory

Delbert Elliott and his associates David Huizinga and Suzanne Ageton (1985) developed a theory that integrates strain theory (anomie and social disorganization), social bonding, and social learning theory. Simply put, their theory argues that anomie, combined with social disorganization and inadequate socialization, sets the stage for weak bonds with social institutions. These weak institutional bonds lead to stronger bonds and greater associations with delinquent peer groups within which the learning of delinquent behaviour is enhanced.

Interactional Theory

interactional theory
Posits that relationships between delinquent behaviour and other variables are not unidirectional, but rather are bidirectional.

Terrence Thornberry (1987) and Thornberry et al. (1991) also integrate social bonding and social learning theory. However, they incorporate aspects of social structure in their **interactional theory** by arguing that social class, race, and community and neighbourhood characteristics affect the social bond and social learning variables. While weakened bonds are the key to delinquent behaviour, the bonds themselves are not enough to produce or prevent delinquency. Rather, delinquency has to be learned and reinforced. Thornberry et al. (1991) refer to their model as "interactional theory" and maintain that it differs from other integrated models in three ways:

> First, it does not assume, as many control-based theories do, that variation in the strength of the bond just happens. This variation is systematically related to structural variables such as social class position and residential area. Second, it does not assume that causal models are stable over the life course. Causal influences vary at different developmental stages and at different stages of criminal careers (i.e., at initiation, maintenance, and termination). Third, it does not assume that causal influences are overwhelmingly unidirectional and that delinquency is merely an outcome variable. Many effects are bidirectional, and delinquency may contribute to the weakening of social bonds as well as being a consequence of weakened social bonds. (p. 9)

As will be discussed in the next chapter, Thornberry and his associates tested their theory on self-reported delinquency and found that low levels of commitment to school and attachment to parents lead to delinquency, but also that delinquent behaviour affects commitment and attachment. So, for example, weak bonds with parents can impact on delinquent behaviour but engaging in delinquent behaviour can also impact on a young person's relationship with her or his parents. Moreover, their research indicates that delinquency has a greater effect on attachment and commitment than commitment and attachment have on delinquency (1991, pp. 29–30).

Radical Conflict, Social Control, and Social Learning

Mark Colvin and John Pauly developed a theory that integrates radical conflict theory, social control theory, and social learning theory. Like other Marxian theorists, Colvin and Pauly (1987) argue that social control in capitalist society is coercive and is designed to support the class structure. However, with regard to understanding delinquency, they point out that these coercive control patterns are reproduced both at home and at school, and that one reinforces the other. Hence, very authoritarian family structures and the use of physical punishment (*coercive control*) are characteristic of homes headed by parents who have jobs without any autonomy or authority and who are monitored and regulated by superiors or supervisors. Coercive control is not conducive to strong bonds between parents and children.

Schools reproduce coercive control through mechanisms and structures that include such things as IQ tests, aptitude testing, and tracking. These mechanisms affect lower- and working-class youth in proportion to the strength of their family bonds. Colvin and Pauly argue that children with weak family bonds are more likely to be identified as potential problem students. As a result of this identification, a self-fulfilling prophecy is set in place. Further, schools that lack the resources to reward students will rely more on coercive controls as well as punishment.

In short, Colvin and Pauly's theory postulates that parents' class position is negatively associated with coercion in the workplace and that this enhances the development of coercive family control structures. Children in this type of family control structure have weak or "alienated" family bonds and are more likely to be placed in a coercive school control structure. Coercive school control in turn leads to increased association with similar peers, thereby predisposing some youth to an involvement in community and neighbourhood opportunities for delinquent behaviour.

SOCIAL CONTROL, STRAIN, AND LIBERAL CONFLICT THEORIES

Theory of Differential Oppression

The theory of differential oppression, developed by Robert Regoli and John Hewitt (1994), integrates strain theory, social control theory, and liberal conflict theory. Instead of viewing social control as always a positive force, Regoli and Hewitt view some aspects of social control as oppressive. They define **oppression** as the unjust use or misuse of authority, which "often results from attempts by one group to impose its conception of order on another group" (p. 206). People who are subject to oppressive measures of control are made into "objects" or are viewed as "things." As a result, they come to view themselves as objects rather than subjects; they become passive and accepting rather than active subjects who exercise autonomy and control over their own lives.

According to Regoli and Hewitt (1994), "children, like women, exist in a socially ordered world created by adults and are defined as 'objects' relative to the adult

oppression
The negative outcome experienced by people due to physical force by an oppressor or structural arrangements (e.g., laws and political policies) that remove or restrict their rights.

subject" (p. 207). Just as women as objects are viewed as inferior to men, children as objects are viewed as inferior to adults. Moreover, they lack any power to change their situation. As Regoli and Hewitt (1994) state,

> . . . compared to parents and teachers, children are relatively powerless and must submit to the power and authority of these adults. When this power is exercised to prevent the child from attaining access to valued resources or to prevent the child from developing a sense of self as a subject rather than an object, it becomes oppression. (p. 208)

While all children are oppressed because of their status relative to adults, their oppression is a "matter of degree, not of kind." Some children are only "minimally oppressed"; others experience severe oppression.

Regoli and Hewitt (1994) describe the theory of differential oppression in terms of the following four principles:

1. Adults emphasize order in the home and school. Children are continually forced to abide by the rules of those in authority and these rules are determined by adults' views about how children should behave.
2. Adults' perceptions establish children as inferior, subordinate, and troublemakers. It is assumed by adults that children must be controlled and that it is being done "for the child's own good." Seldom do adults acknowledge that if children are not controlled they may not necessarily be a threat to themselves, but they are certainly a threat to adult order, or order as it is defined by adults. A child who refuses to obey orders given by an adult is defined as "a problem," "a troublemaker," or "out of control." Children are inferior to the extent it is believed that they are incapable of knowing what to do "for their own good."
3. The imposition of adults' conceptions of order on children often becomes extreme to the point of oppression. While the general oppression of children, through laws and customs, limits their opportunities for autonomy and a sense of value, the most destructive oppression is that which occurs on the individual level. Here the most destructive are those that involve force "as a result of relational coercion." Children most at risk are those who are "obedient out of a fear of losing approval, or of the adult withdrawing affection." When coercion and force become abuse or neglect, children often generalize this abuse of authority to other adults, such as the police or school authorities or shopkeepers.
4. Oppression leads to adaptive reactions by children (pp. 209–210).

Borrowing from Freire (1990, p. 153), Regoli and Hewitt (1994) argue that children who are made to feel impotent and powerless by the oppressive acts of adults will adapt in four ways:

1. *Passive acceptance.* Children who are obedient out of fear behave much like slaves, prison inmates, and battered women. They are "fearful of freedom" and often learn to hate. Their hatred is repressed, which makes them susceptible to low self-esteem, alcoholism, drug addiction, and the like.
2. *Exercise of illegitimate, coercive power.* The child attempts to demonstrate power over adults by engaging in the illicit use of drugs or alcohol, crime, or sexual misbehaviour.
3. *Manipulation of peers.* The child tries to gain power through control of her or his peers. This strategy gives the child a feeling of empowerment.

4. *Retaliation.* Children try to strike back at the people and the institutions that oppress them. School vandalism is one way; assault and murder of teachers or parents is an extreme response. Some children become depressed or commit suicide (pp. 210–211).

No matter what the child's chosen mode of adaptation, the typical response of adults is to enhance his or her oppression, thereby escalating the problem. According to Regoli and Hewitt (1994), solutions to youth crime will not come from justice system reforms. Rather, they will come from changes to the social structure and existing social arrangements that will permit adults to see children as "equally valuable, autonomous, and independent human beings" (p. 211).

OPPORTUNITY THEORY

Another new approach to understanding crime distinguishes between the characteristics of individuals as "causing" crime and the crime itself. This view looks at crime as an event connected to situational factors. Rather than asking why a person committed a crime, the question becomes why a particular **criminal event** happened. In routine activities theory, crime is more than a behaviour that violates the law: it is an event involving the convergence of a motivated offender, a suitable target or targets, and the absence of controls. This perspective represents something of a move away from positivism and a return to the classical school in that it is based on the assumption that people operate on the basis of free will and make rational choices about engaging in criminal activity.

criminal event
An event involving the convergence of a motivated offender, a suitable target or targets, and the absence of controls.

One of the most important contributions of this perspective is the notion that there is not one explanation for crime, but rather that different explanations may be required for different types of crimes. Hence, the decisions or situations that lead to a property crime may be quite different from those leading to an assault. This approach also leads to the recognition that it is as—or more—important to understand why a person stops his or her involvement in criminal activity, as it is to know why he or she began. It is a perspective that provides a rationale for those who would advocate stiffer penalties as a means of deterring criminal activity.

Routine Activity Theory

Cohen and Felson (1979) began the work in routine activity theory tradition based on their observation that there had been an increase in crime rates following World War II, contrary to expectations that times of prosperity should reduce criminal activity. They reasoned that this was likely due to changes in *routine activities* brought about by structural changes. Therefore, the more people who have cars that allow them to travel, have jobs that require them to travel, and have money to spend on activities outside the home, the more opportunities they have for criminal activity, and the more vulnerable they are as targets of criminal activity.

As mentioned above, the convergence of three components is required for a criminal event: *motivated offenders*, *suitable targets*, and the *absence of a capable guardian*. Crime could increase, the authors argue, if all three of these components remained the same but there was a change in routine everyday activities (Cohen & Felson, 1979, p. 589). So for example, youth walking home from school rather than being bussed (a change in routine) increases the chances of "motivated offenders" coming into contact with "suitable targets." Cook (1980) expanded this "opportunity theory" by arguing that motivated offenders are also selective in their choice of targets. Ideal targets are those offering "a high payoff with little effort or risk of legal consequence."

Rational Choice Theory

Clarke and Cornish (1985) and Clarke and Felson (1993) developed opportunity theory further by combining all aspects of the criminal event, the offender, her or his motivation, and situational factors. They argue that offenders rationally assess all information about the potential crime and make a rational choice based on an assessment of consequences. This involves a process that is sometimes very complex when an individual is making decisions about "criminal involvement," either initially, or to continue, or to desist. Other situations involve less complex decision making. These refer to "criminal event" decisions that are tied more specifically to particular situations and/or circumstances. Hence, deciding to deal drugs at school is likely to involve a more complicated decision-making process than shoplifting snacks in a variety store on a "dare" while out with a group of friends.

LIFECOURSE DEVELOPMENTAL THEORY

Two theoretical approaches are developing that offer explanations not only of how youth get involved in criminal activity, but that also incorporate the important fact of why most eventually desist. **Lifecourse developmental theory** posits that children undergo a succession of role and status changes as they grow older. Applied to crime, the theory takes a contextual approach. It looks at criminal behaviour in the context of the course of life, which is characterized by *transitions* (short-term changes), and pathways or *trajectories* (long-term trends or patterns).

lifecourse developmental theory
The theory that children undergo a succession of role and status changes as they grow older.

Sociological lifecourse theory views these trajectories and transitions as embedded in social institutions (Elder, 1985). Pregnancy, for example is a life transition, something that changes the course of one's life, the effect of which sets in motion a particular trajectory depending on the age and gender of a person. The consequence of pregnancy on a career is radically different for women and girls than for boys and men, and equally different for a woman with an already established career than for a teenaged schoolgirl.

Some criminologists have integrated control theory and strain theory with lifecourse theory to explain crime. Sampson and Laub (1993), for example, argue that crime is the product of the amount of informal social control associated with life transitions. Therefore, it is not marriage or employment that increases social control, but emotional and mutual ties that increase both social and self-control, thereby reducing criminality.

social capital theory
The theory that people possess varying degrees of useful and valuable social goods (e.g., supportive family and neighbours and an education or good grades in school).

Lifecourse developmental theory connects family, friends, and school to youth crime by integrating aspects of **social capital theory** (Coleman, 1990; Elder, 1985). *Social capital* refers to investments in institutional relationships such as family, work, and school. "Social capital is productive, making possible the achievements of certain ends that in its absence would not be possible" (Coleman, 1988, p. 98). Hence, Sampson and Laub argue that weak social bonds mean a lack of social capital, and that explaining crime involves identifying the characteristics of social relations that facilitate or impede the development or accumulation of social capital. To use our earlier example, teenaged pregnancy occurring in the context of substantial social capital such as a supportive family network, adequate income, and educational and employment opportunities is not likely to result in problematic behaviours. On the other hand, very different results would be expected in the absence of social capital—a pregnant girl with an abusive family, no marketable labour skills, inadequate income, and little to no education (Matsueda & Heimer, 1997).

Hagan and McCarthy define social capital as

... originating in the socially structured relations between individuals, in families, and in aggregations of individuals in neighborhoods, churches, schools, and so on. These relations facilitate social action by generating a knowledge and sense of obligations, expectations, trustworthiness, information channels, norms, and sanctions. (1997, p. 229)

Social capital and lifecourse development theories explain how some young people get involved in crime while others do not, and why some become uninvolved while others continue to be involved into adulthood. Hagan and McCarthy (1997) used these concepts to explain the behaviour of street youth in Toronto and Vancouver. The youth in their study not only had limited social capital, but they also came from economically marginalized families with limited social capital that provided poor parenting, violence, abuse, and neglect. The youth had also had poor experiences with teachers in school and received low grades.

The authors argue that such a lack of social capital was responsible for the youths in the study ending up on the street, and predicted a continued erosion of social capital. This in itself propels street youth toward the justice system and a further reinforcement, as well as further erosion, of low social capital. In other words, without a major event or transition out of this situation, a criminal trajectory is in the making for many street youth, particularly if their low social capital leads them into an organized criminal network.

THE FEMINIST PERSPECTIVE AND CRITIQUE

Early criminology theorists tended to ignore the behaviour of women and girls in their efforts to explain crime and delinquency. It was not until women began entering the field of criminology that gender issues began to be seriously addressed. In this section of the chapter, we will review early theoretical efforts at explaining female crime and delinquency, examine the feminist critique of this work, and present recent research and theorizing about girls and crime.

The Invisible Girl

Frederic Thrasher's study of gangs in the 1920s (1927) identified some six female gangs. Using **role theory** to explain the rarity of female gangs, Thrasher argued that socially acceptable female behaviour is antithetical to gang activity. Girls who are involved in gang activities are not "girls" but rather "tomboys" who have taken on a male role. Shaw and McKay, who examined more than 60,000 male delinquents, had little to say on the subject of female delinquency. Merton's theory also ignored crime and delinquency among girls in that he did not apply his typology of adaptations to women.

In an early attempt to offer an explanation for female crime, Ruth Morris rejected Merton's assumption that everyone aspires to the same goals, arguing that the fundamental goals of women are different from those of men. According to Morris (1964), women are concerned with *relational goals* such as love, marriage, family, and friends, whereas men are concerned with material goals. She argued that since women's goals are more easily attainable than men's goals, we will find lower rates of crime and delinquency among girls and women. On the other hand, Alison Morris (1987) maintained that women do have the same material goals as men. In applying Merton's typology of adaptations to women, she pointed out that since women do not occupy the same

role theory
Attempts to explain criminal behaviour by understanding the processes whereby individuals acquire and become committed to deviant roles.

status in society as men, they have fewer opportunities to achieve material success. Hence, Merton's theory would hypothesize that women and girls should actually be more delinquent than boys and men. We know from Chapter 3 that this is not the case.

Eileen Leonard (1982) offers a critique of Walter Miller's (1958) argument that delinquency is created by the focal concerns of lower-class culture. "If it is the focal concerns of lower-class culture that 'cause' crime," she asked, "then how do we account for the lower crime rates among girls and women who occupy lower-class positions?"

Albert Cohen regarded delinquency and the delinquent subculture as specifically male phenomena. According to Cohen, the delinquent subculture is an adaptive response to the problems faced by boys. While boys are interested in achievements and in being "male," girls are interested in boys. When Cohen (1955) envisioned girls as delinquent, it was specifically in relation to sexual behaviour: "Sex delinquency is one kind of meaningful response to the most characteristic, most central and most ego-involved problems of the female role: the establishment of satisfactory relationships with the opposite sex" (p. 147). On the subject of male delinquency, he has this to say: "However it may be condemned by others on moral grounds, it has at least one virtue: it incontestably confirms, in the eyes of all concerned, his essential masculinity. The delinquent is the rogue male" (pp. 139–140).

Chesney-Lind and Shelden (1992) responded as follows: "Cohen's comments are notable in their candor and probably capture the allure that male delinquency has had for at least some male theorists and the fact that sexism has rendered the female delinquent irrelevant to their work" (p. 65).

Cloward and Ohlin not only focused on male delinquency, but they also assigned blame to mothers, particularly female-headed households. According to Cloward and Ohlin (1960), in the absence of male role models, boys will have trouble developing a masculine image. This creates a source of strain for male adolescents:

> Engulfed by a feminine world and uncertain of their own identification, they tend to "protest" against femininity. This protest may take the form of robust and aggressive behavior and even of malicious, irresponsible and destructive acts. Such acts evoke maternal disapproval and thus come to stand for independence and masculinity to rebellious adolescents. (p. 49)

As Regoli and Hewitt (1994) comment, "The fact that some girls do become delinquent was apparently of no interest to Cloward and Ohlin" (p. 345).

Sutherland's differential association theory also ignores female delinquency. Sutherland simply attributes the different rates of delinquency for boys and girls to differential associations based on "different standards of propriety and supervision" for boys and girls. As for social control theory, Hirschi tested his theory by administering self-report surveys to some 4,000 boys. Early labelling theories ignored girls and women, but Rosenblum (1980) applied Lemert's theory in her study of prostitution. She showed that the lives of adult female prostitutes are "reorganized around deviance" (p. 115), or what Lemert defined as secondary deviance. Chesney-Lind and Shelden (1992) suggest that "the same processes are likely to be at work in the lives of juvenile prostitutes who resort to 'survival sex' while on the run from home" (p. 69).

Lest we think that the tendency to ignore gender is a thing of the past, an article by Gary Brayton (1996) used gender-neutral or **androgynous** terms in referring to adolescent sex offenders and their victims. Brayton consistently refers to adolescent sex offenders as "adolescents," "perpetrators," or "offenders." What is so insidious about these gender-neutral terms is their implication that boys and girls are equally likely to be offenders or victims. O'Brien and Bera's typology of adolescent sex offenders

androgynous
Describes terms that are assumed to refer to both males and females (e.g., "gangs").

(see Box 3.1 in Chapter 3 on page 82) suggests otherwise: boys are more likely offenders and girls are more likely victims.

The Less-Than-Perfect Girl

An absence of concern about female crime and delinquency in many theories does not mean that there were no explanations of female crime. While the early biological theories of crime and delinquency discussed in the preceding chapter may seem ludicrous by contemporary standards, they did not ignore women. Unfortunately, their perspectives on women and girls are at best stereotypical and at worst misogynous. Yet, these theories continued to be used as explanations of female crime and delinquency well into the 1970s.

Early positivist criminology, as we saw in the last chapter, focused on biology in its search for the causes of crime and delinquency. Most of these early theories shared the assumption that males and females are inherently different. An extension of this assumption was that female crime would be different from male crime. Among the early explanations of female criminality, Lombroso's was perhaps most influential in that we see many of his ideas reflected in today's taken-for-granted and some scholarly views of female crime.

Biology and Physiology

Lombroso and Ferrero (1895) maintain in *The Female Offender* that female criminals are lower on the evolutionary scale than non-criminal females, and that women as a whole are lower on the evolutionary scale than the general male population. According to Lombroso and Ferrero, women are weaker than men, as well as more childlike, more maternal, and less intelligent; further, women's moral sense is inferior to that of men. As described by Lombroso and Ferrero, women are "revengeful, jealous, inclined to vengeances of a refined cruelty . . . [t]heir evil tendencies . . . more varied than men's" (p. 151). Nonetheless, they warn that female criminals, precisely because they are female, are less visible than male criminals:

> Very often, too, in women, the type is disguised by youth with its absence of wrinkles and the plumpness which conceals the size of the jaw and cheek bones, thus softening the masculine and savage features. Then when the hair is black and plentiful . . . and the eyes are bright, a not unpleasing appearance is presented. In short, let a female delinquent be young and we can overlook her degenerate type, and even regard her as beautiful; the sexual instinct misleading us here as it does in making attribute to women more of sensitiveness and passion than they really possess. And in the same way, when she is being tried on a criminal charge, we are inclined to excuse, as noble impulses of passion, an act which arises from the most cynical calculations. (Lombroso & Ferrero, 1895, p. 97)

The themes of male versus female biology and women's sexuality continued to dominate theories of female crime and delinquency after the turn of the century. Freud (1924) argued that female crime and delinquency stemmed from penis envy. During the Oedipal stage of development, children must learn to repress their sexual love for their opposite-sex parent. For girls, the result is an Electra complex. Girls who are unable to deal adequately with this complex will exhibit not only penis envy but also a desire for revenge that will cause them to act out in various ways. In Freud's view, promiscuous sexual behaviour and prostitution were the consequences of girls' failure to cope with the Electra complex.

In 1923, W.I. Thomas published *The Unadjusted Girl*. The book, based on his study of case records from the Cook County Juvenile Court and the Girls' Protective Bureau in Chicago, was one of the first attempts to analyze female delinquent behaviour. Like Lombroso before him, Thomas focused on girls' sexuality, but his explanation was far more sociological in that he emphasized gender roles as a source of female delinquency. According to Thomas, much of human behaviour is driven by wish fulfillment, which in turn is driven by biological instincts. One important biological difference between men and women, Thomas argued, is that women have a greater need for love. Their need to both give and receive love is a source of delinquency (particularly sexual delinquency) for girls because they use their sex to fulfill other more basic needs. As Thomas put it, "[sex] is their capital" (1923, p. 109).

Whereas Freud maintained that sexuality was a source of female problems, Thomas argued that girls' problems stemmed from inadequate families, demoralization, and frustration stemming from social rules and moral codes. "Sexual passion," he wrote, "does not play an important role, for the girls usually become 'wild' before the development of sexual desire, and their casual sexual relations do not usually awaken sex feelings" (1923, p. 109).

The early biological explanations of female crime are most reflected in the work of Otto Pollak (1950). Pollak attributed women's criminal behaviour to their physiology, and he used this same physiology to explain why women have lower rates of crime than men. According to Pollak, women are as criminal as men but use their physiology to hide their criminality.

Women are deceitful, Pollak maintains, and they are deceitful for three reasons: they have less physical strength, they lack a penis, and they menstruate. These physical differences from men require women to take a passive role in sexual relations and enable them to conceal their sexual arousal, while social norms force them to conceal not only menstruation, but also sexual activity. All of these factors encourage women to be deceitful, and a consequence with regard to crime is that women are "instigators" while men are "perpetrators." These same factors, referred to as *precocious biological maturity*, were used by Pollak to explain female sexual delinquency:

> The male has to be active while the female has to be passive. In the active attempt to find satisfaction for the sex urge, physiological precocity does not seem to help the boy very much, but for the girl who has to wait until she is "propositioned," the appearance of sexual maturity furnishes the opportunity for sex delinquencies that do not come the way of her normally developed age mates. (1950, p. 125)

chivalry hypothesis
A belief that crime rates are lower for women and girls because people are less likely to view their behaviour as criminal.

Anticipating what is now known as the **chivalry hypothesis,** Pollak attributes low rates of female delinquency and crime to women's lesser likelihood than men to be caught and processed; he maintains that this is because men and boys who are victimized by women and girls are reluctant to report, and because men in the criminal justice system (e.g., police officers, prosecutors, judges, and juries) are reluctant to prosecute women and girls.

Not all early criminologists accepted biological explanations of crime. Bonger (1916) argued that the low rate of female crime was a result of women's position in society:

> Her smaller criminality is like the health of a hothouse plant; it is due not to innate qualities, but to the hothouse which protects it from harmful influences. If the life of women were like that of men their criminality would hardly differ at all as to quantity, though perhaps somewhat as to quality. (p. 478)

CONTEMPORARY THEORY AND THE SEXUAL GIRL

The theoretical emphasis on female biology and sexuality as an explanation of crime and delinquency continued well into the 1960s and 1970s. As Chesney-Lind and Shelden (1992) point out, "most authors of the early works [1960s and 1970s] on female delinquency assumed that most female delinquency is either 'sexual' or 'relational' rather than 'criminal' in nature, and [were] convinced that social intervention administered by sensitive and informed individuals could help young women with their problems" (p. 61).

Gisela Konopka (1966) posited that sexual behaviour causes girls to get into trouble. Like Freud, she maintained that problems begin in the family with conflicts between mothers and daughters. The emotional instability, loneliness, and low self-esteem that girls experience as a result of these conflicts impel them into abusive and sexually exploitive relationships with boys. Those relationships, in turn, enhance family problems, reinforce low self-esteem and loneliness, and increase sexual delinquency.

The sexuality theme was reiterated by a group of British researchers, John Cowie, Valerie Cowie, and Eliot Slater (1968), who argued that dysfunctional families are the source of female delinquency, which they also saw as primarily sexual. However, their view of female delinquency was far less sympathetic than that offered by Konopka. Reminiscent of Lombroso, Cowie et al. contend that delinquent girls have more psychiatric and health problems than delinquent boys. Moreover, they are "oversized, lumpish, uncouth, and graceless, with a raised incidence of minor physical defects" (Cowie, Cowie, & Slater, 1968, pp. 166–167). In their book *The Delinquent Girl*, the American researchers Clyde Vedder and Dora Somerville state, "when a girl is unable to gain a sufficient degree of acceptance from her home and peers, she seeks to deny this rejection by engaging in sexual acts which she fantasizes to be an expression of another's love" (Vedder & Somerville, 1975, p. 109).

Perhaps characteristic of the attitudes toward women and girls in the 1960s and 1970s, both Cowie et al. and Vedder and Somerville acknowledge the existence of sexual abuse and incest in the lives of the girls they studied, but fail to pursue its connection to girls' behaviour. Cowie et al. (1968, p. 112) merely note that "a disconcerting number of [the girls] say they ran away from home because of sexual advances made by near relatives," while Vedder and Somerville (1975, p. 154) suggest that girls run away because "they fear the incestual consequences of [their] own impulses."

Girls and Their Hormones

The most recent purely biological explanations maintain that hormones have something to do with delinquency. Male delinquency rates are understood to be higher than female delinquency rates because testosterone levels in boys are six times higher and androgen levels twice as high. This argument is further supported by studies reporting that violent female offenders have higher levels of testosterone than non-violent women (see, for example, Dabbs et al., 1988). Premenstrual syndrome (PMS) has also been posited as a cause of aggressive behaviour (particularly criminal behaviour) among women (Ellis & Austin, 1971). However, Karen Pugliesi (1992) and Jessica McFarlane and Tannis Williams (1990) argue that PMS is a socially constructed label and yet another example of the medicalization of problems women experience as a result of their oppressed status in the family and society.

The Liberated Girl

By the 1970s, the women's movement was having an impact on public thinking about the "naturalness" or biological foundations of gender roles. People were beginning to accept the notion that "being a boy" or "being a girl" was a product of the socialization process. Not surprisingly, as attitudes changed so too did the thinking of some theorists on the subject of female crime.

Two works in particular had a major impact on our thinking about women and crime. Rita Simon's *Women in Crime* and Freda Adler's *Sisters in Crime*, both published in 1975, presented what has come to be known as the **liberation hypothesis.** According to this hypothesis, women are becoming more like men in their criminality as a consequence of the women's liberation movement. While Adler and Simon agreed that the spread of liberated attitudes was affecting criminal behaviour among women, they had different views of how these new attitudes were affecting women. Simon argued that liberated attitudes led to greater numbers of women working outside the home, which in turn increased opportunities for women to commit offences that were traditionally male activities, such as fraud, forgery, and embezzlement. Her argument was supported by figures showing that the most dramatic increase in women's crime was in the area of property crime. Adler, on the other hand, argued that liberated attitudes encouraged women to imitate male competitive behaviours, resulting in their growing involvement in masculine types of criminal activity such as gang activities, robberies, and muggings.

Neither argument has been supported by research or statistics on female crime and delinquency since the 1970s. As we saw in Chapter 3, girls are still less involved in delinquency than boys, and their crimes are less serious. Research in the United States on self-reported and official statistics has shown that rates of female delinquency increased throughout the 1960s and into the 1970s, but actually decreased after 1975. Moreover, according to studies comparing delinquent and non-delinquent girls' attitudes, delinquent girls are more traditional in their thinking about "women's place" (Chesney-Lind & Shelden, 1992, pp. 11, 79).

On the basis of this evidence, Chesney-Lind and Shelden (1992, p. 11) suggest that the increases observed by Simon and Adler are likely better explained by the introduction of the baby boomers into the age of delinquency. They and others argue that if liberated attitudes gave rise to behaviour changes among women during the 1960s and 1970s, then the behaviour of people in the criminal justice system was also affected. More specifically, the traditional attitude of paternalism and chivalry (described by Pollak, 1950) gave way to a law-and-order approach and a more gender-neutral treatment of male and female offenders.

liberation hypothesis
A belief that women's and girls' criminal behaviour is becoming more like that of men and boys because of the women's liberation movement.

SORTING OUT WHAT NEEDS TO BE EXPLAINED

By the 1980s, the feminist critique of positivistic theories of crime and delinquency was in full swing. As we have seen, these theories were shown to be negative, sexist, stereotypical, and sometimes misogynist in their view of girls and women. In addition, two important issues surfaced from feminist discourse: (1) the "generalizability problem," which concerns whether or not theories based on the crimes and delinquencies of men and boys apply to women and girls; and (2) the "gender ratio problem," which concerns the ability of existing theories to explain gender differences in crime and delinquency (Daly & Chesney-Lind, 1988, p. 514). Feminist criminologists thus sought to determine if specific theories of female crime needed to be developed or if existing theory could be altered, modified, or integrated in some way that would explain both male and female crime.

According to Eileen Leonard (1982), certain parts of some theories, such as anomie, social control, differential association, conflict, Marxist, labelling, and social learning, may be useful in explaining both female criminality and male/female differences. Alison Morris (1987) suggests that while biological, psychiatric, and women's liberation theories are clearly wrong, "differential opportunity structure, associations, socialization, and social bonding can aid our understanding of crimes committed both by men and women and can take account of differences in the nature and extent of their crimes" (p. 76). For their part, Chesney-Lind and Shelden (1992) maintain that

> . . . if a theory of female delinquency is to emerge, it must draw on the best of a flawed heritage. Theories of boys' delinquency cannot be completely rejected, but their uncritical grounding in male behaviour must be recognized and corrected. Theories of female delinquency must get past common sense constructions of femininity to a broader appreciation of the role of girls' situations and lives in their troubles with the juvenile justice system. (p. 79)

Daly's list of important areas for inquiry for feminist criminology (1998) now includes not only the gender ratio issue but also three new items: gendered pathways into crime, gendered crime, and gendered lives (pp. 94–99). To this end, Christine Alder and Anne Worrall (Worrall, 2004) add that in order to get past common-sense or taken-for-granted understandings of girls' behaviour, understanding femininity is important. This approach leads us to ask two new questions: (1) "Under what material and ideological conditions are girls required to 'do femininities'?" and (2) "What resources are available to girls to perform non-passive femininities and in what ways do they utilize these in their daily routines?" (Worrall, 2004, p. 10). Answers to these questions will be discussed in more detail in the next chapter, but some answers to these questions are offered in the discussion below.

The general answers offered by Alder and Worrall (Worrall, 2004) to their own questions are that socially approved resources are available to girls through the school and family, academic achievement and "domestic docility"—possibly things such as shopping and babysitting. The only socially approved alternative resources available to girls outside of those related to school and family are found in "discourses of victimization." Acting-out behaviours, even those involving violence, are more likely to be afforded greater leniency than those involving risk-taking or resistance, when a girl is most likely to be perceived as behaving "like a boy." Girls' material and ideological conditions are defined by class position, marginalization, and their intersections with race. Ideologies are those attached to race, class, and gender (pp. 11–12), such as patriarchy, capitalism, misogyny, and religion, to name but a few.

Delinquency and Patriarchy

In 1985, John Hagan, A.R. Gillis, and John Simpson (1985; Hagan, Simpson, & Gillis, 1987, 1988) introduced their "**power-control theory** of common delinquent behaviour," which combines conflict and control theories to develop a theory that can explain both male and female delinquency as well as differences in frequency of delinquency for boys and girls.

Power-control theory contrasts gender roles and control mechanisms in patriarchal families with those in egalitarian families. In the patriarchal family, fathers work outside

power-control theory
Attempts to explain class and gender differences in delinquency by the structure of family relations, whether egalitarian or patriarchal.

the home and mothers are restricted to the home and are responsible for socializing and controlling children. In egalitarian families, by contrast, roles inside and outside the home (including child rearing) are shared equally by mothers and fathers, and boys and girls receive the same amount of supervision. According to Hagan et al. (1987), "positions of power in the workplace are translated into power relations in the household and the latter, in turn, influence the gender-determined control of adolescents, their preferences for risk taking, and the patterning of gender and delinquency" (p. 812).

A key difference between patriarchal families and egalitarian families is that, in the former, boys are encouraged to be risk-takers and girls—because they are controlled more rigorously—are raised to be risk-aversive. Hagen et al. (1987) tested their theory through a self-report study of 436 parents of high-school students in the Toronto area. They found that the delinquency rates of girls from patriarchal families were considerably lower than those of boys from patriarchal families. In egalitarian families, delinquency rates for girls and boys were closer.

Tests on larger samples in the United States have failed to support the power-control theory of delinquency (see, for example, Jensen & Thompson, 1990). Morash and Chesney-Lind (1991) found that boys were more delinquent than girls in both types of families, and that the most important predictor of delinquency was the quality of a child's relationship with the mother. The authors also found that

> . . . in some types of families, boys were controlled more than girls. Specifically, if the mother was alone and unemployed, she controlled more of the decisions about boys than about girls, and was more punitive towards boys. A family with an unemployed mother alone also differs from other types in that the children identify less with their mother. (Morash & Chesney-Lind, 1991, p. 371)

Some argue that power-control theory is feminist because it considers power relations and **patriarchy** in developing an explanation for differences in male and female crime and delinquency (Akers, 1994, p. 174). Chesney-Lind and Shelden (1992) suggest otherwise:

patriarchy
A set of structural relations that creates, reinforces, and perpetuates male dominance and control over women.

> Although it is intriguing, this [theory] is essentially a not-too-subtle variation on the "liberation" hypothesis. Now, mothers' liberation or employment causes daughters' crime . . . Hagan and his associations are, however, to be commended insofar as they focussed on the importance of gender and patriarchy in the shaping of both male and female behaviour. (pp. 96–97)

Chesney-Lind and Shelden (1992, p. 97) also point out that, despite increases over the past decade in both the number of female-headed households and women's participation in the labour force, female delinquency, whether measured by self-report data or official statistics, has either remained the same or declined. Some (see Hagan, 1989) have preferred to categorize power-control theory as "structural criminology" because of its focus on power relations and a recognition that power is not linear but relational, in the sense that it exists through people's relations to each other and social institutions. As such, power is related to crime in a variety of ways. In this sense, Hagan, Gillis and Simpson's power-control theory of delinquency is an application of structural criminology to the explanation of delinquency and the gender-gap problem.

Girls and Oppression

Messerschmidt (1986) offers a socialist-feminist explanation of the nature and low incidence of female crime and delinquency. According to Messerschmidt, in a capitalist society, the owners and managers of capital control workers; in a patriarchal society, men control women's labour and their sexuality. Hence, in a patriarchal capitalist society, women experience *double marginality* in that they are controlled not only by capital but also by men.

Regoli and Hewitt (1994) applied their differential oppression theory to explain the gender differential in crime and delinquency as well as the nature of girls' crimes. If children are oppressed in society and viewed by adults as inferior, subordinate, and troublemakers, girls in patriarchal society are *doubly oppressed*. Making use of social learning concepts, Regoli and Hewitt argue that girls are socialized to be dependent and caring, to value themselves through others, and to refrain from risk-taking—all of which means they are less likely to engage in troublesome behaviours. Furthermore:

> . . . adult conceptions in patriarchal societies of the *Girl as Female* (passive, relational, and nurturing) leads to oppression, reinforcing her traditional gender role and, subsequently, to the girl's identity as "object." Treated as an "object," a girl may adapt by developing an identity through relationships with boys: she does not have to "prove" her own worth as long as she is "related" to a proven person. Consequently, her delinquencies may be indirect and relational. Being defined as a female "object" may also reinforce the identity of the girl as a "sexual object." In this case, adaptations may take the form of sexual delinquencies and prostitution. (Regoli & Hewitt, 1994, pp. 348–349)

While recognizing the double oppression of girls, Regoli and Hewitt fail to develop the implications of masculine control of the sexuality and labour power of girls. Two feminist theories of female delinquency elaborate on these relations and identify more specifically what it is about being a girl that leads to delinquency.

FEMINIST THEORIZING ABOUT GIRLS

Ethic of Care

According to Morash and Chesney-Lind (1989), research suggests that women are "predisposed" toward nurturing relationships with their children. The strength of mother–child relationships is the key to delinquent behaviour. In other words, strong bonds created through nurturing will reduce delinquency for both boys and girls. Morash and Chesney-Lind refer to this nurturing as an *ethic of care* and argue that children raised in an ethic of care will develop identities that involve a concern for others (p. 75). Moreover, this **care ethic** need not be restricted to women and girls; any child, male or female, raised by a nurturing parent, mother, or father, will more likely exhibit pro-social behaviour.

Female delinquency, according to Chesney-Lind and Shelden (1992, 1998), is a consequence of the fact that girls are more likely than boys to be victims of family-related sexual abuse. Hence, girls do the caring and are not cared for or about. Further, because women and girls are viewed as sexual objects in patriarchal society, girls are more vulnerable to physical and sexual abuse by male relatives. Girls who attempt to escape this abuse are vulnerable to apprehension by the justice system. If they fail to conform there, or if they "run away," they are then vulnerable to victimization on the streets, where their survival usually depends on petty crime and often prostitution.

care ethic
An ethical or moral standard based on nurturing attitudes of caring for the welfare and well-being of others.

Resistance to Care Lessons

The development of the care ethic in girls is well documented in Reitsma-Street's study of 26 pairs of sisters (1991b). In each pair, one sister was convicted for delinquency, the other was not. Reitsma-Street's work documents how girls learn to care, the costs of this caring, and how girls are policed to care. One of the most significant findings from Reitsma-Street's research centers on what she calls the sisters' *core commonalities*. She states that "of most relevance to women and caring were the core commonalities, which revolved around how the sisters learned to care for themselves and for others, the cost they bore for caring and how they were policed to conform to expectations about caring" (p. 111). Further, "besides being less connected to their fathers and more ambivalent about their mothers, I could not see strong patterns in the sisters' relationships—or anything, for that matter, that could be argued to contribute either to delinquency or conformity" (p. 118).

In learning the lessons of caring, girls are not permitted to develop a range of caring ways, but rather are pressured to care in three particular ways. Girls must

1. learn to be the major and primary providers of love and nurture;
2. learn to restrict caring for themselves to "looking nice and being nice," and, above all, learn to "not make a fuss"; and
3. learn "to make a boyfriend their primary object of caring" (Reitsma-Street, 1991b, p. 119).

Whether girls learn these lessons or not, there are costs to bear: they restrict their interests, they neglect their bodies, and they risk poverty and dependence. Girls who do learn the lessons of caring learn to forfeit their physical, psychological, social, and material health to caring for others. There is an inherent paradox in the economic dependence that caring brings: "While focusing care on a boyfriend is a source of economic vulnerability, continuing such care is critical because a relationship with a male who earns a satisfactory income is the major hope girls have for minimizing the impact of that vulnerability" (Reitsma-Street, 1991b, p. 123). Further, in learning to not care about her own needs, girls pay a "bodily cost":

> Suddenly her body is no longer at her own disposal but has become a zone where others have competing interests—parents and boyfriends and social workers and ad agencies—a territory liable to a whole series of catastrophes: diseases, pregnancy, rape, abortion. (Kostash, 1987, p. 175, cited in Reitsma-Street, 1991b, p. 121)

Citing Donzelot (1979, p. 8), Reitsma-Street argues that lessons of caring involve far more than mere socialization. Rather, girls are policed to learn their lessons through various *techniques of regulation* (1991b, p. 123). There are levels to this policing, each one more intrusive than the last. The first level involves judgments of a girl's reputation, "slut" being the most deadly and effective. The second level involves physical force, or the threat of it, from the men and boys in the girl's life. The third level involves the justice system. The more a girl resists these lessons—the more she struggles against caring for others more than herself—the greater the personal cost. Thus, Reitsma-Street found that delinquent girls were more likely to report having fought against prioritizing "looking nice" or "being nice." They would avoid wearing dresses, they would swear or be loud, and they would often resort to physical fighting as a way to meet their needs. They were also more likely to be sexually active, to want to travel, and to pursue exciting and fun activities.

None of these resistances are "seen in the context of a society that limits the ways that girls can care for themselves and their loved ones and restricts avenues of protest against these limitations" (Reitsma-Street, 1991b, p. 125). Rather, acts of resistance are interpreted by parents, teachers, and others in authority as signs of disturbance. The girls who undertake them are seen as needing help, protection, or correction—anything that will enable them "to act more like a normal girl" (p. 126). Thus, judges tend to be far more lenient with girls who have committed common sorts of delinquencies like theft and burglary (especially if they have done so as accomplices of boyfriends) than with girls who show independence, especially when this independence involves running away from home, a treatment/correctional centre, or foster/group home.

A FINAL NOTE ON FEMINIST CRIMINOLOGY

As we have seen with other theoretical perspectives in criminology, there are many "types" of feminist criminologies and some involve specific theories while others offer something more like a feminist perspective on specific problems related to crime, law, and justice and how these things are mitigated by gender. The body of work in feminist criminology has been differentiated as liberal, radical, Marxist, socialist, and postmodern, and only some of these have addressed issues of crime, law, and justice as they pertain to girls or youth.

Liberal feminism works, such as power-control theory, are not as focused on patriarchy as are other perspectives, and tend to be more concerned with issues of equality and choice. The work of Simon (1975) and Adler (1975), discussed earlier, is characteristic of this approach as is the work of Regoli and Hewitt (1994). Marxist feminist work focuses on patriarchal oppression within structures of capitalism; the Schwendingers' work (1983) provides an example of this.

Socialist feminism combines the Marxist focus on patriarchy and adds gender as an equal source of oppression; Messerschmidt (1986, 1993) takes this type of approach, as does Chesney-Lind (1988, 2004). Radical feminism focuses almost entirely on patriarchy as the source of oppression and in this sense, Reitsma-Street's work (1989–1990, 1991b) could stand as an example. Postmodern feminists address questions of oppression by examining how hierarchies of age, race, class, gender, and sexual orientation are constructed, and usually focus on a micro level of everyday interactions, as do Alder and Worrall (Worrall, 2004).

"NEW" DIRECTIONS IN CRIMINOLOGY

As a reaction to the shortcomings of existing criminological perspectives and theories, some new perspectives have emerged over the last 10 years. While not "theory" in the formal sense of the word, these perspectives are providing frameworks that are making significant contributions to our knowledge of youth and how we respond to them.

Peacemaking Criminology

The peacemaking approach to criminology developed from the work of Hal Pepinski and Richard Quinney (1991) and their concern with the increasing harshness and negative impacts of the criminal justice system, as evidenced by the "war on crime" and related law-and-order rhetoric. This perspective is not interested in understanding or explaining crime. It begins with the view of crime as suffering, and its objective is to address the ways in which this suffering can be reduced. From this perspective come arguments about restorative and transformative justice that involve a focus on not only restoring and transforming individuals but also a focus on laws and justice systems and their policies and practices.

The first step for peacemaking criminologists is to find ways to end the war on crime. Critics of this perspective react to its "idealism" (Bohm, 1997, p. 132). Peacemaking's contribution in youth criminology is in its applications to the youth justice system and how we respond to youth crime, which will become more apparent in later chapters.

Cultural Studies Perspective

To some extent, the cultural studies perspective developed as a reaction to the rigid boundaries that tend to be drawn between different "types" of theories and the limitations this imposes on knowledge production. In this regard, the cultural studies perspective takes a multidisciplinary approach to studying cultures and how these intersect with behaviour. It is particularly useful in youth criminology because it contextualizes youth behaviour in their cultures, allowing analyses of the clashes among these cultures and with the wider adult cultures and society. Because it is multidisciplinary, this perspective allows considerable latitude regarding the questions to be asked, the methods to be taken in its approach, and the issues it will address.

While not necessarily a "new" perspective, work in the area of cultural studies is gaining prominence in criminology because of rising public concerns about youth crime and the justice system. At a social level, we not only responded to these concerns with law reform but with a renewed interest in youth on the part of criminologists. As a result, a body of knowledge sufficient enough to warrant its own place in the field of criminology has developed—youth criminology.

Brown (2005, pp. 39–51) traces the roots of the critical cultural studies focus on youth back to Matza's *Delinquency and Drift* (1964). Ten years later, from the British "Birmingham School" came the defining Marxist-oriented works of Clarke, Hall, Jefferson and Roberts in Stuart Hall and Tony Jefferson's *Resistance through Ritual* (1976), followed by *Policing the Crisis* (Hall et al., 1978). Hall and Jefferson's most important contribution, as Brown (2005) sees it, is their refocusing of the concept of "youth culture" to the more structural concept of "subcultures" and their relationship to "parent cultures." From there it is a simple yet important step to an analysis of dominant culture and struggles between dominant and subordinate cultures. From this school of thought, Angela McRobbie (1976) introduced the world of girls to criminology through her analysis of the friendship groups and popular culture of working-class girls in Britain. These frameworks paved the way for other works to follow.

The work of Hall et al. (1978) introduces us to the concept of youth crisis. Through an analysis of a violent mugging by a black youth in a poor black urban community, and the public panic that followed, they develop the concept and dynamics of "crisis." Through this application to youth crime and corresponding beliefs that such crises need to be controlled through repressive policing, laws, and policies, we are led to an understanding of the "complex linkages between colonial history, state, youth, urbanization, 'Englishness,' class, capital, and the processes and contradictions of the striving of the state for legitimacy and consensus under conditions of economic recession" (Brown, 2005, p. 43).

Meanwhile, Stanley Cohen's work, *Folk Devils and Moral Panics: The Creation of the Mods and Rockers* (1972), in the same place and time frame gave us the concept of "moral panic," as well as an appreciation of the role of the media in defining events and reinforcing and reproducing repression. An important characteristic of media representations of youth crime is that they are produced through a complex set of social relationships among the public, youth, police, and courts. Cohen's work leads to an appreciation of the ways in which youth are demonized in public discourse and become symbols of all that is wrong in adult society. These concepts play an important role in the chapters that follow, as we attempt to understand youth crime in Canada and Canadians' responses to it. To a great extent, the crisis and moral panic concepts have served as a framework for organizing this text.

Subcultural/cultural studies in North America today developed from the classic North American works of Frederic Thrasher, Walter Miller, and Albert Cohen, as well as from the work of the Birmingham School. While media studies often involve textual analyses of pop culture, the tool of choice in cultural studies is ethnography. A recent example of "textual" analysis is Angela McRobbie's use of the film *Bridget Jones Diary* (2004) and the audience's reactions to it to get a better understanding of contemporary messages about the consequences of "being feminist," or at least of being a young woman or "girl" in contemporary society. While Bridget is capable, competent, highly skilled, able to "have men" without being married, free of the constraints of dependency, free to engage in a career of her choosing—in other words, a young woman with choice—she nonetheless pays a price. There are risks associated with her "choices" and she is continually reminded of these risks (to be "partnerless" is to be lonely, isolated, "marginalized from the world of happy couples") and she is continually "overwhelmed by the burden of self-management." The larger point made by McRobbie regards the situated power of the messages. She states, ". . . relations of power are indeed made and remade within texts of enjoyment and rituals of relaxation and abandonment" (McRobbie, 2004, p. 12).

Over the last 20 years, a wealth of knowledge has been developed on youth cultures/subcultures that, while not specifically "about" crime, its focus on youth resistance contributes immensely to our understanding of youth crime and justice. The most significant aspect of this type of work is that it allows us to locate youth "crime" in the context of youths' daily lives and lived experiences, as opposed to trying to develop understandings of deviant behaviour in juxtaposition with adult culture and criminal activity, as is the case in media and public discourse.

Postmodernism Perspective

The postmodernism perspective is also a multidisciplinary one that rejects disciplinary boundaries. It gained prominence (particularly among feminists) as a reaction to the critique that much of our theorizing in North America is devoid of race, class, sexual orientation, and age analysis. Postmodernism originated in France and Germany, where it was developed as a critique of philosophy and modernity. It began to gain a foothold in North America during the 1980s and 1990s in English departments where there was an interest in literary criticism (Curran & Renzetti, 2001, pp. 202–203). The predominance given to language and constructions of meaning in the work of these postmodernists caught the interest of criminologists who were asking questions about the social construction of crime and the processes of criminalization.

Among the most distinguishing characteristics of postmodernism is its rejection of the fundamental assumption underlying the positivistic version of the scientific model—that is, that truth is knowable. For postmodernists, truth is contingent and socially constructed, and a primary objective of postmodernist analysis in criminology is to deconstruct the meanings and social processes associated with crime and justice systems. There is also a focus on power and how it is exercised through language and other cultural forms in the construction and establishment of particular claims of "truth." Important questions concern whose claims to truth are privileged and whose are not. In this manner, a postmodernist perspective sees the "truth" claims of positivism in criminology as having occupied a position of privilege over those whose knowledge is based more on experience—those who have been studied by criminologists using positivistic methods.

In short, the work of postmodernists has challenged the taken-for-granted knowledge of criminology. Much of their work involves analyses of discourse that use **"semiotics"** and **deconstruction** to identify the discursive processes that construct hierarchies of difference. These structural hierarchies of truth, usually presented as dichotomies of difference, are based most often on race, class, gender, sexual orientation, and age. For example, young black men, particularly if they are poor, are portrayed and talked about as "criminal," while young white suburban youth are not.

semiotics
The study of signs and symbols.

deconstruction
A method of interpreting texts, movies, TV programs, and other cultural symbols and practices.

SUMMARY

This chapter documents different directions in thinking about crime and delinquency from those addressed in the last chapter. Some of these directions involve theories based on different assumptions and questions about crime, others involve integrating some of the "old" and now classic theories, and others involve new and recent approaches to crime and justice issues. Some of the theories discussed have taken a critical perspective, while others have moved positivistic theories in new directions.

Among these new developments are the integrative theories. Social learning and social control theories have received more empirical support than has strain theory. As a result of the feminist critique of traditional positivistic approaches to explaining crime and delinquency, attempts have been made to develop theories that explain the crimes of girls as well as boys, and that contribute to an understanding of girls' delinquency from a feminist perspective. The cultural studies perspective has allowed us to locate youth crime in the context of youth cultures and the wider social structure, while postmodernism has offered a challenge to taken-for-granted criminology and offered new understandings of the social construction of crime.

Labelling theory moved sociological theorizing away from a positivistic approach to crime by asking questions about crime rather than about the person. Once we have accepted one of the central tenets of labelling theory—that no act is inherently deviant—we then have to ask questions about why some acts are defined as deviant, who defines them as such, how we respond to those who are labelled, and the impact of labels and definitions.

Critical theory in criminology focuses more on the effect of power relations in the production of crime and delinquency than on attempting to explain the "root causes" of an individual's behaviour. Conflict theory belongs in this tradition. Liberal conflict theory (Sellin, 1938; Turk, 1969; Vold & Bernard, 1986) focuses on value or cultural conflict, while radical conflict theory (Greenberg, 1977; Schwendinger and Schwendinger, 1979) focuses on the various ways in which capitalist forces of production contribute to delinquency.

Integrative theory combines or integrates concepts and propositions from a number of theories to create more general explanations of delinquency. Akers' social learning theory (1985) combines differential association theory and differential reinforcement theory to explain criminal and delinquent behaviour. Other theories that focus on social control and social learning theory include Kaplan's self-derogation theory (1975); Elliott, Huizinga, and Ageton's integrative theory (1985); and Thornberry's interactional theory (1987). Colvin and Pauly (1987) combine radical conflict theory with social control and social learning, while Regoli and Hewitt (1994) combine strain, social control, and liberal conflict theories in their theory of differential oppression.

Another approach to understanding crime that moves away from a strictly positivist tradition is opportunity theory. This approach looks at crime as an event connected to situational factors. Rather than asking why a person committed a crime, the question becomes why a particular criminal event happened. Routine activity theory (Cohen & Felson, 1979) and rational choice theory (Clark & Cornish, 1985) begin with the assumption that people operate on the basis of free will and make rational choices about engaging in criminal activity. This approach leads to the recognition that it is as or more important to understand why a person stops his or her involvement in criminal activity as it is to know why she or he began.

Lifecourse developmental theory as it is applied to crime looks at criminal behaviour in the context of the course of life, which is characterized by transitions (short-term changes), and pathways or trajectories (long-term trends or patterns). Sociological lifecourse theory views these trajectories and transitions as embedded in social institutions. Crime, therefore, can be seen as the product of the amount of informal social control associated with life transitions. "Social capital" refers to investments in institutional relationships such as family, work, and school. Social capital and lifecourse developmental theory is able to explain how some young people get involved in crime while others do not, and why some become uninvolved while others continue to be involved into adulthood.

Most criminology theory that emerged from the positivist tradition between the 1930s and 1960s is androgynous in that it purports to be a general theory of crime and delinquency, but explains only the behaviour of boys and men. Classical theory that did address female criminality tended to sexualize or pathologize women and girls, a tendency that carries through to some contemporary theory and research.

Feminist criminologists agree that theories must be able to account for differences in male and female crime rates (the gender ratio problem) and question whether theories based on the experience of men and boys can be applied to girls and women (the generalizability problem). Some feminist critics believe that old theories can be revised to account for both male and female criminality. Others argue that theories devoted exclusively to female crime need to be developed. Theories of women's and girls' criminality also need to account for gendered pathways into crime, gendered crime, and gendered lives (Daly, 1998). Alder and Worrall (Worrall, 2004) focus on the material and ideological conditions under which girls are required to "do femininities" and the ways in which the resources available to girls to perform non-passive femininities lead to impositions of criminality.

Some new theories of crime and delinquency have attempted to account for the behaviour of boys and girls. Theories that have emerged from the conflict perspective include those of Messerschmidt (1986), who focuses on patriarchy and capitalism and the double marginality of women, and Regoli and Hewitt (1994), who address the oppression of children by adults and the double oppression of girls. Hagan, Simpson, and Gillis (1985, 1987, 1988) combine conflict theory with control theory in their power-control theory of delinquency.

Feminist theorizing about girls' crimes focuses on patriarchy and the process by which masculine control of women, their labour, and their bodies translates into female criminality. Reitsma-Street (1991b) argues that girls are both taught and policed to care. Girls who resist the lessons of caring are subject to sanctions that vary in intensity from name-calling to physical force or the threat of apprehension by social agencies and/or the juvenile justice system. Feminist criminology has been differentiated as liberal, radical, Marxist, socialist, and postmodern, and only some of these have addressed issues of crime, law, and justice as they pertain to girls or youth.

New directions in criminology of relevance to youth criminology come from peacemaking criminology, cultural studies, and postmodernism. Peacemaking criminology views crime as suffering, and its objective is to address ways to reduce this suffering. Primary in this undertaking is the need to end the "war on crime." From this perspective come arguments about restorative and transformative justice that involve a focus on not only restoring and transforming individuals, but also on laws and justice systems and their policies and practices.

Cultural studies are particularly useful in youth criminology because they contextualize youth behaviour in their cultures and allow analyses of the clashes among these cultures and with the wider adult cultures and society. Early theories from this perspective are central to our understanding of youth behaviour and to our responses. For example, Hall and Jefferson (1976) refocused the concept "youth culture" to the more structural concept of "subcultures" and their relationship to "parent cultures." From there it is a simple yet important step to an analysis of dominant culture and struggles between dominant and subordinate cultures. Hall and his colleagues (1978) introduced the concept of youth crisis and its connection to repressive policing, laws, and policies. Stanley Cohen (1973) gave us the concept "moral panic" and an appreciation of the role of the media in defining events and reinforcing and reproducing repression.

Postmodernism is a perspective that challenges taken-for-granted knowledge in criminology and has led to an understanding of discursive processes and their role in casting groups into hierarchical categories of race, class, gender, sexual orientation, and age. Postmodernism rejects the fundamental assumption underlying the positivistic version of the scientific model—that is, that truth is knowable. For postmodernists, truth is contingent and socially constructed. A primary objective of postmodernist analysis in criminology is to deconstruct the meanings and social processes associated with crime and justice systems.

DISCUSSION/CRITICAL THINKING QUESTIONS

1. Does it make sense to have separate theories of crime for girls? Explain your answer.
2. In what ways do theories create boundaries? How are these boundaries crossed?
3. Is it as important to know why a person stops their involvement in criminal activity as it is knowing why they start? Explain your answer.

WEB LINKS

Postmodernism & Liberalism
http://foucault.info/Foucault-L/archive/msg05233.shtml

Feminist Criminology, Female Crime, and Integrated Theory
http://faculty.ncwc.edu/toconnor/301/301lect14.htm

Growing Up Behind Bars: Confinement, Youth Development and Crime
www.doc.state.ok.us/DOCS/OCJRC/Ocjrc96/Ocjrc29.htm

Bad Girls
http://cms.psychologytoday.com/articles/pto-19991101-000037.html

For chapter quizzes and more links, visit this book's accompanying website at
www.bellyoungoffenders3e.nelson.com

CHAPTER SEVEN

Family, School, Peers and the Youth Crime Problem

CHAPTER OBJECTIVES

1. To examine what we know about the effects of family structure and family relationships on youth crime and delinquency.
2. To discuss individual, organizational, and structural factors that link school performance to youth crime and delinquency.
3. To consider how friends and peers impact on young people's involvement in criminal and delinquent activity.
4. To identify and discuss issues associated with the discourse and our understandings of family, school, and peer influences in the production of "youth crime."

KEY TERMS

Microscopic perspective
Family structure
Broken homes hypothesis
Meta-analysis
Criminalize
Etiological
Tracking

Social class
Politics of youth crime
Relational aggression
Zero-tolerance policies
Differentially exposed
Differentially affected
Androcentric

INTRODUCTION

As we saw in the last two chapters and in the historical discussion in Chapter 1 and 2, some factors have consistently emerged in both common understandings and scholarly theorizing about crime and delinquency. The family has been identified as a "causal" factor throughout Canadian history, and youth gangs and peer influences have been linked to crime and delinquency for at least 100 years. In addition, while schools were thought of at the turn of the 19th century as a "solution" to delinquency issues, this seemed to change in the 1980s, and schools are now often presented as a source of many youth crime issues. These factors are also important in that they are primary tools used today to determine if youth are at risk of delinquent and criminal behaviour. Nonetheless, in spite of a consistent academic and professional focus on these factors, there is little agreement as to what is problematic about the family, school, and peers.

Control theory explanations such as Hirschi's make intuitive sense—children not attached to parents will be more delinquent than children who are attached. Yet, whether this explanation is confirmed empirically depends on how one defines "attachment": Is it supervision or affection? In addition, many theories are contradictory. Control theory, for example, argues that strong attachments even to delinquent friends will decrease delinquency, while differential association theory implies that strong attachments to delinquent peers will increase delinquent behaviour. Attempts have been made by criminologists to develop models that sort through some of these contradictions and theoretical gaps, and that specify some of the links between social factors associated with delinquency. Other scholars have focused more on the ways in which our thinking on these issues have been problematic. This chapter reviews important empirical findings and issues related to theories discussed in the last two chapters and ends with a critical discussion of public issues and policies associated with family, school, peers and the youth crime problem.

FAMILY

Reminiscent of concerns in the Victorian era, people at a recent town hall meeting with police officers identified "problem youth" as the community's greatest concern and "blamed parents for the problem." Residents complained that "communities plagued by fearless, disrespectful young people and derelict parents are breeding criminals and poisoning themselves" (Dorey, 2005).

Most research examining the relationship between family factors and youth crime has looked at either the structure of the family or family relationships. These studies have taken a **microscopic perspective** and have examined **family structure** in terms of whether the family is "broken" (divorced or separated) or whether both parents are working. Much of the early research and conceptual understandings adopted a traditional Western model of the family as the "norm"—a "nuclear" family that consists of two heterosexual parents living with their own (birth) juvenile children.

In reality, families have many different structures, and the model of a traditional nuclear family just does not represent the structures of many families today. More recent research has identified as many as nine family "types" (Kierkus & Baer, 2002, p. 429), including single parents, both heterosexual and gay or lesbian, with adopted (or birth) children; elderly parents with married children; and blended families with married parents (heterosexual or gay or lesbian) living with their own juvenile children as well as children from previous marriages, to name just a few. Family structure

microscopic perspective
In sociology and criminology, refers to theoretical approaches that focus on individuals and behaviour in small social settings rather than in the context of larger social structures.

family structure
How families are structured in terms of living arrangements (e.g., a traditional nuclear family or a single-parent family).

studies have assumed a traditional model and begin their research with the premise that anything other than this is a problem. Family relationship studies are not as tied to these assumptions and look at such things as parenting skills, parental supervision of children, parenting styles, and young people's attachments to parents.

Family Structure

broken homes hypothesis
The commonly held proposition that children from divorced and single-parent families are more likely to be delinquent.

There are strong "intuitive" explanations as to why one-parent families may be more likely than two-parent families to produce delinquent children—the **"broken homes hypothesis"** (Kierkus & Baer, 2002, p. 426). One comes from the reality that children in one-parent families, particularly female-headed families, are considerably poorer than those in two-parent families. While this in itself is not necessarily problematic, the additional fact that single parents do not have the support of another adult in the home to assist in child rearing means a potential for less support and supervision for the child, particularly if the lone parent also has to work long hours to provide for the family.

A related assumption, derived from the traditional nuclear family model, is that children need paternal discipline and that boys especially need male (preferably father) role models for healthy development. Research on family structure in the 1970s and 1980s—in particular, 68 studies carried out between 1972 and 1990 (Free, 1991)—seemed to confirm these intuitive positions. Mavis Hetherington (1977), for example, compared broken (defined as "no longer nuclear") families with intact families (defined as "nuclear") and identified three major effects of divorce on women that *may* influence their children's behaviour: (1) single mothers are overburdened from working in the labour force and caring for children; (2) single mothers experience considerable financial stress in that female-headed households earn less than half the income earned in male-headed households; and (3) single mothers experience social isolation, which means they have fewer social and emotional supports.

This of course does not mean that children from divorced homes *are* more problematic than other children, only that these are factors that can contribute to problems. It has been found, for example, that boys from families with a stepfather are more likely to report delinquent behaviour than boys from homes with two birth parents (Johnson, 1986, p. 75). A related common belief is that mothers from two-parent families who work outside the home also contribute to delinquency in that they are overburdened and cannot provide the child rearing supports and supervision that their children need. There is very little evidence that working mothers produce more delinquency, however; less time spent with children does not necessarily mean less quality time. According to Melville (1988), "when working mothers derive satisfaction from their employment and do not feel guilty about its effects, they are likely to perform the mother's role at least as well as non-working women" (p. 352).

meta-analysis
A type of analysis in which the unit of analysis is the research results from other research reports.

In the early 1990s, Edward Wells and Joseph Rankin (1991) conducted a **meta-analysis** of the research on the impact of broken homes on delinquency and found: (1) that the relationship between broken homes and delinquency is weak at best; (2) that this relationship has been empirically demonstrated consistently for more than 50 years; (3) that the relationship is stronger for minor crimes than for serious ones; and (4) to the extent that there are negative effects on children, these effects are greater for boys than girls. A major problem with much of the family structure research through the 1970s and 1980s is that it did not incorporate, for comparative purposes, a comparison group of families that were not divorced. Hence, we had no way of knowing if children from non-divorced families would also experience problems with delinquency.

On the other hand, some of the few studies that did use comparison groups are equally flawed in that they relied on official data. In so doing, they are just as likely to have measured the effect of police and judicial attitudes toward single-parent and female-headed households. Johnson (1986) found that even though girls from single-mother households were no more likely to self-report delinquent behaviour, they were more likely to be arrested and go to court than girls from traditional two-parent families.

Little research has examined the positive effects of single-parenting on children. For example, it could be argued that these children are more independent and have a stronger sense of responsibility than children from two-parent homes. Recently, Strohschein used data from the *National Longitudinal Survey of Children and Youth* (NLSCY) and tracked a group of four- to seven-year-olds who were living with both of their birth parents for a four-year period. She found that levels of depression and antisocial behaviour were very high in families where parents divorced but, most important, she found that depression and antisocial behaviour levels for these children were already higher at the beginning of the study, compared to children whose parents did not divorce over the four-year period. Conversely, she found that the mental health and behavioural problems of children with highly dysfunctional families actually improved after a divorce. Her conclusion with regard to "broken" families was that "most of the damages are done before the divorce" (*The Chronicle Herald*, December 15a, 2005).

Similarly, Sigfusdottir, Farkas, and Silver (2004) tested Agnew's strain theory, measured as stress on children from exposure to arguments and fights at home, and found that this type of exposure is related to depression and anger among adolescents. However, depression had no effect on delinquency, while anger increased levels of adolescent delinquent behaviour. Thus, the bulk of the evidence suggests that single mothers and working mothers do not "cause" delinquent behaviour. Parenting skills, parenting styles, and family dynamics, rather than family structure, might account for the weak relationship identified by some studies.

Parenting

Negative parent–child relationships and poor parenting skills have been identified as significant risk factors for youth criminality (Lipsey & Derzon, 1998). Data from the NLSCY show that children whose parents engage in poor parenting practices are more likely to have behavioural problems than other children (Statistics Canada, 2001). Parenting skills programs are commonly offered to parents whose children are experiencing behavioural difficulties, often as part of diversionary programs for young offenders. Nonetheless, it is a difficult and complicated task to sort out empirically exactly what it is about parenting that contributes to problem behaviours in children and youth.

Dianna Baumrind (1978, 1991) suggested that the two most important aspects of parenting behaviour are (1) the extent to which parents are supportive of their children's needs (*parental responsiveness*) and (2) the extent to which parents are demanding of appropriate behaviour from their children (*parental demandingness*). Hence, parents may be authoritative (i.e., supportive and demanding), authoritarian (rejecting and demanding), indulgent (supportive and not at all demanding), or indifferent (rejecting and not at all demanding). *Authoritative* parents set standards and have expectations that are consistent with their child's age. Such parents discuss

CASE STUDY BOX 7.1

Johnny: A Lost Boy

At the age of 3, shortly after Johnny's parents divorced, Johnny's mother and her new boyfriend moved him away from his father and other family members. By the age of 11, he had endured numerous moves from one town to another, until his family finally settled in an urban community. Diagnosed at the age of seven with attention deficit disorder, Johnny began taking Ritalin. However, he was soon taken off the drug after his mother claimed that it made him violent.

Johnny did not get along with his stepfather, and although Johnny's father promised him that he could move back with him at any time, his mother refused to let him go.

By junior high, he was getting into a lot of trouble in school and at home, so his mother sought the help of social workers. This was not Johnny's first encounter with social services, as the family had had significant involvement with other social service agencies in the past. By Grade 7, Johnny had become the target of bullying as well. After Johnny's mother contacted the police about this matter, he was referred to "Bully Busters," a local program aimed at helping kids to deal with bullies. In response to Johnny's struggles in the classroom, the school performed several assessments on him, diagnosing him with an eye disorder, scotopic sensitivity syndrome, which made reading difficult for him. Shortly after this, Johnny was kicked out of school for the rest of the year.

That summer, Johnny's mother sent him to live with his father. In the fall, he began Grade 7 over again. Yet, by the end of September, Johnny's father had kicked him out and sent him back to live with his mother. He was then enrolled in a different junior high school in the area. Johnny had trouble concentrating in school. Therefore, his behaviour in the classroom only worsened and the school soon threatened to expel him. His mother removed him from the school and attempted to home-school him.

Conflict arose between Johnny, his mother, and his stepfather. Johnny made a complaint to a social worker that his stepfather had grabbed him by the neck and thrown him onto a bed. Johnny was then moved into a group home. A neighbour and friend speak of Johnny, saying, "He wanted to be good at something—he failed at school, he failed with friends, he failed with his father—he wanted to be good at something." It just so happened that Johnny was good at stealing cars.

Sources: *The Coast* [Halifax] (June 16-23, 2005); *The Chronicle Herald* [Halifax] (February 21, 24, 2006). Researched and written by Nicole Landry.

and explain disciplinary matters with their children. *Authoritarian* parents value obedience and conformity. These parents tend to restrict children's autonomy and to favour the use of punitive disciplinary measures.

Indulgent parents allow children considerable freedom, are opposed to control or disciplinary measures, and see themselves more as resources for their children than as disciplinarians. *Indifferent* parents spend little time with their children, know little about their children's activities, and tend to put their own needs above those of their children. In extreme cases, indifferent parents neglect their children. Baumrind reports that delinquent behaviour is most likely to be found among the children of indifferent parents (1991). Canadian research shows that children are involved in far more aggressive behaviour when their parents are rejecting (Baumrind's indifferent type), highly punitive (Baumrind's authoritarian type), and/or limited nurturers (Sprott, Doob, & Jenkins, 2001, p. 7).

Data from the NLSCY survey allow an examination of Canadian parenting styles. In the NLSCY, parenting styles are measured on a continuum from negative— "ineffective/hostile"—to positive—"positive interaction." *Ineffective/hostile* is measured in terms of the frequency of parents telling children they are "bad" or not as good as others, or whether the parents are angry when punishing their children. *Punitive/aversive* refers to parents raising their voices at children or using physical punishment, while *consistent* refers to parents following through with punishment after a warning, or making sure that the child follows orders. *Positive interaction* involves parents laughing and playing with children. The most recent analysis from the survey reports that two-thirds (63 percent) of the children receiving ineffective parenting exhibited aggressive behaviours, such as fighting, bullying, and threatening, compared to only 4 percent of children whose parents rarely used this style (see Figure 7.1) (Statistics Canada, 2001, p. 13).

As for questions about which is more important, family structure or parenting styles, early results from the NLSCY indicate that parenting styles have far more impact on children's behavioural patterns than do family structure or even income levels. Children from two-parent homes with "ineffective" or hostile parents are five times more likely to have "persistent behavioural problems" than are children with an "effective" single parent (Dauvergne & Johnson, 2001; Philip, 1998).

Steven Cernkovich and Peggy Giordano (1987) attempted to ascertain whether structural factors or relationship factors are more important in children's delinquency

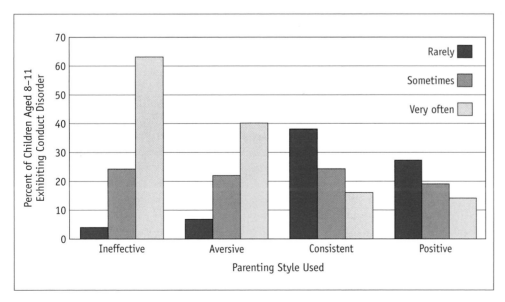

FIGURE 7.1

Parenting Styles: Percentage of Children Aged 8–11 Exhibiting Conduct Disorder

Sources: Statistics Canada, *National Longitudinal Survey of Children and Youth* (1994, 1996), Cycles 1 & 2, Children and Youth in Canada; Statistics Canada Cat. No. 85-F0033MIE (2001), p. 14.

by analyzing a number of factors. Their analysis, based on a sample of 824 adolescents, considered seven family interaction factors: control and supervision, identity support, caring and trust, intimate communication, instrumental communication, parental disapproval of peers, and conflict in the home. In comparing the impact of all of these factors on behaviour with the impact of a "broken family," they found that "internal family dynamics are considerably more important than family structure in affecting delinquency" (Cernkovich & Giordano, 1987, p. 316).

Differential association theory would suggest that the children of criminal parents are more likely to engage in criminal or delinquent behaviour. Notwithstanding Hirschi's contention that "parents with criminal records do not encourage criminality in their children and are as 'censorious' toward their criminality as are parents with no record of criminal involvement" (1983, p. 59), some studies have found a correlation between parent and child criminality (Alksnis & Robinson, 1995; Hawkins et al., 1998). According to West and Farrington (1977), boys with criminal fathers are four times more likely than boys with non-criminal fathers to be involved in delinquent behaviour, and Laub and Sampson (1988) found higher rates of delinquency among children of mothers and fathers who are deviant.

What seems like a contradiction here may be a result of research limitation in that, once again, it is difficult for us to know if such children are actually more delinquent than other children. As with single mothers, it may be that police and courts are more likely to **criminalize** the misdeeds of some children precisely because their parents have criminal records and are known to the police.

criminalize
A term that differentiates between referring to a person as a "criminal" and the process whereby individuals come to be viewed as "criminal."

Most research on family influences on youth crime has focused on family structure and relations or the relationship between the two. Very little has addressed the larger social structure and its impact on particular families. One exception is Hagan, Gillis, and Simpson's study of power relationships in the home between parents and children (1985). Their power-control theory looks at how structural power relations from the workplace are reflected in control mechanisms in the home. They found that family control structures are influenced by whether or not both parents work and whether in their employment they occupy positions of power and authority. Differences in degree of delinquency, and between boys' and girls' delinquency, are based on whether families are structured as patriarchal or egalitarian. Delinquency—especially boys' delinquency—is more strongly correlated with a patriarchal family structure.

Hirschi's control theory has important implications for predicting delinquency. Simply put, from the point of view of family relationships, the control theory hypothesis from Hirschi is that children who are not "attached" to their parents will have higher rates of delinquency. Kierkus and Baer (2002) looked at family structure and self-reported delinquency (ranging from truancy and running away from home to gang fighting and auto theft) among a sample of Ontario students and found that family structure is a predictor of delinquency, regardless of age, gender, or income. However, once parental attachments were considered (measured as supervision, communication, and quality of relationships), the statistical relationship between delinquency and family structure was considerably diminished. In other words, the authors maintained that parental attachments may explain why some research has reported family structure to be an important predictor of delinquency.

Similar results were found by Brannigan, Gemmell, Pevalin, and Wade (2002). Using NLSCY data, they too found that family structure was related to delinquency, but its effect was mediated by more interactive family factors. Furthermore, hyperactivity and hostile parenting were direct contributors to misconduct and aggression (p. 137). Along the same lines, Parker and Benson (2004) found, using national longitudinal data for adolescents in the United States, that high parental support and parental monitoring are related to greater self-esteem and lower risk behaviours (p. 519).

The works of Thornberry, Lizotte, Krohm, Farnworth, and Jang (1991) have been highly influential in promoting the development of family intervention strategies for reducing delinquency (this will be discussed in more detail in later chapters). Thornberry et al. examined the question of parental attachments by looking at interactional effects between family and school experiences, and found that the relationship is more complex than suggested by control theory. A total of 987 seventh and eighth graders enrolled in Rochester City public schools were interviewed three times and asked to report on their delinquent behaviour. In the first interview, they were asked about delinquency over the previous six months; in subsequent interviews, they were asked about delinquency since the first interview.

The researchers found that the relationship between parental attachments and delinquent behaviour is not a simple one. The first stage of testing revealed that low parental attachment increases delinquency and, as expected, that delinquency worsens attachments to parents. However, the last two stages of testing indicated that while delinquency negatively influences attachment to parents, attachment does not have a significant effect on delinquency. According to Thornberry et al., "parental influences in accounting for delinquency diminished considerably over time as adolescents gain independence. Indeed, by middle adolescence, attachment to parents is viewed as an effect of delinquency rather than a cause of it" (1991, p. 30). Thornberry et al. elaborated on the delinquency–attachment relationship and made suggestions regarding its implications for effective responses to delinquent behaviour:

> Because of its reciprocal relationships with the bonding variables, delinquent behaviour contributes, in a very real sense, to its own causation. Once exhibited, delinquency causes a deterioration in attachment and commitment, which, in turn, leads to further increases in delinquency. Treatment agents need to be aware of this causal pattern and should design intervention strategies that reduce or mitigate the negative consequences of delinquency on family and school. If this is not done, then the adolescent's continuing delinquency may simply "undo" the success of intervention programs in improving attachment to family and commitment to school. (1991, p. 31)

The Meaning of Family Attachment

Research on children's attachment to parents suggests that this attachment reduces rates of delinquency when it is measured as "affect," or emotional ties, rather than as supervision. Positive emotional attachments tend to be most effective in reducing delinquency. Children who feel loved, who identify with their parents, and who respect their wishes are less likely to be delinquent than children who come from homes where there is conflict or neglect, or where discipline is lacking, or erratic, or extreme.

Since low attachment seems to start the delinquency process, it is important to know just what it means. In measuring parental attachment, Thornberry et al. (1991) used an 11-item scale that measured, among other things, children's perceptions of warmth, liking, and feelings of hostility between themselves and their "primary caretaker." Thornberry et al. indicated that in 85 percent of the cases in their sample, the primary caretaker was the mother, while in 10 percent of the cases it was a stepmother.

Only 5 percent of the cases involved a caretaker other than a mother or stepmother, such as a father or grandparent (1991, p. 17).

More often than not, mothers are the focus of research on family relationships. Interestingly, ethnographic studies of young offenders often indicate that fathers are particularly disruptive to family life, and that children's "bad" relationships with mothers are frequently due to larger problems in the family setting stemming from the fathers' violence. Data from the U.S. National Crime Victimization surveys, for example, suggest that adults who have been abused and assaulted in the home, most often mothers, have a reduced capacity for supervising and monitoring their children (Mitchell & Finkelhor, 2001, p. 946). One of the first Canadian ethnographic studies of youth was undertaken by Elliott Leyton (1979), who examined all aspects of the lives of a group of young people incarcerated in juvenile facilities in Newfoundland, from family to school to social services and the juvenile justice system. The following three accounts from interviews with these youth focus on fathers' destructive behaviours:

> Father used to come home late in the night drinking. He was cracked, like somebody gone mental. Once he came home and he took off his belt and he hit my sister across the leg for no reason, leaving a great mark. He was drunk, right. He got arrested three or four times up at the house. One Christmas he even caught the place on fire, the fire started in the wardrobe upstairs. He got my mother—she's got false teeth now—and he knocked all her teeth out and he took the phone and ripped it off the wall; and he had a bottle of liquor there, he smashed it and pushed us all around. I, we, told him to get out of the house . . . I don't talk to my father. Sometimes I talk to him. I talk to him any time I want to—my mother won't say nothing—but the rest of my family don't talk to him. He's nice to me all the time. (Leyton, 1979, pp. 42–43)

> When I was younger, my parents fought a lot. Their fights were usually about money or something stupid like that. I didn't like being at home. As I got older I started to drink, I'd come home drunk and I'd usually end up being whipped [by my father] next morning. A couple of times I got locked out of the house. Once I was so cold I wanted to come in, so mom had to phone the police on dad so he'd let me in. Another time I slept in the car because he wouldn't let me in. I almost froze. (Leyton, 1979, pp. 66–67)

> Dad didn't abuse me so much when he was drinking; he was better to me when he was drunk than when he was sober—he was cranky then, you couldn't look at him. Me and him couldn't get along together. He'd always be fighting with me when I was 13 and 14, and when mom would go to work I'd go out and I wouldn't come home 'til she came home because we'd be fighting. We'd fight about any old thing. I'd get in trouble in school or around our neighbourhood. If I was hanging around with a hard bunch, he didn't want me hanging around with them: he was always fighting me about that. They were fist fights. He'd hit me and I'd hit him back or kick him. Then I wouldn't be able to go home. When mom would come home, nothing would be said. He'd only have a fight with mom. (Leyton, 1979, p. 123)

Virtually all of the young people Leyton interviewed tell of violent, angry, and destructive fathers. Unfortunately, as we have seen throughout the book, children in the Victorian era had similar stories, as do some of today's youth. Mark Totten (2000) conducted interviews with marginalized male youth and also found stories of destructive fathers and other male relatives. In one particularly disturbing story, a 17-year-old tells of the severe abuse he experienced and witnessed as a child, and the effect it had on his feelings about himself and about women and girls:

> . . . My real Dad beat my Mom. And I've always been told that he ritually abused me . . . I guess he burned and strapped me a lot. I was too young to remember . . . My Step-Dad's not much better. He's been really violent. He threatens to kick the shit outta me. Once he slapped my mom. She kicked him in the nuts. He's told me lots of times that if a girl hits you or touches you where you don't want to be touched, punch her out. I guess the men in my family don't treat women very well. My Uncle's told me that if you do things for a girl, she's got to fuck you. My Grandfather and my real Dad put women down all the time. They call them "Hey bitch, you goddam whore" all the time. I know my grandfather sexually assaulted two of my cousins . . . I think I'm worthless—like a piece of shit. I guess it's been all the put-downs and physical violence. It gets to you after a while. I've seen psychiatrists . . . I'm on medication . . . They say I'm a manic-depressive . . . I'm pretty fucked up. (pp. 103–104)

To focus on attachments to mothers, or even attachments to parents in general, is to miss the most important **etiological** question about delinquency—namely: What factors are responsible for weak attachments to parents? It is only through ethnographic studies such as Leyton's and interviews such as Totten's that we can begin to understand and perhaps even appreciate why some young people have weak attachments to their parents.

etiological
Having to do with cause or origin.

Consequences of "Bad" Family Relationships

Marc Le Blanc (1992), based on his work with families and young offenders in Quebec, recognizes that "marital variables" have direct links to delinquent behaviour. NLSCY data indicate that Canadian children exposed to physical fighting and violence in the home are more likely to behave aggressively, exhibit emotional disorders, and be involved in property crime (Dauvergne & Johnson, 2001), and they are more likely to engage in bullying behaviour and use indirect forms of aggression such as rallying friends against other children (Statistics Canada, 2001). Girls in custody are particularly likely to have experienced physical abuse, sexual abuse, and a family history of violence (Wallace, 1997).

Childhood victimization increases the risk of violent offending, particularly for male youth, and abused and neglected children are found to begin delinquent careers earlier than non-abused or neglected children (Rivera & Widom, 1990). Studies of juvenile male sex offenders found that, compared to non-sexual offenders, they were more likely to have witnessed family violence (Caputo, Frick, & Brodsky, 1999) and they predominantly came from "multiproblemic families, were abused in early childhood and were exposed to pornographic materials at an early age" (Wieckowski, Hartsoe, Mayer, & Shortz, 1998). Schissel (1997) finds marital discord and parental problems with alcohol and drugs are associated with young offenders' substance abuse and legal problems, such as time spent in custodial facilities and various administrative charges (pp. 96–100).

A survival strategy for many youth in such family conditions is running away from home, and this puts them at greater risk for criminalization (McCarthy & Hagan, 1992). In 2003, most Canadian runaway children were 12–17 years of age; two-thirds were girls and three-quarters were "habitual runners." Parental neglect, family conflict and violence, school problems, and abuse are the primary reasons for running (Dalley, 2004). Hagan and McCarthy (1997) found that 60 percent of Toronto and Vancouver street youth had been physically abused, and 14 percent of girls and 6 percent of boys reported sexual abuse (pp. 23–24).

Canadian studies also report anywhere from 18 to 32 percent of runaway street youth become involved in prostitution (Fisher, 1989; Hagan & McCarthy, 1997, p. 116; Kufeldt & Nimmo, 1987; McCarthy, 1990). Schissel and Fedec (2000) found that Saskatoon and Regina young offenders who had experienced childhood neglect and/or sexual, physical, or psychological abuse were more likely to be involved in prostitution. Among these factors, all were highly significant for Aboriginal youth, but only child-hood sexual abuse was a significant predictor for non-Aboriginal youth involved in prostitution (p. 43).

Those writing from a feminist perspective are well aware of the impact of poor parenting and violence on girls, and they also recognize the connection between rela-tionships and social structure. We have seen in earlier chapters that young women and girls are more likely to be the victims of sexual abuse over a longer period of time, and are more likely to be victimized by a relative. Chesney-Lind and Shelden (1992, 1998), emphasized that a feminist perspective on female crime will not only account for patriarchal social structures, but will contain an explicit concern about physical and sexual abuse of girls and the relationship between the two:

> Unlike young men's victimization, young women's victimization and their response to it is shaped by their status as young women. . . . their vulnerability is heightened by norms that require that they stay at home, where their victimizers have greater access to them. Moreover, . . . females' victimizers (usually males) can invoke official agencies of social control . . . abusers have traditionally been able to utilize the uncritical commitment of the juvenile justice system to parental authority to force girls to obey them . . . many young women on the run from homes characterized by sexual abuse and parental neglect are pushed by the very statutes designed to protect them into life on the streets . . . young girls are seen as sexually desirable . . . [which] means life on the streets and survival strategies are shaped by patriarchal values. (1992, p. 91)

In other words, one cannot understand the crime and delinquency of girls without accounting for the status of women and girls in a patriarchal society and their conse-quent victimization not only in the home but also in the justice system. Similarly, one cannot talk about attachments or commitments to family and parents without recog-nizing that, for some youth, there is good reason for weak attachments. In these cases, one would be reluctant to say that the "cause" of delinquency is weak attachments to mothers or parents.

The "Bad Seed" and Invisible Victims

Tales of "bad" parenting, like those of "bad" children, provide ripe fodder for public dis-cussion and moral panic. While children are blamed for social ills, the most readily accepted "cause" is bad parenting. In a recent court case, Chief Justice Joseph Kennedy of the Nova Scotia Supreme Court addressed both of these issues in sentencing a young man being convicted of a particularly violent crime. Chief Justice Kennedy was cited in a local newspaper as speaking in general about young people as outsiders, as the Other, in today's society and about the role of parents in creating this "menace." The mother had reported for the pre-sentence report that she raised her son with "tough love." The following excerpt is taken from the sentencing hearing and was reported on the first page of a local newspaper under the heading "Judge scolds Wyllie's killers, relatives."

> There is an ever-growing significant number of our society, relatively young, who are not functioning properly . . . and they are a significant segment of a generation . . . They are undisciplined, they are undereducated, they are immoral and they are adrift.[And to the mother] . . . Tough Love, I guess, in this instance was putting a 15-year-old out on the street—that was tough love . . . It didn't work so well . . . these catchphrases that are used to explain the failure of parental responsibility. (Borden-Colley, 2005)

"Tough love" is a parenting style believed to provide a solution for parents with "problem" children. It is also a name commonly given to parental support groups that promote "getting-tough" parenting strategies. Using Baumrind's terminology, it is an authoritarian parenting style possibly fitting into the ineffective/hostile category of the NLSCY surveys. Locking a child out of the house is a common strategy promoted by tough love advocates. It seems to draw its legitimacy by purporting to be "in the child's best interest" and justified as "this will hurt me more than you." In the words of a tough love mother:

> It's called Toughlove because it's very tough on the parents because they love their kids so much that they're going to be tough on those kids because they do love them. And its actually not hard on the kids. It's harder on the parents. It's very tough on the parents. (Hil & McMahon, 2001, p. 104)

Clearly, Justice Kennedy is not impressed with the tough love results that he sees in his courtroom. The quote taken from his sentencing rationale is important because it is not only a reflection of a common sentiment regarding "bad" children and "bad" parents, its significance lies in the blaming—shifting the blame for social ills from children to parents and back again—a vicious spiral that takes us all the way back to the 19th-century Victorian reformers. Just as child blaming leads to repressive policies, "solutions" and laws, so too does parent blaming. Hillian and Reitsma-Street (2003, p. 20) refer to this as the "faulty parenting paradigm," a belief that both children and parents should be held accountable for the misdeeds of the young.

Considerable pressure to increase parental responsibility in the legislation was brought by lobby groups and provinces during the Young Offenders Act reform process. Some provinces, such as Manitoba, Ontario, and British Columbia have legislated parental responsibility by allowing victims of property crime to take civil action against the parents of young offenders. For example, the 2001 Parental Responsibility Act of British Columbia allows such action to be taken unless the parents can prove that they took reasonable supervision measures and discouraged destructive activity (Hillian & Reitsma-Street, 2003, p. 21). This trend is not unique to Canada; parental responsibility "crackdowns" are occurring in Britain, Australia, and the United States, to name a few. For example, McNaught (1998) reports that 17 U.S. states allow for parents to be fined or even jailed for failing to properly supervise their children (cited in Hillian & Reitsma-Street, 2003, p. 21).

One cannot help but wonder about the sense of these laws. It certainly raises questions from a jurisprudential point of view about the legality of holding two people responsible for the same offence or of holding one person accountable twice. What it does is take W.L. Scott's vision for probation (1908) to its widest extension—it potentially brings all families and parents under the surveillance of the justice system. Justice policies no longer stop with the search for at-risk youth: the search is extended to at-risk families. At the very least, such policies are likely to put even more youth at risk, intensify their marginalization, increase their parents' difficulties and possibly even criminalize parents who cannot or will not comply. The concern is best expressed in the words of an astute Australian parent, who also works with street kids:

> Oh, well, that's stupid. All you're going to end up with is 10,000 kids on the street because I know myself, that if my kid went out when he was 14 or something or stole or wrecked a house and I got charged $5000, I would throw him out onto the street. I'd say get out there, go on, go out and earn the money the hard way. That's what will happen to all these kids. I could tell you that now. People on pensions or social security benefits, they're not going to pay it. What can they do? That is an insane idea of making the parents pay for it . . . (Hil and McMahon, 2001, p. 128)

Another problematic aspect of the blame game is what is left out. As we have seen in ethnographic accounts of the family lives of institutionalized youth and in discussions in earlier chapters, child and youth victimization is pervasive, yet it receives little to no public attention other than in the form of "stranger danger" warnings. Public discourse and moral panics do not problematize parental violence; they problematize the stranger. This is clearly seen in educational programs encouraging parents to street-proof their children and in police mall displays encouraging parents to fingerprint or footprint their babies and toddlers. The most pervasive form of child and youth victimization, that occurring in the home, is not a subject for public discourse, not to mention that corporal punishment is a legally sanctioned form of parental discipline in Canada today. In spite of the numbers of fathers responsible for killing their children and brutalizing them in their homes, we have yet to see a newspaper headline that reads "Fathers out of control."

On the other hand, "parent abuse" is a new concept, growing in popularity, that is suitable for public consumption and that does provide fodder for moral panics by furthering the image of immoral youth predators. The parent abuse concept also falls into the same category as "tough love." It is a catch phrase used to blame children for their "bad" behaviour and, as Justice Kennedy claimed about tough love, it also abrogates parental responsibility by shifting a failure of parental responsibility onto children. In addressing solutions to parent abuse, counselling for both parents and children is urged and the primary objective of counselling is to reassert a parent's "natural" right to authority over the child.

> Whatever method is used, the counselling must be grounded in the understanding that the natural hierarchy of the family is for parents to have authority over their children. Teenagers are not adults, they are dependants, and when parents are being abused there is an imbalance of the natural hierarchy. (Cottrell, 2004, p. 128)

And here is the blame game problem in a nutshell: parents have rights, children do not. This is hardly a new idea but, as discussed in Chapter 2, is characteristic of the colonial period in Canada when children were viewed as possessions and objects of parental authority. Like tough love, the parent abuse concept allows parents and adults to deny that children have inherent rights, that they are persons with dignity and rights of their own, and that parents (and the state) have an obligation to provide for those rights (Denov, 2005, pp. 67–68). Importantly, these rights include the freedom of a voice in their own affairs and a right to the fundamentals of survival: food clothing and shelter.

The public blame game accuses parents of abrogating their colonial responsibility to control their children, and the concepts of tough love and parent abuse give parents a rationale for abrogating their primary responsibility in ensuring these rights. Many parents, in particular those involved in the youth justice system, are fearful of the very notion of children's rights and express concern that the "law" (Young Offenders Act [YOA]/Youth Criminal Justice Act [YCJA]), by giving children "rights," makes it impossible for them to control their children because they can't discipline (hit) them anymore (Bell, 1993; Hillian & Reitsma-Street, 2003).

The idea of children participating in decision making in the home was not even considered by many parents of young offenders. When I asked questions in my court research pertaining to decision making, a majority of young offenders' parents asked me to repeat and explain the question of child participation in decision making. They were surprised that such a question would even be asked. After repeated probing and elaboration, most parents answered that they make decisions about such things as how to spend leisure time, not their children (Bell, 1993).

Identifying the blame game as problematic does not deny that parent abuse is a real human tragedy experienced mostly by women at the hands of their children. Nor does it say that Chief Justice Kennedy is wrong. In fact, he was probably very correct in his assessment of the young man and the inappropriateness of his mother's parenting style. Nor is it to say that most young offenders' parents do not love their children and struggle to reach them, get worn out from trying, and resort to last-ditch efforts such as tough love. Adopting tough love is usually one step above parents begging the police or court to put their child or children in jail, as we see in "Johnny's" case (Box 7.1 on page 184).

As mentioned earlier, my research in youth/family court (Bell, 1993) showed me a steady stream of economically disadvantaged parents, mostly mothers, worn well beyond their years, tired and exhausted from trying to keep a family together with meagre resources and from trying to manage children who in fact were not "out of control" in an absolute sense, but out of *their* control. It is quite possible that their children never were "under" their control; the only difference, once they become enmeshed in the justice system, is that their children become too big physically to drag back into the house. Other research has also found that a majority of parents in the youth justice system are deeply concerned about their children's well-being and are highly cooperative in helping the courts find solutions for their children's behaviour (Hil & McMahon, 2001; Hillian & Reitsma-Street, 2003).

So what then is the issue? How are we to understand the "bad" behaviour of youth and children, including violence directed toward their parents, without blaming children and parents and in such a way that recognizes the victimization of children and youth at the hands of their parents? These are not unrelated questions. Answering one provides an answer to the other. Answers may come from recognizing first, as we have in this textbook, that child and youth victimization is largely invisible in our society, while child and youth criminal activity has a very high profile. Victim status must be *"earned"* by children and youth, while their status as offenders is *"eagerly ascribed"* (Brown, 2005, p. 128).

Secondly, as exemplified by the parent abuse counselling solution, we also have longstanding colonial-based views about the role and place of parents and children in the family. Thirdly, both our views of offender and victim as well as parental and child roles are reinforced by equally long-standing punitive attitudes toward children and youth. Sheila Brown (2005) maintains that there is, in Western society, a punitive culture toward children and argues that:

> . . . the punitive culture towards young people must be seen as rooted in a long history in which the "chastisement" of children is the legitimate province of the family as a primary institution of socialization and control. "Discipline" by parents (or rather the lack of it) has so consistently been placed at the forefront of debates about the crime problem that we must consider whether there is a longstanding and deeply ingrained punitiveness towards children and young people which precedes, and frames, our societal insistence upon seeing young people as a problem population who must first and foremost be contained through punishment. (Brown, 2005, p. 128)

SCHOOL

As with positivist and "modern" scientific thinking on youth crime that looks at family factors to explain the criminal behaviour of youth and children, schools are also implicated in many theories and a considerable amount of research has taken place in this tradition in order to isolate factors associated with school that contribute to delinquency. Up until the 1960s, schools tended to be viewed as "solutions" to issues of race and class, in the sense that they were seen as the great equalizers, the source of the "American dream," so to speak. All one needed to do was get an education and social mobility was assured.

School failure was viewed as a major problem because it was linked to delinquent behaviour. Canadian research in the 1980s, for example, showed that both self-reported delinquency and official rates of delinquency were strongly correlated with school failure (Gomme, 1985; Le Blanc, 1983). More recently, Sprott, Jenkins, and Doob (2000) found that schools can be a "protective factor" for at-risk Canadian youth; for example, for children from single-parent families or children who are subject to hostile parenting. The causal chain is assumed to be that school failure is the source of delinquent behaviour and school failure is the result of individual inability to achieve or as a failure of the school system to meet the educational needs of all youth. By the 1980s, as the moral panic about youth gained momentum, public emphasis and concern shifted to schools as a site of youth crime, and educational issues took a back seat to concerns about the schools' ability (or lack thereof) to discipline and control the youth population. In the discussion that follows, we will look at theory, empirical knowledge, and theorizing regarding both of these tracks.

Youth Crime as an Educational Issue

Both Albert Cohen's subcultural theory and control theory suggest that school is a determinant of delinquent behaviour. Cohen (1955), in his version of strain theory, indicated that the delinquent subculture stemmed from *reaction formation*, wherein lower- and working-class youth responded to the frustrations they experienced in a middle-class school system. Control theory simply posits that low levels of school commitment will lead to delinquency.

School Commitment

Much of the contemporary research has focused on school commitment and has not only consistently found a relationship between school commitment and youth crime but also that lack of commitment is related to an early onset of delinquency and the escalation of delinquency to more serious criminal activity (Loeber, Southamer-Loeber, Van Kammen, & Farrington, 1991), with the risk of gang involvement (Bjerregard & Smith, 1993; Esbensen & Deschenes, 1998; Hill, Howell, Hawkins, & Battin-Pearson, 1999). Research has also demonstrated that strategies designed to increase levels of commitment reduce youth criminal activity (Cairns & Cairns, 1994; Maguin & Loeber, 1996).

The NLSCY allows a measure of school commitment through questions about participation in school activities, making friends at school, learning new things, the importance of doing well at school, expressing opinions at school, and showing up on time. Results from an analysis of 12- to 15-year-old Canadian youth in 1998–1999 showed that Canadian girls are more committed to school than are boys, and that girls' commitment to school reduces their involvement in property crime more so than it does for boys.

Low levels of school commitment were also associated with violent crime, and there were no differences between boys and girls (Fitzgerald, 2003, pp. 12–14). Interestingly, Fitzgerald also looked at interconnections between delinquency and self-reported victimization and school commitment, and found that girls seem to have "an increased sensitivity to both factors." More specifically, where both boys' and girls' commitment to school and level of victimization were related to delinquency, girls with high levels of victimization and a low level of school commitment reported more property-related and violence-related delinquency (pp. 12, 16, 18).

Colvin and Pauly (1987) combined the ideas of Cohen's working-class "reaction formation" with control theory notions of school commitment and argue that *coercive controls* in working-class families combine with similar controls in schools to increase the chance of failure among working-class youth in the school system. Hence, some failure explanations focus on the organization of schools and classrooms, others on the role of school in the larger social structure and its impact on particular class and minority groups, and still others focus on an individual's shortcomings.

Individual Failures

IQ Reminiscent of early biological understandings of criminality as a function of "feeblemindedness" are modern claims that a low IQ is predictive of school failure and subsequent delinquent behaviour. This is the view presented by James Q. Wilson and Richard Herrnstein (1985). Based on their studies in the United States and Great Britain, they reported that the IQ of non-offenders was some 10 points higher than that of offenders. They argued that IQ has a direct effect on delinquency, in that young people with low intelligence tend to be impulsive, lacking in moral reasoning, and inclined to think only in terms of immediate gratification. For these youth, school failure encourages delinquency:

> A child who chronically loses standing in the competition of the classroom may feel justified in settling the score outside, by violence, theft, and other forms of defiant illegality. School failure enhances the rewards for crime by engendering feelings of unfairness. (Wilson & Herrnstein, 1985, p. 121)

Hirschi (1969) argues that IQ is related to delinquency indirectly through its effect on grades. IQ affects grades, which in turn affect one's attachment to school. Attachment to school affects one's tolerance of school authority, and tolerance of authority affects one's involvement in delinquency. Although research in the 1960s

> **BOX 7.2**
>
> ## An Example of an IQ Test Question
>
> What should you do if you find a wallet in a store?
>
> (a) Find out whom it belongs to and return it.
> (b) Give it to the storeowner or a police officer.
> (c) Try to find the owner.
> (d) Make believe you didn't see it.
>
> Source: Adapted from Regoli & Hewitt (1994, p. 263).

and 1970s indicated that grades are better predictors of delinquency than IQ, more recent research challenges Hirschi's argument. Liska and Reid (1985), for example, questioned not only the predominance of IQ in Hirschi's model but also the chain of events. They maintained that:

> . . . street delinquency may be correlated with troublesome school behavior in classrooms, school halls and school yards . . . [A]lso, adolescents involved in delinquency simply have less time for school; thus, delinquency, independently of teacher reactions, may decrease school attachment. (p. 557)

Of course, none of the IQ research addresses the cultural bias inherent in IQ tests and its negative effects on students from minority groups. Box 7.2 presents an example of a question from the Wechsler Intelligence Scale for Children (WISC-R), an IQ test used in California. The scores for this question are (a) two points, (b) two points, (c) one point, and (d) no points. What makes the question culturally biased is the high probability that children who have experienced racial prejudice or police harassment will choose (d), based on the assumption that picking up the wallet would make them vulnerable to accusations of theft (Regoli & Hewitt, 1994, p. 263).

Tracking One of the consequences of IQ tests and other forms of testing is that schools "streamline" or "track" students into different types of classes. Students can be tracked into vocational programs, college prep programs, remedial programs, or special ed programs, to name a few. Studies have shown delinquency to be more strongly correlated with **tracking** than with gender or **social class** (Gamoran & Mare, 1989; Kelly, 1975). Based on his Montreal studies, Marc Le Blanc (1993) reported a number of school experiences, including tracking, to be predictors of delinquency. Nonetheless, it is not necessarily IQ or grades that determine students' track allocations. Tracking decisions are often made by counsellors, teachers, and parents, and they are often made on the basis of race and class. Regoli and Hewitt (1994, p. 262) report that, in the United States, African American students are two times more likely than white students to be tracked into special education classes. Not surprisingly, as the proportion of African American teachers increases in schools, the number of African American students in special education programs decreases (p. 263).

In a longitudinal study conducted in the United States, a group of high-school students were interviewed four times over the course of their school experience. The results provided little evidence that delinquency was related to tracking at either the beginning or the end of the high-school career (Wiatrowski et al., 1982). For

tracking
School policies that group and stream students into different programs based on their performance on standardized tests.

social class
Generally refers to one's economic position or standing in a particular social structure or society.

Tanner (1996), an important finding was that 87 percent of the students said they were satisfied with their track allocation. This finding suggested to Tanner that tracking may be related to delinquency only when students are negatively labelled because of it and come to resent being tracked. Given the contradictory research evidence on tracking, Tanner argues that "a reasonable conclusion might be that a sense of fairness about appropriate track allocations reduces delinquency" (1996, p. 102).

School Failures

School Organization Another way of looking at tracking and IQ testing and their impact on delinquency is to consider them as part of the organization of the school and the educational system rather than as factors related to the young offender. By the 1980s, youth problems were being reframed as "the problem of youth" (Acland, 1995) and schools were identified as a part of that problem. And, once again, lack of discipline and control was the issue. A highly influential book at the time was Paul Copperman's *The Literacy Hoax* (1980). Copperman outlined a number of problems associated with schools that are delinquency-producing. Simply put, he argued that school delinquency is created by a lack of teacher authority. This lack of teacher authority is a function of the organization of the school, particularly with respect to school principals. According to Copperman, a school cannot teach students in the absence of a strong principal who is able to exercise authority and concentrate on curriculum and teaching (including the firing of incompetent teachers).

Similarly, a lack of parental support for school systems and teachers reduces teachers' authority in the classroom. If parents do not support and respect teachers, neither will children. Copperman also viewed open classrooms with flexible schedules, electives, and light course loads as problematic. A lack of structure in classrooms translates into teachers' loss of control over students. It is precisely this loss of control, Copperman maintained, that leads to violence, disruption, and drug use in contemporary schools.

An opposite argument comes from those who examine schools and their ability to meet the needs of marginalized students. Schissel (1997), for example, maintains that rigid, punitive, authoritarian school systems exacerbate youth problems, particularly for individuals who are marginalized, at risk, or simply have not had the advantages others have (pp. 120–126). He advocates more flexibility in schools to meet youth needs and a "human rights approach" to youth education (p. 121). Contrary to Copperman, Schissel (1997) advocates for fundamental changes and argues that schools need to develop alternative models of teaching, learning, and curriculum to better serve youth who are marginal and "relatively disadvantaged." He cites Princess Alexandria School and Joe Duquette High School in Saskatoon and St. Peter's College Alternative High School in Muenster, Saskatchewan, as examples of schools that are committed to "egalitarian and non-authoritarian" teaching. All of these schools reject standardized, inflexible curricula; offer a non-judgmental and non-punitive learning environment; reject discipline and punishment; and focus on empowering students in an atmosphere of mutual respect (Schissel, 1997, pp. 120–126). School boards also need to adapt to the needs of street youth by providing educational programs that address their remedial needs and acknowledge the realities of street life in physical learning spaces that are accessible to them (Schissel & Fedec, 2000, p. 52).

Jane Sprott (2004) examined data on Canadian students from the NLSCY to assess the effect of classroom and school climates on delinquent behaviour. She found that delinquency is related to classroom climate and that the classroom climate is more important at reducing levels of violent behaviour than the school climate, measured as management styles. More specifically, an emotionally supportive classroom with favourable social relationships for younger students, aged 10–13, meant lower levels of violent behaviours among the same youth when they were 12 to 15 years old. Classrooms with a strong academic focus had the effect of lowering rates of property offending as youth aged (Sprott, 2004, pp. 553–565).

Structural Failures

Social Class A question lurking behind all of the research regarding, tracking, IQ, and loss of teacher authority is whether or not these factors are related to delinquency because of the class structure of Western society. Greenberg (1977) argues that the regimentation of schools causes delinquency and that regimentation is more likely to be resented by working-class youth. Students who are doing well academically, or who participate in extracurricular activities, may find school rules to be mere annoyance because they find rewards in the school system. However, students who are not actively involved in school life, or who are not doing well academically, will find the same rules to be oppressive because they are not being rewarded by the school system.

Further, Greenberg argues, working-class youth are more affected than middle-class students by worsening job conditions because such conditions force them to stay in school longer than they normally would. Students forced to remain in school will find the school experience particularly degrading and will strike out against teachers and school property in an effort to regain their self-esteem. Perhaps the strongest support for this argument came from American and Canadian research showing that delinquency declines after young people graduate from or drop out of school (Elliott, 1966, pp. 307–314; Elliott & Voss, 1974a, 1974b).

Davies (1994b), in a survey of high-school students in Ontario, challenges the notion that resistance to or rebellion against school systems is a working-class behaviour. He found that resistant attitudes and behaviours, such as drug and alcohol use and disrespect toward police, are associated with tracking and academic problems but unrelated to class background. Rather, the school "stands on its own" as a causal factor in delinquent behaviour among high-school students. On the other hand, there is evidence that school problems and resentment of school have a racial component. Solomon (1992), who documented through ethnography the resistance of black male students in a Toronto high school, argues that this resistance is race-based. For black students, school resistance is a consequence of a conflict between schools' cultural assumptions and rules and their own cultural backgrounds and experiences.

A classic study by Arthur Stinchcombe (1964) puts an interesting twist on Cohen's idea of status frustration. While he agreed with Cohen that status frustration generated by the school system is a source of delinquency, Stinchcombe maintained that it is not working-class students but rather middle-class students who are most likely to be frustrated. Students who are most pressured to do well in school (i.e., middle-class students) are the ones who will be most likely to experience status frustration if they do not meet expectations. These are the students most at risk of delinquency. Based on his study of a California high school, Stinchcombe found (1) that poor grades were related to rebellious behaviour, and (2) that the most rebellious students were male middle-class students with poor grades.

According to Davies (1994a), school failure is related to male delinquency, not female delinquency. Girls leave school not because they are frustrated with school or are failing, but because they have placed "domestic" concerns above academic concerns. Whereas boys leave school as a form of resistance and rebellion, girls leave school because of "marriage and motherhood." Neither response is related to class position. One has to wonder if Davies considered unwanted teen pregnancies a matter of "placing domestic concerns" above academic ones. Boys are not usually pressured to leave school because they get a girl pregnant.

In his review of the literature on school rebellion, Tanner (1996) concludes, "regardless of whether it is called rebellion or resistance, anti-school behaviour has its origins in factors and experiences located inside the school yard gates rather than in the wider world beyond them" (p. 116).

Youth Failure: Schools in Crisis

By the mid 1990s, public discourse on "youth in crisis" was in full swing and schools came to be defined as an important component of the "youth problem." At the same time, youth behaviour at school was presented as evidence of the crisis. Nothing was more dramatic and influential in this regard than school shootings and other forms of serious violence. Once again, newspaper headlines took the lead and provided evidence to an already fearful public that even schools were no longer safe places from youth violence and depredation, nor were they able to control today's youth.

Yet, in 1998, the United States Federal Department of Justice reported that violent crime had been on the decline since 1992, that the number of children bringing weapons to school had declined over that time period, that "a child's chance of dying in school violence was less than one in a million," and that "for every one child killed in a school, 200 were killed in incidents of domestic abuse." On April 20, 1999, the Federal Departments of Justice and Education released a joint report on school safety that reported "a significant decline in school violence" (cited in Wooden & Blazak, 2001, pp. 102–103). That was the day of the Columbine school shootings. Six months later, six students were shot at a school in Fort Gibson, Oklahoma. By the late 1990s, there had also been school shootings in Littleton, Colorado; West Paducah, Kentucky; Pearl, Mississippi; Springfield, Oregon; Jonesboro, Arkansas; Conyers, Georgia; Moses Lake, Washington; and Blackville South Carolina (Wooden & Blazak, 2001, pp. 102–103). Then there was Taber, Alberta.

As violent and tragic as these events were, what is significant about these incidents for an understanding of the **politics of youth crime** is that they did not occur in core area schools or in the inner areas of large cities, nor did they involve visible minority youth or youth gangs. They involved white middle-class boys killing other white middle-class youth and teachers in suburban schools. Hence, the already fearful white adult public was now presented with the message that they were not safe from their very own children.

As with the history of drug legislation in North America, where drug use did not become a moral panic requiring legislation to control its use and possession until white suburban youth became the users and dealers (victims), the same seems to be true of school violence. Wooden and Blazak (2001) tell of a radio interview with black students in Harlem, New York, the day after the Columbine shootings, where all of the youth interviewed were "confused about how the perpetrators evaded metal detectors, heavily monitored surveillance cameras, and police to get the guns into the school" (p. 108).

politics of youth crime
The mechanisms and methods whereby youth activities are socially constructed as criminal; the meanings and imagery attached to these definitions and the types of responses they generate.

I too experienced a similar confusion on a tour of youth and adult prisons in the late 1990s in Louisiana. Our bus had already stopped at a youth prison in the core of New Orleans and then moved on to another stop in the city. Similar to the youth prison, the grey concrete building was surrounded by a three-metre-high chainlink fence topped with barbed and razor wire. The only entry to the building required passage by metal detectors and there were surveillance cameras everywhere, inside and out. It was a cold and dismal place and I thought we were entering another prison, but it was in fact a high school. It was closed temporarily for repainting and the purpose of the stop was to show us prisoners busily repainting the school. For black inner-city youth in New Orleans, there is little difference between their school and the local prison.

Bullying is also a central part of the schools and youth in crisis discourse and panic. It too is a primarily white, middle-class, suburban youth issue. The news media consistently report the most extreme cases of school bullying with an implication that the incidence of bullying is on the rise, as are the severity and consequences of bullying. The latest "discovery" is that youth are using the Internet to broadcast school fights, and boys and girls alike are using chat rooms and e-mail to bully their classmates.

We saw earlier from NLSCY data that more than half of the sampled boys (56 percent) and almost one-third of the girls (29 percent) aged 12 to 13 reported such aggressive behaviour as threatening someone or getting into fights. Equally important is that children who are bullied are also more likely to be aggressive than children who are not bullied (Sprott, Doob, & Jenkins, 2001). Research in the mid-1990s indicated that boys' aggression was instrumental, that is, physically oriented toward power and control, while girls' aggression was more interpersonally oriented and focused on controlling relationships. Hence, girls are said to use indirect forms of aggression such as name-calling, gossip, verbal abuse, and social exclusion—referred to as **relational aggression** (Crick & Grotpeter, 1996).

relational aggression
An indirect form of aggression that is interpersonally oriented and focused on controlling relationships, rather than direct forms of aggression that involve physical force.

Based on surveys of Canadian school children, Artz (2004) did not identify any difference between boys and girls in their use of indirect or relational aggression. She found that among 10- to 12-year-olds who were asked "how they would respond if they were angry with another student because that person had been saying hurtful things about them," boys were more likely than girls to say they would "start rumours about that person to get even." Furthermore, among youth who had been involved in direct forms of violence, there was no difference between boys and girls in their use of indirect violence. Both violent boys and girls engaged in shunning; spreading rumours; using homophobic putdowns, obscene language, blackmail, and threats; and damaging other youths' property. In short, Artz concluded that all boys use name-calling more than girls and that "violent boys use at least as much indirect and relational violence as violent girls and in some cases use even more" (2004, pp. 155–157).

Anne Worrall (2004) maintains that much of what is currently constructed and perceived as "new" girl violence comes from a lack of cultural notions of "normal" uses of violence by girls as we have for boys. We accept "rough play and fighting" among boys but all such behaviours engaged in by girls is defined as "violence" (p. 51). Furthermore, girl-on-girl aggression is more tolerable, while girl-on-boy bullying is viewed as not only criminal violence but also as pathological.

Responding to School Violence

Programs of an educational and preventive nature have been developed in many schools to teach children about the consequences of bullying; constructive ways of responding to threats from other bullying children; and more positive, less destructive ways of responding to other transgressions against them by their schoolmates. Programs are also being aimed at teachers to assist in identifying when "roughhousing becomes bullying." Importantly, it is also being recognized that schools may be more effective sites for preventing and addressing bullying, since parents of bullies are sometimes bullies themselves (Wooden & Blazak, 2001, pp. 45–46).

The more general response in Canadian schools, and elsewhere, to violence has been to cut after-school programs, put police officers in schools, and adopt **zero-tolerance policies,** a policing ideology and attitude imported in the 1990s from the United States. Zero tolerance was adopted in a number of schools but was quickly abandoned, likely because of its potential for targeting minority and already marginalized youth. It now exists as part of more generalized school policies of "codes of conduct."

zero-tolerance policies
Policies related to the intolerance of behaviour that is considered undesirable.

The concept zero tolerance is not in and of itself a punitive one. For example, in the United Kingdom, it was first adopted in Edinburgh, Scotland, as an advertising campaign (with a "Z" logo) to send a message about ending violence against women and children. Nonetheless, it is now widely accepted and adopted throughout the United Kingdom as a policing strategy and is part of the punitive law-and-order rhetoric or, as Brown states, zero tolerance has become "a cultural and rhetorical device of popular authoritarianism" (2005, p. 223). Henry Giroux (2002) sees such policies, including curfews, as an "easy excuse" for punishing children rather than finding ways to work with them and address issues relating to their social, psychological, and economic well-being. It is yet another way of involving the police in criminalizing youth for minor infractions. It is a policy of intolerance (Giroux, 2002, pp. 36–37).

In Canadian schools, zero tolerance has become a defining characteristic of school "codes of conduct" and students are suspended or expelled from school for infractions such as uttering threats, possessing weapons, possessing illegal drugs, or providing alcohol to minors. While zero tolerance is easily palatable as something that will "protect our children," it is also a repressive and potentially criminalizing policy. An eight-year-old boy in Nova Scotia, for example, was suspended for pointing a breaded chicken finger (weapons threat?) at a classmate while saying, "Bang." He reportedly "already had a record" of being suspended for pointing his finger at another student and saying, "Bang" (Grade 2 boy . . . , 2001). Apparently, he is not alone, as an Arkansas boy was also suspended for a similar offence of chicken-finger pointing, except he said, "Pow, pow, pow" (Doob & Cesaroni, 2004, p. 108).

Yet, beyond a few particularly violent events, there is little evidence of an increase in serious violence in schools or of Canadian students feeling more fearful or less safe in schools (Doob & Cesaroni, 2004, pp. 103–108). This is not to say that all children in Canadian schools feel safe. While the numbers may be small, some children do report engaging in more aggressive behaviours than other children. Some of these students feel unfairly treated by teachers, are bullied by other students, or are made to feel like outsiders (Sprott, Doob, & Jenkins, 2001, p. 9). What we should have learned from the incidents of extreme violence in suburban schools is that suspending such students is not a productive response.

As a final comment on policing youth behaviour, a few points about curfews are worthy of note. First, curfews are usually implemented in smaller towns and cities; 15 communities in New Brunswick have them, for example. Curfews are viewed as too difficult to enforce in larger cities, as explained by Toronto's bylaw coordinator (*CBC News Online,* August 19, 2004) and, even though some police forces would like to have curfews and see them as useful "enforcement vehicles," they worry that "imposing time limits on teens could be considered age discrimination" (*CBS News*, March 29, 2005). Indeed, there have been constitutional challenges in the United States (Fried, 2001).

It is also worth noting that in spite of public opinion and police reports that curfews "work," research evaluations of curfews indicate that they do not reduce youth crime levels or youth victimization (Fried, 2001; Lersch & Sellers, 2000), that they may work to reduce only specific offences such as burglary and simple assault, and that any preventive effects are small (McDowall, Loftin, & Wiersema, 1999).

There are less punitive and more creative, positive, and non-punitive ways of addressing school problems. At Joe Duquette High School in Saskatoon, students involved in bullying or violence have a choice: to apologize and convince the victimized student that he or she has nothing to fear in the future or to leave the school. Students are able to return when they are ready to accept the school's standards. It is a policy of choice and respect, rather than censure and punishment (Schissel, 1997, pp. 123–124).

A school in Calgary addresses vandalism problems through a creative use of music. The idea was to make spaces that were most at risk of being vandalized less attractive to potential vandals by piping in "obscure operas, operettas, and classical music." As the school board director explains, "We're making an atmosphere less conducive to people who wouldn't normally enjoy this type of music" (Different note, 1996). The school board reports that this technique has been highly successful in reducing vandalism and that it is an inexpensive solution to a costly problem.

PEERS: FRIENDS AND GANGS

Friends

Empirically, it has been established that the single most important predictor of "official" delinquency is delinquent friends, that peer group experiences are predictors of the seriousness of delinquency (Morash, 1986), and that youth crime is more a function of "companions" than of group behaviour such as gangs (Regoli & Hewitt, 1994, p. 277). The NLSCY data also support these "facts." In 1996, one adolescent in seven reported belonging to a group that did "risky things" and these children were four times more likely to have been in a "fight," seven times more likely to skip school, and nine times more likely to have stolen something (see Figure 7.2) (Statistics Canada, 2001, pp. 12–14).

In considering both family and peer influences on delinquent behaviour, Warr (1993) in his analysis of data from the U.S. *National Youth Survey* concluded that while the amount of time spent with family can reduce and even eliminate peer influences on delinquency, attachment to parents, measured as affective ties between parents and children, has no such direct effect. Instead, attachment to parents affects delinquency indirectly by inhibiting the initial formation of delinquent friendships (p. 247).

Explanations of the relationship between peer relations and youth crime come from variations of Sutherland's theory of differential association and its variations, such as social learning theory (Akers, 1985). Here it is argued that criminal behaviour is learned through group affiliations, such as delinquent friends, that reinforce nonconforming behaviour.

Brownfield and Thompson (1991) add elements of Hirschi's control theory to this argument and ask how attachment to friends affects an individual's involvement in

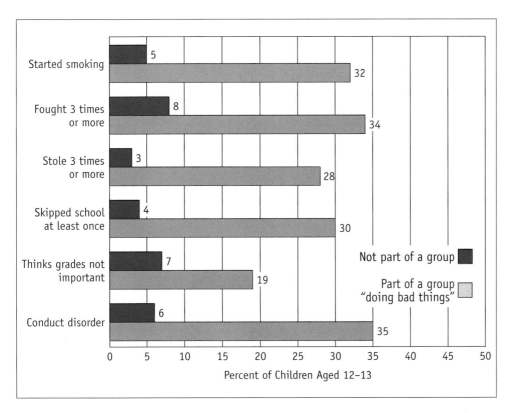

Sources: Statistics Canada, *National Longitudinal Survey of Children and Youth* (1996), Cycle 2, Children and Youth in Canada; Statistics Canada, Cat. No. 85-F0033MIE (2001), p. 14.

FIGURE 7.2

Peer Influence on Risk-Taking Behaviour

criminal behaviour. Based on an analysis of self-reported delinquency data from the *Seattle Youth Study* of male youth, they found support for both social learning and social control theories. Although the strongest relationship was between peer association and self-reported delinquency, "trust in friends and respect for friends [was] negatively associated with self-reported delinquency" (Brownfield & Thompson, 1991, p. 57). In other words, boys who trust and respect their friends are less likely to be involved in crime and delinquency; stated conversely, boys engaged in crime and delinquency are less likely than non-delinquents to trust or respect their friends.

Prior to the late 1980s, when the feminist critique began to exert some influence, no one seemed to notice that the bulk of our theorizing and empirical knowledge was based on boys, that youth criminology boiled down to "youth crime equals male offender." Once academics started to move beyond the "boy zone" (Brown, 2005, p. 142), they discovered that what we thought we knew did not necessarily apply to girls. As the "facts" of girl crime began to be investigated (the gender ratio problem discussed in the last chapter), two conclusions emerged—that boys and girls are **"differentially exposed"** to criminogenic conditions and/or that they are **"differentially affected"** by them.

We find support for both hypotheses. As discussed earlier in this chapter, Fitzgerald (2003) found in her analysis of NLSCY data that girls are affected differently by family violence than are boys, while Morash (1986) found support for differential exposure. Morash interviewed a sample of youth in two Boston communities about their criminal

differentially exposed
Refers to the idea that there is a gender gap in youth crime rates because girls and boys have different exposure to criminogenic conditions.

differentially affected
Refers to the idea that there is a gender gap in youth crime rates because boys and girls are affected differently by criminogenic conditions.

activity and found that gender effects on crime operate through types of friends. Quite simply, she argues that one reason for lower rates of self-reported crime among girls is that their friends are less likely to be delinquent than are the friends of boys.

Sutherland's theory of differential association is a differentially exposed hypothesis, and Mears, Ploeger, and Warr (1998) tested this against Gilligan's theory of moral development, a differentially affected hypothesis. They found, like Morash, that boys are significantly more likely to have delinquent friends than girls (differential exposure), but that this exposure to delinquent peers was more mitigated by moral evaluations for girls than for boys. They argue that "the moral judgements of girls are apparently sufficient to reduce and even eliminate the impact of delinquent peers" (p. 9).

Moving beyond the "boy zone" of traditional theorizing about youth crime also made us aware that our theories and knowledge might not necessarily apply to other male youth populations, such as the children of ethnic minority immigrants. While a considerable amount of attention has been addressed to African American youth in the United States, little attention has been directed toward other groups of youth populations; the same is particularly true of youth criminology in Canada, with the exception of youth of Asian descent. Research on Asian youth has consistently shown lower rates of delinquency compared to Caucasian youth and youth from other ethnic groups in North America (see for example, Bachman et al., 1991). Low rates of delinquency among Chinese, Indian, and Japanese American youth have largely been attributed to cultural differences in parenting practices. Wong (1999) tested this cultural hypothesis against differential association and control theory explanations for the effect of peers on delinquent behaviour with a sample of Chinese Canadian youth in Winnipeg. His results support the cultural hypothesis as well as differential association and control theories.

While finding that rates of delinquency are lower among youth who adhere to Chinese culture than Chinese youth who have acculturated to North American society, the effect of peers was the same for both groups. Similar to Brownfield and Thompson's findings (1991), Wong found that association with delinquent peers increased delinquent activity but attachment to peers reduced delinquency, regardless of peer involvement in delinquency. Contrary to the cultural hypothesis, Chinese youth who associate with Chinese peers are not entirely deterred from delinquent activities, so it cannot be argued that the demise of traditional values and the effect of acculturation to North American values explains the delinquent activities of Chinese Canadian youth. Wong suggests that because his findings challenge the notion of the Chinese as a "model minority," the delinquent activities of Chinese Canadian youth, like those of other ethnic minority groups, need to be understood in terms of the demands put on these youth by "different and sometimes conflicting cultures" (1999, pp. 5–6).

Gangs

As with most youth crime information, a majority of people get their information about gangs from the news media, and most media information on gangs comes from the police. Some critics have argued that defining gangs is a political activity that reflects the interests and agendas of law enforcement, politicians, and the media (Conly, 1993; Spergel & Curry, 1991). As discussed in Chapter 1, Zatz (1987) connects the discovery of a gang problem in Phoenix with "the acquisition of federal funds to create and maintain a gang squad within the Phoenix police department" (p. 153).

Importantly, research in the United States has documented that the identification of young people as gang members has a negative impact on their processing through the justice system (Chambliss, 1973; Morash, 1983; Pearson, 1983; Werthman & Piliavin, 1967; Zatz, 1985). Indeed, gang activity has been identified as an "emerging priority" in Canada, and beginning in 2005, the incident-based *Uniform Crime Reporting* police statistics began collecting information on organized crime activity and street gang activity. Within the next couple of years, we should expect to find increased news reporting of gang activity based on these official statistics, as well as an increase in analyses of gang activity in Canada. With increased police and media focus on gang activities in Canadian cities, it becomes increasingly important to understand gang definitions and how gang status is attributed to individuals.

Definitions and Measurement

As we know from Hollywood Western movies, the term "gangs" used to refer to desperadoes, adult outlaws who spread havoc and violence throughout the American West. After the turn of the century, gangs began to be associated with inner cities in the United States. In his book *The Gang: A Study of 1,313 Gangs in Chicago*, Frederic Thrasher (1927) focused on youth groups, presenting them as localized and organized by territory. Walter Miller's definition of gangs (1980) is closer to police and public conceptions of gangs:

> A youth gang is a self forming association of peers, bound together by mutual interests, with identifiable leadership, well developed lines of authority, and other organizational features, who act in concert to achieve a specific purpose or purposes which generally include the conduct of illegal activity and control over a particular territory, facility, or type of enterprise. (p. 121)

Studies of gangs in Canada are rare, compared to the number done in the United States. Rogers (1945) studied street gangs in Toronto in the 1940s, but little research was done after that until Joe and Robinson (1980) looked at immigrant gangs in Vancouver's Chinatown in the 1970s and found that they were short-lived and not highly organized. Most of the gangs they studied were no longer in existence within five years. Gangs are not new to Canadian cities, however. Young's historical analysis of gangs in Vancouver (1993) showed intermittent periods of heightened activity. During the late 1920s, there were what newspapers referred to as "corner lounger gangs." The late 1940s and 1950s were the period of "zoot suit" and "hoodlum" gangs. The late 1960s and early 1970s were dominated by "park" gangs.

Ruth Horowitz (1990) challenged early definitions of gangs by pointing out that research on youth gangs indicates that not all such gangs are involved in illegal activities; moreover, only some gangs claim a territory, and not all are highly organized with identifiable leadership. Research on U.S. gangs from the 1960s through the 1980s indicated that gang members are more likely to wile away their time than spend it engaging in criminal activities (Hagedorn, 1988; Klein, 1971).

On the question of gang cohesiveness and commitment, gang members observed by Klein (1971) were "dissatisfied, deprived, and making the best of an essentially unhappy situation" (p. 91), and organization and leadership has been found to vary by gang. As early as 1959, Yablonsky (1959) suggested that most gangs would be better conceptualized as "near groups." Near groups have ill-defined membership, limited cohesion, minimal consensus regarding norms and rules, and vague leadership. Matthews' work with youth gangs in Toronto (1993) suggests that "gang/group" is a more accurate term to describe youth groups and that they should be viewed along a continuum of friends who spend time together and occasionally get involved in criminal activity, on the one end, to organized criminal groups on the other.

Based on studies of gang members serving terms in British Columbian prisons, Gordon (1995) offered a method of categorizing gangs and gang activities in Vancouver. According to Gordon, five different groups have frequently been referred to as gangs: youth movements, youth groups, criminal groups, criminal business organizations, and street gangs. The term *youth movements* refer to distinctive modes of dress and activities that serve to set one group of young people apart from another; examples could be the 1950s' "zoot suiters," the 1960s' "mods and rockers," the 1970s' "hippies," and the 1980s' "punk rockers." *Youth groups* are "small clusters of friends" who hang out together in public places. *Criminal groups* are groups of friends who are together specifically for the purpose of committing a crime and who may consist of young people, adults, or a combination of the two. A *criminal business organization*, by contrast, is a "consortium of adults who . . . engage in crime for profit" (Gordon, 1995, p. 313).

All of these groups are different from *street gangs*, which Gordon (1995) defines as "groups of young people and young adults who have banded together to form semi-structured organizations, the primary purpose of which is profitable criminal activity" (p. 313). Street gangs differ from youth groups and criminal groups in that members identify themselves as a gang, adopt a name for themselves, and wear distinctive clothing or tattoos.

Inconsistencies in defining gangs contribute to difficulties and inconsistencies in determining what behaviours constitute gang activity and the levels of that activity. Maxon and Klein's analysis of police departments' definitions of gang activity in Los Angeles and Chicago (1990) points to considerable variation in definitions and attributions. What is considered gang violence in Los Angeles would not be considered as such in Chicago. Chicago police require a gang-related motive before they will consider an incident to be gang activity, whereas both the Los Angeles Sheriff's Department and Police Department require only that victims or accused are known to be gang members.

Other research comparing the self-reported activities of male gang and non-gang member youth in major American cities found that while gang members reported more criminal activities overall, their activities more often involved non-violent offences. Non-gang youth were more involved in assaults (major and minor), robberies, and extortion (Fagan, 1991). Chesney-Lind et al. (1994) found similar results in Hawaii, except that they were comparing youth who were identified by police as gang members with youth not so identified. The two groups of youth were no different in the severity or frequency of their self-reported offences. Where they did differ was in racial composition. Where Filipino and Samoan males were most commonly labelled by police as gang members and were least likely to identify themselves as such (9 percent), most of the self-reported gang members were Hawaiian/part-Hawaiian (42 percent) and were least likely to be identified by police as such (Chesney-Lind et al., 1994, p. 201).

Interestingly, as with research in the United States, Gordon (2001) reports that some Vancouver "gangs" were figments of the imagination of media and police. One group discussed in newspapers as the gang "Back Alley Boys" referred simply to a small group of young offenders who had been bullying high-school students for cash and possessions. Another group of eight youth and young adults were involved in a series of bank and store robberies over a four-month period and were referred to by police and media as the "626 gang" because they used Mazda 626 cars in their heists. Not only had this group not chosen this name, but they did not perceive themselves to be a "gang" (p. 47).

According to Gordon, active street gangs in the 1990s in Vancouver were similar to Canadian gangs in the 1950s (the Alma Dukes and the Vic Gang) and the park gangs of Vancouver in the 1970s (the Clark Park Gang and the Riley Park Gang). Like earlier gangs, these gangs were made up of males aged 14–26 who were interested in lucrative property crime and whose activities tended to involve violent offences such as assault and weapons offences. Some gangs were involved in activities related to drugs and prostitution. As with the findings in American studies, Gordon reported that street gangs tend to be short-lived. In the spring of 1991, there were about 10 street gangs in Vancouver (including the Bacada Boys, Los Diablos, Mara Latinos, and Patook); by the fall of 1993, most of these gangs had disappeared and six new gangs had formed (e.g., Los Cholos and East Van Saints). Groups disband for a number of reasons, including arrests, convictions, and simply loss of interest.

Explaining Gang Membership

Based on interviews with gang members in British Columbia prisons, Gordon (1995, 2001) found that psychological and interpersonal reasons were offered by most for involvement in youth gangs. On the psychological side are "pull" factors, such as the opportunity for material rewards (money, cars, etc.) not readily available through conventional means, and psychological rewards stemming from friendship networks, such as relief of boredom and a sense of independence and autonomy from the adult world. Factors that "push" youth toward gangs involve negative school experiences, such as truancy, fighting, and academic failure, and extremely problematic home lives characterized by drug and alcohol abuse and physical and sexual abuse. Gordon maintains that for many, gang membership was a "haven" in an otherwise "heartless world." Fewer of those interviewed (one-third) offered relief from boredom, a desire for money, and association with friends as their reasons for belonging to a gang.

Theorizing about male crime focuses on masculinities and differences among men in terms of their access to power and resources (Connell, 1987; Messerschmidt, 1986) applies particularly well to many youth gangs. According to these theories, young men create different cultural ideas of dominance, control, and independence—*hegemonic masculinity*—based on their class and race position in the social structure. Young minority males in economically impoverished communities choose public and private displays of aggressive masculinity (intimidation and gang violence) as a source of status and respect because they are "typically denied masculine status in the educational and occupational spheres" (Messerschmidt, 1993, p. 112).

Katz (1988) referred to the public aggressiveness of these males as "street elite posturing," while Connell (1987) called it "doing gender." Horowitz (1987), who studied a Chicano community in Chicago, suggested that in such communities, gang violence is understood and "articulated within the cultural framework of honor" (p. 437). "Doing gender" and masculinity is clearly evident in the Box 7.3 excerpts taken from Mark Totten's interviews with young Canadian male gang members (2000).

VOICES BOX 7.3

Gang Members' Thoughts on . . .

Race

Marty: At the time, it was a high. A power high. It was a feeling of being king shit—no one could touch you. It was like niggers were to blame for everything and we made them pay for everything. They were the reason we had no money, no jobs, no decent place to live. Being part of the gang [white supremacist] gave us a sense of belonging. We felt like we were accepted and someone cared for us. They told us we had an important job to do. We felt important—because we were white—because we were guys.

Dave: Yeah. I would say I'm supposed to be superior. But you know this male superiority thing is a pretty hard thing to do if you're a fucking unemployed Indian on welfare. Am I superior? I don't think so. Am I gonna let her know it? I don't think so. So what do I do? I guess you could say it's like putting on hockey equipment. Then nobody can see how scared shitless you are. It's like I have hockey pads I put on everyday before I see her and I never can let her see beneath my pads. She'd laugh at the real me. Scared shitless and feeling totally worthless. It's weird how treating a girl like that makes you feel better.

Girlfriends

Steve: One time at school I slammed her against a locker. I choked her until she was red. She was making me look stupid with lies and shit. I got sent to the pickle room. I was talked to by the psychiatrist. I almost got suspended. The principal is an asshole. Last year I shoved a girl into a snow bank. There was a big block of ice in it. I rammed her in. I wanted to hurt her . . . Yeah. I've got nothing to hide. Who'd believe it? Locked in a fucking pickle room for just giving my ex what she wanted. I told you that she's weird. She always was wanting me to hit her. It was nothin'. I never even laid a hand on her [long silence].

Steve: It's all about knowing your place in society. Some girls do, but most girls don't know what they're supposed to do. It really pisses me off when I see a girl who pretends that she doesn't have to be in her place. I feel like I have to teach her a lesson. How the fuck are girls ever gonna know that their job is to take care of shit at home—cooking, cleaning, the kids—if we don't tell them? I mean, it's me who's supposed to be making the big bucks to support my family. Where the fuck do girls get off thinking that they can do it too? . . . I've never agreed with hitting a girl and I never will. I think I treat girls really well. In fact, I think I'm doing them a favour. They're gonna find out sooner or later that they can't fuck around with a guy . . . I mean, can you imagine if guys didn't do that—I mean, making sure that women do what they're supposed to be doing instead of fucking around? What a fucked-up world it would be. No, guys need to remind girls that they should be doing what they're supposed to be doing. I mean, all this equal rights bullshit! Women have all the equality they need. The bottom line is that men are more important—we do the necessary things—working, bringing the bacon home, protecting our families—and if a woman's not going to respect that, then fuck her. A guy's gotta take that responsibility and tell'er not to fuck around.

Family and Peers

Carl: Lots of assaults, B and Es, auto theft and shit. And tons of drugs. Hash, all the chemicals. We're always high. And sometimes we just hang out. What the fuck do you want? It's my family. I got nothin' else. It's like I'm divorced from those fuckers who said they were my parents. Now I've got no parents and lots of brothers. It's great. No ass-hole parents to beat you all the time. So yeah. Gang is family . . .

John: What home? I've got nothin'. The old gang was my home. I'm looking for a new one now. I think the new gang will be it . . . Yeah. I've got no other family. I mean I do but they're not my family. Too much violence and shit. Too heavy for me. It's a lot better this way. No one to tell you what the fuck to do.

Paul: Well, I see my Mom occasionally. No one else. They all fucked me too bad. I mean, a guy can only get hurt so much and then he moves on . . . You could say I've been adopted by a bunch of queens [laughing] . . .

Source: Totten (2000).

Girls and Gangs

Once again we find that girls have been absent in the research and theorizing about youth gangs. Nonetheless, the North American media have implanted the notion that "girl gangs" are a growing phenomenon and that their activities are as violent as those of male youth gangs. We are told that not only is bullying pervasive but also that it is a major problem now because even girls are involved. CTV News, for example, reported that "swarming girl gangs" are a "growing criminal problem" in Winnipeg (December, 2004). And in keeping with the spirit of the liberation hypothesis, a police detective, said to be an expert on youth crime, was quoted in *The Globe and Mail* on girl gangs and violence: "We shouldn't be surprised by what's happening . . . what we're looking at is ladies coming of age in the 1990s, and girls are taking on a much more aggressive, violent role" (Vincent, 1998). In response to notions of liberation, Kathleen Daly (1997, p. 37) draws on masculinity/gender theory and asks a very thought-provoking question about girls acting "like boys":

> Would the claim that crime is a "resource for doing femininity"—or [for] women
> and girls "to create differences from men and boys or to separate from all that is
> masculine"—have any cultural resonance? Probably not.

Not surprisingly, most early gang research is **androcentric** in that terms such as "gangs" are presented as gender-neutral (androgynous), when in fact the research being discussed has been based on all-male samples. The resultant knowledge is about male gangs and behaviour but is presented in a so-called generic manner—gangs. In addition, gang activity on the part of male youth is presented as a "normal" response to their "abnormal" circumstances. On the other hand, girl gang members

> . . . typically are portrayed as maladjusted tomboys or sexual chattel, who in either
> case, are no more than mere appendages to boy members of the gang. Collectively
> they are perceived as an "auxiliary" or "satellite" of the boy's group, and their partici-
> pation in delinquent activities (e.g., carrying weapons) is explained in relation to the
> boys. (Joe & Chesney-Lind, 1993, p. 8)

androcentric
Refers to seemingly gender-neutral ideas, concepts, or theories that are actually male-centred.

A few studies go beyond such stereotypical notions of girls (see, for example, Campbell, 1984, 1990; Fishman, 1988; Harris, 1988; Lauderback, Hansen, & Waldorf, 1992; Miller & White, 2004; Moore, 1991; Quicker, 1983). These studies indicate that (1) girls often form gangs after being abandoned by their children's fathers and/or after living in abusive and controlling relationships with boyfriends, partners, or parents/guardians; (2) while girl gang members are disproportionately from dysfunctional families, the strongest predictive variable among this group was having a girlfriend, boyfriend, or sibling in a gang; (3) gang membership provides a source of support for girls, sometimes financial, but mostly familial and emotional; and (4) many girl gangs are attached to male gangs or are mixed male/female (male-dominated), but just as many girl gangs engage in independent activity. Joe and Chesney-Lind (1993), who interviewed 48 self-identified gang members in Honolulu, identified four common themes that cross gender and ethnic lines:

1. *Gangs provide a social outlet.* Girls like to dance and sing, boys like to cruise in cars; both like to drink and fight, but boys more so than girls.
2. *Gangs serve as an alternative family.* Both boys and girls use the gang as a replacement for deceased or absent parents.
3. *Gangs help members to deal with family problems and family violence.* Both boys and girls experienced physical abuse at home, but for different reasons—the girls for being away from home too much or too late, the boys for their crimes and delinquencies.
4. *Gang activities compensate for impoverished community life.* Both boys and girls use the gangs to escape the "boredom" of their impoverished lives.

Joe and Chesney-Lind (1993) argue that in order to understand girls' participation in gangs, we must place that participation

> . . . within the context of the lives of girls, particularly young women of color, on the economic and political margins. Girl gang life is certainly not an expression of "liberation," but instead reflects the attempts of young women to cope with a bleak and harsh present as well as a dismal future. One fifteen year old Samoan girl captured this sense of despair, when in response to our question about whether she was doing well in school she said, "No, I wish I was, I need a future. [My life] is jammed up." (p. 35)

And this takes us back to the question raised by Daly, because a central issue when attempting to explain girls' delinquent, criminal, or gang activity is whether we should be engaging in a "search for equivalence" with boys (Worrall, 2002). Where Daly answers, "No," Christine Alder and Anne Worrall (Worrall, 2004) offer a "tentative Yes" (p. 11). They argue that we should not be interpreting girls' behaviour as attempts to be "more like boys" but need to recognize that girls, as youth, have limited resources that are further limited by their social position as "adolescent feminine." In this position, girls have a choice of academic achievement or "domestic docility"—good girls who do well in school and/or help out in the home.

Whenever girls step outside this "place," they are defined, as we see in the media and public discourse, as being a threat and as being violent. These are the girls who are choosing alternative ways of being girls. They are occupying public spaces, street corners, neighbourhood parks, and shopping malls, but not for shopping. They give priority to female relationships and loyalty to female friends, rather than to boys and domestic pursuits. Put in the context of the fact that more girls are behaving aggressively than even 20 years ago, they are perceived in public discourse as "behaving like boys."

Alder and Worrall maintain that since there is no societal tolerance or latitude for girls' resistance against "being girls," their alternative behaviours are constructed in terms of "crime," "disorder," and "violence" (Worrall, 2004, p. 11). Hence, alternative girl behaviour, whether delinquent, violent, or gang-related, should be viewed as girls' efforts to claim (or reclaim) whatever limited resources are available to them (their youth, their energy, their sexuality, their peers, their mobility relative to children, etc.) as a demonstration of their "difference" from boys—they are "girls being girls."

SUMMARY

The family, school, friends, and peers have consistently been identified by theorists and in public discourse as sources of youth crime and delinquency. This chapter reviews the recent history of public concerns, the trends in research, the state of empirical knowledge, and the latest public issues revolving around youth crime and the family, school, friends, and peers.

Control theory has generated a considerable volume of research on the effect of family structure and family dynamics in "producing" delinquency. Family structure, measured as a "broken home" or a home with a working mother, has consistently been identified empirically as a factor in delinquency. However, the evidence suggests that parenting styles, the quality of family relationships, and internal family dynamics are far more important factors than family structure. According to power-control theory, differences in degree of delinquency, and between boys' and girls' delinquency, are based on whether families are structured as egalitarian or patriarchal. Tests of interactional theory have shown that low parental attachment increases delinquency, which in turn worsens attachments to parents. However, as adolescents age, parental influences diminish; delinquency lessens parental attachments, not vice versa.

Public discourse and moral panics blame parents as well as children for the problem of youth crime. A new ingredient in the public blame game is "parent abuse," yet child victimization at the hands of parents is not a public issue. Most family research focusing on parental attachments has ignored child and youth victimization and continues to define the problem as one of lack of attachments. The blame game and its components are indicative of a colonial way of thinking about the status of children and youth relative to parents, and our Western culture continues to promote a punitive disciplinary model of parenting roles and responsibilities.

School research has tended to focus on Cohen's and Hirschi's theories, with most attention still devoted today to levels of school commitment and delinquency. Research has demonstrated that grades and low commitment to school are better predictors of delinquency than IQ scores. However, while low commitment leads to delinquency, delinquency also reduces commitment to school. The organization of schools and classrooms and the class structure of Canadian society are also seen as a source of delinquency. Contrary to Cohen's suggestion that a middle-class school system creates status frustration for working-class boys (1955), research has shown that middle-class boys with poor grades are more likely to behave in delinquent ways and to rebel against schooling. School resistance on the part of black students is a consequence of a conflict between schools' cultural assumptions and rules and these students' own cultural backgrounds and experiences. Classroom climates have a greater impact on delinquency than do the management styles of the school.

While schooling used to be viewed as part of the solution to youth crime issues, by the 1990s it became viewed as part of the problem. Violence in schools, based on isolated, atypical, and extreme incidents of school shootings, became a defining symbol of "youth gone mad." Bullying, along with other forms of serious school violence, is a largely white, middle-class, suburban "problem." Boys and girls are not very different in their use of indirect relational aggression against their peers. Schools have responded to youth violence with repressive and potentially criminalizing policies such as "zero tolerance," rather than restructuring and refocusing priorities on the well-being of children and youth.

The single most important predictor of "official" delinquency is having delinquent friends. Research findings indicate that boys and girls are both "differentially exposed" to and "differentially affected" by criminogenic conditions. Both the cultural hypothesis as well as differential association and control theories may explain delinquency among youth from different ethnic backgrounds.

Information on gangs varies depending on how "gang" is defined and how gang activity is measured. Definitions of both are politically motivated and reflect the interests of researchers and the agendas of law-enforcement agencies, politicians, and the media. Research on youth gangs indicates that not all such gangs are involved in illegal activities, that members do not spend much time on criminal activities, that their activities tend to be no more severe or frequent than those of non-gang youth, that only some gangs claim a territory, and that not all gangs are highly organized with identifiable leadership.

Research indicates that street gangs in Canada today are not much different from those in the 1970s. Canadian street gangs tend to be short-lived and composed of males aged 14–26 who are primarily interested in lucrative property crime. Boys and girls seem to join gangs for the same reasons: gang membership provides a social outlet, escape from an abusive or neglectful family life, and compensation for an impoverished community life. In contrast to the liberation hypothesis, some scholars argue that a "search for equivalencies" is not a useful way of understanding girls' behaviours. Rather their behaviours should be understood as "girls being girls," as acts of resistance to claim or reclaim femininity from the grasp of domesticity.

DISCUSSION/CRITICAL THINKING QUESTIONS

1. How do the vestiges of colonialism affect our thinking about children's rights?
2. Is it justifiable to suspend a child from school for threatening someone with a breaded chicken finger? Why or why not?
3. In what ways is "girls being girls" the same as, or different from, "boys being boys"? Why is it important to recognize the difference between the two?

WEB LINKS

Canadian Incidence Study of Reported Child Abuse and Neglect: Final Report
http://dsp-psd.pwgsc.gc.ca/Collection/H49-151-2000E.pdf

Developmental trajectories of boys' delinquent group membership and facilitation of violent behaviors during adolescence
www.socio.umontreal.ca/personnel/documents/Lacourseetal.
delinquentgroup2003.pdf

The Causes of Delinquency
http://nmsc.state.nm.us/download/wp/wpn31.pdf

For chapter quizzes and more links, visit this book's accompanying website at
www.bellyoungoffenders3e.nelson.com

CHAPTER EIGHT

First Contact: Police and Diversionary Measures

CHAPTER OBJECTIVES

1. To examine the initial stages of youth involvement in the youth justice system.
2. To detail factors and issues associated with police discretion in decision making.
3. To outline principles and rules regarding diversion and extrajudicial measures and sanctions under the Youth Criminal Justice Act (YCJA) and discuss how these compare to diversion under the Young Offenders Act (YOA).
4. To examine provincial differences in the administration of diversionary measures and in types of programs.
5. To identify and discuss issues associated with diversionary programs.

KEY TERMS

Diversion

Discretion

Surveillance

Extralegal factors

High-risk youth

Stigmatization

Alternative measures

Principle of least
    possible interference

Extrajudicial measures

Extrajudicial sanctions

Reconciliation

Mediation

Restitution

Net widening

INTRODUCTION

In this chapter and in the next two chapters, we discuss the various stages of the youth justice system, focusing particular attention on how the stages are organized, how decisions are made, and which factors affect decision making at each stage. A youth's involvement with the justice system begins with a police investigation to determine whether or not an offence has taken place. The police or the Crown have the option in most provinces to divert youth from the courts through extrajudicial measures provisions in the YCJA, a practice dating back to the Juvenile Delinquents Act (JDA) era that was formalized through alternative measures provisions under the YOA.

These diversionary provisions became even more formalized with the YCJA. While the YOA provided for diversionary programs and regulations around their use, the YCJA also encourages police to consider issuing a warning for first-time offenders involved in non-violent offences. This has created an additional level to diversion. As a result of these diversionary provisions, if a youth successfully completes an extrajudicial measures program, his or her involvement with the justice system ends. While there are a number of justifications and benefits to **diversion** for both the young offender and the justice system, the concept and the practice are criticized by some. This chapter discusses the structure and process of diversion, beginning with police contact, as well as current issues.

diversion
A practice based on a philosophy that justice, rehabilitation, and reintegration are better served by keeping most people out of the formal justice system.

CASE STUDY BOX 8.1

Johnny: Police Interaction and Diversion

According to Sergeant John Langille, an RCMP officer and head of the auto-theft unit in the Halifax–Dartmouth area, Johnny went on a "rampage" in the spring of 2004, allegedly "racking up" dozens of motor vehicle-related charges. He had been arrested six times in the months of May and June, so the police officers in the area were quite familiar with him. Johnny had also been referred by the police to a restorative justice program after stealing a car. He was expected to complete 60 hours of community clean-up work and attend seven weekly anger-management sessions, but he dropped out of the program after attending two of the therapy sessions.

Police Accountability

While the police pursuit that took place on the day of the accident in which Theresa McEvoy was killed was not a priority in the Nunn inquiry, there was some discussion surrounding police accountability during the inquiry. Johnny's lawyer, Warren Zimmer, told the court that he believed the police were in the wrong to begin a pursuit of a stolen vehicle in a quiet, residential neighbourhood. According to the two police officers involved in the chase, the pursuit did not fall under the definition of "high-speed," as the vehicles were not travelling more than 20 kilometres over the posted speed limit. In addition, the officers claimed that the police had ceased the pursuit before the actual crash occurred. Other testimony revealed that the police had stopped chasing Johnny a mere 17 seconds before the crash.

At the time of the accident, Johnny was facing 24 charges for incidents in the Halifax–Dartmouth area. Just two days before the accident, he had been released from custody by a Windsor, Nova Scotia, court on charges resulting from an earlier high-speed pursuit, even though a justice of the peace in Dartmouth had issued

(continued)

Box 8.1 continued

a warrant for his arrest. After obtaining a copy of the warrant, the Halifax RCMP claimed that a package was put together, including the arrest warrant, a copy of the outstanding charges, a copy of the new Windsor charges, and a document recommending that he be remanded for a bail hearing on these charges. The Halifax RCMP claimed that an attempt was made to fax these papers to the Windsor court before Johnny was to appear there, but the fax machine at the Windsor court was apparently broken. Johnny's defence lawyer argued, "There is no reason why, when you get a document in your hands and you realize it's important for the court to have, to say I couldn't fax it through!"

Constable Harvey O'Toole claimed that Johnny was arraigned by telephone and, apparently, most of the information concerning Johnny's outstanding charges in Halifax–Dartmouth had been transmitted to the Windsor RCMP detachment. Corporal Mary Jo DeLuco of the Windsor RCMP detachment argued that she assumed that the Halifax Regional Police would be at the Windsor court to execute the arrest warrant before Johnny left the courthouse, and also that there would be a transfer order in court that day, authorizing Johnny's return to Halifax for a bail hearing on his charges in Halifax. Corporal DeLuco contended that the Windsor detachment was never asked by the Halifax police to execute the warrant.

Source: *The Chronicle Herald* [Halifax] (January 17, 18, 26, 30; February 1, 2006).
Researched and written by Nicole Landry.

POLICE CONTACT AND DECISION MAKING

A young person's involvement in the justice system may begin with police contact in a public setting or with a complaint laid by parents, school authorities, or someone who has been victimized. A majority of youth crime comes to police attention through complaints (Carrington & Schulenberg, 2005, p. 157). Police have a considerable amount of **discretion** in making decisions about how to proceed with suspicious or accused youth. The YCJA requires a police officer to consider if warning or cautioning a youth is sufficient (see Box 8.2), but section 6(2) of the act clearly suggests that it is not a violation of youths' legal rights if the police fail to do so. Sections 7 and 8 allow provinces to formalize these warnings and cautions. Nova Scotia, for example, has a formal letter that is issued to all youth so warned by police. Therefore, an individual officer has the power, freedom, and autonomy to choose from a number of courses of action including:

discretion
The decision-making power that police and other criminal justice personnel (e.g., judges and Crown prosecutors) have to make decisions with minimal legal requirements.

1. issuing a warning (formal or informal) to the young offender about his or her behaviour and then letting the person go;
2. taking the young person home for a talk with parents or guardians;
3. arresting and holding the youth in police custody (parents/guardians must be notified);
4. taking the young person to the police station for questioning before releasing her or him;
5. writing up a report on the young person before release;
6. charging the young person with an offence;

BOX 8.2

YCJA Guidelines for Police

Section 6(1) of the YCJA requires police officers to consider if a warning is a sufficient response to a youth's behaviour:

> **Section 6(1)** A police officer shall, before starting judicial proceedings or taking any other measures under this Act against a young person alleged to have committed an offence, consider whether it would be sufficient, having regard to the principles set out in section 4, to take no further action, warn the young person, administer a caution, if a program has been established under section 7, or, with the consent of the young person, refer the young person to a program or agency in the community that may assist the young person not to commit offences.

> **Section 6(2)** The failure of a police officer to consider the options set out in subsection (1) does not invalidate any subsequent charges against the young person for the offence.

7. (in some provinces) referring the young person to a diversionary program or youth justice committee; or
8. holding the young person in detention (maximum 24 hours) for further judicial processing, beginning with a "bail" hearing.

Police officers can have a significant impact on young people's futures, depending on how the officers choose to exercise their discretionary power. Ontario police statistics for 1992 indicated that 26,412 young people who had not been charged with an offence were in police records; this amounted to almost one-third of the number of young people charged by police that year (Doob, Marinos, & Varma, 1995, p. 94). In 1993, informal police processing of apprehended youth ranged from one-half to less than 20 percent, depending on jurisdiction (Report on the Federal–Provincial–Territorial Task Force on Youth Justice, 1996).

Canadian and British studies of policing indicate that police **surveillance** of youth is disproportionately high compared to surveillance of adults. This discrepancy does not necessarily translate into high rates of criminalization. Rather, most criminal cases involving young offenders are handled informally (Ericson & Haggerty, 1997; Loader, 1996; Meehan, 1993). Nonetheless, the YOA did result in dramatic increases in the formal charging of young offenders (Schissel, 1993, 1997), which suggests a substantial decrease in the use of discretion by police with youth.

Between 1993 and 1997, there was little change in the rate of informal case handling by the police, and then the rate declined until 2000. Since then, the rate of youth cleared by police without the laying of a charge has also been declining. The Department of Justice (2005) reports that the YCJA has resulted in increased use of diversionary measures by police since its introduction, and *Uniform Crime Reporting* (UCR) statistics from the first two years of the YCJA (2003 and 2004) suggest that sections 6 through 8 have had an impact on police charging practices and on the numbers of cases going before the courts. The rate of youth charged by police decreased by 16 percent in 2003, the most significant decrease since 1977. For the same year, the rate of youth cleared by means other than police laying a charge increased by 30 percent, a rate considerably higher than the decrease in charge rates. It dropped again in 2004, but by only 4 percent (Sauve, 2005, p. 1; Wallace, 2004, pp. 1, 14). The youth

surveillance
Mechanisms and processes by which the state keeps track of people and monitors their behaviour.

court caseload dropped by 17 percent in the first year of the YCJA, when it was one-third (33 percent) lower than it was in the early 1990s (Thomas, 2005, p. 1). Almost three-quarters (71 percent) of the informal measures reported by the police involved verbal warnings and 6 percent were referrals to a community-based program or agency. The remaining cases involved formal cautions (12 percent) and formal referrals to diversionary programs or committees (Wallace, 2004, p. 14).

This raises the question as to why some youth are charged and others are not. Research has shown that there are legal and **extralegal factors** associated with police discretion. Legal factors refer to legal requirements or to things generally considered relevant or pertinent in criminal justice matters. Extralegal factors are those that are not necessarily or usually considered legitimate or relevant in justice decision making. For example, it would be considered discriminatory or even illegal to hold someone in pretrial detention because of the colour of his or her skin; doing so because of the seriousness of the offence would not be considered as such. In this example, skin colour is an extralegal factor and offence seriousness is a legal factor.

extralegal factors
Factors affecting criminal or youth justice processing that are outside the jurisdiction of law.

Legal Factors Affecting Police Discretion

Research on police discretion, most of which until recently has been done in the United States, began more than 20 years ago. This research confirms what we might expect—that the seriousness of an offence and prior arrest records influence police decisions to lay a charge (Krisberg & Austin, 1978; Lundman, Sykes, & Clark, 1978; Piliavin & Briar, 1964). In 2002, Carrington and Schulenberg (2005, p. 164) interviewed 300 police officers from 95 police departments across Canada and found that the most important consideration in laying a charge for almost all of the officers (98 percent) was the seriousness of the offence; whether weapons were involved and the extent of harm or damage done were close seconds (88 percent).

This does not mean that police discretion is not operative in serious offences, however. Sellin and Wolfgang (1964), in an examination of Philadelphia police records, found that in cases where youth were involved in offences that led to the hospitalization or death of a victim, only about half resulted in arrests or charges. In Chapter 3, we saw that charge rates are highest for serious offences; however, for some offences, such as sexual assault, only 48 percent resulted in charges and only half of the major thefts resulted in charges. The majority of youth offences that resulted in charges were not serious ones; therefore, relying solely on the seriousness of the offence would not take us very far in understanding the factors that lead to police charging.

Another important factor affecting the use of discretion is prior police contact. Cicourel (1968) argued that simply being in contact with police was often enough to increase the probability of police charging a youth. He suggested that having police attention drawn to oneself would lead to being known by the police. This contact would be remembered, thereby increasing the chance of arrest in future encounters. Similarly, the tendency of police to arrest certain "types" of youth helps to create a police record for some youth, which in turn increases the chance of future arrest and processing through the system. Terry (1967) showed that offenders without police records made up 38 percent of police arrests and only 7 percent of court referrals. On the other hand, youth with extensive records made up 20 percent of arrests and 60 percent of referrals to court.

According to a Department of Justice report on the impact of the YCJA, police are now more likely to detain youth who have prior convictions and who have previously breached a probation order (2005). Carrington and Schulenberg (2005) found that almost all (96 percent) of the police officers they surveyed reported this to be a major factor in their decision making, and that it was one of the factors they used to determine the "seriousness" of an offence. Interestingly, they did not differentiate between a record for a criminal offence or diversionary measures (pp. 165–166).

Extralegal Factors Affecting Police Discretion

Race

While there is considerable evidence that legal factors have an effect on police charging, it is extremely difficult to separate some of these factors, particularly prior record, from extralegal factors. Recent research has shown that both legal and extralegal factors are related to race. Minority youth are more likely to be arrested by police and to have a record. This suggests that race may very well be a more important factor than a police record (Dannifer & Schutt, 1982). In other words, if police are more likely to keep records on minority youth, we should not be surprised to find that minority youth are more likely than white youth to be processed by police (Huizinga & Elliott, 1987; Smith & Visher, 1981). This idea would certainly be supported by Carrington and Schulenberg's data, which indicated that, even though police unanimously reported that race is never a factor in their decision to lay a charge, a prior record of any kind is of primary significance (2005, pp. 166, 169).

While the race differential in police processing is clear, the reasons for it are not. It is easy to conclude that police may be biased, but other factors may also be at work. Black and Reiss (1970), for example, found that whether or not a case proceeds to court has a lot to do with complainants and their wishes. Based on their finding that police complied in every case in which a complainant requested that a youth not go to court, they suggest that African American youth may have higher arrest rates because complainants are less likely to ask for leniency in their cases.

Doob and Chan (1995) found that the victim's request was an important factor in police charging in Canada, and Carrington and Schulenberg reported that more than half (56 percent) of the police in their survey reported that victim preference was an important factor in their decision to lay a charge. Others have argued that racial bias in the justice system is the most important factor in explaining differences in police arrest and charging (Dannifer & Schutt, 1982; Fagan, Slaughter, & Hartstone, 1987). One important factor that intersects with race in police decision making is demeanour.

Demeanour and Race

One factor that has consistently been found to affect the outcome of youth encounters with police is a young person's demeanour. A youth's appearance and attitude, and how that youth behaves with a police officer, will influence how the officer will use her or his discretion (Black & Reiss, 1970; Cicourel, 1968; Hohenstein, 1969; Morash, 1984; Smith & Visher, 1981; Winslow, 1973). Youth who fit a stereotypical image of delinquents—that is, who exhibit a disrespectful, uncooperative, or defiant manner—are more likely to be arrested.

The significance of demeanour depends on the seriousness of the offence (Piliavin & Briar, 1964), but also on race. According to Ferdinand and Luchterhand (1970), African American youth expect the worst from police and therefore are more likely to behave in a defiant manner. Police, in turn, see African American youth as more threatening and hostile than other youth. Canadian police seem to concur. Nearly three-quarters (71 percent) of the police surveyed by Carrington and Schulenberg (2005, pp. 166, 169) reported that a youth's demeanour is an important factor, particularly in relation to a decision to use diversionary measures.

A study of police–minority youth relations in Metropolitan Toronto and York Region illustrates and confirms the type of encounters described by Ferdinand and Luchterhand. Neugebauer-Visano's interviews with Toronto youth (1996) clearly indicated that young people, regardless of colour, believe that black youth are a focus of police harassment:

> It's like this. They hassle anybody who is young and looks out of place. With me they'll talk about me being on a joyride thing. But with blacks they call it car theft. No big deal. What sounds worse in court? Joyride is having fun. But stealing cars is breaking the law. (Georgette, white, age 18, p. 294)

> White kids are lucky. They can always pretend to be afraid of the police. Cops believe them. Cops see some bonds with them. All a white kid has to do is fake it. They can play better. My brothers and sisters can't play along. They don't know how. They're too hurt. Too suspicious of the cop. African Canadians are never trusted anytime. Even when they're innocent they're guilty. They are made to feel guilty. I'm not saying that white kids love the police or the cops like all the white kids. All I'm saying is that black kids have a hell of a time connecting with the cop. It's deep. Really deep. Cops don't get it. (Amanda, black, age 17, p. 295)

> What kind of dumb fucks do they think we are. Piss on us and then expect us to respect that shit [community policing]. Times are changing. I think that is what the cops want. They want us to declare war. They want me to be mouthy. They want something on me. Why give them an excuse to fuck you. Just be cool. Take the heat. (Manley, black, age 16, p. 300)

Citing a 1976 report on police attitudes toward visible minorities in Toronto, Neugebauer-Visano states, "In response to the police slogan 'to serve and protect,' the feeling among blacks is that the motto of some police officers may as well be 'to harass and oppress'" (1996, p. 302). Recent allegations of "racial profiling" on the part of police in major cities across the country would suggest that the situation has not changed. In Halifax, for example, there are currently two cases before the Human Rights Commission that have been launched against the Halifax Regional Police for their treatment of black youth. Both incidents occurred in the summer of 2005. In one, a Grade 12 African Canadian student maintains that he was harassed by police as he walked home from a friend's house at 2:30 A.M. The officers in one police car pulled up beside him and began questioning him, while a second police car followed him. He answered the police questions, but kept walking; within minutes, a third police car arrived and drove in front of him to cut him off. Shortly thereafter, a police van joined the procession and all four vehicles trailed him home. According to the youth, at least five police officers were at the scene. As for the interrogation, he said that the police officer:

> . . . just kept making snide remarks . . . I asked him what the problem was, I was just trying to go home. The guy told me that there were a lot of cars being stolen at that time of night. I asked him if I was in a car right now and he said, "No, not yet." (Stewart, September 27, 2005)

In the other case, a black woman maintains that her 14-year-old son was beaten by the police during an arrest. She has charged the police with racism and being violent. A neighbour who witnessed the incident states:

> I saw the cop grab [the boy], put his hands behind him and bang his head onto the step . . . they hammered him . . . they shouldn't have done that. (Arsenault, December 21, 2005)

Studies of Aboriginal youth in Canadian cities have shown similar kinds of problems. Native youth in cities tend to be located in areas where there are high levels of policing, thereby increasing their chances of arrest (Schissel, 1993). In addition, some police hold stereotypical views of Native peoples. Hylton (1981), who studied police and public attitudes toward Aboriginal youth in Regina, found a relationship between negative attitudes toward Native peoples and a fear of crime. The Aboriginal Justice Inquiry of Manitoba reports that Aboriginal youth have more charges laid against them, are more likely to be held in detention prior to court, and are more likely to be denied bail (Hamilton & Sinclair, 1991). According to Fisher and Janetti (1996):

> Aboriginal people perceive the justice system as discriminatory and culturally insensitive . . . [A]boriginal people perceive themselves to be subjects of the system, rather than informed, empowered and accepted participants in the system. When the system is perceived as fundamentally unjust, the end products are lack of trust and alienation. A justice system that may be difficult to understand and that both in appearance and reality treats aboriginal peoples differently may not offer them justice at all. (p. 247)

Carrington (1998a) examined the details of 94,221 incidents reported by police forces in seven jurisdictions for the years 1992 and 1993. He found that, when other legal and extralegal factors that are known to be related to charge rate differentials were controlled, the effect from Aboriginal status remained. In other words, charge rates were significantly higher for Aboriginal youth than for non-Aboriginal youth.

For their part, police spokespeople maintain that racial profiling is not an official or even an informal policy or practice, that most officers do not use or accept racial profiling, and that incidents that do occur are the result of individual officers acting on their own beliefs (see Box 8.3).

VOICES BOX 8.3

Racial Profiling

Ronald Melchers, a criminologist at the University of Ottawa, questioned issues about racial profiling raised by a series of articles in October 2002 in the *Toronto Star*. The series resulted in the Toronto police suing the newspaper. Melchers (2003) challenged the newspaper's use of aggregate data to conduct its analysis, arguing that spurious relationships were drawn along with a number of other methodological errors. His conclusion was:

> . . . while it is highly plausible that, once all legally relevant factors have been accounted for, differences in the treatment of groups according to race will remain, even this in and of itself may not be evidence of actual discriminatory practices, as opposed to any number of equally valid explanations of these differences. The best research can conclude in such cases is the modest statement that the possibility of discrimination cannot be excluded. In the absence of compelling evidence, to make any more ambitious statement goes against the scientific ethic.

Meanwhile, heavyweight boxer Kirk Johnson, a young black Nova Scotian, had been stopped by the Halifax police 29 times in one month. Johnson took his case to the Nova Scotia Human Rights Commission and, in 2003, it was ruled that the police officer in question had in fact discriminated against Johnson when he was wrongfully pulled over and his car was seized during one of those stops.

(continued)

Box 8.3 continued

Dr. Wanda Thomas-Bernard, an African Nova Scotian political activist who testified at Johnson's Human Rights Commission hearing, spoke to a United Baptist Church congregation on International Day for the Elimination of Racial Discrimination. While maintaining that "Nova Scotians are very polite" and Halifax Regional Police have made "great strides" in recruiting members of visible minorities, she stated that "We want unwarranted police stops and searches to stop . . . we want racial profiling to stop. We want racial discrimination to end . . . we could stay here all night and pray but when we wake up tomorrow and we go out into the world, we know that we're going to experience some form of racism." Institutions must be examined for policies and practices that "hide, support and condone racism."

Halifax Regional Police Chief Frank Beazley said the force has formed a diversity advisory committee to re-examine its practices. Since the Johnson inquiry, the city's police officers have gone through a "cultural competency" training course. Further, the police chief maintained, if police officers are engaging in racial profiling, "It's invisible . . . they're certainly not showing it, let's put it that way."

Sources: Melchers (2003); *The Chronicle Herald* (March 20, 2006).

Class and Marginalization

Evidence on social class and police discretion can come only from research, and the results are mixed and not recent. According to Sampson (1986), youth who live in poor neighbourhoods with high crime rates have higher arrest rates than youth living in middle-class neighbourhoods. On the other hand, Shannon (1963) and Bodine (1964) argued that differences in charge and arrest rates by neighbourhoods can be explained by type of offence and police records. Thornberry (1973), who questioned this argument, found that lower-class youth were treated more severely regardless of their offence and prior record; he also found that class differences in charges were greatest when the offence was more serious.

Based on research conducted in Toronto, Hagan, Gillis, and Chan (1978) found that police attitudes toward or perceptions of crime-prone areas, coupled with citizen complaints, were strong predictors of delinquency rates. They noted that "actual class differences in the experience of juvenile crime are amplified by underclass housing conditions and complaint practices, and, in turn, even more so by police perceptions" (p. 100). According to Ericson's study of police patrols in Ontario (1982), young men of lower socioeconomic status are disproportionately stopped, searched, questioned, and recorded; they are referred to in police culture as "pukers"—that is, people requiring "extra surveillance." Sampson (1986, p. 881) found that social class, race, and having delinquent friends accounted for roughly one-third of the variation in police responses to youth.

Research on homeless youth in Canada confirms high rates of criminal activity compared to domiciled youth (Gaetz, 2004; Hagan & McCarthy, 1997; Tanner & Wortley, 2002). While these behaviours are largely understood as situational, of increasing concern is the criminalization of homeless youth through the growth of repressive enforcement measures. Increasingly, in response to pressures from business groups and public complaints, municipal governments are targeting survival behaviours of homeless youth and passing legislation and implementing policies that are designed to increase police surveillance and thereby further the marginalization and criminalization of homeless youth (Gaetz, 2004, p. 447). An example is the Ontario Safe Streets Act implemented in 1999 that makes squeegeeing and panhandling illegal. The sentiment expressed in the Attorney General's speech to the Ontario Legislative Assembly when the act was introduced provides a clear justification for increasing police surveillance—homeless youth are dangerous people to be feared:

> Our Government believes that all people in Ontario have the right to drive on the roads, walk down the street or go to public places without being or feeling intimidated. They must be able to carry out their daily activities without fear. When they are not able to do so, it is time for government to act. (Cited in Gaetz, 2004, p. 447)

Age and Gender

Research on the effect of gender on police encounters generally shows that girls are treated more leniently (G. Armstrong, 1977; Chesney-Lind, 1970; Elliott & Voss, 1974b). However, other research shows that gender differences in charging depend on type of offence. Teilmann and Landry (1981) and Horowitz and Pottieger (1991) demonstrated that police are more likely to respond harshly to girls involved in minor offences, but less likely to arrest girls for more serious offences. DeFleur (1975) and Visher (1983) both found that police are reluctant to arrest female suspects who behave in stereotypical feminine ways, such as crying. Girls who did not adhere to middle-class behavioural standards for a traditional female were not afforded leniency or chivalry by police officers.

Age also has a bearing on police discretion in that younger girls seem to be treated more harshly. Visher (1983) found that police were more likely to arrest younger girls, but that age had no bearing on their use of discretion with respect to boys. While only 1 percent of the police in Carrington and Schulenberg's survey reported that gender was a factor in their decision making, 28 percent said that age was important (2005, p. 168). Age differences overall are certainly reflected in crime and court statistics: charge rates and rates of youth going to court are higher for older youth but the opposite is true for girls. Younger girls are more likely charged and to go to court than are younger boys and the converse is also true: older girls are less likely to be charged and to go to court than are older boys (Sauve, 2005; Thomas, 2005). Some attribute this difference to shoplifting charges, which are most often levied against girls and which have a high charge rate compared to other offences (Carrington, 1998b).

As we saw in earlier chapters, charge rates are also exceedingly high for prostitution offences. Surveys of young Canadian women who work the streets have indicated that many have good relations with the police, while others (most often Aboriginal) have reported racism, sexual and physical assault, and harassment. Others are just generally fearful of police and will not go to them for assistance (Nixon & Tutty, 2003, p. 77). In the words of one young woman: "If you have had a bad date on the street, the cops won't offer you much. They'll jack you up and haul your ass down to the police station." (2003, pp. 77–78).

Family and Community

Both the family and the community have an impact on police discretion. When parents are interested in and concerned about their children's behaviour and appear to be cooperative with police, a warning is more likely to be given to a young offender. Similarly, when a community has youth centres, safe houses, and other facilities offering programs or safe living space for young people, then police have choices. Community options are particularly important in cases where parents are less than interested in their children's behaviour or well-being.

As we will see later in this chapter, extrajudicial measures programs affect police decisions to the extent that police have a choice other than total release or processing through the justice system. Unfortunately, this third choice may lead to more rather than fewer police charges. Parental involvement was the one extralegal factor that a sizeable number (42 percent) of Canadian police officers said was important in their decision making. If a parent was felt to be "on board," police were more likely to use discretionary measures or in the case of charges for serious offences, to release youth to their parents than hold them for a bail hearing. On the other hand when parents "minimized the seriousness of the situation" or "denied that their son or daughter could have committed the crime" or "wanted nothing to do with the young person," police were more likely to lay a charge, release the youth on strict conditions or detain her or him for a bail hearing (Carrington & Schulenberg, 2005, p. 168).

Police Departments

A study of Canadian cities in the 1970s showed considerable variation in charges by city; for example, while only 17 percent of youth were being charged by police in Hamilton, 96 percent were being charged in Calgary (Conly, 1978). Under the JDA, there were no restrictions on police discretion, since the YOA, the amount of discretion used by a police officer is limited by law, as in the case of diversionary measures under the YOA that restricted these options to first-time offenders. Decisions to charge also vary depending on whether individual police departments have developed their own diversionary programs. It is also limited by provincial policies and the policies of the departments and municipalities within which officers do their work, as well as by the attitudes and characteristics of individual officers.

Wilbanks (1975), who looked at the relationship between departmental policy and police officers' decision making, found that the best predictor of police decisions was the personal views of police officers, rather than department policy. However, other research (Sundeen, 1972; Wilson, 1968) suggests something more complex. The extent to which police officers are able to make decisions based on their personal views and beliefs depends on the organization of the police department—that is, on whether it is characterized by close supervision or centralized management. According to Wilson (1968), whether or not police officers send youth to court depends on how much they are expected to be involved in the case and whether they will have to appear in court. Goldman (1963) found that officers who were paid a fee for serving as witnesses in court were more likely to send youth to court than were those who were required to use their own unpaid time for court appearances.

high-risk youth
Youth with characteristics and/or living circumstances that are known to be criminogenic.

Some Canadian police departments have adopted risk-management programs for **high-risk youth** in their jurisdictions (Ericson & Haggerty, 1997). These programs involve intensive police supervision of a youth and his or her family, which sometimes lasts as long as two years. When improvement is not apparent, the youth graduates to a more intrusive surveillance program, such as Police Attending Youth (PAY). The PAY program involves more intensive investigation of the youth's activities, record-keeping, and coordination of efforts toward criminal prosecution and "appropriate" sentencing (Ericson & Haggerty, 1997, pp. 270–271). When these youth are arrested, their files are stamped "PAY" and specialized investigators and prosecutors are brought in. In the words of one police officer:

> . . . we can provide the information on that kid from day one, from the first time he was reported missing when he was aged eight all the way through the gambit. There's often twenty or thirty pages of information that we can provide the court. (Ericson & Haggerty, 1997, p. 273)

On the other hand, many police departments and RCMP detachments have developed programs that are designed to enhance successful diversion and reduce criminalization. One such example is Operation Help in Saskatoon—a program that won international acclaim and awards in 2002 for "... being a brilliant new way of dealing with the problem of the abysmal lives of those working in the sex trade" (Green & Healey, 2003, p. 224). Prior to this program, most children and youth involved in the sex trade were charged and sentenced to custody.

Operation Help is an outreach program that involves a team consisting of three police officers, a lawyer, a social worker, a street outreach worker, a former sex-trade worker, an Aboriginal elder, an Aboriginal court worker, and a worker to do follow-up. The team works to provide an "environment of support and encouragement for the young person." When the police do their "stings" and pick up girls from the streets, the girls are met at the police station by the Operation Help team with "coffee and cookies," and no charges are laid for "communicating for the purpose of prostitution" or for breach of probation (pp. 221–224). The social worker on the team describes the girls' reactions:

> They're shocked . . . they're shocked that they aren't going to be charged . . . they can't believe they're going home with [a] plan . . . and we're there to support them . . . some of the toughest are shocked because they are used to being looked down upon . . . the way they describe it . . . there's love and caring . . . because we don't judge, they have to be out there for one reason or another. (Cited in Green & Healey, 2003, pp. 222–223)

Research Summary on Police Discretion

Research on police discretion with respect to youth in the United States can be summarized as follows:

1. Police departments vary considerably in their policies and practices with respect to release or referral of people with whom they have contact.
2. Most youth apprehended by police are reported by citizen complaints, rather than on police initiative.
3. Police handling of serious offences is based chiefly on legalistic criteria, rather than on social class or racial distinctions.
4. With less serious offences, decisions to arrest are based principally on complainant preference, but what is defined as offensive behavior is influenced by other extralegal factors. (Regoli & Hewitt, 1994, p. 374)

Canadian research results are not much different. Doob and Chan (1995), who studied factors affecting police decisions in Toronto, found that the four most significant factors were offence seriousness, previous contacts with police, a young person's demeanour when apprehended, and the victim's request. The results of Carrington and Schulenberg's 2000 survey (2005) are almost the same. The rank order of factors that half or more of the officers reported as important in decision making were: seriousness of the offence, amount of harm done, whether a weapon was involved, history of prior contacts with the police, the youth's demeanour, the victim's preference, and parental involvement (2005, p. 169).

DIVERSIONARY MEASURES

No specific provisions for diversionary measures were included in the JDA. Young people were kept out of the justice system solely through the exercise of police or prosecutorial discretion (Bala et al., 1994, p. 77). During the 1970s, labelling theory raised concerns about **stigmatization**, and critical theorists raised awareness of the

stigmatization
The detrimental consequences for an individual of having a negative label or definition attached to his or her behaviour.

alternative measures
A variety of programs under the YOA, such as mediation, designed to prevent future crime and divert youth from the courts.

principle of least possible interference
The principle that whatever action is taken should have the least impact on a youth's freedom.

extrajudicial measures
Under the YCJA, refers to processing accused young offenders by means other than through the youth or adult justice system.

extrajudicial sanctions
Used under the YCJA when cases proceed to court and the provisions provide for specific sanctions and rules regarding the use of more formal diversionary programs.

criminalization that often results from formal processing in the justice system. One consequence of these concerns was the development of numerous programs aimed at diverting young people from the formal justice system. In 1977, for example, Quebec passed the Youth Protection Act, which combined juvenile delinquency cases and child welfare cases in services designed to meet both needs. Diversion is a key component of this legislation. Police are required to refer all young people to an intake officer who decides whether to take further action through the court, divert the young person to another aspect of the system, or take no action (Bala et al., 1994, p. 78).

As we saw in Chapter 2, the notion of diversion was expressed in s. 3(1)(d) of the Young Offenders Act, which stated, ". . . where it is not inconsistent with the protection of the public, taking no measures or taking measures other than judicial proceedings should be considered for dealing with young persons who have committed offences." This principle, along with its resultant policies and programs, was referred to as **alternative measures** and was complemented by the **principle of least possible interference** contained in s. 3(1)(f) of the YOA.

While diversion as alternative measures (AM) is not a formal principle of youth justice in the YCJA, both the principle of diversion and the concept and practice of AM have now been formalized to an even greater degree under the concept **extrajudicial measures,** which is defined in the YCJA as ". . . measures other than judicial proceedings under this Act used to deal with a young person alleged to have committed an offence." Extrajudicial measures are presented as a set of principles (s. 4) and objectives (s. 5) (see Boxes 8.4 and 8.5) with accompanying rules regarding sanctions, **extrajudicial sanctions** (s. 10), and a formalized set of regulations regarding the police role in this process (s. 6) (see Box 8.2 on page 217).

This is a significantly different approach to diversion than under the YOA in that it actively promotes the diversion of youth from formal police processing and the courts, as well as provides a framework for the implementation of restorative justice

---

BOX 8.4

Principles of Extrajudicial Measures under the YCJA

Section 4. The following principles apply in this Part in addition to the principles set out in section 3:

(a) extrajudicial measures are often the most appropriate and effective way to address youth crime;

(b) extrajudicial measures allow for effective and timely interventions focused on correcting offending behaviour;

(c) extrajudicial measures are presumed to be adequate to hold a young person accountable for his or her offending behaviour if the young person has committed a non-violent offence and has not previously been found guilty of an offence; and

(d) extrajudicial measures should be used if they are adequate to hold a young person accountable for his or her offending behaviour and, if the use of extrajudicial measures is consistent with the principles set out in this section, nothing in this Act precludes their use in respect of a young person who

(i) has previously been dealt with by the use of extrajudicial measures, or

(ii) has previously been found guilty of an offence.

BOX 8.5

Objectives of Extrajudicial Measures under the YCJA

Section 5. Extrajudicial measures should be designed to

(a) provide an effective and timely response to offending behaviour outside the bounds of judicial measures;

(b) encourage young persons to acknowledge and repair the harm caused to the victim and the community;

(c) encourage families of young persons—including extended families where appropriate—and the community to become involved in the design and implementation of those measures;

(d) provide an opportunity for victims to participate in decisions related to the measures selected and to receive reparation; and

(e) respect the rights and freedoms of young persons and be proportionate to the seriousness of the offence.

Section 10(2) of the YCJA outlines the necessary criteria for using extrajudicial sanctions in a given case:
An extrajudicial sanction may be used only if

(a) it is part of a program of sanctions that may be authorized by the Attorney General or authorized by a person, or a member of a class of persons, designated by the lieutenant governor in council of the province;

(b) the person who is considering whether to use the extrajudicial sanction is satisfied that it would be appropriate, having regard to the needs of the young person and the interests of society;

(c) the young person, having been informed of the extrajudicial sanction, fully and freely consents to be subject to it;

(d) the young person has, before consenting to be subject to the extrajudicial sanctions, been advised of his or her right to be represented by counsel and been given a reasonable opportunity to consult with counsel;

(e) the young person accepts responsibility for the act or omission that forms the basis of the offence that he or she is alleged to have committed;

(f) there is, in the opinion of the Attorney General, sufficient evidence to proceed with the prosecution of the offence; and

(g) the prosecution of the offence is not in any way barred at law.

principles. Section 4 establishes that diverting youth from police action in courts is not "doing nothing," but rather that it is an appropriate way of ensuring that young people are held accountable for their behaviour or, in the words of the YCJA, that there are "meaningful consequences" for their behaviour, if the offence is a non-violent one. It does not preclude diversion for repeat offenders in the program or even for those who may already have gone through the courts for another offence.

Section 5 further provides for the realization of restorative justice principles and a more holistic approach to youth justice by recognizing that a criminal offence is a harm not only to a victim but also to the community. This section underscores the importance of victim, family, and community involvement in responding to youth. As we saw earlier, section 6 of the YCJA adds another level to diversion by encouraging police officers to offer warnings and cautions to youth or to refer them to community-based programs rather than charge and process them through the formal justice system.

While the concept and philosophy of alternative measures is renamed "extrajudicial measures" (EM) in the YCJA, alternative measures programs are renamed as "extrajudicial sanctions" (ES). Hence, EM is the broader concept with principles and objectives, and it allows police to issue warnings or cautions or to refer the youth to a community program. ES provide for specific sanctions and rules regarding their use. Together, they create a two-tiered diversionary structure of informal and formal measures and sanctions.

These rules and regulations regarding extrajudicial sanctions are identical to those for alternative measures [YOA, s. 4(1)]. The YCJA sections 10(3) through 10(6) are also identical to the YOA in the requirement that extrajudicial sanctions may not be used if a youth denies participation in the offence or prefers to have her or his case addressed by the court. Two "notice" conditions were added in this part of the YCJA. Section 11 requires ES administrators to notify parents that an ES has been undertaken, and s. 12 specifies that victims have a right to be informed (if they so request) not only of an ES action, but also of the identity of the young person.

After the YOA was implemented, all provinces eventually had alternative measures programs. Ontario was one of the last to establish such a program, with the greatest restrictions on its use. These programs varied in terms of how they were administrated, who made the decision to refer a youth to alternative measures, and when this decision was made, either before or after a charge is laid (pre- or post-charge). Although programs were generally restricted to youth accused of minor offences who did not have prior records, Quebec and some Aboriginal communities operated alternative measures for more serious repeat offenders (Bala et al., 1994, p. 79).

Extrajudicial measures in the YCJA, given their similarity to alternative measures provisions in the YOA, seem to be following the same practices, except that there is more use of police-based diversionary programs and Youth Justice Committees (Bala, 2005, pp. 188–190). One change implemented by some provinces is the use of a "Crown Caution." Manitoba implemented this program in 2002, in anticipation of the YCJA, and it applies to first-time offenders involved in property offences where restitution was not an issue. A letter is sent to the parents by a Crown attorney, advising them of their child's involvement in the offence and explaining that the decision has been made to leave "the imposition of consequences to the parent." The Manitoba Attorney General's office reports that since 2002, 90 percent of the youth referred to the Crown Caution program have not reoffended (private correspondence, 2005).

Diversionary Programs

By the mid 1990s, alternative measures programs across the country involved three types of programming (Schrader, 1994). Under **reconciliation/mediation,** offenders and victims are brought together; apologies, either verbal or written, and the writing of essays or letters are among the program's elements. The second type of program, *retributive/restitutive*, is more punitive, involving **restitution** through such things as fines, financial compensation to (or actual work for) victims, or community service. The third type of program is *rehabilitative/educational* and is exemplified by the StopLift Education Program in Saskatoon run by the John Howard Society and continues to be used in many cities. This anti-shoplifting program is for young people involved in petty theft. The program is designed

> . . . to create an awareness in the young person of the effects of his or her actions on themselves, the victim, the community and society at large, and to provide an opportunity for the young person to reflect on his or her development, discuss values and

reconciliation
An important component of the mediation/healing process, based on the belief that a productive response to crime is to encourage all affected parties to participate in conflict resolution.

mediation
A form of conflict resolution that involves a third party, usually a person with professional skills, to assist two parties with a grievance or unresolved matter to reach a mutually agreeable solution.

restitution
Payment in money or kind to compensate victims for their loss.

focus on issues such as self-esteem, peer pressure and decision making skills. (John Howard Society pamphlet on StopLift, cited in Schrader, 1994, p. 167)

Similar programs, such as the Mino-Pamatezwin Program in Winnipeg, have been developed as preventative educational programs for youth who have been involved in auto-theft offences.

There has been little change from AM programs to programming offered through ES in areas where programs were designed to address the "underlying circumstances" of the offence. Some provinces such as Ontario prefer a non-interventionist approach and will not allow programs with a therapeutic orientation on the grounds that these more intrusive approaches are best left to the courts to decide (Bala, 2005, p. 191).

By the mid- to late 1990s, restorative justice principles had gained some prominence, and programs based on these principles began to develop. With the YCJA's emphasis on reintegration, victim involvement, and harm reduction, there is now a greater emphasis on, and proliferation of, programs that facilitate greater involvement of victims and community members. These programs usually involve meetings of the offenders, their supporters, the victims and/or their supporters, community members such as a police or school representative, and a trained community facilitator. The purpose of the meetings is to develop a reparation agreement and promote restoration from the harm done by the behaviour of the young offender.

Hence, a fourth type of program has emerged—restorative interventions. These programs vary in their focus and can involve community conferencing, family conferencing, or healing circles. An example is the Valley Restorative Justice Society in Nova Scotia, which offers conferencing sessions and healing circles designed to address the harm caused by a youth's behaviour and to develop a reparation plan for the youth. Similarly, Onashowewin Inc., a community-based organization in Winnipeg, offers community justice forums, peacemaking circles, and conciliation sessions that are non-retributive and designed to "restore, heal and transform relationships in the community."

The RCMP played a major role in the implementation of family group conferencing across the country. Inspired by Judge Lilles of the Yukon Territorial Court and by conferencing developments in Australia and New Zealand (the Wagga Wagga model) that are based on ancient Maori traditions, the RCMP found these community justice forums consistent with the force's philosophy of community policing and so adopted community forums as its "preferred restorative tool."

In early 1997, the RCMP launched its Restorative Justice Initiative and began a cross-country training program with the objective of "training the trainer." The force sees its role as that of a catalyst in training key community people to become trainers and facilitators to assist communities in developing their own community conferencing programs. By the end of 1998, the RCMP had trained 1,700 people across the country in the skills of conducting community conferencing. A subsequent evaluation of almost 500 community conferencing participants (Chatterjee, 1999) reported high levels of satisfaction for both offenders and victims or victim supporters (whose participation was voluntary) and that the outcomes/agreements reached in these sessions were fair. Offenders had complied with the agreement in almost all of the cases, victims felt the sessions helped them to heal and regain a sense of control over their lives, and both indicated they felt that "harmony had been restored" (Chatterjee & Elliott, 2003, pp. 352–353).

Police continue to play an active role in diversion as gatekeepers to programs and as supporters of community-based justice across the country. In this way, police work becomes peacekeeping and is an important and vital component in the creation of peaceful communities (Elliott, 2005).

Usually, provincial governments managed referrals to alternative measures programs, through either social services or correctional services departments, and are continuing to do so for extrajudicial sanctions. In most cases, the programs are implemented by social agencies or specially mandated agencies such as the Community Justice Society in Nova Scotia. The John Howard Restorative Justice Society in Nova Scotia is one of many agencies contracted by the Nova Scotia Department of Justice to offer a Restorative Justice Program and deliver a Community Service Order Program. They receive pre-charge referrals from the police and post-charge referrals from the Crown.

In some provinces, administration is shared. In Alberta, correctional staff (usually probation) handle approximately 60 percent of referrals for programs; the remaining are dealt with by either the Social Services Department in major cities or Youth Justice Committees, or through contracts with Native service providers (Schrader, 1994, p. 136). Prince Edward Island and Quebec administer programs through government, while Saskatchewan, British Columbia, Ontario, and Nova Scotia tend to contract to social service agencies, community agencies, and various service providers.

One of the key differences in the implementation of diversionary measures stems from the distinction between pre- and post-charge referrals. As we have seen, extrajudicial measures allow police to issue warnings or cautions, or to refer the youth to a community program. This is the informal side of EM and is normally done without a charge being laid; it can also be done without an admission of guilt. Youth must agree with the choice of a referral and must be informed that they have the right to a lawyer before agreeing. Police have a choice about keeping records of these measures, but the records cannot be used as evidence in the future.

Extrajudicial sanctions are used when warnings, cautions, and referrals are considered not to be adequate, and that the young person should be held accountable because of the seriousness of the offence, the number of previous offences, or other circumstances (YCJA s. 10). It is the formal side of EM and can be done pre- or post-charge. Some provinces and territories, such as Saskatchewan, Nova Scotia, and the Yukon, have both pre- and post-charge programs. In some provinces, there are arrangements where program referrals, such as Operation Help in Saskatoon, are almost entirely pre-charge, while other provinces, such as Ontario, are almost entirely a post-charge system in that charges are generally laid before a case can go to ES (Bala, 2005, p. 189).

In most provinces and territories, the police are the gatekeepers to referrals for ES; they make the first decision to refer to the Crown or justice committee. In other cases, ES decisions are made by a committee. In Whitehorse, for example, the RCMP refer all charged cases to the Youth Justice Panel, which decides whether to send cases to youth court or divert them to ES. In Manitoba and Alberta, police refer all charges to the Crown, which makes decisions for referral to ES (see Figure 8.1, for examples). In post-charge systems, a caution is part of the formal system and can be made only by the Crown (Sauve, 2005, p. 12).

The YCJA affords youth the right to consult with a lawyer before agreeing to an EM or ES referral to a program, as well as the right to refuse to participate in any aspect of EM or ES and insist that the case go to court. Extrajudicial sanctions may involve a period of supervision with conditions and also such things as writing an essay, an apology, personal service or restitution to victims, community service, donations to charity, or participation in a community intervention or counselling program. A two-year police record is associated with ES, and information can be used in sentencing reports in future cases. In most provinces, youth who fail to comply with EM agreements, contracts, or

FIGURE 8.1

Northwest Territories and Alberta Youth Extrajudicial Measures

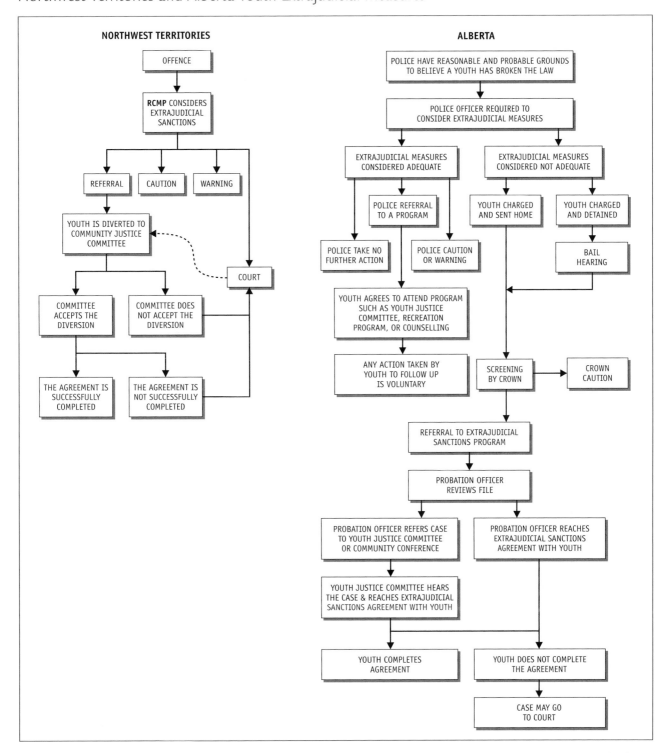

Sources: Northwest Territories, Department of Justice, *Community Justice Policies and Procedures Manual* (2005), p. 4; John Howard Society and the Alberta Law Foundation, *YCJA Handbook* (2003), p. 12.

VOICES BOX 8.6

Essay by a Young Offender Who Participated in a Diversionary Program

Life's Too Short

Well, it has been a rough year for me. I imagine for teenagers like myself, there is nothing "unrough" about getting involved with drugs, alcohol, sex, . . . and the list goes on.

During the last year of my life I have faced it all. I got into smoking dope and drinking every day. I started hanging around the wrong crowd and this was the major downfall of everything that went wrong in my life.

I started shop-lifting mainly because my friends were and at first I got away with it. That ended real soon. I was caught and charged. I received a punishment for it.

I've been living on my own for over a year, and believe me, don't be in a hurry to move out. It's hard worrying about a job and having money to live. I also haven't talked to my family in a year because of my mistakes.

I'm not saying I know it all because I don't. I've had to make some big changes in my life and because of it I've grown up a lot. I have some good people in my life now and I plan on keeping in the positive side of life! It's far too easy to let yourself fall back down.

"Life's too short to grow up too fast!" Enjoy life's good things! Take care!

Source: *Youth Alternative Society Newsletter* (1997, January/February).

---

programs are referred back to court, but pre-charge referrals are not. In Ottawa, for example, police may, at the pre-charge stage, refer 12- to 15-year-olds who are not involved in a violent offence to the Preventive Intervention Program (PIP). Charges are not laid if the young person fails to complete the program.

Youth Justice Committees

The Youth Justice Committee concept was established by the YOA and is maintained by the YCJA.

> **Section 18(1):** The Attorney General of Canada or a province or any other minister that the lieutenant governor in council of the province may designate may establish one or more committees of citizens, to be known as youth justice committees, to assist in any aspect of the administration of this Act or in any programs or services for young persons.

The YCJA is more specific than the YOA about the role and function of the committee and, unlike the YOA, does not require Youth Justice Committee members to perform their duties without "remuneration." Section 18(2) outlines the functions of a Youth Justice Committee:

1. give advice on appropriate extrajudicial measures;
2. provide support to victims and facilitate reconciliation between young offenders and their victims;
3. ensure community support is available to youth;
4. help coordinate youth services with activities of the justice system;

5. advise federal and provincial governments on the justice system's compliance with the act and various policies and procedures of youth justice; and
6. provide public information on the act and the youth justice system.

The definition of "Youth Justice Committee" in the YCJC is sufficiently vague that, in practice, it includes a variety of activities that involve family group conferences, community/neighbourhood accountability panels, victim/offender mediation/reconciliation sessions, multidisciplinary case management conferences, and Aboriginal sentencing and healing circles (Markwart, 2000). Youth Justice Committees were underused in most of the country under the YOA but their use is increasing with the YCJA and its emphasis on reintegration and the growth of the restorative justice philosophy. How these committees are used in EM varies—a committee might be the primary decision maker on referrals to ES or the body responsible for deciding on an ES program, or both—and there are a number of issues associated with their use that will be discussed later in the chapter.

Youth Justice Committees have been used extensively in Manitoba, Alberta, New Brunswick, Newfoundland and Labrador, and the Northwest Territories for some time, most often in Aboriginal communities. In Manitoba and the Northwest Territories (see Figure 8.1), under the YCJA, a community youth justice team receives all Crown referrals and makes decisions on an appropriate ES program. Other individual community Youth Justice Committees are responsible for particular programming. In Alberta and New Brunswick, probation officers decide whether to use a Youth Justice Committee to decide on an appropriate ES program. In 2003, Alberta had about 98 Youth Justice Committees operating across the province (Nuffield, 2003, p. 34).

British Columbia uses Youth Justice Committees in a citizen advisory capacity rather than for EM; Ontario has a similar arrangement. British Columbia currently has approximately 25 such committees that use community accountability programs to work with ES and EM referrals in the development and implementation of diversionary agreements (Hillian, Reitsma-Street, & Hackler, 2004, pp. 349–351). In Nanaimo, for example, the RCMP makes recommendations to the Crown and approved cases are then referred to the John Howard Society. The society consults with a Neighbourhood Accountability Board, which assists in developing a young person's reparation agreement.

The province's South Island Tribal Council program takes a more active role. Under this program, a young person who has committed an offence meets with members of the Tribal Court and a diversion coordinator. The coordinator conducts an interview with the youth and makes recommendations to the Tribal Court. If the Tribal Court decides to accept the youth into a counselling/supervision program, it outlines a contract for the youth. The youth is then supervised and counselled by an elder from the community (Jackson, 1988).

Similarly the Youth Conference Committee of the Ridge Meadows Youth and Justice Advocacy is a neighbourhood community-based organization in Maple Ridge, British Columbia, that has been running diversion programs since 1994. Referrals come from the Crown or RCMP, and a conference is called with the youth, parents, victim(s), and a group of community volunteers to decide on a "meaningful consequence" for the youth. Once agreement is reached, a committee person is assigned as a mentor to work with the youth through the duration of her or his ES term. The Ridge Meadows Youth Conference Committee reports that it has not changed its program as a result of the YCJA (private correspondence, 2005).

In Newfoundland and Labrador, Youth Justice Committees strive to create a sense of ownership and empowerment among community members with respect to youth justice matters. The 32 committees in the province decide whether cases should proceed with ES or go to court. The process begins with a committee conducting an intake interview with the young person, his or her parents or guardian, and the victim of the offence. On the basis of this interview, the committee determines how best to proceed. Some provinces, such as Nova Scotia, do not use Youth Justice Committees to screen for referral to ES; the police and the Crown make these decisions.

Referral and Success Rates

Rates of referral to diversionary measures vary across the country. Nova Scotia's average referral rate, calculated as a percentage of numbers of youth apprehended from 1987 to 1995, was 24 percent (Montgomery, 1997). Quebec reported a five-year average of 36 percent; New Brunswick, 35 percent (1992–1993); Saskatchewan, 22 percent (1991–1992); Alberta, 17 percent (1992–1993); and British Columbia, 16 percent (1993) (Schrader, 1994). Since 2000, perhaps in anticipation of the introduction of the YCJA, youth courts have reported statistics on admissions to alternative measures and ES programs and crime statistics reports on offences cleared through EM and ES programs.

As discussed earlier, there was a 30 percent increase in the rate of police clearance through alternative measures just prior to the YCJA; the rates are now levelling or showing small decreases. These rate statistics are probably not reliable as trend indicators because there have been changes to the reporting systems and a number of jurisdictions have not been reporting over the last few years. Similarly, admissions to AM programs have been fluctuating since 1997–1998 and show an overall decrease of 19 percent in rate of admissions since then (Marinelli, 2004, p. 18).

Diversionary measures programs are highly successful. Nova Scotia reported success rates ranging from 92.9 percent in 1992 to 98 percent in 1996 (Montgomery, 1997, p. 109). Over a five-year period, Quebec reported an average success rate of 97 percent; Manitoba, 86 percent; Alberta, 94 percent; New Brunswick, 91 percent; British Columbia, 89 percent; and Saskatchewan, 80 percent (over a two-year period) (Schrader, 1994). The overall success rate across the country in 1998–1999 was 93 percent (Engler & Crowe, 2000, p. 11). The Department of Justice in Nova Scotia conducted a study comparing first-time offenders in alternative measures programs with those going through the courts for similar offences. First-time offenders going through court had a higher rate of recidivism than those going through alternative measures programs (Montgomery, 1997). This pattern seems to be continuing: in 2001–2002, three-quarters (77 percent) of the youth admitted to AM across the country successfully completed their agreements, and in 2002–2003, 86 percent did so (Marinelli, 2004, p. 18).

Diversionary Measures Issues

In this section, we consider four diversionary measures issues: **net widening** consistency and accountability; mediation, reconciliation, and conferencing; and administration, control, and inequality of access.

Net Widening

Supporters of diversion maintain that diverting offenders out of the youth justice system is in the best interests of both offenders and taxpayers. If nothing else, diversion prevents problems associated with reintegration after incarceration, reduces the risk of further criminalization associated with imprisonment, and provides an alternative to high-cost court proceedings and dispositions. Legislators have clearly attempted, through the YCJA, to increase the use of diversion by adding another level

net widening
A tendency for policies seemingly designed to reduce the number of people in the justice system to inadvertently result in more people under state control.

to diversion prior to that of diversionary programs. They insist that this is an appropriate way to deliver "meaningful consequences" and for young offenders to be held accountable for their behaviour. One could reasonably assume that many minor offences that would have been processed through alternative measures under the YOA will now simply receive a warning, and other offenders who might have gone to court will now receive a caution or an extrajudicial sanction.

Critics have long argued, however, that formalizing diversion results in more people going into the system, thereby effecting a "widening of the net" (Cohen, 1985). More specifically, it is argued that in the absence of diversionary measures, youth with a minor offence and no prior record would likely be "let go" with a warning. In this view, adding a warning letter amounts to formalizing procedures for those who would have been "let go," particularly if this warning becomes part of a record. In the case of a Crown caution, there is a record that can be used in future reports for sentencing.

Others suggest that diversionary measures, particularly ES, are not an alternative to court, but rather an alternative to police discretion. In other words, discretion is merely shifted from police to the Crown prosecutor (Montgomery, 1997). Since the YCJA specifies that extrajudicial measures may not be used if a youth denies participation in the offence or prefers to have her or his case addressed by the court, this particular type of net widening remains and may even be exacerbated by the more formal cautioning system. Furthermore, since a failure to meet the conditions of EM or ES may result in a return to court, youth who otherwise simply might have been let go with a warning may end up in the system for "violations."

This may be a very real concern since the Department of Justice (2005, p. 3) reports that, while there was not a significant increase in the number of youth being brought into the youth justice system in 2003, there have been "instances where net widening appears to have occurred in the use of extrajudicial measures programs." The report indicates that, compared to pre-YCJA years, police are now more likely to impose conditions and also to impose an increased number of conditions on youth they release. Maclure, Campbell, and Dufresne (2003) suggest that police are likely to bypass formal ES processing because they then forfeit any say in sanctions and thereby lose control over the outcomes for any particular youth (p. 144).

A related concern is that the combination of pre-charge and post-charge diversion in any one jurisdiction creates a two-tiered system of diversion that produces a "revolving door" situation. EM as a pre-charge system is the first tier of diversion and, because of the discretionary latitude afforded to different professional groups in the system, there may be more than one round of diversion at this stage for any one youth. ES creates a second tier to the program and can start a second round of two or more diversions for the same youth. Hence, by the time a youth gets to court for something that may have begun as a minor offence, there is now a lengthy record and the potential for the youth to be seen as a "loser," as someone who needs a "crack down" (Maclure, Campbell, & Dufresne, 2003, p. 146).

The net-widening issue was one of the main reasons for Ontario refusing initially to participate in AM and then, once it did adopt an AM program, for significantly restricting its use, compared to other provinces. Ontario's requirement that all cases have at least one court appearance before alternative measures are considered can be seen as an attempt to sidestep some of these net-widening issues (Bala, 2005, pp. 178–179).

Some have questioned whether diversionary programs can be truly voluntary, when the consequence of non-participation is for a youth to go to court. Questionable

VOICES BOX 8.7

Diversionary Measures in British Columbia

British Columbia's practice of not prosecuting youth for failure to complete diversionary measures agreements stems from a Supreme Court decision in a case where such a prosecution occurred. According to then-Chief Justice Anderson, prosecution in this context is illegal, contrary to the philosophy of diversion, and useless as a deterrent:

> Only the Courts have the right to impose sentence and the Crown cannot create an administrative program inherently coercive in nature, whereby the accused accepts "diversion" on terms fixed by the Crown, subject to its control, retaining the discretion to revive the criminal proceedings if the accused fails to adhere to the terms. The Crown cannot thwart the role of the law in this way . . . [Such a] diversion agreement amounts to a pre-trial probation order. The exercise of such power by the Crown constitutes a direct and unlawful interference with the proceedings of the Criminal Courts and amounts to an abuse of process . . .
>
> Even if I am wrong in respect of the conclusions I have reached, it would seem unwise to prosecute in cases of default. Some of the purposes of "diversion" are to avoid expense, publicity and legal entanglements. It is readily apparent that such purposes will not be achieved by proceeding against a defaulting accused on "revived" charges . . . [V]ery little will be accomplished by the use of "default" sanctions. I do not think it cynical to say that the threat of sanctions will not deter those who are bent on a career of crime. An accused who violates his undertaking is likely to return to the courts in respect of some other offence in any event.

Source: *R. v. Jones* [1979] 4 C. R. (3D).

too is the fact that, in most provinces, court proceedings result when a youth fails to fulfill any agreement reached through diversionary measures. British Columbia and the Ottawa-based Preventive Intervention Program avoided charges of coerced participation by not proceeding with prosecution if a youth did not participate or did not successfully complete a diversion program.

In Box 8.7, we see the legal rationale for the pre-charge based system in British Columbia. In a nutshell, then-Chief Justice Anderson argued that prosecution for failing to complete a diversionary program (or "default sanctions") is illegal, contrary to a diversion philosophy, and useless as a deterrent. His "bottom line" was that if a person is not sufficiently motivated to complete a program designed in his or her best interests, then that person will more than likely end up back in court for another offence anyway.

Proponents of prosecution for a failure to complete diversionary agreements argue that there needs to be an incentive (or a threat) in order for diversionary measures to work. However, the success–failure rates that are available, as we have seen, do not suggest any difference in success between programs with or without sanctions for non-compliance—British Columbia's success rates were as high as those of other provinces. Nonetheless, the success rates reported for these programs are problematic because it is impossible to know if successes are due to the diversionary measures programs themselves or the fact that mostly minor cases—that is, youth who probably would not reoffend after police contact and warnings—are processed through diversionary measures.

Some provinces and groups lobbied for changes to the YOA eligibility criteria so that more serious offences and offenders with prior records could be included in diversionary measures programs. The YCJA does not preclude using extrajudicial measures for repeat offenders or even for youth who have prior convictions; these decisions are left up to provinces. It does, however, restrict extrajudicial measures to non-violent offences.

Consistency and Accountability

The Supreme Court of Canada in 1992 [*R. v. T.(V.)*] ruled unanimously that decisions regarding referral to extrajudicial sanctions (AM at that time) are almost entirely a matter of prosecutorial discretion and, with the exception of extremely limited circumstances, are not subject to a court review. As discussed throughout this chapter, a number of people are involved in making decisions about whether a youth will be diverted through EM or ES provisions. The problem is that no one is publicly accountable for these decisions (Maclure, Campbell, & Dufresne, 2003, pp. 144–145).

Justice David Cole of the Ontario Court of Justice refers to "non-transparent discretionary decisions" and points out that, based on his experience in court, there are a number of problems with this set of arrangements. First, is the question of accountability. Justice Cole points out that, unlike his decisions as a judge, prosecutors are not required to justify their diversion decisions in open court; therefore, there is no way to assess if a decision to divert (or not) and specifics regarding the imposition of sanctions are appropriate, fair, or even consistent with other similar cases (Harris et al., 2004, pp. 377–380).

Similarly, the rationale for EM and ES decisions and sanction arrangements made by prosecutors and other criminal justice professionals working on youth cases are not indicated in court and are therefore not publicly accountable. While the judge is accountable for her or his decisions "to the public in attendance [in the courtroom], to the media, and to the appellate courts," other criminal justice professionals are not when it comes to the terms of extrajudicial sanctions (Harris et al., 2004, pp. 377–380).

Justice Cole stated that his second, and related, concern is one of consistency—which youth get which measures and under which circumstances. With regard to police decisions to refer youth, Justice Cole maintains that there are questions about why one youth merely has to attend a StopLift program and another, "similarly situated" with a "similar offence," has to perform hours of community service. Furthermore, these informal sanctions often involve lawyers working out EM arrangements without input from probation officials, who know from experience what it is reasonable to expect of a young person. A case in point is a 13-year-old youth who agreed to 100 hours of community service in exchange for not being charged (Harris et al., 2004, pp. 377–380). Justice Cole "confesses" that in circumstances such as this:

> I sometimes feel like searching out the young person in the halls of the court building to tell them, "Look, why don't you plead guilty to the charge. True, you will have a criminal record for a time, but I will likely impose only 30 hours of community service for this offence!" (p. 380)

Mediation, Reconciliation, and Conferencing

A major problem in mediation programs concerns the role of victims. Successful mediation requires the participation of both the accused and the accuser, but many victims of crime are reluctant to face the accused. Supporters of mediation argue that it is equally difficult for an accused to face her or his accuser and, further, that the most important part of the healing process is for both parties to come to see each other as people—to understand why the incident occurred and how each person and the incident affected and continues to affect the other. A solution to this dilemma has been to use the victim's "supporters" in sessions or, as a last resort, a volunteer who assumes the victim's role.

Although most diversionary measures programs do report a high level of victim participation, problems arise when the accuser is a business. Many businesses, particularly large department stores, will not participate in mediation programs, arguing that it costs them too much to take employees away from their job. Some stores (Zellers and The Bay, for example) have even launched civil suits against offenders by sending a bill for their costs. Thus, offenders who have accepted responsibility and "paid" for their offence according to the justice system, face a potential civil penalty as a result of action by the stores. The legality of this practice has been successfully challenged in court by some adult offenders (Bell, 1995, p. 20). In general, victims and offenders who have participated in mediation programs report a high level of satisfaction (78 and 74 percent, respectively), while negotiated arrangements were acceptable to both parties (92 percent) (Umbreit, 1995). Box 8.8 presents an example of the views of

---

VOICES BOX 8.8

Participant Views on Diversionary Measures Mediation

A Parent
This is a marvellous intervention for first offenders. The non-judgmental and non-threatening attitude and atmosphere were very unexpected. The volunteer allowed us to verbalize our feelings and emotions and discuss whatever was on our minds while keeping us on track to meet the objective of the meeting. It even expedited the healing process between parent and child. I am sincerely thankful for a such a program. I wish more parents would take the interest in accompanying their child to such a meeting. (John Howard Society alternative measures report, April 1994, cited in Schrader, 1994, p. 183)

Youth and Victim: Before
Head bowed, voice lowered, eyes avoiding contact, she twists the corner of her jacket nervously. Across from the 15-year-old sits the security officer for the department store. He asks again, why did she try to leave the store without paying for the make-up? The question is asked directly, but not harshly. She hesitates, then shrugs. After a brief silence, a third person, seated between them, speaks. The mediator, a skilled professional, suggests that perhaps they can come back to that question a little later.

Youth and Victim: After
The 15-year-old smiles, stuffing her carefully folded agreement into her back pocket as she heads for the door. She still can't believe that the security guard accepted her offer. He had seemed like kind-of-a-jerk the first time they met, but now she is almost looking forward to helping him on a Saturday afternoon.

The security guard sips his coffee, slowly shaking his head. The girl had been much more likeable and responsible than he had expected, and had offered to do three times more work to make amends than he ever would have expected. Although he had come to the meeting planning to demand an essay and an apology from the teenager, he likes the idea of her working for him. He wonders what the Saturday afternoon security tagging will be like. (Pate & Peachey, 1988, pp. 105, 118–119)

participants in mediation programs. Even though the examples are from a few years ago, they are nonetheless representative of the timely essence of the issues faced by youth in trouble, their parents, and victims.

Issues associated with the application and implementation of restorative justice principles in general and, in particular, conferencing, are more numerous and complex. Elliott (2005) and Chatterjee and Elliott (2003) point to problems associated with the statutory imposition of restorative justice that stem from attempts to implement restorative justice principles within a retributive model of justice. Here the issues revolve around matters of attempting a healing process.

A major impetus for government and justice department support for community-based interventions is that they are relatively cost-effective compared to a reliance on institutionally based program delivery. Nonetheless, cost effectiveness and justice delivery require time lines. The YCJA emphasizes that timely interventions and processing are important aspects of "meaningful consequences" for youth, and governments have placed restrictions on the time frames for EM and ES. Alberta, for example, requires that EM and ES be completed within three months. While this may be appropriate when thinking in justice terms of consistency and fairness of sanctions, or in retributive terms of punishment for an offence, it makes little sense from a restorative justice framework.

Elliott and Chatterjee (2003) point to the questions raised by Zehr (2002, p. 21) that demonstrate inherent tensions between these competing models of justice, as well as the reasons why conferencing attempts to repair and heal harms is easily thwarted by retributive statutory requirements and bureaucratic policies. In restorative justice, the questions are: "Who has been hurt?" "What are their needs?" "Whose obligations are these?" These questions are inclusive of the offender, victim, and community. The questions of concern in a retributive model focus on the offence and the offender: "What laws have been broken?" "Who did it?" "What do they deserve?" Clearly, effectively addressing the first set of questions cannot be time-lined; no doubt the second set of questions can be addressed within three months or less.

Perhaps one of the most critical issues associated with conferencing interventions is the matter of shaming, a concept promoted by Braithwaite (1989) as central to family group conferences and as a result, many programs are implemented around this concept. While Braithwaite argued that shaming could be a powerful tool for reintegration (reintegrative shaming) it could also, if not used appropriately, have a disintegrative effect (disintegrative shaming).

Elliott (2005, pp. 257–259) and Chatterjee and Elliott (2003, pp. 355–357) point out that the difference between reintegrative shaming and disintegrative shaming is highly significant for conferencing outcomes. From a restorative perspective and for healing to occur, shaming, as a "self-derived emotion," should be experienced through a process of reflection on hearing the thoughts and experiences of others. Furthermore, there is an opportunity in restorative conferencing for all participants—for the collective not just the offender—to feel this emotion. In these cases, the collective assumes responsibility for healing; it is not the responsibility of the offender alone. In a retributive model, shaming is a punishment, something done to the offender. This is disintegrative shaming.

Elliott (2005) and Chatterjee and Elliott (2003) maintain that disintegrative shaming is counterproductive to the principles of restorative justice and conferencing in a variety of ways. First and most important is that it may exacerbate violence, precisely because punishment is intended to generate feelings of shame and humiliation: "The basic psychological motive of violent behaviour is the wish to eliminate the feeling of shame and humiliation . . ." (Gilligan, 2001, as cited in Chatterjee & Elliott, 2003, p. 356). Hence, conferencing based on motives of punishment can, in and of itself, inadvertently induce offenders' ". . . need[s] to respond to humiliation in defence of their honour" (p. 357), as can agreements that are overly punitive. This can be particularly acute for youth who have already been humiliated by adult authority.

Disintegrative shaming also violates principles of restorative justice and is counterproductive to healing to the extent that it places participants in the position of being "active agents in harm-doing." Furthermore, the idea of shaming is appealing to those adhering to a retributive model of justice and looking for punishment. Elliott (2005) maintains therefore that a cultivation of empathy is perhaps a more effective and positive goal of conferencing than shaming, precisely because empathy is a concept that is not so conducive to punishment (pp. 258–259).

Administration, Control, and Inequalities of Access

The issue of administration and control concerns the role of the community in deciding who is diverted and when, and how committed governments are to providing resources for community-based diversionary measures programming. The overriding issue here with regard to youth justice is one of "inequality of access" to diversionary programs, and who controls who goes where. As we have seen, some provinces are firmly committed to community involvement in youth justice processes and have established Youth Justice Committees as active participants in diversionary measures programs; in some Aboriginal communities, the committees operate as a sentencing circle. However, only Newfoundland and Labrador involves the committee in deciding what cases will actually be diverted to diversionary measures on a province-wide basis. Hence, the control and autonomy afforded community committees will vary not only by province, but also within provinces (Report of the Federal–Provincial–Territorial Task Force on Youth Justice, 1996, pp. 52–54; Schrader, 1994).

Tobin (1987) notes that mediation programs can be either community-based or justice-based. Only community-based mediation—in circumstances where disputes are handled by community committees before police involvement—is truly diversionary. An example of this type of mediation is the Community Boards Program in San Francisco: complaints are initiated by community people who contact the agency, report a dispute, and ask for assistance in reaching a resolution (Tobin, 1987, p. 114). Elliott (2005) points out that communities may not wish to handle their own problems and cites Judge Barry Stuart's description of a "911 mentality"—". . . the tendency of people to call in external, professionalized enforcement for most problems . . ." (p. 256).

The legal profession is the main opponent to community-based programs. Its opposition stems from concerns about people practising law who are not qualified to do so (Tobin, 1987). On the other hand, a justice-based system of mediation has its own major weakness—namely, that program success depends on an acceptance of diversion philosophy on the part of individual police officers, Crown prosecutors, and their departments. Furthermore, government has driven and controlled the growth, structure, and implementation of youth justice services, leaving little opportunity for communities to challenge discrepancies with what they would like to accomplish.

Some communities would like to address more serious offences through EM but are prevented from doing so by legislation and provincial policies. The Manitoba Department of Justice, for example, lists the following offences as being appropriate "warning offences": first offence property crimes (under $5,000), motor vehicle theft, provincial statute offences, city bylaw offences, possession of housebreaking instruments, false pretences, and simple possession. The department considers second offences after a previous warning or caution, along with more serious first offences (common assault, mischief, theft over $5,000, arson, break and enter, communication for the purpose of prostitution, possession of weapons, and public mischief) as being appropriate for EM and ES.

On the other hand, the Saskatchewan *Policy and Procedures Manual* excludes the following offences from ES diversion: use of a weapon, violence against a person, child sexual abuse, perjury, driving while disqualified, all family violence cases, and any offence other than Criminal Code ones (this would include YCJA offences and therefore those with previous ES experience).

Under the YOA, there was considerable variation between types and number of alternative measures programs offered across the country, including variation within provinces and in diversion rates by police departments (Schrader, 1994). There was also variation in diversion rates and programs by regions. All of which means that not all young offenders had access to the same services. Much of this diversity continues under the YCJA and is a matter of resources and funding. Urban areas have far more resources to support diversionary measures programs than do rural and isolated areas. A study by the federal Department of Justice reports that rural and isolated communities are "... places of real hardship, especially when it comes to the delivery of services such as youth justice" (Nuffield, 2003, p. 1).

The most common problems cited by provincial and territorial officials for offenders are a lack of diversionary measures programs and specialized services, difficulties in getting to appointments and accessing services, and removal from families and communities. The major problem cited in regard to diversion programs is the "in-between" cases, those requiring more than police warnings and something less than custody. It is also difficult to find supervisory level employees within local populations and equally difficult to attract and keep professionals in isolated communities. There is also a high burnout rate and rapid turnover of workers. For their part, those working in the system report being overworked and unable to have anything but minimal contact with young offenders and victims because of physical distance and heavy caseloads (Nuffield, 2003, pp. i–ii, 17).

A related issue concerns the availability of resources for Aboriginal youth. Both Alberta and Saskatchewan recognized the problems associated with low rates of diversionary measures referrals for Aboriginal youth and have addressed this inequity by increasing the number of Aboriginal service providers in their respective provinces.

None of these access issues are likely to change under YCJA provisions for extrajudicial measures because provinces maintain control of the administration of extrajudicial measures, including its programs. Ontario, for example, initially resisted introducing alternative measures and eventually came to use courts rather than the police as entry points for diversionary programs in many jurisdictions. Since Ontario has also repeatedly requested that the federal government move youth justice procedures and sentences closer to those found in the adult system, it is unlikely, with the vagueness of section 10 of the YCJA, that Ontario will change its diversionary practices in the near future.

On the other hand, provinces currently working toward implementing restorative justice principles in the youth justice system, such as Nova Scotia and Prince Edward Island, have been provided more latitude to do so with the YCJA. The YCJA also assumes that all communities have an "equivalent capacity" to create and deliver services. Rural and isolated communities expressed concern that this increased emphasis on diversion in the YCJA would place an even greater burden on their struggles to deliver diversionary programs because of increased numbers of youth requiring services and a change in this population to youth who "present more serious needs."

Those who work in the youth justice system have reported that the "YCJA expands options but it also makes the community take a stronger role and if communities can't deliver, it will be a problem" and in a related sense, "The YCJA doesn't change [the] fabric of community" (Nuffield, 2003, pp. 21–22). While a primary programming question in the latter part of the 20th century was "Rehabilitate to what?" an important question now at the beginning of the 21st century, as posed by Hillian, Reitsma-Street, and Hackler (2004, p. 362), is "Reintegrated into what?"

SUMMARY

A young person's involvement with the youth justice system begins with police contact. Except in cases involving the most serious offences, police have considerable discretionary power with regard to charging the youth with a criminal offence. A number of factors, both legal and extralegal, have been found to influence police decision making. The police and Crown are empowered under extrajudicial measures and extrajudicial sanctions provisions in the YCJA and through provincial regulations to divert young offenders from the courts. Diversionary measures programs vary across the country, both within and between provinces.

The most important legal factors influencing police discretion are offence seriousness and prior record of the offender. Minor offences offer more latitude for police discretion. Police contact in itself also increases the chances of future arrest. Race, class, gender, age, demeanour, homelessness, and complainant preference have all been identified as significant factors affecting police decision making. Other important extralegal factors include family, community, neighbourhood, and the structure and organization of police departments. The extent to which the personal views and beliefs of individual police officers affect their decisions depends to a great extent on the organization of their departments.

Extrajudicial measures as expressed in the YCJA are based on the philosophy that diversion is the most appropriate and effective way to address non-violent youth crime. The YCJA requires that, in every case, an extrajudicial sanction should be proportionate to the offence and provide an effective, timely opportunity for young offenders to acknowledge and repair the harm their behaviour has caused for victims and communities. Diversionary measures programs are usually restricted to first-time offenders charged with minor offences. Some provinces are lobbying to follow Quebec's lead in including more serious offences.

Diversionary measures programming can be categorized as reconciliation/mediation, retributive/restitutive, rehabilitative/educational, or restorative interventions. In most provinces, police make referrals for diversionary measures. Only Ontario uses a post-charge system, in which all youth are required to go to court before entering diversionary programs. Most provinces use both a pre- and post-charge referral system. In some provinces, Youth Justice Committees made up of citizens participate in these decision-making processes. Province by province, anywhere from 16 to 36 percent of apprehended youth have been referred to diversionary measures; success rates range from 80 to 98 percent.

Critics charge that diversionary measures are a net-widening mechanism because programs are largely restricted to minor offences by youth with no prior record and because, in most provinces, failure to comply may result in court processing. The usefulness and effectiveness of mediation is also questionable if victims are not willing to participate in the process, while the use of shaming in conferencing can be counter-productive to the restorative justice principles on which conferencing is based. Equally problematic is the question of who should control or administer diversionary measures and the extent to which governments are willing to adequately fund programs. Important questions have also been raised about the lack of accountability for referral decisions and the resulting potential for lack of consistency and unfair decisions. Some argue that to be truly diversionary, programs should be community-based and administered independently of the justice system.

DISCUSSION/CRITICAL THINKING QUESTIONS

1. Is the use of extrajudicial measures and sanctions equivalent to "doing nothing" or a "slap on the wrist"? Explain your answer.
2. In a restorative model of justice, does it make sense to have police as the "gatekeepers" of diversion? Explain your answer.
3. Does the term "meaningful consequences" imply punishment or reconciliation, harm reduction, and healing? Explain your answer.

WEB LINKS

Speech given by Armand P. La Barge, Chief of York Regional Police, Ontario
www.operationspringboard.on.ca
On the Operation Springboard home page at the above URL, click on "Site Search" and then, in the search window, insert "Speech given by Armand."

RCMP Youth Site
www.deal.org

An Examination of the Toronto Police Service Youth Referral Program
http://canada.justice.gc.ca/en/ps/yj/research/examen/index.html

Police Discretion with Young Offenders
http://canada.justice.gc.ca/en/ps/yj/research/carrington-schulenberg/report.html

For chapter quizzes and more links, visit this book's accompanying website at www.bellyoungoffenders3e.nelson.com

CHAPTER NINE

Going to Court

CHAPTER OBJECTIVES

1. To provide a statistical profile of the youth court population and show how it has changed through the Juvenile Delinquents Act (JDA), the Young Offenders Act (YOA), and the Youth Criminal Justice Act (YCJA).
2. To examine pretrial procedures and decision making associated with bail, detention, and the questions around adult sanctions for youth.
3. To discuss the role of legal professionals in youth court.
4. To identify rights provisions under the YCJA and the issues that surround them.
5. To discuss sentencing principles and provisions in youth court and examine how they have changed from the JDA to the YOA and YCJA, and how these principles and provisions compare to those for adult sentencing.

KEY TERMS

Interim release
Pretrial detention
Presumptive offence
Presumptive transfer
Extrajudicial sanctions
Jurisprudence
Legal advocate
Guardian
Sentencing conference
Retribution

Proportionality principle
Deterrence
Incapacitation
Rehabilitation
Restoration
Reconciliation
Reintegration
Gendered expectations
Median sentence length

INTRODUCTION

In Canada, more is known about the youth court than any other aspect of youth justice. Because of the creation of the Youth Court branch of the Canadian Centre for Justice Statistics, information has been readily available for discussion and analysis since the inception of the YOA. Not all of this information is comparable over time because of the time delay in introducing 16- to 17-year-old youth to the system, because not all provinces initially participated in sending their court statistics to Ottawa, and because of the introduction of the YCJA and important procedural and substantive changes. Nonetheless, researchers have been able to identify trends in the application of YOA principles; considerable debate accompanied these analyses, some of which influenced YOA reform and the resulting YCJA. At the time this book was written, statistics were available for only one year of YCJA operation, so at this point, we are able to make only general observations of change, rather than conclusive statements about impact. Judicial decisions and media coverage of individual cases provide examples of emerging issues, as judges and lawyers grapple with implementing the new legislation.

CASE STUDY BOX 9.1

Johnny: Court and Sentencing

In response to Johnny's case, as Theresa McEvoy was killed during police pursuit of a stolen vehicle, the Justice Minister at the time, Michael Baker, launched a public crusade, announcing he would fight for tougher youth laws for motor vehicle theft and arguing that stealing a car should be considered a violent crime. In opposition, Brian Stephens, a Legal Aid lawyer in Halifax, argued, "It's not uncommon for youths to steal cars, and by and large you don't have these kinds of chases. You're talking about property offences that immature youths do."

The media, however, capitalized on Minister Baker's crusade by continually criticizing the YCJA for taking away a judge's ability to detain youth in cases where they have not committed violent offences. Even Johnny's mother was critical of the youth criminal justice system, arguing, "No one should have the opportunities that my son had to keep walking away. Auto theft is a violent offence, and kids are getting too many chances. Thank God he was arrested." One reporter wrote, "How long is the public going to put up with teens repeatedly committing crimes only days after their release from custody on other criminal charges?"

Sharing Minister Baker's sentiments, Crown prosecutors Gary Holt and Eric Taylor were prepared to make an example of Johnny's case by seeking an adult sentence. Judge James Burrill agreed with the Crown and, on January 11, 2006, 16-year-old Johnny was sentenced as an adult to $5\frac{1}{2}$ years, which was consequently reduced to $4\frac{1}{2}$ years due to the one year he had served on remand. Johnny could apply for day parole within nine months, and he would be eligible for full parole after serving 18 months.

Under the YCJA, Johnny will serve his sentence at the Waterville Youth Detention Centre until he turns 20. At the age of 18, however, either he or the youth facility can apply for his transfer to an adult institution.

Sources: *The Chronicle Herald* [Halifax] (December 15, 2005; January 12, 26, 2006; February 23, 2006); B. Hayes (February 8, 2006); D. Jeffrey (December 20, 2005).

This chapter begins with a profile and analysis of the types of cases appearing before youth courts and proceeds to a discussion of the various stages of court decision making, including judicial discretion. Pretrial decisions regarding bail, detention, changes regarding transfers of youth to adult court, and the application of adult sentences to youth are addressed, along with the associated issues of net widening, deterrence, and children's legislative rights and potential violations. The chapter moves on to a discussion of sentencing practices in youth court. Following a review of the allowable sentences and the principles that support them, we consider how relevant adult sentencing principles are to youth court sentencing; how race, class, and gender affect sentencing decisions in youth court; whether youth court sentences under the YOA amounted to anything more than a "slap on the wrist," and whether this has changed under the YCJA.

THE COURT

A Profile

In 2003–2004, the first year of the YCJA, the youth court processed 70,465 cases and 191,302 charges—a 17 percent decrease in cases from the previous year and a 33 percent decrease from 1991–1992 (Thomas, 2005, pp. 1, 16). Much of this decrease is attributable to the YCJA because, as we saw in the last chapter, police charges also decreased dramatically during that period, and caseloads are directly impacted by changing police practices. Nonetheless, not all of the decline is attributable to changing legislation, because these declines began long before the new legislation. Court caseloads increased 20 percent in 1986–1987, when the YOA was fully implemented, and did not begin to show declines until 1994–1995 (Hendrick, 1997; Statistics Canada, 1998, pp. i, xii). Most of this caseload growth came from increases in administrative and YOA offence cases; failure to appear cases increased by 10 percent and YOA cases increased by 33 percent (Sudworth & deSouza, 2001, p. 3).

After the mid-1990s, the overall caseload steadily decreased; administrative cases fluctuated and continued to show some increases until 1999–2000, after which the number of cases began to decline to a low of 10 percent of all cases in 2003–2004. Administrative cases have dropped by 10 percent since 2000 and by 16 percent since 1991 (Robinson, 2004, p. 14; Thomas, 2005, pp. 13, 16).

Part of the long-range court caseload decrease is also attributable to a steady decline in cases coming before the court for property crimes. Property cases in 2003–2004 were less than half (58 percent) of what they were in 1991–1992 (see Table 9.1). They decreased the most—one-fifth (21 percent)—when the YCJA was implemented (Thomas, 2005, p. 16). This decrease is probably attributable to more use of extrajudicial measures for minor property offences. Similarly the effect of extrajudicial measures is also apparent with violent offence cases. This category of cases decreased for four years out of six between the 1998–1999 and 2003–2004 reports, but the greatest decrease was in 2003–2004 (9 percent compared to a range of 0.2 to 3.3). Nonetheless, the number of violent offences in 2003–2004 was still 14 percent higher than it was twelve years previously. While administrative cases have decreased over time, the number of YOA/YCJA cases appearing before the court was almost 30 percent higher in 2003–2004 than it was in 1991–1992 (Robinson, 2004, p. 14; Thomas, 2005, p. 16).

Table 9.1 also shows that the most common youth court cases (37 percent) involved property offences. Of these offences, the most common was theft under

TABLE 9.1

Number and Percentage of Cases in Youth Court, 2003–2004, by Type of Offence and Percentage Change from 1991–1992

Offence Category	Number of Cases	Percentage	% Change from 1991–1992
Property offences	25,663	37	−58.0
Violent offences	20,416	29	13.9
Administration of justice	6,784	10	−16.1
Other Criminal Code	3,896	6	−41.0
YOA/YCJA offences	7,692	11	34.6*
Other federal offences	4,893	7	**

*2003–2004 youth court statistics report only federal offences, including YOA/YCJA offences, which make up two-thirds of the federal offence cases for that year. Total federal offences increased for this 12-year period by 27.1 percent. This figure of 34.6 percent is for YOA/YCJA case changes for the period 1991–1992 to 2002–2003.

**A percentage change in "Other federal offences" cannot be calculated because YOA/YCJA offences are included in this category.

Source: Adapted from Statistics Canada (2004d, 2005e), *Juristat*, Cat. No. 85-002, 24(2), 25(4).

$5,000 (13 percent of the total number of court cases). Violent cases made up 29 percent of the cases, and combined administrative and YOA/YCJA offences accounted for 21 percent. Two-thirds of the cases were processed in four months and only 7 percent took longer than a year. While the number of charges heard by the court was almost three times the number of cases, 44 percent of the cases involved only one charge and 21 percent involved more than three (Thomas, 2005, pp. 4–5, 13).

Approximately 80 percent of youth court cases involved male youth; of these youth, 42 percent were under 16 years of age; one-third of the boys were 17 (Thomas, 2005, p. 4). The proportionate number of girls going to court increased from 18 percent in 1992–1993 to 21 percent in 2003–2004 and they were younger than the boys: 53 percent of the girls were under 16, and 15-year-old girls made up the largest category at 23 percent.

While the number of cases going to court has decreased since 1992–1993, the absolute number of girls going to court increased from 20,775 to 21,507 in 1999–2000, an increase largely accounted for by administrative and violence offences. Over this time period, girls increased their share of YOA charges from 21 to 26 percent and of violent charges from 18 to 22 percent. Their share of other Criminal Code charges also increased from 21 to 25 percent (Sudworth & deSouza, 2001, pp. 5–6).

Since the YOA was implemented, the number of girls in court for failure to comply charges increased as a proportion of all girls' charges: from 6.1 percent in 1985–1986 to 27.3 percent in 1995–1996 (Reitsma-Street, 1999, p. 338). From 2000–2005, the number of girls appearing in court decreased to 14,915 and their proportionate representation increased to 21 percent. This increase is largely accounted for by YOA/YCJA offences, which made up one-third of the cases. Girls were also over-represented in other administrative cases (24 percent), where they made up one-third of the failure to appear cases and "other" categories and almost one-quarter of the violent cases (24 percent). In the latter category, girls were mostly over-represented in the minor assault category.

In any one year, repeat offenders make up about one-third of court cases. The most recent statistics report that 35 percent of the convicted cases in 1999–2000 were repeat offenders; about 10 percent of the convictions were "persistent" offenders, that is, youth with three or more prior convictions. Repeat offenders were more involved in property crime (53 percent of all property cases) than in violent offences (25 percent). More boys in court were repeat offenders than girls (37 percent vs. 29 percent); 11 percent of the male cases were persistent offenders, while only 5 percent of the girls fell into this category (Sudworth & deSouza, 2001, p. 10).

A Statistics Canada study that traced 59,000 young offenders from 1991 to 2003 found that offenders who had been referred to court two to four times accounted for about 28 percent of all cases (Most young offenders . . .). An analysis of repeat offender data, or recidivists, from 1999–2000, shows that slightly more than two-thirds (62 percent) of convicted young adults between 18 to 25 years of age had at least one previous youth court conviction and, among these, almost 40 percent (38.7 percent) had multiple prior youth court convictions (Thomas, Hurley, & Grimes, 2002, pp. 4, 16). This does not mean that repeat young offenders necessarily go on to adult court, only that a large proportion of adult offenders have youth court records. Interestingly, this is the very observation that precipitated the process to reform the JDA almost 45 years ago.

Pretrial Detention

interim release
Provisions that allow an arrested person to be released into the community, under specific conditions, while waiting for a court appearance; commonly referred to as "bail."

Both the YCJA and Criminal Code provisions regarding judicial **interim release** apply to young offenders. The YCJA requires that young people held in detention prior to trial be detained separately from adults [s. 30(3)], unless no youth facility is available or it would be unsafe to do so [s. 30(3)(a) and (b)]. This does not apply to youth who are between 18 and 20: the YCJA allows for them to be held in adult provincial facilities [s. 30(4) and (5)].

The judicial interim release provisions of the Criminal Code require that a young person be brought before a youth court judge or justice of the peace within 24 hours. At this hearing, the prosecutor must show why the accused should be held in custody. The Criminal Code provides two reasons for **pretrial detention:** primary grounds and secondary grounds. Primary grounds are invoked when the court is convinced that custody is necessary to ensure that the youth will appear in court. Secondary grounds are invoked when the court believes that custody is necessary for public protection (Bala et al., 1994, p. 88; Doob, Marinos, & Varma, 1995, p. 101).

pretrial detention
The holding of an accused person in a prison or detention facility prior to a court appearance or trial, or while awaiting sentence; sometimes referred to as "remand."

An important difference for young offenders created by the YCJA is the required presumption in the YCJA that pretrial detention is not necessary under certain conditions. When considering secondary grounds for detention (that is, whether detention is necessary for the protection of society (s. 515(10)(b) of the Criminal Code), section 29(2) of the YCJA requires the court to presume that pretrial detention is not necessary if, on a conviction, the young person could not be sentenced to custody because of YCJA restrictions on committal to custody (s. 39(1)(a), (2)(c), as discussed below). One of the important restrictions on committal to custody that is different from the YOA is on the grounds of social welfare considerations. In other words, the YCJA specifically prohibits placing a young offender in pretrial detention "as a substitute for appropriate child protection, mental health or other social measures" [s. 29(1)].

Pretrial facilities vary considerably across the country. Some youth are detained in group homes and detention facilities that offer school, recreational, and counselling programs. Some jurisdictions do not offer programs in detention facilities, while other jurisdictions do not even have detention facilities. Sometimes youth are detained in custodial facilities for young people serving sentences (Bala et al., 1994, p. 89). Morin (1990) and Hamilton and Sinclair (1991) report that youth in Aboriginal communities are often removed from their communities because of a lack of detention facilities.

The number of young persons held in pretrial detention increased substantially under the YOA. Between 1986 and 1994, there was a 33 percent increase in the number of young people remanded in custody across the country (Foran, 1995). During this period, only Manitoba, the Yukon, and Prince Edward Island showed decreases in numbers of youth held in remand; all other provinces showed increases. In Ontario between 1985–1986 and 1988–1989, the number of 16- and 17-year-old youth in detention increased by 38 percent, there was a 71 percent increase in the number of bail hearings for 12- to 15-year-olds, and the number of pretrial detentions in 1989 was 30 percent higher than in 1985–1986 (Kenewell, Bala, & Colfer, 1991, p. 160).

In 2002–2003, 14,580 youth were detained in pretrial detention; this amounts to 61 percent of custody admissions: 33 percent were related to property offences and 31 percent were violent offence charges. This represents a 21 percent increase in remand admissions since 1993–1994. Use of remand continues to be highest for Manitoba and lowest for Prince Edward Island, New Brunswick, Quebec, and British Columbia. Much of the increase in remand use since 1993–1994 is due to increases in Newfoundland and Labrador, Nova Scotia, Manitoba, and Saskatchewan. All other provinces have shown declines in the use of remand (Reitano, 2004, pp. 2, 3). The federal Department of Justice reports that by 2005, the number of admissions to detention had decreased from YOA levels, and fewer youth with minor offence charges and breach of probation charges were being detained (Department of Justice, 2005, pp. 3–4).

The majority of youth admitted to pretrial detention are 16 and 17 years of age, but more 14- and 15-year-old girls are detained than boys in that age group (34 percent vs. 20 percent). Girls are also detained more often with minor offences. Similarly, Aboriginal youth are far more likely to be held in detention than non-Aboriginal youth and are more likely to be held for minor offences, especially Aboriginal girls. Twenty-six percent of admissions to detention are Aboriginal youth and 36 percent of girls admitted are Aboriginal. The average length of stay is 21 days, with one-half being released in less than one week. Seventeen percent of youth in remand are there from one to six months (Reitano, 2004, pp. 2–6; Statistics Canada, 2000b, pp. 1–18).

The court may decide to release a young offender if it is satisfied that a responsible person is willing to assume responsibility and control of the youth. This responsible person, who could be a parent, some other adult relative, or a family friend, makes an application for release and is examined by the court to determine if he or she is a suitable alternative to custody for the young person. A youth may also be released if a responsible person agrees to forfeit money or some security if the young offender violates the conditions of release.

The YCJA allows an accused youth to refuse this type of release. The YOA introduced the "responsible person" option to the courts and the YCJA [(s.31(2)] has turned it into an obligation of the court. Before the court can detain a young person, it is now mandatory that the court investigate as to the availability of a responsible person. Release conditions may include such things as a curfew, a specified place of residence, requirements to attend school, and a list of persons with whom the youth is not to associate. A youth who does not follow the direction of the person into whose custody she or he has been released, or who fails to comply with the conditions of release (YOA/YCJA offences) may be returned to the custody of the court (Hak, 1996, pp. 57–58).

Overall, under the YOA, this alternative method of release was highly underutilized (Report of the Federal–Provincial–Territorial Task Force on Youth Justice, 1996, p. 178). Doob's cross-country survey of youth court judges (2001) found that the "responsible person" option was not raised in almost one-quarter of detention cases overall and that there was considerable variation across the country. British Columbia judges were most likely to investigate this option, and Ontario judges were least likely to do so. Varma's observations of pretrial detention hearings (2002) found that not one of 118 bail hearings in Ontario involved a discussion of the "responsible person" option. The main reason offered by judges is that these youth are already ". . . out of the control of their parents and/or child protection agencies."

It is too early to know if there will be more or less use of the "responsible person" option under the YCJA, but recent media attention to pretrial release could foreshadow changes to come and has the potential to become a point of focus in the "youth-out-of-control" discourse and possible law reform. We have seen in the boxed "Johnny" case details throughout the text (including Box 9.1 on page 245) that the accidental death of a woman during a joyride in a stolen vehicle has largely been attributed to the fact that the young offender had been released to his mother's custody rather than held in detention pending trial. Similarly, as this book is being written, three other incidents that occurred in one week are unfolding in the Nova Scotia media. One involves a 15-year-old youth charged with a total of nine offences, including assault and uttering threats at his school. He has been released to his mother's custody while he waits for a court appearance. In another, a 13-year-old boy and a 14-year-old boy are together facing charges of motor vehicle theft. In the third case, the 13-year-old is also facing 23 other motor vehicle charges. These boys were all released pending their court appearances.

The main focus of these media stories has been, as in Johnny's case, pretrial release. All of the stories emphasize that the boys had initially been released to the custody of parents and offer chronologies of their criminal activities after their release, as well as details of the release conditions that were violated. In all three cases, the boys are now also facing YCJA charges for violating their bail conditions and failing to abide by their release conditions. In one case, the youth was charged with an assault offence the same day he was released by the court to his mother's custody, and was still returned to his mother's custody by the police. Interestingly, one father is cited, similar to Johnny's mother, as being critical of the YCJA because it prevents parents from using corporal punishment as a method of controlling their children (Boy facing assault charges released, 2006).

Widening the Net

Pretrial detention contributes to net widening by increasing the number of youth in custody and, as seen in the examples above, by escalating charges for young people through rules associated with violations of release conditions. Gandy (1992), who examined transcripts of bail hearings in three Ontario cities, argued that bail hearings often set youth up for further offending, thereby assuring custodial dispositions for some. He found that, contrary to the rules (secondary grounds), most young people detained in pretrial custodial facilities were initially charged with non-violent offences. According to Gandy:

> . . . the courts have created a situation, through very restrictive conditions of release,
> in which "out of control" is an almost inevitable outcome. It may be that the court

should consider imposing the fewest conditions that are compatible with the protection of the public. It would appear that in establishing the conditions of release some judges use a shotgun approach to try to anticipate all contingencies. (1992, p. 75)

Some youth are adversely affected by the use of pretrial detention and the rules and regulations concerning bail release. The use of pretrial detention is particularly problematic for homeless youth, for Aboriginal youth, for those whose friends or relatives are not likely to be considered responsible by the court, and for those with poor parental relationships. Many youth end up in custody not because they committed a serious crime, but because (1) they did not follow the direction of the court or their parents or (2) they do not have parents, adults, or relatives who are willing or able to assume responsibility for them (Gandy, 1992). Section 31(2) of the YCJA addresses this issue by directing the court to attempt to find a responsible person in instances where a youth would be detained in custody if no such person is immediately available.

The federal Department of Justice reports that while the use of detention is showing declines under the YCJA, the proportion of youth detained at bail hearings has not changed. Furthermore, pre-trial detention is still being used in some jurisdictions to address social welfare needs, in contravention of subsection 29(1) of the YCJA (Department of Justice, 2005, pp. 3–4).

Transfer to Adult Court

For those committed to youth justice reform, one of the most contentious aspects of the YOA was s. 16, which allowed judges to transfer youth (over 14 at the time of the offence) to adult court for trial if they had been charged with a serious indictable offence. Transfer was not automatic initially, and applications for transfer were made by the Crown or the young person. When the YOA was first implemented, the decision to transfer required the court to strike a balance between "the interest of society" and "the needs of the young person." In practice, there was considerable variation in how judges interpreted s. 16. Manitoba and Alberta, both with a relatively high transfer rate, placed a greater emphasis on the "interest of society." Ontario, Quebec, and Saskatchewan, on the other hand, placed a greater emphasis on the "needs of the young person," as reflected in their much lower rates of transfer (Bala et al., 1994, pp. 101–102). As a result of discrepancies such as these, the YOA, and the test for transfer, were twice modified—first in 1992 and again in 1995.

The first amendments specified more clearly what should be done if principles could not easily be balanced. As we see in Box 9.2, YOA s. 16(2) required the court to consider a number of factors in making its decision. One of the most important of these factors was "the availability of appropriate treatment and correctional resources" in the youth system, compared to available resources in the adult system. Thus, if the court decided that the protection of society and the rehabilitation of the young person could not be reconciled under the YOA, the youth could be transferred to the adult system for trial.

One young offender successfully argued to have his youth custody sentence changed to adult custody. Convicted of manslaughter in the stabbing of a cabdriver, the youth was sentenced in 1996. He was to serve $1^1/_2$ years at the Nova Scotia Youth Centre, two years in a provincial jail, and the remainder of his sentence in a federal penitentiary. At the original sentencing, Justice Suzanne Hood expressed concern that the young offender would be "badly influenced" by an adult penitentiary culture. At the custody hearing, corrections officials maintained that the young offender, then

BOX 9.2

YOA Provisions for Transfer

Section 16(2) of the YOA outlined the factors that the court was required to consider in making decisions about transfer. These factors were to be considered in the context of the principles laid out in s. 3 of the YOA:

(a) the seriousness of the alleged offence and the circumstances in which it was allegedly committed;

(b) the age, maturity, character and background of the young person and any record or summary of previous findings of delinquency;

(c) the adequacy of this Act, and the adequacy of the Criminal Code or any other Act of Parliament that would apply in respect of the young person if an order were made under this section to meet the circumstances of the case;

(d) the availability of treatment or correctional resources;

(e) any representations made to the court on behalf of the young person or by the Attorney General or his agent; and

(f) any other factors that the court considers relevant.

Under the 1995 revision, subsection 1.1 was added. It stated:

> In making the determination referred to in Subsection (1), the youth court, after affording both parties and the parents of the young person an opportunity to be heard, shall consider the interest of society, which includes the objectives of affording protection to the public and rehabilitation of the young person, and determine whether those objectives can be reconciled by the youth being under the jurisdiction of the youth court.

19, had successfully completed all of the programming offered by the youth facility and that it would be a "recipe for disaster" to keep him there or move him to a provincial facility. Only the penitentiary system, they argued, could give the youth what he needed, that is, "more advanced educational programming and more intensive psychiatric counselling and addiction treatment" (Armstrong, 1997).

A major concern at transfer hearings therefore was whether the young person was likely to be rehabilitated within the duration of the sentence allowed in the youth court. Initially, the maximum sentence in youth court for first-degree murder was three years. In adult court, the choice for young offenders was a life sentence with a minimum of 25 years before eligibility for parole. Hence, judges or juries were reluctant to sentence youth in the same manner they would adults. Hak (1996) tells of the case of a young person who had been involved in a fatal driving accident: "[Given] the age of the young offender and the lack of a prior record, it was unlikely that the adult court would sentence the youth to more than three years. As that sentence was available in youth court, transfer to adult court would have had little meaning" (p. 63).

The disparity between youth and adult sentences was reduced considerably in 1992. Amendments allowed the youth court to impose a murder sentence of five years less a day. For those transferred to and convicted in adult court, a life sentence meant eligibility for parole after five to ten years. Amendments also permitted adult courts to determine whether the young person would be sent to an adult federal penitentiary, an adult provincial facility, a youth custody facility, or any combination of the three. The second set of changes, in 1995, lengthened youth court sentences and shortened youth sentences in adult court, thereby bringing the two closer together. Changes included the following:

- Youth court sentences for first- and second-degree murder were increased to ten years and seven years, respectively;
- Young offenders charged with murder who were to be tried in youth court were given the choice of trial by judge and jury or trial by judge alone;
- For youth transferred to adult court, eligibility for parole was increased to ten and seven years, respectively, for first- and second-degree murder; and
- Sixteen- and seventeen-year-old youth charged with murder, attempted murder, manslaughter, aggravated sexual assault, or aggravated assault were to be automatically transferred to and tried in adult court unless an application was granted for the young person's case to be heard in youth court [section 16(1.01)].

With the latter change, another reverse onus situation was created. The onus was on a 16- or 17-year-old offender to demonstrate to a judge why she or he should be tried in youth court rather than adult court. In justifying this change, then-Minister of Justice Allan Rock stated:

> . . . public protection is a primary concern and this is best achieved through community-based crime prevention programs for children at risk and through rehabilitation, wherever possible. At the same time, we must ensure that young people understand that violence is not acceptable and that there are serious consequences for violent behaviour. (Minister of Justice, 1994)

Transfer Issues

Issues surrounding transfer included whether it would reduce youth crime (deterrence), whether it would increase the number of youth in the adult system (net widening), and whether it was "fair" to young offenders (due process). While there was (and still is) no shortage of groups lobbying for more young offenders to be processed through adult courts, there is little evidence to suggest that transfer will actually have a deterrent effect on youth crime. According to two American studies, changes that allowed automatic transfers in New York and Idaho did not result in a decrease in serious youth crime (Jensen & Metsger, 1994; Singer & McDowall, 1988). Notwithstanding this finding, young offenders in a study conducted in New York reported being more afraid of adult court than youth court (Glassner et al., 1983).

McGuire (1997, pp. 197–198) argued that lengthy sentence provisions resulting from 1995 changes to the YOA (Bill C-37) were likely to result in fewer transfers to the adult system rather than more. She based this argument on the major differences between adult and youth facilities with respect to treatment and rehabilitation programs. She refers to *R. v. James Albert C.* (T) [1991], where the court noted:

> . . . this phase I facility [Syl Apps Secure Custody Facility] has twenty treatment beds and is based on Milieu Therapy in which each part of the youth's day from the moment he wakes until the end of the day is focused on treatment . . . Warkworth Institution [an adult federal penitentiary] has a mental health staff of four psychologists to deal with an inmate population of approximately 700, a ratio of 175:1. The only therapy that the psychologists provide is crisis management, as the vast majority of their time is spent doing risk reports prior to parole hearings.

Justice Lucien Beaulieu (1994) raised some serious legal concerns about transfer provisions in the YOA. In his argument, he points out that since the primary focus of transfer hearings is to determine the type of sentence that a young person would get in youth court versus adult court, a fundamental and "cherished principle of criminal common law" is compromised. Our justice system requires that an accused be presumed innocent until proven guilty in a court of law. However, in transfer hearings for young people, we are forced to "presume innocence but assume guilt." All of the information considered in a transfer hearing—predisposition reports, medical reports, psychological reports, and the like—reflects an assumption of the guilt of the accused. Beaulieu (pp. 338–339) suggested that since some exceptional cases of young offenders might be better transferred to the adult court for sentencing, the legislation should be altered so that transfer to the adult system for sentencing would take place after a young person had been found guilty in youth court. Both the Federal–Provincial–Territorial Task Force and the Standing Committee on Justice and Legal Affairs recommended that the YOA be revised so that transfer provisions would be imposed after a finding of guilt (Cohen, 1997, p. 65; Report of the Federal–Provincial–Territorial Task Force, 1996, pp. 305–306). This turned out to be one of the important aspects of the YCJA.

Adult Sentences and the YCJA

Legislators responded to these concerns about transfer by sidestepping the whole issue of a transfer hearing in the YCJA: all youth charges will be heard in youth court. The issue under the YCJA is one of liability for an adult sentence, not transfer. There are now provisions in the legislation giving youth court the power to impose adult sentences (see Box 9.3) rather than have to face the arduous task of deciding to transfer a youth to adult court. This was accomplished through the creation of the **presumptive offence** (see Box 9.4), in combination with new sentencing provisions for "serious offences" and "serious violent offences." Quite simply, whether a youth is liable to an adult sentence depends on the nature of the offence, the youth's age, and prior record, and whether the offence would make an adult liable for imprisonment for a term of more than two years.

Basically, there are three situations in which youth are liable to an adult sentence. First, the YCJA requires an adult sentence for youth 16 and over who are found guilty of murder, attempted murder, manslaughter, or aggravated sexual assault. The presumptive offence rule applies to youth aged 14 and 15, unless a province changes the minimum age to 15 for its jurisdiction.

Second, section 64(1) further strengthens the court's ability to impose adult sentences by extending these powers to also include serious violent offences. In these instances, the onus is on the attorney general to request an adult sentence and for the accused youth to challenge such a request, or for a young offender to apply for the court to order that she or he is not liable to an adult sentence and for the attorney general to challenge. Furthermore, s. 42(9) allows the youth court to determine that an offence is a serious violent one, and while the act defines a serious violent offence as "an offence in the commission of which a young person causes or attempts to cause serious bodily harm [s. 2(1)], it does not define "serious offences." Third, there is now a "three-strike rule," so youth who have committed (or are alleged to have committed) a serious violent offence who already have two prior convictions for serious violent offences are also liable to an adult sentence.

The Quebec government has challenged the constitutionality of a number of YCJA provisions, but most were rejected; the exceptions were those relating to presumptive offences. More specifically, the Quebec Court of Appeal maintained that it is a violation of the Canadian Charter of Rights and Freedoms for the onus to be on a

presumptive offence
Under the YCJA, a serious violent offence, or any other violent offence for which an adult would be liable to a prison sentence of more than two years.

BOX 9.3

YCJA Provisions for Adult Sentences

Section 62 of the YCJA outlines the conditions under which the youth court has the power to impose an adult sentence on a young offender, and s. 72(1) outlines the factors that the court must consider in making a decision as to a youth's liability for an adult sentence:

Section 62 An adult sentence shall be imposed on a young person who is found guilty of an indictable offence for which an adult is liable to imprisonment for a term of more than two years in the following cases:

(a) in the case of a presumptive offence, if the youth justice court makes an order under subsection 70(2) (youth does not request a youth sentence) or paragraph 72(1)(b) [see below]; or

(b) in any other case, if the youth justice court makes an order under subsection 64(5) (youth does not oppose an adult sentence) or paragraph 72(1)(b) [see below] in relation to an offence committed after the young person attained the age of fourteen years.

Section 72 (1) In making its decision on an application heard in accordance with section 71(hearing for adult sentence), the youth justice court shall consider the seriousness and circumstances of the offence, and the age, maturity, character, background and previous record of the young person and any other factors that the court considers relevant, and

(a) if it is of the opinion that a youth sentence imposed in accordance with the purpose and principles set out in subparagraph 3(1)(b)(ii) and section 38 would have sufficient length to hold the young person accountable for his or her offending behaviour, it shall order that the young person is not liable to an adult sentence and that a youth sentence must be imposed; and

(b) if it is of the opinion that a youth sentence imposed in accordance with the purpose and principles set out in subparagraph 3(1)(b)(ii) and section 38 would not have sufficient length to hold the young person accountable for his or her offending behaviour, it shall order that an adult sentence be imposed.

youth to convince the court that a youth sentence should be imposed. A consequence of an adult sentence is that the youth is no longer entitled to a publication ban, and the Quebec court also ruled this to be a violation of the Charter. The federal government under Jean Chrétien announced plans to revise the YCJA so that it would be consistent with the appeal court ruling (Bala & Anand, 2004, p. 264). Subsequent changes in government have delayed these reforms.

These new provisions for adult sentencing have solved the legal dilemma raised by Justice Beaulieu but they also have created new problems, the nature of which depends on the model of juvenile justice that is adopted. Crime control advocates, particularly Conservative MPs, are still advocating for the age of eligibility to be lowered from age 14 (Hogeveen & Smandych, 2001, pp. 161–162), while welfare and restorative justice advocates are concerned that these new provisions will result in far too

BOX 9.4

YCJA Definition of Presumptive Offence

The YCJA defines a presumptive offence as:

2.1 (a) an offence committed, or alleged to have been committed, by a young person who has attained the age of 14 years, or, in a province where the Lieutenant Governor in Council has fixed an age greater than 14 years under section 61, the age so fixed, under one of the following provisions of the Criminal Code:

    (i)   Section 231 or 235 (First Degree Murder or Second Degree Murder within the meaning of Section 231),

    (ii)   Section 239 (Attempt to Commit Murder),

    (iii)   Section 232, 234, or 236 (Manslaughter), or

    (iv)   Section 273 (Aggravated Sexual Assault),

  (b) a serious violent offence for which an adult is liable to imprisonment for a term of more than two years committed, or alleged to have been committed, by a young person after the coming into force of section 62 (adult sentence) and after the young person has attained the age of 14 years, or in a province where the Lieutenant Governor in Council has fixed an age greater than 14 years under section 61, the age so fixed, if at the time of the commission or alleged commission of the offence at least two judicial determinations have been made under subsection 42(9), at different proceedings, that the young person has committed a serious violent offence.

many 14- and 15-year-old youth in the adult system—a regressive return to pre-JDA years. Similarly, these same advocates foresee greater numbers of youth overall in the adult system, thereby undermining the very reason for a youth justice system—to keep them out of the adult system. This too is a main reason for Bloc MPs' opposition to the YCJA: these automatic adult sentences effectively undermine the welfare and restorative justice aspects of Quebec's Youth Protection Act (Hogveen & Smandych, 2001, pp. 163–164). Already, we have seen the new Conservative government introduce a bill to add "street racing" to the Criminal Code as a violent offence. This will undoubtedly increase the number of youth liable to adult sentences.

According to 1999–2000 court statistics, 7,103 youth were charged with violent offences more serious than minor assault. Taking away the 15 percent that are 12 and 13 years of age, roughly 6,000 youth could potentially be eligible for an adult sentence under YCJA rules—a significantly greater number than the 52 cases that were actually transferred under the YOA rules (Sudworth & deSouza, 2001, pp. 7, 14, 16). As we will see later in this chapter, adult sentences also mean adult rules. Young offenders with adult sentences, some potentially as young as 14, will now come under the jurisdiction of the Corrections and Conditional Release Act, including the Parole Act and decision-making powers of the Parole Board—legislation that governs adult federal corrections.

Another question relates to the future of youth in the adult system—taking us right back to the issue addressed in Box 9.6 and by McGuire (1997)—whether adult facilities have programs and staff that can address the needs of young offenders. Anand (2003) and Doob and Cesaroni (2004, pp. 187–188) maintain that the YCJA changes to transfer provisions does only two new things: it reduces the age limit of automatic or **"presumptive transfer"** to the adult system to age 14 and expands the list of offences for automatic transfer. To this we can add that, now, no youth cases are tried in adult court.

presumptive transfer
Under the YCJA, the automatic transfer of a youth case to adult sentencing provisions.

BOX 9.5

Maximum Penalty for First-Degree Murder under the YOA

In Youth Court

- Ten-year sentence of six years' custody and four years' conditional supervision in the community.
- Custody term served in youth facility. Transfer to adult provincial facility possible at age 18.

In Adult Court

- Mandatory life sentence with parole eligibility after 10 years.
- Sentence served in youth facility, provincial adult facility, federal penitentiary, or a combination of the three.

BOX 9.6

Maximum Penalty for First-Degree Murder under the YCJA in Youth Court

Section 42(2) of the YCJA reads: . . . if the offence is first degree murder or second degree murder within the meaning of section 231 of the Criminal Code, the court shall . . . :

42(2) (q) order the young person to serve a sentence not to exceed
   (i) in the case of first degree murder, ten years comprised of
      (A) a committal to custody, to be served continuously, for a period that must not, subject to subsection 104(1) (Continuation of Custody), exceed six years from the date of committal, and
      (B) a placement under conditional supervision to be served in the community in accordance with section 105, and
   (ii) in the case of second degree murder, seven years comprised of
      (A) a committal to custody, to be served continuously, for a period that must not, subject to subsection 104(1) (Continuation of Custody), exceed four years from the date of committal, and
      (B) a placement under conditional supervision to be served in the community in accordance with section 105;
   (r) make an intensive rehabilitative custody and supervision order in respect of the young person
      (ii) that is for a specified period that must not exceed, in the case of first degree murder, ten years from the date of committal, comprising
         (A) a committal to intensive rehabilitative custody, to be served continuously, for a period that must not exceed six years from the date of committal, and
         (B) subject to subsection 104(1) (Continuation of Custody), placement under conditional supervision to be served in the community in accordance with section 105, and

(continued)

Box 9.6 continued

     (iii) that is for a specified period that must not exceed, in the case of second degree murder, seven years from the date of committal, comprising

      (A) a committal to intensive rehabilitative custody, to be served continuously, for a period that must not exceed four years from the date of committal, and

      (B) subject to subsection 104(1) (Continuation of Custody), a placement under conditional supervision to be served in the community in accordance with section 105;

If the youth is to receive an adult sentence, he or she would receive the same sentence as an adult.

Parole eligibility is different for youth, depending on age. Whereas adults serving murder sentences are not eligible for parole for 10 to 25 years, youth aged 14 to 15 are not eligible for 5 to 7 years, and those 16 to 17 are not eligible for 7 to 10 years (Doob & Sprott, 2005, p. 238).

VOICES BOX 9.7

Positions on Youth Incarceration in Adult Facilities

Clinical Social Worker at a YOA Transfer Hearing

The culture in a federal institution is based on physical power and intimidation, not on cooperation and earning good will such as is found in the community. A young offender who is not sufficiently tough will be abused physically, sexually . . . [I]f he refuses the protection and homosexual advances from the tougher, older inmate, then he will be raped and abused until he accepts that protection.

  The only protection which can be afforded a young offender is to place him in segregation . . . Anyone who is put in segregation for reasons other than punishment is labelled, rightly or wrongly, as a possible informer and therefore life becomes very dangerous when he re-enters the general prison population.

Forensic Scientist at the Same Hearing

I can guarantee after ten years we'll have the worst frustrated and angry man. I can guarantee that the damage that the penitentiary system will do will be far worse than anything you've ever seen.

Source: *R. v. G.J.M.*, April 21, 1992, unreported (Alta. Q.B.): T.P. 33.

The Reality of Transfer Decisions

In 1994–1995, 123 cases were sent to adult court; 67 percent involved violent offences and 24 percent involved property offences. The highest rate of transfer occurred in Manitoba, where 58 cases (47 percent of all transfer cases) were transferred to adult court. According to youth court reports, young people in Manitoba were choosing to transfer to adult court as a means of avoiding a sentence to a youth custody facility (Doherty & deSouza, 1996, p. 7). It appears that McGuire's prediction (1997) may have been correct, in that only 74 cases were transferred to adult court in 1995–1996. While 92 youth were transferred in 1996–1997, the numbers of transfers have declined since then to a low of 30 in 2002–2003, the last year for which YOA statistics appear (Robinson, 2004, p. 5; Statistics Canada, 1998, p. vii). In 2003–2004, 8 cases were transferred because the proceedings had begun under the YOA (Thomas, 2005, p. 5). Statistics are not reported for youth receiving an adult sentence.

Over the years of the YOA, the majority of transfers involved older male youth charged with violent offences such as robbery, serious assault, and sexual assault. However, Doob and Cesaroni's analysis of transfer cases from 1998–2000 (2004) points out that the majority of the most serious offences, such as murder and aggravated assault, were handled in youth court. Equally important, many cases transferred to adult court did not involve serious offences but rather property offences and administrative offences, among others (pp. 180–181).

Transfers to adult court have led to considerable variation in consequences for youth, particularly after the 1995 YOA modifications. In 1997, two teens were transferred to adult court in Edmonton and convicted of fatally stabbing a mother of two. One was convicted of second-degree murder and sent to the federal penitentiary in Prince Albert, Saskatchewan, to serve a life sentence. He was not eligible for parole for seven years. The other youth was convicted of manslaughter and served $4^{1}/_{2}$ months of a four-year sentence in the Edmonton Young Offenders Centre before being transferred to an Alberta adult penitentiary. He was eligible for parole after two years (Teens who killed . . . , 1997).

COURT PROCEEDINGS

Youth court trials begin with a plea. Most young offenders plead guilty. In 2003–2004, 57 percent of youth court cases involved a finding or plea of guilt, a figure slightly lower than the previous eight years, when the rate fluctuated from 67 to 60 percent (Robinson, 2004, p. 15; Thomas, 2005, p. 17). In spite of overall decreases in guilty cases, the rate of guilty findings for girls increased from 1991–1992 to 1999–2000. Sprott and Doob (2003) argue that percentage increases for girls do not mean that more girls are being found guilty, but rather that boys' rates are declining due to decreases in guilty findings for boys charged with property offences (p. 79).

If a young person pleads guilty, the court proceeds directly to sentencing; if she or he pleads not guilty, the case goes to trial. A youth court trial is the same as an adult court trial, with two exceptions. Initially, under the YOA, there was no preliminary hearing and no jury trial in youth court, but the 1995 revisions (Bill C-37) allowed young offenders to opt for a jury trial in murder cases only. The YCJA changed these rules considerably, allowing a youth to elect a trial when an application has been made for an order for an adult sentence, when a young offender is subject to an adult sentence, or when he or she is facing a murder charge. This is also the case when the charge is one that would entitle an adult to a jury trial. YCJA section 67(2) outlines the instructions that the judge must put to the young person in all of these cases:

> You have the option to elect to be tried by a youth justice court judge without a jury and without having had a preliminary inquiry; or you may elect to have a preliminary inquiry and to be tried by a judge without a jury; or you may elect to have a

preliminary inquiry and to be tried by a court composed of a judge and jury. If you do not elect now, you shall be deemed to have elected to have a preliminary inquiry and to be tried by a court composed of a judge and jury. How do you elect to be tried?

Young offenders in Nunavut have the right to be tried by the Nunavut Court of Justice [s. 67(4)]. Youth may not elect for a jury trial if they are subject to a youth sentence, unless the charge is murder (s. 66).

Preliminary inquiries must now be conducted in the same manner as they are for adults, except where this might be inconsistent with the YCJA. In addition, s. 67(6) gives the attorney general the power to require a young person be tried by a judge and jury, even in cases where a young person elects to be tried without a jury.

In 2003–2004, it took an average of 134 days to process a case with only one charge (Thomas, 2005, p. 5). Processing a case through youth court is a complex affair and the YCJA has made the process longer and more complex than it was under the YOA. Bloomenfeld and Cole (2005) explain that case processing involves not only the accused and a judge, but also police, Crown prosecutors, judges other than the trial judge, a justice of the peace, and defence and duty counsel, as well as probation officers, youth workers, and a variety of other non-legal professionals.

The YCJA requires some processes and lays the groundwork for provincial choices in others, such as judicial conferencing (see the discussion of sentencing conference in the "Court Sentencing" section later in this chapter). This means that processing may vary from province to province. Bloomenfeld and Cole (2005) provide the following hypothetical scenario for court processing in Ontario. After the police have decided to lay a charge, the case goes to court for a trial judge to decide on pretrial release. Prior to this and after the Crown receives the police charge, the evidence and information presented must be weighed for a decision by the Crown as to whether to process the case through court or, when there is a guilty plea, whether to apply **extrajudicial sanctions.** If the decision is to go to court, decisions must then be made in meetings with defence counsel about guilty pleas and potentially reducing charges in terms of number or severity. This stage often involves an informal judicial pretrial (JPT) meeting, where the Crown and defence counsel meet with a judge other than the scheduled trial judge to discuss the viability of particular sentences for a plea or finding of guilt (Bloomenfeld & Cole, 2005, pp. 203–216):

> . . . neither the crown nor defence are obligated to go along with what may have been agreed to at a JPT. What both parties get out of a judicial indication of what sentence will be imposed is certainty, in exchange for compromise. (p. 212)

If the case goes to trial and there is a guilty plea or a finding of guilt, the judge will then involve probation officers and other professionals to assist in determination of sentence through a variety of psychological, medical or community assessments, and pre-sentence reports. In cases where youth are liable for adult sentences (presumptive offences), a pre-sentencing hearing is held with all parties to determine if an adult sentence will be applied to the case. Hence, 134 days from start to finish for one case may, in simple cases where all parties are in agreement, translate into 1 to 4 full court days to complete (Bloomenfeld & Cole, 2005, p. 211). In other words, a lot of behind-the-scenes work is required by policy, law, and **jurisprudence** (pp. 211, 217). More complex cases take longer than a year, and in 2003–2004, there were 4,932 of these (7 percent of the court cases) (Thomas, 2005, p. 4).

extrajudicial sanctions
Used when cases proceed to court and the provisions provide for specific sanctions and rules regarding the use of more formal diversionary programs.

jurisprudence
The science and philosophy of law and its practice.

Legal Representation

Only with the introduction of the YOA (s. 11) did youth have the right to legal representation in court. Four types of representation are available to a young offender: privately retained lawyer, Legal Aid lawyer, duty counsel (i.e., a lawyer on duty each day in the court), or a court-appointed/funded lawyer. Court-appointed lawyers are not available in adult court. Young offenders who are unable to retain the services of a private lawyer or a Legal Aid lawyer have the right to request that the court provide them with a lawyer—a policy that has been criticized as something that gives "inexperienced" lawyers an opportunity to learn on the job (Hak, 1996, p. 54).

Under the YCJA, s. 25, young people are still entitled to a private, Legal Aid, or court-appointed lawyer. If the court has a sense that the interests of a young person and the interests of a parent are in conflict, the judge is required to ensure that a young person is represented by counsel, independent of his or her parents [s. 25(8)]. Subsection (10) allows provinces to establish a program that would recover the cost of a young person's counsel, either from the young person or the parents of the young person. Of concern here is that parents may coerce their children to plead guilty to avoid having to pay legal fees. In addition, lawyers have expressed concern regarding tensions between youth receiving legal counsel and those paying their legal bills. Parents and other legal guardians of youth appearing in court, such as foster parents and institutions, are not always in agreement about what they consider to be the best interests of the youth relative to the young person's instructions to the lawyer (Bloomenfeld & Cole, 2005, p. 210). If the court believes that these interests are in conflict, it has the power to ensure independent counsel for the youth (Doob & Cesaroni, 2004, p. 36).

Whether a young offender has a lawyer does seem to make a difference. A survey of major cities across the country just prior to implementation of the YOA indicated that the presence of a lawyer and the type of representation did have an influence on the likelihood of conviction and/or type of conviction. Duty counsel lawyers were found to be considerably less "successful" than private lawyers. In fact, duty counsel cases were comparable in outcome to cases with no legal representation. Private lawyers were found to be better than duty counsel at negotiating to have charges dropped and in defending not-guilty pleas (Carrington & Moyer, 1990, p. 633). Both Bell (1994a) and Schissel (1993), who studied individual YOA youth courts in 1986, reported that type of representation made a difference, and that the effect of representation varies by race, class, and gender of the accused. Schissel (1993) also found that Aboriginal youth do not benefit as much from private and Legal Aid lawyers as do non-Aboriginal youth.

The Role of Lawyers

A young person's right to legal representation introduced with the YOA has continued with the YCJA. The YCJA and the Canadian Charter of Rights and Freedoms maintain that youth should be provided with ample opportunities for legal advocacy and advice before any court sanctioning and that access to lawyers should be available at pretrial stages and at all stages of the court process.

Most young offenders do not have a lawyer when they first appear in court and this is where duty counsel can step in. In Ontario, duty counsel lawyers are either private lawyers paid by the Ontario Legal Aid Plan or employees of the plan. They work in the court waiting rooms to provide advice to youth and their parents about what to expect when they go into court, and speak to the court on the youth's behalf. They will also talk to youth about release and supervision, and contact people who might agree to supervise the youth or, in the case of extrajudicial sanctions, discuss options with the youth and negotiate sanctioning terms with the Crown and probation services. Duty counsel lawyers also make submissions and present arguments to the court judge about release conditions, extrajudicial sanctioning agreements, and sentencing if the youth has decided to plead guilty at his or her first court appearance. Beyond the first appearance, private, Legal Aid, or court-appointed counsel takes over these functions (Bell, 1994a; Bloomenfeld & Cole, 2005, pp. 208–209).

There is some debate over what role lawyers should play in youth court. Should they act in the best interest of the child, or should they merely offer legal representation? In other words, should a lawyer assume a **legal advocate** role or a **guardian** role? The Law Society of Upper Canada advises lawyers to serve as advocates:

> There is no place . . . for counsel representing the child to argue what is in his opinion in the best interest of the child. Counsel should not be deciding whether training school would be "good" for the child . . . It is advice with respect to the legal rights of the child which is being provided, and that advice is being provided to the child, not to the parents, not to the court, and not to society, but to the child. (1981, cited in Bala et al., 1994, p. 83)

Lawyers who assume a legal advocate role will advise young clients of their rights to remain silent, suggest that they not cooperate with police, provide a legal defence, and try to prevent a conviction; in the case of conviction, they try to get the most lenient disposition possible (Milne, Linden, & Kueneman, 1992, p. 329).

Lawyers who assume a guardian role are primarily concerned about what they believe to be the "best interests" of the young offender. As one Manitoba lawyer puts it, "My attitude to the practice of law is not adversarial. I am aware of the legal issues and the fact that I am a lawyer, but I am concerned with rehabilitation. I do take the role of a stern parent" (cited in Milne, Linden, & Kueneman, 1992, p. 333). In the event of a conviction, this kind of lawyer will be primarily concerned about what he or she thinks the young offender requires for rehabilitation. Bloomenfeld and Cole (2005) maintain that most defence counsel ". . . likely combine elements of both of these approaches to best address their client's needs and requirements" (p. 211).

Legal Rights

A fundamental principle underlying a separate justice system for youth is that they are of a different level of maturity than adults and as such have special needs and require special protections. To this end, the YOA and now the YCJA specify these rights and the procedures to ensure them. Beyond the right to counsel and the right to a court-appointed lawyer, the YCJA provides youth the right to be informed, through a variety of means, of these legal rights [s. 25(9)] and of provisions specific to youth regarding the admissibility of statements they make to the police. These latter provisions, in addition to the ones provided to adults (such as the right to not make a statement), include the right to consult a parent or other person as well as a lawyer and a requirement that statements to police be made in the presence of counsel and any other person requested by the youth [s. 146(2)(b)(iii, iv)]. The YCJA also requires that rights regarding police statements be "clearly explained . . . in language appropriate to his or her age and understanding" [s. 146(2)(b)].

These latter requirements, also included in the YOA [s. 56(b)] sparked controversy because police "technical" mistakes could lead to acquittals and were eventually accepted as "overly prescriptive." The YCJA provides more leeway for the courts in

legal advocate
The role of a lawyer in making decisions and acting in the best interests of his or her client, to ensure that the client has every possible legal advantage.

guardian
A person who has been given legal authority over and responsibility for another person.

deciding if a youth's rights regarding statements were upheld. More specifically, the court can decide to uphold a young person's statement even when it has determined that required procedures were not followed when the youth waived his or her right to not make a statement. The court must satisfy three conditions to uphold this type of statement: The court must be satisfied that procedures were not followed because of a "technical violation," that the young person was informed of his or her rights and waived them voluntarily, and that admitting the statement ". . . would not bring into disrepute the principle that young persons are entitled to enhanced procedural protection" to ensure their rights [s. 146(5–6)]. It is interesting to note that the YCJA does not define what constitutes a "technical violation" (Bala, 2003).

From a strictly legal perspective, there are questions about whether young people understand the rights that are provided to them by law. While a youth may understand that she or he "has" rights, the fundamental question concerns whether any particular individual understands the meaning of these rights. A case decision in August 2005 raised this question about provisions protecting youth rights in police questioning, more specifically YCJA s. 146 (2)(b). Judge Pam Williams ruled in a Nova Scotia youth court that a videotaped confession from a 15-year-old boy charged with dangerous driving causing bodily harm was inadmissible because the ". . . police didn't follow the guidelines properly" and ". . . she was not convinced beyond a reasonable doubt the boy understood his rights." The defence had argued that the police should engage teens in a conversation and then write down their explanation of the youths' rights ". . . to make sure they understand." The boy's mother testified that her son had a learning disability and ". . . was probably too proud to tell his interviewers that he didn't understand."

In responding to the judge's ruling and in keeping with the YCJA procedural requirements, the Crown prosecutor maintained that the ". . . police will have to do more than simply read from a form outlining young people's rights and then ask them if they understand . . ." (Hayes, 2005). In this case, "technical violations" were not set aside and more weight was given to assessing the youth's ability to understand his rights. Viewed in terms of how young people experience their world, Feld (2000) maintains that rights are seen by youth as something you are allowed to do, rather than as something you are entitled to exercise (p. 147). Young people's understandings of rights then is befitting of their status in society. They seem to not feel empowered nor to have agency and choice; rather, rights are like privileges, something that people in authority give them.

The question of young people's understanding of their rights to silence and to legal representation was put to the test by Abramovitch, Peterson-Badali, and Rohan (1995) and Abramovitch, Higgins-Biss, and Biss (1993) by comparing a sample of Toronto high-school students aged 11 to 18 with a university student population. They found that youth over 16 understand their rights better than younger youth and that older youth are more like university students in this regard. An important difference between the groups is that younger youth are more likely to assert their right to silence if they perceive strong evidence of guilt in the case and are more likely to assert their right to a lawyer if the evidence of guilt is perceived as weak. The researchers conclude that university students are less naive than young high-school students in that, for them, the guilt or innocence of accused persons has no bearing on their assertion of their rights.

In separate surveys of young people in primary grades and high school (Grades 6 to 13), Abramovitch et al. (1993) found that younger youth were more likely to report that they would give a statement to the police if they were asked to do so. With regard to rights to legal representation, including the right to instruct counsel themselves, the authors found that most youth did not fully understand what it meant to waive their right to a lawyer. They did not understand that a waiver meant that no one but the police would be present when they were questioned (cited in Doob & Cesaroni, 2004, p. 37). The central issue then is the extent to which protections are provided for youth who waive their rights, given that they may not understand the meaning of the rights themselves and the consequences of their waiver. With the exception of statements given to the police, it is not clear that the YCJA has provided sufficient protections.

One final legislative means to ensure the protection of young people in the justice system comes from restrictions on the disclosure of information about a young offender. Because of the media and its reporting of crime, most people are aware that the media is not permitted to publish the names of young offenders. This publication restriction surfaces periodically as a debate over the "public's right to protection" versus a young offender's "right to privacy." The latter is defended as an important tool to assist in the rehabilitation of young offenders and their reintegration into society. The protection of a young person's identity has been entrenched in the juvenile justice system since its inception in 1908, when JDA privacy regulations stipulated ". . . no report . . . in which the name of the child or of its parents or guardian is disclosed . . . shall, without the special leave of the judge, be published in any newspaper or other publication . . ." [JDA 1908 s. 10(3)]. In addition, s. 10 stipulated that hearings were to be closed to the public and s.8 allowed parents or guardians to attend, while s. 20 prevented siblings from doing so.

Over the last 100 years, changes to privacy provisions in the juvenile/youth justice system have made the regulation of privacy considerably more complex by increasing the amount of information about a young offender and youth court cases that is private, while at the same time eroding protections by decreasing limitations to the sharing of young offender information. While there were a few modifications to the JDA, most of the change began with the YOA and has continued through the YCJA. The main section on privacy is contained in s. 38 of the YOA which stipulated that ". . . any information serving to identify . . ." a young offender or a youth victim or witness was private. No longer is information about parents or guardians stipulated as being private.

Another important change was that the court was no longer closed to the public (YOA s.39). Other sections concerning the sharing of information were stipulated throughout the YOA (MacIntyre, 2006). The YCJA is even more complex, with Part 6 (s. 110 through s. 129) being devoted entirely to disclosure of information. Once again, changes increased the amount of information that is private, such as DNA information, while at the same time decreasing limitations by making information more available. So, for example, while the names of all offenders in the youth justice system are not to be made public, this protection is no longer afforded to youth who are liable to an adult sentence. Furthermore, young offenders' rights are further eroded by s. 75(3), which allows the court to decide if it will permit publication of the names of youth who receive youth sentences for presumptive offences.

sentencing conference
A meeting of a group of professionals to make recommendations to the court about appropriate sentences for individual cases.

COURT SENTENCING

The YCJA makes sentencing a far more complex process than it was under the YOA by adding **sentencing conferences** to the process, providing general sentencing principles, restricting the use of custody, and providing for a greater range of sentencing options. Section 19 of the YCJA allows for a sentencing conference to act as an advisory body with regard to sentences, sentence reviews, extrajudicial measures, conditions for interim release, and reintegration plans. These committees are to consist of a youth court judge, the provincial director, a police officer, a justice of the peace, and a prosecutor or youth worker. Before sentencing, the court is required to consider recommendations from a sentencing committee (if these have been established by the province), pre-sentence reports, and any other information submitted by parents or counsel.

In particular, before imposing a custodial sentence, s. 39(6) of the YCJA requires the youth justice court to consider a pre-sentence report and "any sentencing proposal made by the young person or his or her counsel," unless the young person or his or her counsel indicates a preference to not have a pre-sentence report [s. 39(7)]. In the latter case, the onus is on the court to ascertain if the report is not necessary.

Section 40 of the YCJA outlines what should be contained in a pre-sentence report. These reports are generally prepared by a probation officer, who compiles information about the youth's background, including a history with the YOA court and/or alternative/extrajudicial measures and sanctions; results from an interview with the victim; the recommendation of a sentencing conference; and information from the youth's parents, extended family, social workers involved with the family, and school officials. The reports also often contain judgments about the emotional development, attitude, maturity, and character of the youth, as well as information about her or his insight into the offence, willingness to make amends, and plans for the future, particularly with regard to changing her or his behaviour (see Box 9.8 for an example).

VOICES BOX 9.8

Excerpts from Pre-Sentencing Reports, Ontario

1. [This woman is] despondent and somewhat tired of the burden of raising adolescents.
2. In order to try to understand Paul better and to control him, his mother has attended several tough love sessions. Her attitude is "I've made up my mind I'm not going to let him beat me." . . . It would appear Paul's position in the house is very precarious.
3. Before the court, Your Honour, is a twelve-year-old Native youth whose history of truancy problems surfaced [five years ago] and has not lost momentum since that time. George's truancy appears to be a symptom of an underorganized family system. It was earlier identified in [an] assessment that George's truancy arose as a result of increasing family disorganization as well as anger at his mother for her inability to take charge of the family. It would seem that interventions have had very little impact on helping to alleviate the multi-issues presented by the various members of this family . . . Although a great deal of court and agency history has preceded . . . [the] current court situation, it is important that its impact not cloud or colour the present need to continue to try to plan for this youth.

Source: Bell (1993).

TABLE 9.2

Juvenile Justice Models and Sentencing

Juvenile Justice Model	Sentencing Principle	Court Sentence	Correctional Programming
Welfare	Rehabilitation	Probation with conditions Treatment orders Community service order Conditional discharge	Treatment Rehabilitation
Justice	Retribution Proportionality	Range of sanctions proportional to offence	All sanctions proportional to offence Voluntary
Crime control	Punishment Incapacitation Deterrence	Fine or custody Lengthy sentence	Prisons Tighter security Longer sentences
Restorative	Reintegration Restoration Reconciliation	Mediation, conferencing Sentencing circle	Victim and community participation Reparation Crime prevention Promotion of responsibility for action

retribution
Punishment for an offence committed.

proportionality principle
Maintains that a sentence should be proportional to the offence that a person is guilty of committing.

deterrence
The theory that certain and speedy punishment will discourage or prevent future criminal behaviour, both in a general and a specific manner.

incapacitation
Basically means to deprive a person, so to put someone in prison is to incapacitate her or him in an absolute and fundamental manner.

Sentencing Principles

Four basic principles govern sentencing in adult criminal cases: retribution, deterrence, incapacitation, and rehabilitation (see Table 9.2). **Retribution** is based on the notion of moral accountability and the idea that persons who intentionally harm others should suffer negative consequences so that wrongs can be righted. An additional component of this principle is the **proportionality principle**—the belief that justice is best served if the consequence is in proportion to the crime. So, for example, the death penalty would be an inappropriate sentence for car theft or shoplifting. For advocates of crime control, retribution is interpreted as punishment, and the proportionality principle often means vengeance or "an eye for an eye."

Deterrence is a theory that originated in the 18th century. It is based on the assumption that people will not engage in certain activities if the potential costs of doing so are greater than the potential gains. Deterrence may be general or specific/individual, meaning that negative consequences directed at an individual may be designed to dissuade all members of a society from engaging in similar actions (general). Sanctions may also be designed to prevent a particular person from reoffending (specific/individual). **Incapacitation** refers to measures taken, such as a prison sentence, to deprive a person of the opportunity to commit an offence (Bala et al., 1994, pp. 30–34). **Rehabilitation** philosophies began to emerge toward the latter part of the 19th century and are based on the assumption that people can change their behaviour if given an opportunity to do so. Rehabilitation may or may not involve particular treatment strategies or programs.

The restorative justice principles of **restoration, reconciliation,** and **reintegration** are relatively new concepts just beginning to work their way into sentencing discourse and practice. While some of the "older" principles, such as deterrence and incapacitation, are based on assumptions that punishment and retribution are the most effective means of stopping criminal behaviour, restorative justice principles assume the most effective response to crime involves policies and practices that attempt to repair the harm done to the individual and the community by criminal activity. As we will see in the discussion that follows, new sentencing options in the YCJA are incorporating these principles as objectives in their own right, but also in a way that serves to redefine the meaning of the older principles. An important long-standing issue concerns the extent to which adult sentencing principles are appropriate in youth justice systems, a discussion we will return to at the end of this chapter.

YCJA Sentencing Principles

Section 38 of the YCJA presents a significant change from YOA sentencing provisions in that it sets out the purpose and principles for youth sentencing, along with factors to be considered in all sentencing deliberations, something that did not exist under the YOA. While the general principles of s. 3 apply to youth sentences (as they did under the YOA), s. 38 principles are also to be used by the court in determining sentences. Under the YOA, the only directive provided to the court regarding disposition decisions was for the court to strike a balance between the interests of society and the needs of the young offender.

Interestingly, as with the s. 3 principles, no one justice model is reflected in s. 38. An examination of these principles and requirements (Box 9.9) reveals an interesting combination and prioritizing of the different justice models (see Table 9.2 on page 266 in this chapter and Table 2.1 in Chapter 2 on page 40). Justice principles of retribution [subsections (1)(2)(d)(iii) and (3)(a), (b)] and proportionality [subsection (2)(a), (b), (c)] are paramount. These sections make it clear that the purpose of sentencing is to hold a young person accountable and to impose "meaningful consequences." More importantly, from a justice perspective, these consequences must be proportional to other youth sentences for similar offences and not any more severe than an adult sentence for a similar offence in similar circumstances. The court is also required to look beyond the offence and consider the youth's intention, degree of involvement in the offence, and degree of harm caused by the action.

Nonetheless, subsection (1) also speaks of "protection of the public," a crime control objective, and subsection (2)(a) speaks of punishment. While stated in the negative, that punishment should not exceed that appropriate for an adult, this subsection nonetheless explicitly presents punishment, rather than proportionate sanctions, as an important principle of juvenile justice. Welfare principles are also evident. Subsection (2)(d)(i) reintroduces the minimal interference principle of the YOA and applies it specifically to sentencing; subsection (2)(d)(ii) incorporates the principle of rehabilitation from both the JDA and YOA; and subsection (1) presents rehabilitation as a primary objective of "just sanctions." In addition, restorative justice principles are introduced through subsections (1)(d)(ii) and (iii), as well as (3)(c). Reintegration is stated as a primary objective and guiding principle for sentencing decisions.

rehabilitation
A correctional philosophy based on the belief that appropriate treatment programs can reform or change an individual.

restoration, reconciliation, reintegration
In the context of a restorative justice framework, these related concepts refer to restoring balance by repairing harms.

BOX 9.9

The Purpose and Principles of Sentencing under the YCJA (Section 38)

Purpose

(1) The purpose of sentencing under section 42 (youth sentences) is to hold a young person accountable for an offence through the imposition of just sanctions that have meaningful consequences for the young person and that promote his or her rehabilitation and reintegration into society, thereby contributing to the long-term protection of the public.

Principles

(2) A youth justice court that imposes a youth sentence on a young person shall determine the sentence in accordance with the principles set out in section 3 and the following principles:

   (a) the sentence must not result in a punishment that is greater than the punishment that would be appropriate for an adult who has been convicted of the same offence committed in similar circumstances;
   (b) the sentence must be similar to the sentences imposed in the region on similar young persons found guilty of the same offence committed in similar circumstances;
   (c) the sentence must be proportionate to the seriousness of the offence and the degree of responsibility of the young person for that offence; and
   (d) subject to paragraph (c), the sentence must
      (i) be the least restrictive sentence that is capable of achieving the purpose set out in subsection (1),
      (ii) be the one that is most likely to rehabilitate the young person and reintegrate him or her into society, and
      (iii) promote a sense of responsibility in the young person, and an acknowledgment of the harm done to victims and the community.

Factors to Be Taken into Account

(3) In determining a youth sentence, the youth justice court shall take into account

   (a) the degree of participation by the young person in the commission of the offence;
   (b) the harm done to victims and whether it was intentional or reasonably foreseeable;
   (c) any reparation made by the young person to the victim or the community;
   (d) the time spent in detention by the young person as a result of the offence;
   (e) the previous findings of guilt of the young person; and
   (f) any other aggravating and mitigating circumstances related to the young person or the offence that are relevant to the purpose and principles set out in this section.

However, while it might appear that this act, like the YOA before it, is establishing all of the justice models as guiding principles, it does not. Section 38(1) includes all models in a manner that gives priority to accountability and protection of the public, and subsection (2)(d) clearly states that welfare and restorative justice principles apply only *after* consideration of proportionality and responsibility principles. Hence, justice and crime control principles are paramount, with welfare and restorative justice principles as secondary.

The prominence of proportionality is apparent in a ruling in the first year of the YCJA that addressed the matter of sentence length. In *R. v. D.L.C.* (2003), Judge Gorman examined sentencing objectives and stated:

> Any sentence of custody imposed must be of sufficient length so that a proper assessment and rehabilitative plan can be developed. In this region of the Province, this will take approximately six–eight weeks. In addition, it must be of sufficient length to allow a young person who is not susceptible to counselling in a non-custodial environment to benefit from the program offered to young persons in custody. Otherwise, the young person's rehabilitation and reintegration will not be promoted. However, the length of the period of custody imposed must be proportionate to the offence committed and to a young person's "reduced level of maturity." In other words, the period of custody imposed cannot be artificially high for the purpose of promoting rehabilitation. (Para. 77, as cited in Bala & Anand, 2004, p. 259)

Bala and Anand (2004) maintain that in light of this argument, we should expect that under the YCJA ". . . judges should be reluctant to impose short custodial sentences (a "short, sharp shock") that are unlikely to achieve any rehabilitative purpose (p. 259). On the other hand, Judge Daniel Pahl in *R. v. L.M.F.* (para. 21, 2003) uses accountability as a rationale for imposing short custodial sentences:

> In my opinion, non-custodial sentences would not adequately reflect the very serious nature of these offences. I therefore find that a period of custody is necessary to promote a sense of responsibility in these young men and as well, to acknowledge the harm done to their victims . . . (Cited in Bala & Anand, 2004, pp. 259–260)

Youth Sentences

Section 42(2) of the YCJA allows for a wide range of youth sentences, from a simple reprimand to the most severe (as measured in terms of loss of freedom)—intensive rehabilitative custody with community supervision. The youth court has far more sentencing options than were available under the YOA [s. 20(1)] and judges can choose any one or a combination of sentences for a convicted youth.

Data were not yet available from the youth court on these new YCJA options when this book was being written. The most recent youth court data, 2003–2004 does reflect YCJA sentencing decisions, but they are reported in YOA categories. New YCJA sentences are contained in the "other" sentencing category (Thomas, 2005, p. 3). The major sentencing and dispositional categories from the YOA that remain for YCJA sentencing are absolute and conditional discharge, fine, community service order, probation, treatment order, and custody. They are discussed below, along with the new YCJA options. In some cases, particularly for the lesser non-custodial sentences, the most recent available statistics are those for 1999–2000.

Non-Custodial Sanctions

Reprimand A reprimand is new with the YCJA and simply involves a stern lecture from the judge; it technically does not constitute a "sentence." A reprimand would likely be considered suitable for first-time offenders facing a minor charge, where it is believed that experience with police processing and the court is sufficient to meet accountability requirements (Thomas, 2005, p. 7). It, along with the absolute discharge does not result in a criminal record. This means that a youth would not appear in a criminal record check.

Absolute Discharge An absolute discharge is also a sentence with no criminal sanctions. As with the reprimand, the young person, even though found guilty, is free to leave the court with no penalty. This disposition is also given most often for very minor offences when the young person has no prior record. In 1999–2000, 2 percent of court cases resulted in an absolute discharge (1,363 cases) (Sudworth & deSouza, 2001, p. 16).

Conditional Discharge The 1995 YOA amendments, Bill C-37, introduced a new disposition—the conditional discharge—and it is retained by the YCJA. The conditional discharge has always been available as a sentencing option in the adult system, where it is generally viewed as similar to probation, but more lenient. The conditional discharge provides for conditions similar to those outlined in a probation order. After successful completion of the terms of the order, however, the person's criminal record is "erased"; in other words, the person is discharged without a conviction on his or her record. Such a person who applies for employment and is asked about any prior convictions can legally respond in the negative. In the youth system, a conditional discharge similarly erases a person's criminal record so that she or he can no longer be viewed as a convicted offender. It is most commonly used in combination with probation orders. In 1999–2000, less than 2 percent of sentences were conditional discharges (Sudworth & deSouza, 2001, p. 8).

McGuire (1997, pp. 198–202) argued that the conditional discharge can work to a youth's disadvantage in some circumstances. A conditional discharge may be revoked at any point if a young person is convicted of another offence. The court may then impose another disposition while denying the right to appeal with respect to the original sentence. In every other instance, courts are not permitted to impose a greater intervention for young offenders following original sentencing (i.e., when dispositions are reviewed). Because the conditional discharge allows for greater intervention with respect to young offenders, it should be viewed, McGuire suggests, as something more punitive than probation, but less intrusive and less punitive than custody.

Fine The court may impose a fine not to exceed $1,000, but it must consider the youth's ability to pay. Under a fine option program, young people can elect to do community service work if they are unable to pay a fine. The percentage of cases resulting in a fine (6 percent) was the same in 2003–2004 as it was in 1999–2000 but, as we would expect with decreasing numbers of cases going through the courts, the number of cases in 2003–2004 was about one-half of the 1999–2000 level. Fines are still often used in traffic-related Criminal Code offences (76 percent impaired driving), where the mean was $462 in 2003–2004 (Sudworth & deSouza, 2001, pp. 8, 16; Thomas, 2005, p. 9). It seems that monetary inflation has also affected court fines, since 10 years ago. only 2 percent of the court fines in youth court were over $500 (Statistics Canada, 1998, p. x).

The YCJA also offers the court a range of fine-related sanctions: compensation to be paid for loss of property, income, or support (with different rules in the province of Quebec); restitution involving an order to restore or replace stolen or damaged property; restitution that encompasses an order to pay someone who may have purchased stolen property from the young offender; and compensation in kind for loss, damage, or injury caused by the young offender. Seizure or forfeiture of property can also be imposed as a disposition separately from a fine under the YCJA.

Community Service Order　The court may order young people to perform unpaid and supervised community service for a period not to exceed 240 hours, with 12 months allowed for completion. Community service orders (CSOs) are often operated through probation offices. Arrangements are made for young people to work for food banks or other charitable or non-profit organizations such as the Society for the Prevention of Cruelty to Animals. Most commonly, a CSO is attached to another more serious sentence. It is used most often for property and drug offences (32 percent and 35 percent, respectively). As in 1999–2000, 28 percent of all convictions received a CSO in 2002–2004. In 1999–2000, only 7 percent of the court dispositions were for community service orders alone (a total of 4,772 cases) (Sudworth & deSouza, 2001, p. 8; Thomas, 2005, p. 15).

VOICES BOX 9.10

Court Transcript of Discussions Preceding Sentencing

Young offender Susan was found guilty of shoplifting and has a prior record of similar offences. Susan lives in a very impoverished section of the city and is supported by her mother, a "single mom" on welfare.

Judge to Susan:

J.　Susan, why do you take these things?
S.　[pause] Well, 'cause I want the stuff.
J.　Because you want the stuff, well, is that a good reason?
S.　No.
J.　Pardon?
S.　No.
J.　No? OK so you went out and stole in March and got caught. Why didn't you stop then? A month later, you were out stealing again. Why?
S.　I don't know.
J.　You don't know? We'll have a family court clinic assessment [psychiatric assessment] and this case will be adjourned for a month.

Judge's questioning of Susan's mother:

J.　Mother, what would you like to say, please?
M.　Well, I certainly don't want her to be taken out of her home. Other than her shoplifting she doesn't cause any problems. She is handable.
J.　She is what?
M.　She is [pause]—I can handle her and when she was brought home by the police it was a total surprise to me.
J.　Why should it be such a surprise to you? She's been out of control now . . . as long as I can remember, hasn't she? How many times have you been here with your two daughters, especially Susan?
M.　Yeah, well, I [pause] I think she is making progress.
J.　Is she?

(continued)

Box 9.10 continued

M. At this new school like I don't think that if the program was interrupted it would be very good for Susan, maybe open custody or—

J. Well for all I know they probably will put her in open custody. That's the way they do it these days.

M. I know she was very depressed and frustrated when she wasn't keeping up in the normal school in the Grade 8 because she was going to the general learning disability class where she wasn't supposed to be in. I placed her in the special school. Ever since then she has been more happier, the depression has ceased. So I thought that maybe, well, that was one thing I did, placing her in this special program and other than that—

J. And that seems to be working more or less?

M. Yes.

Later, the judge resumes his discussion with Susan's mother:

J. What I am thinking of is six months' open custody followed by a year's probation. Mrs. C., do you want to comment on that?

M. Mmmmm, it just seems like a very long time, half a year.

J. Well, you know she has been in trouble over and over again, hasn't she?

M. I don't really—

J. Just say it, whatever is on your mind.

M. I [pause] I don't really know if she'll respond to that, maybe she will [pause] she's not responding right now. She doesn't seem to realize—

J. In truth, she hasn't responded to anything favourable, has she?

M. [No response]

J. Has she?

M. Well . . .

J. How long have you been looking up and seeing her in front of me?

M. That's true, that's true.

J. Isn't that right?

M. Mmmmm—

J. It's always the same story. She's back again with more offences, doesn't cooperate with probation. Isn't that right?

M. I don't know if she will stay if she goes to open custody.

J. If she doesn't stay she will get locked up. Maybe that is what she needs, some control. She has no control—she does what she wants.

M. She is rather hard to handle right now.

J. Yes, and her sister is not a very good influence on her, is she?

M. No.

J. All right, please sit down. If there is anything else you'd like to say you will be given a chance.

At sentencing the judge says:

. . . six months' open custody, followed by 12 months' probation, concurrent. What are you crying for, Susan? This is the best thing that ever happened here. We should have done this a long time ago.

Source: (Bell, 1993).

Probation The most common sentence or disposition in youth court is probation, which is most commonly administered for sexual offences, assault, drug offences, theft, and arson. In 2003–2004, 63 percent of the convicted court cases resulted in a probation disposition. This was lower than it had been for the previous five years, when the proportions ranged from a low of 64 in 1999–2000 to a high of 70 percent in 2002–2003 (Robinson, 2004, p. 16; Thomas, 2005, p. 15). Probation after release was often attached to a custody sentence under the YOA, so we should expect to see a decrease in probation sentences because of the new YCJA requirement that custody sentences have a period of supervision after release as part of the sentence. In addition, some minor cases that formerly received a probation order may have been diverted by extrajudicial measures or sanctions.

A probation order is a means of controlling and supervising a young person's behaviour while he or she is in the community. There are sanctions for non-compliance with the conditions of probation, in that breach of probation constitutes a Criminal Code offence. Under the YOA, there were two mandatory conditions in all probation orders: to "keep the peace" and "be of good behaviour," and to appear in court as required. The YCJA adds two new mandatory conditions: prohibition from possessing or purchasing weapons, ammunition, and explosive substances, and any other conditions necessary to "secure the young person's good conduct" and prevent further criminal activity. In addition, young people may be required to report to a probation officer on a regular basis, maintain employment, go to school, reside at a particular residence, report any change in address, and/or remain within the court's jurisdiction. The court often orders a youth not to associate with certain people and to avoid certain neighbourhoods, obey a curfew, abstain from drugs and alcohol, and/or attend treatment or counselling programs. Prohibition orders can also be imposed under the YCJA independently of a probation order. Community service orders are often included as a condition of probation.

The maximum term for probation is two years. In 2003–2004, 25,261 cases resulted in probation. Slightly more than half (58 percent) of these probation orders ranged from 7 to 12 months: 16 percent were for 6 months or less, and 26 percent were for more than 12 months (Thomas, 2005, p. 9). Compared to the later YOA years (Sudworth & deSouza, 2001, p. 9), there are fewer short-terms and more long-term probation orders under the YCJA. Since longer terms of probation are generally attached to more serious offences, it would appear that the YCJA has changed the youth probationer population to youth who have been involved in more serious offences than in the past.

Treatment Order/Intensive Support and Supervision Order Section 22 of the YOA allowed the court to order youth detained in a hospital or other facility for the purpose of treatment, providing he or she gave consent. The requirement of consent for treatment was a contentious aspect of the YOA (Leschied & Jaffe, 1991), and the 1995 amendments to the YOA (Bill C-37) repealed sections 22 and 20(1)(i) of the act. Treatment as a disposition was no longer allowed under the YOA after that date.

Fetherston (2000) argue that YCJA principles move the youth justice system even further from a welfare model by requiring similar sentences for similar offences and sentences proportionate to the offence (pp. 111–112). Nonetheless, the act does promote rehabilitation as a sentencing principle and provides a new sentencing option that is potentially rehabilitative: an intensive support and supervision program. This disposition is similar to probation in that it is served in the community and comes with conditions attached. The difference is that this sentence is intended to provide closer monitoring and more support and services than probation. Unlike probation, the YCJA allows provinces to decide if they wish to offer this option (Thomas, 2005, p. 7).

Non-Residential Attendance Order Under the YCJA, a youth may also be ordered to attend a non-residential program for up to 240 hours. This too is a potentially rehabilitative sentence and other conditions may be attached to the order, such as to refrain from alcohol or to not associate with certain persons. As with the intensive support and supervision order, these two dispositions, as sentences, sidestep the thorny issue of consent to treatment. For 2003–2004, both of these dispositions were included in the "other" sentencing category. As with probation, there are sanctions attached to non-compliance with the orders of the sentence, but here the charge is "failure to comply." Provisions for the use of these sentences by the court will be discussed in the next chapter.

Custodial Sanctions

Under the YOA, custody sentence options were limited to two choices: the court could sentence a young offender to one of two levels of custody—open or secure—which differed in terms of restrictions on freedom of movement, level of supervision, and access to the community. The YCJA has considerably expanded these choices, perhaps because, as we will see in the next chapter, the use of custody under the YOA was a contentious issue. Those advocating a crime control or justice model wanted more and longer custody sentences for some young offenders, while welfare and restorative justice model advocates expressed alarm over the excessive use of custody by the courts. The YCJA has addressed this issue in a number of ways. First, s. 39(1) of the YCJA specifies that a young person cannot be sentenced to custody unless she or he has committed a violent offence, has already received a non-custodial sentence and failed to comply with that, has committed an indictable offence for which an adult would receive a federal prison term, or has committed an indictable offence. In this latter case, the court is required to argue that there are aggravating circumstances that justify a custody sentence and that a non-custodial sentence would violate the sentencing principles of s. 38.

Second, s. 39(2) specifies that when any of the conditions in subsection (2) are met and a custody sentence is allowed, the court must then consider all non-custodial alternatives and determine that there is no reasonable alternative before imposing a custodial sentence. Section 39(3) outlines the factors that the court must consider regarding non-custodial alternatives, including the availability of alternatives to custody, the likelihood based on previous experience and sentences that the young person will comply with a non-custodial sentence, and whether alternatives have already been used or what alternatives have been used with people who have committed similar offences under similar circumstances. The court is also prohibited from using custody "as a substitute for appropriate child protection, mental health or other social measures" [s. 39(5)], and is not prohibited from using a non-custodial sentence in circumstances where a young offender is a repeat offender [s. 39(4)]. Importantly, these provisions do not preclude a non-custodial sentence in convictions for violent offences, nor is custody an allowable sentence for non-violent offences.

Finally, in all cases where a judge imposes a custody sentence, the court must state the reasons why a non-custodial sentence was not appropriate. If a case and its circumstances are considered to be exceptional, the court is required to state why a non-custodial disposition is not appropriate for a non-violent offence and also state the reasons why a case is considered to be an exceptional one [s. 39(9)]. These are the provisions that are blamed for the incidents leading to the tragic death of Theresa McEvoy in the Johnny case studies throughout the text and the reason for attempts to have motor vehicle theft and joyriding reclassified as "potentially harmful to the public"; such offences could then be reclassified as violent offences with custodial sanctions.

Types of custody sentences have also changed. Judges no longer make determinations about level of custody; rather, they have a range of sentencing choices about types of custody. These include a deferral of custody and supervision (except for presumptive offences), custody with supervision in the community, custody with conditional supervision, and intensive rehabilitative custody and supervision. All custody sentences are now accompanied by some type of supervision order after release. The differences among these custody sentences will be discussed in the next chapter.

Although the Criminal Code provides for a mandatory minimum to the length of custody sentences for certain types of offences committed by adults, the YOA did so only for first- and second-degree murder. The YCJA keeps these same minimums (see Box 9.6 on page 257) and specifies a two-year maximum for all other youth sentences, except where the offence would warrant a life sentence for an adult or is a presumptive offence. These carry a three-year maximum youth sentence.

Overall, administrative offences are more likely to result in a custody sentence than any other offence category (37 percent compared to crimes against the person at 23.7 percent). Not surprisingly, a charge of being unlawfully at large is more likely to result in a custody term (79 percent) than any other offence, even homicide (57.9 percent) (Thomas, 2005, p. 15). Of course, it would be misleading to interpret these figures to mean that people committing the most serious offences are not very likely to get a custody sentence. The most serious offences occur in such small numbers that they would not have a great impact on the overall percentage in the violent category receiving custody sentences. Again, there have been dramatic increases for girls. Over the latter part of the YOA, the number of girls committed to custody increased by 26 percent, while male committals increased by only 4 percent. Many of these committals stem from a higher rate of charges against girls for breach of a community service order (Report of the Federal–Provincial–Territorial Task Force on Youth Justice, 1996, p. 614). The reasons for this discrepancy will be considered in Chapter 11.

Since 1991–1992, the use of shorter custody sentences has increased annually. In 2003–2004, the average sentence length was 67 days (Thomas, 2005, p. 18). In 1991–1992, the average length of secure custody sentences was 95 days and 90 days for open custody; by 2002–2003 (the last year of the YOA), sentences had reduced to an average of 68 and 66 days, respectively (Robinson, 2004, pp. 9, 16). Another way of looking at changes is to compare percentages. In 2003–2004, almost one-half (49 percent) of all custody sentences were for a period of less than one month, a considerable increase from five years previously, when only one-third (33 percent) of the custodial sentences were for one month or less. On the other hand, only 6 percent of the custodial sentences in both 2004–2005 and 1999–2000 were for more than six months (Robinson, 2004, pp. 9, 16; Thomas, 2005, p. 18).

Toward the latter years of the YCJA, judges appeared to be favouring this "short, sharp shock" approach to custody sentences, and this type of sentencing continued into the first year of the YCJA. Nonetheless, since average custody terms are longer for serious offences than for minor ones (99 days for violent offences versus 69 days for property ones), the YCJA may be resulting in shorter sentences only for more minor offences.

Sentence Review There are no changes in the YCJA from the YOA regarding review orders. All custody sentences of greater than one year in length must be reviewed each year by the youth court, and the youth or a parent may request a review after six months. When the custody term is less than one year, the youth or parent may request a review after one-third of the sentence (minimum 30 days). Reviews of non-custodial sentences and of the level of custody imposed may also be requested (s. 87(1) and s. 94), and they must be initiated by the youth, parent, or Crown or provincial director after six months of the sentence has been served (or earlier, with permission from a youth court judge).

Section 94(6) of the YCJA outlines the grounds for reviewing a young offender's sentence: the youth has shown progress with respect to rehabilitation; the circumstances that led to the youth's sentence have changed materially; new services or programs are available that were not available at the time of the youth's sentence; the opportunities for rehabilitation are now greater in the community; or any other ground that the youth justice court considers appropriate.

The sentence review involves a hearing and is mandated to consider the "needs of the young person" as well as "the interests of society." The judge has three options in making a final decision, all of which involve a lesser or equal sentence: (1) transfer the young offender to a less secure custody level, or from custody to conditional supervision or probation; (2) release the youth from a non-custodial disposition or vary the disposition in some way (e.g., the court might omit a curfew or change a condition in a probation or supervision order); or (3) confirm the existing disposition and make no change.

SENTENCING ISSUES

In this section, we consider three sentencing issues that have been addressed by academics and practitioners: (1) the extent to which adult sentencing principles are relevant to the youth justice system; (2) the extent to which extralegal factors—race, class, and gender—affect court dispositions; and (3) the severity of youth court sentencing relative to adult court sentencing and sentencing under the Juvenile Delinquents Act and YOA.

Relevance of Adult Sentencing Principles to Youth Court

Retribution and Incapacitation

As we have seen in this and the last chapter, the principle of retribution, viewed as moral accountability, is an integral aspect of youth justice under the YCJA. However, given that young people lack the moral development, intellectual and emotional capacity, and judgment of adults, it would be unreasonable to apply an adult standard in making them accountable for their actions (Bala et al., 1994, pp. 30–31). Those who advocate transferring youth to adult court and subjecting youth to adult sentences do in fact hold youth to an adult standard of accountability—a position at odds with the spirit of a youth justice system.

Incapacitation refers to removing offenders from the community—generally by putting them into an institution—so that they can no longer pose a threat (Bala et al., 1994, pp. 34–35). While most would agree that young offenders who have committed serious violent crimes should be removed from the community, there is no agreement as to where they should be held in custody, for how long, and under what conditions. Some people maintain that youth facilities are "holiday camps" and should be more like places of punishment. Others think ahead to the time that young offenders will be released back into the community and worry that custodial institutions may be "schools of crime" or a "recipe for disaster." This latter view was expressed by Chief Judge Lilles of the Yukon Territorial Court:

> Affording protection to the public is not synonymous with incarceration. In the long term, society is best protected by the successful rehabilitation of the offender. Society is not protected if a youth emerges institutionalized from a federal penitentiary, or having learned additional criminal skills that would make him more dangerous. Unnecessary or unproductive incarceration of a youth or young adult in the federal system will rarely be in the interests of society. (*R. v. M. T.*, April 15 [1993], Yukon Territorial Court, cited in Bala et al., 1994, p. 35)

Although the YCJA seems to have addressed this issue through its strict requirement for the use of custody and increased emphasis on extrajudicial measures and sanctions, along with provisions for sentencing conferences, some judges are concerned that these practices will not change (Harris, Weagant, Cole, & Weinper, 2004).

Rehabilitation

In the classical sense of the term, rehabilitation attempts to "change" the offender through the use of various types of programs such as behaviour modification or group therapy. The ultimate goal is to reintegrate the offender back into society. Rehabilitation is viewed as particularly attractive for young offenders because "it is assumed they will be more amenable to rehabilitation than adults" (Bala et al., 1994, p. 36).

The problem with applying the principle of rehabilitation to youth sentencing is that it can be viewed as counterproductive to the proportionality principle contained in the YOA and also in the YCJA. A 1993 Supreme Court decision upheld a two-year open-custody sentence because of concerns about the youth's "depressing home conditions." In his decision, Justice Cory addressed the issue of proportionality as follows:

> It is true that for both adults and minors the sentence must be proportional to the offence committed. But in the sentencing of adult offenders, the principle of proportionality will have a greater significance than it will in the disposition of young offenders. For the young, proper disposition must take into account not only the seriousness of the crime but also all the other relevant factors . . . Intolerable conditions in the home indicate both a special need for care and the absence of any guidance within the home.
>
> The situation in the home of a young offender should neither be ignored nor made the predominant factor in sentencing. Nonetheless, it is a factor that can properly be taken into account in fashioning the disposition. (*R. v. J. J. M.* [1993], C. S. J. 14.)

In the first year of the YCJA, the precedential value of this decision was challenged in Manitoba by Judge Wesley Swail's argument that proportionality and accountability are now of prime importance:

> Now by virtue of section 38(2) of the *Youth Criminal Justice Act*, a sentence imposed on a youth ". . . must be proportionate to the seriousness of the offence and the degree of responsibility of the young person for that offence . . ." Insofar as the J.J.M. case indicates that a proper disposition "must take into account not only the seriousness

of the crime but all the other relevant factors," perhaps the inclusion of subsection 38(2)(c) above does not change the sentencing of a young offender under the *Youth Criminal Justice Act*. It does mean, however, that proportionality of sentencing of a youth in relation to the seriousness of the youth's offence is a very basic and important factor for the court to proceed from in sentencing that youth: no doubt more so than was the situation under the *Young Offenders Act*. (Para. 26, cited in Bala & Anand, 2004, p. 258)

The YCJA is clearer about proportionality than was the YOA in that it specifies that youth sentences must not exceed adult sentences for similar offences, there must be parity across the country, and that a sentence must be proportionate to the seriousness of an offence. Furthermore, Anand (2003) maintains that the YCJA has also rejected the Supreme Court's decision in *R. v. J.J. M.* by insisting that youth custody cannot be justified solely on the social and welfare needs of the youth. He predicts that youth will receive a "rehabilitative discount" on the length of a proportional sentence. Nonetheless, Roberts and Bala (2003, p. 409) argue that precisely because rehabilitation is subject to proportionality considerations in the YCJA, the issue will continue and we should expect that "more tension between rehabilitation and proportionality will arise at the youth justice court level."

Deterrence

On the issue of general deterrence—which is based on the assumption that one young offender's sentence will deter others from engaging in similar crimes—judges were clearly divided in their opinions of the YOA provisions. In the Alberta Court of Appeal, Justice William Stevenson wrote:

> . . . in any event, deterrence to others does not, in my view, have any place in the sentencing of youth offenders. It is not one of the principles enumerated in the catalogue in section 3 of the Act, which declares the policy for young offenders in Canada. Indeed, I note that in regard to secure custody, section 24(5) prohibits committal unless necessary for the protection of society. [*R. v. G. K.* [1985], 21 C.C.C. (3D) 558 (Alta. C.A.)]

One year later, Justice John Brooke of the Ontario Court of Appeal disagreed with this decision. In *R. v. O.*, he wrote:

> . . . with the greatest deference, we do not agree with that statement. We think it is too broad. The principles under section 3 of the Young Offenders Act do not sweep away the principle of general deterrence. The principles under that section enshrine the principle of protection of society and this subsumes general and specific deterrence. It is perhaps sufficient to say that in our opinion the principle of general deterrence must be considered but it has diminished importance in determining the appropriate disposition in the case of a youthful offender. [*R. v. O.* [1986], 27 C.C.C. (3D) 376 (Ont. C.A.)]

The principle of individual deterrence is based on an assumption or belief that people make decisions on the basis of rational choice. The rational choice model of decision making requires that a youth who is considering engaging in criminal activity will

1. think about the consequences of his or her behaviour;
2. give some thought to the chances of getting caught;
3. know what the penalty is for the offence;

4. take the chances of apprehension into account; and
5. weigh the cost of the sanctions/penalty against what can be gained from the offence.

Doob, Marinos, and Varma (1995) maintain that contemplation of all of these things is highly unlikely, particularly on the part of adolescents. They cite the work of Weagant and Milne (1992) who argue, on the basis of their direct contact with young offenders, that

> . . . teenagers seldom contemplate the consequence (i.e., punishment or sanction by the court) when they intentionally engage in criminal behaviour. This is because of one basic principle which we have learned through our experience: teenagers willingly engage in criminal behaviour when they think they are going to get away with it. If they think they are going to be apprehended they don't do it. The last thing the teenage girl thinks before pocketing that cassette tape is what happened to a friend who got caught and went to youth court. The only thing running through that girl's mind is: where is the security guard. (Cited in Doob, Marinos, & Varma, 1995, p. 63)

Deterrence is still not a stated principle of youth justice in Canada. In *R.. v. K.D.* (para. 14), Justice Lynch states, "When I look at the *Youth Criminal Justice Act*, deterrence is not something that is given high or any profile." And in *R. v. H.A.M.* (para. 34), Judge Swail says that it is a "principle . . . not to be considered in a *Youth Criminal Justice Act* sentencing" (cited in Bala & Anand, 2004, p. 260).

Race, Class, and Gender

Research conducted in the United States indicates that race, class, and gender characteristics affect what happens to young offenders in the justice system. The effect of these factors is not always straightforward, since they usually interact with each other and with legal variables, such as a prior record. Unfortunately, there has been very little Canadian research on this subject, although some work has been done on the experiences of First Nations and Aboriginal youth in the justice system. Beyond this, Schissel's work in an Edmonton court (1993) and Bell's work in a southwestern Ontario court (1994a) shed some light on the effects of race, class, and gender in Canadian youth courts.

With regard to race, Aboriginal youth are more likely than non-Aboriginal youth to be convicted and more likely to receive a custody sentence or probation. In addition, without a parent or guardian in court, Aboriginal youth are more likely to receive more severe dispositions (Schissel, 1993, pp. 99–102). A lack of resources or detention facilities in Aboriginal communities also means that more Aboriginal youth are removed from their communities (Hamilton & Sinclair, 1991; Morin, 1990). To the extent that justice officials define and assess "responsible parents or guardians" in non-Native terms, Aboriginal youth are also less likely to be released either without charges or on bail (LaPrairie, 1983; Stevens, 1990).

Generally, most girls in court are two years younger than boys (age 15 versus 17) (Schissel, 1993, pp. 37–38). As Duffy (1996) puts it, "It appears that courts are most offended by young girls (15 years of age) who are 'already' in trouble with the law and by older boys (17 years old) who are 'still' in trouble. The harshest sentences go to older males and younger females" (1996, p. 214).

The findings on gender of Bell (1994a), Schissel (1993), and Duffy (1996) elaborate on the complex ways in which gender, class, and family factors influence court outcomes. According to Bell, girls are treated more leniently than boys only if their offences are the traditional criminal offences of property crime and crime against the person. Girls charged with administrative offences and with mischief or disturbing the peace are treated more severely than are boys. Both boys and girls are treated leniently if their only parent is a single mother—provided that she is not a professionally employed mother. When parents (particularly mothers) are professionals, and when fathers appear in court, young offenders are treated more severely (Bell, 1994a, pp. 45–54). Thus, for girls, sentencing is something of a "double whammy." Not only are they judged in terms of their ability to conform to the stereotype of the "good daughter," but they are also judged by their parents' ability to conform to **gendered expectations** of "good parenting."

gendered expectations
What is expected of a person because of his or her biological sex characteristics.

Because race, class, and gender interact and intersect with legal factors to affect what happens to youth in the justice system, a number of recent scholars have focused their work (as we saw in Chapters 3 and 4) on street youth and homelessness, where the most marginalized among the youth population are to be found (Baron, 1995; Gaetz, 2004; McCarthy & Hagan, 1992; Miller, Donahue, Este, & Hofer, 2004). Through an examination of this population, we most clearly see how the justice system, through policy, law, and practice, further marginalize youth who are already dispossessed and disadvantaged.

Some policies and legislative procedures and programs are more likely than others to criminalize marginalized youth. As we have seen in this and other chapters, administrative offence charges, often referred to as "technical violations" to differentiate them from behaviours considered to be "criminal," increased dramatically through the YOA years and are still high relative to other offences. Moreover, these technical violations are more likely than other offences to result in a custody/prison sentence, and girls, Aboriginal, and black youth are disproportionately represented among these charges. The most problematic technical violations, including YOA/YCJA offences, are those pertaining to breach of probation or failure to comply with conditions of an order, pre- or post-sentence.

Youth who are homeless are not living on the streets because they are criminal; rather, because they are homeless, they are more likely to be criminalized. Green and Healy (2003) write from their experiences as lawyers working in the youth court and argue that the very nature of administrative offences (and, in particular, how violations are sanctioned) explains to a great extent the over-representation of marginalized children in the justice system and in custody.

There are a number of reasons for this. First is the tendency to view a person who has breached the conditions of an order as a "repeat" offender. This conceptualization makes little sense, Green and Healy (2003) point out, when the reality of the breach is that a young person has simply returned home past a specified curfew time. Nonetheless, as far as the official statistics and court records indicate, the youth has been in court and therefore "offended" more than once, and the likelihood of a more severe sentence is increased. Related to this are the actual conditions of the orders and how likely it is that some youth will be able to abide by them. The authors maintain that, for example, they would expect few 12- or 13-year-old youth to understand the legal definition of such concepts as "keep the peace" or "good behaviour."

Similarly, another concern is the assumption that children and youth are all equal in their ability to abide by conditions. For some children and youth, it would be very difficult to comply with an order of regular school attendance or to reside in a particular residence. Green and Healy point out that in cases of family conflict or dysfunction, young people often find themselves in situations where a parent will leave the home or they themselves are forced to leave for their own safety. School attendance is also extremely difficult for youth who may already be disadvantaged by a learning disability or fetal alcohol syndrome/effects, for example a 15-year-old boy with a Grade 3 level in reading or math skills. They maintain that ". . . many of these conditions ask too much from the youth, and too little from the community" (2003, pp. 44–46).

The final problem that Green and Healy raise relates to the fact that probation always comes with conditions and sanctions are attached to the violation of these conditions. This is the source of criminalization and further marginalization for many youth and there is no good reason to continue the counterproductive liaison between probation conditions and sanctions for technical violations. It would be a simple matter in the case of a breach of minor conditions to leave a youth in the community and provide more social supports or, if a youth is considered "a risk to society," to hold her or him in remand pending a review of the original sentence or order (2003, pp. 47–48). The authors sum up the issue through the words of an Aboriginal youth's response to a question regarding how he would change the youth justice system:

> Probation. That's just like being locked up again. Obviously, not one person in the whole world is not going to be breach once in a while, like a curfew. Regarding probation, I wouldn't have so many rules. I'd ask the kids what they wanted: a job, school, counselling, whatever. I'd want them to do that. I wouldn't go too hard on a curfew. I wouldn't really tell them what to do, that just gets them mad. It doesn't let them do what they want. If you try this, they just say "fuck them." (Cited in Green & Healy, 2003, p. 45)

Is Youth Court Sentencing a "Slap on the Wrist"?

According to a public survey in Ontario, 86 percent of those surveyed believed that youth court sentences were too lenient (Doob, Sprott, Marinos, & Varma, 1998, as cited in Doob & Cesaroni, 2004, p. 22). Yet, for a number of reasons, the majority of those who have studied or worked in the youth justice system do not believe that youth sentences amount to a "slap on the wrist." As we will see in the next chapter, a major reason is that, from 1986–1987 to 1993–1994, there was a 41 percent increase in the number of custody dispositions meted out in the youth courts (Foran, 1995, p. 7) and daily counts and rates of incarceration did not begin to show consistent decreases until the late 1990s (Statistics Canada, 2000, pp. 48–49). Of course, various interest groups who lobby for tougher sentencing measures take a very different view of the youth justice system. For them, it is too lenient.

Bala (1988) suggests that how one views the YOA-based justice system depends on the object of comparison. If the YOA-based system is compared with the adult justice system and with sentencing guidelines of the Criminal Code, a different view emerges than if it is compared with the Juvenile Delinquents Act. As Bala states:

> . . . the YOA [and now the YCJA] does not have a single, simple underlying philosophy; there is no single, simple philosophy that can deal with all situations in which young persons violate the criminal law. When contrasted with the child welfare oriented philosophy of the JDA, the YOA emphasizes due process, protection of society, and limited discretion. In comparison to the adult criminal code, however, the YOA emphasizes the special needs and limited accountability of young persons. (1988, p. 15)

Compared with the JDA, then, the YOA and the YCJA look tough. Compared with the adult system, however, the YOA appears lenient. The YCJA, with its added emphasis on diversion and non-custodial sentences, looks even more lenient than the YOA, but its creation of the presumptive offence and automatic adult sentences make it far tougher than the YOA. As we will see in the discussion that follows, comparisons of legal provisions and sentencing practices for specific offenders suggest that the issue is more complex.

What Is Being Compared?

It is fairly clear that the youth justice system is more lenient than the adult system for youth under age 14 with respect to particularly violent offences (including murder). Such is not always the case when it comes to other offences. For example, while adults are eligible for parole and may be released after serving one-sixth of a sentence or are entitled to statutory release after serving two-thirds of a sentence, young offenders lack the benefit of these provisions. In lieu of parole or early release, the young offender has conditional supervision, but even this is not automatic.

Doob, Marinos, and Varma (1995) compared custody dispositions from youth court in 1992–1993 with dispositions from six adult provincial courts. They found that the percentage of cases resulting in custody is roughly the same for youth and adults charged with mischief offences, theft under $1,000, failure to comply with a disposition or probation order, and assault. Offences for which adults are more likely to receive a custodial sentence include failure to appear in court, robbery, and sexual assault (p. 65).

median sentence length
A statistical term meaning that sentences in half the cases are above the median sentence length and half are below.

Bell and Smith (1994), who compared **median sentence length** for Nova Scotia youth and adults sentenced to custody during the period 1992–1994, found that for some offences, young offenders were getting longer custody terms than adults. Their comparison of broad categories of offences, and some specific offences, revealed that the median sentence length (in days) was longer for young offenders. Of offenders with no previous record, young offenders received longer or equal custody terms for theft, mischief, serious assault, and common assault. Of offenders with a previous custody record, young offenders received longer sentences than adults for theft, mischief, sexual assault, and common assault (Bell & Smith, 1994). Similarly, a Statistics Canada comparison of youth and adult custody sentences for the entire country found that in 1998–1999, youth received longer custody terms than adults for theft, serious and minor assault, break and enter, mischief, drugs, weapons charges, and failure to appear (Sanders, 2000, p. 11).

Statistics Canada data on mean (average) and median lengths of custody sentences for both adult and youth courts show that in 2003–2004, youth received the same sentences for both common and major assaults, as well as for theft. As is to be expected because of legislative differences, youth receive lesser custody terms for the most serious crimes against the person. Of major concern is that young offenders received longer custody terms for traffic offences, administrative offences, and prostitution.

The most glaringly different custody terms are for prostitution. Here, the mean and median number of days for adults is 53 and 3 days, respectively, while for youth the corresponding figures are 147 and 150, respectively (J. Thomas, 2005, p. 18; M. Thomas, 2004, p. 13). Since prostitution offences almost entirely involve women and girls, it is likely that these cases are mostly women and girls. The fact that the mean and median are almost the same for girls, while the mean is higher for women than the median, means that only a few women are receiving custody sentences longer than three days and half the girls are receiving sentences of longer than 5 months. It is probably also safe to surmise from this data that almost all girls charged with prostitution are getting custody terms considerably longer than the three days that half of the women receive. Furthermore, this differential in custody terms has been a consistent pattern for at least the last six years, regardless of the level of custody. Importantly, it is clear from this data that prostitution charges are a major avenue for the criminalization of girls.

These comparisons are suggestive rather than conclusive (Doob, Marinos, & Varma, 1995). Given that different sentencing principles underlie the youth and adult justice systems, we should not expect—or even want—outcomes to be the same. The fact that adults have parole means that while their sentences may be longer than those of youth, their time served may be shorter. On the other hand, youth sentences that are longer than those for adults will be even longer when time served is considered. It may also be the case that adult offences and youth offences are viewed differently by courts. A break and enter or a robbery committed by an adult may be seen as a professional activity but more as experimentation if engaged in by a juvenile.

Such differences aside, the evidence suggests that youth court sentencing cannot easily be dismissed as a "slap on the wrist." Conversely, for those who argue that more youth should receive adult sentences, it cannot be assumed that stiffer penalties would be the end result. Maybe some youth know more than the general public and this is why, as we saw earlier in this chapter, young offenders in Manitoba were opting for transfers to the adult court as a way out of the youth justice system. It is also possible that some youth know that the adult system sometimes offers programming better suited to their needs than the youth system does, as we will see in the next chapter.

SUMMARY

The first year to show a decrease in youth court caseload since the YOA was implemented was 1994–1995 and the caseload has decreased every year since then—most dramatically when the YCJA was implemented. Most youth court cases involve male youth and the most common offences are property crimes. Girls going to court tend to be younger than boys. Under the YOA, there was an increase in the number of youth held in pretrial detention, which critics charge is a net-widening mechanism. YCJA provisions requiring the court to assume that pretrial detention is not necessary may halt this increase and reduce the numbers of youth in detention.

Transferring a youth to adult court was one of the most contentious, complicated, and legally problematic aspects of the YOA because the transfer occurred before a finding of guilt. The YCJA has sidestepped many of these problems through the creation of the presumptive offence, requiring an automatic adult sentence for any youth aged 14 or older convicted of serious violent offences, as well as other "serious" offences committed by youth aged 16 and 17. Youth facing adult sentences also have adult legal rights that are not available to those receiving youth sentences—they can elect a jury trial and are entitled to a preliminary hearing.

Private lawyers have been found to be more successful than duty counsel in defending clients. Lawyers who assume a "guardian" role are primarily concerned with the "best interests" of their clients. Lawyers who assume a "legal advocate" role are more concerned with their clients' legal rights. The YCJA allows the court to order young offenders or their parents/guardians to pay for court-appointed representation. The youth justice system offers special legal protections and rights, and it is not at all clear that youth understand the meaning of these rights. A major concern then is the extent to which youth are protected when they waive their rights.

The most common sentences in youth court are probation and custody. Custody rates skyrocketed under the YOA in spite of restrictions and provisions for diversion. The YCJA strengthens these restrictions by requiring a conviction for a violent offence for custody to be considered and a justification for a custodial sentence for a non-violent offence conviction. There is reason to believe that attaching conditions to sanctions and then charging youth with violations of those conditions is a major reason that so many youth are in custody.

Sentencing principles from all juvenile justice models have been incorporated into the YCJA. Nonetheless, justice principles of proportionality and retribution, along with the crime control principle of punishment, take precedence over the welfare principle of rehabilitation and the restorative justice principles of reintegration and reparation. The general principles governing adult sentencing are retribution, deterrence, incapacitation, and rehabilitation; all except deterrence have been established by the YCJA. There has been no consensus among youth court judges regarding the application of rehabilitation and deterrence principles. Retribution and incapacitation are generally seen as appropriate in the youth justice system, as long as they are not applied in the same way in which they are applied in the adult system.

Race, class, and gender characteristics affect what happens to young offenders in court. Aboriginal youth, girls charged with non-traditional offences, and youth with professional parents (especially professional mothers) are treated more harshly than other youth. Technical violations are a major reason for the criminalization of marginalized youth.

Juvenile justice under the YOA appeared tough when compared with juvenile justice under the JDA and "lenient" when compared with the adult system. However, actual comparisons of adult and youth sentences suggest that sanctions in the adult system are not always tougher than sanctions in the youth system and there is no reason to expect any difference with the YCJA. Furthermore, given the different philosophy underlying the youth justice system, we should neither expect nor desire identical outcomes in the two systems.

DISCUSSION/CRITICAL THINKING QUESTIONS

1. Thinking in terms of law reform, why and how are pretrial rules and decisions so crucial in general and specifically to potential reforms of the YCJA?
2. To what extent are youth rights in the youth justice system mitigated by their status in Canadian society and the intersections of race, class, and gender?
3. How is juvenile justice related to youth marginalization?
4. Is the youth justice system a "slap on the wrist" for young offenders? Explain your answer.

WEB LINKS

A Comparison of Case Processing under the Young Offenders Act and the First Six Months of the Youth Criminal Justice Act
http://canada.justice.gc.ca/en/ps/yj/research/moyer/index.html

Youth Court Judges' Views of the Youth Justice System: The Results of a Survey
http://canada.justice.gc.ca/en/ps/yj/research/doob/index.html

Parents' Involvement in Youth Justice Proceedings: Perspectives of Youth and Parents
http://canada.justice.gc.ca/en/ps/yj/research/petersonbadali-broeking/index.html

For chapter quizzes and more links, visit this book's accompanying website at
www.bellyoungoffenders3e.nelson.com

CHAPTER TEN

Youth Corrections: Going to Jail

CHAPTER OBJECTIVES

1. To trace the history of juvenile institutions in Canada from prisons to industrial training schools and correctional centres.
2. To profile the use of custody and examine Youth Criminal Justice Act (YCJA) provisions for using custody.
3. To discuss different types of correctional programs, along with their objectives and philosophies.
4. To examine issues associated with program and legislative philosophies.

KEY TERMS

Correctional services
Remand
Training schools
Secure custody
Open custody
Conditional supervision order
Deferred custody and
    supervision order
Intensive rehabilitative custody
    and supervision order
Aftercare

Corrections
Correctional programming
Cognitive skills
Life skills
Boot camp
Rehabilitative treatment
Rehabilitation
Multisystemic therapy
Indeterminate sentences
Determinate sentences

INTRODUCTION

The number of youth involved in the system that is commonly referred to as **"correctional services"** can be measured in a number of different ways. Statistics Canada reports rates of youth in the system per 10,000 youth population (aged 12–17) and by the number of youth in the correctional system. The latter are reported in three ways: as average daily counts, as a monthly average of daily counts, and as total number of admissions. *Counts* give us an indication of how many youth are in the system on any one day or in any one month. *Admissions* refers to the number of youth who have gone through the system in any one year. So, for example, for the year 2002–2003 (the most recent statistics available), a total of 26,200 youth were admitted under supervision as a result of a probation sentence. In any one month, though, there were 26,400 youth under supervision. Meanwhile, the rate of probation is 121 per 10,000 youth 12–17 years of age (Reitano, 2004, pp. 3–4).

These differences are important in understanding and interpreting the statistics. Admissions will always be higher than daily or monthly averages because people are always coming into the system and leaving the system on a day-to-day basis. Admission figures are therefore a measure of how many youth are moving through custody, receiving programs, and experiencing the system. Counts tell us about capacity and are of use to the correctional institutions and probation officials for administrative and operational purposes. Rates are a reflection of the youth population as a whole and make sense when we are interested in police crime statistics. Correctional rates are compared with crime rates to understand how young offenders are sanctioned or to compare changes from year to year or between jurisdictions to see if some provinces or territories are more or less likely than others to use custody or probation. As shown in the next paragraph, these rates also enable statements about how many from the entire Canadian youth population are locked up or are under probation supervision in a given period of time.

In 2001–2002, 1.4 percent of the Canadian youth population between the ages of 12 and 17 were in custody or on probation. Overall, 12,291 boys and 2796 girls were admitted to a term in custody, with an average daily count of 3,420 youth in custody, or 0.1 percent of Canada's total youth population. A total of 6,415 were 15 years of age or younger, and girls were considerably younger than boys. Fifty-eight percent of the girls admitted were under 15, while only 38 percent of the boys were under 15. The proportion of younger girls admitted to custody was higher than for **remand,** and both remand and custody rates were higher than the proportion of girls admitted to probation supervision (Marinelli, 2004, pp. 3, 7, 12).

Disproportionate admissions are also found for Aboriginal youth, who in 2002–2003 accounted for 8 percent of the youth population, yet they accounted for 46 percent of the sentenced admissions to custody and 44 percent of the admissions to remand. Aboriginal girls are even more over-represented in that they constitute 25 percent of the girls admitted to custody, while Aboriginal boys account for 21 percent of the boys' admissions. On any given day, 850 youth were being held in remand, and one-quarter of these were Aboriginal youth. One-third (32 percent) of the girls admitted to remand were Aboriginal, and 23 percent of the boys were Aboriginal. In 2001–2002, approximately, 38,261 youth were under supervision in the community on a probation order, girls were younger than boys, and Aboriginal youth were over-represented (Marinelli, 2004, pp. 3, 7, 12; Reitano, 2004, pp. 2, 4, 6).

Custody is an expensive undertaking: it costs an average of $80,000 per year to keep a young person in custody. Actual costs vary by province and also depend on the facility's

correctional services
Custodial institutions and probation services for youth offenders in Canada.

remand
To hold an accused person in a prison or detention facility prior to a court appearance, trial, or while awaiting sentence; sometimes also referred to as "pretrial detention."

CASE STUDY BOX 10.1

Johnny: Custody

On January 18, 2005, Johnny was admitted to Nova Scotia's Waterville Youth Detention Centre on remand. A youth worker told the court that many of the other youth at the facility treated Johnny badly because they knew what he had done, and said things like "He killed that lady, he should be punished." The worker also said that it was common for the youth at the facility to brag to one another about the crimes that they had committed, and he had overheard Johnny talking about the enjoyment he got from stealing cars.

Dr. Mark Johnston, a Halifax psychiatrist at the IWK Children's Health Centre, regularly met with Johnny at the Waterville facility during his time on remand. The doctor argued it was "unlikely" that two years would be enough to rehabilitate Johnny, saying, "He should be considered a significant threat to safety and has made limited to no progress. I would say that it would take another two or three years at least and even then it may not happen." In the same breath, Dr. Johnston also argued that time and maturation are essential to Johnny's rehabilitation. While the doctor recommended to the court that Johnny should continue on at Waterville, he also remarked, "I'm not saying it's the end of the world if he goes to adult jail."

Sources: *The Chronicle Herald* [Halifax] (December 15b, 16a, 2005); D. Jeffrey (December 20, 2005). Researched and written by Nicole Landry.

level of security. Reported figures from Atlantic Canada indicate that community-based residential custody expenses range from $8,000 to $12,000 per year. The range of annual average costs of low- and high-security facilities are $55,000–$70,000 and $70,000–$120,000, respectively (Eckstein, 2005, p. 80; Newfoundland and Labrador, October 1994, p. 1). Not surprisingly, cost estimates run higher in Ontario, where low-security facilities cost $93,000 per year and high-security facilities cost $126,000 (Campbell, 2005b, p. 265). Supervising a young offender in the community through programs such as probation is considerably cheaper: approximately $600 to $700 per person (Newfoundland and Labrador, October 1994, p. 1). Leschied and Cunningham report that their community-based program, involving intensive family intervention and support systems for 380 youth, costs $6,000–$7,000 per youth (2002, p. 65).

The practice of keeping adults and young people in separate correctional facilities began about 140 years ago. This chapter begins with a discussion of the history of youth corrections in Canada. Next, it examines YCJA provisions for youth custody, followed by a discussion of contemporary facilities and programs. A discussion of some of the critical issues in corrections today rounds out the chapter.

HISTORICAL FOUNDATIONS

The foundation for the practice of institutionalizing Canadian youth separately from adults was laid in 1857 with the passage of the Act for Establishing Prisons for Young Offenders. The first institution was opened at Isle aux Noix on the Richelieu River in October 1858, and the second at Penetanguishene on Georgian Bay in August 1859. Both institutions had formerly been used as army barracks. The intention was to provide a better environment for youth than was to be found in adult penitentiaries.

While both boys and girls were sent to Isle aux Noix, only boys were detained at Penetanguishene (Carrigan, 1991, pp. 405–406). Notwithstanding all of the good intentions, both institutions reportedly "fell short of expectations" and became "primarily institutions of work and punishment" (Carrigan, 1991, p. 406).

From Reformatories to Industrial Schools

In 1867, J.M. Langmuir was appointed as Ontario's first Inspector of Prisons, Asylums, and Public Charities. He began with a campaign to change correctional philosophy and policy regarding youth. His efforts were instrumental in changing Penetanguishene from a "reformatory prison" to a "reformatory for boys," with a mandate to foster the "education, industrial training and moral reclamation of juvenile delinquents" (Langmuir, cited in Carrigan, 1991, p. 407).

Meanwhile, efforts were under way in other parts of the country to provide institutions that would serve as places of reform for all children in need—the poor and the neglected, as well as the delinquent. Children in need would be prevented from becoming criminals, it was argued, if they received care and education, and were taught a trade through industrial training. Halifax was one of the first cities to develop an institution that provided those things. The Halifax Protestant Industrial School (established 1864) and the St. Patrick's Industrial School for Catholic Boys (established 1865) were followed by the Monastery of the Good Shepherd, an Industrial School for Roman Catholic Girls. Ontario's first industrial schools were the Victoria Industrial School for Boys (established 1887) and the Alexandra Industrial School for Girls (established 1892).

By 1927, 24 industrial schools were spread across the country: nine in Quebec, five in Ontario, four in Nova Scotia, two in British Columbia, two in Manitoba, and one each in Saskatchewan and New Brunswick (Carrigan, 1991, p. 422). All had similar routines: half of each day was spent in school and half in learning a trade. Boys typically received training in carpentry, shoemaking, cooking and baking, and farm and garden work; girls were taught sewing, knitting, crocheting, dressmaking, shoemaking, and domestic science (Carrigan, 1991, p. 422; Sutherland, 1976, p. 137).

Training Schools

Officially designated as "industrial training schools" at the turn of the century, these institutions came to be known as simply **training schools.** Not surprisingly, as more industrial schools were built, their use increased. In 1922, 8.5 percent of children convicted in juvenile court were sentenced to industrial schools. That figure rose to 11.5 percent in 1932, 13.1 percent in 1945, and 14.4 percent in 1949 (Carrigan, 1991, p. 426; Hackler, 1978, p. 104). Thereafter, the numbers declined. By 1968, the number of youth sentenced to training schools had dropped to 8 percent; by 1973, custody sentences made up 2.3 percent of convictions (Hackler, 1978, pp. 104–106). A Canadian criminologist writing in the late 1970s reported that "there has probably been no increase in the use of training schools in the last few years . . . [T]here is a general indication that the juvenile justice system in Canada has not been opting for an increased use of institutional care" (cited in Hackler, 1978, pp. 105–108).

One of the major reasons for declining rates in the use of training schools was that provinces began to restrict their use. In the early 1970s, British Columbia abolished the use of secure custody and then, as if anticipating the Young Offenders Act (YOA), reintroduced it in 1977; this reintroduced custody was to be used only for "hard-core" offenders and for the purpose of "protection of society." Ontario also restricted the use of training schools; only youth who had committed an offence for which an adult

training schools
A common term for juvenile correctional institutions before the introduction of the Young Offenders Act.

would be sentenced to prison could be sentenced to custody. The development of community programs and group homes in the 1970s further reduced the use of training schools (Markwart, 1992, p. 232).

Youth Centres

secure custody
A form of youth custody under the YOA that required more restrictions on movement, both within and outside an institution, than was required for open security.

open custody
A form of youth custody under the YOA that required fewer restrictions on movement, both within and outside an institution, than was required for secure custody.

Correctional systems for young people underwent structural and procedural changes with the introduction of the YOA. Two levels of custody were established, **secure** and **open,** and the court was required to set the level of custody at sentencing. When sentenced for a murder conviction in youth court, a set period of community supervision was also required after a youth was released from custody. While the court established level of custody, provinces were given the power to designate which of their facilities would classify as open (limited restrictions on movement) or secure (maximum restrictions on movement). Hence, there was considerable variation in facilities across the country.

In Newfoundland and Labrador, for example, the Department of Social Services Division of Youth Corrections was responsible for carrying out the sentence of the court. This department has two divisions—Community Correctional Services, and

---

VOICES BOX 10.2

A Young Person's Thoughts about Detention

I went to court
all dressed up
in high heeled shoes
and a deadly suit
for the whole four days
Sitting in that court room
knowing I was guilty
and lying through my teeth
—only made it harder
The threat of their time
—too much to bare
I wish for death
but each morning
when I wake
I'm pleased
and stay pleased until night hits
But left alone I feel like
a beast that can't sleep
& bang my head against the wall
pacing up and down
like a tiger
Knowing I'm really
a cub
that's been deserted.
n.g.

Source: From *Heroes and Villains,* an anthology of poems by young people in detention. (1994). Adelaide, Australia: Via Magenta.

Secure Custody and Remand Services. Community Correctional Services was responsible for alternative measures, non-custodial supervision programs, and open-custody services and facilities. Newfoundland and Labrador's open-custody facilities consisted of eight group homes, three assessment centres, and foster homes. There were two facilities for secure custody and remand—the Newfoundland and Labrador Youth Centre in Whitborne and the Pleasantville Youth Centre in St. John's. In 1994–1995, funding was allocated for an additional regional youth centre in Corner Brook (Newfoundland and Labrador, 1996).

In British Columbia, youth institutions and other young offender programs such as probation and alternative measures came under the jurisdiction of the Ministry for Children and Families. British Columbia had five secure-custody centres—one on Vancouver Island, one in Vancouver, one in the Fraser Valley, one in the Interior, and one in the North Region. There were seven open-custody facilities, one in each region and three in Vancouver. There were also three community-based residential centres (CBRCs) in the province.

Ontario and Nova Scotia are unique in that the implementation of the YOA created a split jurisdiction over young offenders, resulting in 12- to 15-year-olds being processed differently from 16- to 17-year-olds. In both provinces, 16- to 17-year-olds remained under the jurisdiction of adult corrections and 12- to 15-year-old youth under the jurisdiction of the youth system. Courts were also operated separately. Youth under 15 were processed under the family court, as they had been under the Juvenile Delinquents Act (JDA). Youth aged 16–17 were processed in adult court under YOA restrictions; the court was referred to as "youth court" when young offender cases were heard. Both provinces have since moved to have all young offenders processed through the family court.

Since August 1994, all youth corrections processes in Nova Scotia have been under the jurisdiction of the Department of Justice, but youth institutions continued to be separated by age and/or gender until the advent of the YCJA. All secure-custody sentences for males aged 16–17 were served in the Nova Scotia Youth Centre, while 12- to 15-year-olds served their sentences at the Shelburne Youth Centre. All female young offenders sentenced to secure custody were held at Shelburne regardless of age. Since implementation of the YCJA, all youth serving secure custody sentences, regardless of age or gender, do so at the Nova Scotia Youth Centre.

With already declining daily counts from shorter youth custody sentences for non-violent offences and the YCJA's emphasis on extrajudicial measures and sanctions and restrictions on the use of custody, many other provinces have been closing youth institutions over the last few years. In Ontario, Phase I youth (12- to 15-year-olds) were under the jurisdiction of the Ministry of Community and Social Services and Phase II youth (16- to 17-year-olds) were handled by the Ministry of the Solicitor General and Correctional Services. Jurisdictions in some areas were combined for female offenders; for example, in Hamilton, Brantford, Niagara, and the Haldimand–Norfolk regions, the Ministry of Community and Social Services also provided detention for Phase II female youth. This change resulted from (1) the closing of secure-custody/detention facilities for 16- to 17-year-old female youth at the Hamilton–Wentworth Detention Centre in June 1995, and (2) recommendations contained in the Women's Issues Task Force Report (Ontario Ministry of the Solicitor General and Correctional Services, 1995b). Ontario has since subsumed Phase I and II youth under the Ministry of Children and Youth Services (Campbell, 2005, ff. p. 288).

The YCJA does not require the youth court to specify a level of custody for young offenders. Rather, s. 85(1) requires only that provinces have at least two levels of custody for young persons and that levels be distinguished by the degree of restraint of the young persons in them. It is still the Lieutenant Governor in Council who determines facility custodial levels, but it is now the provincial director who determines the level of custody to be served by each young person rather than the court. While custody was addressed in the YOA in terms of two levels of security (open and secure), the YCJA paves the way for individual custodial sentences and provincial facilities to be differentiated by multiple security levels and a variety of programs and intervention methods. Provinces are not likely to change YOA facilities in any major ways in the foreseeable future. What did change is the concept of custody and its lack of links with community corrections.

Custody Provisions under the YCJA

The whole concept of custody, as a sanction for the criminal offences of youth, changed under the YCJA. With the YOA, custody was mostly perceived and used as an end in itself, leading to a number of aftercare issues to be discussed later in the chapter. With the YCJA, custody is no longer an entity unto itself, but rather exists as part of a larger system of programs and community supervision designed to rehabilitate and reintegrate young offenders back into the community as law-abiding people. This represents an important shift in emphasis regarding the purpose of custody. The YCJA refers to custody as "the custody and supervision system" and it is clear that its purpose is a welfare and restorative one: to carry out the sentence of the court and assist in the reintegration and rehabilitation of youth. Still, the ultimate objective is one of crime control: to "contribute to the protection of society" (see Box 10.3). Interestingly, these are also the purposes of the adult correctional system as mandated by the Corrections and Conditional Release Act.

New sentencing options under the YCJA create two new aspects of youth correctional programs: the conditional supervision order and intensive rehabilitation custody and supervision. Youth serving a custody sentence are now required to serve the latter portion of their sentence in the community under supervision. Section 105 of the YCJA outlines the regulations regarding the conditions of a **conditional supervision order** and the powers of the provincial director regarding required and discretionary conditions. Under this section, the provincial director is required to bring a young person to the youth justice court before the custodial portion of her or his sentence expires, for the court to set the specific conditions of the youth's conditional supervision. The necessary conditions of the conditional supervision order include:

conditional supervision order
Requires a person under supervision to abide by particular conditions set by the court (e.g., attend drug or alcohol rehabilitation programs).

- keep the peace and be of good behaviour;
- appear before the youth justice court when required;
- be under the supervision of the provincial director or designate;
- inform the provincial director when arrested or questioned by the police;
- report to the police as instructed;
- advise the provincial director of any change in address, employment, vocational or educational training, volunteer work, family or financial situation, and any changes that might affect the young person's ability to comply with the conditions of the order;
- not own, possess, or have the control of any weapon, ammunition, prohibited ammunition, prohibited device, or explosive substance; and,
- comply with any reasonable instructions that the provincial director considers necessary.

BOX 10.3

Purpose of Custody and Supervision

Section 83 of the Youth Criminal Justice Act outlined the purpose and limitations of the custody and supervision system:

(1) The purpose of the youth custody and supervision system is to contribute to the protection of society by
   (a) carrying out sentences imposed by courts through the safe, fair and humane custody and supervision of young persons; and
   (b) assisting young persons to be rehabilitated and reintegrated into the community as law-abiding citizens, by providing effective programs to young persons in custody and while under supervision in the community.

(2) In addition to the principles set out in section 3, the following principles are to be used in achieving that purpose:
   (a) that the least restrictive measures consistent with the protection of the public, of personnel working with young persons and of young persons be used;
   (b) that young persons sentenced to custody retain the rights of other young persons, except the rights that are necessarily removed or restricted as a consequence of a sentence under this Act or another Act of Parliament;
   (c) that the youth custody and supervision system facilitate the involvement of the families of young persons and members of the public;
   (d) that custody and supervision decisions be made in a forthright, fair and timely manner, and that young persons have access to an effective review procedure; and
   (e) that placements of young persons where they are treated as adults not disadvantage them with respect to their eligibility for and conditions of release.

In addition, the court may impose any number of additional conditions regarding where the youth will live, including with whom; what efforts the youth will make to get a job, attend school or other place of training or recreational program; restrictions on moving out of the court's jurisdiction; and any other conditions the court considers appropriate to promote the youth's reintegration. Related to this is the court's option to defer a custody term. The **deferred custody and supervision order** is a new sentence option that permits a judge to sentence a youth to a term in custody and also to specify that this sentence will be deferred in favour of the youth serving the duration of the sentence under conditional supervision in the community. A violation in these cases does not involve a new charge of breach, but rather the possibility that the youth will be incarcerated.

The **intensive rehabilitative custody and supervision order** is reserved for youth convicted of the most serious violent offences—murder, attempted murder, manslaughter, aggravated sexual assault—or a youth who is a repeat offender and has been convicted of a serious violent offence for which an adult would be liable to a prison term of more than two years. In addition, s. 42(7) of the YCJA also requires the court to establish three other conditions:

(b) the young person is suffering from a mental illness or disorder, a psychological disorder or an emotional disturbance;

deferred custody and supervision order
A sentence option created by the YCJA that is similar to "house arrest" sentences for adults.

intensive rehabilitative custody and supervision order
A term created by the YCJA that refers to a sentence of the court whereby a youth must serve a custody term in a facility designated as a rehabilitation institution.

(c) a plan of treatment and intensive supervision has been developed for the young person, and there are reasonable grounds to believe that the plan might reduce the risk of the young person repeating the offence or committing a serious violent offence; and

(d) the provincial director has determined that an intensive rehabilitative custody and supervision program is available and that the young person's participation in the program is appropriate.

Two other aspects of the YCJA complement and strengthen the rehabilitative and reintegrative mandate of s. 83(1): youth workers and reintegration leave. Under the YOA, youth workers' duties and functions were connected to community dispositions such as probation and conditional supervision. The YCJA (s. 90) requires that a youth worker be assigned to every youth sentenced to custody. This worker is responsible for developing plans for the youth's reintegration into the community that include the most effective programs for the young person, as well as supervising and providing support to the youth when she or he is released from custody and is under supervision in the community.

The YOA allowed for temporary absences and day release (escorted or unescorted) from custody for a period of up to 15 days. These releases were granted by the provincial director for medical, compassionate, humanitarian, or rehabilitative reasons, or to allow a youth to attend school, find a job or work, or participate in training or treatment programs. The YCJA refers to this type of release [s. 91(1), (2)] as "reintegrative leave," allows release for the same reasons as the YOA, and extends such a release to a 30-day period that can be renewed any number of times.

YOUTH CUSTODY ISSUES

A total of 23,900 youth were admitted to custodial facilities in 2002–2003, and two-thirds of these (61 percent) were remanded to custody to await trial or sentencing (Reitano, 2004, p. 2). Although property offences predominate among sentenced admissions, their proportion declined from 46 percent in 1991–1992 to 42 in 1998–1999. Over the same period, the proportion of sentence admissions for YOA and administrative offences increased from 12.2 percent to 19 percent, while the proportion of sentenced admissions for violent offences increased from 16 percent to 22 percent. As Table 10.1 shows, this trend continued to 2003. Sentenced admissions for property offences have continued to decline and admissions for violent offences have continued to increase. The decline in sentenced admissions for administrative offences may be levelling off. It is difficult to do any more than observe these trends at this time because statistics are now being recorded differently. A few more years' data will be required to assess the impact of the YCJA.

The recording of remand admissions has not changed over time and remands appear to have been steadily increasing for the last 10 years. In 2002–2003, remand admissions were highest for both property and violent offences (33 percent and 31 percent, respectively), twice as high as they were 10 years ago and a 21 percent increase since 1993–1994. Not only are more youth being held in remand, but they also are spending more time there. Half of the youth in remand were held for one week or less and 1.4 percent (178 youth) for six months or more. In 1997–1998, 56 percent spent less than one week and 0.8 percent more than six months (Marinelli, 2004, pp. 17, 19; Reitano, 2004, pp. 2–3; St. Amand & Greenberg, 1996, p. 9; Statistics Canada, 2000b, pp. 20–21). Judges' increased preference for short sentences is also reflected in custody release figures. In 2001–2002, half of the youth released had

TABLE 10.1

Distribution of Custodial Admissions by Offence Type, 1998–1999, 2002–2003*

Offence Type	Secure % of Cases 1998–99	Open % of Cases 1998–99	All Custody % of Cases 2002–03	Remand % of Cases 1998–99	Remand % of Cases 2002–03
Violent	22	22	30	23	31
Property	42	43	34	37	33
Other CC[1, 2]	12	10	13	18	14
Other[3]	22	23	20	22	23

*In 1998–1999, YOA offences were recorded as a separate category, but in 2002–2003, they were included as "Other"; for comparative purposes, YOA offences have been included in "Other" in this table for 1998–1999. Similarly, as of 2002–2003, secure and open custody categories were combined, reflecting changes to come in the reporting of YCJA statistics.

[1]YOA offences include failure to comply with a disposition, failure to comply with an undertaking, contempt against youth court, and other YOA dispositions.

[2]Other Criminal Code offences include impaired operation of a motor vehicle, escape from custody, being unlawfully at large, failure to appear, failure to comply, and disorderly conduct/nuisances.

[3]Other offences include Narcotics Control Act offences, Food and Drug Act offences, YOA and other federal statute offences.

Sources: Statistics Canada, *Juristat*, (2000), Cat. No. 85-002, pp. 12–13, 20–21, 30–31; (2004), Cat. No. 85-002, 24(9), pp. 4–5.

served one month or less and only 9 percent had served six months or more (Marinelli, 2004, p. 19). With the YCJA's emphasis on serious and violent offences, these trends are expected to continue.

Changing Use of Custody

One of the interesting effects of the YOA is that its implementation reversed the declining JDA trend in the use of custody. Most research comparing the uses of incarceration under the JDA and the YOA has concluded that the YOA created an increase in the use of custody for young offenders (Leschied & Jaffe, 1987, 1988, 1991; Leschied, Jaffe, & Willis, 1991; Markwart & Corrado, 1989). Some of this research was considered problematic because it had not considered age differences before and after legislative change. Nonetheless, when age is considered, the results regarding increased use of custody were astounding. From 1984–1985 to 1989–1990, virtually every province increased its use of custody. Of course, increases varied across the country, so for example, between the last year of the JDA and the third year of the YOA, youth custody use in British Columbia increased by 85 percent, while adult admissions to custody in British Columbia decreased by 12 percent; in Manitoba, the youth population sentenced to custody increased by 148 percent (Markwart, 1992, pp. 236–238, 242).

Leonard, Smandych, and Brickey's research (1996) confirmed this trend reversal in Manitoba over the period 1968 to 1990: admission rates, discharge rates, and daily population rates showed an increased use of custody after the YOA was implemented. From 1968 to the mid-1970s, custody rates declined and then increased dramatically in 1984. According to the authors, the average daily rate of incarceration under the JDA was 4.7 youth per 10,000 in custody, while the YOA average was 10.3 youth per 10,000—a 219 percent increase (Leonard, Smandych, & Brickey, 1996, pp. 132–133).

Remarkably, this trend continued through to the mid-1990s. From 1991–1992 to 1993–1994, there was a 10 percent increase in the average daily count of youth in Canadian custodial facilities, and a 5 percent increase in 1994–1995 (Foran, 1995, p. 9). From 1990 to 1995, there was a 15 percent increase in the number of youth in secure custody and a 24 percent increase in the number of youth in open custody (St. Amand & Greenberg, 1996, p. 5). Daily counts and rates of incarceration did not begin to show consistent decreases until the latter part of the 1990s (Statistics Canada, 2000b, pp. 48–49). Interestingly, as discussed earlier in this chapter, the use of custody under the JDA also declined in its waning years.

Provincial Variation

While custody trends were fairly consistent across the country, there were and are provincial variations. All provinces showed increases between 1990 and 1995 in the number of youth in custodial facilities (the Yukon and Northwest Territories were exceptions). Increases ranged from 3 percent in Prince Edward Island to 58 percent in Newfoundland and Labrador. Alberta showed a 39 percent increase and British Columbia a 29 percent increase, while increases in other provinces ranged from 8 percent to 18 percent (St. Amand & Greenberg, 1996, p. 6). Youth court statistics for 1994–1995 show that Saskatchewan and Manitoba at 37.4 and 31.7 percent respectively, had the highest overall custody rates, while Quebec at 10.5 percent had the lowest. In fact, Quebec consistently appears to be low (St. Amand & Greenberg, 1996, p. 9).

As Table 10.2 shows, by 2002–2003, with the exception of Newfoundland and Labrador and the Northwest Territories, all provinces and territories were showing decreases in their incarceration rates, and most have been consistently declining since 1994–1995. Alberta's rates declined consistently, from a rate of 26.9 per 10,000 youth in 1994–1995 to 11.8 in 2002–2003; New Brunswick's rates declined from 31.2 to 18.1, and British Columbia's declined from 14.1 to 6.7. Ontario's declines were less dramatic: from 23.4 in 1994–1995 to 22.2 in 1998–1999. Among the provinces, Saskatchewan and Manitoba have maintained the highest rates. Manitoba's rate was 31.6 in 1994–1995 and 25.5 in 2002–2003. Saskatchewan, on the other hand, did not show decreases until after 1998–1999: rates increased from 36.9 in 1994–1995 to 41.2 in 1998–1999 and then dropped to 34.1 in 2002–2003.

The Yukon and Northwest Territories had the highest rates of incarceration, but by 2002–2003 the Yukon showed a dramatic decline to levels closer to the national average. Incarceration rates for the Northwest Territories are still fluctuating and are difficult to interpret. The drop in 1998–1999 was likely due to the creation of Nunavut as a territory in April 1999. Prior to that time, Nunavut custody statistics were included in those for the Northwest Territories.

A majority of youth in custody in Manitoba, Saskatchewan, and the territories are Aboriginal, both boys and girls. In 1998–1999, 74 percent of youth admitted to custody in Manitoba were Aboriginal, and 90 percent of the girls admitted were Aboriginal. For Saskatchewan, the figures were 70 percent and 71 percent, respectively; for the Yukon, 51 percent and 69 percent, respectively; and for the Northwest Territories, 76 percent and 83 percent, respectively (Statistics Canada, 2000b, pp. 24, 34). When over-representation is considered by comparing the proportion

TABLE 10.2

Provincial Incarceration Rates per 10,000 Youth: 1994–95, 1998–99, and 2002–03

Province	1994–1995	1998–1999	2002–2003
Newfoundland and Labrador	26.9	23.0	24.2
Prince Edward Island	30.0	18.8	12.2
Nova Scotia	22.5	19.3	17.0
New Brunswick	31.2	23.3	18.1
Quebec	11.2	10.5 (1995–96)	7.2
Ontario	23.4	22.2	—
Manitoba	31.6	31.1	25.5
Saskatchewan	36.9	41.2	34.1
Alberta	26.9	17.8	11.8
British Columbia	14.1	11.3	6.7
Yukon	48.1	49.2	21.1
Northwest Territories	137.2	80.7	109.4
Nunavut	—	—	37.9

—Not available.

Sources: Statistics Canada, *Juristat* (2000), Cat. No. 85-226-XIE, pp. 48–49; (2004), Cat. No. 85-002 24(9), p. 12.

of Aboriginal youth admitted to their proportion of the population, we find that Aboriginal youth are most over-represented in Manitoba, Saskatchewan, and Alberta. In Atlantic Canada, with the exception of Prince Edward Island, there was no Aboriginal youth over-representation.

In 2000, the Department of Justice undertook a project to ascertain how many Aboriginal youth were in custody and their experiences with the system. This study involved a "snapshot" of youth custody facilities across the country on one day in May/June 2000 (Bittle, Quann, Hattem, & Muise, 2002) and May/July 2003 (Latimer & Foss, 2004). The one-day snapshot gives a somewhat different picture of Aboriginal youth in custody because it measures the actual number of youth in custody on a particular day rather than average daily or monthly counts. Latimer and Foss (2004) argue that this is a better measure than admissions or average counts because it focuses on individuals and eliminates the multiple counting of individuals who move in and out of the system more than once over a year, or in and out of remand during a single court case, or have their level of custody changed (p. 1).

Bittle et al. (2002, p. 5) found that Ontario had the highest proportion of "in-count" Aboriginal youth incarcerated, 24 percent. Saskatchewan and Manitoba followed closely, with 23 percent of their custody population being Aboriginal. Nova Scotia, Nunavut, Prince Edward Island, and Newfoundland and Labrador all report Aboriginal populations of 1 percent or less; Alberta reported 11 percent,; British Columbia, 8 percent; and the Northwest Territories, 7 percent.

These studies also indicate that there were "substantial reductions" in the number of Aboriginal youth in custody from 2000 to 2003: from 1,128 to 720. All provinces and territories showed reductions, except for Nova Scotia and Nunavut. An examination of cities shows that custodial reductions were greatest in Winnipeg

(60 fewer youth), followed by Prince Albert (27 fewer), down to 1 fewer in Calgary. The only increases were for Regina and Saskatoon (3 more youth) (Latimer & Foss, 2004, p. 6).

Green and Healey (2003, pp. 94–95) refer to the work of LaPrairie (2002) and maintain that levels of education have a lot to do with variations in custody rates of Aboriginal youth. They point out that cities with the highest levels of education among Aboriginal peoples—Halifax, Montreal, and Toronto—also have the lowest rates of Aboriginal youth incarceration. As for type of custody, Aboriginal youth were over-represented only in secure-custody cases and youth incarcerated for serious violent offences, and were serving longer sentences for serious offences. Seventy-eight percent of the youth were First Nations; 16 percent, Métis; and 3 percent, Inuit; 75 percent were Status Indian (Latimer & Foss, 2004, pp. 7–11). We will return to a discussion of these figures in the next chapter.

Explaining Changes and Interprovincial Variation

When increases in the use of custody were first noticed, they were largely understood to be a result of the new philosophy of the YOA. It was argued that judges were favouring crime control principles over welfare principles (Leschied & Jaffe, 1991). This interpretation was supported by the fact that more youth were going into custody for shorter periods of time, with the greatest increases occurring for sentences of three months or less—a trend that is also reflected in more recent statistics (Statistics Canada, 1998, p. ix). It seemed that judges were shifting toward a "short, sharp shock" style of sentencing. However, Leonard, Smandych, and Brickey (1996) suggest that these increases were due more to changes in sentencing practice and the consequence of these changes than to the adoption of a new philosophy. They argue that shorter sentences ultimately give youth more opportunity to commit crimes; the result is an increase in the number of offenders, some of whom are being committed to custody three times or more in a single year.

The other problem requiring explanation is the variation in rates across the country. In spite of reporting consistent increases, not all provinces are using custody at the same rate. According to Doob and Sprott (1996, p. 411), we "need look no further than the courthouse door" for explanations of provincial and jurisdictional variation. It is not youth behaviour that is different across the country, but rather "the behaviour of provincial criminal justice personnel" (p. 411). It appears that type and length of sentence are fairly consistent for serious offences. Where inconsistencies in sentencing arise is in regard to less serious charges. Variation may be a function, then, of the number of less serious charges being brought to court by police and Crown prosecutors. Similarly, Carrington and Moyer's research (1994b) suggests that interprovincial variation can be explained by the "level of police activity" and by judicial "decision as to length of custodial sentence" (p. 288). Once the YCJA has been in effect for a few years, we should expect to see reductions in the amount of provincial variation in rates of incarceration.

Youth Facility Location

Controversy over the location of youth facilities is sometimes based on the NIMBY (Not In My Back Yard) syndrome. While community residents or homeowners will sometimes object to a facility in their town or neighbourhood, community business leaders and politicians will often vie for custodial facilities because of the money and jobs they bring to a community. Correctional facilities contribute to local economies through the dollars that are spent on food and other maintenance costs for prisoners; more indirectly, they contribute through salaries paid to employees. In addition, some facilities provide community access to their pools and gymnasiums. Institutions may also organize projects to raise money for volunteer organizations within the community, thereby helping to ensure good public relations.

Low-security custodial facilities are often more contentious than high-security facilities because—with the exception of wilderness camps and facilities located in other rural settings—they are intended to be located in residential neighbourhoods. Institutional locations are often the result of politically expedient decisions, precisely because they can provide employment opportunities in areas where job opportunities are limited. Hence, many youth (and adult) institutions are located some distance from major urban centres. This places undue hardship on poorer families who must travel a distance to visit their children and do not have the means or resources to do so. This also limits family contact for disadvantaged youth. Volunteer organizations, such as the John Howard Society, often run programs that offer transportation services to youth institutions for family visits.

Youth Serving Adult Sentences

As with the YOA, the YCJA requires young people who are sentenced to custody to be held separately and apart from adults, but it does not require this for youth with adult sentences and youth sentenced to adult facilities. When a youth has been sentenced to youth custody and reaches the age of 18, the provincial director has the power to request that the remainder of the youth sentence be served either in a provincial correctional facility for adults or in a penitentiary, if the court considers it to be in the best interests of the young person or in the public interest, or the youth has two years or more remaining on his or her custodial sentence [s. 92(2)]. This section of the act essentially allows the youth justice court to authorize a provincial director to place a youth serving a youth sentence in a federal penitentiary.

More specifically, subsection (5) of s. 92 allows for young persons committed to custody under a youth sentence, who may also have an adult sentence, to serve this sentence in a youth custody facility, in a provincial correctional facility for adults, or if the unexpired portion of the sentence is two years or more, in a penitentiary. For youth serving a sentence in a youth custody facility who reach age 20, s. 93 also allows for the young person to be transferred to a provincial correctional facility for adults or to a penitentiary if the court considers it to be in the best interests of the young person or the public interest and two or more years of the sentence are still to be served. When a young person is transferred to the adult system to serve the remainder of a youth sentence, s. 93(3) requires that the Prisons and Reformatories Act and the Corrections and Conditional Release Act (legislation regulating adult corrections) be applied, except for the protection that youth have in the YCJA regarding publication of records and information.

YCJA requirements for a portion of a youth's custody sentence to be served in the community makes the custody sentence similar to adult parole entitlements. As in the adult system, a youth who violates the conditions of his or her supervision may be returned to custody to serve the remainder of the sentence. The difference is that, in the youth system, the court sets the length and conditions of custody and supervision, rather than a parole board, and the attorney general [YCJA s. 98(1)] may apply to the court to keep a youth in custody for a longer period of time (see Box 10.4).

BOX 10.4

Extending a Period of Custody

YCJA section 98(4) outlines the factors to be considered by the youth court in deciding if a youth should remain in custody for a longer portion of her or his sentence. These factors include:

(a) evidence of a pattern of persistent violent behaviour and, in particular,
  (i) the number of offences committed by the young person that caused physical or psychological harm to any other person,
  (ii) the young person's difficulties in controlling violent impulses to the point of endangering the safety of any other person,
  (iii) the use of weapons in the commission of any offence,
  (iv) explicit threats of violence,
  (v) behaviour of a brutal nature associated with the commission of any offence, and
  (vi) a substantial degree of indifference on the part of the young person as to the reasonably foreseeable consequences, to other persons, of the young person's behaviour;
(b) psychiatric or psychological evidence that a physical or mental illness or disorder of the young person is of such a nature that the young person is likely to commit, before the expiry of the youth sentence the young person is then serving, a serious violent offence;
(c) reliable information that satisfies the youth justice court that the young person is planning to commit, before the expiry of the youth sentence the young person is then serving, a serious violent offence;
(d) the availability of supervision programs in the community that would offer adequate protection to the public from the risk that the young person might otherwise present until the expiry of the youth sentence the young person is then serving;
(e) whether the young person is more likely to reoffend if he or she serves his or her youth sentence entirely in custody without the benefits of serving a portion of the youth sentence in the community under supervision; and
(f) evidence of a pattern of committing violent offences while he or she was serving a portion of a youth sentence in the community under supervision.

CORRECTIONAL PROGRAMS

Correctional programs are a vital aspect of youth justice, since they are an important component in the rehabilitation and reintegration process designed to prevent future criminal behaviour when a youth completes his or her sentence. Correctional programming involves institutional programs as well as **aftercare** or follow-up programming that assists in reintegrating young offenders back into their homes and communities. It also involves programming for youth who have been given a community sentence such as probation or community service.

Many low-security custodial facilities are operated through contractual arrangements with private organizations such as the Salvation Army and the John Howard Society. Specialized programs for offenders in this type of facility are often provided

aftercare
Any range of programming and services provided after a young person has completed his or her court-imposed sentence or extrajudicial measures contract.

through contracts with community-based professionals who provide such services as academic life skills training, anger management, counselling, and more specialized programs, such as those for substance abuse and sex offenders. Many facilities offer in-house programs.

High-level security facilities provide programming developed by in-house professional staff and youth workers. Often a multidisciplinary team will develop a case management plan for each youth, based on an assessment of his or her individual needs. These teams usually consist of a social worker, a psychologist, a chaplain, one or two teachers, a recreational officer, a manager and supervisor, and a number of youth workers. All custodial facilities begin the correctional process with an initial assessment to determine the needs and appropriate management strategies for each youth. Custodial facilities rely on volunteer-based specialized programs, such as those provided by the John Howard Society and the Elizabeth Fry Society.

Types of Programs

The YCJA sets the parameters for juvenile **corrections**. However, since the provinces are responsible for implementation, there is considerable variation in philosophical orientations to **correctional programming.** Toward the end of the YOA era, some provinces experimented with disciplinary crime control programs (e.g., boot camps in Alberta and Ontario), while others, such as Newfoundland and Labrador, were developing interventionist service delivery programs designed to minimize the use of custody. Although provincial correctional philosophies do change (particularly when there is a change in the governing political party), there is a certain amount of consistency in the types of programs offered to young offenders, both in custodial facilities and in the community.

corrections
The part of the justice system that is responsible for carrying out the sentence of the court and/or alternative and extrajudicial measures.

correctional programming
A range of structured activities within a correctional system, designed to rehabilitate, educate, train, and otherwise facilitate a person's reintegration into society.

VOICES BOX 10.5

Differing Views of a High-Security Custodial Facility for Young Offenders

Administration

Most of the boys have gone through probation, alternative measures, they've been before the court two, three, four times and this is the last alternative . . . Sometimes the first time a kid comes in he may have been in trouble for a serious offence, the next time it may have changed to more of a property-related offence. It's a small gain. We don't look for miracles.

Basically, [facility programming involves] making a person stop and think rather than reacting emotionally, and understanding why they think the way they do and understanding the consequences of their actions, understanding they have choices . . . When [young offenders] go from there to an environment where their old peer group exists, they don't have the controls any more . . . the slippage can be considerable.

Victims

You take them and you put them in this [facility] that is like a hotel—there's swimming pools, I guess there's nothing that they could want . . . [A]re they really being punished?

(continued)

Box 10.5 continued

Young Offenders

Convicted of Break and Enter:

[In the first institution] you'd sit around, smoke cigarettes and watch TV . . . [In this facility, the programs] help me, like, stop and think about problems before I do things. Before I didn't care. I always thought about myself, not other people. I was self-centred . . . but now I think about other people and what I did to them. The people I stole from, I wouldn't want to feel what they would feel.

Your freedom's gone. It's a jail because when you're in your room, your door's locked at night.

Convicted of Murder:

I feel remorse for what I did. But I've gotta work on myself while I'm here, so I won't repeat things I've done in the past and be back in a place like this.

In some ways [this facility is] the best thing to happen to me. Not how I got here but what it did for me, because if I hadn't come here, things probably would have just got worse. I know I hurt my family and a lot of other people with what I did, so I don't want to be like that. I don't want to be the way I was anymore. I want to change.

Involved in Drugs, Convicted of Break and Enter:

[About leaving the facility] I'm kind of worried about that. I'm scared to get into the same old areas. It'll be a good chance to see how much willpower I got.

Suicidal Youth Convicted of Theft:

Drugs change the way I'd relate to my folks, the way I'd talk to them. I just wanted to run away. I have flashbacks now of everything bad I did.

Convicted of Assault and Break and Enter:

[About drug treatment] I resisted it a bit because I didn't really want it, but I needed it and I didn't get enough of it, especially at the Centre. [It] was more or less volunteer and you could do pretty much what you wanted. [At this facility] they teach us to stop and think about the consequences, how to say no and stick to your word. They give you a lot of help here, a lot more than the other places. They teach us this is the last stop here. It's the Big House next time . . . [About being a crook] It's not really worth it, because I was just robbing myself, wasting my life. You might not wake up and realize it until you're thirty, sitting in a jail. That's not gonna be me . . . I'm not going back to crime. You may as well realize it while you're young.

Convicted of Robbery

Losing your freedom is hardly the worst of it . . . I came out in good shape in spite of the system . . . at the end of the day, do we really believe that locking people in prison and all the things we do to control people actually helps them? I don't.

Source: Dorey (1996); Trichur (2004).

There are three types of correctional programs: general, offence-specific, and offender-specific. General programs usually apply to all offenders and include such things as **life skills,** education, recreation, and counselling programs. Offence-specific programs target specific offences; examples are the StopLift program for shoplifters and sex offender programs. Offender-specific programs target the offender's problems and behaviours and are exemplified by substance abuse programs, leisure time programs, and anger management. Some facilities are specifically designed to provide programming for special needs such as substance abuse.

Programs are also offered to youth serving sentences in the community. Community programming is often provided through services contracted by governments. So, for example, the Pacific Legal Education Association contracts with the Province of British Columbia to provide volunteer supervision for young offenders accused of sex offences and intensive supervision for youth serving probation sentences. The organization also provides support in employment, independent living, anger management, and other special-needs services. (British Columbia Ministry of the Attorney General, Corrections Branch, 1995).

Most institutions offer programming in the areas of education, counselling, life skills, and recreation. In most cases, programs are developed on an individual basis to meet young offender needs through the initial assessment process. Behaviour modification programs, or a token economy system, are most often used as a method of reinforcing program objectives. With behaviour modification, offenders are rewarded or punished by earning or losing points for various privileges. Privileges include such things as contact or home visits with parents and family, movies, or longer hours in TV or games rooms. Punishments involve a removal of some or all privileges, cell confinement, or extra household duties.

Some newer high-security youth centres are designed to facilitate small-group living arrangements and interaction. Living areas consist of a group of small cottages, and youth are responsible for cleaning, cooking, and laundry—activities that are viewed as part of life skills training. Facilities such as the Nova Scotia Youth Centre in Waterville, Nova Scotia, assign youth to cottages on the basis of programming needs. While some cottages focus on academic education, others emphasize vocational training or substance abuse.

Substance Abuse

Substance abuse is considered a major risk factor in delinquent and aggressive behaviour and recidivism, so an important first step in programming is for the young offenders to work successfully through a substance abuse program. These programs are designed to provide the resources, encouragement, and support that a young person will need to overcome physical, emotional, and/or psychological addictions to alcohol and/or drugs. Substance abuse programs are seen as a starting point for youth to learn how to overcome their addictions. An important part of substance abuse programming is to involve community support systems and groups (such as Narcotics Anonymous and Alcoholics Anonymous), so that follow-up assistance can be provided when young offenders are released into the community.

Based on a literature review of substance abuse programs, Dowden (2003) maintains that programs should target multiple needs related to schooling, employment, and peer and family relationships. Ideally, such programs should be delivered in a community setting. However, since this is not possible for incarcerated youth, institutional programs and residential programs need to incorporate aftercare and advocacy

life skills
The behavioural, emotional, and philosophical skill set that one acquires to enable functioning in the social world.

components for youth when they return to their communities (p. 25). Regardless of setting, effective substance abuse programs will:

- be delivered in correctional settings with low staff turnover and a rehabilitative rather than retributive philosophy;
- identify and target a youth's strengths;
- provide extended rather than short-term programs;
- incorporate relapse prevention into the program design and content; and
- systematically address HIV/AIDS concerns. (Dowden, 2003, pp. 25–26)

Education

Educational programming is an important part of correctional programming because many youth have experienced failure in the regular school system and are poorly motivated with respect to academic studies. Educational programs aim to address self-esteem, motivation, and overall reading and writing skills, as well as academic subjects and vocational training. Some students work on academic credits through correspondence courses. Others are granted an educational temporary absence for the purpose of attending local schools. Some institutions offer computer classes in which young offenders are able to learn basic word processing and some software applications. Youth facilities sometimes arrange with local community colleges to provide instruction in specialized vocational studies.

Cognitive Skills and Life Skills

cognitive skills
In the field of corrections, refers to the ability of people to develop cognitive solutions to their problems rather than to react emotionally and physically.

Many young offenders are seen to have failed to acquire the **cognitive skills** that are essential to effective interpersonal relations. Problems with interpersonal relations are seen to stem from a lack of parental guidance, a poor home environment, and negative peer group influences. Life skills and social skills programs attempt to provide young offenders with an opportunity to develop appropriate cognitive skills and self-esteem, and to replace anger, hostility, and aggression with pro-social attitudes and behaviour. This type of programming is designed to help youth to think about why they got into trouble with the law, how they might have avoided such an outcome in the past, and how they will avoid problems in the future.

Cognitive skills programming focuses on rational self-analysis, self-control, means/end reasoning, critical thinking, and interpersonal cognitive problem solving.

1. *Rational self-analysis:* The objective is to teach the youth to pay attention to and critically assess his or her own thinking.
2. *Self-control:* Involves teaching youth to stop, think, and analyze the consequences of their behaviour before they act.
3. *Means/End reasoning:* The aim is to teach youth to think about appropriate pro-social means of satisfying their needs before they act.
4. *Critical thinking:* Requires teaching youth how to think logically, objectively, and rationally as opposed to externalizing blame and overgeneralizing or distorting facts and information.
5. *Interpersonal cognitive problem solving:* The objective is to teach youth how to analyze interpersonal problems, how to recognize how their own behaviour affects other people and why others respond to them as they do, and how to understand and consider other people's values, behaviour, and feelings. (Nova Scotia Department of Corrections, 1994)

Working through the development of cognitive skills provides an avenue for addressing more specific problems such as anger management, employment strategies, stress management, and decision making. Life skills programs focus on communication skills, family and peer relationships, sex education, and personal hygiene.

One specific program that combines a number of cognitive and skills training methods is aggression replacement training (ART). Campbell (2005b) describes ART as a program that focuses on a combination of skills training (referred to as "skill-streaming"), anger control training, and moral reasoning. The skill-streaming aspect of the program involves role-playing, feedback, and practical applications to develop and enhance pro-social skills. Anger control training teaches youth to use their self-control to reduce and control their anger and aggression. They are taught to recognize anger triggers and to recognize their own physiological cues to anger arousal, along with ways to reduce and defuse triggers. Moral reasoning training is designed to raise youth to higher moral levels through exposure to a variety of moral dilemmas in a group setting (Campbell, 2005b, pp. 281–282).

Recreation

Recreational facilities and programs, particularly those that feature swimming pools and gymnasiums built into youth facilities, are viewed by some public-interest groups as bringing a "holiday camp" atmosphere to youth corrections. Those responsible for administrating youth facilities and programs have a different view. They see recreational programs as an integral part of the rehabilitation process and emphasize the therapeutic benefits of recreation. Many facilities offer arts and crafts programs in addition to their sporting and physical fitness programs. All of these programs are designed to teach young offenders to make productive use of their leisure time and to assist youth in improving their interpersonal and communications skills and ability to work cooperatively. Other program objectives include providing youth with a sense of accomplishment and well-being, and giving them an opportunity to explore their individual talents and interests.

Some facilities offer wilderness survival programs. Project DARE in Northern Ontario and the Youth Asset Building Adventure program in British Columbia are based entirely on an Outward Bound philosophy. These programs are designed to enhance self-awareness, foster a sense of self-reliance and trust, and help youth develop goal-setting and problem-solving abilities. Some programs, such as aquatics, are run as a vocational training program. Temporary absences are often granted to allow youth to attend and/or participate in community-based recreational activities.

Work Activities and Incentives

Daily work routines are another part of institutional programming. These programs are designed to meet institutional needs (e.g., cleaning the facility) and at the same time give young offenders opportunities to develop good work habits. Institutions usually offer an allowance program as a positive behavioural incentive. For example, under the Incentive Allowance Program, the Nova Scotia Department of Correctional Services pays one dollar per day to all youth in custodial facilities. The allowance, which is not automatic but must be earned, is credited to a trust account held for each youth (Nova Scotia Department of Corrections, 1994).

Boot Camps

Two provincial governments (Ontario and Alberta) implemented boot camps for young offenders. **"Boot camp"** refers to facilities or programs that emphasize military-style discipline, physical conditioning, teamwork, and punishment in attempting to rehabilitate young offenders; educational and life skills programs are sometimes also involved.

boot camp
In the corrections system, a place of confinement where programming follows a militaristic regime.

People who believe that youth today lack discipline and respect for authority tend to be attracted to the idea of boot camps. For governments, boot camps offer a cheap alternative to incarceration. It would appear that these programs are being adopted for political, financial, and ideological reasons, not because of any demonstrated success.

In 1992, the U.S. Department of Justice implemented the first boot camp programs for juveniles—one in Cleveland, Ohio; one in Denver, Colorado; and one in Mobile, Alabama. The programs involved a three-month residential program for youth, followed by six to nine months of community programming. The primary motivation for the camps was financial; the diversion of "less serious" youth offenders from institutions to boot camps provided a cheap solution to overcrowded juvenile institutions (Bourque et al., 1996).

Each of the three U.S. boot camps was evaluated over a two-year period. They were found to be cheaper (at an average per resident cost of $26,000 (U.S.) per year) than other types of institutions, but no more effective than probation or custody in reducing recidivism rates. In Cleveland, recidivism rates were actually higher for boot camp participants than for youth in state correctional facilities (Peterson, 1996). Importantly, boot camps produced cost savings only when compared with secure custody; a 90-day stay in boot camp cost as much as the same length of stay in open custody. Completion rates for the boot camp part of the program were very high (80 to 94 percent). In contrast, completion rates for community aftercare ranged from 26 to 49 percent. The major reason for youth not completing the community aftercare part of the program was arrest for a criminal offence (20 to 33 percent) (Bourque et al., 1996, p. 5).

While evaluation of any program is a difficult undertaking and results are often difficult to interpret (Zhang, 1998), these evaluations revealed a number of problems with boot camps that are useful for future endeavours. These included community resistance to the location of the boot camps, aftercare facilities and programs, and the fact that aftercare program locations were not always accessible by public transportation. Other problems included inappropriate placements, tensions between the military-minded staff and the staff operating rehabilitation programs, high staff burnout and turnover; an overly abrupt transition from boot camp structure to aftercare supervision, and lack of consistent philosophy between staff and between different phases of the program.

Project Turnaround was Ontario's attempt at establishing a "strict discipline" boot camp program. It was opened in Barrie in 1997 and has since closed. Nonetheless, the Ministry of Corrections had the program evaluated and announced the program's success in a press release that reported boot camp participants to have a considerably lower recidivism rate than a comparison group of young offenders. Doob and Cesaroni (2004) reviewed this evaluation and found it to be fraught with methodological errors. Their analysis of the data found that boot camp outcomes were consistent with results from other studies. More specifically, they found no statistically significant differences in rates of recidivism between the boot camp participants (whether they completed the program or not) and the comparison group, regardless of the elapsed time of release. The authors concluded that there "was no evidence of any overall beneficial psychological or academic impact of the boot camp experience over a standard correctional institution." (pp. 256–258). Others have found that boot camps can have a negative impact for youth with histories of abuse, compared to traditional institutions (MacKenzie, Wilson, Armstrong, & Gover, 2001).

Peterson (1996) and Bourque et al. (1996) argue that a militaristic discipline and structure can be useful for some youth. Youth who need a highly structured and controlled environment can benefit if boot camp is combined with rehabilitative programs designed to meet the youths' educational, psychological, and emotional needs. Hence, if boot camps are to be designed for these youth in the future, Peterson and Bourque provide the following program and design recommendations:

1. There should be community acceptance of boot camp, combined with a commitment and involvement in aftercare facilities and programs.
2. Given that recidivism rates were highest for youth who had been held in custody in the past and for those involved in the least serious offences, boot camps would be more successful for young people involved in moderately serious offences who have not been in custody in the past.
3. There should be careful screening and selection of staff at the beginning of the program, as well as ongoing staff training. Activities of staff in all phases of the program must be coordinated, as should program philosophy.
4. The transition between boot camp and aftercare should be less abrupt. At least in the beginning, aftercare should be more structured and disciplined and should also provide some form of required participation.
5. There should be coordination among the various community agencies involved in aftercare, as well as an understanding and commitment to the program philosophy and procedures of the boot camp aftercare.
6. All staff and all agency participants should have a clear understanding of the rationale for the various aspects and activities of the program. (Bourque et al., 1996, pp. 7–9; Peterson, 1996)

Scared Straight

Scared Straight is another program with widespread public appeal. Numerous Scared Straight programs were implemented throughout the United States in the late 1970s and early 1980s, and many people are still intrigued by the idea. A well-known and highly publicized Scared Straight program was implemented at the New Jersey Rahway State Prison 30 years ago. The purpose of the program was to expose young offenders to the "realities" of life in adult prisons by having them participate in confrontation sessions with adult male prisoners. Between 1976 and 1981, over 13,000 young offenders attended confrontation sessions at the Rahway State Prison, a maximum-security prison for men. According to the 1978 film documentary *Scared Straight!*, 90 percent of the youth who participated in the program did not become involved in further delinquency (Bortner, 1988, pp. 295–296).

Scared Straight! is a disturbing film that documents how participating youth were subjected to intensive verbal abuse and threats of physical abuse and assault. Contrary to the documentary's claims of success, later assessments of the Scared Straight program suggest that it did not deter young people from delinquency. Finckenauer (1982, p. 135) found that 41.3 percent of the juveniles who attended the Scared Straight sessions committed new offences within six months after their visit to the prison; comparable juveniles who had not attended or participated in these sessions had a recidivism rate of only 11.4 percent. Similarly, another review of the Scared Straight (or prison visitation) programs conducted between 1967 and 1992 found that the program had harmful effects and led to increased crime and delinquency (Petrosino, Turpin-Petrosino, & Finckenauer, 2000). What proponents of the scared straight philosophy seem to have overlooked is the harsh reality of many young offenders' lives. Young offenders who have grown up in an environment of violence and abuse and have been on the receiving end have already demonstrated that this tactic does not work as a deterrent.

Programming Issues

No discussion of correctional programming would be complete without a consideration of the issues associated with the very idea of **rehabilitative treatment** or **rehabilitation.** These concepts tend to be used interchangeably, as both refer to the objectives of correctional programs. The term "treatment" is often used to refer to psychiatric and psychological programs that involve individual or group counselling or psychotherapy and whose purpose is to change a person's behaviour or attitudes. The term "rehabilitation" also refers to programs designed to effect change; these programs may involve educational and vocational training, as well as various types of life skills programming.

Most treatment programs are geared toward a particular type of offender, as exemplified by sex offender treatment programs. "Rehabilitation" usually refers to a philosophical approach to correctional programming. The variety of programs through which it seeks to correct or change stands in contrast to programs that are based on the principles of retribution or incapacitation. Campbell (2005b) adds the idea of "interventions" to this discussion, a term used in rehabilitation literature from Quebec that is increasingly appearing in recent treatment and programming literature. Campbell speaks of "rehabilitative interventions" in a manner that encompasses all types of programming, both institutional and community, and may even be more appropriate for newer programs that involve combinations of therapy and training directed at youth or at both youth and their families, such as aggression replacement training and **multisystemic therapy** (MST) (pp. 264–265). With respect to treatment, rehabilitation, or rehabilitative interventions, the most important issue is whether programs are successful.

Does Treatment/Rehabilitation Work?

The question of whether treatment programs are effective is difficult to answer because, until recently, most correctional programs were not rigorously evaluated using a scientific testing model with control groups. Rather, programs tended to be evaluated by the people running them; these evaluations are fraught with methodological errors, the most common of which is failing to include people who do not complete the program, as in the evaluation of the Project Turnaround in Ontario. Seldom is follow-up information available regarding how people have fared over time after leaving correctional programs, and most evaluation studies report relatively low success rates (see, for example, the discussion of multisystemic therapy later in this chapter). While some people therefore conclude that more people are not changed by correctional programming than are changed (Ekstedt & Griffiths, 1988), others have a more positive attitude and maintain that the literature suggests that "some rehabilitation programs work with some offenders in some settings when applied by some staff" (Antonowicz & Ross, 1994, p. 1).

The debate regarding the efficacy of treatment began with a now-classic study published in the 1970s that had a profound impact on attitudes and thinking about correctional programming. Robert Martinson (1974) examined all of the research that had been done to evaluate treatment programs and concluded from the results that "nothing works." Not surprisingly, correctional workers and treatment providers took issue with this finding. Some treatment advocates scrutinized Martinson's work and concluded that he was wrong in his conclusion. When Martinson (1979) later reexamined his earlier work, his critics reported that he had retracted his "nothing works" conclusion (Gendreau & Ross, 1987). However, Doob and Brodeur (1989) later pointed out that Martinson's critics had misrepresented both his original and later

rehabilitative treatment
Rehabilitative programs based on assumptions of correcting individual pathologies.

rehabilitation
A correctional philosophy based on the belief that appropriate treatment programs can reform or change an individual.

multisystemic therapy
A form of rehabilitative integration that focuses on the entire family, not just on an individual.

work. Although Martinson conceded in his re-examination that some programs had a modest success rate, his most significant finding—and one ignored by his critics—was that some programs had negative consequences for participants.

An important lesson to be learned from Martinson's findings is that, even though our intentions are good and we want to help a person, we cannot assume that the person will actually benefit from rehabilitative interventions. There are many reasons why programs may not have the positive effects that are intended. One reason is quite simply that short sentences afford limited time in which to affect change. More fundamentally problematic is the setting itself: an institutional setting may not be conducive to rehabilitation (Rothman, 1980). It may be unreasonable to expect that removing people, especially young people, from their families and communities and subjecting them to an institutional environment and non-voluntary participation in a variety of programs will somehow equip them for reintegration back into these communities. This is a problem also identified by both the people who work in institutions and the youth who live there. Anger management programs are a case in point. Barron (2000), from her research at the Willingdon Youth Detention Centre in British Columbia, reported the views of the senior officer of correctional programming on the transitory nature of anger management programming:

> In here kids deal with their anger, they don't act out. So when I see this I think a lot of them do have ways of managing their behaviour. But the problem with any programming done inside this building is there is no opportunity for them to practice the skills they learn. They often go back to everything they ever came from, and there's no one to point out to them when to use the skills. (p. 99)

The youth themselves are only too aware of the violence that is commonplace in their lives outside the institution and the ineffectiveness of their anger management "training." In Katie's words:

> I've been ordered to go to so much anger management and they're all the same. All it does is make you aware of the technical terms, like different kinds of abuse. If someone is coming at you, ready to hit you, you don't say, "Oh, I'll be the bigger man and walk away." It doesn't work.

And, according to Tara, anger management training is

> . . . awful. This guy just said, "Crumple your anger up and put it in your back pocket and take a deep breath" and I was like, "That's just not going to work." It was really patronizing. (Barron, 2000, pp. 98–99)

Over the last few years, programs have been subject to more stringent evaluations, and meta-analysis has been used to analyze research results from an entire literature. One example comes from a project undertaken by Latimer, Dowden, and Morton-Bourgon (2003) to conduct a meta-analysis of all published program evaluations that have taken place over the last 25 to 30 years. Unlike many other evaluations and meta-analytical reviews, the authors limited their analysis to programs for youth under 18 who had committed a criminal offence.

The overall result was a 9 percent reduction in recidivism for youth who had been involved in treatment programs, compared to those who were in "control groups." This corresponds to earlier evaluations that reported low success rates and to those done by Lipsey (1995) and Dowden and Andrews (1999), who reported a 10 percent reduction in youth recidivism. Interestingly, most types of programming showed success rates; the highest was for multi-focused and family-focused (compared to individual-focused) programs and the lowest was for group-focused programs. There were two exceptions, however: boot camps and wilderness programs had a negative outcome, which means that these programs actually resulted in a higher recidivism rate than the control groups (Latimer, Dowden et al., 2003, pp. 11–12).

Results such as these are encouraging, because they indicate that some programs do work, but they are also disappointing in that program successes are consistently low. For some, these findings simply underscore the need for intervention before young people find themselves "in trouble," while others fear that institutions are merely serving as costly warehouses for young people, as a last resort of state-imposed social control, rather than as agents of positive change.

Others take a less benign view and point to the violent nature of some youth institutions. In 1997, for example, a youth died from injuries inflicted on him by another youth while in segregation in the Wellington Detention Centre in Guelph, Ontario (Trichure, 2004).

BRIDGING THE GAP: AFTERCARE AND COMMUNITY REINTEGRATION

A major stumbling block exists for young offenders and correctional efforts at rehabilitation when youth reach the end of their sentences. As we have seen, positive change evidenced through program participation in an institution may not continue once the youth is released into the community and reintegration as a law-abiding citizen is not realized. In a welfare/rehabilitation-oriented justice system with **indeterminate sentences,** as we had under the JDA, youth were not released into the community until it was decided that they were ready for release. In the adult system, parole turns a prison sentence for a definite time period into something indefinite: it is not clear how long a person will spend in prison because he or she might get out on parole.

indeterminate sentences
Sentences that are not absolute or definite.

Under the YOA and now the YCJA, with **determinate sentences,** there is a predetermined time frame in which to work in a rehabilitative manner with youth. A short sentence may serve to disrupt school programming for youth who are in school, and may allow only a minimal exposure to institutional programs. Whatever positive behavioural/attitudinal changes may occur can quickly be undermined when youth return to their homes, neighbourhoods, friends, and "old" ways. Youth who made some progress in their programs may have nowhere to go on release except back to the streets or to families that have been a major source of their problems.

determinate sentences
Sentences with a stated minimum or maximum term.

In order to effect lasting change and promote successful reintegration, both time and a continuation of programs and support services are required after young people are released from an institution or come to the end of their community sentences. The YCJA's requirement of community supervision after a term in custody (conditional supervision and intensive supervision) is a step in the right direction toward aftercare, but the sentence does end, regardless of the likelihood that a youth's needs for support, rehabilitative interventions, and supervision may continue.

While there is general consensus on the need for aftercare, there is debate over which branch of government (if any) should pay for it. Some jurisdictions have developed aftercare programs but others are less likely to do so, particularly in light of government cutbacks on social spending. The federal government has addressed this issue by providing funding for communities and non-government organizations to implement programs for youth through its national crime prevention program.

Aftercare Programs

Many communities have developed aftercare programs through existing community organizations. These programs are often rehabilitative and skill-based. The Stop and Think program in Halifax is an example of such a program and it involved two stages that could begin on release or in the institution and then continue after release. First-stage programming focused on programs related to sexuality, drugs, family relationships, leisure education, self-analysis, and motivation/goal identification. After this first phase, the focus switched to programming more specific to community living, such as academic upgrading for school preparation or literacy instruction, career planning, and pre-employment training that involved work placements. Once youth completed the actual aftercare program, the aftercare continued because of linkages that had been established with other support systems in the community, such as alcohol and drug counselling groups. Following its first year in operation, Stop and Think reported that two-thirds of the youth who successfully completed the program did not engage in further criminal activities.

Another program example is the John Howard Society's WrapAround Project (WP), which is designed to assist in the reintegration of young offenders released from custody after serving sentences for serious crimes. One WP program involves a partnership of the Youth Services Bureau of Ottawa–Carleton, Carleton University, and over 50 other community organizations, agencies, and representatives in a combined effort to provide individualized support and services for youth within the context of their families and communities. These support and service areas include educational, vocational, cultural, spiritual, family, physical/mental health, and leisure (Caputo et al., 2000; Totten, 2000, March 14).

Other programs have been designed specifically for delivery in the community, most often the family home, rather than in an office or community facility. One such program is (MST) multisystemic therapy. MST is an intervention strategy based on a family preservation service delivery model with a demonstrated effectiveness for delinquency prevention. Leschied and Cunningham describe MST as ". . . more an amalgam of best practices than a brand-new method" (2002, p. 110). The intervention involves one person (a trained MST therapist) delivering services to family members identified as in need of intervention, not just to the young offender.

MST directly addresses the fact that social interventions cannot last forever and is therefore designed to be of short, intense duration. Hence, the interventions take place over a relatively short period of time (one to four months), are delivered in the home, and are available 24 hours a day, seven days a week. The intervention strategy involves a focus on problem behaviours with the young offender and parents, siblings, and friends, including substance abuse, assaultive behaviours, non-compliance with family rules, poor parenting skills, lack of supervision, and antisocial values. The process involves developing strategies to eliminate these behaviours by building on the strengths of the youth and family members (Leschied & Cunningham, 2002, pp. 9, 116–117). The ultimate goal of MST interventions is family empowerment, more specifically:

> . . . to empower the family to take responsibility for making and maintaining gains. An important goal in this process is to foster in parents the ability to be good advocates for their children and themselves with social service agencies and to seek out supportive services and networks. In other words, parents are encouraged to develop the requisite skills to solve their own problems rather than to rely on professionals. (Leschied & Cunningham, 2002, p. 116)

The MST therapist is considered ultimately responsible for positive outcomes, not youth or their families, and a "case is considered closed when the family-defined goals have been attained" (Leschied & Cunningham, 2002, pp. 115, 117).

MST was developed at the Family Services Research Center of the Department of Psychiatry and Behavioural Sciences of the Medical University of South Carolina, and was designed to meet the needs of chronic or violent young offenders. The first clinical trials of MST were conducted in South Carolina in the late 1990s. Since then, MST has been implemented and tested in a number of settings and identified as more effective at reducing recidivism than other programs by a number of state organizations, including the Office for Juvenile Justice and Delinquency Prevention in Utah and the Washington State Institute for Public Policy. It has also been endorsed by the Surgeon General of the United States as an exemplary approach to treatment for children with serious emotional and behavioural problems (Leschied, Cunningham, & Hawkins, 2000, p. 12).

With the support of the Ontario Ministry of Community and Social Services and funding from the National Crime Prevention Centre, MST was tested in four Ontario communities (London, Mississauga, Ottawa, and Simcoe County) over a four-year period beginning in 1997. The project involved approximately 400 youth who were already chronic offenders or at high risk and a control group of similar youth assigned to regular programs and services offered in the community. Preliminary results were disappointing and not much different from evaluations of other types of programs. In short, youth in the program fared no better with regard to criminal activity during the course of the project than did the control group in regular community programming. Youth who had no prior convictions prior to MST interventions had no priors at the first evaluation after two years, and those who had lengthy records at the beginning of the study tended to have multiple convictions during the interventions (Leschied & Cunningham, 2002, pp. 25–26).

The good news about MST is that it is far cheaper than custody and cheaper than processing youth through the justice system. Over the first three years of this program, Leschied and Cunningham estimated that the 380 youth who had been convicted of no more than 400 offences involving victims cost the Canadian taxpayer $5.8 million in custody costs and that $1 million had been spent on incarceration for administrative offences (2002, p. 65). If the costs of processing these youth through the justice system (police, courts, legal fees, etc.) are totalled, a conservative estimate puts the figure at $25,000 per offence and the total justice cost exceeds $43 million. In the words of Leschied and Cunningham, ". . . it is plain to see that even a small group of young offenders can have an enormous fiscal impact" (2002, p. 26). It remains to be seen whether other MST projects will be funded. The $6,000 to $7,000 cost per youth per year is a tremendous incentive for community-based correctional programming; however, it is still 10 times the cost of probation supervision at $600 to $700 per youth per year.

Other community reintegration projects have a larger scope and have been adopted by some provincial governments as a means of coordinating existing programs and services in order to provide an overarching philosophy for a "continuum of care" as youth either move from custody to the community or serve sentences in the community under supervision orders. While MST may not meet evaluation criteria as a "stand-alone" program, its value as a model for intervention perhaps lies in its ability to provide an overarching plan of community supervision and aftercare.

An example of a multisystemic therapy program in action comes from New Brunswick, where, in response to high rates of custody and the impending emphasis on community alternatives and custodial supervision under the YCJA, the province, through its Community and Correctional Services Division of the Department of Public Safety, implemented an Intensive Support Program (ISP). It is built on the principles of rehabilitation and reintegration and is designed to enhance diversion by providing the youth court with a viable alternative to the custody sentence, a concrete program to attach to conditional orders that go with probation and deferred custody sentences, and to provide for the community component of custody and supervision sentences. It is estimated that ISP will result in 40 to 60 youth per year being diverted from custody (Eckstein, 2005, pp. 79, 81, 87). This is a significant reduction for a province with an average daily custodial count of 118 youth and 400 yearly admissions to custody in 2001–2002 (Marinelli, 2004, pp. 12, 16).

Targeted "at risk for custody" youth who, along with their families, are interested in participating in ISP will be sentenced to supervised probation or deferred custody with the condition of participation in ISP. While a major portion of ISP services and interventions will be provided by community organizations, ISP views the family as an essential component of successful intervention and is committed to an MST model. ISP will involve specific programs such as anger control and cognitive/life skills, as well as interventions through Family Support Services. A trained facilitator will work with youth in their "natural environment," and try to empower parents by developing their parental skills and resources, along with a support network of positive relationships in the extended family and community (Eckstein, 2005, pp. 81, 87, 92, 94–95).

Hence, while rehabilitative and reintegrative goals, as measured through recidivism rates, may not have been realized in Ontario with interventions based on direct applications of multisystemic therapy, the model is of use as a component of larger crime prevention strategies of diversion and aftercare. Furthermore, evaluation criteria need to also consider positive outcomes in terms other than recidivism. Perhaps the value of MST principles and interventions is best summed up in a letter written by the father of a young offender whose family was a participant in the Ontario project:

> When I look back on all that [my son] went through a few years ago, there is one thing I am certain I would change. I would not abandon him to the "justice system" again . . . What I believe now is this: if parents, with the aid of support systems, can bring a troubled child to believe in a sense of responsibility to their community and vice versa, the benefit to everyone, including bean counters, will manifest itself. If a child enters the maze of the legal system, reaching them becomes much more difficult. The larger truth I learned was that it is never too late for a parent to gain the heart of their child. (Cited in Leschied & Cunningham, 2002, p. 23)

Clearly, this is a parent who is feeling empowered.

SUMMARY

The groundwork for the practice of institutionalizing Canadian youth separately from adults was laid in 1857 with the passage of the Act for Establishing Prisons for Young Offenders. The first institution was opened at Isle aux Noix on the Richelieu River in October 1858, and the second at Penetanguishene on Georgian Bay in August 1859. Both institutions were looked upon as "reformatories"—places offering education and industrial training. Within a decade, industrial training schools were opening across the country. With the YOA came a change in terminology that continues under the YCJA. Youth institutions are now referred to as "detention centres," "youth correctional centres," or "community-based residential facilities." The YCJA made youth corrections more like the adult system by adding conditional supervision to all custody sentences and creating a new "house arrest" sentence. The purpose of youth corrections under the YCJA is rehabilitation and reintegration in order to protect society.

Admissions to industrial training schools as a percentage of children convicted in juvenile court increased in the decades leading up to the World War II, but declined thereafter. The introduction of the YOA reversed this declining trend. Between 1990 and 1995 alone, there was a 15 percent increase in the number of youth in secure custody and a 24 percent increase in the number of youth in open custody. By the end of the 1990s, custody rates were on the decline again in most provinces. The YCJA restrictions on the use of custody should continue this trend.

Some attribute the increase in the use of custody to a shift among judges to a "short, sharp shock" style of sentencing. Others suggest that shorter sentences give youth more opportunity to commit crime, resulting in an increase in the number of repeat offenders, who are more likely than first-time offenders to receive custody sentences. Interprovincial variations in the use of custody stem from differences in levels of police activity and judicial discretion.

It costs anywhere from $55,000 to $126,000 per year to keep one young offender in custody. Actual costs vary across the country and depend on the facility's level of security. Overall, 0.1 percent of the Canadian youth population is currently serving a custodial sentence—an average daily count of 3,420.

There are three types of correctional programs: general, offence-specific, and offender-specific. Most institutions offer programming in the areas of education, counselling, life skills, and recreation. Behaviour modification programs are most often used as a method of reinforcing program objectives. Some newer secure-custody facilities are designed to facilitate small-group living arrangements. Boot camps are cheaper to maintain than secure-custody correctional institutions, but about the same as open-custody facilities in terms of cost. Boot camps have been found to be no more effective in reducing recidivism than probation or other forms of custody.

Treatment and rehabilitation have been contentious issues since the implementation of the YOA. At issue under the YOA was whether or not young people should have the right to refuse treatment; this was sidestepped in the YCJA through the creation of sentences that involve treatment/rehabilitation programs. Of continued concern is the question of the effectiveness of treatment/rehabilitation programs. One important reason programs do not always have the intended positive effects is that institutional settings may not be conducive to rehabilitation.

More important than treatment or rehabilitation programs is the aftercare that occurs when youth are released into the community or finish serving their community sentences. Institutional programs such as boot camps often fail because there is no continuity of support and programming in the community. Important new models of programming, such as multisystemic therapy allow us to move away from thinking of rehabilitation in terms of programs designed to address a specific individual need and to think in terms of interventions that not only assist rehabilitation but also community reintegration.

DISCUSSION/CRITICAL THINKING QUESTIONS

1. Does treatment work? Explain your answer.
2. New supervision provisions in the YCJA in combination with restorative justice philosophies hold great promise for more effective responses to youth crime than in the past. Why might we be skeptical that results will be any different than in the past?

3. Recalling Johnny's story as it has unfolded throughout the book, how might his fate and that of Theresa McEvoy have been different if he had not simply been abandoned to the justice system?

4. Some might argue that variations in the use of custody over time are a result of changes in the criminal behaviour of young people. What are other possible explanations?

WEB LINKS

Youth Risk/Need Assessment: An Overview of Issues and Practices
http://canada.justice.gc.ca/en/ps/rs/rep/2003/rr03yj-4/rr03yj-4.html

The John Howard Society of New Brunswick: Promoting and Supporting Alternatives to Youth Custody: Final Report
www.jhsnb.ca/report.htm

Standing Senate Committee on Aboriginal Peoples: Urban Aboriginal Youth: An Action Plan for Change
www.turtleisland.org/news/absenuayrpt.pdf

For chapter quizzes and more links, visit this book's accompanying website at www.bellyoungoffenders3e.nelson.com

CHAPTER ELEVEN

Perpetuating Social Injustice

CHAPTER OBJECTIVES

1. To document how and why correctional programs fail girls and Aboriginal youth.
2. To understand why equal treatment perpetuates social injustice.
3. To examine different ways of thinking about correctional programming for girls and Aboriginal youth.
4. To discuss examples of correctional programs designed specifically for girls and Aboriginal youth.

KEY TERMS

Reintegration

Eurocentric

Equality

Reverse discrimination

Minorities

Social injustice

Monolithic

Healing principle

Reconciliation

Sentencing circle

INTRODUCTION

Section 3(1)(b) of the Youth Criminal Justice Act (YCJA) establishes that the youth criminal justice system must be separate from the adult system, and while accountability is an integral part of this system, s. 3(1)(b)(ii) makes accountability contingent on "the greater dependency of young persons and their reduced level of maturity." In other words, they are not adults, and so they must be treated differently from adults in criminal justice matters. This is a fundamental principle of juvenile justice, which implicitly acknowledges that justice would not be served if youth received the same justice as adults.

The Young Offenders Act (YOA) did not acknowledge that in some ways the needs of Aboriginal youth, girls, and other minority youth differed from the needs of Euro-Canadian boys, the dominant group in the juvenile justice system. Section 3(1)(c)(iv) acknowledges that there are important sociohistorical, cultural, gender, and other differences between young Canadians and instructs that within the youth justice system, all measures taken should "respect gender, ethnic, cultural and linguistic differences and respond to the needs of Aboriginal young persons and of young persons with special requirements." The YCJA also recognizes that the special circumstances of Aboriginal youth should be acknowledged in decision making.

As we saw in earlier chapters, theories of youth crime and delinquency developed with boys in mind failed to explain girls' offences. The same is true of law, the administration of justice, and correctional programming. To the extent that these things are not developed with girls or Aboriginal youth in mind, justice is not served for many of these youth. For them, in particular, youth justice is an injustice. This does not mean that the youth justice system has a positive impact on all boys, but rather that we need to critically examine how the system affects girls and Aboriginal youth, precisely because of their status in Canadian society. Professor Patricia Monture-OKanee, in her submission to the Royal Commission on Aboriginal Peoples, argued that the oppression of youth of all races will continue until the contradictions of colonialism, racism, and sexism are exposed (1993, p. 118).

This chapter focuses on correctional programming and its impact on Aboriginal youth and girls. It discusses how corrections under the YOA failed to meet the needs of many youth from these groups and how we might rethink correctional responses to Aboriginal youth and girls. Examples of programs designed specifically for these groups are presented.

ABORIGINAL YOUNG OFFENDERS

Correctional Issues

One of the first comprehensive analyses of Aboriginal people and the justice system came from a public inquiry undertaken by the Manitoba provincial government. In their report on the results of this inquiry, Associate Chief Justice A.C. Hamilton and Associate Chief Judge C.M. Sinclair identified two correctional problems: (1) the overuse of custody for Aboriginal youth and (2) inappropriate programming. They stated that "the present system of dealing with Aboriginal young offenders, by removing them from their communities, warehousing them and then returning them to their communities, is both ineffective and inconsistent with the principles of the YOA" (Hamilton & Sinclair, 1991, p. 566). The 1996 Royal Commission on Aboriginal Peoples added to this list of correctional issues the problem of detaining Aboriginal youth separately from adults in remote locations.

Overuse of Custody

As we saw in the last chapter, overuse of custody for Aboriginal youth takes three forms: they are disproportionately sentenced to custody or held in remand, their custody sentences are longer, and they are disproportionately held in secure custody. High rates of pretrial detention are due in part to the criteria used by judges in determining whether to grant bail. These criteria include whether the youth has a job or is going to school, has family stability, and has parent(s) or guardians who are employed. Also of concern is whether drug or alcohol problems have been experienced by the youth or her or his family. All of these factors are directly linked to the economic and social marginality of Aboriginal peoples in Canadian society. For this reason, Hamilton and Sinclair (1991) argued that decision making based on such criteria constitutes discrimination against Aboriginal youth.

Interestingly, section 718.2(e) of the Criminal Code, introduced in 1996, directs judges to consider alternatives to prison for Aboriginal offenders. It states that

> . . . all available sanctions other than imprisonment that are reasonable in the circumstances should be considered for all offenders, with particular attention to the circumstances of Aboriginal offenders.

What is interesting about this section of the Criminal Code is that it applies only to adults. In spite of numerous revisions to the YCJA and specific submissions recommending that such a provision be included in the YCJA, by the summer of 2001, no such clause had appeared in the YCJA, only a promise by the Justice Minister to introduce amendments (Roach & Rudin, 2001, pp. 381–383). This meant that Aboriginal youth would not receive the same standard of fairness from the courts as Aboriginal adults unless they were charged with a serious or presumptive offence and subject to an adult sentence. A last-minute amendment by the Senate in January 2002 to s. 38 of the YCJA, (requiring that all available sanctions other than custody should be considered for all young persons), added the requirement that "particular attention" be directed "to the circumstances of Aboriginal young persons" [s. 38(2)(d)].

There were mixed reactions to this addition. From the Department of Justice, Richard Barnhorst maintained that the provision was not needed because the need to consider and respect the needs of Aboriginal youth is stated as a principle in section 3 of the act (Pereira, 2003). On the other hand, Johnathan Rudin, program director of the Aboriginal Legal Services of Toronto, argued that YCJA provisions were not sufficient to ensure "full protection" from custody for Aboriginal youth (Pereira, 2003). A youth worker at the Toronto Native Canadian Centre saw it as a "good thing" only if the alternatives were sufficient to hold youth accountable for their actions, but he hoped it would not be necessary in the future. He stated:

> There is a [Native] teaching called the "seven generations" that says the seventh generation will bring healing and new life to our people. If you look at the history, the seventh generation is here. It's my generation. (Cited in Pereira, 2003, p. 21)

Meanwhile, at the time the amendment was introduced, the then-Canadian Alliance Party justice critic, Vic Toews, maintained that he was "offended" and saw the change as just one more flaw in an overall bad law. He stated:

> I don't think as Canadians we can accept a law that tells judges you have to look at the colour of a person's skin. I find that objectionable. (New Youth Justice Act clears . . . , 2002)

This is a view that places race at the forefront of an issue that is not about race. Rather, the legislation and other government policies and reform strategies, such as the federal Aboriginal Justice Strategy discussed in the "Changing Directions in Correctional Responses for Aboriginal Youth" section later in this chapter, is a response to colonialism and its legacy in the contemporary reality of the marginalization and impoverishment of First Nations and Aboriginal peoples. It is also partially a response to international pressure. The UN Committee on the Rights of the Child has urged the Canadian government to continue to "pursue its efforts to address the gap in life chances between Aboriginal and non-Aboriginal children" (Denov, 2005, p. 77).

This is not to say that racism in Canadian society and in the justice system is not an issue that affects Aboriginal peoples and other visible minorities. Indeed, Aboriginal youth do talk about their experiences of racism, both covert and overt, in the justice system by criminal justice professionals, about being made to feel "dirty" and suspect because they are Aboriginal (Latimer & Foss, 2004, p. 15). Instead, these policies and strategies are an attempt to stop the devastating impact of colonialism. A standard "joke" among some First Nations leaders in response to academic descriptions of "postcolonial" society, is "What, it's gone?"

It is too soon to know how these legislative provisions will play out in sentencing Aboriginal youth. And, as we will see in the section on girls in the justice system later in this chapter, a lesson to be learned from an analysis of the history of juvenile justice reform in Canada is that we should be cautious about judging legislation at face value—"rhetoric is not always reality" (Sangster, 2002, p. 178). Chartrand (2005) reports on a case in Saskatchewan (*R. v. M.B.*) that began on a promising note but reverted to old practices. The case involved an Aboriginal youth convicted of two armed robberies. Defence counsel and the Crown recommended a two-year custodial sentence, but the judge in the case (Justice Mary Ellen Turpel-Lafond) suspected that the youth had fetal alcohol spectrum disorder and ordered an assessment that confirmed her suspicion.

Judge Turpel-Lafond then ordered a circle sentencing conference to explore alternatives to custody that had not been previously investigated by counsel or the youth worker. As a result, the youth was sentenced to 18 months probation with a number of conditions. In passing sentence, Justice Turpel-Lafond addressed the YCJA as well as a lack of funding from governments to support such court initiatives and alternatives. She stated:

> The YCJA, through the conferencing provisions, and its guiding principles, encourages those administering the Act to "prevent crime by addressing the circumstances underlying a young person's offending behaviour." This requires a very different approach than has been taken in the past . . . The court is on its own in attempting to implement this legislation and conduct conferences without adequate or meaningful supports from government. Compounding this is the fact that no additional resources have been assigned to support the additional work required by the legislation to look at the circumstances underlying a young person's offending behaviour. (Cited in Chartrand, 2005, pp. 328–329)

Most disheartening for those who would hope for change in the sentencing of Aboriginal youth is that the 18 month probation sentence was overturned by the Saskatchewan Court of Appeal, where the youth received a sentence of 22 months in custody.

Lack of Facilities and Programming
A lack of young offender facilities and programs in Aboriginal communities has also been cited as a reason for the overuse of custody for Aboriginal youth (Nuffield,

2003). In 2001, one-quarter (23 percent) of the Aboriginal youth in custody came from reserves, half (53 percent) came from cities, and the remainder lived in smaller towns. Girls are more likely to be from reserves than are boys (Bittle et al., 2002, pp. 9–10).

Generally smaller rural and isolated communities simply do not have the resources for community options to custody. Some communities do provide options, such as the Wet'suwet'en Nation's Unlocking Aboriginal Justice program in northwest British Columbia. In other communities, youth are sent into custody simply because there are no alcohol and drug treatment programs, or because the communities cannot offer an intensive support and supervision program (Nuffield, 2003, pp. 17–18). In addition, because Aboriginal youth are often sent from their communities to serve custody sentences, successful community **reintegration** when they are released is undermined because a lack of such programs for aftercare in their home communities increases the risk of the youth reoffending.

Another barrier to reintegration for some Aboriginal youth is that First Nations communities have the right to use a Band Council Resolution to ban people from the community, and sometimes use this right to ban youth convicted of crimes because of concern for the victims of these crimes. The youth are then often forced to move to cities, and all too often begin a downward spiral, back into a life of crime (Nuffield, 2003, pp. 18–19, 24). When Aboriginal youth are allowed to return to their communities after serving their sentences, they usually do so as "outsiders"; this alienation from their culture can contribute to an escalation of legal problems (Fisher & Janetti, 1996, p. 248). Hamilton and Sinclair (1991) summed up the problem:

> The fact that existing correctional facilities are situated far from aboriginal communities is a problem. Successive governments have refused to consider establishing appropriate facilities for youth who reside in Northern Manitoba. Most young people from the north have no contact with their family or friends during their incarceration. Because of distances and cost, these young people do not have the opportunity to visit their homes and to prepare for their eventual release. This is a lesser problem for aboriginal families in the south, but even they have trouble visiting family members who are in custody. (pp. 566–568)

Rethinking Correctional Responses to Aboriginal Youth

Equality and Social Justice

At the core of the correctional system's failure with respect to the treatment of many Aboriginal youth is a justice system whose philosophies and practices serve as a reflection of the wider **Eurocentric** society. Central to Canadian thinking about what is fair and just is the liberal notion of **equality**—the belief that everyone should be treated equally and that to do otherwise is to discriminate. These arguments were heard in the House of Commons regarding Criminal Code s. 718.2(e). Both Reform (now Conservative) members and the Bloc Québécois argued that Aboriginal offenders should be treated the same as non-Aboriginal offenders—that to do otherwise is **reverse discrimination** (Roach & Rudin, 2001, pp. 379–380). Hence, the importance of the Supreme Court's interpretation in the *R. v. Gladue* (1999) case:

> The fact that a court is called upon to take into consideration the unique circumstances surrounding these different parties is not unfair to non-aboriginal people. Rather, the fundamental purpose of s. 718.2(e) is to treat aboriginal offenders fairly by taking into account their difference.

reintegration
A correctional concept referring to policies and programs designed to introduce offenders back into their communities as productive, participating, law-abiding members.

Eurocentric
Beliefs, attitudes, theories, philosophies, and practices that are specific to the European experience, thinking, and worldviews.

equality
A liberal-based philosophy or belief that all is, or should be, the same.

reverse discrimination
Occurs when policies designed to end discrimination against one group inadvertently create discrimination against another group.

Herein lies the problem with correctional responses to female and Aboriginal young offenders. To the extent that Canada fails to specifically acknowledge—through its laws and their administration, and through correctional policies and practices—that the life experiences of **minorities** differ from those of the dominant group, then **social injustice** is perpetuated, particularly when peoples are oppressed, marginalized, and dispossessed. In the case of Aboriginal youth, injustice is also perpetuated when Canadian laws, social policy, and practices fail to recognize fundamental cultural differences that separate Aboriginal young offenders from the principles that form the basis of Canada's justice system.

Role of Culture

This is not to suggest that Aboriginal culture is unified or **monolithic.** Aboriginal societies are culturally diverse in a variety of ways. Nonetheless, certain common aspects of Aboriginal culture and their clashes with the dominant Euro-Canadian legal system have been identified by a number of scholars and reports (see, for example, Chartrand, 2005; Crow, 1994; Goff, 1997; Hamilton & Sinclair, 1991; LaPrairie, 1983, 1988, 2002; Law Reform Commission of Canada, 1991; Ross, 1992, 1994; Royal Commission on Aboriginal Peoples, 1996; Schissel, 1993). The most important commonality is Native spirituality—this lies at the heart of cultural differences that differentiate Aboriginal societies from non-Native society.

Four particular aspects of Aboriginal cultural difference are of significance in justice administration and correctional programming: a principle of not burdening others with one's problems, an orientation to the present and future rather than to the past, a focus on the collective rather than the individual, and an emphasis on **healing** and **reconciliation,** rather than on punishment.

Throughout the 1990s, various alternative justice initiatives took place in a number of Aboriginal communities that provided more culturally relevant and more effective mechanisms for crime prevention, and also furthered Aboriginal self-government. Chartrand (2005), based on Clairmont and Linden's work in Aboriginal communities (1998), listed three principles common to those initiatives that are still in practice. First is the principle of holistic understanding, which is based on the belief that all things are connected. From this perspective, it makes no sense to focus only on a criminal act and adjudge an appropriate response to this act—healing must focus on the individual, not the act.

A second principle is based on the belief that everyone (not just the victim and the offender) has a right and obligation to voice their views on the matter—inclusive decision making. Consensus must be reached by all decision makers. Crime as a sickness is the third area of commonality. This view is that crime is not something inherently "bad" but rather is more like a "sickness" that needs to be healed. Furthermore, the individual is viewed as being separate from the illness. Discussions and decisions are not about punishment in proportion to an offence but rather about how the sickness can be cured (Chartrand, 2005, pp. 323–324).

As we saw in the last chapter, therapy and counselling are common ingredients of correctional programming. They involve talking about one's problems and, in particular, dwelling on one's past experience and the behaviour that led to criminal charges and sanctions. According to Ross (1992) and others, these activities are culturally unacceptable to some Aboriginal peoples (see Box 11.1 and Box 11.2). The two points of cultural difference—not wanting to burden others and an orientation to the present and future—are suggestive of reasons why Eurocentric programming may be unsuccessful with many Aboriginal offenders. The other two points of

minorities
Groups of people who do not form the political, social, and/or cultural majority.

social injustice
A situation in which specific groups of people are disadvantaged relative to others because of societal laws, policies, or practices.

monolithic
A single, uniform, undifferentiated idea or structure.

healing principle
A principle of justice based on the philosophy that crime is an injury requiring the healing of severed relations among the offender, the victim, their families, and the community.

reconciliation
An important component of the mediation/healing process, based on the belief that a productive response to crime is to encourage all affected parties to participate in conflict resolution.

VOICES BOX 11.1

Different Views on Therapeutic Intervention

On Burdening Others

A young Native offender was brought into court one day to be sentenced on a number of serious charges . . . It was clear that this young man had many unresolved emotional problems, for he had constantly been in trouble with the law and had already been placed in a number of different institutions. That formed part of the court's dilemma, for we wanted to find a place that showed the greatest promise of involving him in some successful therapy. We spent a considerable amount of time talking about what he needed when he suddenly interrupted our discussion. He said that he'd been through different kinds of therapy already but that it didn't work. Therapy would fail, he said, not because he was embarrassed to talk about [his problems] but because it wasn't right to talk about them. It wasn't right to "burden" other people in that way . . .

In the mainstream culture, we are virtually bombarded with magazine articles, books and television talk shows telling us how to delve into our psyches, how to explore our deepest griefs and neuroses, how to talk about them, get them out in the open, share them, and so on. At times it seems as if the person who can't find a treatable neuroses deep within himself must for that reason alone be really neurotic!

The Native exhortation, however, seems to go in the opposite direction . . . It forbids the burdening of others. It is almost as if speaking about your worries puts an obligation on others to both share and respond, an obligation difficult to meet, given the prohibition against offering advice in return.

Even the act of concentrating privately on your feelings seems to be discouraged. Such self-indulgence seems to be viewed as a further source of possible debilitation which poses a threat to the survival of the group.

I suspect that the number of psychiatric misdiagnoses must be staggering, for we cannot see their behaviour except through our own eyes, our own notions of propriety. To us, the person who refuses to dig deep within his psyche and then divulge all that he sees is someone with serious psychological problems. At the very least, he is someone who, we conclude, has no interest in coming to grips with his difficulties, no interest in trying to turn his life around . . . Unable to see beyond our own ways we fail to see that there are others, and we draw negative conclusions about the "refusal" or "failure" or "inability" of other people to use our mode of behaviour.

Source: Ross (1992, pp. 32–34).

---

difference—a focus on the collective and an emphasis on healing—suggest ways in which correctional programming might be made more positive for some Aboriginal youth.

Changing Directions in Correctional Responses for Aboriginal Youth

Hamilton and Sinclair (1991) argue that correctional responses to Aboriginal youth need to be more consistent with Aboriginal cultural values. To accomplish this:

VOICES BOX 11.2

Different Views on Correctional Philosophy

On Orientation to the Present and Future

Could it be that we view people as being defined not by essential strength and goodness but by weakness and, if not outright malevolence, then at least indifference to others? Our judicial lectures and religious sermons seem to dwell on how hard we will have to work not to give in to our base instincts. Is that how we see ourselves, and each other?

. . . The Elders of Sandy Lake (and elsewhere) certainly do not speak from within that sort of perspective. At every step they tell each offender they meet with not about how hard he'll have to work to control his base self but instead how they are there to help him realize the goodness that is within him.

In short, the Elders seem to do their best to convince people that they are one step away from heaven instead of one step away from hell. They define their role not within anything remotely like the doctrine of original sin but within another, diametrically opposed doctrine which I will call the Doctrine of Original Sanctity . . .

The freely chosen responses to criminal activity illustrate the differences which flow from adopting each of the two perspectives. If it is your conviction that people live one short step from hell, that it is more natural to sin than to do good, then your response as a judicial official will be to use terror to prevent the taking of that last step backward. You will be quick to threaten offenders with dire consequences should they "slide back" into their destructive ways. In fact, a Band Councillor once asked me directly why our courts came into his community when all we wanted to do was, in his words, "terrorize my people with jail and fines." If, by contrast, it is your conviction that people live one step away from heaven, you will be more likely to respond by coaxing them gently forward, by encouraging them to progress, to realize the goodness within them. The use of coercion, threats or punishment by those who would serve as guides to goodness would seem a denial of the very vision that inspires them. And that, I suggest, is how Elders see it.

Source: Ross (1992, pp. 168–169).

. . . young offenders should be left in their home communities, except in the most extreme situations. Efforts should be directed to determining the reason for their unacceptable conduct, and at helping the youth and the parents to deal with the reason for the offence and to avoid any repetition of it. The main objective should be to restore harmony in the community . . . (p. 566)

For those youth who may require more structure, Hamilton and Sinclair recommended open-custody homes that would allow them to find or keep employment and continue schooling. They also recommended the establishment of wilderness camps— particularly in Aboriginal communities—that would provide various programs such as education, recreation, counselling, and instruction in Aboriginal culture and life skills; work programming in these camps would be designed to provide skills training useful for future employment (Hamilton & Sinclair, 1991, p. 569). For serious offenders who may require secure custody and some form of institutional programming, the following recommendations were proposed:

1. a focus on dispute resolution, healing wounds, and restoring social harmony (Dickson-Gilmore, 1992);
2. an emphasis on spiritual ceremonies to assist in healing processes;
3. a recognition that people must be viewed as "participants in a large web of relationships" rather than as isolated individuals (Ross, 1994, p. 262);
4. a central place for community elders as both teachers and healers; and
5. the hiring of facility or program staff who can speak Aboriginal languages (Hamilton & Sinclair, 1991, pp. 588–589).

Where there is a general acceptance that programming for Aboriginal youth must be culturally appropriate if it is to be useful and effective rather than counterproductive, policymakers have two choices: to create separate programming for Aboriginal youth within the existing system, or to develop mechanisms that will allow the development of youth programming as part of a separate Aboriginal justice system. Governments are divided on this question.

The federal position, which was first presented by former Justice Minister Kim Campbell, rejected the notion of a separate Aboriginal justice system in favour of an incorporation of Aboriginal values into the broader legal system. The Liberal government under Jean Chrétien recommended that Aboriginal peoples play a more central role in sentencing Aboriginal offenders and in developing alternatives to prison (Goff, 1997, p. 84). To this end, the federal government set up, through the Justice

BOX 11.3

The Origins of Sentencing Circles in Sentencing Practice

The practice known as "community peacemaking circles" has its roots in innovative sentencing decisions. An early example involved a 1978 case heard in British Columbia by Judge Cunliffe Barnett . . . The case involved a 14-year-old boy who committed armed robbery after a string of other offences. The boy was clearly becoming more threatening and dangerous, and there seemed little choice but to impose a prison sentence. However, community members felt the boy had much to contribute if his energies could be rechannelled, and knew that potential would be lost if he went to jail. So his uncle and other community leaders asked Judge Barnett to sentence the boy instead to a period on a remote island within the band's reserve (and where his uncle went regularly in his work, so the boy was not abandoned). Judge Barnett had long been dissatisfied with the legal system's limitations, and gladly ordered the recommended sentence . . . [In the end] the community was right. The boy came back from his experience transformed and was never in trouble again. He became a leader in British Columbia's Aboriginal communities, and helped many other young persons stay out of trouble with the law (Cunliffe Barnett, 1996, as cited in Sharpe, 1998, p. 37).

. . . Territorial Court Judge Barry Stuart saw in 1981 that the system he represented was hindering local communities from solving the problems in their midst. So he began asking the community to help him find meaningful sentences that might encourage rehabilitation in the community. He sat with community members in a circle, following native custom, and the term "circle sentencing" stuck. The term gained official legal status in 1991 (Sharpe, 1998, p. 37).

Department, an Aboriginal Justice Strategy program that provided funding, cost-shared with provincial and territorial governments, to support and further develop community-based justice programs in Aboriginal communities.

In 1993, Manitoba adopted a system that would "combine Aboriginal methods of conflict resolution with rules and procedures of the existing system," under which Aboriginal judges and paralegals handle summary convictions and youth cases. On the other hand, Saskatchewan moved in the direction of a separate, parallel system by establishing a Justice of the Peace Program on northern reserves (Goff, 1997, p. 84). Nova Scotia has adopted a similar approach on some reserves by establishing Aboriginal **sentencing circles.** Alberta has developed "community sentencing panels" in a number of communities (Price & Dunnigan, 1995).

Aboriginal Justice and Programs

Aboriginal "justice" now varies across the country and ranges from separate and semi-independent systems of decision making in reserve communities to specialized programs and services offered in the core areas of major cities.

Aboriginal Justice Systems

> Mao logotinetj otjit apigsigtoagan ola egtotanminag "Lets work together to promote forgiveness in the community." (cited in Reid, 2005, p. 101)

An example of an Aboriginal justice system working within the confines of the larger justice structure, comes from Elsipogtog (Big Cove) First Nation, one of the two largest Native communities in New Brunswick. This is a Mi'kmaq community of 2,484 Aboriginal people and inhabitants of the Richibucto Reserve, spanning over 4,120 acres of land, that was established in 1805. In 1995, the community held a justice Awareness Day that resulted in a commitment to create a justice alternative. According to Reid:

> Elsipogtog was a community in crisis. It was losing its children at a phenomenal rate, if not by suicide, by the significant overrepresentation of its youth in the traditional court system. Rather than blame the system, the children or the community, Elsipogtog took on the commitment to build a system that would provide responsibility for actions and applicable, appropriate consequences—one that was made by the community, for the community and as a result, of the community. (p. 114)

The Elsipogtog Restorative Justice Program has developed community-based, culturally appropriate programs that include a pre- and post-charge diversion system, mediation and group conferencing programs, and sentencing circles. This program is designed to allow the community to "decide what [is] best for itself in terms of resolving wrongdoing . . . by striving to resolve the effects of an offender's behaviour" (Reid, 2005, p. 104). It has accomplished this through developing partnerships with Crown prosecutors, police, judges, and other service providers. For example, the police are encouraged to refer youth to the Elsipogtog diversion program before making decisions on whether or not to charge.

Cultural Rediscovery Programs

Rediscovery camp programs for Aboriginal youth have been developed in British Columbia. Fashioned along the lines of the Outward Bound philosophy, they are intended to reconnect Aboriginal youth with the land and their cultural roots. Sometimes used to introduce youth to traditional hunting and fishing, these programs usually involve the teaching of traditional skills, dances, legends, and songs, as well as

sentencing circle
Often used in Aboriginal communities; judges sit with community members to decide on an appropriate sentence for an individual case.

VOICES BOX 11.4

Aboriginal Youth Views on . . .

Custodial Staff

I have been told by staff that I am a loser and a lowlife and some praise me and have hope for me.

Some of the staff have good personalities, make me laugh, make me feel good about myself.

Staff seem to have no hope or trust in us, they keep on saying that we will be back right away. I feel like they are not trying to help me, they are putting me down.

They write down everything, and it gets put on your file and everyone reads it and I don't want that getting around and everyone knowing my business.

Suicide

When I tell staff how I am feeling they stick me in isolation . . . and sticking me in the hole makes me feel more depressed.

Cultural Programming

I would like to live with the Aboriginal culture I was raised with.

I would like more teachings, classes to tell me about the history, spiritual stuff, something to learn more about my culture.

I am more happy and energetic and healthy . . . after a sweat lodge.

There are no sweat lodges for the girls . . .

Mentoring Programs

I would rather go somewhere to talk to someone that I can trust, the certificate or degree doesn't matter, I would rather someone who will understand.

I would like to access a mentor . . . that volunteers . . . someone to be there for me because they are not getting paid.

General Programming

I would like a transition place . . . where when I get out I will be able to do programs, get recreation and life skills for free . . . where I will be able to make a better life.

Remand youth are treated like the bottom of the barrel . . .

Source: Latimer (2004).

the provision of environmental education (Fisher & Janetti, 1996, pp. 251–252). As a measure of the programs' success, the Rediscovery International Foundation was established in 1985; its purpose is to expand the programs to Aboriginal communities around the world (Henley, 1989). Nunavut has developed a correctional program that allows youth in custody to go on escorted hunting day-trips (Weber, 2005). And yes, everyone—youth and guards—carry hunting rifles on these trips.

Education and Skills Training through Mentoring Mentoring has shown some success as a programming style for Aboriginal youth, both in institutions and in the community (Latimer & Foss, 2004). An example of such a program is the Manitoba Aboriginal Youth Career Awareness Committee (MAYCAC). This committee was formed in 1987 by a group of Aboriginal professionals with a vision to provide Aboriginal mentors to Aboriginal youth. It has since expanded to involve a number of different types of activities, including an internship program focused on Aboriginal and black youth in inner-city high schools and a community and custody-based program that works with youth gang members. The core of the work involves assembling volunteers to work as mentors and role models on a one-to-one relationship basis with youth. MAYCAC now lists 650 volunteers in their role model profile (Green & Healey, 2003, pp. 195–197).

Community Healing Ross (1994) compared three programs in Manitoba that have taken different approaches to community involvement in healing processes. The Hollow Water Reserve has chosen to modify the existing Western justice system in developing its Community Holistic Healing Program. This program for sex offenders is staffed by a team made up of volunteers from the community and RCMP officers.

The process begins with disclosure of the abuse to the community team. Criminal charges are laid, but the offender has the option of participating in the healing program or proceeding with the charge in a court of law. In either case, the charge goes to court. However, if the offender agrees to participate in the healing program, the community team will, at sentencing, present to the judge a report detailing the person's progress in the healing program. The community team is in principle opposed to recommendations for prison sentences.

At the Sandy Bay Reserve in Manitoba, a panel of elders from the community works with a judge or justice of the peace to determine an appropriate sentence for offenders. The sentences are most often community work or restitution. If the Aboriginal offender fails to fulfill the terms of the community sentence, the panel of elders "banishes" him or her to the judgment of the Western legal system.

In the Atawapiskat community in Ontario, a panel of elders, independent of the justice system, hears cases and determines sentences. If an offender fails to abide by a community-imposed sentence, his or her case is then turned over to the provincial court (Ross, 1994, p. 249).

GIRLS AND CORRECTIONS

Correctional Issues

Overuse of Custody

Well aware of the injustices heaped layer upon layer on girls in Canadian society through the criminalization of girls for their poverty and attempts to resist violence in the home and survival on the streets, reformers hailed the YOA as a positive step for girls because it eliminated the "status offence" (Sangster, 2002, p. 178). Their hopes were quickly dashed, though, as we saw in earlier chapters—justice professionals found new ways of criminalizing the same girls for the same "offences." Under the YOA, "slapping a mother," which under the Juvenile Delinquents Act (JDA) was "incorrigibility," is now "assault"; struggling with the police to avoid apprehension is "assaulting police officers"; ignoring a curfew is "breaching probation"; and street survival skills become "soliciting for the purposes of prostitution" and "robbing" schoolmates of lunch money." Now all of these "criminal offences" bring girls into the formal justice system.

Furthermore, not only are girls disproportionately processed for these "status" and "survival" offences, but there are a disproportionate number of First Nations girls and young women of colour also in the justice system (Bourne, McCoy, & Smith, 1998; Canadian Association of Elizabeth Fry Societies and Correctional Services of Canada, 1990; Chunn, 1998; LaPrairie, 1995; Leah, 1995).

If we knew little about girls and crime and delinquency prior to the 1980s, we know even less about girls in correctional settings. We do know, from statistics reviewed in earlier chapters, that girls are more likely than boys to be confined for less serious offences and at younger ages. There is also evidence that girls are more likely than boys to be sentenced to custody for breach of probation or community service orders and administrative offences. A survey of all incarcerated girls in British Columbia over an 18-month period, from April 1998 to October 1999, found that almost one-half (44.8 percent) were serving time for breaches of court orders. Only one-quarter (27 percent) had committed a violent offence. In addition, girls were spending significantly more time in custody for these "status" type offences than for other types of offences.

Even more striking is that a one-year follow-up of the girls revealed that two-thirds had been returned to custody, 80 percent for non-violent offences, and almost 80 percent of these (78.3 percent) were charged with administrative offences within three months of their release (Corrado, Odgers, & Cohen, 2000, pp. 196–198). As we have seen, these YOA patterns have not yet changed with the YCJA.

Inappropriate Programming and Facilities

Once in the system, similar to Aboriginal youth, girls find themselves being processed through a youth justice system that is designed to address the needs of Euro-Canadian boys. There are few exceptions to the "all-boy system," the Vanier Centre in Ontario is one example. As with women in the adult system, girls are considered "too few to count" (Adelberg & Currie, 1988) to warrant facilities and programs that are appropriate for girls. The Federal–Provincial–Territorial Task Force on Youth Justice states in its recommendations for reforming the YOA:

> . . . to some extent, young female offenders suffer from the greater degree of social conformity of their female peers—if they offend, their minority representation in the youth justice system inhibits the development of specialized programs, especially in respect of custody and alternatives of custody . . . [S]imply put, there are numerous financial and practical obstacles to developing specialized programs, precisely because of small numbers. For example, it would be impractical, or prohibitively expensive, to develop a specialized alternative program for females in a small or mid-sized town. (Report of the Federal–Provincial–Territorial Task Force on Youth Justice, 1996, p. 617)

The girls themselves are well aware of this injustice. As one young incarcerated woman stated, "Women [girls] are placed in jail without any choice. They're forced to be with men [boys]. It doesn't make sense that there's . . . only one [system] for youth" (Totten, 2000, p. 47).

A university student making a first trip to a youth institution described the girls' daily activities there as: "The girls wake up at the crack of dawn, clean house, eat, sit, eat, sit, eat, shower and sleep" (Holsinger & Ayers, 2004, p. 367). Others have described girls' recreational activities as "watching the boys play sports." In a 2001 case (*R. v. L.B.*) involving a transfer hearing to adult court for a young woman, the judge expressed concerns about the choice of facilities and appropriate programming in both adult and youth facilities in Manitoba. The adult provincial facility for women was said to be so overcrowded that "programming was impossible" and had been for over two years, parenting courses were not offered, and young women with children could not be accommodated. Furthermore, the judge stated that the evidence suggested that the prison had done little but warehouse women. As for youth facilities available to the young woman, "The sad truth is that the facilities for incarcerated youth in this province are woefully inadequate and do not differentiate in any meaningful way between remand, open custody, or secure custody" (cited in Boyle et al., 2002, p. 416).

In a 2002 Alberta case (*R. v. A.J.S.*) the judge pointed to a problem related to a more general issue of incarcerating youth in adult facilities: a lack of appropriate programming because the female offender was younger than most in the adult prison. This general issue is even more aggravated in the women's system, which also has inadequate programming. Not only are girls "too few to count" to warrant their own facilities and programming, but they are too few to count even in the women's system. This issue will be further aggravated by the YCJA's presumptive offence rules.

Paternalism and the "Feminine"

The tendency to use custody as a response to non-criminal behaviour is generally understood to stem from a paternalistic desire to protect girls for "their own good," and from widely shared, sometimes misogynist notions about "bad" girls in relation to femininity—how it is used against them and how alternative forms of femininity also lead to negative attributions. These views are reflected in the common complaint heard from many professionals working in the corrections side of the justice system that "girls are difficult to work with" (see Box 11.5). Their views clearly present a picture of probation far different from that envisioned by W.L. Scott a hundred years ago.

VOICES BOX 11.5

Probation Officers' Views of Girls on Their Caseloads

They play the system real well. Girls play the system better than boys do. They're manipulative. They, you know: "Pity poor me. I'm the innocent bystander and nobody's listening to me." They play the role as if they're so helpless . . . and the majority of the judges are male and they fall into that trap every single time.

You just don't see a lot of girls in here [intensive probation]. And to be honest with you we groan when we have one . . . you know, the issues. I don't know why you groan—maybe because they're definitely a lot needier.

They're more like criers. Girls will do that. They'll break down and you'll be in the sympathy thing for awhile you know, but then you realize what they're doing.

They feel like they're the victim. They try from "Mom kicked me out" to "Mom's boyfriend molested me" to "My brother was sexually assaulting me." They'll find all kinds of excuses to justify their actions. Because they feel if I say I was victimized at home that justifies me being out on the streets . . . Or while they were out there they got raped. Or, they were mistreated. Personally, I think 98% is false . . . 98% of the girls say the exact same story, so it's as if they just get together on the units and think up these things.

(continued)

Box 11.5 continued

I don't feel like you can just say that this program works for girls or whatever—they're children. Some of them are ready and some of them aren't. Whether they be boys or girls.

[There are] girls on our caseload who are kind of macho girls. They're not the normal, everyday girl that you deal with.

They're not your typical girls . . . you know, the fingernails, the make-up, the Ms. Prissy. They're just like the boys. They're worse than some boys. They go out and they prove themselves like they're not feminine. You know they don't want anybody to think . . . well, I'm helpless. I can take care of myself, so they play the role as portraying to be something that they're not.

Girls are much more difficult to case manage. Their affect is different—they will push you away when really they want to come closer. They will make your life miserable—whereas boys will just sort of go along with the program . . . A lot of it, I think, in my opinion, is hormones. In fact, when I had a lot of girls on a caseload, you could almost watch the ebb and tide. When their hormones are on the move and they're ovulating, you couldn't stand to be around them.

Source: Gaarder, Rodriguez, and Zatz (2004).

Corrado et al. (2000) found paternalism to be alive and well among probation officers who commonly offer a paternalistic rationale for charging a young woman with breaching her probation.

> . . . I breach her for her safety . . . her probation runs out in September and we are worried that she will become street entrenched . . . what else can we do? . . . she won't leave the streets, and she is in some very real and immediate danger. (p. 203)

> . . . short of a custodial disposition, which is not desirable at this point, the writer is at a loss as to how to control or assist this defiant young girl in the community . . . her history reflects a continuous cycle of refusal to cooperate with treatment attempts and running away . . . It is the fear of this writer that this youth is in grave danger of further victimization and self-harm if no action is taken. (p. 200)

The same paternalism is also often found in judges' sentencing decisions. For example, in *R. v. R.L.R.* (2001), the judge sentenced a teen to a term of probation on condition that she live with her parents. The judge justified this sentence by expressing general concern about "teens who cannot get along with their parents and are in danger of ending up living on the streets or living with dangerous boyfriends," and that the girl in this case had chosen to live with her boyfriend. The judge stated that the girl "needed protection, in my view . . ." (Boyle et al., 2002, p. 396). And again, the girls going through the courts are aware of this paternalism. One 14-year-old said, "I'm here because of drugs . . . the judge wants me off the streets . . . he thinks that I am a danger to myself" (Corrado et al., 2000, p. 200).

Judges have also sentenced girls because of their motherhood or impending motherhood. In *R. v. A.D.* (2001), the judge did not sentence a girl, who had a child at age 12, to custody because she was a "dedicated and responsible parent" whose child was the "focus of her life." In another instance (*R. v. S.H.*, 2001), a 17-year-old girl's sentence, for breach of probation, was due to the fact of her pregnancy. The judge stated:

> The only way I can see of protecting them both [mother and child] . . . is to order three months of secure custody followed by twelve months' probation . . . The sooner that you're in a warm place, with three meals a day, and people to help you with the baby, the better it's going to be. (Cited in Boyle et al., 2002, p. 418)

Note that in this case, the young woman received a lengthy, high-security custodial sentence for a breach of probation—for her protection.

Rethinking Correctional Responses to Girls

Constitutional and Legislated Rights

In itself, protecting girls from victimization on the streets sounds like a worthy goal, but acting on that sympathy raises questions about the constitutional and legislated rights of girls in Canadian society and the YCJA (the dilemma raised by Justice Sharon McCully in Box 11.6). There are a number of ways in which girls' rights are violated in justice decision-making processes. The YOA, for example, promoted "minimal interference" with the rights and freedoms of youth, thereby implying that probation and custody should be the last options, rather than the first as is the case for many girls in the system.

We have seen that for at least some probation officers and judges, protection has been used as a justification for infringement of young female offenders' rights. Nonetheless, the emphasis in the YCJA on extrajudicial measures, restrictions on the use of the justice system to address child welfare matters, and restrictions on the use of custody, combined with a stated principle that decision making should consider gender, has the potential to reduce the overuse of custody (and probation) for girls. However, restrictions regarding welfare matters already existed under the YOA and paternalism was still used in decision making for girls; these attitudes are deeply ingrained in our society. There is still a considerable amount of discretion allowable for judges to invoke a variety of principles in justifying their decisions. Without considerable changes in attitude and/or court challenges to set precedent, there may be little change.

VOICES BOX 11.6

A Judge's Point of View on Girls in Detention

Protective detention seems to be utilized more often for girls than for boys in the juvenile system, reflecting the paternalistic traditions of juvenile justice. Most juvenile court judges, including women, are unwilling to let girls be used, abused, and subjected to numerous indignities on the streets. While I share those concerns, and I personally abhor ingrained attitudes and traditional roles of our society which subject women in general to such atrocities, I cannot justify subjecting girls to yet another loss of personal control and liberty by placing them in secure correctional facilities to protect them from their own choices . . . [A]lternatives must be developed to assist courts in releasing such girls to placements outside secure correctional settings. We are stretching the bounds of constitutional acceptance by using detention as a holding facility for promiscuous, prostituting, street-walking juvenile girls.

Source: McCully (1994, p. 17).

Girls can be apprehended for their own protection through child welfare legislation and other child-protection laws. All provinces and territories have child and family services legislation and while such legislation varies considerably in details and procedures, almost all provinces and territories allow police and social workers to apprehend and detain children "in need of protection." Examples of such children are those who are being sexually abused or sexually exploited, or those who are involved in prostitution or use alcohol or drugs. A court order is not required, nor are warrants for searches. Apprehended children normally cannot be held in detention or facilities designed for young offenders (Busby, 2003, pp. 105–106).

In spite of these powers, some provinces have attempted to enact additional legislation that focuses exclusively on prostitution and protecting girls from their own actions. Saskatchewan and Ontario have tried unsuccessfully to pass legislation, while Alberta and British Columbia have been successful in passing the Protection of Children Involved in Prostitution Act (PCIP, 1998, amended 2002) and the Secure Care Act (2002), respectively. Alberta's PCIP is worthy of focus because it has been challenged in court. PCIP allows police and social workers to apprehend anyone under 18 who is involved in prostitution, with or without a warrant in "emergency situations." Children may be held for up to 5 days and two additional periods of 21 days each with a court order, for a total of 47 days. During this time, they are subjected to a battery of assessments and tests, including tests for drug use, sexually transmitted diseases, HIV, and pregnancy.

Under the Alberta PCIP, if youth are confined without a warrant, there must be a court hearing where social workers are required to justify the apprehension and detention. The youth is entitled to legal representation at the hearing. Most have been released after the initial apprehension, but many have been apprehended repeatedly, including one girl who was apprehended 17 times. The policy is intended to apply "equally" to boys and girls, but in the first year of operation, it had been used 343 times against 66 girls, but only twice against boys. Almost all of the girls are apprehended on an "emergency" basis, meaning that no warrant is issued for their apprehension (Bell, 2001; Busby, 2003, pp. 106–107).

These laws define prostitution as sexual abuse, so proponents argue that they are designed to protect children and youth from "pimps and johns," not to punish them. Nonetheless, a lawyer representing two 17-year-old girls in Alberta successfully challenged the law as a violation of the girls' rights under the Canadian Charter of Rights and Freedoms (*Alberta v. K.B. and M.J.*, 2000). The court determined that the PCIP was "unconstitutional in its lack of procedural safeguards." The law was subsequently amended in 2002 and has not been challenged since (Busby, 2003).

While there is little objection to providing the assistance that children and youth need to get them off the streets, the fact that the act permits confinement of girls and medical testing for their own protection constitutes violations of their rights, regardless of the use of tricky legal terminology to circumvent this conclusion. Some argue that the act puts girls at further risk of violence and criminalization: girls who have been "apprehended for their own protection" report severe beatings once they were back on the street. The girls also report that PCIP forces their activities underground to avoid police apprehension, and that they believe they are safer out in the open on the streets:

> You're going to push the prostitutes so far into an isolated area that bad stuff is going to end up happening again. So perhaps that is what is going to happen to these girls, they're going to go out there and the cops won't see them, and then they're going to

get screwed up just because of that . . . young girls . . . have left town many more times than they would have normally. They are being circulated a lot more; they're underground. (Busby, 2003, p. 121)

Poverty and Marginalization

It is now generally recognized that one of the most important programming needs for girls is to receive the skills training necessary for economic survival and independence. A survey of girls in custody in Nova Scotia revealed that 15 percent of the respondents were mothers (Nova Scotia Department of Community Services, 1993, p. 14) and in British Columbia, a majority of girls in prison had been on their own from a very early age. Almost 90 percent of the girls in custody had been kicked out of their family homes or had left of their own volition. Only 37 percent were living at home at the time of the offence that brought them to prison (Corrado et al., 2000, p. 196).

Girls are far more likely to enter the justice system from the child welfare system and as a result of "status offences." A sample of institutionalized girls from across Canada indicated that almost all of the girls had initially encountered the youth justice system on charges related to prostitution and running away—both child welfare matters (Totten, 2002). Programs related to economic independence need to be considered as essential for such girls.

Vocational programs are generally less successful than work programs in reducing delinquency. This is likely because vocational programs do not offer what many youth want and need most—real employment experience. The programming challenge for female youth is to provide non-traditional vocational and employment programs and to convince staff and potential employers that girls are as capable as boys when it comes to performing non-traditional jobs. In the survey of girls in Nova Scotia institutions cited earlier, respondents reported being offered vocational programming in a number of areas, including baby-sitting, woodworking, computer use, hospitality management, cooking, and driver's education. Although the report that resulted from the survey recommended that girls be offered male programming such as work and life skills training, as well as some academic programs accessible only to male youth, no consideration was given to non-traditional vocational programming (Nova Scotia Department of Community Services, 1993).

Abuse and Sexual Exploitation

Programming for girls needs to reflect a recognition that many young female offenders have been victims of abuse at the hands of those in positions of trust—parents, relatives, friends, neighbours, and boyfriends. Contrary to what some probation officers might think, girls do not get together and conspire to make up abuse stories (Box 11.5 on page 329). We have seen throughout this textbook, from a variety of sources, that most girls "in trouble" and "in the system" have lived lives of violence and abuse. The Nova Scotia survey indicated that 63 percent of the girls in custody had been abused; one-third reported sexual abuse and another third physical abuse (Nova Scotia Department of Community Services, 1993, p. 5).

Unfortunately, these findings are fairly typical. In the British Columbia survey, 67 percent of the girls had been physically abused and 52 percent had been sexually abused (Corrado et al., 2000, p. 199). This is not to say that boys have not also experienced abuse, or that some boys do not need similarly focused programs. The problem lies in the failure to provide girls with programming that recognizes these issues as central in their lives. More specifically, for girls, the effectiveness of any programming—particularly that which stresses economic independence—may depend on programs that address abuse issues.

Foster care is often used as a means of getting children out of unsafe homes. All too often, though, children have been abused and/or neglected in these placements. Totten's interviews with a sample of institutionalized girls indicated that all of the participants experienced an escalation of violence while in child welfare facilities and while in custody (Totten, 2002).

Although group homes seem to be less problematic than foster homes and are generally viewed as more desirable than institutional sentences, it is not clear that they are a positive experience for girls. A study of three group homes in Ohio found that girls in these placements had less success than boys. This is not to say that girls cannot benefit from an application of the group home concept, but rather that group home programming must be assessed for its appropriateness for girls. Similar problems can be seen with Outward Bound wilderness programs. The question here is whether counsellors and workers in these programs "rely on male models of physical challenge and risk taking as metaphors for success in life . . . [and whether] the programs explicitly [are] enforcing traditional gender scripts" (Chesney-Lind & Shelden, 1992, p. 198).

Many family therapy and counselling models are based on the notion that keeping families intact is all-important. This view is especially problematic with respect to both boys and girls who have been physically and sexually abused by family members. In such cases, family therapy is not a positive approach to take unless the young person is provided with programs and services that allow her or him to live separately from the family (Chesney-Lind & Shelden, 1992, pp. 192–193; Herman, 1981).

Too Few to Count

The "too few to count" argument also needs to be considered in relation to the number of Aboriginal and black young women in the justice system. Since minority girls' gender experiences are different from those of white girls, as are their experiences with dominant institutions, programs also need to be rooted in specific cultures (Chesney-Lind, 2001, p. 44).

An important question arising from the small numbers of girls in corrections is whether to provide separate programming for girls or to include girls in programming designed for boys. As suggested earlier, the federal government position is that considerable resources would be required to provide separate facilities and separate programs for girls, and provinces seem only too eager to agree with this opinion. Nonetheless, Hamilton and Sinclair (1991) maintain that designing programming and facilities for young offenders on the basis of economic factors is "abhorrent"; in their view, "Young people should not be mistreated by the justice system because of a lack of resources" (p. 567). A national survey of institutionalized girls indicated that they too see this as problematic and that it is a source of injustice. One young woman summarized the problem when she poignantly stated:

> . . . the first time I was [institutionalized] with boys, they used to harass me and everything . . . I was the only girl . . . Like, (they said) I'll see you in your bedroom tonight, and stuff like that. *I stayed scared.* (Totten, 2000, p. 41) [Italics added]

A related issue concerns male staff in institutions and for programming. Evaluation studies have found individual counselling to be the least effective type of intervention program for girls (Lipsey, 1990). Group therapy is likely best conducted in groups of girls with the same histories, rather than in general groups or coed groups, but seems to be problematic for girls when counsellors are male. One female youth stated:

> . . . there was not . . . ever one woman psychologist for us. It was always these men psychologists . . . When you are just coming off the street, and you're dealing with pimps and johns and stuff like that, the last person you want to talk to is some guy about it. (Totten, 2000, p. 47)

Positive Directions in Programming for Girls

With respect to gender-appropriate, culturally sensitive programming, particularly in a climate where governments are unwilling to provide separate facilities for girls, a critical question is whether to provide coeducational programming or separate programming for boys and girls. There are strong arguments for both positions. Past experience indicates that the institutional experience and its programming has benefited boys more than it has girls, which lends strong support to the argument for programming designed specifically for girls. On the other hand, some take the position that coeducational programming better reflects everyday life, brings a "degree of normalcy" to institutional life, and improves social skills (Nova Scotia Department of Community Services, 1993, p. 12). The comments of one girl in Totten's study gives cause for reflection on the benefits of exposure to "everyday life" in a coed youth facility:

> . . . Guys would be fighting over girls . . . I would see guys whacking off . . . they'd sit there and fart and spit . . . Some guys would fight with girls . . . It's a big time tease. I felt like people were fucking with my sexual emotions. (2000, p. 40)

A middle-of-the-road position might be to assess all programs in terms of their gender-appropriate nature and to offer some programs only for girls. One institution in Nova Scotia offers a program called So He Says He Loves You. This eight-week program addresses abuse survival and victimization and is restricted to girls, although a similar coed program is also offered. Other specific-needs programs might address such topics as pregnancy, parenting, and date rape.

A related issue is whether the staff in female institutions should include men. According to the Nova Scotia report on female offenders, there should be male staff in female institutions because "it is unhealthy . . . to foster a perception amongst the female residents that men are present only when physical containment or discipline is necessary" (Nova Scotia Department of Community Services, 1993, p. 18). The report further recommends a partner approach, whereby male staff would be paired with female work partners. It also recommends that female young offenders be given the right to request female doctors, psychologists, or psychiatrists (p. 19). On the other hand, Faith (1993) points out that women and girls who have been physically and sexually abused do not feel comfortable with men who have institutionalized power over them. Rather, they are more likely to benefit from other women who have shared experiences and have "subsequently learned to forgive, honour and love themselves" (Faith, 1993, p. 164). The girls themselves seem to agree:

> When you are involved in a restraint . . . to have a bunch of men jump on you and drag you somewhere . . . You see your friends being jumped by men and they're screaming . . . (Totten, 2000, p. 47)

> When I was on my period I asked the [male] guards for something and they wouldn't get me anything, they told me to use toilet paper. (Totten, 2000, p. 41)

Research results tend to support girls' views of the efficacy of all-female staff and counsellors. Professionals, both male and female, who work with girls in mixed gender settings are the ones most likely to express the negative and destructive attitudes we saw earlier in Box 11.5. They tend to focus on boys' concerns and progress and report that "girls are more difficult to work with, verbally aggressive, hysterical and manipulative" (cited in Totten, 2004, p. 3). In contrast, women who work only with girls focus more on girls' needs and concerns, such as sexual health, parenting, and sexual abuse. Young women report feeling safer and more willing to engage in therapeutic programming with women staff (Bloom, 2003; Bloom & Covington, 2001; Totten, 2004, p. 3).

Totten (2004), based on a review of programming and interviews with incarcerated girls across Canada, offers the following as essential components of gender-responsive programs and services for girls:

1. A safe, supportive, nurturing female-centred environment, including a positive gender-responsive work environment;
2. Staff that reflect the gender, race, and sexual orientation of the institutionalized girls;
3. Program approaches based on girl-centred theories that focus on girls' strengths and assets, with building skills as an objective;
4. Opportunities to develop skills in a range of educational and vocational areas;
5. Therapeutic models that address issues such as healing from abuse, family relationships, eating disorders, assertiveness skills, parenting education, and child development;
6. Education and counselling on issues related to health, such as pregnancy, stress management, HIV/AIDS, STDs, and mental health;
7. An overall emphasis and focus on empowerment, self-respect, and positive self-perception; and
8. Women role models and mentors that reflect the racial and ethnic backgrounds of the girls.

Chesney-Lind cautions against the standard "issue-specific" approach to programming, anger management, drug abuse, etc., and suggests that girls' programming should be multifaceted, work to empower girls, and advocate for change that will benefit them. Hence, programs need to not only work on girls' "strengths, skills and creativities to develop their voices and their abilities to assert themselves, but also [work at] identifying and challenging barriers that girls, particularly marginalized girls, face in our society" (2001, p. 44).

Changing Directions in Correctional Responses for Girls

New initiatives for girls are developing and being implemented, ranging from prison/detention design to community-based programs to preventive programs aimed at individual girls as well as training programs for staff.

Gender-Specific Prison/Detention Facilities

While it seems like a contradiction to speak of prisons for girls in the context of appropriate gender-specific programming and not wanting to advocate prisons for girls, courts will continue to sentence girls to prison terms, so alternative prison models need to be considered. For example, the Department of Youth Services (DYS) in Massachusetts has, since the mid 1990s, been housing girls in a 19th-century facility built for boys. Responding to research indicating that girls do not do well in detention and educational models designed for boys, the DYS attempted to deliver gender-specific programming, counselling, job training, physical recreation, trauma work, and parenting skills. However, it became apparent that the institutional environment was not conducive to such programming—taking a boys' institution and "painting it pink" did not make the system work better for girls.

As a result, the DYS spearheaded an initiative to design and build a gender-specific high-security detention and custodial facility. Now in the construction phase, the institution will be a 45,500-square-foot building on a hospital campus with a capacity to hold 60 girls aged 12 to 18. It will be a secure, locked facility with a perimeter fence, controlled interior and exterior entrances, a fenced-in outdoor recreation area, and closed-circuit monitoring of the institution. Nonetheless, the design of the public space aims to create a "high-school/boarding school" atmosphere with aesthetically pleasing visual lines. For example, there will be ample natural light, clear views to the outdoors, and windows that are four panes wide and six panes high, designed to look like windows in a home instead of the standard prison windows with vertical steel security bars. In the new building, the dividers between the window-panes are the security bars.

Efforts are also being made to reduce the chance of girls harming themselves, by installing sprinklers, coat hooks, air supply and exhaust grills, and door hardware that cannot be used in suicide attempts; for example, the bedroom walls are designed with slopes to keep sprinkler heads out of reach. Also, the girls will have real glass mirrors in their rooms, but the mirrors will be covered with a plastic substance to make them unbreakable. For personal decorative touches, portions of the rooms' walls will be treated to allow the girls to tape up personal photos, posters, pictures, and mementos. Recognizing that girls have a greater need for privacy than boys, bathroom areas are designed to maximize privacy and grooming needs, and cameras will not be installed in bathrooms, bedrooms, or classrooms.

In an effort to meet girls' enhanced medical needs because of histories of trauma, body concerns, pregnancy, and birth control issues, the facility design incorporates direct access for the girls to the medical centre in the facility. In an effort to meet the girls' relational needs, the institution is designed with four "wings" for the girls' living spaces, rather than large dormitories or "units." Each wing will hold 15 girls (Morton & Glynn, 2005, pp. 88–92).

While this model holds considerable promise when compared to antiquated male institutions, a word of caution is in order regarding the "great experiment" in reforming women's prisons. Similar efforts were expended in Canada and in Britain to create environmentally supportive environments and, within months of opening, some women were being shipped back to male institutions because they were a "security risk," and the institutions were being remodelled to enhance security concerns and contain the women in more secure spaces. Reformers' concerns about the increasing number of women being sent to prison by the courts *because* there were now special facilities with specialized programming seem to have been realized, as rates of imprisonment increased for women after the new prisons were opened (Faith, 1993; Hannah-Moffat & Shaw, 2000). This too is a potential negative consequence of appropriate programming.

Independent Living

Supportive Housing for Young Mothers is a new program in Halifax that provides safe, stable, long-term housing with support services for young single mothers aged 16 to 19.

More specifically, the program is targeted for young women who would otherwise be on the streets or in shelters with their babies. The project is designed to assist young mothers to "organize themselves, learn how to cope with having a baby, and get themselves situated in a community . . . where they can get involved and make friends and have resources for them and their children. It helps them grow up and learn how to be an adult with a child." The facility is designed to provide 8 to 10 apartment living spaces (Lambie, January 18, 2006).

Mentoring and "Walk and Talk"

As with Aboriginal youth program, mentoring programs are something to which youth, including girls, respond, particularly when the programs involve matching youth with volunteers who are seen by youth as "someone who cares" rather than "someone who is paid to do a job." Mentoring is seen as particularly appropriate for girls because it is a "relationally oriented" program. Often, as with the MAYCAC program in Manitoba, the programs are partnered with universities and university students work with youth as mentors. MAYCAC is partnered with the University of Manitoba.

While MAYCAC works with inner-city youth, mentoring programs are also used in institutional settings and for youth released to the community on probation. One such program operates through a criminology program at the University of Missouri–Kansas City. It involves young women enrolled in a course (commonly referred to as "the mentoring class") working with the girls. For credit, the students write a paper on their experiences and the knowledge they gained about the girls and their treatment as well as their own personal insights. The program is designed to be an enriching educational experience for the students and to provide beneficial services to institutionalized girls who would not otherwise have such programming (Holsinger & Ayers, 2004, pp. 351–352).

A related program is the Walk and Talk program in Alberta. This program is based on attachment theory and the idea of positive benefits from therapeutic alliances. Volunteers go for walks with "at-risk" schoolchildren and offer them examples and instruction on new coping strategies and life skills, encourage them to explore alternative behavioural choices, and help the children feel better about themselves. This too is a relational approach to counselling (Doucette, 2004, p. 373).

Participatory Staff Development

Participatory staff development involves gender-sensitive training for staff. This program focuses on the process of developing training programs that are inclusive, and is primarily concerned with the needs of both workers and youth. Informed by theoretical and empirical knowledge about gender, culture, and normative and atypical adolescent behaviour, researchers, line staff, and youth workers work together to develop gender-sensitivity training modules for institutional staff and youth workers (Artz, Nicholson, & Rodriguez, 2005, pp. 304–305).

SUMMARY

Aboriginal youth in the justice system are disproportionately held in remand, sentenced to custody, and placed in secure custody. Girls who find themselves in court are more likely than boys to be sentenced to custody for less serious offences, and at younger ages. Because Euro-Canadian boys constitute the majority of youth in the justice system and custodial institutions, programming is most often devised to meet their specific needs. Sending Aboriginal youth away from their communities to serve custody sentences undermines successful community reintegration on their release.

As we have seen throughout this textbook, youth issues are individualized and decontextualized. We have argued that youth behaviour is best understood in the context of youth cultures/subcultures, and the same is true for Aboriginal youth who have run afoul of "the law." The behaviours that bring them into the justice system and the negative impact that this contact and experience has on them needs to be viewed in the context of the status of Aboriginal peoples and the status of youth in Aboriginal communities and Canadian cities.

Governments have attempted to address the consequences of colonialism and marginalization by providing resources for community initiatives and development in the administration of justice and delivery of services. Changes that have been made to the YCJA also recognize diversity in the youth population coming into the justice system and the unique position of Aboriginal youth in the system. Nonetheless, these changes have occurred in the context of cutbacks to other social services, and legislative reform may not change judicial interpretation and prioritization of the principles of sentencing.

Efforts at cultural programming and service provision are piecemeal and not consistent across the country. Some communities and jurisdictions have made considerable strides while others have not. Many of the "old" problems, inequities, and injustices continue across the county not only with regard to Aboriginal youth, but also in a failure to address the inequities and social changes required to beneficially alter the life circumstances of other minority youth. Inequities for girls and visible minority youth continue to be justified on the grounds that it would be too expensive to provide separate programming and facilities. In spite of efforts to provide services and programs for girls, many institutions continue to do little more than offer programs designed for boys or ones that do not meet the needs of girls and visible minority youth. The juvenile justice system thus perpetuates the inequities already experienced by these youth.

Central to the Canadian justice system is the notion that "equality" is the cornerstone of fairness and justice. However, treating people who are already oppressed and marginalized as equal before the law, or failing to recognize important aspects of cultural and social diversity, only serves to perpetuate social injustice. The Supreme Court of Canada has argued that treating Aboriginal peoples differently in the justice system does not constitute reverse discrimination. Nonetheless, legislative changes in the YCJA, while intended to allow for consideration of the special circumstances of Aboriginal youth, may not be realized in practice by justice professionals.

Four aspects of Aboriginal cultural difference are of significance to justice administration and correctional programming: the principle of not burdening others with one's problems, an orientation to the present and future rather than the past, a focus on the collective rather than the individual, and an emphasis on healing rather than punishment. Numerous changes have been made over the last 10 years in developing community-based justice, and programming for Aboriginal youth has incorporated aspects of earlier recommendations. These include a focus on dispute resolution, an emphasis on spiritual ceremonies, a central role for community elders, and the hiring of staff who speak Aboriginal languages. Central components shared by most Aboriginal justice systems include a principle of holistic understanding that is based on the belief that all things are connected; inclusive decision making based on consensus; and a view that crime is not something inherently "bad" but rather is more like a "sickness."

Overuse of custody is a primary concern for girls in the system. Girls are more likely than boys to be confined because of a paternalistic desire to protect them "for their own good." Contributing to this injustice are widely shared, sometimes misogynist notions about "bad" girls in relation to femininity—how it is used against them and how alternative forms of femininity lead to negative attributions. Girls are usually confined in male facilities and denied gender- and culture-appropriate programming because they are seen as being too few in number to justify separate facilities and programs. All of these factors raise questions of girls' constitutional rights being violated. In spite of YCJA provisions to recognize the needs of youth on the basis of gender and ethnicity, such attitudes are likely to continue to influence decision making in the justice system.

Programs for girls need to be grounded in theories that are gender-specific, that recognize that girls' paths to delinquency and their needs are different from those of boys. Some types of programming, such as individual counselling and group homes, are not effective for girls. Effective programming for girls requires female staff and professionals who are sensitive to and supportive of the girls' needs, and should take place in a supportive women/girl-centred environment. Programming needs include education and employment and vocational skills training, advocacy, and ongoing support systems, as well as skills training and counselling on such issues as health, parenting, family relationships, HIV/AIDS and STDs, pregnancy, eating disorders and abuse. Such programs will explicitly recognize the gendered nature of family life and the unique problems that this creates for girls.

Models of gender-specific detention and custodial facilities have been designed specifically for girls. Independent-living programs that allow young mothers to live with their children are an example of innovative programming for girls. Mentoring programs are appropriate for girls, and efforts are being made to develop gender and culturally sensitive training for staff and youth workers in institutions.

DISCUSSION/CRITICAL THINKING QUESTIONS

1. Why or why not is it racist (or reverse discrimination) to develop separate policies and programs for marginalized groups?
2. Is it possible to develop an Aboriginal justice system that is completely autonomous from the state's justice system? Why or why not?
3. Why or why not should girls be locked up and/or subject to medical procedures "for their own protection"? How is this "fair" or "just"?
4. Should girls have separate facilities from boys? Explain your answer.

WEB LINKS

Justice for Girls
www.justiceforgirls.org/index.html

Elizabeth Fry Society: Young Women and Violent Offences
www.elizabethfry.ca/violent/ywomen.htm

Social Issue: Who killed Garrett Campiou?
www.albertaviews.ab.ca/issues/2001/mayjun01/mayjun01social2.pdf

Centre for Gender and Justice
www.centerforgenderandjustice.org

For chapter quizzes and more links, visit this book's accompanying website at
www.bellyoungoffenders3e.nelson.com

CHAPTER TWELVE

A Century after the Fact: What Do We Know? Where Are We Going?

CHAPTER OBJECTIVES

1. To summarize what we have learned in the text about youth crime and justice through the last century, and to develop an appreciation of how this helps us understand today's issues.
2. To discuss current ideas about youth crime and justice system practices, and to review proposals and ideas for reform to consider their strengths, limitations, and implications for the future.
3. To re-examine the Youth Criminal Justice Act (YCJA) as policy and in practice to identify ongoing and new issues, and to weigh the implications of both for future reform.
4. To consider, in light of what we know now and from the past, whether new reforms and proposals are likely to constitute positive directions in youth justice reform or will simply perpetuate current injustices.

KEY TERMS

Neoliberal
Prevention
Racialized
Hegemonic
Restorative justice model

Peacemaking circle
Transformative justice model
Community change model
Law reform

INTRODUCTION

A century ago, Canadians thought poverty, neglect, and poor parenting were the sources of youth crime. Creating a juvenile justice system was their solution. Family courts were the cornerstone of this system, and they were supported by probation, supervision, and institutions that would teach morals and trade skills to neglected and delinquent children. Today, many academics, policymakers, and members of the public still think that the family is the source of youth crime, and we still rely on probation and institutions to solve the problem.

While some things have not changed, others have. An important structural change came with the Young Offenders Act (YOA) and the introduction of alternative measures, a change that is maintained and strengthened with the extrajudicial measures of

---

CASE STUDY BOX 12.1

Johnny: Blame and Responsibility

When in police custody, Johnny wrote a letter to the McEvoy family, apologizing for the death of Theresa McEvoy in a collision with Johnny's stolen vehicle during a police pursuit:

> Hi, I'm sorry for your loss. I wish it was me that died in that car today. I can't stop thinking about it. I can't sleep or close my eyes, not for a second, or I can see my car hit her car. I will never get over this. It never should have happened today . . . It will stay in my nightmares forever and forever.

Staff at the Waterville Youth Detention Centre testified that Johnny had shown little remorse for his crime and felt that he was unlikely to change. Yet, in a police cell, on the day of the accident, Johnny was heard muttering to himself, "I can't believe I killed her. I can't even curse at somebody I don't know, let alone murder them." In court, Dr. Mark Johnston claimed that this was not necessarily remorse, but rather it was Johnny trying to put himself in a good light. Regardless of how others perceive his remorse—or lack of it, for that matter—it is evident that Johnny will have to learn to live with the fact that his love of stealing cars caused him to take another's life.

While Johnny and the "experts" working with him grapple with issues of remorse and blame, the issue for the legal professionals involves lines of responsibility and blame-shifting between the persons who administer youth justice and the legislation itself. While it seems evident that there was a major communication breakdown between the various sectors of youth justice, namely the police and the courts, everyone seems to be passing the buck during the McEvoy inquiry. Even the education system takes a turn at spinning the wheel of blame; as the principal of the junior high school that Johnny attended testified in court, "We did the best with what we had." He recalled an incident when Johnny was suspended from school and drove around the school grounds on his bicycle during a frozen-rain storm "because his mother wouldn't allow him back into the house." Yet, no matter how many fingers are pointed, all blame is directed at youth justice legislation and how it seemingly failed us, yet again.

Sources: *The Chronicle Herald* [Halifax] (December 15, 17, 2005; February 7, 21, 22, 2006); B. Hayes (February 9, 2006). Researched and written by Nicole Landry.

the YCJA. And, as we saw in previous chapters, there have been some innovations in how we respond to youth crime. Unfortunately, the YCJA has also introduced a structural change with provisions for adult sentences, eroding the fundamental precept of a juvenile justice system—its separateness from the adult system.

Important changes have also occurred in how we conceptualize and think about young people and their involvement in criminal activity, which also contributes to this erosion. A hundred years ago, youth were talked about in public discourse first as "delinquents" and then as "young offenders"; now they're called "youth criminals." Indeed, the publisher of this edition of the text suggested changing its title to *Youth Criminals and Juvenile Justice*.

Where we go from here in creating a system that responds positively to youth crime issues depends on how we use the wealth of theoretical, empirical, and research knowledge that has been accumulated over the past century. If we are to move ahead in positive directions, we need to consider what we know about youth crime and our responses to it, and we need to learn some lessons from the past in order not to repeat mistakes. In this chapter, we will review the important things that we have learned over the last century and consider how it is useful to our understanding of young offenders and juvenile justice and our efforts to respond productively to both. We will also address what is new on the youth justice scene, as well as the issues that Canadians have been dragging along with them for at least one hundred years.

RETHINKING JUVENILE JUSTICE

What We Know

Moral panic still rages as the public continues to be warned about new and frightening dangers and threats. Now we are to worry about toddlers. The newspaper headline "Toddlers taken by Children's Aid after trashing Ontario home" warned people in Listowel, Ontario, of the impending danger of "rampaging" two-year-olds. According to the article, the toddlers "wandered" from their home, entered a neighbouring home, and were later found "standing in a sea of destruction." They had apparently "ransacked" a bedroom, "dumped" the contents of a refrigerator, smashed a large sheet of drywall that was leaning against a wall, poured water into an electric guitar, knocked over plants, pulled a wind chime from a high perch in the kitchen, and "one tot's diaper found its way into a basement aquarium" (Davis, 2005).

The homeowners apparently found it "hard to believe" that the children did this on their own. They pointed out that two-year-olds would not have the attention span to do hours of damage; could not physically do some of the things, like reach high places and smash drywall; are not likely to entirely empty a fridge of its contents and not eat anything; or ignore rather than eat readily available candy lying around in dishes. The investigating police officer apparently saw a different picture:

> If there was any evidence to support the (homeowner's suspicions), we'd be pursuing it. He's just having a hard time accepting that two-year-olds can do that. He's never met these two-year-olds. There's absolutely nothing there that's beyond the realm of possibility with these kids. (Davis, 2005)

One objective of this book has been to locate today's issues about youth crime and justice in a historical context, so that we might unearth the myths, rhetoric, and ideologies behind current discourse about these issues. Related to this is a second objective: to understand the central role that the media play in this discourse, through a deconstruction of media images of youth crime by contrasting them to the facts. The "facts" of youth crime, as gleaned from wading through two full chapters of official statistics, tell us, quite simply, that very few young people in Canada are actually involved in criminal activity and the justice system, and that a majority of the offenders are involved in minor offences. Our look at the history of youth crime told us that these facts have not changed much throughout Canadian history, and that youth crime always seems to be an issue to every new generation of adults.

This then leads us to other questions about youth crime—and also about the media—that revolve around why youth crime is a public issue, what role the media play in defining and perpetuating the issue, what messages are sent by these images, and whether these messages have changed over time. How do these messages compare to the "social facts" of youth crime and the reasons and explanations for youth crime, as gleaned from research findings, youth voices, ethnographies, theories of youth crime, and statistical profiles?

This book is also about the juvenile justice system, so another objective has been to locate today's justice system in the context of youth justice reforms over the 20th century so as to understand the nature and dynamics of the system and current issues that revolve around it. Our examination of the history of juvenile justice and its structure tells us that there is a persistent cycle of juvenile justice, that reform has been an integral part of juvenile justice and also an issue, largely because there has always been a number of consistent yet conflicting principles and philosophies supporting the system. Our examination of research, case files, and voices from the system tells us that "Youth justice is a confusing and messy business" (Muncie & Hughes, 2004, p. 15) and, for far too many children and youth, it is also an injustice.

A lesson we should have learned from an examination of the history of juvenile justice and continued reform efforts is that our system is failing Canadian children and youth. As a society, we are failing to provide young people with the care and protection they need, and should be entitled to by the UN *Convention on the Rights of the Child.*

Bernard Schissel, a Canadian youth advocate, criminologist, and social reformer, speaks about his work in the following manner:

> When I hear stories about an elementary school child who works after school to buy clothes and food for his siblings; or who, after spending a sleepless night traumatized by drunken partying and fighting by adults, gets breakfast for her siblings, makes their lunches and gets them and herself to school, albeit in a disoriented and anxious state; or who, at the age of eleven, turns a trick and shares her bounty with other children to buy things at the 7–11, I am both humbled and ashamed. I am humbled by the strength, kindness and benevolence of children, especially in dire circumstances, and ashamed by a society that fails to provide for the families and the children who live on the margins and by the venomous adult public rhetoric surrounding youth that is unfounded, false, political and patently hateful. (1997, p. 127)

We should also have learned from the history of youth justice and youth crime that supervision and institutionalization are punitive, repressive control measures and are not the solutions to youth crime. At best, these are merely piecemeal efforts that focus on children, youth, and their parents as the source of problems. At worst, because they direct reform efforts from a focus on the kinds of issues raised by Schissel—marginalization and the ideologies that support it—supervision and institutionalization become mechanisms and tools that perpetuate injustices. Now we are faced with questions about why the justice system changed the way that it did;

why policies, practices, and programs that do more harm than good remain as part of the system; and, above all, whether contemporary advocates, reformers, and academics are doing anything in the continual reform process that will move the juvenile justice cycle in new and positive directions.

Answering the Questions

Answers to some of these questions were offered throughout this textbook through discussions of a variety of perspectives, traditions, and schools of thought. From the social constructionist perspective comes the view that "crime," "criminal," "dangerous," and myriad other labels associated with young people and their actions are social constructions, products of social activity and enterprise. The British cultural studies of the Birmingham School informed us about the specifics, dynamics, and consequences of these constructions: that public discourses about youth crime and justice are moral panics, and that youth are the measuring stick of all that is "good" about our society and all that adults hope and dream for regarding the future. At the same time, youth and children are scapegoats for all that is wrong in society and for all that adults fear about themselves. From this come the constant comparisons, from each new generation of adults, to the "good old days" when children and youth were not so "bad," "disrespectful," "criminal," "disobedient," and "out of control."

These labels are all moral statements about what adults fear, as opposed to what they value and wish for. Canadian filmmaker Michael Moore addressed these adult fears in his film *Bowling for Columbine*. Moore may be correct in the view that Canadians are not as fearful as Americans because we tend not to "lock our doors," but his film misses the larger point about fear. While Canadian adults may not be as fearful about their personal safety, they are as fearful about the future of their cherished values, beliefs, and way of life and any threat to it, as are Americans. There are many perceived threats, and a significant one is youth crime and the inability of the youth justice system to control it—this is the "youth crisis." We also have many examples of the news media as a powerful force in defining, shaping, and reinforcing these moral panics.

Media Texts The Birmingham School and, more recently, feminists, postmodernists, and other critical criminologists have made us aware that there are specific and consistent "texts" in public discourse: moral panics and "youth crisis" fears. These consistent texts revolve around intersections of race, class, gender, sexuality, and colonialism. These fears and sources of danger are not generalized—they are about poor black male youth, the male children of Asian immigrants, girls who transgress the boundaries of appropriate femininity, and Aboriginal youth who are members of gangs in core areas of major cities, to name but a few. And the discourse and constructions are not about behaviour that is problematic; they are about who is engaging in the behaviour or who is at the receiving end of the behaviour and why both are signals of danger.

Violence in itself is not considered a problem by most people, as is clearly evidenced by the amount of violence in contemporary Western culture that is eagerly shared in a variety of ways as "entertainment." Violence is constructed as problematic when white middle-class girls and boys are seen to engage in it and when the victims are white and middle-class, or adults, or the elderly. Child and youth victimization by adults is not problematized unless it is perpetrated by a stranger. While a "youth crisis" seems to arise with each new generation, the crisis changes when dominant hierarchies based on classism, racism, sexism, and heterosexism are challenged. Hence, as a backlash to feminism, the crisis of violent girls in public discourse has shifted focus from the dangerous girls of the 1990s, who were said to be more vicious than boys and men, to the nasty, mean, backstabbing, too assertive/aggressive girls of the 2000s (Chesney-Lind & Irwin, 2004). A case in point comes from a recent book by James Garbarino, *See Jane Hit* (2006), the cover of which features a little girl, 8 or 10 years old, reddish-blond hair in "pig-tails," blue eyes, very white/pinkish skin, and freckles, reminiscent of Anne of Green Gables. Unlike Anne, this little girl looks very mean and nasty. Her eyes are squinted and she has a scowl on her face. Inside, Garbarino warns of the dangers lurking as girls today move away from the "stifled femininity of the past." He states:

> Unless we see the trends emerging in the thinking and feeling of the new girl, the empowered girl, the unfettered girl, we shall not see her as she is. When she is good, she is very, very good. But when she is bad, she can be lethal. (2006, p. 193)

Locating Change: Global Context The juvenile justice system is a system of governance designed to set rules about how youth are to be governed, regulated, and managed. While this system is informed by moral panics and youth crisis discourse, it is also influenced and informed by larger changes at national and global levels. For example, as the international community moved toward establishing legal standards for human rights and then children's rights, so too did the Canadian government. This was reflected in the introduction of legal protections in the YOA and similar appropriate modifications in the YCJA, such as restrictions on the use of custody and a more legally correct mechanism for transferring more and younger youth to the adult system. These were changes that balanced international standards with the interests of Canadian lobby groups.

As Western governments responded to global political and economic forces, they also moved to a **neoliberal** form of governance, which some have referred to as more actuarial and managerial modes of governing and regulating (Garland, 1996, 2001; Rose, 1989, 1996). These modes entail setting targets and performance indicators to enable an auditing of efficiency and effectiveness, a costing and testing of all activities to ensure value for money (Muncie & Hughes, 2004, p. 5). Hence, as governing philosophies changed from a welfare orientation, with a rehabilitation focus, to a liberal orientation, with a justice/rights focus, to a neoliberal orientation, the juvenile justice system changed from the Juvenile Delinquents Act (JDA) to the YOA to the YCJA. With these changes also came a change in how we talk and think about youth and justice—from rehabilitating delinquents, to reintegrating young offenders, to the accountability of youth criminals, to concerns about "youth at risk" (concern for youth crime and its consequences or because handling such offences is a costly undertaking for government?) and the need for crime **prevention**/control (for public safety or to save money?).

As a case in point, it is worth noting that, since 2000, the Canadian Centre for Justice Statistics has been changing police reporting of statistics, collecting different kinds of information, such as on gang-related crime, and breaking youth apprehensions into categories of "charged" and "cleared otherwise." It is also changing how the information is distributed. Library branches of Statistics Canada are closing in some cities and information that used to be readily accessible, with librarian assistance, is now available only online in a condensed form or for a fee.

For its part, the federal government is busy funding Justice Department research projects about subjects of interest to governance, such as meta-analyses of "what works" in the area of therapeutic interventions and independent pilot tests of intervention programs with strict evaluation criteria. An integral part of these evaluation

neoliberal
A form of government that prioritizes setting targets and performance indicators to audit program efficiency and cost-effectiveness.

prevention
Policies and programs designed to curtail certain behaviours (e.g., criminal acts).

criteria is a cost of delivery analysis. Many of these government works have been used in this book to inform our understanding of youth crime, the justice system, and correctional programs. While the amount of information now available is impressive and useful, (albeit only to some), it also means that we have more information that is government-controlled than ever before. Stated differently, in the absence of independent academic research, the federal government controls what is known about crime and justice, more so now than ever before.

Locating Change: Criminological Context   Meanwhile, North American schools of criminology gave us a tradition of theory and research that offered an understanding of why youth engage in criminal and delinquent behaviours. A considerable amount of research activity revolved around testing these theories, mostly control and association theories, for their ability to predict rates of delinquency. Nonetheless, little effort was devoted to specific applications for developing programming from this work, other than three large-scale projects discussed in Chapters 5 and 6. First, from disorganization theory came the Chicago Area Project, which operated through the 1940s and 1950s under the direction of sociologists Clifford Shaw, its founder, and co-researcher Henry MacKay. The detached street worker was considered the most unique and promising feature of this project.

Next, from opportunity theory came the Mobilization for Youth Project in New York in the 1960s, which involved communities organizing for self-help, and in the 1970s, the California Youth Services Bureau, where community leaders and agencies hired professionals to deliver services to youth in their communities. The programming feature considered most important of the Youth Services Bureau activities was its (largely unsuccessful) attempts at developing diversionary programs (Krisberg, 2004, pp. 45–53).

Canadian programming efforts have tended to borrow bits and pieces of these projects, as well as of other small-scale experiments in the United States. Our history, similar to most of the United States outside of the large projects mentioned above, has been one of a hodgepodge of single-factor, single-agency approaches to programming (Krisberg, 2004, p. 129) based on a "flavour of the month" (Elliott, 2005, p. 244), that is, whatever appealed to staff in any particular agency. Most Canadian experiments in programming are still borrowing techniques from the United States; for example, multisystemic therapy applications have been imported from North Carolina. A primary reason for American leadership in this field is that American universities have an infrastructure to support large-scale criminology research projects that also includes generous government and corporate funding.

By the 1970s, Martinson's "nothing works" critique (1974), combined with the growing influence of labelling theory, paved the way for a philosophy of radical non-intervention (Schur, 1973) and diversionary policies and programs. Not only had "treatment" been demonstrated to be ineffective, but the fallout from the large-scale urban projects also contributed to notions that community restoration projects such as the Chicago Area Project were a wasted effort. Furthermore, the predominant view was that "leaving these juveniles alone most certainly would have been just as effective and far less expensive" (Lundman, 1993, p. 244). Non-intervention was seen as a good idea because it would keep most young people out of prisons or institutions, thereby reducing the contribution that prisons make to further criminalizing youth. Hence, the late 1970s and 1980s, in both Canada and the United States, became the era of community-based programming delivered through group homes and a variety of "residential" facilities.

Then came the large-scale, government-funded, longitudinal research agendas of the early 1990s, involving teams of American researchers such as Thornberry, Lizotte, Krohm, Farnworth, and Jang (1991), Thornberry, Huizinga, and Loeber (1995), and Kelley, Thornberry, and Smith (1997) that were based on their efforts at developing integrative theories to predict delinquency. Their work demonstrated that there are "multiple paths" to delinquency, opened the door to more developmental life course approaches to understanding delinquency "causation," and ended the single-factor approach to programming. They advocated for a "comprehensive community-wide approach" to programming that would involve "multiple aspects of a child's life" (Krisberg, 2004, pp. 128–129). These were the seeds for the multisystemic intervention approach to delinquency control and the end of a single-focus, single-program pattern of programming.

Control Texts The work of the teams of U.S. researchers in the 1990s also sowed the seeds for a new way of thinking and talking about delinquency control. In the history of delinquency theory, there has always been a gap between theory, the research that accompanies it, and actual programming for youth. Often, programs are developed in response to a need, such as probation developing in response to a need for supervision. While changing directions in programming may come from "flavour of the month" preferences, new directions, as we have seen, also come from innovative "border crossings," from theoretical and research directions that cross the boundaries between disciplines and perspectives.

Krisberg (2004, pp. 129–130) attributes the new directions of the 21st century to the work of David Hawkins and Richard Catalano (1992), who, by integrating concepts from the medical/health field with delinquency causation research, were able to bridge the gap between causation theory and programming. They argued that we all understand the notion of "risk" factors for disease, genetics, smoking, fatty foods, life style, etc., and also understand that there are "protective" factors against disease—steps to take to lower risks. By analogy then, delinquency causation theory could be used to identify risk and protective factors, and programming then becomes a simple matter of reducing risk factors and building and promoting protective factors.

Hawkins and Catalano (1992) developed a community planning model to accomplish these objectives: the Communities That Care model. This model borrows from control and attachment theory and social development theory, as well as empirical evidence regarding economic deprivation, parenting, and family conflict to develop a "risk" checklist. The checklist includes community risk factors such as the availability of drugs and weapons, economic deprivation, and low neighbourhood attachment, as well as family indicators and individual factors related to school and peers.

Many community- and justice-based organizations are using this checklist and its variations to make decisions about diversion and to develop programs, and some have carried the medical analogy to the level of "triage" programming. Some probation services departments, for example, use risk-level assessment to manage caseloads in a triage fashion. Simply put, high-risk youth receive more probation services than low-risk youth (Hillian & Reitsma-Street, 2003). Delinquency programming "talk" has finally moved away from theory into a realm conducive to neoliberal governing styles.

Science of Prevention As we enter the 21st century, we find ourselves in an era of "crime-prevention" discourse, not treatment and rehabilitation, and we talk about "at-risk youth," "resiliency," and "protective factors." In a climate of neoliberal governing strategies, crime prevention is the flavour of the era. To the extent that we do talk about remnants of other periods—treatment and reintegration and rehabilitation—it is done in the context of crime-prevention goals. We no longer treat youth for the purpose of rehabilitation, but rather to protect against risk factors and increase protective factors, both designed to enhance resiliency to the crime "disease," and, these interventions can occur in community or institutional settings.

It appears that a new science is developing—the science of crime prevention (Krisberg, 2004, pp. 125–144). A great deal of research energy and government (taxpayer) money is now devoted to developing assessment tools that allow an identification of high or low risk levels for individual youth. Programming strategies are designed and evaluated for their potential to reduce the risk of crime for individual youth and for communities.

A body of research is also beginning to develop around the cost-effectiveness of programming relative to criminal activity. The RAND Corporation in the United States is an example of an organization (noted for its conservative agenda) that sponsors evaluation research, and much of the focus of this research is on the relative costs of programming. For example, a graduation incentive program, where youth from low-income backgrounds are paid cash and other incentives to graduate, was evaluated and the results indicated that "graduation incentives save enough in averted crime costs to pay for the entire program." By way of contrast, home interventions would save enough in crime costs to pay for 20 to 40 percent of the program costs. Hence, home intervention is seen as a costly program (Greenwood et al., 1996, as cited in Krisberg, 2004, p. 141). Canadian programs funded through the federal crime prevention programs are required to provide similar cost-benefit analyses, as we saw with the multisystemic therapy program discussed in Chapter 10.

Martinson's (1974) legacy, in the context of neoliberal governance, is also found in the popularity of meta-analysis in the area of programming. This has become a useful tool for assessing the utility of programs and particularly for governments in deciding which project proposals will receive government funding for implementation. It too is a central component of the crime-prevention era, in that most program evaluation uses recidivism rates as its primary measure of "success."

Lip service is often paid to alternative outcomes, such as improved relationships with family members or improved self-esteem. The bottom line is that if these successes do not result in a reduction of criminal activity, the programs are considered a failure. Meta-analysis not only helps to identify "what works" in terms of risk reduction, but also how long it takes to reduce risk. In other words, Martinson's question has now become "How can we reduce crime in the cheapest way?" While crime-prevention talk is conducive to goals of restoration, it just as readily lends itself to the crime control agenda of more policing. Measuring program success in terms of recidivism feeds the crime control/law-and-order agenda.

Box 12.2 provides an example of the latest meta-analysis project from the federal Department of Justice, Research and Statistics Division, on "what works" in young offender programming. This government report, based on a literature review of all research evaluations of young offender programs that involved an independent evaluation and a control group (a requirement now of government-funded projects) makes a number of recommendations that are designed to ". . . provide direction to key decision makers, program developers and program funders" regarding programming for "youth in conflict with the law" (Latimer, Dowden, & Morton-Bourgon, 2003, p. i).

BOX 12.2

Recommendations for Successful Programming: What Works—30 Years after Martinson

1. Program:
   - treatment in a therapeutic environment using multiple forms of counselling (individual, group, and family);
   - limit program length to six months;
   - maximum 20 hours of programming for low-risk youth—"increase treatment dosage" for high-risk youth;
   - develop program manuals, measure "program compliance," provide staff training and supervision.

2. Behavioural/skill targets:
   - anger—provide anger management training;
   - antisocial attitudes—teach respect for authority and institutions of the justice system;
   - cognitive skills—problem solving, perspective taking, and goal setting;
   - social skills—training in communication strategies, how to work in groups.

3. Family skills:
   - positive communication skills (warmth, respect, honesty) within families;
   - teach parents appropriate skills to monitor and supervise youth;
   - meaningful family participation in programs.

4. Employment skills:
   - increase employment potential;
   - offer specific vocational training;
   - provide training in résumé writing and interviewing for jobs.

5. Community (where appropriate):
   - involve schools/educators in treatment programs and target school performance;
   - involve police, community leaders, and community agencies.

6. Ambiguous/less promising targets (include on a case-by-case basis, where appropriate):
   - address antisocial peers, substance abuse, psychological well-being;
   - leisure and recreation;
   - community functioning;
   - relapse prevention;
   - other non-criminogenic needs.

7. What does not work (does not reduce recidivism):
   - victim involvement;
   - general family therapy and non-specific family targets;
   - non-specific employment and school targets;
   - wilderness programs and boot camps (increase reoffending).

Source: Latimer, Dowden, & Morton-Bourgon. (2003), pp. 20–21.

The recommendations are based on 154 studies that met the criteria of involving independent evaluation and a control group, and were conducted over the period of 1964 to 2002 in Canada, the United States, the United Kingdom, and Australia. Most studies meeting the criteria for inclusion in the meta-analysis were from the United States, mostly involving male youth in urban areas. Missing from these evaluations (and, consequently, the recommendations for "what works") is a consideration of race, class, gender, and sexuality. The neoliberal language of crime prevention is apparent in the recommendations—"risks," "targets," "length of delivery"—as is the medical talk of "triage," "therapeutic environments," and "treatment dosages."

WHERE ARE WE GOING?

A third objective of this textbook has been to present juvenile justice as something other than a structure of laws, procedures, processes, and practices designed to respond to and control youth criminal behaviour, as is implied by the title of the youth justice system's legislation—the Youth Criminal Justice Act. Juvenile justice is more than law and its administration and system of governance. It is also a package that includes youth, their behaviour, and how we respond to it, both legally and informally, as well as the assumptions, beliefs, and philosophies that underlie both law and a system of governance and the laws, policies, and practices that develop from these.

The YCJA, for example, comprises merely the rules and regulations that provide a structure, objectives, procedures, and rules for the application of the Criminal Code and of sanctions to young people who have been accused or suspected of Criminal Code violations and a select few "special" YCJA violations. Understanding the YCJA and assessing how it is working involves an analysis of the beliefs, assumptions, and philosophies that underlie all of these aspects of the youth justice system.

With this in mind and with the foundation of what we know, we can now assess the directions we are pursuing in our efforts to understand youth crime and the directions in which youth justice is headed under the YCJA. An important part of this assessment involves a consideration of whether these directions are regressive or positive. Regressive policies and practices are ones that take us back to old practices or are "more of the same," keeping us exactly where we are or have been, but under the guise of new names and labels (Rothman, 1980). Positive policies will take us in new directions and hold promise for positive change in the lives of children and youth. Regressive policies perpetuate hierarchies of domination and injustice, while positive policies challenge and break down these hierarchies and offer solutions to injustice. For this assessment, we will look again at what is being done now in the thinking, practice, policy, and reform efforts.

Philosophy and Assumptions

Youth Scripts

While British youth criminology has always been focused on race and class, North American work, particularly that in the United States, tended to be more classless, with occasional references to "working-class" boys, and race was largely addressed in terms of "problem" visible minorities. As we saw in Chapters 5 and 6, the focus of discussion in North American youth criminology at one time was "youth," but the theoretical and empirical knowledge was largely about white working-class (or classless) boys. Both British and North American works were silent on "girl" questions. That has all changed. The feminist discussion about whether we need gender-specific theories has spilled over to other perspectives and traditions in criminology, and a trend in

VOICES BOX 12.3

Youth Reflections on the Consequences of Their Criminal Actions: Excerpts from Youth Letters Written as Part of Extrajudicial Measures Agreements

On Theft

When I was caught stealing . . . I was going through many different emotions, embarrassed to be in front of everyone at a time like that. I kept thinking, God help me, I really didn't mean to do it . . . I was mad at myself for putting this situation on me. I hurt my family, friends and especially myself.

If anybody ever reads this essay, and is thinking about stealing, take my advice and don't bother. Just walk away . . . I hope I never get into this kind of trouble again because it is not very nice to be worried all the time about dealing with the police, especially when you are 14 years old.

On Assault

If anybody ever tells me or dares me to do something I know isn't right, I'm not going to do it and neither should anybody else because you could get arrested, you could be sent to a home away from your family, you could get charged, you could lose your friends and might have a criminal record and won't get a very good job because people would be afraid of you . . . [T]he kid you beat up could have been a very good friend until you hurt him. I know now that I will never hurt anybody on purpose again . . . [W]hen I think of how the boy must have felt, I really get upset at myself . . . [N]obody likes to feel pain and somebody like me who gets beat up a lot should know that. Maybe I thought if I beat somebody else up instead of the other way around, it would make me feel tougher, but instead I felt stupid . . . I just take it a day at a time and wait for him to forgive me for what I did to him. I am really sorry for what I did to him and his parents and wish that it would never have happened.

To Victims

I am writing to you to apologize about the incident which occurred in your home. I feel extremely bad for what I did. I wish I had thought about what I was doing. I hate carrying around this guilt. I guess it's part of my punishment. I hate thinking about what I did. The more I think about it, the worse I feel. I'm trying to put myself in your shoes. I now realize how both of you must have felt, having a stranger come into your home and take something belonging to you. If ever anybody were to do something like that to me, I would find it extremely hard to forgive them for what they did. Nothing gave me the right to take something not belonging to me. I would understand if you can't forgive me. But I hope one of these days, you will find it somewhere in your hearts to accept my apology.

I am very sorry for all the pain I have caused in your life. Please forgive me!!! I have learned my lesson in all of this. I have changed my life right around. I spent time with my grandparents, my family and I am hanging around with a very good crowd. I would like to give a special thanks to the Y.A.S. [Youth Alternative Society] for giving me a chance, and most of all GOD.

Source: Youth Alternative Society files, Halifax/Dartmouth, Nova Scotia (n.d.).

criminology now is the search for the conditions under which a particular theory, hypothesis, or program will be effective. These "conditions" are most often defined in terms of race and gender, with class scripts assumed for both. "Black youth," for example, is still mostly assumed to mean "male and poor."

The significance of these former omissions for "new directions" lay in how criminologists are now attempting to correct them. Those whose work focuses on questions of omission, or what is missing, are now pointing our thinking in some illuminating directions. Still almost completely absent in thinking about youth is youth sexuality, in that "youth heterosexuality" is assumed in public and academic discourse.

The focus of youth sexuality, if it is addressed, is whether they are "active" or not. In neoliberal society, this is important information because to be "active" is to be in the "at-risk" category, and corrective measures of a preventive nature can come into play—preventing pregnancy or HIV/AIDS/STDs. Yet, we know from youth ethnographies and youth telling their experiences that, all too often, it is their alternative sexual orientation that led to being forced out of their homes and onto the streets. This does put these youth at risk of criminalization, but the corrective/preventive measures required are not so simple or cost-effective. That is, unless these measures involve repressive/punitive measures designed to pathologize and demonize anything other than heterosexuality. Opposition to same-sex marriage is a case in point. More productive and positive responses here would mean providing safe homes for youth and opportunities for affordable independent living. Yet, with cost-cutting measures as a government priority, this type of resource is few and far between and usually only available to youth in large cities, if at all (Balla & Balla, 2000, pp. 43–47).

Sexuality is present in the thinking about (assumed) heterosexual girls, but the discourse continues to sexualize girl behaviour and understand "girl crime" in terms of "promiscuity" or "vulnerability" to men and older boys who would exploit their sexuality by getting girls "hooked on drugs" or involved in criminal activity. While girls may be involved in prostitution to support drug habits and may be involved in crime to support their boyfriends, what is telling about the dominant discourse is that the reasons why girls are vulnerable are not problematized. Some of the most interesting work today comes from a socialist feminist and postmodern perspective, largely because it focuses on intersections of race, class, and gender and uncovers what is missing in the current discourse about girls. Reena Virk's murder and how it was talked about by the news media (see Box 12.4) is a case in point.

Femininity and "Erasing Race" A number of scholars analyzed the discourse (court trials and news coverage) about Reena Virk over the years that the accused youth were processed through the courts (Batacharya, 2004; Chakkalakal, 2000; Jiwani, 1999). The fundamental finding from this research is that, while overt discussions of race were absent in the discourse, what happened at the Gorge and how it was talked about were about race. It was a **racialized** discourse.

Explanations of "girl violence" usually stem from assumptions about what is essentially feminine; simply put, girls are not supposed to be violent. Explanations must focus then on ascertaining how "violent" girls are different from girls who are not: she is a sociopath, shows no remorse (the "bad" girl); she has herself been a victim of violence (the victim); or she is behaving like a boy (liberation or "too masculine"); or something more misogynist: girls when "aroused"/not controlled are "more vicious than boys." Kadi (1996, p. 64) maintains that these types of explanations are attempts ". . . . to make simple something that is not simple" and, further, that "girl violence is

racialized
A concept that allows an understanding of racism that goes beyond overt expressions and discriminatory actions of individuals, referring more to underlying assumptions in discourse and practice.

CASE STUDY BOX 12.4

Reena Virk and the Media

On November 22, 1997, the body of 14-year-old Reena Virk was found in a tidal inlet at the Gorge Waterway in Victoria, British Columbia. Drowning was offered as the official cause of her death, but she had also been severely beaten before drowning and had suffered "... internal injuries more common to a car accident than a teen fight ..." A 16-year-old boy and 15-year-old girl were accused and subsequently convicted, in adult court, of second-degree murder in her death. In addition, six other teenaged girls, aged 14 to 16, were charged with aggravated assault and convicted in youth court for their part in Reena's final ordeal. These youth were all part of the same friendship/peer network; they were not strangers to each other.

A number of explanations were offered in the news for this "girl violence." Some of the accused were said to be "wannabe" gang members, all were reported to have long histories of violent behaviour, one was said to display "all the elements of sociopathic conduct," another was described as having an "omnipotent attitude," and, as a group, the girls were said to be a "criminal clique." One girl's mother is reported to have called her daughter "a habitual troublemaker utterly lacking in remorse."

Even Reena and her behaviour were scrutinized in the media, and she was both pitied and blamed as the author of her own fate. She is reported to have lived in a foster home, to have been sexually abused by her father, and to have attempted suicide. At the same time, the same media reported that Reena ran away from home, according to her parents, "to gain more freedom," that she had lied about the sexual assaults attributed to her father, that she was self-conscious about her weight, and that she was caught in a "... downward spiral of plummeting self-esteem."

Early academic analyses of Reena's murder, while acknowledging the horrific manner in which she died, did little more than trivialize girls' lives and experiences, as attempts were made to understand and explain what happened. One girl was said to have stubbed out a cigarette on Reena earlier on the day of her murder and DeKeseredy (2000) asked, "Why would anyone want to socialize with such a cruel person?" His answer was that "... many young girls ... feel the need to be able to fit in and be part of the popular crowd" and that "many Canadian adolescent women ... are afraid of losing friends, having no friends, not having the 'right' friends, or not having enough friends. The 'reason' for Reena's death is that unfortunately the 'cool kids' did not want her friendship, and ... they made their position clear in a terrifying and deadly manner" (p. 2).

Source: Bell (2001).

---

an empty concept." It is based on a good girl/bad girl dichotomy that vilifies the "bad" girl and sexualizes the "good" girl as a "passive female." These are views that all fail to locate the "bad girls" as negotiating their survival within a context of violence.

The good girl/bad girl dichotomy was used as a defence in the Virk trials. The lawyer representing the young woman who was found guilty of Reena's murder used notions of white femininity as a defence. She was portrayed as "a person who loves animals, had positive and caring relationships with her family and friends, and posed a low risk to society in general" (Jiwani, 1999, p. 1)—all constructions of white femininity as non-aggressive, the dominant definition of "girl" in Western culture (Batacharya, 2004, p. 62). Hence, the implication was that this type of violence for her was "unimaginable as a white middle-class girl," she had merely fallen into "bad" company (Batacharya, 2004, pp. 75–76). We also see this dichotomy in the news discussions of Reena (Box 12.4).

This dichotomous view of girls ignores context and in so doing is a view that "erases race" (Jiwani, 1999, p. 3). According to Batacharya, (2004, pp. 62–63), such discourses fail to address "how racism, sexism, classism, ableism and heterosexism place girls in dominant and subordinate relationships to one another." Furthermore, she maintains that:

> Reena Virk was not a "bad girl." It is crucial to acknowledge her agency as she tried to negotiate between family, friends, teachers, and social workers in an effort to cope with the violence to which she was subjected. She was never only a victim and never only an agent (Handa, 1997, p. 78) but a young South Asian woman "caught between omissions" (1997, p. 58), trying to maneuver between various systems of oppression and the violence that was, and continues to be, simultaneously virulent and invisible. Labelling [the young woman convicted of murdering Reena] . . . as a "bad girl" is also problematic because her act of murder becomes defined through **hegemonic** notions of female deviance rather than analyzed with respect to her position of racial and class dominance. (Batacharya, 2004, p. 77)

hegemonic
Refers here to belief systems about power differences and how they are maintained and reinforce the interests of the powerful.

This analysis of the discourse on Reena Virk's murder has important implications for the current trend in justice systems, supported by the principles of the YCJA, to ensure that justice decisions and youth programs are sensitive to the needs of youth with regard to culture, gender, race, and ethnicity. While on the surface this is a potentially positive move in the direction of ending the perpetuation of injustice, it can easily turn into "more of the same" if the reasons or foundations for such programming are absent or misunderstood. In this sense, directives for "sensitive" programming become hollow rhetoric if the programs are not viewed in the context of an understanding of hierarchies of dominance. More specifically, teaching "bad" white middle-class girls how to be "good" white middle-class girls will do little more than perpetuate hierarchies of dominance and thereby perpetuate injustices against all girls. Such directives, devoid of understanding, easily lead to a "politically correct" diatribe and backlash.

Youth Justice

Two years after the introduction of the YCJA, when everything about youth crime was on the decline (police arrests; youth crime, particularly violent crime; use of courts; and the use of custody), a defence lawyer tried to use these statistics—including those indicating that Canada has one of the highest rates of youth incarceration among Western countries—at a sentencing hearing for a 14-year-old who was facing an "escape custody" conviction. The judge, Robert White, seemed unimpressed and is quoted in a newspaper article as saying:

> There are lies, damn lies, and statistics . . . It's funny, I hear the statistics, but in my 22 years as a judge, I've noticed just the opposite . . . These kinds of things [assaults, assaults by "females," violent offences, home invasions] have flowered since I've been a judge . . . I've heard the statistics, I know what people are saying. It just hasn't

proven true in my experience . . . you have to jump through hoops to get someone in court . . . all I can go by is my own experience . . . Maybe I'm too long in the tooth. (Fairclough, 2004)

In thinking about "where we are going," this is a quotation to ponder, as its implications are far-reaching regarding any efforts to effect change. It underscores the reality that changing laws and models of justice will not necessarily change practices, attitudes, beliefs, or philosophies, and that assumptions play a large role in the practices of the juvenile justice system and in any attempts to reform the system. As a side note, it seems clear that this judge has not considered how changes in police charging practices and the YCJA's introduction of extrajudicial measures provisions have likely affected what he sees in his court—more "serious" offences.

As we learned in earlier chapters, a different philosophy has worked its way into the justice system through a restorative model of justice (see Chapter 2, Table 2.1). Based on an assumption that crime harms the victim, the offender, and the wider community, the central philosophy underlying the restorative model is one of healing and peacemaking. The model is based on a belief that the central objective of justice should be one of repairing harms through a reconciliation of victims, offenders, and communities. This is a philosophy new to formal juvenile justice systems but one that has roots stretching back to the precolonial era. Liz Elliott (2005), in tracing the origins of **restorative justice,** maintains that it was used as a means of conflict resolution in communities throughout Europe prior to the development of the formal justice systems that we are familiar with today. In Canada, and prior to colonization, community-based justice was practised in Aboriginal communities as part of an overall holistic way of life, and these traditional practices are now being revived (Elliott, 2005, pp. 244–246).

The resurrection of traditional justice practices in Aboriginal communities began in the mid-1980s in Hollow Water, Manitoba, by a group of mostly Aboriginal women concerned about youth behaviour in the community. In the non-Aboriginal community, restorative justice principles began in 1974 in the Kitchener–Waterloo area of Ontario through the work of the Mennonite Central Committee and a probation officer who used the principles with youth who were vandalizing property. This initial project spread across Canada to other communities with Mennonite traditions and became known as the Victim–Offender Reconciliation Program (VORP). The program involves a meeting with a trained community mediator and the wrongdoer(s) and victim(s) to bring about a "greater understanding of the offence and to come to a restitution agreement." VORP was limited to minor offences and first-time offenders (Elliott, 2005, pp. 244–246). Box 8.8 in Chapter 8 provides an example from a VORP session.

VORP evolved in the late 1980s into a program that would include mediation for people affected by serious sexual assaults, robberies, and homicides, led by the Community Justice Initiative Association in Langley, British Columbia (Elliott, 2005, pp. 244–246). The initial non-Aboriginal restorative practices worked parallel to the existing justice system as a diversionary measure, began prior to the YOA and were eventually supported by alternative measures principles in the YOA. The Langley initiative is different in that it is not a diversionary program: it operates post-sentencing and can take months or years of working with offenders and victims before bringing them together for mediation.

Peacemaking The restorative justice philosophy has been reinforced by YCJA principles and is being practised through extrajudicial measures and provisions for sentencing

restorative justice model
A justice model that focuses on the harm caused by crime and seeks through responses to repair the damage done to offenders, victims, and communities.

peacemaking circle
An alternative method of resolving criminal conflicts, based on a healing philosophy.

conferences and Youth Justice Committees that act in an advisory capacity. The principal tool of restorative justice as practised today is the **peacemaking circle,** which is grounded in the belief that the responsibility for crime rests partly with the community, not solely with the offender and his or her family (Sharpe, 1998, p. 37). It is differentiated from more formal justice system decision making in that it is non-hierarchical in structure and is based on core values of equal support to all parties, equal power in decision making for all concerned parties, and the fostering of individuals' capacities for productive participation in the community.

In theory, peacemaking circles are structured so that all participants "share equal responsibility for the process and its outcome . . . [and] outcomes are decided by consensus" (Sharpe, 1998, p. 40). Three types of peacemaking circles are currently in practice in Canada in both Aboriginal and non-Aboriginal communities: the healing circle, the sentencing circle, and the community peacemaking circle (Stuart, 1997, p. 12). Healing circles work outside the formal justice system and bring people together to solve problems before criminal incidents occur; they also provide support for people already serving sentences.

Sentencing circles work inside the formal justice system. They are supported by and referred to in the YCJA as "sentencing conferences" and in some discussions as "circle sentencing." All refer to an alternative to standard sentencing practices, where the Crown and the defence make recommendations at sentencing hearings or make a "joint submission" to the court based on former meetings and agreements. The sentencing circle brings the Crown, defence, judge, court workers, and a number of other relevant professionals together, possibly with the offender and family members, for as many meetings as might be necessary. The purpose of these meetings is to gather information that will be useful in making decisions about sentences that will assist in the rehabilitation and reintegration of the youth. An example is the case heard by Justice Turpel-Lafond discussed in the last chapter.

Some Aboriginal communities, such as those in the Sto:Lo First Nation territory in the Fraser Valley in British Columbia, use sentencing circles that are part of formal justice proceedings but attempt to give responsibility for resolution to the community. This is done by involving community members in the circle meetings and having either a respected community elder or court judge chair the circle process (Hillian, Reitsma-Street, & Hackler, 2004, p. 350). Many other Aboriginal communities, such as the Elsipogtog First Nation in New Brunswick (Reid, 2005), are pressing their provincial governments for agreements that will allow community-based sentencing circles.

The third type of peacemaking, the community circle, is used in cases where criminal charges have or might be laid, and usually take place as a pre-plea form of conferencing, such as family conferencing. We have already seen the police activity in this regard that began before the YCJA, but now, because of YCJA provisions, some judges [for example, in York Region (Newmarket, Ontario)] are using this type of gathering in their courts.

While the YCJA allows for and promotes this new practice, how it is organized and structured is left to provincial governments and sometimes to local jurisdictions. In York Region, proceedings are recorded but the sessions are closed to the public and information provided by the youth is not permitted to be entered into proceedings if the case ends up in a court trial. Sessions are used as a mediation and conflict resolution tool and involve the offender and victim, their supporters, court officials and other professionals.

Some judges see this as a highly useful and productive form of "conferencing" because it allows them to make decisions about diversion or accepting a guilty plea with a full knowledge of the youth, the circumstances of the offence, and community resources available for assistance with rehabilitation and reintegration. Most important, according to Justice Fern Weinper, is that "the young person accepts responsibility for the behaviour and agrees with the conference plan knowing that the resolution was decided by consensus and a genuine concern for rehabilitation" (Hillian, Reitsma-Street, & Hackler, 2004, p. 386).

The sentencing circle is the most important of these peacekeeping circles because it is promoted by the YCJA as an integral part of the youth justice system and its principles of promoting rehabilitation, reintegration, "meaningful consequences," and community and victim involvement in these processes. It is not yet widely used, even in Aboriginal communities, because it is a costly undertaking that involves far more court time and use of "professional" time (Chartrand, 2005, p. 329; Hillian, Reitsma-Street, & Hackler, 2004, p. 350).

As we saw in earlier chapters, some have expressed concerns about net widening and how the practice of shaming is often used in a disintegrative way rather than as an integrative tool for restoration and integration. Others have pointed to concerns about the potential for professionals to bring long-standing practices into play in the circles. Sharpe (1998, p. 93) cautions that non-hierarchal structures can be undermined by professional domination if, because of the training, skills, and experience of professionals, they begin to dominate conferencing sessions, or for them and others to think that the professional "knows best." Similarly, to the extent that professionals are involved in conflict resolution on a regular basis, their participation may become routinized and the uniqueness of each case can be lost.

Perpetuating Injustice There is also a concern that these initiatives can too easily sustain and perpetuate existing injustices. Without government funding, careful planning, community resources, and community commitment to restorative justice principles, peacemaking circles are likely to develop only in some areas, be restricted to dominant languages, or exclude people who are not "easy" to serve, such as women with children who need baby-sitting services or people without money for transportation to sessions. Some people may be reluctant to participate if circles and meetings use language, vocabulary, and practices that are unfamiliar or uncomfortable, or if professionals and other community participants are drawn only from privileged groups (Sharpe, 1998, pp. 94–98).

An important challenge for peacemaking circles is to ensure that "vulnerable" individuals or groups are not subject to the tyranny of more powerful community individuals and groups (Griffiths & Hamilton, 1996, p. 188). Others do not trust or are not optimistic about the potential benefits of programs based on healing and restorative justice principles. In Nova Scotia, for example, women's groups successfully lobbied to have sexual offences excluded from the restorative justice process. Also, some Aboriginal women have insisted that Aboriginal men, including chiefs and elders, must be held accountable in the Canadian justice system for the harms they have perpetrated on women and children. Leaders of the Native Women's Association of Canada have also expressed reservations about First Nations self-government, fearing that women and children in First Nations communities will not be protected if local chiefs and national leaders do not address violence in their communities (Faith, 1993, pp. 200–201; Hamilton & Sinclair, 1991, p. 485). Within this context then, peacemaking circles and the healing philosophy have been problematized.

Koshan (1998) expresses concern about a perpetuation of injustice if victims feel compelled to participate in peacemaking circles because of community pressure to do so or because there are no other available options for recourse. Furthermore, she maintains that the issue of continued victimization of Aboriginal women and children needs to be addressed before practices based on a healing philosophy can be fully accepted and be effective. Furthermore, Nahanee (1995) argues that healing philosophies that bring benefit to Aboriginal offenders through lenient sentences violate the human rights of Aboriginal women who have been victimized. The issue is further racialized by Koshan (1998) when she states:

> Aboriginal women perceive as too lenient, and indeed racist, the "culturally sensitive" sentencing of Aboriginal men convicted of crimes of violence. Sentences which allow a violent offender to remain in his community are seen as imposing very serious risks for survivors and potential victims . . . Political and judicial support for community sentencing combined with the apathy or outright tolerance of some Aboriginal community leaders and elders towards violence against women may exacerbate these risks. (Koshan, 1998, pp. 40–41, as cited in Chartrand, 2005, p. 323)

While speaking specifically about Aboriginal women and children, as in the specific analysis of "girl violence" discourse, the larger issue raised here is that of perpetuating injustice through practices that perpetuate hierarchies of dominance and violence. Until these hierarchies and the hegemonic ideologies that support them are deconstructed and dismantled, peacemaking strategies, in spite of being a promising alternative to formal retributive systems of justice, become another tool of oppression.

Transformative Justice Just as Mennonite communities, through the Mennonite Central Committee, played a key role in bringing restorative justice principles to the practice of justice in Canada, people with a Quaker background have also played a central role in justice reforms, particularly with regard to prisons. Quakers have been advocating and working toward prison reform in North America since the 19th century when prisons were first developed and institutionalized through legislation as a means of responding to crime. Contemporary Canadian Quakers, through the Quaker Committee on Jails and Justice, represent the first religious body in the world to unanimously endorse prison abolition. Ruth Morris, now deceased, is, through her works and the people she inspired, a contemporary reformer working from this tradition (Morris, 2000).

With two graduate degrees in criminology and the experience of two justice system jobs, Morris's justice reform work began with prison reform. She explains the difference between Mennonite and Quaker reform work in the 1970s in Canada as one of Mennonites working "on the seeds of victim offender reconciliation and other ways of saying 'yes' to healing justice, [while] we Quakers were focused on saying 'no' to all that was wrong with the criminal justice system" (2000, p. 18).

Morris explains that in her prison work, she became aware of a "revenge spirit" that was at the core of the retributive crime control system then in practice. She was intrigued by the work of Mennonite friends in Kitchener–Waterloo, Dave Worth and Mark Yantzi, who were busy creating a victim–offender reconciliation program and talking about "something they called 'restorative justice'" (Morris, 2000, p. 18). What she found particularly intriguing was their insistence that reconciliation was "the spirit behind all true alternatives." From there, she began her crusade for restorative justice, one supported by Howard Zehr's *Changing Lenses* (1990), which she describes as the "Bible of the restorative justice movement."

It is the focus on bringing victims and communities into the justice system and bringing them together with offenders for reconciliation and healing that makes restorative justice an alternative to retributive justice. This is what drew Ruth Morris to restorative justice and kept her committed. Nonetheless, her experience of working with restorative justice for a few years made her dissatisfied with it as a "true" alternative and she became "disturbed" by "defects" in its theory and practice. She explains:

1. The very word restorative was unhealthy for victims. A victim's first instinct is to want the world back as it was. Until a victim is ready to move on from this, to recognize they can *transform* the world positively from their pain, but they can't *restore* the world as it was, their healing is blocked. Restorative justice . . . in practice encouraged victims in imagining that you can restore a past, before some trauma changed life forever.

2. Restorative theory did not take into account the enormous structural injustices at the base of our justice systems, and the extent to which they function mainly to reinforce racism and classism. Any theory or method that ignores the racism and classism that are basic to retributive justice is missing something very vital, and will serve to reinforce that racism and classism further, by not challenging it.

3. Related to both these points, the idea of restoring justice implied we had had justice, and lost it. In fact, distributive justice abounds everywhere, and most offenders are, more than the average person is, victims of distributive injustice. Do we want to restore offenders to the marginalized, enraged, disempowered condition most were in just before the offence? This makes no sense at all! (Morris, 2000, p. 19)

The most telling evidence of her critique came from her observations of "revenge-oriented" justice officials coopting the language of restorative justice and using healing in punitive ways. For example, a common expression among justice professionals was "I'm going to VORP that kid" (p. 19).

Critics of former justice system philosophies have asked, "Rehabilitate to what?" "Reintegrate to what?" The new question on the table is "Restore to what?" This takes us back to Aboriginal women's critique and rejection of the restorative model and an understanding of why they would argue that violence against women and children must be addressed before healing can begin. For them, the world before the violence began is the world before colonialism.

Transformative Processes There are successes in the application of restorative justice in practices of family and community group conferencing in Aboriginal peacemaking circles and now in sentencing circles. Ruth Morris (2000) saw these too and found that the successes involve not restoration but transformation. These were the instances where all the victims' needs were met, where the offender and offence were viewed in a social context, where communities were empowered, and both distributive injustices and the injustice of being victimized by a crime were addressed.

From these observations then comes the **transformative justice model**. This model sees crime as an "opportunity to build a more caring, more inclusive, more just community" (Morris, 2000, p. 21) and, importantly, issues surrounding crime are not separated from issues of distributive injustice. While healing is still an important component, it is not viewed as the end result, but as part of the path to

transformative justice model
Entails addressing the social inequities that existed before a crime was committed.

transformation. "Creative listening" is a critical tool for transformative justice. To truly "hear" what someone is saying requires empathy, caring, and a will to hear what is being said. Morris maintains that, contrary to the views of many justice officials, the more serious the offence, the more likely victims and offenders are to want to talk to each other.

While creative listening is a central tool, the key to the transformative process is "forgiveness." Transformation cannot occur until people let go of their anger, their rage, their desire for revenge. The difficulty of doing this explains why many victims refer to forgiveness as "the 'F' word." No one can know the extent and intensity of grief and pain experienced by victims and the families who are also victims, and many resent extremely those who "preach" forgiveness. Nonetheless, Morris maintains that forgiveness is more often given than not (2000, p. 202). In defence of finding paths and processes to forgiveness, she reminds us that "If we expect [offenders] . . . to deal maturely with their injustices, we need to use processes that enable all of us to do just that" (p. 203). Forgiveness involves commitment to a process of goodwill.

Victims' needs are central to the transformative model, not just needs that are a result of the offence, but also those that arise from events occurring after the offence. These needs are addressed in specific terms. For example, there is a need for "recognition of wrong," that their community recognizes that an injustice has occurred to them and that they are not to blame. This is particularly acute in instances of media coverage of crimes. Victims also want to feel safe again, and need reassurances from the offender and her or his community, family, and friends that they will be safe in the future. Restitution is also important, particularly for the most serious offences, but not in the sense of remaking the past—paying back what was stolen. This clearly is not possible for all offences, but even when it is, money or service is never sufficient. The victim needs the sense of restoration provided by a caring and secure community, whether that be a parent, welcoming family, or friends. For some victims, it comes from the offender's family and community (2000, pp. 10–13).

Most important are the questions to which all victims want answers: "Why me?" "Why my child?" "Why did my daughter get into your car?" or even: "Why did you take my computer and not the television?" Answers help in developing a sense of safety, that these things are preventable in the future, and in establishing that they were wronged and were not to blame. As Morris also explains, some questions are particularly painful ones. Family members, as victims, want to know about their loved ones' experiences, even if these are horrific. The answers give some sense of peace and closure even in these cases (Morris, 2000, pp. 9–10). More than any other victim need, this one requires talking with the offender(s).

In the McEvoy case that we have been following throughout the text, in the retributive system, the best that the family and community of Theresa McEvoy can do is request a public inquiry for answers to their questions. And, as we saw in Box 12.1, the best that the young offender Johnny could do was write a letter about his feelings, only to have them discounted by professionals. In both cases, justice professionals control the questions and the answers.

The last stage in transformation for the victim is "significance." After all is said and done and grief has gone as far as it can, there is a need to find meaning, or what Morris calls "significance." Victims need to feel there was some purpose or significance in what happened. This, she maintains, is when true healing begins. Most commonly, victims want to use their pain and grief to build a better world for others. The organization of Mothers against Drunk Driving (MADD) is an example. Often though, while finding significance is a healing and transformative process for the victim, the activities and organizations that flow from them work against transformative justice. MADD policies and lobby efforts to toughen sentencing for drunk drivers again stands as an example of organizational activities that focus on punishing offenders (Morris, 2000, pp. 13–14).

Community Change Model While the transformative model offers a significant and valuable critique of the limitations and potential pitfalls of restorative justice, one other model—community change—focuses on the role of community as a change agent. This **community change model** complements the transformative model because it too addresses issues of distributive justice and injustice. A difference between the two is that the community model looks more at the specific ways in which a community can address these inequities and injustices and has less of a focus on offenders. The view in this model is that preventing crime is the responsibility of communities, and that communities are also the source of crime: youth behaviour is seen as a product of life circumstances within communities. More specifically, this model assumes that people are active agents in their behaviour, that they make choices, including choices to behave in criminal ways, and that these choices are made "in the context of current possibilities and historical constraints" (Hillian & Reitsma-Street, 2003, p. 21). Reform is seen as the responsibility of communities, as is the development of effective responses to youth issues. In this model, community is seen as a societal community and also as a local community (see Reid & Zuker, 2005, p. 96) or as combinations of the two.

> **community change model**
> Looks at the specific ways in which a community can address inequities and injustices, and has less of a focus on offenders.

Hillian, Reitsma-Street, and Hackler (2004) and Hillian and Reitsma-Street (2003) have looked at the ways in which government and communities have worked together to affect change. They identify the ways in which the community is uniquely poised to meet needs (such as those of parents of victims and young offenders) that have not been addressed by the formal justice system, as well as the barriers to such community reform efforts. They point out, for example, that while a community model is apparent in the YCJA in that it is named as a participant in extrajudicial measures and Youth Justice Committees, governments often set barriers to realizing community involvement.

While many communities are eager to take on this role and some government bureaucrats are eager to work with community members, barriers can arise if governments are unable or unwilling to fund community initiatives. Hillian et al (2004) point out that it is not a simple matter of the amount of money involved, but that it is also one of funding arrangements; consequently, reform efforts often need to be directed specifically at government bureaucracy and policy. For example, caps on federal funding provided to provinces have a profound effect on programming for youth. Whereas the federal government used to fund 50 percent of the cost of custodial and non-custodial costs for youth, it now pays only 30 percent of these costs. Furthermore, there are issues around the jurisdiction and distribution of costs between custodial and non-custodial programs. The Standing Committee on Justice and Legal Affairs, in its report to government on youth justice as part of the YOA reform process in the late 1990s, recommended that 80 percent of these "shareable" costs should be allocated to non-custodial programs. Similarly, how government is structured also impacts on the distribution of resources at the community level.

Of importance here, Hillian and Reitsma-Street (2003) suggested, is whether youth justice is the purview of justice departments or child and family service departments. Justice departments are primarily oriented toward adults and matters of justice, while child and family service departments' primary objectives are matters of family and community. Clearly, community change reforms are more likely to be able to move beyond crime prevention and address issues of diversity, injustice, and inequity if they are working through government branches outside of a justice department.

Another shortcoming of the YCJA is that, while it promotes and encourages community participation and coordination of health, education, and social services, it does not require such linkages and leaves the responsibility of such matters up to provinces; hence, the importance of federal transfer payments and cost-sharing arrangements with provinces. Furthermore, while the federal government provides considerable amounts of funding for communities to start up crime-prevention programs, it does so in the context of reducing spending on social programs. Funding for social programs has been on the decline since the mid-1990s; for example, in British Columbia, all departments have had their budgets and staff cut by 30 percent since 2001 (Hillian & Reitsma-Smith, 2003, pp. 36–37); Hillian, Reitsma-Street, & Hackler, 2004, p. 361). Often community agencies struggle to sustain these programs and waste their scarce resources trying to do so rather than on delivering their programs.

Stepping Stone, an organization in Halifax that provides services for street sex-trade workers, has to struggle each year to maintain its government funding. Year after year, the organization has gone through a cycle of shutting its doors and closing down operations because the provincial government reduces its funding to inadequate levels or has cut its funding altogether. This is then followed by a flurry of news coverage, stories about "needy girls," "drug addiction," "pimps," and an assorted array of "expert" and "man/woman on the street" opinions, followed by increased and/or restored government funding.

In a similar issue related to significant cutbacks in government funding to agencies providing support for women and children's needs, Bill Estabrooks, an NDP MLA and Education critic, joined the public debate by suggesting that perhaps women should be looking after their own needs. Focusing on a prominent woman in government, he argued that women with government salaries *and* "wealthy" husbands should give up their salaries to support women's shelters.

System Reform

While youth justice is "messy business," so too is reform. More than one Canadian reformer, including Ruth Morris, has lost her or his job because of taking a stand or working from within organizations to try to change policy. People are often quietly "replaced" when new management enters the organization or, in the case of government bureaucrats, lose their jobs when there is a change in government as a result of elections and the philosophical and policy changes that flow from shifting governments.

While people attempting reforms can lose their jobs, reforms sometimes fail simply because of the amount of time and energy involved in a reform effort. Even change for something that is "obviously" problematic requires dedication, sustained effort, energy, and commitment from people and organizations. One such small-scale reform effort occurred in London, Ontario, and stands as but one of many examples of the complexity of reform on a small scale.

In London, a group of community people, brought together by the John Howard Society, worked to improve conditions for youth held in detention cells in the basement of the courthouse. The group consisted of people from a range of community organizations, including the Council of Women, the Black Congress of Women, the Catholic Women's League, and the Home and School Association. The concerns—things that reformers felt should have been "obvious" if for no reason other than that some of the practices were prohibited by the YOA—were that girls were detained in cells with women, boys aged 12 were in cells with boys aged 18, and no supervision and no activities were provided—just warehousing. More to the point, "psychic and sexual intimidation and assaults were common." Apparently, no one would take responsibility for change. Alternative detention arrangements were considered "financially prohibitive" and, it seems, no one from the court bureaucracy or politicians or government ministries wanted to take responsibility (*John Howard Society Magazine*, 2000, pp. 6–7).

The reform committee began its work in 1991; it took eight years for change to be effected. After the committee persuaded a member of the Office of the Child and Family Advocacy to "visit" the cells, the provincial government announced it would pay for the construction of six more cells to facilitate the separation of youth from adults and smaller boys from "bigger ones." The committee celebrated "a reserved" victory in 1999, even though the matters of lack of supervision and activities were not addressed. A side effect of the committee's effort was a policy change that gave detained youth with complaints easier access to the advocacy office. The then-executive director of the John Howard Society of London described her experience with this particular reform effort to change one very small (but not insignificant) thing as

> . . . the most frustrating thing I've ever been through. Strategy after strategy fell through. Sometimes they didn't believe us. The other thing is, we were talking about young offenders, and people don't care about them. (*John Howard Society Magazine*, 2000, pp. 6–7)

Ongoing Issues

Age and Privacy As we have seen, attitudes and philosophies about youth crime and justice play a major role in precipitating reform efforts and in the directions that reforms will move. On the other hand, these factors also play a role in keeping some issues alive and ensuring that others never go away. One issue that has been with us since the JDA is that of age of jurisdiction. The question of whether children and youth involved in serious crimes should be treated as adults was an issue under the JDA as early as the 1920s (Sangster, 2002, p. 175). As we have seen, with every successive **law reform,** the age of responsibility has changed, and provinces have retained jurisdiction over setting age differences within the 12 to 17 age range, thereby perpetuating inequities across the country.

law reform
The processes by which laws are changed.

While the YCJA has satisfied the law-and-order lobby to some extent by making transfer of youth to the adult system easier and by extending it to youth as young as 14, pressure remains to lower the minimum age from 12 to 10 and the maximum age from 17 to 16. Youth advocates and those concerned with inequity, injustice, and children's rights see the current age changes and proposals for lowering these ages as a significant erosion of the fundamental principle of juvenile justice and a significant step away from the UN *Convention on the Rights of the Child*.

A related rights issue is that of the loss of privacy protections, limited as they already are, when youth are subject to adult sentences; the public naming of young offenders is a particular issue. While youth advocates are concerned about the erosion of these rights in the YCJA, through adult sentencing provisions, the law-and-order lobby to lower minimum and maximum ages is one that would further erode the privacy provisions for even more youth.

Naming children and youth who have been convicted of Criminal Code offences is a purely punitive and repressive approach to reform. While promoted under principles of "deterrence," "protection of society," and the "rights of people to safety," there is no reason to believe that any positive outcomes would result from such a practice. Publishing young people's names is not likely to deter youth from crime, particularly if they are already marginalized—these youth already know that "people/adults don't like them"—they are already "Other."

If naming is an attempt at shaming, it is not likely to be effective because many youth in trouble are continually shamed, sometimes by their very existence, as is the case with street youth. This type of shaming has no reintegrative qualities and is clearly disintegrative. Nor is the threat or actual public naming of children likely to make parents act or feel more accountable. As a source of shame for parents, publicly naming their children as offenders would have disintegrative effects similar to those that it has for children. As the Canadian Criminal Justice Association sees it, "Parents who care for their children are [already] devastated when [their children] engage in crime, and those who have given up on their children, could not care less" (n.d., p. 8).

Johnny, whom we have been following throughout the book, is an unfortunate case in point. He, "the lost boy," is, and has been for most of his young life, living on the periphery of every aspect of his community. He is on the margins of his parents' lives and he is on the margins of the school community. The "only" thing he is good at and can enjoy is "stealing cars," so he is also on the margins of the law. It hardly seemed necessary to identify him publicly. His community already knew him—the school as "a failure with a learning disability," the police and courts as "a frequent flyer," and child and social services as a child in "need" and "at risk." It makes no sense to think that naming him in newspapers and television and radio newscasts, as was done once he was deemed liable to an adult sentence, will serve any protective or deterrent function for Canadian people as a whole. It probably has further humiliated him—an example of disintegrative shaming. Furthermore, people in Nova Scotia and far beyond, thanks to the extensive news coverage, now also know Johnny's mother.

Parental Responsibility Another issue that has been dragged along through 100 years of reform is that of parental responsibility. The law-and-order lobby advocates retribution and punishment for the parents or guardians of young offenders. The JDA allowed for a $500 fine and/or up to two years' imprisonment for parents or guardians of juvenile delinquents under two conditions: (1) if they knowingly failed or neglected to provide "that which would prevent the child being or becoming a juvenile delinquent," and (2) removing "conditions that render or are likely to render the child a juvenile delinquent" [JDA s. 33(2)]. The Commission on Juvenile Delinquency addressed the matter in its 1965 report and recommendations for reform of the JDA—the report that set in motion the 25 years of reform leading to the YOA. The commissioners recommended removing these provisions from the JDA, as they were firmly against submissions of proposals to "punish the parent," arguing that such laws would be ineffective and unproductive (Sangster, 2002, p. 175).

As we saw in Chapter 2, this seemed to be the predominant view of judges through the JDA era, as section 33(2) was seldom used and provisions for parental responsibility were dropped in the YOA. It seems that the law-and-order lobby has been trying to revive them ever since. As well as the now-defunct Reform and Alliance parties, other groups favouring parental responsibility laws include Victims of Violence and the Canadian Police Association (Groundswell against youth crime . . . , 1996; Manitoba parents . . . , 1997). Failing at the federal level, as the YCJA makes parents responsible only for their children's legal fees, the law-and-order lobby has had more success at provincial levels. British Columbia, Manitoba, and Ontario have all adopted parental responsibility legislation. If more provinces follow their lead, the issue in the future may become a legal one on matters of jurisprudence—something like "double jeopardy."

And again, there is no reason to expect that such laws will make parents any more responsible than they already are or feel that they are. There are at least two problems with wanting to "make" parents more responsible with threats of punishment. First, fining or otherwise penalizing parents for their children's behaviours is likely to intensify already negative family relationships or further penalize those already dispossessed. Such laws simply heap more injustices onto families already struggling with meagre resources, particularly single-parent families headed by women.

Johnny's mother is one of the parents that parental responsibility reform proposals want to penalize, and her story is all too typical. She is a woman who was as "responsible" as she possibly could be, given her life circumstances. She behaved "responsibly," even to the point of withdrawing her agreement to her son's "responsible person undertaking" and "begging" the courts to lock up her child. Newspaper youth crime stories are also full of similar stories from parents of young offenders, usually mothers. If we listen to these parents in the caring and empathetic manner that Ruth Morris advocated, we hear tales of anger and frustration and sorrow, not only about what their children have done, but about how the justice system and social services have failed them in their efforts to be responsible parents (Bell, 1993; Hillian & Reitsma-Street, 2003).

Similar to Johnny's mother's story, yet another Halifax mother whose son has been in and out of court for a number of violent offences, ranging from uttering threats, serious assaults, and attempted murder was featured in a news story. This mother reportedly wrote a letter to the court when her son appeared on the uttering threats charges "pleading for her son to be held in custody or treated at a hospital." She is quoted as saying: "Our pleas didn't mean anything . . . My biggest thing is that I would like people to know that the system didn't help him . . . I do believe that people choose the things that they do, but you do get cases where people do need help" (Arsenault, December 30, 2005).

New Issues

Parental Rights/Supports People caught up in the "blame the parents" component of the perceived youth crisis hear only an abdication of responsibility in these parent's stories. Blaming parents, blaming children, blaming children for abusing their parents (which also implicitly blames parents for not parenting their children to "natural hierarchies of authority") are all part of the "faulty parenting paradigm"—a paradigm that reinforces and perpetuates already existing injustices.

Viewing the issue of parental responsibility from the point of view of the community change model, Hillian and Reitsma-Street (2003) see a different problem. For them, the issue is not one of parents abdicating responsibility in parenting their children, but the justice system's abdication of responsibility in supporting the majority of parents who are trying, to the best of their abilities, resources, and circumstances, to be "good" parents. The YCJA offers nothing by way of actual support to parents who want to work with the system to have their children's needs met, albeit as a last resort. In fact, the history of youth justice gives testimony to stories of impoverished parents 100 years ago who, like Johnny's mother, willingly turned their children over to the justice system in the belief that it would give them a better chance in life.

The YCJA gives parents the right to be informed that a child has been apprehended or is to appear in court and also to read a pre-sentencing report. The act does not, however, address their needs or capabilities during these processes—it simply presupposes parental duties. Something seemingly as simple as not having a parent appear in court can have a negative impact on a youth's sentence (Bell, 1993; Hillian & Reitsma-Street, 2003). Hillian and Reitsma-Street tell the story of one single mother unable to attend court because she had no car and was required at home to care for a blind autistic daughter. Her son suffered because his mother was not in court—evidence of a "bad" parent.

Clearly, assumptions are being made about "good/bad" parenting by a parent's participation in the justice process. Yet, for their part, parents who do try to participate in the process tell stories of "feeling alone, ashamed, humiliated, and blamed," of "spending days on the phone" trying to secure appointments with various agencies and professionals. They complain about a lack of support for their activities, constraints on their participation, being left out, and being ignored. An example of the latter is a parent who was unable to secure probation services for a child because probation officers' time for casework is allocated according to a child's assessment of risk (Hillian & Reitsma-Street, 2003).

Parents' stories about their experiences in the formal justice system suggest new directions for reform, such as convincing provincial governments to provide supports and resources to parents who want to "be responsible." This requires thinking of responsibility as more than just control and discipline; the supports, services, and resources that address inequities are crucial. Parents continually speak of exhausting efforts to support their children and a lack of resources both in their own lives and in the justice system for them to do so. Legal reform—specifically, parents' rights in the system—is another important area for possible reform. The YCJA has opened doors with the potential inclusion of parents in conferencing and sentencing circles, and also in section 94(3), which allows parents the right to have their child's custody sentence reviewed after a specified period.

Release Conditions Release conditions comprise another critical area in need of reform that is likely to surface on the national scene as a result of the Nunn inquiry into the McEvoy case in Nova Scotia. Furthermore, we have seen that the number of youth in the system for administrative offences continues to escalate, and these youth are most likely to end up in custody. Again, Johnny is a case in point. As opposed to viewing administrative offences in terms of "bad children" or "bad parents," and directing reform toward punitive parenting responsibility legislation, perhaps a more positive approach would be to view this issue as one of "bad" release conditions (Green & Healey, 2003).

Regarding some common release conditions, it seems to make little sense to require youth to maintain a curfew if parents are not around to see that it is enforced or if, for whatever reason, parents are not able to enforce it with their children. Similarly, requiring youth to attend school when they are failing or are already alienated and marginalized is not likely to work. In this context, the YCJA provisions for intensive supervision combined with appropriate programming holds the potential for a more appropriate response than a custodial sentence for youth who breach probation, fail to appear in court, escape custody, or run from detention. It also has the potential to address the over-representation of Aboriginal youth, girls, and other visible minority youth in custody.

In the light of information unfolding from the Nunn inquiry into Johnny's case, and remembering Justice Turpel-Lafond's experience in trying to find out what would work in terms of releasing a youth to the community, reform in the area of release conditions would appear to require changes in at least three areas: the practice and process of release conditions; the lack of supports and resources for parents and the community; and lack of supports and resources provided to the court and other justice professionals. Such reforms would also encourage or require a cooperative/collaborative approach involving the justice system and the social, health, and educational branches of government.

Interestingly, in the federal government's law reform process (discussed in Chapter 2) the task force recommended a coordination of youth services (Report of the Federal–Provincial–Territorial Task Force on Youth Justice, 1996, pp. 630–631), but the standing committee failed to do so. Nonetheless, some provinces are coordinating services. Ontario and British Columbia combine education and social services, while the Yukon combines health and human resources. Quebec never abandoned a coordinated approach to youth issues. What is needed in a more general sense is a commitment on the part of government to short-term crisis intervention and long-term support for youth and their families and communities. Simply coordinating government departments is not sufficient; government efforts need to be integrated with the community in ways that make all parties equal partners. Again, Youth Justice Committees provide a mechanism to make this happen, but community effort is required to establish such committees.

Furthermore, reforms must focus on involving youth in both the community and in the justice system as more than "offenders" so that they develop a sense of being genuine stakeholders. One community-developed program to involve youth is the Youth Empowerment and Success Program in Whitehorse. Early in the program's development, community youth were asked what help they needed. It was their idea to have a resource centre rather than a drop-in centre. They wanted a place where they could participate in literacy programs and programs designed to prepare them for jobs. At the centre, youth are also involved in social activities and have organized a "talking circle" and their own youth magazine (Bula, 1996).

Of course, the definition of "community involvement" is open for debate. Does it mean bringing professionals into community activities? Or does it mean empowering community members to take responsibility for, and control of, their own problems? Empowerment of community members is required if such initiatives as Youth Justice Committees and community sentencing circles are to offer true alternatives to punishment and the revenge motive. What is of interest regarding such initiatives is that they are not new. Community-based reform and involvement were tried 50 years ago in the Chicago, California, and New York delinquency projects and were considered "failures." Nonetheless, they are relevant once again because important lessons can probably be learned by revisiting these early efforts at community empowerment and involving young people in reform processes.

CYCLE OF JUVENILE JUSTICE

Finally, in thinking about juvenile justice reforms, it is useful to be reminded again of what Thomas Bernard (1992) said about reforming juvenile justice—that it is a cycle, ever moving from punishment to leniency and back to punishment, where the cycle begins again. To this we now can add that reform is also something like a spiral; we do make some progress. In other words, while the system may progress from a retributive punishment model to a more "lenient" restorative model, continued pressures from the law-and-order lobby will draw the system back toward the retributive model, but not all the way. Not all youth are back in the adult system—yet. The challenge for reformers who work for positive change, one that moves away from retribution and is geared to stopping harms and injustices, is to block the regression and put reforms back on the track to positive change.

Bernard (1992) also argues that juvenile justice is a cycle because people believe that policy causes crime. Lenient policy is believed to raise crime rates because it is "a slap on the wrist" and "get-tough" policies are believed by others to cause crime because "they teach young people how to be better criminals" and sometimes provide motivation toward crime. Hence, it is important to realize that no justice-related policy is ever going to change perceptions about crime—some people will always be unhappy about the justice system.

Social policy changes are needed to change criminal activity and this requires changing people's beliefs, assumptions, and philosophies about crime, changing the focus of thinking about crime issues. Some reform models, for example, do not focus on crime at all, as we see in the transformative justice model. Given that we are not likely to ever "stop" crime, reforms and policies that refocus thinking toward stopping the harms and injustices will make a positive difference in many people's lives. Graduation incentives, for example, do help some young people to stay in school. Stay-in-school allowances would probably also keep kids in school. Focusing on stopping harms and injustices will also make it more difficult for regressive reform proposals to gain a strong hold and begin the reversal of the cycle.

This means changing the questions that are asked about youth crime and how we respond to it. Instead of asking, "How can we stop crime?" and thinking in terms of crime prevention, we need to ask, "What do we need to do to improve people's lives?" And any answers need to go beyond skills training for the individual or the family. Answers need to come in forms that will reconnect people and their communities. This is the promise of the restorative, transformative, and community change models of justice. Restorative ideas as reflected in the YCJA's Youth Justice Committees have potential for immediate positive changes, while the transformative model alerts us to the weaknesses, pitfalls, and limitations of the restorative model and can assist in preventing cooptation by the retributive model. The community change model offers ways of thinking that promote a level of community caring that goes beyond risk assessment and triage responses to youth and their families who are in trouble. Both the community change and transformation models requiring thinking about responses that go beyond the justice system and crime prevention.

Anti-bullying programs in schools are a case in point. Positive reforms in the area of bullying require "crime prevention" in the community and not in the form of simple school expulsions of a child into a community that also does not want him or her (as we saw in the "Johnny" case studies). Crime-prevention policies need to be restorative and transformative. Rather than teach kids how to "cope" with violence and punish those who behave in violent ways, children need to learn how to live together in harmonious ways, how to be peacemakers themselves. Alternatives need to be a part of the response to ensure that all children are included, especially those already damaged by violence and depredation. School policy needs to go beyond teaching children and youth "anti-bullying and management skills" and stepping up security to make schools safer places for middle-class children. Responses to "bullying" need to make schools more caring places that respond to the needs of all children.

Above all, only the transformative and community change models allow us to address what is still missing from youth justice system reform—youth marginalization; child poverty; homeless youth, children, and their families—all issues of distributive justice/injustice.

In this regard, there are two absolute essentials that must be addressed in youth justice reform. The first takes us back to Schissel's point about alternative schools (1997), which is not so say that we need more alternative schools, but rather that we need fundamental changes in the school system. Such changes will have to start in the community through school boards. What makes Princess Alexandria School and Joe Duquette High School in Saskatoon and St. Peter's College Alternative High School in Muenster, Saskatchewan, stand apart as true alternative school models is that they are youth-centered, they adopt a human-rights approach to children, and they are designed to meet the needs of the youth they serve. This is a switch in focus from looking at education as "teaching and learning" to one of looking at schools as part of the community's service to youth. In Schissel's words:

> . . . these schools are . . . simple and effective; they are profound in their egalitarianism, wisdom and understanding towards disadvantaged and abused youth; and they are proactive, they reach out to the youths and the community to help personal and community healing . . . they are based on empowering youth through the ideals and practices of respect, community and concern for the future.
> (1997, p. 120)

The other essential focus for reform efforts is the Safe Homes for Kids concept advocated by Whitbeck et al. (2001, pp. 1200–1202). No matter what other programs are implemented, residential facilities must be provided for abused and neglected children and for young people who, for whatever reason, are not able to live with their families. These alternative living arrangements must not follow a corrections model, as they have in the past, with strict rules and punishments for violations. Rather, homes for children and youth must provide a caring, supportive environment. As with the alternative school model, they must be youth-centered, based on a human-rights approach to children, and designed to meet the needs of children and youth.

Runaway and homeless youth are the most victimized, the most vulnerable, and the most in need of protection, not only from the street, but also from uncaring, insensitive, adult authority figures. Young people (and their families, where appropriate) need to be protected from the life-threatening dangers of the streets and, in addition to shelter and independent living arrangements, also require street workers and outreach agencies (Miller et al., 2004, pp. 752–754; Schissel & Fedec, 1999, pp. 51–52; Webber, 1991, pp. 239–248).

SUMMARY

In thinking about how to respond positively to youth crime and in wondering if the YCJA will contribute anything positive to the cycle of juvenile justice reform, we might begin by contrasting the view expressed earlier in the chapter by Justice Robert White of Kentville, Nova Scotia, who believes that youth violent offences have "flowered" and is concerned that "you have to jump through hoops to get someone in court"

(Fairclough, 2004) with the view of Justice Fern Weinper of York Region (Newmarket, Ontario), who says:

> The young people of this country are our future. How we respond to this important legislation—whether we act decisively and deliver sensible justice for youth who never asked to be brought before us, whether we just pay lip service—will determine the type of society we convey to future generations. (Harris, Weagant, Cole, & Weinper, 2004, p. 386)

An important lesson to be learned from the history of juvenile justice in Canada is that supervision and control by means of probation and institutionalization have not solved youth crime problems. In order to achieve genuine reform in the juvenile justice system, we need to stop recycling programs that have failed in the past and start thinking about alternative solutions. Alternative solutions will be those that focus on all aspects of child and youth issues, not just criminal activity. They will also involve a coordinated approach to services that goes beyond the boundaries of the justice system and that addresses the "whole child."

Most importantly, alternative solutions will bring to the forefront of the reform agenda the issues of marginalization, colonization, child poverty, children's rights, homelessness, and violence against children and youth. These solutions will be developed to meet the needs of youth and children, rather than to fit into the limited and potentially regressive crime-prevention paradigm. This will be a far more rewarding reform effort for all concerned than one with a goal to stop crime—something that is not likely to ever happen.

Now that we have new legislation that is based on what Canadians knew 10 years ago when this last law reform project started, we want to know how it is working and where it still needs to go. We have seen throughout the text that the YCJA has kept elements of the previous two youth law reform efforts, and it has also set the stage for new restorative directions. Small-scale reform efforts will continue to push the system ahead in the direction of restoration or back in the direction of "older" models. Since there are principles from many models in the YCJA, how far we go in the direction of the new model, restoration, will depend on the strength of conviction of those working in the justice system and of reformers. The key question for all of these parties in their day-to-day decision making involves a juggling of principles and boils down to "How important is safety relative to restoration and healing?"

The larger question in terms of reform comes from considering our goals. If the objective of the last reform that introduced restorative justice principles into the system is to repair harms and restore a sense of justice to all parties, then the critical question is "Restore to what?" Stated differently, the key question is whether restorative efforts aimed at offenders, victims, and their families can work to repair harms. In some cases the answer may be "yes" but in many others, the answer will be "no" because an individual or family has been struggling for far too long for survival in a hostile and damaging environment. In these instances, we cannot expect restorative intervention to work and need alternative models to continue moving in positive directions—transformative reform directions.

Much about youth crime and justice could not covered in this text, simply because there is not enough book space or course time to cover it all. The most important omission is the one that locates these issues in the global context, the discussion of the politics of reform and crime prevention. We were able to merely touch on these earlier in this chapter and elsewhere in the text. Nonetheless, it is important to know that it is not only Canadians who are struggling with these issues. Many Western countries are working through the same issues, and for the same reasons. Western governments everywhere are facing similar pressures as they move to neoliberal governing strategies, including the United States, Britain, Australia, and New Zealand. The cycle of juvenile justice propels the reform process everywhere, and we continue to influence and be influenced by reforms in other countries.

Moral panics and "youth crisis" media texts revolve around intersections of race, class, gender, sexualities, and colonialism. The discourse and constructions are about who is engaging in the behaviour or who is at the receiving end of the behaviour and why both are signals of danger. Violence is constructed as problematic when white middle-class girls and boys are seen to engage in it and when victims are white and middle-class or adult or elderly. Child and youth victimization by adults is not problematized unless it is perpetrated by a stranger. The "youth crisis" changes when dominant hierarchies based on classism, racism, sexism, and heterosexism are challenged.

As a system of governance, the juvenile justice system is informed by moral panics, youth crisis discourse, and broader changes at a global level. Western governments have moved to a neoliberal form of governance, one involving more actuarial and managerial modes of governing and regulating (Garland, 1996; Rose, 1989, 1996). There is now more information about youth crime and its administration than ever before, but more of this information is now controlled by the federal government than ever before.

North American schools of criminology gave us a tradition of theory and research, some of which was applied in large-scale delinquency prevention projects in the United States: the Chicago Area Project in the 1940s and 1950s, the Mobilization for Youth projects in New York in the 1960s, and the California Youth Services Bureau in the 1970s. All were considered "failures." Canadian programming has tended to borrow bits and pieces of American efforts, which has amounted to a hodgepodge of single-factor, single-agency approaches to programming. Large-scale, government-funded, longitudinal research agendas of the early 1990s in the United States sowed the seeds for the current multisystemic intervention approach to delinquency control.

The terms "at risk," "resiliency," and "protective factors," all part of crime-prevention discourse, can be traced to American researchers who applied medical/health concepts to delinquency causation theory. This work is all part of a new "science of crime prevention" that involves research to develop assessment tools to identify "risk levels" for individual youth, to evaluate the cost-effectiveness of programming relative to criminal activity, and to carry out meta-analyses of program evaluation research. Programming strategies are designed on the basis of meta-analysis of "what works" and evaluated for their potential to reduce the "risk" of crime for individual youth and for communities in a cost-effective manner.

Still almost completely absent in thinking about youth in general is youth sexuality. Generally heterosexuality is assumed of youth in public and academic discourse. Sexuality is still not absent in thinking about (assumed) heterosexual girls in discourses that continue to understand girl behaviour in sexualized ways. Some of the most interesting work today comes from a socialist, feminist, and postmodern perspective. "Girl violence" is largely understood in public discourse as a good girl/bad girl dichotomy that ignores context and "erases race" (Jiwani, 1999, p. 3). Directives for "sensitive programs" can easily turn into a "politically correct" diatribe and backlash without an understanding of hierarchies of dominance.

The principal tool of restorative justice as practised today is the peacemaking circle. It is differentiated from more formal justice system decision making in that it is non-hierarchical in structure. There are three types of circles: healing, sentencing, and community circles. Circles are commonly referred to as "conferences" or "conferencing." Community circles take place outside the formal system and work best in relation to diversionary measures, while sentencing circles work inside the formal justice system and are being used to develop sentences that are geared to an individual's needs. Some warn that peacemaking circles can too easily become tools of oppression. Other critics of restorative justice argue that it is unable to meet victims' primary need for healing, does not take structural injustices into account, reinforces classism and racism, and fails to recognize that restoration is not possible for many victims and offenders.

Two alternative justice models, transformative justice and community change, borrow what is productive and positive about the restorative justice model. Transformative justice is offered as a true alternative to retributive justice. This model sees crime issues as issues of distributive justice and crime as an opportunity to address these issues. Healing is the beginning of the transformation process. Creative listening and forgiveness are the critical tools for transformative justice. Victims' needs are central to the transformative model and include a need for a recognition of wrong; a need to feel safe; a need for restitution; a need for answers; and a need for significance. The community change model also addresses issues of distributive justice and injustice, and focuses on the specific ways that community can address these inequities and injustices. It has less of a focus on offenders. The view in this model is that preventing crime is the responsibility of communities and that community is also the source of crime.

Ongoing reform issues include minimum and maximum age limits, privacy protection, and parental responsibility. New issues include parental rights and needs, including an active involvement in the justice system decision-making processes involving their children. Release conditions and their role in escalating youth involvement in the justice system have yet to be addressed and are an area that requires reform. Other important issues that are central to positive justice system reforms are youth marginalization, child poverty, and homelessness. Essentials in a positive reform process are alternative schools, safe houses for youth, and street services.

DISCUSSION/CRITICAL THINKING QUESTIONS

1. When are girls presented in discourse as vulnerable and when are they not? What are the policy implications of these views?
2. What are the implications of assessing and evaluating the costs of crime prevention? What is gained? What is lost?
3. What does "alternative" mean in the area of justice reform?
4. Why is the question "Restore to what?" such a significant one?

WEB LINKS

Hope Now for Youth
www.hopenow.org/history

Youth Justice: Tell us what you think/Online discussions for students
www.epals.com/projects/justice/justice2.tpl

Justice for Children and Youth
www.jfcy.org

Community Plan on Vulnerable Youth in London, 2004
www.london.ca
In the site's Search window at the top of the screen, enter the words "Vulnerable
Youth." The title of the above document is in the list that will appear.

For chapter quizzes and more links, visit this book's accompanying website at
www.bellyoungoffenders3e.nelson.com

GLOSSARY

(Numbers in parentheses refer to the chapter(s) containing the main discussion of the term.)

Administrative charges – Charges laid for behaviours that are not generally considered to be criminal (e.g., failure to appear in court). (3)

Administrative offences – These are offences that involve interference with the administration of justice. (3)

Aftercare – Any range of programming and services provided after a young person has completed his or her court-imposed sentence or extrajudicial measures contract. (10)

Aggregated – Statistics on crime and other social behaviour are deemed aggregated when they are grouped into categories that make it impossible to match individuals on other characteristics. (3)

Alternative measures – A variety of programs under the YOA, such as mediation, designed to prevent future crime and divert youth from the courts. (8)

Androcentric – Refers to seemingly gender-neutral ideas, concepts, or theories that are actually male-centred. (7)

Androgynous – Describes terms that are assumed to refer to both males and females (e.g., "gangs"). (6)

Anomie – A term coined by Émile Durkheim, referring to a state of "normlessness" or no rules. (5)

Antisocial personality – Psychological classification of people with traits of impulsivity, insensitivity to their own pain or the pain of others, and a lack of guilt or remorse. (5)

Behaviourism – A branch of psychology based on a set of behavioural principles first developed by B.F. Skinner. (5)

Bifurcated – Divided into two parts. (2)

Birth cohorts – A group of people born in the same time period. (4)

Boot camp – In the corrections system, a place of confinement where programming follows a militaristic regime. (10)

Broken homes hypothesis – The commonly held proposition that children from divorced and single-parent families are more likely to be delinquent. (7)

Care ethic – An ethical or moral standard based on nurturing attitudes of caring for the welfare and well-being of others. (6)

Child savers – A term used to refer to 19th-century North American middle-class reformers who were instrumental in the creation of a separate system of justice for juveniles. (2)

Chivalry hypothesis – A belief that crime rates are lower for women and girls because people are less likely to view their behaviour as criminal. (6)

Classical school of criminology – The school of thought that assumes people are rational, intelligent beings who exercise free will in choosing criminal behaviour. (5)

Clearance rates – Refers to statistics that indicate the rate at which police process criminal incidents as charged offences. (3)

Cognitive – Having to do with mental processes and how we develop knowledge about and understanding of ourselves and the world around us. (5)

Cognitive skills – In the field of corrections, refers to the ability of people to develop cognitive solutions to their problems rather than to react emotionally and physically. (10)

Community change model – Looks at the specific ways in which a community can address inequities and injustices, and has less of a focus on offenders. (12)

Concept – A general or abstract term that refers to a class or group of more specific terms (e.g., "crime" refers to any number of specific behaviours). (3, 5)

Conditional supervision order – Requires a person under supervision to abide by particular conditions set by the court (e.g., attend drug or alcohol rehabilitation programs). (10)

Conditioned – In behaviourist theory, refers to behaviours that have been patterned to repeat or stop by a regime of rewards or punishments. (5)

Consensus theory – In criminology, refers to a group of theories based on a fundamental assumption that people are essentially law-abiding. (5)

Control theory – Refers to a group of theories premised on an assumption that people will operate on the basis of self-interest unless constrained. (5)

Correctional programming – A range of structured activities within a correctional system, designed to rehabilitate, educate, train, and otherwise facilitate a person's reintegration into society. (10)

Correctional services – In this text refers to custodial institutions and programs as well as probation supervision and services for young offenders. (10)

Corrections – The part of the justice system that is responsible for carrying out the sentence of the court and/or alternative and extrajudicial measures. (10)

Crime control model – A theoretical model representing a retributive set of beliefs and philosophies about crime and justice. (2)

Crime index – Statistics Canada categorization scheme for classifying police crime statistics as property, violent, and "other" index crimes. (3)

Criminal event – An event involving the convergence a motivated offender, a suitable target or targets, and the absence of controls. (6)

Criminalization – The process whereby a person comes to be officially and/or publicly known as a "criminal." (6)

Criminalize – A term that differentiates between referring to a person as a "criminal" and the process whereby individuals come to be viewed as "criminal." (7)

Critical perspective on crime – Refers to the group of theories that begins with the assumption that structures of power and oppression are the source of crime (i.e., race, class, gender, and to some extent, age structures in society). (6)

Cycle of juvenile justice – Refers to the tendency toward a never-ending cycle of juvenile justice reform common in Western society. (2)

Cycle of violence – The theory that when children witness or experience violence, they are more likely to experience or initiate violence as they get older. (4)

Decarceration – The practice of moving individuals from institutional settings into community facilities and programs. (6)

Deconstruction – A method of interpreting texts, movies, TV programs, and other cultural symbols and practices. (6)

Decontextualize – Remove something from its context. (1)

Deferred custody and supervision order – A sentence option created by the YCJA that is similar to "house arrest" sentences for adults. (10)

Delinquent subculture – A concept used in early criminology theory to explain youth crime. (5)

Demographics – The basic or vital statistics of a group, usually factors such as age, gender, ethnicity, marital status. (1)

Denied adulthood – Refers to the notion that youth, because of their legal dependency in Western society, are prevented from attaining the things that many adults take for granted, such as the right to make decisions about their own lives and the right to express their views. (1)

Determinate sentences – Sentences with a stated minimum and maximum term. (10)

Deterrence – The theory that certain and speedy punishment will discourage or prevent future criminal behaviour, both in a general and specific manner. (9)

Development theory – Focuses on states of development and posits inadequate development or failure to progress to higher states in explaining criminal and delinquent behaviour. (5)

Differentially affected – Refers to the idea that there is a gender gap in youth crime rates because boys and girls are affected differently by criminogenic conditions. (7)

Differentially exposed – Refers to the idea that there is a gender gap in youth crime rates because girls and boys have different exposure to criminogenic conditions. (7)

Discourse – How things are talked about and understood, both orally and in written form, including formal talk such as theory; professional talk such as reports, books, and media; and conversations. (1)

Discretion – The decision-making power that police and other criminal justice personnel (e.g., judges and Crown prosecutors) have to make decisions with minimal legal requirements. (8)

Diversion – A practice based on a philosophy that justice, rehabilitation, and reintegration are better served by keeping most people out of the formal justice system. (8)

Empirical – An adjective describing knowledge that is based on observation, experience, or experiment rather than on theory or philosophy. (3, 5)

Equality – A liberal-based philosophy or belief that all is, or should be, the same. (11)

Ethnicity – A person's group of origin, where origin is usually thought of in terms of geographical place and/or elements of culture (e.g., language, style of dress, behavioural patterns, social customs). (4)

Ethnographic method – A research method that involves richly detailed descriptions and classifications of a group of people or behaviours. (4)

Etiological – Having to do with cause or origin. (7)

Eugenics – A branch of science based on a belief in genetic differences between groups that result in superior and inferior strains of people. (5)

Eurocentric – Beliefs, attitudes, theories, philosophies, and practices that are specific to European experience, thinking, and world views. (11)

Extrajudicial measures – Under the YCJA, refers to processing accused young offenders by means other than through the youth court or adult justice system. (8)

Extrajudicial sanctions – Under the YCJA, refers to provisions that provide for specific sanctions and rules regarding the use of more formal diversionary programs when cases proceed to the court level. (8, 9)

Extralegal factors – Factors affecting criminal or youth justice processing that are outside the jurisdiction of law. (8)

Fact – In everyday terms, a fact is usually something that is considered to be true. In a scientific sense, a fact is something that has been established through the research process. (5)

Family structure – How families are structured in terms of living arrangements (e.g., a traditional nuclear family or a single-parent family). (7)

Field research – A method in which research is conducted outside of a laboratory, in the setting where the behaviour of interest is occurring. (3)

First Nations – Compared to the term "Aboriginal," "First Nations" has clear political connotations because it defines a group in historically specific terms. It means the first people who were a nation (i.e., a people with legal and political standing). (4)

Gender – The socially constructed aspects of a person's biological sex. (4)

Gendered expectations – What is expected of a person because of his or her biological sex characteristics. (9)

Guardian – A person who has been given legal authority over and responsibility for another person. (9)

Healing principle – A principle of justice based on the philosophy that crime is an injury requiring the healing of severed relations among the offender, the victim, their families, and the community. (11)

Hegemonic – Refers to belief systems about power differences and how they are maintained and reinforce the interests of the powerful. (12)

High-risk youth – Youth with characteristics and/or living circumstances that are known to be criminogenic. (8)

Human ecology – A branch of behavioural science that examines the relationship between people and their physical environment. (5)

Incapacitation – Basically means to deprive a person, so to put someone in prison is to incapacitate her or him in an absolute and fundamental manner. (9)

Indeterminate sentences – Sentences that are not absolute or definite. (10)

Indictable – In the Canadian Criminal Code, refers to offences that are of a serious nature; the maximum sentence is never less than two years. (2)

Intensive rehabilitative custody and supervision order – A term created by the YCJA that refers to a sentence of the court whereby a youth must serve a custody term in a facility designated as a rehabilitation institution. (10)

Interactional theory – Posits that relationships between delinquent behaviour and other variables are not unidirectional, but rather are bidirectional. (6)

Interim release – Provisions that allow an arrested person to be released into the community, under specific conditions, while waiting for a court appearance; commonly referred to as "bail." (9, 10)

Jurisprudence – The science and philosophy of law and its practice. (9)

Justice model – Refers in this text to a philosophy and orientation to criminal justice that posits the rule of law as the primary means of achieving a "just" justice system. (2)

Juvenile delinquent – A concept popularized in the Victorian era, referring to children and youth who were considered problematic for a variety of reasons. (1)

Juvenile justice system – A system of laws, policies, and practices designed under the guiding philosophy that children and youth, because of their age and maturity, should not be subject to criminal law in the same manner as adults. (1)

Law reform – The processes by which laws are changed. (12)

Legal advocate – The role of a lawyer in making decisions and acting in the best interests of his or her client, to ensure that the client has every possible legal advantage. (9)

Liberation hypothesis – A belief that women's and girls' criminal behaviour is becoming more like that of men and boys because of the women's liberation movement. (6)

Lifecourse developmental theory – The theory that children undergo a succession of role and status changes as they grow older. (6)

Life skills – The behavioural, emotional, and philosophical skill set that one acquires to enable functioning in the social world. (10)

Limited accountability – Children and youth are held accountable by the justice system, but in a limited manner compared to adults. (2)

Longitudinal studies – A research method in which data on a group of people are collected over a number of time periods, rather than at only one point in their lives. (4)

Marginalized – A condition in which people are excluded from mainstream society. This exclusion can be economic, social, cultural, political, or all four. (1)

Median sentence length – A statistical term meaning that sentences in half the cases are above the median sentence length and half are below. (9)

Mediation – A form of conflict resolution that involves a third party, usually a person with professional skills, to assist two parties with a grievance or unresolved matter to reach a mutually agreeable solution. (8)

Meta-analysis – A type of analysis in which the unit of analysis is the research results from other research reports. (7)

Microscopic approach – In sociology and criminology, refers to theoretical approaches that focus on individuals and behaviour in small social settings rather than in the context of larger social structures. (7)

Minorities – Groups of people who do not form the political, social, and/or cultural majority. (11)

Modified justice model – A particular model of criminal or juvenile justice that is not in strict adherence to a pure justice philosophy. (2)

Monolithic – A single, uniform, undifferentiated idea or structure. (11)

Moral panic – Refers to situations where people, groups, circumstances, or events are defined and perceived to be a threat to security and public order. (1)

Multisystemic therapy (MST) – A form of rehabilitative integration that focuses on the entire family, not just on an individual. (10)

Neoliberal – A form of government that prioritizes setting targets and performance indicators to audit program efficiency and cost-effectiveness. (12)

Net widening – A tendency for policies seemingly designed to reduce the number of people in the justice system to inadvertently result in more people under state control. (8)

Official crime – Offender and offence data based on information collected for administrative purposes by justice agencies such as the police, courts, and correctional institutions. (1)

Open custody – A form of youth custody under the YOA that required fewer restrictions on movement, both within and outside an institution, than was required for secure custody. (10)

Oppression – The negative outcome experienced by people due to physical force by an oppressor or structural arrangements (e.g., laws and political policies) that remove or restrict their rights. (6)

Parens patriae – A doctrine based on English common law that gives the state the power to take on a guardian or parenting role for children. (2)

Patriarchy – A set of structural relations that creates, reinforces, and perpetuates male dominance and control over women. (6)

Peacemaking circle – An alternative Aboriginal method of resolving criminal conflicts. (12)

Penitentiary – A 19th-century term for prisons based on a philosophy of penitence and punishment to atone for wrongs. (1)

Politics of youth crime – The ways in which youth crime is understood and talked about, both formally and informally, and the actions, laws, and policies that usually derive from this discourse. *Also,* the mechanisms and methods whereby youth activities are socially constructed as criminal; the meanings and imagery attached to these definitions and the types of responses they generate. (1, 7)

Positivist – An 18th-century philosophical, theoretical, and methodological perspective positing that only that which is observable through the scientific method is knowable. (5)

Postmodernists – Those who reject or challenge all that has been considered to be modern. (5)

Power – The ability of a person or group to force others to do what they wish. (6)

Power-control theory – Attempts to explain class and gender differences in delinquency by the structure of family relations, whether egalitarian or patriarchal. (6)

Presumptive offence – Under the YCJA, a serious violent offence, or any other violent offence for which an adult would be liable to a prison sentence of more than two years. (9)

Presumptive transfer – Under the YCJA, the automatic transfer of a youth case to adult sentencing provisions. (9)

Pretrial detention – The holding of an accused person in a prison or detention facility prior to a court appearance or trial, or while awaiting sentence; sometimes also referred to as "remand." (9, 10)

Prevention – Policies and programs designed to curtail certain behaviours (e.g., criminal acts). (12)

Primary data – Research information gathered directly from the original source. (1)

Principle of least possible interference – The principle that whatever action is taken should have the least impact on a youth's freedom. (8)

Probation – A sentence of the court that involves supervision in the community and set conditions that must be adhered to if the person is to remain in the community. (2)

Problematize – A process whereby something, someone, or some group is defined as a problem. (1)

Proportionality principle – Maintains that a sentence should be proportional to the offence that a person is guilty of committing. (9)

Public issues – Matters of public concern that are debated in a variety of forums and involve demands for action. (1)

Race – A socially constructed category based on beliefs about biological differences between groups of people that have no basis in scientific evidence. (4)

Racializes/Racialized – A concept that allows an understanding of racism that goes beyond overt expressions and discriminatory actions of individuals, referring more to underlying assumptions in discourse and practice. (4, 12)

Reconciliation – An important component of the mediation/healing process, based on the belief that a productive response to crime is to encourage all affected parties to participate in conflict resolution. (8, 11)

Reformatories – A 19th-century term for juvenile prisons that were based on a belief in the ability of prisons to reform or change an individual. (1)

Rehabilitation – A correctional philosophy based on the belief that appropriate treatment programs can reform or change an individual. (9, 10)

Rehabilitative philosophy – A belief that the right treatment can change a person's attitudes, values, and/or behaviour. (1)

Rehabilitative treatment – Rehabilitative programs based on assumptions of correcting individual pathologies. (10)

Reintegration – A correctional concept referring to policies and programs designed to introduce offenders back into their communities as productive, participating, law-abiding members. (2, 9, 11)

Relational aggression – An indirect form of aggression that is interpersonally oriented and focused on controlling relationships, rather than direct forms of aggression that involve physical force. (7)

Reliability – In behavioural science, refers to the extent to which variable measurement and research findings can be or have been repeated. (3)

Remand – To hold an accused person in a prison or detention facility prior to a court appearance, trial, or while awaiting sentence; sometimes also referred to as "pretrial detention." (10)

Remedial solutions – Programs designed to help overcome a weakness as opposed to correct a problem. (4)

Reparation – In restorative justice models, this involves offenders making amends in any of a variety of ways to their victims for the harm done by the offence. (2)

Research – A systematic process of information gathering, analysis, and reporting of findings. (5)

Restitution – Payment in money or kind to compensate victims for their loss. (8)

Restoration, reconciliation, reintegration – In the context of a restorative justice framework, these related concepts refer to restoring balance by repairing harms. (9)

Restorative justice model – A justice model that focuses on the harm caused by crime and seeks to repair the damage done to offenders, victims, and communities. (2, 12)

Retribution – Punishment for an offence committed. (9)

Reverse discrimination – Occurs when policies designed to end discrimination against one group inadvertently create discrimination against another group. (11)

Role theory – Attempts to explain criminal behaviour by understanding the processes whereby individuals acquire and become committed to deviant roles. (6)

Secondary data – Research information or data that was originally collected for another purpose. (1)

Secure custody – A form of youth custody under the YOA that required more restrictions on movement, both within and outside an institution, than was required for open security. (10)

Self-fulfilling prophecy – A prediction or assumption that, in being made, actually causes itself to become true. (3)

Self-report surveys – Criminology questionnaire surveys, in which individuals are asked to report on their involvement in criminal or delinquent activities. (3)

Semiotics – The study of signs and symbols. (6)

Sentencing circle – Often used in Aboriginal communities; judges sit with community members to decide on an appropriate sentence for an individual case. (11)

Sentencing conference – A meeting of a group of professionals to make recommendations to the court about appropriate sentences for individual cases. (9)

Social bond – The social ties that hold people together, cause people to care about each other. (5)

Social capital theory – The theory that people possess varying degrees of useful and valuable social resources (e.g., supportive family and neighbours and an education or good grades in school). (7)

Social class – Generally refers to one's economic position or standing in a particular social structure or society. (7)

Social control agencies – Usually government agencies mandated to perform various functions in the justice system, such as police courts and correctional institutions. (3)

Social injustice – A situation in which groups of people are disadvantaged relative to others because of societal laws, policies, or practices. (11)

Social learning theory – Attempts to explain crime and delinquency through notions of imitation and modelling. (6)

Social order – Refers to assumptions about society as free of disorder. (6)

Socioeconomic status – Similar to social class, but specifically refers to a person's social standing or position in terms of education, occupation, income. (4)

Status offences – Behaviours considered to be illegal only because of the age status of the individual (e.g., truancy). (2, 4)

Stigmatization – The detrimental consequences for an individual of having a negative label or definition attached to his or her behaviour. (8)

Strain theory – A group of theories that argue in a variety of ways that blocked opportunities are a cause of problem behaviours. (5)

Structural – Refers to how something is ordered and organized, how its parts relate and connect to each other and to the whole. (1)

Surveillance – Mechanisms and processes by which the state keeps track of people and monitors their behaviour. (8)

Telescoping – A problem faced by researchers conducting self-report or victimization surveys: people tend to lump offences that may have occurred several years ago into something that occurred "last year." (3)

Theory – Integrated sets of propositions that offer explanations for some phenomenon. (5)

Tracking – School policies that group and stream students into different programs based on their performance on standardized tests. (7)

Training schools – A common term for juvenile correctional institutions before the introduction of the Young Offenders Act. (10)

Transformative justice model – Entails addressing the social inequities that existed before a crime was committed. (12)

Unfounded offences – Events investigated by the police as potentially criminal offences that are determined not to be offences. (3)

Validity – Refers to the extent to which research variables have been measured in a way that is consistent with the theoretical concept, or what was intended. (3)

Victimization survey – A survey questionnaire that asks individuals whether they have been victimized over a particular time period, and in what ways. (3)

Welfare-based juvenile justice system – A model of juvenile justice based on a rehabilitative philosophy. (2)

Zero-tolerance policies – Policies related to the intolerance of behaviour that is considered undesirable. (3, 7)

REFERENCES

Abramovitch, M., Peterson-Badali, M., & Rohan, M. (1995). Young People's Understanding and Assertion of Their Rights to Silence and Legal Counsel. *Canadian Journal of Criminology, 37*, 1–19.

Abramovitch, R., Higgins-Bliss, K.L., & Biss, S.R. (1993). Young persons' comprehension of waivers in criminal proceedings. *Canadian Journal of Criminology, 35* (3), 309–322.

Acland, C.R. (1995). *Youth, Murder, Spectacle: The Cultural Politics of "Youth Crisis."* Boulder: Westview Press.

Adelberg, E., & Currie, C. (1988). *Too Few to Count.* Vancouver: Press Gang Publishers.

Adler, C., & Worrall, A. (2004). A Contemporary Crisis? In C. Adler & A. Worrall, (Eds.), *Girls' Violence: Myths and Realities.* Albany: State University of New York Press.

Adler, F. (1975). *Sisters in Crime.* New York: McGraw-Hill.

Adler, F. (1981). *The Incidence of Female Criminality in the Contemporary World.* New York: New York University Press.

Agnew, R. (1985a). Social Control Theory and Delinquency. *Criminology, 23*, 47–61.

Agnew, R. (1985b). A Revised Strain Theory of Delinquency. *Social Forces, 64*, 151–167.

Agnew, R. (1990). Adolescent Resources and Delinquency. *Criminology, 28*, 535–566.

Agnew, R. (1992). Foundation for a General Strain Theory of Crime and Delinquency. *Criminology, 30*, 47–88.

Agnew, R. (1993). Why Do They Do It? An Examination of the Intervening Mechanisms Between "Social Control" Variables and Delinquency. *Journal of Research in Crime and Delinquency, 28*, 126–156.

Agnew, R. (2001). Building on the Foundation of General Strain Theory: Specifying the Types of Strain Most Likely to Lead to Crime and Delinquency. *Journal of Research in Crime and Delinquency, 38* (4), 319–361.

Akers, R. (1973). *Deviant Behavior: A Social Learning Approach.* Belmont, CA: Wadsworth.

Akers, R. (1977). *Deviant Behavior: A Social Learning Approach* (2nd ed.). Belmont, CA: Wadsworth.

Akers, R. (1985). *Deviant Behavior: A Social Learning Approach* (3rd ed.). Belmont, CA: Wadsworth. (Reprinted 1992. Fairfax, VA: Techbooks.)

Akers, R. (1994). *Criminological Theories: Introduction and Evaluation.* Los Angeles: Roxbury Publishing.

Albonetti, C. (1991). An Integration of Theories to Explain Judicial Discretion. *Social Problems, 38*, 247–266.

Alksnis, C., & Robinson, D. (1995). *Childhood Victimization and Violent Behaviour among Adult Offenders.* Ottawa: Correctional Service of Canada.

Allen, R. (1991). Preliminary Crime Statistics–1990. *Juristat, 11* (9). Ottawa: Statistics Canada, Canadian Centre for Justice Statistics.

Alvi, S. (1986). Realistic Crime Prevention Strategies through Alternative Measures for Youth. In D. Currie & B. Maclean, (Eds.), *The Administration of Justice.* Saskatoon: University of Saskatchewan, Department of Sociology.

Anand, S. (1999). The good, the bad and the unaltered: An analysis of Bill C-68, the Youth Criminal Justice Act. *Canadian Criminal Law Review, 4*, 249–270.

Anand, S. (2003). Crafting Youth Sentences: The roles of rehabilitation, proportionality, restraint, restorative justice and race under the *Youth Criminal Justice Act. Alberta Law Review, 40* (4), 943–963.

Anderson, K. (1996). *Sociology: A Critical Introduction*. Scarborough, ON: ITP Nelson.

Andrews, D.A., & Bonta, J. (1994). *The Psychology of Criminal Conduct*. Cincinnati, OH: Anderson.

Annual Report of the Several Departments of the City Government of Halifax, Nova Scotia, for the Municipal Year 1898–99. Report of Chief of Police, 76.

Antonowicz, D.H., & Ross, R.R. (1994). Essential components of successful rehabilitation programs for offenders. *International Journal of Offender Therapy and Comparative Criminology, 38*, 97–104.

Archambault, R.O. (1986). Young Offenders Act: Philosophy and Principles. In R.A. Silverman, J.J. Teevan, & V. F. Sacco, (Eds.), *Crime in Canadian Society* (3rd ed.). Toronto: Butterworths.

Armstrong, F. (1997, September 30). Cabbie's killer chooses prison. *The Chronicle Herald* [Halifax], A6.

Armstrong, G. (1977). Females Under the Law—Protected but Unequal. *Crime and Delinquency, 23*, 109–120.

Arsenault, D. (2005, December 21). Mom: Cops slammed son's head on steps—Woman launches complaint about handling of teen's arrest. *The Chronicle Herald* [Halifax], B5.

Arsenault, D. (2005, December 30). Accused killer's mom: Boy needs help—Teen arrested six times for weapons, drugs but "every time ... they let him go." *The Chronicle Herald* [Halifax], A1.

Artz, S. (1998). *Sex, Power, and the Violent School Girl*. Toronto: Trifolium Books.

Artz, S. (2004). Violence in the Schoolyard: School Girls' Use of Violence. In C. Alder & A. Worrall, (Eds.), *Girls' Violence: Myths and Realities*. New York: State University of New York Press.

Artz, S., Nicholson, D., & Rodriguez, C. (2005). Girl delinquency in Canada. In K. Campbell, (Ed.), *Youth Justice in Canada*. Toronto: Pearson Education.

Asquith, S. (2004). Justice, retribution and children. In J. Muncie, G. Hughes, & E. McLaughlin, (Eds.), *Youth Justice: Critical Readings*. London, UK: Sage Publications Ltd.

AuCoin, K. (2005). Children and Youth as Victims of Violent Crime. *Juristat, 25* (1). Ottawa: Statistics Canada, Canadian Centre for Justice Statistics.

Augimeri, L.K., Goldberg, K., & Koegl, C.J. (1999). *Canadian Children Under 12 Committing Offences: Police Protocols*. Ottawa: Department of Justice, Canada.

Austin, G., Jaffe, P., Peter, G., Leschied, A., &. Sas, L. (1985). A Model for the Provision of Clinical Assessment and Service Brokerage for Young Offenders. *Canadian Psychology, 25*, 54–62.

Awad, G. (1991). Assessing the Needs of Young Offenders. In A. Leschied, P. Jaffe, & W. Willis, (Eds.), *The Young Offenders Act: A Revolution in Canadian Juvenile Justice*. Toronto: University of Toronto Press.

Bachman, J.G., Wallace, J.M., Jr., O'Malley, P.M., Johnston, L.D., Kurth, C.L., & Neighbors, H.W. (1991). Racial/ethic differences in smoking, drinking, and illicit drug use among American high school seniors, 1976–89. *American Journal of Public Health, 81*, 372–377.

Bailey, I. (1995, July 27). "Violence panic" hitting nation. *The Chronicle Herald* [Halifax], A11.

Bala, N. (1988). Young Offenders Act: A Legal Framework. In J. Hudson, J.B. Hornick, & B. Burrows, (Eds.), *Justice and the Young Offender in Canada*. Toronto: Wall and Thompson.

Bala, N. (1989). Transfer to Adult Court: Two Views as to Parliament's Best Response. *Criminal Reports, 69* (3), 172–177.

Bala, N. (1992). The Young Offenders Act: The Legal Structure. In R. Corrado, N. Bala, R. Linden, & M. Le Blanc, (Eds.), *Juvenile Justice in Canada: A Theoretical and Analytical Assessment.* Toronto: Butterworths.

Bala, N. (1994). What's Wrong with the YOA Bashing? What's Wrong with the YOA? Recognizing the Limits of the Law. *Canadian Journal of Criminology, 36,* 247–270.

Bala, N. (2003). *Youth Criminal Justice Law.* Toronto: Irwin Law.

Bala, N. (2005). Community-Based Responses to Youth Crime: Cautioning, Conferencing, and Extrajudicial Measures. In K. Campbell, (Ed.). *Understanding Youth Justice in Canada.* Toronto: Pearson Education Canada Inc.

Bala, N., & Anand, S. (2004). The First Months under the Youth Criminal Justice Act: A Survey and Analysis of Case Law. *Canadian Journal of Criminology and Criminal Justice,* 251–271.

Bala, N., & Clarke, K.L. (1981). *The Child and the Law.* Toronto: McGraw-Hill Ryerson.

Bala, N., Hornick, J., McCall, M.L., & Clarke, M.E. (1994). *State Responses to Youth Crime: A Consideration of Principles.* Ottawa: Department of Justice, Canada.

Bala, N., & Kirvan, M. (1991). The Statute: Its Principles and Provisions and Their Interpretation by the Courts. In A. Leschied, P. Jaffe, & W. Willis, (Eds.), *The Young Offenders Act: A Revolution in Canadian Juvenile Justice.* Toronto: University of Toronto Press.

Bala, N., & Mahoney, D. (1994). *Responding to Criminal Behaviour of Children under 12: An Analysis of Canadian Law and Practice.* Ottawa: Department of Justice, Canada.

Balla, M.J., & Balla, S.C. (2000). *Forty Years of Community Commitment.* Ottawa: The Youth Services Bureau.

Bandura, A. (1977). *Social Learning Theory.* Englewood Cliffs, NJ: Prentice-Hall.

Barber, J., & Doob, A.N. (2004, April). An Analysis of Public Support for Severity and Proportionality in the Sentencing of Youthful Offenders. *Canadian Journal of Criminology and Criminal Justice,* 327–342.

Barnhorst, R. (2004). The Youth Criminal Justice Act: New Directions and Implementation Issues. *Canadian Journal of Criminology and Criminal Justice,* 231–250.

Baron, S.W. (1995). Serious Offenders. In J.H. Creechan & R.A. Silverman, (Eds.), *Canadian Delinquency.* Scarborough, ON: Prentice Hall Canada.

Baron, S.W. (2001). Street Youth Labour Market Experiences and Crime. *Canadian Review of Sociology and Anthropology/Andropology, 38* (2), 189–216.

Baron, S.W., Forde, D.R., & Kennedy, L.W. (2001). Rough Justice: Street Youth and Violence. *Journal of Interpersonal Violence, 16* (7), 662–678.

Barron, C.L. (2000). *Giving Youth a Voice: A Basis for Rethinking Adolescent Violence.* Halifax: Fernwood.

Barron, C., & Lacombe, D. (2005). Moral Panic and the Nasty Girl. *Canadian Review of Sociology and Anthropology, 42* (1), 51–69.

Baseball bat boy often misbehaves, born addicted to crack, court told. (2003, July 4). *The Daily News* [Halifax], 3.

Batacharya, S. (2004). Racism, Girl Violence, and the Murder of Reena Virk. In C. Adler & A. Worrall, (Eds.), *Girls' Violence: Myths and Realities* (pp. 61–80). Albany: State University of New York Press.

Baumrind, D. (1978). Parental Disciplinary Patterns and Social Competence in Children. *Youth and Society, 9,* 239–276.

Baumrind, D. (1991). Parenting Styles and Adolescent Development. In R. Lerner, A. Peterson, & J. Brooks-Gunn, (Eds.), *Encyclopedia of Adolescence.* New York: Garland Publishing Company.

B.C. anticipates tougher Young Offenders Act. (1997, December 8). *The Chronicle Herald* [Halifax], A15.

Beaulieu, L. (1994). Youth Offenses—Adult Consequences. *Canadian Journal of Criminology, 36,* 329–341.

Beccaria, C. (1819). *On Crimes and Punishments* (2nd ed.). (Edward Ingraham, Trans.). Philadelphia: Philip H. Nicklin.

Becker, H. (1963). *Outsiders: Studies in the Sociology of Deviance.* New York: Free Press.

Bell, S.J. (1993). *Family Court under the Young Offenders Act: The Site of a Power Struggle.* Paper presented at meetings of the American Society of Criminology, Phoenix, AZ.

Bell, S.J. (1994a). An Empirical Approach to Theoretical Perspectives on Sentencing in Young Offender Court. *Canadian Review of Sociology and Anthropology, 31* (1), 35–64.

Bell, S.J. (1994b). *Young Offenders and Family Violence: Implications for Justice Reform.* Paper presented at the 29th annual meeting of the Atlantic Association of Sociology and Anthropology, Halifax.

Bell, S.J. (1995). *Young Offenders and Juvenile Justice in Nova Scotia: An Overview of the Young Offender Symposium.* Halifax: Atlantic Institute of Criminology.

Bell, S.J. (2001). . . . and when she was bad, she was very, very bad: Canadian Girls in Trouble. In B. Schissel & C. Brooks, (Eds.), *Critical Criminology in Canada: Breaking the Links Between Marginality and Condemnation.* Halifax: Fernwood Publishing.

Bell, S.J., & Smith, P. (1994). *Youth and Adult Custody in the Province of Nova Scotia: A Test of the Assumptions Underlying "Get Tough" Proposals.* Paper presented at meetings of the Canadian Sociology and Anthropology Association, Calgary.

Berlin teen arrested in killing of neighbour. (2005, August 31). The Associated Press, 7.

Bernard, T.J. (1987). Testing Structural Strain Theories. *Journal of Research in Crime and Delinquency, 24,* 262–290.

Bernard, T. (1992). *The Cycle of Juvenile Justice.* Toronto: Oxford University Press.

Besserer, S., & Trainor, C. (2000). Criminal Victimization in Canada, 1999. *Juristat, 20* (10). Ottawa: Statistics Canada, Canadian Centre for Justice Statistics.

Bibby, R. (1995). *The Bibby Report: Social Trends Canadian Style.* Toronto: Stoddart Publishing.

Biron, L. (1980). An Overview of Self-Reported Delinquency in a Sample of Girls in the Montreal Area. In A. Morris & L. Gelsthorpe, (Eds.), *Women and Crime.* Cambridge: Institute of Criminology.

Bittle, S., Quann, N., Hattem, T., & Muise D. (2002). A One-Day Snapshot of Aboriginal Youth in Custody Across Canada. Ottawa: Department of Justice, Canada.

Bjerregard, B., & Smith, C. (1993). Gender differences in gang participation, delinquency, and substance use. *Journal of Quantitative Criminology, 9* (4), 329–355.

Black, D., & Reiss, A. (1970). Police Control of Juveniles. *American Sociological Review, 35,* 63–77.

Bloom, B. (Ed.). (2003). *Gendered Justice: Addressing Female Offenders.* Durham, NC: Carolina Academic Press.

Bloom, B., & Covington, S. (2001). *Effective Gender-Responsive Interventions in Juvenile Justice: Addressing the lives of delinquent girls.* Paper presented at the 2001 Annual Meeting of the American Society of Criminology, Atlanta, Georgia.

Bloom, B., Owen, B., Deschenes, E.P., & Rosenbaum, J. (2002). Improving juvenile justice for females: A statewide assessment of California. *Crime & Delinquency, 50* (2).

Bloomenfeld, M., & Cole, D. (2005). The Roles of Legal Professionals in Youth Court. In K. Campbell, (Ed.), *Understanding Youth Justice in Canada.* Toronto: Pearson Education Canada Inc.

Bodine, G. (1964). *Factors Related to Police Dispositions of Juvenile Offenders.* Paper presented at annual meeting of the American Sociological Association.

Bohm, R.M. (1997). *A Primer on Crime and Delinquency.* Belmont, CA: Wadsworth Publishing.

Bonger, W. (1916). *Criminality and Economic Conditions*. (Reprinted 1969. Bloomington, IN: Indiana University Press).

Bonnell, G. (2005, December 16). Girls drowned alcoholic mom. *The Chronicle Herald* [Halifax], A6.

Borden, S. (1998, May 14). YOA changes "right approach." *The Chronicle Herald* [Halifax], A8.

Borden-Colley, S. (2005, June 29). Judge scolds Wyllie's killers, relatives. *The Chronicle* [Halifax], A1.

Boritch, H. (1997). *Fallen Women: Female Crime and Criminal Justice in Canada*. Toronto: ITP Nelson.

Bortner, M. (1988). *Delinquency and Justice: An Age of Crisis*. Toronto: McGraw-Hill Ryerson.

Bourne, P., McCoy, L., & Smith, D. (1998). Girls and Schooling: Their Own Critique. *Resources for Feminist Research*, *26* (1 & 2): 55–68.

Bourque, B.B., Cronin, R.C., Felker, D.B., Pearson, F.R., Han, M., &. Hill, S.M. (1996). *Boot Camps for Juvenile Offenders: An Implementation Evaluation of Three Demonstration Programs*. Washington, DC: National Institute of Justice, Research in Brief, May 1996.

Bowker, M.M. (1986). Juvenile Court in Retrospective: Seven Decades of History in Alberta (1913–1984). *Alberta Law Review, 24* (2), 234–274.

Boy charged with mother's murder. (2001, October 14). The Canadian Press.

Boy facing assault charges released. (2006, February 27). *The Chronicle Herald* [Halifax].

Boyle, C., Fairbridge, S., Kinch, K., Cochran, P., Smyth, R. & Chunn, D. (2002). Commentaries—The Criminalization of Young Women: An Editor's Forum. *Canadian Journal of Women and the Law, 14*, 389–428.

Bradley, S. (2006, January 18). Cop chase wrong, lawyer says. *The Chronicle Herald* [Halifax], A1.

Braga, A.A., Kennedy, D.M., Waring, E.J., & Piehl, A.M. (2001). Problem-Oriented Policing, Deterrence, and Youth Violence: An Evaluation of Boston's Operation Ceasefire. *Journal of Research in Crime and Delinquency, 38* (3), 195–225.

Braithwaite, J. (1989). *Crime, Shame, and Reintegration*. Cambridge: Cambridge University Press.

Braithwaite, J., & Mugford, S. (1994). Conditions of Successful Reintegration Ceremonies: Dealing with Juvenile Offenders. *British Journal of Criminology, 34*, 138–171.

Brannigan, A. (2000). The Adolescent Prostitute: Policing Delinquency of Preventing Victimization. In J.A. Winterdyk, (Ed.), *Issues and Perspectives on Young Offenders in Canada* (2nd ed.). Toronto: Harcourt.

Brannigan, A., Gemmell, W., Pevalin, D.J., & Wade T.J. (2002). Self-control and social control in childhood misconduct and aggression: The role of family structure, hyperactivity, and hostile parenting. *Canadian Journal of Criminology*, 119–142.

Brayton, G. (1996). Adolescent Sexual Offenders. In John Winterdyk, (Ed.), *Issues and Perspectives on Young Offenders in Canada*. Toronto: Harcourt Brace & Company.

Brezina, T., Piquero, A.R., & Mazerolle, P. (2001). Student Anger and Aggressive Behaviour in School: An Initial Test of Agnew's Macro-Level Strain Theory. *Journal of Research in Crime and Delinquency, 38* (4), 362–386.

British Columbia Ministry of the Attorney General, Corrections Branch. (1995, February). *Inventory of Alternative Measures and Diversion Programs*.

British Columbia Ministry of the Attorney General, Corrections Branch. (1996). *Annual Reports*, 1995–1996.

Brodbeck, T. (2002, February). Easier Time for Youth Crime. *Reader's Digest*, 113–114.

Brodeur, J. (1989). Some Comments on Sentencing Guidelines. In L. Beaulieu, (Ed.), *Young Offender Dispositions*. Toronto: Wall and Emerson.

Bromberg, W. (1953). American Achievements in Criminology. *Journal of Criminal Law, Criminology and Police Science, 47*, 166–176.

Brown, S. (2005). Understanding Youth and Crime: Listening to Youth? (2nd ed.). England: Open University Press.

Brownfield, D., & Thompson, K. (1991). Attachment to Peers and Delinquent Behaviour. *Canadian Journal of Criminology, 33*, 46–60.

Bula, F. (1996, April 2). Teenagers are victims of crime more often than cause of them. *The Vancouver Sun*, B2.

Burgess, R.L., & Akers, R. (1966). A Differential Association–Reinforcement Theory of Criminal Behaviour. *Social Problems, 14*, 128–147.

Busby. K. (2003). The Protective Confinement of Girls Involved in Prostitution. In K. Gorkoff & J. Runner, (Eds.), *Being Heard: The Experiences of Young Women in Prostitution*. Nova Scotia: Fernwood Publishing.

Byles, J.A. (1969). *Alienation, Deviance and Social Control: A Study of Adolescents in Metro Toronto*. Toronto: Interim Research Project on Unreached Children.

Bynum, J., & Thompson, W. (1992). *Juvenile Delinquency: A Sociological Approach*. Toronto: Allyn and Bacon.

Cairns, R.B., & Cairns, B.D. (1994). *Lifelines and Risks: Pathways of Youth in Our Time*. Cambridge: Cambridge University Press.

Campbell, A. (1984). *The Girls in the Gang*. Oxford: Basil Blackwell.

Campbell, A. (1990). Female Participation in Gangs. In C. Ronald Huff, (Ed.), *Gangs in America* (pp. 163–182). Newbury Park, CA: Sage.

Campbell, K. M. (2005a). Introduction: Theoretical Overview. In K. Campbell, (Ed.), *Understanding Youth Justice in Canada*. Toronto: Pearson Education Canada Inc.

Campbell, K. M. (2005b) Rehabilitation Revisited: The Changing Nature of "Intervention" in Juvenile Justice. In K. Campbell, (Ed.). *Understanding Youth Justice in Canada*. Toronto: Pearson Education Canada Inc.

Campbell, K., Dufresne, M., & Maclure, R. (2001). Amending youth justice policy in Canada: Discourse, mediation and ambiguity. *Howard Journal, 40*, 272–284.

Campbell, M. (1998, October 30). A perfect carnival of juvenile horrors. *The Globe and Mail*, A6.

Canada, Department of Justice. (1991). *Aboriginal People and Justice Administration—A Discussion Paper*. Ottawa: Department of Justice.

Canadian Association of Elizabeth Fry Societies and Correctional Services of Canada. (1990). *Creating Choices: The Report of the Task Force on Federally Sentenced Women*. Ottawa: Correctional Services Canada.

Canadian Criminal Justice Association. (n.d.). *Comments on "Strategy for the Renewal of Youth Justice."* Retrieved November 11, 2001, from http://home.istar.ca/~ccja/angl/youth.htm.

The Canadian Press. (2001, October 27). Nfld. Girl convicted of killing grandmother.

The Canadian Press. (2005, December 15). Damage to kids "done before the divorce"—study.

Caputo, A.A., Frick, P.J., & Brodsky, S.L. (1999). Family violence and juvenile sex offending: The potential mediating role of psychopathic traits and negative attitudes toward women. *Criminal Justice & Behavior, 26* (3), 338–356.

Caputo, T.C. (1987). The Young Offenders Act: Children's Rights, Children's Wrongs. *Canadian Public Policy, 13* (2), 125–143.

Caputo, T., & Bracken, D. (1988). Custodial Dispositions and the Young Offenders Act. In J. Hudson, J. Hornick, & B. Burrows, (Eds.), *Justice and the Young Offender in Canada*. Toronto: Wall and Thompson.

Caputo, T., Crichlow, W., Kelly, K., Lundy, C., & Totten, M. (2000, March 13). Youth in Conflict with the Law Project. Community–University Research Alliance.

Caputo, T., & Goldenberg, S. (1986). Young People and the Law: A Consideration of Luddite and Utopian Responses. *The Administration of Justice.* Saskatoon: University of Saskatchewan, Department of Sociology.

Caron, R. (1978). *Go-Boy!* Toronto: McGraw-Hill Ryerson.

Carrigan, O.D. (1991). *Crime and Punishment in Canada: A History.* Toronto: McClelland & Stewart.

Carrington, P.J. (1995). Has Violent Youth Crime Increased? Comment on Corrado and Markwart. *Canadian Journal of Criminology, 37,* 61–74.

Carrington, P.J. (1998a). Changes in Police Charging of Young Offenders in Ontario and Saskatchewan after 1984. *Canadian Journal of Criminology, 36* (1), 1–28.

Carrington, P.J. (1998b). Factors affecting police diversion of young offenders: A statistical analysis. Report to the Solicitor General, Canada.

Carrington, P. J. (1999). Trends in Youth Crime in Canada. *Canadian Journal of Criminology, 41* (1), 1–32.

Carrington, P., & Moyer, S. (1990). The Effects of Defence Counsel on Plea and Outcome in Juvenile Court. *Canadian Journal of Criminology, 32,* 621–637.

Carrington, P., & Moyer, S. (1994a). Trends in Youth Crime and Police Response, Pre- and Post-YOA. *Canadian Journal of Criminology, 36,* 1–28.

Carrington, P., & Moyer, S. (1994b). Interprovincial Variations in the Use of Custody for Young Offenders: A Funnel Analysis. *Canadian Journal of Criminology, 36,* 271–290.

Carrington, P., & Moyer, S. (1998). *A Statistical Profile of Female Young Offenders.* Ottawa: Department of Justice, Research and Statistics Division/Policy Sector.

Carrington, P.J., & Schulenberg, J.L. (2005). Police Decision-Making with Young Offenders: Arrest, Questioning, and Dispositions. In K. Campbell, (Ed.), *Understanding Youth Justice in Canada.* Toronto: Pearson Education Canada Inc.

Castellano, T.C. (1986). Justice Model in the Juvenile Justice System: Washington State's Experience. *Law and Policy, 8,* 479–506.

CBC News. (2002, March 26). B.C. girl convicted in school bullying tragedy.

CBC News. (2004, August 19). Curfews: Do you know where your children are?

CBC News. (2005, March 29). Curfew proposed for Halifax teens.

Cernkovich, S., & Giordano, P. (1987). Family Relationships and Delinquency. *Criminology, 25,* 295–321.

Chakkalakal, T. (2000). Reckless Eyeballing: Being Reena in Canada. In R. Walcott, (Ed.), *Rude: Contemporary Black Cultural Criticism* (pp. 161–167). Toronto: Insomniac Press.

Chambliss, W. (1973). The Saints and the Roughnecks. *Society, 11,* 24–31.

Chang, J. (1996). A comparative study of female gang and non-gang members in Chicago. *Journal of Gang Research, 4* (1), 9–18.

Chartrand, L.N. (2005). Aboriginal Youth and the Criminal Justice System. In K. Campbell, (Ed.), *Understanding Youth Justice in Canada* (pp. 313–333). Toronto: Pearson, Prentice-Hall.

Chatterjee, J. (1999). A report on the evaluation of RCMP restorative justice initiative: Community justice forum as seen by participants. Ottawa: Research and Evaluation Branch, Community, Contract and Aboriginal Policing Services.

Chatterjee, J., & Elliott, L. (2003). Restorative Policing in Canada: The Royal Canadian Mounted Police, Community Justice Forums, and the Youth Criminal Justice Act. *Police Practice and Research, 4* (4), 347–359.

Chesler, P. (1972). *Women and Madness.* New York: Doubleday.

Chesney-Lind, M. (1970). Judicial Paternalism and the Female Status Offender. *Crime and Delinquency, 23,* 121–130.

Chesney-Lind, M. (1988). Girls in Jail. *Crime and Delinquency, 34,* 151–168.

Chesney-Lind, M. (February 2001). What about the girls? Delinquency Programming as if Gender Mattered. *Corrections Today,* 38–45.

Chesney-Lind, M., & Irwin, K. (2004). From Badness to Meanness: Popular Constructions of Contemporary Girlhood. In A. Harris, (Ed.), *All about the Girl: Culture, Power, and Identity.* New York: Routledge.

Chesney-Lind, M., Rockhill, A., Marker, N., & Reyes, A. (1994). Gangs and Exploring Police Estimates of Gang Membership Delinquency. *Crime, Law, and Social Change, 21,* 201–228.

Chesney-Lind, M., & Shelden, R. (1992). *Girls, Delinquency and Juvenile Justice.* Pacific Grove, CA: Brooks/Cole.

Chesney-Lind, M., & Shelden, R. (1998). *Girls, Delinquency and Juvenile Justice.* Belmont, CA: West/Wadsworth.

Chisholm, P. (1997, December 8). Bad Girls: A Brutal B.C. Murder Sounds an Alarm about Teenage Violence. *Maclean's.*

The Chronicle Herald [Halifax]. (2004, April 1). What's up? Behind bars: Is locking kids up the solution to youth crime?

———. (2004, December 2). Judge bucks stats in teen's sentencing: Disagrees youth crime is declining and violent offences are fewer.

———. (2005, March 28). "Swarmers could be future killers," warns cousin of 15-year-old victim.

———. (2005, June 3). 11-year-olds arrested in attack on boy, 5.

———. (2005, June 9). Youth crime project makes progress.

———. (2005, June 29). Judge scolds Wyllie's killers, relatives.

———. (2005, June 30). Student gets life for chilling murders of parents.

———. (2005, July 23). Boys charged in beating: Yarmouth pair held in attack on hotdog vendor.

———. (2005, August 31). Berlin teen arrested in killing of neighbour, 7.

———. (2005, September 27). Teen unnerved by late-night encounter with police officers.

———. (2005, October 14). Teenage killer gets maximum sentence: 3 years.

———. (2005, October 25). Parents blamed for troubled youth woes.

———. (2005, December 15a). Damage to kids "done before the divorce"—study.

———. (2005, December 15b). Teen killer unrepentant hearing told.

———. (2005, December 16a). McEvoy killer considered "significant threat."

———. (2005, December 16b). Girls drowned alcoholic mom.

———. (2005, December 17a). Girl charged in toddler's death.

———. (2005, December 17b). Lethal driver's mother sees new attitude.

———. (2005, December 21). Mom: Cops slammed son's head on steps—Woman launches complaint about handling of teen's arrest.

———. (2005, December 26). Using hunting to reduce youth crime: Nunavut gambles on old ways.

———. (2006, January 6). Toronto mom turns in son after finding AK-47 in his room.

———. (2006, January 12a). Boy could get out in 18 months.

———. (2006, January 12b). Teen jailed in McEvoy death: Joyrider gets $4^1/_2$ years for fatal crash.

———. (2006, January 14). McEvoy inquiry set to start Monday.

———. (2006, January 17). "Lots of warning signs."

———. (2006, January 18). Ex-school may be used to house teen moms.

———. (2006, January 19). Youth laws lax, lawyer tells inquiry.

———. (2006, January 20). Youth no stranger to courts.

———. (2006, January 21). Policy Primer: Where do the parties stand on issues affecting Atlantic Canadians?

———. (2006, January 22). Nunn ruling to have broad impact.

———. (2006, January 27). Teen hits speeds of 170 to 180 km/h.

———. (2006, January 30). A failure to communicate: McEvoy inquiry has to focus on why teen freed despite warrant.

———. (2006, January 31). Warrant was in order.

———. (2006, February 1). Mountie feeling weight of tragedy.

———. (2006, February 6). Justice official, cop differ on status of arrest warrant.

———. (2006, February 7). Fax foul-ups led to bail for teen, McEvoy inquiry told.

———. (2006, February 15). Lax laws failed son, McEvoy, says mom.

———. (2006, February 21). Social worker tells inquiry of boy's troubled home life.

———. (2006, February 22). Inquiry told education system failed McEvoy's killer.

———. (2006, February 23). Youth act not doing its job—Nunn.

———. (2006, February 24). Facility for troubled youth needed, inquiry hears.

———. (2006, March 20). End racial profiling.

———. (2006, March 29). Fewer youths jailed under new act.

Chunn, D. (1998). *Whiter than White: Sexual Offences, Law and Social Purity in Canada, 1885–1940*. Paper presented at the Western Association of Sociology and Anthropology, Vancouver, May 15.

Cicourel, A. (1968). *The Social Organization of Juvenile Justice*. New York: John Wiley.

City Marshal. (1909–1910). *Annual Reports*. City of Halifax: Nova Scotia Provincial Archives.

Clairmont, D., & Linden, R. (1998). Developing and evaluating justice projects in Aboriginal communities: A review of the literature. Ottawa: Aboriginal Corrections Policy Unit, Solicitor General of Canada.

Clark, B., & O'Reilly-Fleming, T. (1993). Implementing the Young Offenders Act in Ontario: Issues of Principles, Programmes, and Power. *Howard Journal of Criminal Justice, 32*, 114–126.

Clark, B., & O'Reilly-Fleming, T. (1994). Out of the Carceral Straightjacket: Under Twelve and the Law. *Canadian Journal of Criminology, 36*, 305–327.

Clark R., & Cornish, D. (1985). Modeling Offenders Decisions. In N. Morris & M. Tonry, (Eds.), *Crime and Justice, 6* (pp. 147–185). Chicago: University of Chicago Press.

Clark, R., & Felson, M. (1993). *Routine Activity and Rational Choice*. New Brunswick, NJ: Transaction Books.

Clarke, J. (2004). Whose Justice? The politics of juvenile control. In J. Muncie, G. Hughes, & E. McLaughlin, (Eds.), *Youth Justice: Critical Readings*. London, UK: Sage Publications Ltd.

Cloninger, C., & Gottesman, I. (1987). Genetic and Environmental Factors in Anti-Social Behavior Disorders. In J. Mednick, T. Moffitt, & S. Stack, (Eds.), *The Causes of Crime: New Biological Approaches*. Cambridge: Cambridge University Press.

Cloward, R., & Ohlin, L. (1960). *Delinquency and Opportunity*. New York: Free Press.

The Coast [Halifax]. (2005, June 16–23). About a boy.

Coflin, J. (1988). The Federal Government's Role in Implementing the Young Offenders Act. In J. Hudson, J. Hornick, & B. Burrows, (Eds.), *Justice and the Young Offender in Canada*. Toronto: Wall and Thompson.

Cohen, A.K. (1955). *Delinquent Boys*. New York: Free Press.

Cohen, L., & Felson, M. (1979). Social Change and Crime Rate Trends: A Routine Activity Approach. *American Sociological Review, 44,* 588–608.

Cohen, S. (1972). *Folk Devils and Moral Panics.* London, UK: Granada Publishing.

Cohen, S. (1985). *Visions of Social Control: Crime, Punishment and Classification.* Cambridge: Polity Press.

Cohen, S. (MP). (1997). *Renewing Youth Justice.* Thirteenth Report of the Standing Committee on Justice and Legal Affairs. Canada: Queen's Printer.

Cohill, M., Jr. (1991). Why Do I Like Broccoli? (*De gustibus non est disputandum*). *Journal of Criminal Law and Criminology, 82,* 125–130.

Coleman, J.S. (1988). Social Capital in the Creation of Human Capital. *American Journal of Sociology, 94,* 95–120.

Coleman, J.S. (1990). *Foundation of Social Theory.* Cambridge, MA: Harvard University Press.

Colvin, M., & Pauly, J. (1987). A Critique of Criminology. *American Journal of Sociology, 89,* 513–551.

Conly, C. (1993). *Street Gangs, Current Knowledge and Strategies.* Washington, DC: National Institute of Justice.

Conly, D. (1978). *Patterns of Delinquency and Police Action in the Major Metropolitan Areas of Canada during the Month of December 1976.* Ottawa: Solicitor General, Canada.

Connell, R.W. (1987). *Gender and Power.* Stanford, CA: Stanford University Press.

Conrad, Rick. (2005, October 13). Students call for action on bullying. *The Chronicle Herald* [Halifax].

Conway, J. (1992). Female Young Offenders, 1990–91. *Juristat, 12* (11). Ottawa: Statistics Canada, Canadian Centre for Justice Statistics.

Cook, P. (1980). Research in Criminal Deterrence. In N. Morris & M. Tonry, (Eds.), *Crime and Justice, 2.* Chicago: University of Chicago Press.

Copperman, P. (1980). *The Literacy Hoax.* New York: Morrow.

Corrado, R. (1992). Introduction. In R. Corrado, N. Bala, R. Linden, & M. Le Blanc, (Eds.), *Juvenile Justice in Canada: A Theoretical and Analytical Assessment.* Toronto: Butterworths.

Corrado, R., & Markwart, A. (1988). The Prices of Rights and Responsibilities: The Impacts of the Young Offenders Act in British Columbia. *Canadian Review of Family Law, 7* (1), 93–115.

Corrado, R., & Markwart, A. (1992). The Evolution and Implementation of a New Era of Juvenile Justice in Canada. In R. Corrado, N. Bala, R. Linden, & M. Le Blanc, (Eds.), *Juvenile Justice in Canada: A Theoretical and Analytical Assessment.* Toronto: Butterworths.

Corrado, R., & Markwart, A. (1994). The Need to Reform the YOA in Response to Violent Young Offenders: Confusion, Reality or Myth? *Canadian Journal of Criminology, 36,* 343–378.

Corrado, R., & Markwart, A. (1995). Processing Serious Cases in British Columbia. In J. Creechan & R. Silverman, (Eds.), *Canadian Delinquency.* Scarborough: Prentice Hall Canada.

Corrado, R.R., Odgers, C., & Cohen, I.M. (2000). The Incarceration of Female Young Offenders: Protection for Whom? *Canadian Journal of Criminology, 42* (2), 189–207.

Costly Problem: Expensive to Lock Kids Up for Long. (1995, April 18). *Daily News* [Halifax].

Cottrell, B. (2004). *When Teens Abuse Their Parents.* Halifax: Fernwood Publishing.

Covell, K., & Howe, R.B. (1996). Public Attitudes and Juvenile Justice in Canada. *The International Journal of Children's Rights, 4,* 345–355.

Covell, K., & Howe, R.B. (2001). *The Challenge of Children's Rights for Canada.* Waterloo, ON: Wilfrid Laurier University Press.

Cowie, J., Cowie, V., & Slater, E. (1968). *Delinquency in Girls*. London, UK: Heinemann.

Cox, W. (1995, August 3). Law-breaking by young continues to decrease. *The Chronicle Herald* [Halifax], A2.

Craig, W. (2004). Bullying and Fighting. *Young People in Canada: Their health and well-being*. Health Canada.

Creechan, J. (1995). How Much Delinquency Is There? In J. Creechan & R. Silverman, (Eds.), *Canadian Delinquency*. Scarborough, ON: Prentice Hall Canada.

Crick, N., & Grotpeter, J. (1996). Children's treatment by peers: Victims of relational and overt aggression. *Development and Psychology, 8*, 367–380.

Critcher, C. (2003). *Moral Panics and the Media*. Buckingham, UK: Open University Press.

Cross, B. (1998, February 12). A killing lights a prairie fire. *The Globe and Mail*, A2.

Crow, C. (1994). Patterns of Discrimination: Aboriginal Justice in Canada. In N. Larsen, (Ed.), *The Canadian Criminal Justice System: An Issues Approach to the Administration of Justice*. Toronto: Canadian Scholars Press.

CTV News. (2004, December 5). Swarming girl gangs a crime problem in Winnipeg.

CTV News. (2006, January 18). YCJA: You can't jail anybody.

Curran, D.J., & Renzetti, C.M. (Eds.). (2001). *Theories of Crime* (2nd ed.). Toronto: Allyn & Bacon.

Dabbs, J., Frady, R., Carr, T., & Besch, N. (1987). Testosterone and Criminal Violence in Young Prison Inmates. *Psychosomatic Medicine, 49*, 174–182.

Dabbs, J., Ruback, R., Frady, R., Hooper, C., & Sgoutas, D. (1988). Saliva Testosterone and Criminal Violence Among Women. *Personality and Individual Differences, 9*, 269–275.

The Daily News [Halifax]. (2001, October 17). Youth sentenced to three years for violent pizza robbery.

———. (2001, October 27). Nfld. Girl convicted of killing grandmother.

———. (2002, September 12). Stabbing-case boy denied bail.

———. (2003, July 4). Baseball bat boy often misbehaves, born addicted to crack, court told.

———. (2003, July 18). Neighbourhood's nightmare: Out-of-control youths spread fear, and it took a 13-year-old boy to stand up to it.

Dalley, M. (2004). *National Missing Children Services, 2003 Reference Report*. Ottawa: Minister of Public Works and Government Services.

Daly, K. (1997). Different ways of conceptualizing sex/gender in feminist theory and their implications for criminology. *Theoretical Criminology, 1* (1), 25–51.

Daly, K. (1998). From gender ratios to gendered lives, women and gender in crime and criminological theory. In M. Tonry, (Ed.), *The handbook of crime and justice*. Oxford: Oxford University Press.

Daly, K., & Chesney-Lind, M. (1988). Feminism and Criminology. *Justice Quarterly, 5*, 497–538.

Danger of the street: Where lieth responsibility? (1908, January 11). *Evening Mail* [Halifax], 16.

Dannifer, D., & Schutt, R. (1982). Race and Juvenile Justice Processing in Court and Police Agencies. *American Journal of Sociology, 87*, 1113–1132.

Dauvergne, M. (2005). Homicide in Canada–2004. *Juristat, 25* (6). Ottawa: Statistics Canada, Canadian Centre for Justice Statistics.

Dauvergne, M., & Johnson, H. (2001). Children Witnessing Family Violence. *Juristat, 21* (6). Ottawa: Statistics Canada, Canadian Centre for Justice Statistics.

Davidson, W., & Redner, R. (1988). The Prevention of Juvenile Delinquency: Diversion from the Juvenile Justice System. In R. Price, E. Cowen, R. Orion, & J. Ramos-McKay, (Eds.), *Fourteen Ounces of Prevention*. Washington, DC: American Psychological Association.

Davies, L. (1994a). In Search of Resistance and Rebellion Among High School Drop-Outs. *Canadian Journal of Sociology, 19* (3), 331–350.

Davies, L. (1994b). Class Dismissed? Student Opposition in Ontario High Schools. *Canadian Review of Sociology and Anthropology, 31* (4), 422–445.

Davis, B. (2005, November 10). Toddlers taken by Children's Aid after trashing Ontario home. *The Chronicle Herald* [Halifax], A10.

Davis, J. (1990). *Youth and the Condition of Britain: Images of Adolescent Conflict.* London, UK: Althone Press.

Davis, N. (1999). *Youth Crisis: Growing up in the High-Risk Society.* New York: Greenwood.

Defective Children Discussed at Annual Conference in Buffalo. (1909, June 8). *Morning Chronicle* [Halifax].

DeFleur, L. (1975). Biasing Influences on Drug Arrest Records, *American Sociological Review, 40,* 88–101.

DeKeseredy, W. (2000). *Women, Crime and the Canadian Criminal Justice System.* Cincinnati, OH: Anderson.

Dell'Olio, J.M., & Jacobs, P.H. (1991). The CHILD Inc. of Delaware Experience. In I. Schwartz & S. Orlando, (Eds.), *Programming for Young Women in the Juvenile Justice System.* Ann Arbor, MI: Center for the Study of Youth Policy.

Denov, M.S. (2005). Children's Rights, Juvenile Justice, and the UN Convention on the Rights of the Child: Implications for Canada. In K. Campbell, (Ed.), *Understanding Youth Justice in Canada.* Toronto: Pearson Education Canada Inc.

Department of Justice, Canada. (2005). *Youth Criminal Justice Act 2005: Annual Statement Executive Summary.* Ottawa: Department of Justice.

de Souza, P. (1995). Youth Court Statistics, 1993–94 Highlights. *Juristat, 15* (3). Ottawa: Statistics Canada, Canadian Crime Statistics.

Dickson-Gilmore, J. (1992). Finding the Ways of the Ancestors: Cultural Change and the Invention of Separate Legal Systems. *Canadian Journal of Criminology* 34(3–4), 479–502.

Different note. (1996, September 30). *The Chronicle Herald* [Halifax], C1.

Doherty, G., & de Souza, P. (1996). Youth Court Statistics, 1994–95 Highlights. *Juristat, 16* (4). Ottawa: Statistics Canada, Canadian Crime Statistics.

Donzelot, J. (1979). *The Policing of Families.* (Robert Hurley, Trans.). New York: Pantheon Books.

Doob, A. (1989). Dispositions under the Young Offenders Act: Issues without Answers. In L. Beaulieu, (Ed.), *Young Offender Dispositions.* Toronto: Wall and Emerson.

Doob, A. (1991). Workshop on Collecting Race and Ethnicity Statistics in the Criminal Justice System. Toronto: University of Toronto, Centre of Criminology.

Doob, A. (1992). Trends in the Use of Custodial Dispositions for Young Offenders. *Canadian Journal of Criminology, 34,* 75–84.

Doob, A. (2001). *Youth court judges' views of the youth justice system: The results of a survey.* Toronto: *Centre for Criminology, University of Toronto.*

Doob, A., and Beaulieu, L. (1992). Variation in the Exercise of Judicial Discretion with Young Offenders. *Canadian Journal of Criminology, 34,* 35–50.

Doob, A., & Beaulieu, L. (1995). The Exercise of Judicial Discretion. In J. Creechan & R. Silverman, (Eds.), *Canadian Delinquency.* Scarborough, ON: Prentice Hall Canada.

Doob, A., & Brodeur, J. (1989). Rehabilitating the Debate on Rehabilitation. *Canadian Journal of Criminology, 31,* 179–192.

Doob, A., & Cesaroni, C. (2004). *Responding to Youth Crime in Canada.* Toronto: University of Toronto Press.

Doob, A., & Chan, J.B.L. (1995). Factors Affecting Police Decisions to Take Juveniles to Court. In J. Creechan & R. Silverman, (Eds.), *Canadian Delinquency*. Scarborough, ON: Prentice Hall Canada.

Doob, A., Marinos, V., & Varma, K. (1995). *Youth Crime and the Youth Justice System in Canada: A Research Perspective*. Toronto: University of Toronto, Centre of Criminology.

Doob, A., & Sprott, J.B. (1996). Interprovincial Variation in the Use of the Youth Court. *Canadian Journal of Criminology* (October), 401–412.

Doob, A., & Sprott, J.B. (1998). Is the "quality" of youth violence becoming more serious? *Canadian Journal of Criminology, 40* (2), 185–194.

Doob, A., & Sprott, J.B. (2004). Changing models of youth justice in Canada. In M. Tonry & A.N. Doob, (Eds.), *Crime and Justice, Youth Crime and Youth Justice: Comparative and Cross-National Perspectives: A Review of Research, 31* (pp. 185–242). Chicago: University of Chicago Press.

Doob, A., & Sprott, J.B. (2005). Sentencing under the Youth Criminal Justice Act: An Historical Perspective. In K. Campbell, (Ed.), *Understanding Youth Justice in Canada* (pp. 221–241). Toronto: Pearson Prentice Hall.

Doob, A., Sprott, J.B., Marinos, V., & Varma, K.N. (1998). An exploration of Ontario residents' views of crime and the criminal justice system. Toronto: Centre of Criminology, University of Toronto.

Dorey, B. (1996, April 20). On the inside, looking out. *The Chronicle Herald* [Halifax], C1.

Dorey, B. (1997, November 22). Justice for kids. *The Chronicle Herald* [Halifax], B2.

Dorey, B. (2005, October 25). Parents blamed for troubled youth woes. *The Chronicle Herald* [Halifax], B4.

Doucette, P.A. (2004). Walk and Talk: An Intervention for Behaviorally Challenged Youths. *Adolescence, 39* (154), 373–88.

Dowden, C. (2003). *The Effectiveness of Substance Abuse Treatment with Young Offenders*. Department of Justice, Canada.

Dowden, C., & Andrews, D.A. (1999). What works in young offender treatment: A meta-analysis. *Forum on Corrections Research, 11* (2), 21–24.

Drucker, S., & Hexter, M. (1923). *Children Astray*. Cambridge, MA: Harvard University Press.

Duffy, A. (1996). Bad Girls in Hard Times: Canadian Female Juvenile Offenders. In G. O'Bireck, (Ed.), *Not a Kid Anymore*. Scarborough, ON: ITP Nelson.

Dugdale, R. (1888). *The Jukes: A Study in Crime, Pauperism, Disease and Heredity* (4th ed.). New York: Putnam.

Durkheim, E. (1893). *The Division of Labour in Society*. (George Simpson, Trans.). (Reprinted 1933. London, UK: Free Press of Glencoe).

Durkheim, E. (1897). *Suicide*. (John A. Spaulding & George Simpson, Trans.). (Reprinted 1951. New York: Free Press).

DuWors, R. (1992). *Report on the Involvement of Children under 12 in Criminal Behaviour*. Ottawa: Statistics Canada, Canadian Centre for Justice Statistics.

Eckstein, B. (2005). New Brunswick Intensive Support Program. In B. Morrison, C. Doucet, & M. LeBlanc, *New Brunswick Perspectives on Crime Prevention: Promising Practices for Children, Youth and Families*. Nova Scotia: Gaspereau Press.

Edwards, P. (1992, February 17). Reform school was a nightmare: woman recalls brutal girlhood behind bars. *Toronto Star*, A8.

Ekstedt, J., & Griffiths, C. (1988). *Corrections in Canada: Policy and Practice*. Toronto: Butterworths.

Elder, G.H., Jr. (1985). Perspectives on the Life Course. In G.H. Elder Jr., (Ed), *Life Course Dynamics* (pp. 23–49). Ithaca: Cornell University Press.

Elder, G.H., Jr. (2000). Symposium on John Hagan & Bill McCarthy's *Mean Streets: Youth Crime and Homelessness* (Cambridge: Cambridge University Press, 1997): Extreme Situations in Young Lives. *Theoretical Criminology, 4* (20), 208–215.

11-year-olds arrested in attack on boy, 5. (2005, June 3). The Associated Press.

Elliott, D. (1966). Delinquency, School Attendance and Dropout. *Social Problems, 13,* 307–314.

Elliott, D., Huizinga, D., & Ageton, S. (1985). *Explaining Delinquency and Drug Use*. Beverly Hills, CA: Sage.

Elliott, D., & Voss, H. (1974a). School Alienation and Delinquency. *Crime and Delinquency, 24,* 355–370.

Elliott, D., & Voss, H. (1974b). *Delinquency and Dropout*. Lexington, MA: Lexington Books.

Elliott, L. (2003, May 7). When justice means restoring the moral bond of community. *The Vancouver Sun*.

Elliott, L. (2005). Restorative Justice in Canadian Approaches to Youth Crime: Origins, Practices, and Retributive Frameworks. In K. Campbell, (Ed.), *Understanding Youth Justice in Canada*. Toronto: Pearson Education Canada Inc.

Ellis, D., & Austin, P. (1971). Menstruation and Aggressive Behaviour in a Correctional Center for Women. *Journal of Criminal Law, Criminology, and Police Science, 62,* 388–395.

Engler, C., & Crowe, S. (2000). Alternative Measures for Youth in Canada. *Juristat, 20* (6). Ottawa: Statistics Canada: Canadian Centre for Justice Statistics.

Enriquez, V. (1990). *Hellside in Paradise: The Honolulu Youth Gang*. Honolulu, HI: University of Hawaii at Manoa, Center for Philippine Studies.

Ericson, R. (1982). *Reproducing Order: A Study of Police Patrol Work*. Toronto: University of Toronto Press.

Ericson, R.V., & Haggerty, K.D. (1997). *Policing the Risk Society*. Toronto: University of Toronto Press.

Erikson, E. (1950). *Childhood and Society*. New York: Norton.

Erikson, E. (1968). *Identity: Youth and Crisis*. New York: Norton.

Esbensen, F., & Deschenes, E.P. (1998). A multisite examination of youth gang membership: Does gender matter? *Criminology, 36* (4), 799–828.

Eysenck, H. (1977). *Crime and Personality* (2nd ed.). London, UK: Routledge & Kegan Paul.

Fagan, J. (1991). Social Processes of Delinquency and Drug Use among Urban Gangs. In C.R. Huff, (Ed.), *Gangs in America*. Newbury Park, CA: Sage.

Fagan, J., Slaughter, E., & Hartstone, E. (1987). Blind Justice? The Impact of Race on the Juvenile Justice Process. *Crime and Delinquency, 33,* 224–258.

Fairclough, I. (2004, December 2). Judge bucks stats in teen's sentencing: Disagrees youth crime is declining and violent offences are fewer. *The Chronicle Herald* [Halifax], B7.

Faith, K. (1993). *Unruly Women*. Vancouver: Press Gang Publishers.

Farrington, D.P. (2001). The Nature and Extent of Youth Crime. In R.C. Smandych, (Ed.), *Youth Crime: Varieties, Theories, and Prevention*. Toronto: Harcourt Canada.

Farrington, D.P. (2004). Understanding and preventing youth crime. In J. Muncie, G. Hughes, & E. McLaughlin, (Eds.), *Youth Justice: Critical Readings*. London, UK: Sage Publications Ltd.

Fasiolo, R., & Leckie, S. (1993). *Canadian Media Coverage of Gangs: A Content Analysis*. Ottawa: Solicitor General, Canada.

Fetherston, D. (2000). The Law and Young Offenders. In J.A. Winterdyk, (Ed.), *Issues and Perspectives on Young Offenders in Canada* (2nd ed.). Toronto: Harbour Canada, 93–118.

Fedorowycz, O. (1997). Homicide in Canada—1996. *Juristat, 17* (9). Ottawa: Statistics Canada, Canadian Centre for Justice Statistics.

Fedorowycz, O. (1999). Homicide in Canada—1998. *Juristat, 19* (10). Ottawa: Statistics Canada, Canadian Centre for Justice Statistics.

Fedorowycz, O. (2000). Homicide in Canada—1999. *Juristat, 20* (9). Ottawa: Statistics Canada, Canadian Centre for Justice Statistics.

Feld, B.C. (2000). Juveniles' waiver of legal rights: Confessions, Miranda, and the right to counsel. In T. Grisso & R.G. Schwartz, (Eds.), *Youth on Trial: A developmental perspective on juvenile justice.* Chicago: University of Chicago Press.

Ferdinand, T.N., & Luchterhand, E.G. (1970). Inner-City Youth, the Police, the Juvenile Court, and Justice. *Social Problems, 17* (Spring), 510–527.

Finckenauer, J.O. (1982). *Scared Straight! and the Panacea Phenomenon.* Englewood Cliffs, NJ: Prentice Hall.

Fingard, J. (1989). *The Dark Side of Life in Victorian Halifax.* Nova Scotia: Pottersfield Press.

Finkelhor, D., & Dziuba-Leatherman, J. (1993). *Children as Victims of Violence: A National Survey.* Durham, NH: University of New Hampshire, Family Research Laboratory.

Finkelhor, D., & Dziuba-Leatherman, J. (1994). Victimization of Children. *American Psychologist, 49,* 173–183.

Fisher, J. (1989). *Missing Children's Research Project: Findings of the Study Executive Summary.* Ottawa: Solicitor General of Canada.

Fisher, L., & Janetti, H. (1996). Aboriginal Youth in the Criminal Justice System. In John Winterdyk, (Ed.), *Issues and Perspectives on Young Offenders in Canada.* Toronto: Harcourt Brace & Company.

Fisherman Murdered. (1995, July 16). *Sunday Daily News* [Halifax].

Fishman, L. (1988). *The Vice Queens: An Ethnographic Study of Black Female Gang Behaviour.* Paper presented at the annual meetings of the American Society of Criminology.

Fishman, M. (1978). Crime Waves as Ideology. *Social Problems, 25,* 531–543.

Fitzgerald, R. (2003). *An examination of sex differences in delinquency.* Ottawa: Statistics Canada, Canadian Centre for Justice Statistics.

Flynn, A. (1995, July). Youth to face adult court in drive-by slaying case. *The Chronicle Herald* [Halifax].

Fogel, D. (1988). *On Doing Less Harm.* Chicago: University of Illinois at Chicago.

Foran, T. (1995). Youth Custody and Probation in Canada, 1993–94. *Juristat, 15* (7). Ottawa: Statistics Canada.

Fottrell, D. (2000). One step forward or two steps sideways? Assessing the first decade of the children's convention on the rights of the child. In D. Fottrell, (Ed.), *Revisiting children's rights.* London, UK: Kluwer Law International.

Fowler, K. (1993). Youth Gangs: Criminals, Thrillseekers or the New Voice of Anarchy? In T. Fleming and B. Clark, (Eds.), *Youth Injustice: Canadian Perspectives.* Toronto: Canadian Scholars Press.

Frank, J. (1991). Violent Offence Cases Heard in Youth Courts, 1990–91. *Juristat, 11* (16). Ottawa: Statistics Canada, Canadian Centre for Justice Statistics.

Frank, J. (1992). Violent Youth Crime. *Canadian Social Trends.* Ottawa: Statistics Canada.

Free, M.D., Jr. (1991). Clarifying the relationship between the broken home and juvenile delinquency: A critique of the current literature. *Deviant Behavior, 12* (2), 109–167.

Freire, R. (1990). *Pedagogy of the Oppressed.* New York: Continuum.

Freud, S. (1924). *A General Introduction to Psychoanalysis.* New York: Boni and Livelight. (Reprinted 1953. New York: Permabooks).

Fried, C.S. (2001). Juvenile curfews: Are they an effective and constitutional means of combating juvenile violence? *Behavioral Sciences & the Law, 19* (1), 127–141.

Friedlander, K. (1947). *The Psychoanalytic Approach to Juvenile Delinquency.* London, UK: Kegan Paul.

Frith, S. (1985). Sociology of Youth. In Michael Haralabos, (Ed.), *Sociology: New Directions*. Ormskiek: Causeway Press.

Gaarder, E., Rodriguez, N., & Zatz M.S. (2004). Criers, Liars, and Manipulators: Probation Officers' Views of Girls. *Justice Quarterly, 21* (3), 547–578.

Gabor, P., Greene, I., & McCormick, P. (1986). The Young Offenders Act: The Alberta Youth Court Experience in the First Year. *Canadian Journal of Family Law, 5*, 301–319.

Gabor, T. (1999). Trends in Youth Crime: Some Evidence Pointing to Increases in the Severity and Volume of Violence on the Part of Young People. *Canadian Journal of Criminology, 41* (3), 385–392.

Gaetz, S. (2004). Safe Streets for Whom? Homeless Youth, Social Exclusion, and Criminal Victimization. *Canadian Journal of Criminology and Criminal Justice*, 423–455.

Gaffield, C. (1991). Labouring and Learning in Nineteenth-Century Canada: Children in the Changing Process of Family Reproduction. In R. Smandych, G. Dodds, & A. Esau, (Eds.), *Dimensions of Childhood: Essays on the History of Children and Youth in Canada*. Winnipeg: University of Manitoba, Legal Research Institute.

Gagnon, M., & Doherty, G. (1993). *Offences Against the Administration of Youth Justice in Canada*. Ottawa: Statistics Canada, Canadian Centre for Justice Statistics.

Gaines, D. (1993). *Teenage Wasteland: Suburbia's Deadend Kids*. New York: Harper Collins.

Gamoran, A, & Mare, R. (1989). Secondary School Tracking and Educational Inequality. *American Journal of Sociology, 94*, 1146–1183.

Gandy, J. (1992). *Judicial Interim Release (Bail) Hearing That Resulted in Detention Prior to Trial of Youths Charged Under the Young Offenders Act in Three Ontario Cities*. Toronto: Policy Research Centre on Children, Youth, and Families.

Gannon, M., & Mihorean, K. (2005). Criminal Victimization in Canada–2004. *Juristat, 25* (7). Ottawa: Statistics Canada, Canadian Centre for Justice Statistics.

Garbarino, James. (2006) *See Jane Hit: Why girls are growing more violent and what we can do about it. New York: Penguin Press.*

Gardner, M.H. (2005, June 9). Youth crime project makes progress. *The Chronicle Herald* [Halifax], B3.

Garland, D. (1996). The Limits of the Sovereign State. *British Journal of Criminology, 36* (4), pp. 445–471.

Garland, D. (2001). *The Culture of Control*. Oxford: Oxford University Press.

Gartner, R., & Doob, A. (1994). Trends in Criminal Victimization, 1988–93. *Juristat, 14* (13). Ottawa: Statistics Canada, Canadian Centre for Justice Statistics.

Gelsthorpe, L., & Morris, A. (2004) Restorative youth justice: the last vestiges of welfare. In J. Muncie, G. Hughes, & E. McLaughlin, (Eds.), *Youth Justice: Critical Readings*. London, UK: Sage Publications Ltd.

Gendreau, P., Paparozzi, M., Little, T., & and Goddard, M. (1993). Does "Punishing Smarter" Work? An Assessment of the New Generation of Alternative Sanctions in Probation. *Forum on Corrections Research, 5*, 31–34.

Gendreau, P., & Ross, R. (1987). Revivication of Rehabilitation: Evidence from the 1980s. *Justice Quarterly, 4* (3), 349–407.

Genesee Justice. (1995). *Instruments of Law, Order, and Peace*. Batavia, NY: Genesee County Sheriff's Office.

Gilligan, C. (1982). *In a Different Voice*. Cambridge, MA: Harvard University Press.

Gilligan, C. (2001). *Preventing Violence*. London, UK: Thames and Hudson.

Gillingham, R. (2005, June 16–23). About a boy. *The Coast* [Halifax], p.1.

Giordano, P. (1978). Girls, Guys, and Gangs: The Changing Social Context of Female Delinquency. *Journal of Criminal Law and Criminology, 69*, 126–132.

Girl charged in toddler's death. (2005, December 17). The Canadian Press.

Girl, 12, charged in triple slaying. (2006, April 25). *Calgary Herald*, A1, A3.

Giroux, H.A. (2002). The War on the Young: Corporate Culture, Schooling, and the Politics of "Zero Tolerance." In R. Strickland, (Ed.), *Growing up Postmodern: Neoliberalism and the War on the Young*. Oxford: Rowman & Littlefield Publishers, Inc.

Glassner, B.N., Ksander, B., & Berg, B, & Johnson, B.D. (1983). A Note on the Deterrent Effect of Juvenile versus Adult Jurisdiction. *Social Problems, 31* (2), 219–221.

The Globe and Mail. (1997, November 8).

The Globe and Mail. (1999, November 17).

Glueck, S., & Glueck, E. (1950). *Unravelling Juvenile Delinquency*. Cambridge, MA: Harvard University Press.

Glueck, S., & Glueck, E. (1956). *Physique and Delinquency*. New York: Harper.

Glueck, S., & Glueck, E. (1959). *Predicting Delinquency and Crime*. Cambridge, MA: Harvard University Press.

Goddard, H. (1912). *The Kallikak Family*. New York: Macmillan.

Godin, R. (1993, January 16). Crime puts squeeze on businesses. *Mail Star*, A4.

Goff, C. (1997). *Criminal Justice in Canada*. Scarborough, ON: ITP Nelson.

Gold, A.D., & Harvey, E.B. (2003, February). Executive summary of presentation on behalf of the Toronto Police Service. Toronto: Toronto Police Service. Available at www. torontopolice.on.ca.

Goldman, N. (1963). *The Differential Selection of Juvenile Offenders for Court Appearance*. New York: National Council on Crime and Delinquency.

Goldson, B. (2004). New punitiveness: The politics of child incarceration. In J. Muncie, G. Hughes, & E. McLaughlin, (Eds.), *Youth Justice: Critical Readings*. London, UK: Sage Publications Ltd.

Gomes, J.T., Bertrand, L.D., Paetsch, J.J., & Hornick, J. (2003). Self-reported Delinquency among Alberta's Youth: Findings from a Survey of 2,001 Junior and Senior High School Students. *Adolescence, 38* (149), 75–91.

Gomme, I. (1985). Predictors of Status and Criminal Offences among Male and Female Adolescents in an Ontario Community. *Canadian Journal of Criminology, 27* (2), 147–160.

Gomme, I. (1995). Theories of Delinquency. In J. Creechan & R. Silverman, (Eds.), *Canadian Delinquency*. Scarborough ON: Prentice Hall Canada.

Gomme, I., Morton, M., & West, G. (1984). Rates, Types and Patterns of Male and Female Delinquency in an Ontario Community. *Canadian Journal of Criminology, 26* (3), 313–324.

Gordon, R.A. (1987). SES versus IQ in the Race–IQ Delinquency Model. *International Journal of Sociology and Social Policy, 7*, 29–96.

Gordon, R.M. (1993). *Incarcerated Gang Members in British Columbia: A Preliminary Study*. Victoria, BC: Ministry of the Attorney General.

Gordon, R.M. (1995). Street Gangs in Vancouver. In J. Creechan & R. Silverman, (Eds.), *Canadian Delinquency*. Scarborough, ON: Prentice Hall Canada.

Gordon, R.M. (2001). Street Gangs and Criminal Business Organizations: A Canadian Perspective. In R.C. Smandych, (Ed.), *Youth Crime: Varieties, Theories, and Prevention*. Toronto: Harcourt Canada.

Gorham, B. (1993, February 7). Island of Despair. *Province* [Vancouver], A34.

Gorkoff, K., & Runner, J. (Eds.). (2003). *Being Heard: The Experiences of Young Women in Prostitution*. Nova Scotia: Fernwood Publishing.

Gottfredson, M., & Hirschi, T. (1990). *A General Theory of Crime*. Palo Alto, CA: Stanford University Press.

Gottlieb, B. (1993). *The Family in the Western World: From the Black Death to the Industrial Age*. New York: Oxford University Press.

Grade 2 boy suspended for poultry prank. (2001, May 31). *National Post*, A1, A10.

Gray, B., & Tchir, J. (2004, December 17). Toronto police chief says teens are out of control. *Canoe Network* (www.canoe.ca).

Green, G. R., & Healy, K.F. (2003). *Tough on Kids: Rethinking Approaches to Youth Justice*. Saskatchewan: Houghton Boston.

Greenberg, D. (1977). Delinquency and the Age Structure of Society. *Contemporary Crises: Crime, Law, and Social Policy, 1*, 189–223.

Greenberg, P. (1992). Youth Property Crime in Canada. *Juristat, 12* (14). Ottawa: Statistics Canada, Canadian Centre for Justice Statistics.

Greenwood, P., Model, K., Rydell, C.P., & Chiesa, J. (1996). *Diverting Children from a Life of Crime: What Are the Costs and Benefits?* Research Brief: RAND Public Safety and Justice Program. Santa Monica, CA: RAND Corporation.

Griffiths, C.T., & Hamilton, R. (1996). Sanctioning and Healing: Restorative Justice in Canadian Aboriginal Communities. In B. Galaway & J. Hudson, (Eds.), *Restorative Justice: International Perspectives*. New York: Criminal Justice Press.

Groundswell against youth crime seeks to make bad parenting illegal. (1996, May 14). *The Vancouver Sun*, A7.

Hackler, J. (1978). *The Prevention of Youthful Crime: The Great Stumble Forward*. Toronto: Methuen.

Hackler, J. (1991). Good People, Dirty System: The Young Offenders Act and Organizational Failure. In A. Leschied, P. Jaffe, & W. Willis, (Eds.), *The Young Offenders Act: A Revolution in Canadian Juvenile Justice*. Toronto: University of Toronto Press.

Hagan, J. (1989). *Structural Criminology*. New Brunswick: Rutgers University Press.

Hagan, J., Gillis, A.R., &. Chan, J. (1978). Explaining Official Delinquency: A Spatial Study of Class, Conflict and Control. *Sociological Quarterly, 19*, 386–398.

Hagan, J., Gillis, A., & Simpson, J. (1985). The Class Structure of Gender and Delinquency: Toward a Power-Control Theory of Common Delinquent Behavior. *American Journal of Sociology, 90*, 1151–1178.

Hagan, J., & Leon, J. (1977). Rediscovering Delinquency: Social History, Political Ideology and the Sociology of Law. *American Sociological Review, 42*, 587–598.

Hagan, J., & McCarthy, B. (1997). *Mean Streets: Youth Crime and Homelessness*. Cambridge: Cambridge University Press.

Hagan, J., & McCarthy, B. (2000). Symposium on John Hagan and Bill McCarthy's *Mean Streets: Youth Crime and Homelessness*. (Cambridge: Cambridge University Press, 1997). The Meaning of Criminology. *Theoretical Criminology, 4* (2), 232–242.

Hagan J., Simpson, J., & Gillis, A. (1987). Class in the Household: A Power-Control Theory of Delinquency. *American Journal of Sociology, 92*, 788–816.

Hagan J., Simpson, J., & Gillis, A. (1988). Feminist Scholarship, Relational and Instrumental Control and a Power Control Theory of Gender and Delinquency. *British Journal of Sociology, 39* (3), 301–336.

Hagedorn, J. (1988). *People and Folks: Gangs, Crime and the Underclass in Rustbelt City*. Chicago: Lakeview Press.

Hak, J. (1996). The Young Offenders Act. In John Winterdyk, (Ed.), *Issues and Perspectives on Young Offenders in Canada*. Toronto: Harcourt Brace & Company.

Hall, S., Critcher, C., Jefferson, T., J. Clarke, J., & Roberts, B. (1978). *Policing the Crisis: Mugging, the State, and Law and Order*. London, UK: Macmillan.

Hall, S., & Jefferson, T. (Eds.). (1976). *Resistance through Rituals: Youth Subcultures in Post-War Britain*. London, UK: Hutchinson.

Hamilton, A.C., & Sinclair, C.M. (1991). *Report of the Aboriginal Justice Inquiry of Manitoba. Volume 1: The System and Aboriginal People.* Winnipeg: Queen's Printer.

Handa, Amita. (1997). Caught Between Omissions: Exploring "Culture Conflict" among Second Generation South Asian Women in Canada. Ph.D. thesis. Toronto: University of Toronto, Graduate Department of Sociology and Education.

Hannah-Moffat, K., & Shaw, M. (2000). *An Ideal Prison? Critical Essays on Women's Imprisonment in Canada.* Halifax: Fernwood Publishing.

Hare-Mustin, R.T. (1983). An Appraisal of the Relationship between Women and Psychotherapy. *American Psychologist, 38,* 593–601.

Harris, A. (Ed.). (2004). *All about the Girl: Culture, Power, and Identity.* New York: Routledge.

Harris, Mary. (1988). *Cholas: Latino Girls and Gangs.* New York: AMS Press.

Harris, P., Weagant, B., Cole, D., & Weinper, F. (2004). Working "In the Trenches" with the YCJA. *Canadian Journal of Criminology and Criminal Justice,* 367–389.

Hartnagel, T.F., & Baron, S.W. (1995). It's Time to Get Serious: Public Attitudes toward Juvenile Justice in Canada. In J.H. Creechan & R.A. Silverman, (Eds.), *Canadian Delinquency.* Scarborough, ON: Prentice Hall Canada.

Harvey, L., Burnham, R., Kendall, K., & Pease, K. (1992). Gender Differences in Criminal Justice. *British Journal of Criminology, 32,* 208–217.

Hatch, A., & Faith, K. (1991). Female Offenders in Canada: A Statistical Profile. In R. Silverman, J. Teevan, & V. Sacco, (Eds.), *Crime in Canadian Society* (4th ed.). Toronto: Butterworths.

Hathaway, S., & Monachesi, E. (1953). *Analyzing and Predicting Juvenile Delinquency with the MMPI.* Minneapolis: University of Minnesota Press.

Havemann, P. (1992). Crisis Justice for Youth: Making the Young Offenders Act and the Discourse of Penalty. In D. Currie & B. MacLean, (Eds.), *Rethinking the Administration of Justice.* Halifax: Fernwood.

Hawkins, D., & Catalano, R. (1992) *Communities That Care: Action for Drug Abuse Prevention.* San Francisco: Jossey-Bass.

Hawkins, J.D., Herrenkohl, T.L., Farrington, D.P., Brewer, D., Catalano, R.F., & Harachi, T.W. (1998). A review of predictors of youth violence. In Rolf Loeber & David P. Farrington, (Eds.), *Serious and Violent Juvenile Offenders: Risk Factors and Successful Interventions.* Thousand Oaks, CA: Sage Publications, Inc.

Hayes, B. (2005, August 26). Victim's mom sobs: Ruling "isn't fair.". *The Chronicle Herald* [Halifax], B4.

———. (2006, January 12). Teen jailed in McEvoy death: Joyrider gets $4^{1}/_{2}$ years for fatal crash. *The Chronicle Herald* [Halifax], A1.

———. (2006, January 19). Youth lax, lawyer tells inquiry. *The Chronicle Herald* [Halifax], B1.

———. (2006, January 20). Youth no stranger to courts. *The Chronicle Herald* [Halifax], B1.

———. (2006, January 22). Nunn ruling to have broad impact. *The Chronicle Herald* [Halifax], A5.

———. (2006, January 26). Fax foul-up preceded teen's release, fatal crash. *The Chronicle Herald* [Halifax], A1.

———. (2006, January 27). Teen hits speeds of 170 to 180 km/h. *The Chronicle Herald* [Halifax], B1.

———. (2006, January 30). A failure to communicate: McEvoy inquiry has to focus on why teen freed despite warrant. *The Chronicle Herald* [Halifax], A1.

———. (2006, January 31). Warrant was in order. *The Chronicle Herald* [Halifax], A1.

———. (2006, February 1). Mountie feeling weight of tragedy. *The Chronicle Herald* [Halifax], A1.

————. (2006, February 6). Justice official, cop differ on status of arrest warrant. *The Chronicle Herald* [Halifax], B1.

————. (2006, February 7). Fax foul-ups led to bail for teen, McEvoy inquiry told. *The Chronicle Herald* [Halifax], B4.

————. (2006, February 8). Repeated teen crimes upon release upsets Nunn. *The Chronicle Herald* [Halifax], B4.

————. (2006, February 9). Teen's transfer "slipped my mind." *The Chronicle Herald* [Halifax], A1+.

————. (2006, February 15). Lax laws failed son, McEvoy, says mom. *The Chronicle Herald* [Halifax], A1.

————. (2006, February 21). Social worker tells inquiry of boy's troubled home life. *The Chronicle Herald* [Halifax], B4.

————. (2006, February 22). Inquiry told education system failed McEvoy's killer. *The Chronicle Herald* [Halifax], B2.

————. (2006, February 23). Youth act not doing its job—Nunn. *The Chronicle Herald* [Halifax], B3.

————. (2006, February 24). Facility for troubled youth needed, inquiry hears. *The Chronicle Herald* [Halifax], B5.

————. (2006, February 28). Teen allegedly violated bail—Boy, 14, charged in multiple joyrides. The Chronicle Herald [Halifax], B3.

Hayes, B., &. Bradley, S. (2006, January 12). Boy could get out in 18 months. *The Chronicle Herald* [Halifax], A1.

Healy, W., and A. Bronner. (1936). *New Light on Delinquency and Its Treatment.* New Haven, CT: Yale University Press.

Heimer, K. (2000). Symposium on John Hagan and Bill McCarthy's *Mean Streets: Youth Crime and Homelessness.* (Cambridge: Cambridge University Press, 1997). A Model for Criminology in the Next Century. *Theoretical Criminology, 4* (2), 215–221.

Heitgerd, J.L., & Bursik, R.J., Jr. (1987). Extra-Community Dynamics and the Ecology of Delinquency. *American Journal of Sociology, 92,* 775–787.

Hendrick, D. (1991). Youth Court Statistics, Preliminary Data, 1990–91 Highlights. *Juristat, 11* (14). Ottawa: Statistics Canada, Canadian Centre for Justice Statistics.

Hendrick, D. (1997). Youth Court Statistics, 1995–96 Highlights. *Juristat, 17* (10). Ottawa: Statistics Canada, Canadian Centre for Justice Statistics.

Henley, T. (1989). Rediscovery, Ancient Pathways: New Directions. *A Guide to Outdoor Education.* Vancouver: Western Canada Wilderness Committee.

Herman, J.L. (1981). *Father–Daughter Incest.* Cambridge: Harvard University Press.

Hetherington, M. (1977). *Review of Child Development Research.* New York: Russell Sage Foundation.

Hil, R., & McMahon, A. (2001). *Families, Crime & Juvenile Justice.* New York: Peter Lang Publishing, Inc.

Hill, K.G., Howell, J.C., Hawkins, J.D., & Battin-Pearson, S.R. (1999). Childhood risk factors for adolescent gang membership: Results from the Seattle Social Development Project. *Journal of Research in Crime and Delinquency, 36* (3), 300–322.

Hillian, D., & Reitsma-Street, M. (2003). Parents and Youth Justice. *Canadian Journal of Criminology and Criminal Justice, 45* (1), 19–41.

Hillian, D., Reitsma-Street, M., & Hackler, J. (2004). Conferencing in the Youth Criminal Justice Act of Canada: Policy Developments in British Columbia. *Canadian Journal of Criminology and Criminal Justice, 46* (3), 343–366.

Hindelang, M. (1979). Sex Differences in Criminal Activity. *Social Problems* 27, 143–56.

Hindelang, M., Hirschi, T., & Weis, J. (1981). *Measuring Delinquency*. Beverly Hills, CA: Sage.

Hindelang, M., & McDermott, J. (1981). *Analysis of National Crime Victimization Survey Data on Study Serious Delinquent Behavior.* (Monograph 2). Washington, DC: U.S. Department of Justice, Office of Juvenile Justice and Delinquency Prevention.

Hirschi, T. (1969). *Causes of Delinquency*. Berkeley, CA: University of California Press.

Hirschi, T. (1983). Crime and the Family. In James Q. Wilson, (Ed.), *Crime and Public Policy*. San Francisco: Institute for Contemporary Studies Press.

Hirschi, T. (1989). Exploring Alternatives to Integrated Theory. In S. Messner, M. Krohn, & A. Liska, (Eds.), *Theoretical Integration in the Study of Deviance and Crime*. Albany, NY: State University of New York Press.

Hoare, E. (1995, September 21). Copycat assault worries parents. *The Chronicle Herald* [Halifax], A6.

Hogeveen, B. (2001). Winning Deviant Youth Over by Friendly Helpfulness; Transformations in the Legal Governance of Deviant Children in Canada, 1857–1908. In R. C. Smandych (Ed.), *Youth Justice: History, Legislation and Reform* (pp. 43–63). Toronto: Harcourt Canada, .

Hogeveen, B. (2005). History, Development, and Transformations in Canadian Juvenile Justice, 1800–1984. In K. Campbell, (Ed.), *Understanding Youth Justice in Canada*. Toronto: Pearson Education Canada Inc.

Hogeveen, B., & Smandych, R.C. (2001). Origins of the Newly Proposed Canadian Youth Criminal Justice Act: Political Discourse and the Perceived Crisis in Youth Crime in the 1990s. In R.C. Smandych, (Ed.), *Youth Justice: History, Legislation and Reform* (pp. 144–168). Toronto: Harcourt Canada.

Hohenstein, W. (1969). Factors Influencing the Police Disposition of Juvenile Offenders. In T. Sellin & M. Wolfgang, (Eds.), *Delinquency: Selected Studies*. New York: John Wiley & Sons.

Holsinger, K., & Ayers, P. (2004). Mentoring Girls in Juvenile Facilities: Connecting College Students with Incarcerated Girls. *Journal of Criminal Justice Education, 15* (2), 351–372.

Homeless Youth in Perspective. (1994). Halifax: Dalhousie University, Nova Scotia Public Interest Research Group.

Hood-Williams, J. (2001). Gender, Masculinities and Crime: From Structures to Psyches. *Theoretical Criminology, 5* (1), 37–60

Horowitz, R. (1987). Community Tolerance of Gang Violence. *Social Problems, 34* (5), 437–450.

Horowitz, R. (1990). Sociological Perspectives on Gangs: Conflicting Definitions and Concepts. In C. Ronald Huff, (Ed.), *Gangs in America*. Newbury Park, CA: Sage.

Horowitz, R., & Pottieger, A. (1991). Gender Bias in Juvenile Justice Handling of Seriously Crime-Involved Youth. *Journal of Research in Crime and Delinquency, 28* (1), 75–100.

Houston, S. (1972). Victorian Origins of Juvenile Delinquency: A Canadian Experience. *History of Education Quarterly, 12*, 254.

Houston, S. (1982). The "Waifs and Strays" of a Late Victorian City: Juvenile Delinquents in Toronto. In J. Parr, (Ed.), *Childhood and Family in Canadian History*. Toronto: McClelland and Stewart.

Howe, R. (2003, July 18). Neighbourhood's nightmare: Out-of-control youths spread fear, and it took a 13-year-old boy to stand up to it. *Daily News* [Halifax], 22.

Hubler, A. E. (2002). Female Adolescence and its Discontents. In R. Strickland, (Ed.), *Growing Up Postmodern: Neoliberalism and the War on the Young*. Oxford: Rowman & Littlefield Publishers, Inc.

Hudson, Annie. (2004). "Troublesome girls": Towards alternative definitions and policies. In J. Muncie, G. Hughes, & E. McLaughlin, (Eds.), *Youth Justice: Critical Readings.* London, UK: Sage Publications Ltd.

Huizinga, D., & Elliott, D.S. (1987). Juvenile Offenders: Prevalence, Offender Incidence, and Arrest Rates by Race. *Crime and Delinquency, 33* (April), 206–223.

Human Rights Watch. *Children's Rights: Human Rights Developments.* Retrieved on April 2, 2003, from www.hrw.org/wr2k/Crd.htm.

Hylton, J. (1981). Some Attitudes Towards Natives in a Prairie City. *Canadian Journal of Criminology, 23*, 357–363.

Hylton, J. (1994). Get Tough or Get Smart? Options for Canada's Youth Justice System in the Twenty-First Century. *Canadian Journal of Criminology, 36*, 229–246.

Jackson, M. (1988). *Locking Up Natives in Canada: A Report of the Committee of the Canadian Bar Association on Imprisonment and Release.* Ottawa: Canadian Bar Association.

Jackson, S. (1999). Family Group Conferences and Youth Justice: The New Panacea? In B. Goldson, (Ed.), *Youth Justice: Contemporary Policy and Practice* (pp. 127–147). Aldershot, UK: Ashgate.

Jankowski, M. (1991). *Islands in the Street: Gangs and American Urban Society.* Berkeley, CA: University of California Press.

Jeffrey, D. (2005, December 17). Lethal driver's mother sees new attitude. *The Chronicle Herald* [Halifax], A1.

Jeffrey, D. (2005, December 20). No time to grieve for McEvoy's sister. *The Chronicle Herald* [Halifax], B3.

Jeffrey, D. (2006, January 14). McEvoy inquiry set to start Monday. *The Chronicle Herald* [Halifax], A1.

Jeffrey, D. (2006, February 7). Out to scare girl with sex talk, man testifies. *The Chronicle Herald* [Halifax], A1.

Jensen, E.L., & Metsger, L.K. (1994). A Test of the Deterrent Effect of Legislative Waiver on Violent Juvenile Crime. *Crime and Delinquency, 40*, 96–104.

Jensen, G., & Thompson, K. (1990). What's Class Got to Do with It? A Further Examination of Power-Control Theory. *American Journal of Sociology, 95*, 1009–1023.

Jiwani, Y. (1999). Erasing race: The story of Reena Virk. *Canadian Women's Studies, 19* (3), 178–184.

Joe, D., & Robinson, N. (1980). Chinatown's Immigrant Gangs. *Criminology, 18*, 337–345.

Joe, K., & Chesney-Lind, M. (1993). *Just Every Mother's Angel.* Paper presented at meetings of the American Society of Criminology, Phoenix, AZ, October 1993.

John Howard Magazine. (2000). [*1* (1)]. Kingston, ON: The John Howard Society in Canada.

Johnson, H. (1986). *Women and Crime in Canada.* TRS NO9. Ottawa: Solicitor General of Canada, Communications Group.

Johnson, H. (1995). Children and Youths as Victims of Violent Crimes. *Juristat, 15* (15). Ottawa: Statistics Canada, Canadian Crime Statistics.

Johnson, H., & Lazarus, G. (1989). The Impact of Age on Crime Victimization Rates. *Canadian Journal of Criminology, 31*, 309–318.

Johnson, Sara (2003). Custodial Remand in Canada, 1986/87 to 2000/01. *Juristat, 23* (7). Ottawa: Statistics Canada, Canadian Centre for Justice Statistics.

Johnson, Sylvia. J. (December 1998). Girls are in trouble: Do we care? *Corrections Today*, 136–141.

Jolly, S. (1983). *Our Children Are Hurting: Fact Sheet on the Disproportionate Involvement of Indian Young People in the Juvenile Justice and Child Welfare Systems of Ontario.* Ontario Native Council on Justice.

Jones, A. (1988). Closing Penetanguishene Reformatory: An Attempt to Deinstitutionalize Treatment of Young Offenders in Early Twentieth-Century Ontario. In R.C. MacLeod, (Ed.), *Lawful Authority: Readings in the History of Criminal Justice in Canada.* Toronto: Copp Clark Pitman.

Joyce, G. (2000, March 11). Friend of accused tells of attack on Virk, *The Chronicle Herald* [Halifax], D32.

Justice for Girls. (2001). *Statement of Opposition to the Secure Care Act.* Available from www.justiceforgirls.org/publications/pos_securecareact.html.

Kadi, J. (1996). *Thinking class: Sketches from a cultural worker.* Boston: Southend Press.

Kaihla, P. (1994). Kids Who Kill. *Maclean's, 107* (33), 32–39.

Kaminski, L. (1993). *The Welfare Supervision Board: The Eugenic Argument and the Report on Juvenile Delinquency in Manitoba, 1934–35: Welfare vs. Justice.* University of Manitoba, Child and Family Research Group.

Kaminski, L. (1994). *Children, Delinquency and the Community.* Unpublished paper. Manitoba: University of Manitoba, School of Social Work.

Kandel, E., & Mednick, S. (1991). Prenatal Complications Predict Violent Offending. *Criminology, 29,* 519–520.

Kaplan, H.B. (1975). *Self-Attitudes and Deviant Behavior.* Pacific Palisades, CA: Goodyear.

Kappeler, V.E., Blumberg, M., & Potter, G.W. (1996). The Mythology of Crime and *Criminal Justice* (2nd ed.). Prospect Heights, IL: Waveland.

Katz, J. (1988). *Seductions of Crime.* New York: Basic Books.

Keane, C., Gillis, A.R., & Hagan, J. (1989). Deterrence and Amplification of Juvenile Delinquency by Police Contact: The Importance of Gender and Risk-Orientation. *British Journal of Criminology, 29* (4), 336–352.

Keating, L.M., Tomishima, M.A., Foster, S., & Alessandri, M. (2002). The Effects of a Mentoring Program on At-Risk Youth. *Adolescence, 37* (148), 717–734.

Keiser, L.R. (1969). *The Vice Lords.* New York: Holt, Rinehart and Winston.

Kelley, B.T., Thornberry, T.P., & Smith, C.A. (1997). *In the Wake of Childhood Maltreatment.* Washington, D.C.: U.S. Department of Justice, Office of Justice Programs, Office of Juvenile Justice and Delinquency Prevention.

Kelly, D. (1975). Status Origins, Track Position, and Delinquent Involvement. *Sociological Quarterly, 16,* 264–271.

Kelso, J.J. (1907a). Delinquent Children. *Canadian Law Review, 6,* 106–110.

Kelso, J.J. (1907b). Children's Courts. *Canadian Law Times and Review, 26,* 163–166.

Kenewell, J., Bala, N., & Colfer, P. (1991). Young Offenders. In R. Barnhorst and L.C. Johnson, (Eds.), *The State of the Child in Ontario.* Toronto: Oxford University Press.

Kierkus, C.A., &. Baer, D. (2002). A social control explanation of the relationship between family structure and delinquent behavior. *Canadian Journal of Criminology, 44* (4), 425–458.

King, A., Boyce, W., & King, M. (1999). *Trends in the Health of Canadian Youth. A World Health Organization Cross-National Study.* Ottawa: Health Canada.

Klein, M. (1971). *Street Gangs and Street Workers.* Englewood Cliffs, NJ: Prentice-Hall.

Kohlberg, L. (1964). Development of Moral Character and Moral Ideology. In M. Hoffman and L. Hoffman, (Eds.), *Review of Childhood Development Research, 1.* New York: Russell Sage Foundation.

Kohlberg, L. (1969). Stage and Sequence. In D. Goslin, (Ed.), *Handbook of Socialization and Theory.* Chicago: Rand McNally.

Kong, R. (1994). Urban/Rural Criminal Victimization in Canada. *Juristat, 14* (17). Ottawa: Statistics Canada, Canadian Crime Statistics.

Kong, R. (1998). Canadian Crime Statistics 1997. *Juristat, 18* (11). Ottawa: Statistics Canada, Canadian Crime Statistics.

Kong, R., Johnson, H., Beattie, S., & Cardillo, A. (2003). Sexual Offences in Canada. *Juristat, 23* (6). Ottawa: Statistics Canada, Canadian Centre for Justice Statistics.

Konopka, G. (1966). *The Adolescent Girl in Conflict.* Englewood Cliffs, NJ: Prentice-Hall.

Koshan, J. (1998). Aboriginal Women, Justice and the *Charter:* Bridging the Divide. *University of British Columbia Law Review, 32,* 23–54.

Kostash, M. (1987). *No Kidding: Inside the World of Teenage Girls.* Toronto: McClelland and Stewart.

Kracke, K. (1996, June). *Safe Futures: Partnerships to Reduce Youth Violence and Delinquency* (Fact Sheet 38). Washington, DC: U.S. Department of Justice, Office of Juvenile Justice and Delinquency Prevention.

Krisberg, B. (1975). *The Gang and the Community.* San Francisco: R & E Research Associates.

Krisberg, B. (2004). *Juvenile Justice: Redeeming our Children.* Newbury Park, CA: Sage

Krisberg, B., & Austin, J.F. (1978). *The Children of Ishmael: Critical Perspectives on Juvenile Justice.* Palo Alto, CA: Mayfield.

Krisberg, B., & Austin, J.F. (1993). *Reinventing Juvenile Justice.* Newbury Park, CA: Sage.

Kueneman, R., Linden, R., & Kosmick, R. (1992). Juvenile Justice in Rural and Northern Manitoba. *Canadian Journal of Criminology, 34,* 435–460.

Kufeldt, K., & Nimmo, M. (1987). Youth on the Street: Abuse and Neglect in the Eighties. *Child Abuse and Neglect, 11,* 531–543.

Lambie, C. (2006, January 18). Ex-school may be used to house teen moms. *The Chronicle Herald* [Halifax], B7.

Lambie, C. (2006, March 20). End racial profiling. *The Chronicle Herald* [Halifax], A1.

LaPrairie, C.P. (1983). Native Juveniles in Court: Some Preliminary Observations. In T. Fleming & L.A. Visano, (Eds.), *Deviant Designations: Crime, Law, and Deviants.* Toronto: Butterworths.

LaPrairie, C.P. (1988). The Young Offenders Act and Aboriginal Youth. In J. Hudson, J. Hornick, & B. Burrows, (Eds.), *Justice and the Young Offender in Canada.* Toronto: Wall and Thompson.

LaPrairie, C.P. (1994). *Seen But Not Heard: Native People in the Inner City.* (Reports 1–3). Ottawa: Department of Justice, Canada.

LaPrairie, C.P. (1995). Seen but Not Heard: Native People in Four Canadian Inner Cities. *The Journal of Human Justice, 6* (2), 30–45.

LaPrairie, C.P. (2002). Aboriginal over-representation in the criminal justice system: A tale of nine cities. *Canadian Journal of Criminology, 44,* 181–208.

LaPrairie, C.P., & Griffiths, C.T. (1982). Native Indian Delinquency: A Review of Recent Findings: Native People and Justice in Canada. *Canadian Legal Aid Bulletin, 5* (1) (Special Issue, Part 1), 39–45.

Latimer, J. (2001). A meta-analytic examination of youth delinquency, family treatment, and recidivism. *Canadian Journal of Criminology,* 237–253.

Latimer, J., & Foss, L.C. (2004). *A One-Day Snapshot of Aboriginal Youth in Custody Across Canada: Phase II.* Ottawa: Department of Justice, Canada.

Latimer, J., Dowden, C., Morton-Bourgon, K.E., Edgar, J., & Bania, M. (2003). *Treating Youth in Conflict with the Law: A New Meta-Analysis.* Ottawa: Department of Justice, Canada.

Laub, L., & Sampson, R. (1988). Unraveling Families and Delinquency. *Criminology, 26,* 355–380.

Lauderback, D., Hansen, J., & Waldorf, D. (1992). Sisters Are Doin' It for Themselves: A Black Female Gang in San Francisco. *The Gang Journal, 1,* 57–72.

Law Reform Commission of Canada. (1991). *Report on Aboriginal Peoples and Criminal Justice.* Ottawa: Minister of Justice.

Leah, R. (1995). Aboriginal Women and Everyday Racism in Alberta. *The Journal of Human Justice, 6* (2), 10–29.

Le Blanc, M. (1983). Delinquency as an Epiphenomenon of Adolescents. In N. Corrado, M. Le Blanc, & J. Trepanier, (Eds.), *Current Issues in Juvenile Justice*. Toronto: Butterworths.

Le Blanc, M. (1992). Family Dynamics, Adolescent Delinquency and Adult Criminality. *Psychiatry, 55*, 336–353.

Le Blanc, M. (1993). The Prediction of Male Adolescent and Adult Offending from School Offence. In E. Vallieres & P. McDuff, (Eds.), *Canadian Journal of Criminology, 33* (4), 459–478.

Le Blanc, M., & Tremblay, R.E. (1988). Homeostasis: Social Changes Plus Modifications in the Basic Personality of Adolescents Equal Stability of Hidden Delinquency. *International Journal of Adolescence and Youth, 1* (3), 269–291.

Legge, L. (1996, April 20). Last hope for the lost boys. *The Chronicle Herald* [Halifax], C1.

Lemert, E. (1951). *Social Pathology*. New York: McGraw-Hill.

Lemert, E. (1967). *Human Deviance, Social Problems and Social Control*. Englewood Cliffs, NJ: Prentice-Hall.

Leon, J.S. (1977). The Development of Canadian Juvenile Justice: A Background for Reform. *Osgoode Hall Law Journal, 15*, 71–106.

Leonard, E.B. (1982). *Women, Crime and Society: A Critique of Theoretical Criminology*. New York: Longmans.

Leonard, T. (1993). Youth Court Statistics. *Juristat, 13* (5). Ottawa: Statistics Canada, Canadian Centre for Justice Statistics.

Leonard, T., Smandych, R., & Brickey, S. (1996). Changes in the Youth Justice System. In John Winterdyk, (Ed.), *Issues and Perspectives on Young Offenders in Canada*. Toronto: Harcourt Brace & Company.

Lerner, R. (1986). *Concepts and Theories of Human Development* (2nd ed.). New York: Random House.

Lersch, K.M., & Sellers, C.S. (2000). A comparison of curfew and noncurfew violators using a self-report delinquency survey. *American Journal of Criminal Justice, 24* (2), 259–269.

Leschied, A., & Cunningham, A. (2002). *Seeking Effective Interventions for Serious Young Offenders: Interim Results of a Four-Year Randomized Study of Multisystematic Therapy in Ontario, Canada*. Ontario: Centre for Children and Families in the Justice System.

Leschied, A., Cunningham, A., & Hawkins, L. (2000). *Clinical Trials of Multisystematic Therapy in Ontario, 1997 to 2001*. Ontario: Centre for Children and Families in the Justice System.

Leschied, A., & Jaffe, P. (1987). Impact of the Young Offenders Act on Court Dispositions: A Comparative Analysis. *Canadian Journal of Criminology, 29*, 421–430.

Leschied, A., & Jaffe, P. (1988). Implementing the Young Offenders Act in Ontario: Critical Issues and Challenges for the Future. In J.P. Hudson, J. Hornick, & B. Burrows, (Eds.), *Justice and the Young Offender in Canada*. Toronto: Wall and Thompson.

Leschied, A., & Jaffe, P. (1991). Dispositions as Indicators of Conflicting Social Purposes Under the JDA and YOA. In A. Leschied, P. Jaffe, and W. Willis, (Eds.), *The Young Offenders Act: A Revolution in Canadian Juvenile Justice*. Toronto: University of Toronto Press.

Leschied, A., Jaffe, P., Andrews, D., & Gendreau, P. (1992). Treatment Issues and Young Offenders: An Empirically Derived Vision of Juvenile Justice Policy. In R. Corrado, N. Bala, R. Linden, M. Le Blanc, (Eds.), *Juvenile Justice in Canada: A Theoretical and Analytical Assessment*. Toronto: Butterworths.

Leschied, A., Jaffe, P., & Stone, G. (1985). Differential Response of Juvenile Offenders to Two Detention Home Environments as a Function of Conceptual Level. *Canadian Journal of Criminology, 27*, 467–476.

Leschied, A., Jaffe, P., & Willis, W. (Eds.). (1991). *The Young Offenders Act: A Revolution in Canadian Juvenile Justice*. Toronto: University of Toronto Press.

Leschied, A., & Thomas, K. (1985). Effective Residential Programming for "Hard-to-Serve" Delinquent Youth. *Canadian Journal of Criminology, 27*, 161–177.

Lethal driver's mother sees new attitude. (2005, December 17). *The Chronicle Herald* [Halifax], A1.

Leyton, E. (1979). *The Myth of Delinquency: An Anatomy of Juvenile Nihilism*. Toronto: McClelland & Stewart.

Li, Peter S. (1990). *Race and Ethnic Relations in Canada*. Toronto: Oxford University Press.

Life's Too Short. (1997, January/February). *Society News*. Youth Alternative Society of Halifax, Nova Scotia.

Limber, S.P., & Nation, M.M. (1998). Bullying Among Children and Youth. In J. Arnette & M. Walsleben, (Eds.), *Combating Fear and Restoring Safety in Schools*. Washington, D.C.: Office of Juvenile Justice & Delinquency Prevention.

Linden, R., & Fillmore, C. (1981). A Comparative Study of Delinquency Involvement. *Canadian Review of Sociology and Anthropology, 18*, 343–361.

Lipscombe, K. (2006, January 17). "Lots of warning signs." *The Chronicle Herald* [Halifax], A1.

Lipsey, M.W. (1990). *Juvenile Delinquency Treatment: A Meta-Analytic Inquiry into the Variability of Effects*. New York: Russell Sage Foundation.

Lipsey, M.W. (1995). What do we learn from 400 research studies on the effectiveness of treatment with juvenile delinquents? In J. McGuire, (Ed.), *What Works:Reducing Reoffending—Guidelines from Research and Practice* (pp. 63–78). Chichester, England: John Wiley and Sons.

Lipsey, M.W., & Derzon, J.H. (1998). Predictors of Violent or Serious Delinquency in Adolescence and Early Adulthood. In Rolf Loeber & David P. Farrington, (Eds.), *Serious and Violent Juvenile Offenders: Risk Factors and Successful Interventions*. Thousand Oaks, CA: Sage Publications, Inc.

Liska, A., Krohn, M.D., & Messner, S.F. (1989). Strategies and Requisites for Theoretical Integration in the Study of Crime and Deviance. In Steven F. Messner, Marvin D. Krohn, & Allen E. Liska, (Eds.), *Theoretical Integration in the Study of Deviance and Crime*. Albany, NY: State University of New York Press.

Liska, A., & Reid, M. (1985). Ties to Conventional Institutions and Delinquency. *American Sociological Review, 50*, 547–560.

Liska, A., & Tausig, M. (1979). Theoretical Interpretations of Social Class and Racial Differentials in Legal Decision-Making for Juveniles. *The Sociological Quarterly, 20*, 197–207.

Loader, I. (1996). *Youth, Policing and Democracy*. London, UK: Macmillan.

Loeber, R. (1988). *Families and Crime*. Washington, DC: U.S. Department of Justice.

Loeber, R., & Stouthamer-Loeber, M. (1999). Juvenile Aggression at Home and at School. In D.S. Elliot, B.A. Hamburg, & K.R. Williams, (Eds.), *Violence in American Schools*. New York: Cambridge.

Loeber, R., Stouthamer-Loeber, M., Van Kammen, W.B., & Farrington, D.P. (1991). Initiation, escalation and desistance in juvenile offending and their correlates. *Journal of Criminal Law and Criminology, 82*, 36–82.

Logan, R. (2000). Crime Statistics in Canada. *Juristat, 21* (8). Ottawa: Statistics Canada, Canadian Centre for Justice Statistics.

Lombroso, C., & Ferrero, W. (1895/1959). *The Female Offender*. New York: Peter Owen.

Lundman, R. (1993). *Prevention and Control of Juvenile Delinquency* (2nd ed.). New York: Oxford University Press.

Lundman, R., Sykes, R.E., & Clark, J.P. (1978). Police Control of Juveniles: A Replication. *Journal of Research in Crime and Delinquency, 15* (January), 74–91.

MacDonald, A. (2002, September 12). Stabbing-case boy denied bail. *The Daily News* [Halifax], 3.

MacDonald, A. (2003, April 6). Act expected to staunch flow of public information on youth crime. *The Sunday Daily News* [Halifax], 8.

MacDonald, Jo-Anne. (1994, September 4). 15 Years Old and Flush with Cash. *Sunday Daily News* [Halifax], 6.

MacDonald, Jo-Anne. (1994, September 5). Judging the Children. *Daily News* [Halifax], 6.

MacDonald, Jo-Anne. (1994, September 6). Locked Down. We're Treating Them as Human Beings. *Daily News* [Halifax], 4.

MacIntyre, M. (2006). *Canada's Little Secret: An examination of governance practices within Youth Justice System Privacy Regulations.* Unpublished MA thesis.

MacKenzie, D.L., Wilson, D.B., Armstrong, G.S., & Gover, A.R. (2001). The Impact of Boot Camps and Traditional Institutions on Juvenile Residents: Perceptions, Adjustment, and Change. *Journal of Research in Crime and Delinquency, 30* (3), 279–313.

MacKinlay, S. (1995, July 26). Teens Charged in "Brutal Attack." *Daily News* [Halifax], 3.

Maclure, R., Campbell, K., & Dufresne, M. (2003). Young Offender Diversion in Canada: Tensions and Contradictions of Social Policy Appropriation. *Policy Studies, 24,* 135–150.

Maguin, E., & Loeber, R. (1996). Academic performance and delinquency. In M. Tonry, (Ed.), *Crime and Justice: A Review of Research.* Illinois: University of Chicago Press.

Manitoba parents can be responsible for youth crime. (1997, September 23). *The Chronicle Herald* [Halifax], A26.

Margolin, G. (1998). Effects of Domestic Violence on Children. In P.K. Trickett & C.J. Schellenbach, (Eds.), *Violence against Children in the Family and the Community.* Washington, DC: American Psychological Association, 57–101.

Marinelli, J. (2004). Youth Custody and Community Services in Canada, 2001/2002. Statistics Canada: *Juristat, 24* (3).

Markwart, A. (1992). Custodial Sanctions Under the Young Offenders Act. In R. Corrado, N. Bala, R. Linden, & M. Le Blanc, (Eds.), *Juvenile Justice in Canada: A Theoretical and Analytical Assessment.* Toronto: Butterworths.

Markwart, A. (2000). *Conferencing under the YCJA.* Unpublished discussion paper. Ottawa: Ministry of Children and Family Development.

Markwart, A., & Corrado, R. (1989). Is the Young Offenders Act More Punitive? In L. Beaulieu, (Ed.), *Young Offender Dispositions: Perspectives on Principles and Practice.* Toronto: Wall and Thompson.

Marron, K. (1993). *Apprenticed in Crime: Young Offenders, the Law, and Crime in Canada.* Toronto: Seal Books.

Martinson, R. (1974). What Works? Questions and Answers About Prison Reform. *The Public Interest, 35* (Spring), 22–54.

Martinson, R. (1979). New Findings, New Views: A Note of Caution Regarding Sentencing Reform. *Hofstra Law Review, 7,* 243–258.

Matsueda, R.L., & Heimer, K. (1997). A Symbolic Interactionist Theory of Role-Transitions, Role-Commitments, and Delinquency. In T. Thornberry, (Ed.), *Developmental Theories of Crime and Delinquency.* New Brunswick, NJ: Transaction Books, 163–213.

Matthews, F. (1993). *Youth Gangs on Youth Gangs.* Ottawa: Department of Justice, Canada.

Matza, D. (1964). *Delinquency and Drift.* New York: Free Press.

Maxon, C., Gordon, M.A., & Klein, M. (1985). Differences Between Gang and Non-Gang Homicides. *Criminology, 23,* 209–222.

Maxon, C., & Klein, M. (1990). Street Gang Violence: Twice as Great or Half as Great? In C. Ronald Huff, (Ed.), *Gangs in America.* Newbury Park, CA: Sage.

Mayor's Report. (1862). *Annual Reports.* City of Halifax: Nova Scotia Provincial Archives.

McCarthy, B., & Hagan, J. (1992). Mean Streets: The Theoretical Significance of Situational Delinquency Among Homeless Youths. *American Journal of Sociology, 98* (3), 597–627.

McCarthy, B., Felmlee, D., & Hagan, J. (2004). Girl Friends are Better: Gender, Friends, and Crime Among School and Street Youth. *Criminology, 42* (4), 805–835.

McCarthy, W. (1990). *Life on the Street: Serious Theft, Drug Selling and Prostitution among Homeless Youth.* Ph.D. dissertation, University of Toronto.

McCormack, A., Janus, M.D., & Burgess, W.A. (1986). Runaway Youths and Sexual Victimization: Gender Differences in an Adolescent Runaway Population. *Child Abuse and Neglect, 10*, 887–895.

McCrossin, S. (1994). *Juvenile Justice and Youth Crime in Nova Scotia.* A research and discussion paper. Nova Scotia Youth Secretariat, Halifax.

McCully, S. (1994). Detention Reform from a Judge's Viewpoint. In I.M. Schwartz & W.H. Barton, (Eds.), *Reforming Juvenile Detention: No More Hidden Closets.* Columbia: Ohio State University Press.

McDougall, D. (1992, August 27). No more slap on the wrist. *The Chronicle Herald* [Halifax], A1.

McDowall, D., Loftin, C., & Wiersema, B. (2000). The impact of youth curfew laws on juvenile crime rates. *Crime & Delinquency, 46* (1), 76–91.

McEachern, R., & Bauzer, R. (1967). Factors Related to Dispositions in Juvenile Police Contacts. In M. Klein, (Ed.), *Juvenile Gangs in Context.* Englewood Cliffs, NJ: Prentice-Hall.

McFarlane, J., & Williams, T. (1990). The Enigma of Premenstrual Syndrome. *Canadian Psychology, 31*, 95–108.

McGuire, M. (1997). C-19: An Act to Amend the Young Offenders Act and the Criminal Code Getting Tougher. *Canadian Journal of Criminology*, (April), 185–214.

McIlroy, A. (1998, March 16). Ottawa poised to revamp Young Offenders Act. *The Globe and Mail*, A3.

McIlroy, A. (1998, May 13). McLellan proposes youth justice changes. *The Globe and Mail*, A3.

McNaught, A. (1998). *Parental Responsibility Legislation and Young Offenders.* (Backgrounder 2). Toronto: Ontario Legislative Library.

McRobbie, A. (1976). Girls and Subcultures. In S. Hall & T. Jefferson, (Eds.), *Resistance Through Rituals.* London, UK: Hutchinson.

McRobbie, A. (2004). Notes on Postfeminism and Popular Culture: Bridget Jones and the New Gender Regime. In A. Harris, (Ed.), *All about the Girl: Culture, Power, and Identity.* New York: Routledge.

Mears, D.P., Ploeger, M., & Warr, M. (1998). Explaining the gender gap in delinquency: Peer influence and moral evaluations of behavior. *Journal of Research in Crime and Delinquency, 35* (3), 251–267.

Medel, B. (2005, July 23). Boys charged in beating: Yarmouth pair held in attack on hotdog vendor. *The Chronicle Herald* [Halifax], B2.

Mednick, S., Gabrielli, W., & Hutchings, B. (1987). Genetic Factors in the Etiology of Criminal Behaviour. In S. Mednick, Terrie E. Moffitt, & Susan A. Stack, (Eds.), *The Causes of Crime.* Cambridge: Cambridge University Press.

Meehan, A.J. (1993). Internal Police Records and the Control of Juveniles: Politics and Policing in a Suburban Town. *British Journal of Criminology, 33* (4), 504–524.

Meissner, D. (2006, February 9). Mom sensed toddler's fear of violent uncle, inquest told. *The Chronicle Herald* [Halifax], A6.

Meissner, D. (2006, February 10). Nobody should have been in my care—Man who beat niece to death testifies at coroner's inquest. *The Chronicle Herald* [Halifax], *A6.*

Melchers, R. (2003). Do Toronto Police Engage in Racial Profiling? *Canadian Journal of Criminology and Criminal Justice, 45* (3), 347–366.

Meloff, W., & Silverman, R. (1992). Canadian Kids Who Kill. *Canadian Journal of Criminology, 34,* 15–34.

Melville, K. (1988). *Marriage and the Family Today* (4th ed.). New York: Random House.

Merton, R.K. (1938). Social Structure and Anomie. *American Sociological Review, 3,* 672–682.

Merton, R.K. (1968). *Social Theory and Social Structure.* New York: Free Press/Macmillan.

Messerschmidt, J. (1986). *Capitalism, Patriarchy, and Crime: Toward a Socialist Feminist Criminology.* Totowa, NJ: Rowman & Littlefield.

Messerschmidt, J. (1993). *Masculinities and Crime.* Lanham, MD: Rowman & Littlefield.

Miller, J., & White, N.A. (2004). Situational Effects of Gender Inequality on Girls' Participation in Violence. In C. Adler & A. Worrall, (Eds.), *Girls' Violence: Myths and Realities.* Albany: State University of New York Press.

Miller, P., Donahue, P., Este, D., & Hofer, M. (2004). Experiences of Being Homeless or At Risk of Being Homeless Among Canadian Youths. *Adolescence, 39* (156), 735–755.

Miller, W. (1958). Lower-Class Culture as a Generating Milieu of Gang Delinquency. *Journal of Social Issues, 14,* 5–19.

Miller, W. (1980). American Youth Gangs. In Abraham Blumberg, (Ed.), *Current Perspectives on Criminal Behavior.* New York: Knopf.

Milne, H., Linden, R., & Kueneman, R. (1992). Advocate or Guardian: The Role of Defence Counsel in Youth Justice. In R. Corrado, N. Bala, R. Linden, & M. Le Blanc, (Eds.), *Juvenile Justice in Canada: A Theoretical and Analytical Assessment.* Toronto: Butterworths.

Milner, T. (1995). Juveniles' Understanding of Legal Language. In J. Creechan & R. Silverman, (Eds.), *Canadian Delinquency.* Scarborough, ON: Prentice Hall Canada.

Minister of Justice. (1994, June 2). *Department of Justice News Release.* Ottawa: Government of Canada.

Mitchell, K.J., & Finkelhor, D. (2001). Risk of Crime Victimization among Youth Exposed to Domestic Violence. *Journal of Interpersonal Violence, 16* (9), 944–964.

Mitterauer, M. (1992). *A History of Youth* (G. Dunphy, Trans.). Blackwell Publishers.

Moffitt, T., McGee, R., & Silva, P. (1987). Self-Reported Delinquency, Neuropsychological Deficit, and History of Attention Deficit Disorder. Paper presented at annual meeting of the American Society of Criminology, Montreal.

Montgomery, A. (1997). *Alternative Measures in Nova Scotia: A Comprehensive Review.* Nova Scotia Department of Justice.

Monture-OKanee, P.A. (1993). Reclaiming Justice: Aboriginal Women and Justice Initiatives in the 1990s. *Aboriginal Peoples and the Justice System: Report of the National Round Table on Aboriginal Justice Issues.* Ottawa: Royal Commission on Aboriginal Peoples, 105–132.

Moogk, P.N. (1982). Les Petits Sauvages: The Children of 18th-Century New France. In J. Parr, (Ed.), *Childhood and Family in Canadian History.* Toronto: McClelland and Stewart.

Moore, D.B., & O'Connell, P.A. (1994). Family Conferencing in Wagga Wagga: A Communitarian Model of Justice. In C. Alder & J. Wundersitz, (Eds.), *Family Conferencing and Juvenile Justice: The Way Forward or Misplaced Optimism?* Canberra: Australian Institute of Criminology.

Moore, J. (1991). *Going Down to the Barrio: Homeboys and Homegirls in Change.* Philadelphia: Temple University Press.

Morash, M. (1983). Gangs, Groups and Delinquency. *British Journal of Criminology, 23,* 309–335.

Morash, M. (1984). Establishment of a Juvenile Police Record: The Influence of Individual and Peer Group Characteristics. *Criminology, 22* (February), 97–111.

Morash, M. (1986). Gender, Peer Group Experiences and Seriousness of Delinquency. *Journal of Research in Crime and Delinquency, 23* (1), 43–67.

Morash, M., & Chesney-Lind, M. (1989). Girls' Crime and Women's Place: Toward a Feminist Model of Female Delinquency. *Crime and Delinquency, 35,* 5–29.

Morash, M., & Chesney-Lind, M. (1991). A Reformulation and Partial Test of the Power Control Theory of Delinquency. *Justice Quarterly, 8,* 347–377.

More dressing than meat. (1998, May 14). *The Chronicle Herald* [Halifax], C1.

Morin, B. (1990). Native Youth and the Young Offenders Act. *Legal Perspectives, 14* (4), 13–15.

Morris, A. (1987). *Women, Crime and Criminal Justice.* New York: Basil Blackwell.

Morris, R. (1964). Female Delinquencies and Relational Problems. *Social Problems, 43,* 82–88.

Morris, R. (2000). *Stories of Transformative Justice.* Toronto: Canadian Scholars' Press Inc.

Morrison, B., Doucet, C., & Le Blanc, M. (2005). New Brunswick Perspectives on Crime Prevention: Promising Practices for Children, Youth and Families. Nova Scotia: Gaspereau Press.

Morton, B., & Glynn, L. (August 2005). Meeting the Distinct Needs of Girls: Progressive, Gender-Specific Design for Girls' Detention. *Corrections Today,* 88–108.

Most young offenders have one brush with law: Study dispels image that minority go on to become chronic criminals. (2005, November 22). The Canadian Press.

Motiuk, M. (1995). Secure Detention and Short-Term Custody Youth Centres: A Social Service Perspective. *Forum of Corrections Research, 7* (1), 28–30.

Moyer, S. (1992). Race, Gender, and Homicide: Comparisons Between Aboriginal and Other Canadians. *Canadian Journal of Criminology, 34,* 387–402.

Moyer, S., & Carrington, P. (1985). *The Attitudes of Canadian Juvenile Justice Professionals Towards the Young Offenders Act.* Ottawa: Ministry of the Solicitor General.

Muehlbauer, G., & Dodder, L. (1983). *The Losers: Gang Delinquency in an American Suburb.* New York: Praeger.

Muncie, J., & Hughes, G. (2004). Modes of youth governance: Political rationalities, criminalization and resistance. In J. Muncie, G. Hughes, & E. McLaughlin, (Eds.), *Youth Justice: Critical Readings.* London, UK: Sage Publications Ltd.

Muncie, J., Hughes, G., & McLaughlin, E. (Eds.). (2004). *Youth Justice: Critical Readings.* London, UK: Sage Publications Ltd.

Myers, M. (2000). Symposium on John Hagan and Bill McCarthy's *Mean Streets: Youth Crime and Homelessness.* (Cambridge: Cambridge University Press, 1997). Toward Theoretical Integration. *Theoretical Criminology, 4* (2), 221–225.

Myrskog, F. (1995, August 3). Canada Becoming a Safer Place. *Daily News* [Halifax], 8.

Nahanee, T. (1995). *Marriage As an Instrument of Oppression in Aboriginal Communities.* Unpublished keynote address to the National Association of Women and the Law's 11th Biennial Conference, St. John's, Newfoundland, May 13, 1995.

Nelson, J. (1994). *Kids Who Kill Kids.* Los Angeles: Storm Publishing Company.

Neugebauer, R. (1992). Misogyny, Law and the Police: Policing Violence Against Women. In K. McCormick & L. Visano, (Eds.), *Understanding Policing.* Toronto: Canadian Scholars Press.

Neugebauer-Visano, R. (1996). Kids, Cops, and Colour: The Social Organization of Police–Minority Youth Relations. In G. O'Bireck, (Ed.), *Not a Kid Anymore.* Scarborough, ON: ITP Nelson.

Newburn, T. (2004). The contemporary politics of youth crime prevention. In J. Muncie, G. Hughes, & E. McLaughlin, (Eds.), *Youth Justice: Critical Readings.* London, UK: Sage Publications Ltd.

Newfoundland and Labrador. (1994, January). *An Overview of the Alternative Measures Process for Young Offenders in Newfoundland and Labrador.* Division of Youth Corrections, Department of Social Services.

Newfoundland and Labrador. (1994, October). *Intensive Intervention Program.* Division of Youth Corrections, Department of Social Services.

Newfoundland and Labrador. (1996). *Annual Report, 1994–95.* Division of Youth Corrections, Department of Social Services.

Newfoundland girl convicted of killing grandmother. (2001, October 27). *The Daily News,* 14

New Youth Justice Act clears Parliament; opposition unimpressed. (2002, February 5). *CBC News.*

NiCarthy, G. (1983). Addictive Love and Abuse: A Course for Teenage Women. In S. Davidson, (Ed.), *The Second Mile: Contemporary Approaches in Counselling Young Women.* Tucson, AZ: New Directions for Young Women.

Nicoll, C. (2001, October 17). Youth sentenced to three years for violent pizza robbery. *The Daily News* [Halifax], 10.

Nixon, K., & Tutty, L.M. (2003). That Was My Prayer Every Night— Just to Get Home Safe: Violence in the Lives of Girls Exploited through Prostitution. In K. Gorkoff & J. Runner, (Eds.), *Being Heard: The Experiences of Young Women in Prostitution. Halifax: Fernwood and RESOLVE.*

Nova Scotia Department of Community Services. (1993). *Report of the Female Young Offender Review Committee.*

Nova Scotia Department of Corrections. (1994, October). *Nova Scotia Department of Justice, Department of Corrections, Policy and Procedures, Young Offender Institutions.*

Nova Scotia Youth Secretariat. (1993). *Juvenile Justice and Youth Crime in Nova Scotia.*

Nuffield, J. (2003). *The Challenges of Youth Justice in Rural and Isolated Areas in Canada.* Department of Justice, Canada, Research and Statistics Division.

Nye, F., & Short, J. (1957). Scaling Delinquent Behavior. *American Sociological Review, 22,* 326–332.

O'Brien, D. (1984). Juvenile Diversion: An Issues Perspective from the Atlantic Provinces. *Canadian Journal of Criminology, 26,* 217–231.

O'Brien, M. J. & Bera, W. H. (1986). Adolescent Sexual Offenders: A Descriptive Typology. *Preventing Sexual Abuse, 1,* 1–4.

Ogrodnik, L. (1994). Canadian Crime Statistics, 1993. *Juristat, 14.* Ottawa: Statistics Canada, Canadian Centre for Justice Statistics.

O'Hanlon. (1998, October 30). Justice ministers split on YOA. *The Chronicle Herald* [Halifax], D14.

Ontario Ministry of the Solicitor General and Correctional Services. (1995a, June 22). *Government of Ontario, Ministry of the Solicitor General and Correctional Services Information Paper.* Correctional Services Division.

Ontario Ministry of the Solicitor General and Correctional Services. *Women's Issues Task Force Report.* (1995b, June 22). Ministry of the Solicitor General and Correctional Services information paper, Correctional Services Division.

Oosterom, N. (1995, July 25). Drive-by shooter kills boy, 13. *The Chronicle Herald* [Halifax], 3.

Owram, K. (2003, January 13). Kids are all right: youth crime rate on the drop. *The Varsity Online:* www.thevarsity.ca.

Palmer, T. (1974). The Youth Authority's Community Treatment Project. *Federal Probation, 38,* 3–14.

Pate, K., & Peachey, D. (1988). Face-to-Face: Victim–Offender Mediation under the Young Offenders Act. In J. Hudson, J. Hornick, & B. Burrows, (Eds.), *Justice and the Young Offender in Canada.* Toronto: Wall and Thompson.

Parker, J.S., & Benson, M.J. (2004). Parent-Adolescent Relations and Adolescent Functioning: Self-Esteem, Substance Abuse, and Delinquency. *Adolescence, 39* (155), 519–530.

Patterson, G. (1980). Children Who Steal. In T. Hirschi & M. Gottfredson, (Eds.), *Understanding Crime.* Beverly Hills, CA: Sage.

Pearson, G. (1983). *Hooligan.* London, UK: Macmillan.

Pearson, J. (1991). Legal Representation under the Young Offenders Act. In A. Leschied, P. Jaffe, & W. Willis, (Eds.), *The Young Offenders Act: A Revolution in Canadian Juvenile Justice.* Toronto: University of Toronto Press.

Pepinsky, H., & Quinney, R. (Eds.). (1991). *Criminology as Peacemaking.* Bloomington: Indiana University Press.

Pereira, D. (2003, March). New youth justice act sends mixed messages. *Windspeaker, 21.*

Peterson, E. (1996, June). *Juvenile Boot Camps: Lessons Learned* (Fact Sheet 36). Washington, DC: U.S. Department of Justice, Office of Juvenile Justice and Delinquency Prevention.

Peterson, M. (1988). Children's Understanding of the Juvenile Justice System: A Cognitive Developmental Perspective. *Canadian Journal of Criminology, 30,* 381–396.

Petrosino, A., Turpin-Petrosino, C., & Finckenauer, J.O. (2000). Well-meaning programs can have harmful effects! Lessons from experiments of programs such as Scared Straight. *Crime & Delinquency, 46* (3), 354–379.

Phelps, R.J. (1982). *Wisconsin Juvenile Female Offender Project.* Madison: Youth Policy and Law Center, Wisconsin Council on Juvenile Justice.

Philip, M. (1998, October 29). Parenting style matters more than family income, study says. *The Globe and Mail,* A9.

Piaget, J. (1932). *The Moral Judgement of the Child.* London, UK: Kegan Paul.

Piliavin, I., & Briar, S. (1964). Police Encounters with Juveniles. *American Journal of Sociology, 70,* 206–214.

Platt, A. (1969a). *The Child Savers.* Chicago: University of Chicago Press.

Platt, A. (1969b). The Rise of the Child-Saving Movement: A Study in Social Policy and Correctional Reform. *The Annals of the American Academy of Political and Social Science, 381,* 21–38.

Police target black drivers. (2002, October 20). *Toronto Star,* A1.

Polk, K. (1983). Curriculum Tracking and Delinquency. *American Sociological Review, 48,* 282–284.

Pollak, O. (1950). *The Criminality of Women.* New York: Barnes.

Pollack, W. (1998). *Real Boys: Rescuing Our Sons from the Myth of Boyhood.* New York: Random House.

Pollock, L. (1983). *Forgotten Children: Parent–Child Relations from 1500 to 1900.* Cambridge: Cambridge University Press.

Porterfield, A. (1946). *Youth in Trouble.* Fort Worth, TX: Leopotishman Foundation.

Price, R.T. & Dunnigan, C. (1995). *Toward an Understanding of Aboriginal Peacemaking.* Victoria: University of Victoria Institute of Dispute Resolution.

Prison Report. (1881, 1889–99). *Annual Reports.* City of Halifax: Nova Scotia Provincial Archives.

Pugliesi, K. (1992). Pre-Menstrual Syndrome: The Medicalization of Emotion Related to Conflict and Chronic Role Strain. *Humboldt Journal of Social Relations, 18,* 131–165.

Purvis, A. (1997, December 8). Fury of Her Peers: A Teenager's Brutal Assault and Drowning Raise Questions in a Quiet Canadian Town. *Time,* 1–3.

Quicker, J. (1983). *Homegirls: Characterizing Chicana Gangs.* Los Angeles: International University Press.

Rains, P., & Teram, E. (1992). *Normal Bad Boys: Public Policies, Institutions, and the Politics of Client Recruitment.* Montreal and Kingston: McGill–Queen's University Press.

Rankin, J., & Wells, E. (1990). The Effect of Parental Attachments and Direct Controls on Delinquency. *Journal of Research in Crime and Delinquency, 27* (2), 140–165.

Ratner, R.S. (1996). In Cultural Limbo: Adolescent Aboriginals in the Urban Life-World. In G. O'Bireck, (Ed.), *Not a Kid Anymore*. Scarborough, ON: ITP Nelson.

Reckless, W. (1953). The Etiology of Delinquent and Criminal Behavior. *Social Science Research Council Bulletin No. 50*. New York: Social Science Research Council.

Reckless, W. (1961). *The Crime Problem* (3rd ed.). New York: Appleton-Century-Crofts.

Redl, F., & Wingman, D. (1956). *Children Who Hate*. New York: Free Press.

Reduced sentences sought for boys who killed toddler. (1996, April 18). *The Chronicle Herald* [Halifax], D8.

Regan, G. (1995). *A Report on Youth Issues from the Town Hall Meeting Held in Bedford, Nova Scotia*. Submission to the Standing Committee on Justice and Legal Affairs.

Regoeczi, W.C. (2000). Adolescent Violent Victimization and Offending: Assessing the Extent of the Link. *Canadian Journal of Criminology, 42* (4), 493–505.

Regoli, R., & Hewitt, J. (1994). *Delinquency in Society: A Child-Centered Approach*. New York: McGraw-Hill.

Reid, L. (2005). Elsipogtog Restorative Justice Program. In B. Morrison, C. Doucet, & M. Le Blanc, (Eds.), *New Brunswick Perspectives on Crime Prevention: Promising Practices for Children, Youth and Families*. Nova Scotia: Gaspereau Press.

Reid, S.A. (2005). Youth Crime and the Media. In K. Campbell, (Ed.), *Understanding Youth Justice in Canada*. Toronto: Pearson Education Canada Inc.

Reid, S.A., & Reitsma-Street, M. (1984). Assumptions and Implications of New Canadian Legislation for Young Offenders. *Canadian Criminology Forum, 7*, 1–19.

Reid, S.A., & Zuker, M.A. (2005). Conceptual Frameworks for Understanding Youth Justice in Canada: From the Juvenile Delinquents Act to the Youth Criminal Justice Act. In K. Campbell, (Ed.), *Understanding Youth Justice in Canada*. Toronto: Pearson Education Canada Inc.

Reid-MacNevin, S. (1991). A Theoretical Understanding of Current Canadian Juvenile-Justice Policy. In A. Leschied, P. Jaffe, & W. Willis, (Eds.), *The Young Offenders Act: A Revolution in Canadian Juvenile Justice*. Toronto: University of Toronto Press.

Reid-MacNevin, S.A. (1996). *The media portrayal of troubled youth*. Unpublished manuscript. Guelph, ON: University of Guelph.

Reid-MacNevin, S.A. (2003). *Bad, bad . . . youth: The media portrayal of youth*. Paper presented at the Crime and Media Symposium, October 2003, St. Thomas University, Fredericton, New Brunswick.

Reitano, J. (2004). Youth custody and community services in Canada, 2002/03. *Juristat, 24* (9). Ottawa: Statistics Canada, Canadian Centre for Justice Statistics.

Reitsma-Street, M. (1984). Differential Treatment of Young Offenders. *Canadian Journal of Criminology, 26*, 199–217.

Reitsma-Street, M. (1989–1990). More Control Than Care: A Critique of Historical and Contemporary Laws for Delinquency and Neglect of Children in Ontario. *Canadian Journal of Women and the Law, 3* (2), 510–530.

Reitsma-Street, M. (1991a). A Review of Female Delinquency. In A. Leschied, P. Jaffe, & W. Willis, (Eds.), *The Young Offenders Act: A Revolution in Canadian Juvenile Justice*. Toronto: University of Toronto Press.

Reitsma-Street, M. (1991b). Girls Learn to Care, Girls Policed to Care. In C. Baines, P. Evans, & S. Neysmith, (Eds.), *Women's Caring*. Toronto: McClelland and Stewart.

Reitsma-Street, M. (1993a). *Fifteen Years in the Lives of Canadian Girls in Conflict with the Law*. Ottawa: Canadian Association of Elizabeth Fry Societies.

Reitsma-Street, M. (1993b). Canadian Youth Court Charges and Dispositions for Females Before and After Implementation of the YOA. *Canadian Journal of Criminology, 35,* 437–458.

Reitsma-Street, M. (1999). Justice for Canadian Girls: A 1990s Update. *Criminal Journal of Criminology, 41* (3), 335–363.

Report of the Federal–Provincial–Territorial Task Force on Youth Justice. (1996). *A Review of the Young Offenders Act and the Youth Justice System in Canada.* Ottawa: The Task Force.

Riley, B. (1995, July 15). Boy, 7, Called Accomplice in Brutal Death of Youngster. *Daily News* [Halifax], 13.

Rivera, B., & Widom, C.S. (1990). Childhood victimization and violent offending. *Violence & Victims 5* (1), 19–35.

Roach, K., & Rudin, J. (2001). Gladue: The Judicial and Political Reception of a Promising Decision. *Canadian Journal of Criminology, 42* (3), 355–388.

Roberts, J.V., & Bala, N. (2003). Understanding Sentencing under the *Youth Criminal Justice Act. Alberta Law Review, 41* (2), 395–423.

Robinson, P. (2004). Youth Court Statistics, 2002/03. *Juristat, 24* (2). Ottawa: Statistics Canada, Canadian Centre for Justice Statistics.

Rogers, K. (1945). *Street Gangs in Toronto: A Study of the Forgotten Boy.* Toronto: Ryerson Press.

Rose, N. (1989). *Governing the Soul.* London: Routledge.

Rose, N. (1996). Governing "Advanced" liberal democracies. In Andrew Barry, Thomas Osborne, & Nikolas Rose, (Eds.), *Foucault and Political Reason.* Chicago: University of Chicago Press.

Rose, T. (1994). *Black Noise: Rap Music and Black Culture in Contemporary America.* New York: Routledge.

Rosenbaum, J.L. (1996). A violent few: Gang girls in the California Youth Authority. *Journal of Gang Research, 3* (3), 17–23.

Rosenblum, K. (1980). Female Deviance and the Female Sex Role: A Preliminary Investigation. In S. Datesman & F. Scarpitti, (Eds.), *Women, Crime and Justice.* New York: Oxford University Press.

Ross, R. (1992). *Dancing with the Ghost: Exploring Indian Reality.* Markham, ON: Octopus Publishing Group.

Ross, R. (1994). Duelling Paradigms, Western Criminal Justice versus Aboriginal Community Healing. In R. Gosse, Y. Youngblood Henderson, & R. Carter, (Eds.), *Continuing Poundmaker and Riel's Quest.* Saskatoon: Purich.

Rothman, D. (1980). *Conscience and Convenience.* Toronto: Little, Brown.

Royal Commission on Aboriginal Peoples (1996). *Bridging the Cultural Divide: A Report on Aboriginal People and Criminal Justice in Canada.* Ottawa: Minister of Supply and Services, Canada.

Rubington, E., & Weinberg, M. (1981). *The Study of Social Problems: Five Perspectives* (3rd ed.). New York: Oxford University Press.

Rush, Peter. (1992). The government of a generation: The subject of juvenile delinquency. *The Liverpool Law Review, 14* (1), 3–41.

Ryan, G., & Lane, S. (Eds.). (1991). *Juvenile Sexual Offending: Causes, Consequences, and Corrections.* Lexington, MA: Lexington Books.

Ryant, J., & Heinrich, C. (1988). Youth Court Committees in Manitoba. In J. Hudson, J. Hornick, & B. Burrows, *Justice and the Young Offender in Canada.* Toronto: Wall and Thompson.

Sampson, R.J. (1986). Effects of Socioeconomic Context on Official Reaction to Juvenile Delinquency. *American Sociological Review, 51* (December), 876–885.

Sampson, R.J., & Laub, J.H. (1993). *Crime in the Making: Pathways and Turning Points through Life.* Cambridge University Press.

Sandberg, D. (1989). *The Child Abuse–Delinquency Connection.* Lexington, MA: Lexington Books.

Sanders, T. (2000). Sentencing Of Young Offenders In Canada, 1998/99, Highlights. *Juristat, 20* (7). Ottawa: Statistics Canada, Canadian Centre for Justice Statistics.

Sangster, J. (2002). *Girl Trouble-Female Delinquency in English Canada.* Toronto: Between the Lines.

Sapers, H., & Leonard, C. (1996). Young Offenders Act Amendments—Principled Reform? In John Winterdyk, (Ed.), *Issues and Perspectives on Young Offenders in Canada.* Toronto: Harcourt Brace & Company.

Sauvé, J. (2005). Crime Statistics in Canada—2004. *Juristat, 25* (5). Ottawa: Statistics Canada, Canadian Centre for Justice Statistics.

Savelsberg, J.J. (2000). Symposium on John Hagan and Bill McCarthy's *Mean Streets: Youth Crime and Homelessness.* (Cambridge: Cambridge University Press, 1997). Linking *Mean Streets* with Adverse Culture. *Theoretical Criminology, 4* (2), 225–232.

Savoie, J. (1999). Youth Violent Crime. *Juristat, 19* (13). Ottawa: Statistics Canada, Canadian Centre for Justice Statistics.

Schissel, B. (1993). *Social Dimensions of Canadian Youth Justice.* Toronto: Oxford University Press.

Schissel, B. (1995). Trends in Official Juvenile Crime Rates. In J. Creechan & R. Silverman, (Eds.), *Canadian Delinquency.* Scarborough, ON: Prentice Hall Canada.

Schissel, B. (1997). *Blaming Children: Youth Crime, Moral Panics and the Politics of Hate.* Halifax: Fernwood.

Schissel, B. (2001). Youth Crime, Moral Panics, and the News: The Conspiracy against the Marginalized in Canada. In R.C. Smandych, (Ed.), *Youth Justice: History, Legislation, and Reform.* Toronto: Harcourt Canada.

Schissel, B., & Fedec, K. (1999). The Selling of Innocence: The Gestalt of Danger in the Lives of Youth Prostitutes. *Canadian Journal of Criminology, 41*(1).

Schrader, K. (1994). *Community Alternatives and Youth Justice: Needs, Interests, and Obstacles.* Master's thesis. Ottawa: Carleton University.

Schulenberg, J.L. (2003). The Social Context of Police Discretion with Young Offenders: An Ecological Analysis. *Canadian Journal of Criminology and Criminal Justice,* (April), 127–157.

Schur, E. (1973). *Radical Non-Intervention: Rethinking the Delinquency Problem.* Englewood Cliffs, NJ: Prentice-Hall.

Schwartz, I.M. (1989). *Justice for Juveniles.* Lexington, MA: Lexington Books.

Schwartz, I.M. (1991). Delinquency Prevention: Where's the Beef? *Journal of Criminal Law and Criminology, 82* (1), 132–140.

Schwartz, I.M. (1992). *Juvenile Justice and Public Policy: Toward a National Agenda.* Lexington, MA: Lexington Books.

Schwartz, I.M. (1994). What Policy Makers Need to Know about Juvenile Detention Reform. In I.M. Schwartz & W.H. Barton, (Eds.), *Reforming Juvenile Detention: No More Hidden Closets.* Columbus: Ohio State University Press.

Schwartz, I., & Orlando, S. (1991). *Programming for Young Women in the Juvenile Justice System.* Ann Arbor: Center for the Study of Youth Policy.

Schwartz, I.M., & Barton, W.H. (1994). *Reforming Juvenile Detention: No More Hidden Closets.* Columbus: Ohio State University Press.

Schwendinger, H., & Schwendinger, J. (1979). Delinquency and Social Reform. In E. Lamar, (Ed.), *Juvenile Justice.* Charlottesville, VA: University of Virginia Press.

Scott, W.L. (1908). The Juvenile Delinquent Act. *Canadian Law Times and Review, 28*, 892–904.

Scraton, P., & Haydon, D. (2004). Challenging the criminalization of children and young people: Securing a rights-based agenda. In J. Muncie, G. Hughes, & E. McLaughlin, (Eds.), *Youth Justice: Critical Readings*. London, UK: Sage Publications Ltd.

Sellin, T. (1938). *Culture and Conflict in Crime*. New York: Social Science Research Council.

Sellin, T., & Wolfgang, M. (1964). *The Measurement of Delinquency*. New York: John Wiley & Sons.

Shahar, S. (1990). *Childhood in the Middle Ages*. London, UK: Routledge.

Shannon, L. (1963). Types and Patterns of Delinquency Referral in a Middle-Sized City. *British Journal of Criminology, 4*, 24–36.

Sharpe, S. (1998). *Restorative Justice: A Vision for Healing and Change*. Edmonton: Edmonton Victim–Offender Mediation Society.

Shaw, C.R., & McKay, H.D. (1931). *Social Factors in Juvenile Delinquency*. Chicago: University of Chicago Press.

Shaw, C., & McKay, H.D. (1942). *Juvenile Delinquency and Urban Areas*. Chicago: University of Chicago Press.

Sheldon, W.H. (1949). *Varieties of Delinquent Youth*. New York: Harper.

Sherr, S.A. (1996). *Our Children, Our Enemies: Media Framing of Children-at-Risk*. Paper presented at the Images of Youth in the Nineties Conference, Ryerson University, Toronto.

Shkilnyk, A.M. (1985). *A Poison Stronger Than Love: The Destruction of an Ojibway Community*. New Haven, CT: Yale University Press.

Shoemaker, D. (1990). *Theories of Delinquency: An Examination of Explanations of Delinquent Behavior* (2nd ed.). New York: Oxford University Press.

Sigfusdottir, I.D., Farkas, G., & Silver, E. (2004). The Role of Depressed Mood and Anger in the Relationship between Family Conflict and Delinquent Behavior. *Journal of Youth and Adolescence, 33* (6), 509–522.

Silverman, R. (1990). Trends in Canadian Youth Homicide: Some Unanticipated Consequences of a Change in Law. *Canadian Journal of Criminology, 32* (4), 651–656.

Silverman, R., & Kennedy, L.W. (1993). *Deadly Deeds: Murder in Canada*. Scarborough, ON: ITP Nelson.

Simon, R. (1975). *Women and Crime*. Lexington, MA: Lexington Books.

Simon, R., & Landis, J. (1991). *The Crimes Women Commit, the Punishments They Receive*. Lexington, MA: Lexington Books.

Simone, M.V. (1985). Group Home Failures in Juvenile Justice: The Next Step. *Child Welfare, 64*, 4.

Simourd, L., & Andrews, D. (1996). Correlates of Delinquency: A Look at Gender. In R. Silverman, J. Teevan, & V. Sacco, (Eds.), *Crime in Canadian Society*. Toronto: Harcourt Brace and Company.

Singer, S.I., & McDowall, D. (1988). Criminalizing Delinquency: The Deterrent Effects of the New York Juvenile Offender Law. *Law and Society Review, 22*, 521–535.

Singled out. (2002, October 19). *Toronto Star*, A1.

Skinner, B.F. (1938). *The Behavior of Organisms*. New York: Appleton.

Skinner, B.F. (1953). *Science and Human Behavior*. New York: Macmillan.

Smandych, R. (1995). Changing Images of Childhood and Delinquency. In J. Creechan & R. Silverman, (Eds.), *Canadian Delinquency*. Scarborough, ON: Prentice Hall Canada.

Smandych, R. (2001a) Accounting for Changes in Canadian Youth Justice: From the Invention to the Disappearance of Childhood. In R. Smandych, (Ed.), *Youth Justice: History, Legislation and Reform*. Toronto: Harcourt, 4–23.

Smandych, R. (2001b). Rethinking System-Based Responses to Young Offenders: International Trends and Perspectives. In R. Smandych, (Ed.), *Youth Justice: History, Legislation and Reform*. Toronto: Harcourt, 191–195.

Smandych, R. (2001c). Youth Crime: Theoretical Perspectives, Introduction. In R. Smandych, (Ed.), *Youth Crime: Varieties, Theories, and Prevention*. Toronto: Harcourt Canada.

Smandych, R. (2001d). *Youth Crime: Varieties, Theories, and Prevention*. Toronto: Harcourt Canada.

Smandych, R. (Ed.). (2001e). *Youth Justice: History, Legislation, and Reform*. Toronto: Harcourt.

Smith, A. (1997, May 3). Locking up youth not the answer, judge says. *The Chronicle Herald* [Halifax], B8.

Smith, D.A., & Visher, C.A. (1981). Street-Level Justice: Situational Determinants of Police Arrest Decisions. *Social Problems, 29* (December), 167–177.

Smith, R.B., Bertrand, L.D., Arnold, B.L., & Hornick, J.P. (1995). *A Study of the Level and Nature of Youth Crime and Violence in Calgary*. Calgary: Calgary Police Service.

Snyder, H., & Sickmund, M. (1995). *Juvenile Offenders and Victims: A Focus on Violence*. Pittsburgh, PA: National Center for Juvenile Justice.

Solomon, P. (1992). *Black Resistance in High School: Forging a Separatist Culture*. Albany, NY: State University of New York Press.

Spergel, I. (1992). Youth Gangs. *Social Service Review, 66*, 121–140.

Spergel, I., & Curry, D. (1991). The National Youth Gang Survey: A Research and Development Process. In A. Goldstein & C.R. Huff, (Eds.), *Gang Intervention Handbook*. Champaign-Urbana, IL: Academic Press.

Sprott, J.B. (1996). Understanding Public Views of Youth Crime and the Youth Justice System. *Canadian Journal of Criminology, 38* (3), 271–290.

Sprott, J.B. (2004). The Development of Early Delinquency: Can Classroom and School Climates make a Difference? *Canadian Journal of Criminology and Criminal Justice, 46* (5), 553–572.

Sprott, J.B., & Doob, A.N. (2000). Bad, Sad, and Rejected: The Lives of Aggressive Children. *Canadian Journal of Criminology, 42* (2), 123–133.

Sprott, J.B., & Doob, A.N. (2003). It's All in the Denominator: Trends in the Processing of Girls in Canada's Youth Courts. *Canadian Journal of Criminology and Criminal Justice*, 73–80.

Sprott, J.B., Doob, A.N., & Jenkins, J.M. (2001). Problem Behaviour and Delinquency in Children and Youth. *Juristat, 21* (4). Ottawa: Statistics Canada, Canadian Centre for Justice Statistics.

Sprott, J.B., Jenkins, J.M., & Doob, A.N. (2000). Early offending: Understanding the risk and protective factors of delinquency. Human Resources Development Canada: Applied Research Branch, Strategic Policy.

Stackhouse, J. (2001, November 4). Welcome to Harlem on the prairies. *The Globe and Mail*.

St. Amand, C., & Greenberg, P. (1996). Youth Custody and Probation in Canada. *Juristat, 16* (5). Ottawa: Canadian Crime Statistics.

Standing Committee on Justice and the Solicitor General. (1993). *Crime Prevention in Canada: Toward a National Strategy*. Ottawa: Queen's Printer.

Stansell, C. (1986). *City of Women: Sex and Class in New York, 1789–1860*. New York: Alfred A. Knopf.

Statistics Canada. (1947). *Canada Year Book*. Ottawa: Canadian Centre of Statistics.

———. (1981). Juvenile Delinquents, 1980. *Juristat, 1* (2). Ottawa: Canadian Crime Statistics.

———. (1984). Data from the Juvenile Courts–1982. *Juristat, 4* (3). Ottawa: Canadian Crime Statistics.

———. (1990a). Violent Offences by Young Offenders, 1986–87 to 1988–89. *Juristat, 10* (5). Ottawa: Canadian Crime Statistics.

———. (1990b). Youth Crime in Canada, 1986–1988. *Juristat, 10* (12). Ottawa: Canadian Crime Statistics.

———. (1990c). Youth Court Statistics Preliminary Data, 1989–90 Highlights. *Juristat, 10* (13). Ottawa: Canadian Centre for Justice Statistics.

———. (1992a). Crime Trends in Canada, 1962–1990. *Juristat, 12* (7). Ottawa: Canadian Crime Statistics.

———. (1992b). Teenage Victims of Violent Crime. *Juristat, 12* (6). Ottawa: Canadian Centre for Justice Statistics.

———. (1993). *Youth Court Statistics,* 1992–93 Ottawa: Canadian Crime Statistics.

———. (1995). Canadian Crime Statistics. *Juristat, 15* (12). Ottawa: Canadian Crime Statistics.

———. (1996). *Youth Court Statistics,* 1994–1995. Ottawa: Canadian Centre for Justice Statistics.

———. (1997a). Canadian Crime Statistics, 1996. *Juristat, 17* (8).

———. (1997b). Youth Court Statistics, 1995–96 Highlights. *Juristat, 17* (10). Ottawa: Canadian Centre for Justice Statistics.

———. (1998). *Youth Court Statistics, 1996–1997.* Ottawa: Canadian Centre for Justice Statistics.

———. (1999a). *Canadian Crime Statistics, 1998* Ottawa: Canadian Centre for Justice Statistics.

———. (1999b). Sex Offenders. *Juristat, 19* (3). Ottawa: Canadian Centre for Justice Statistics.

———. (2000a). Crime Statistics in Canada. *Juristat, 21* (8). Ottawa: Canadian Centre for Justice Statistics.

———. (2000b). *Youth Custody and Community Services Data Tables,* 1998–99. Ottawa: Canadian Centre for Justice Statistics.

———. (2001). *Children and Youth in Canada.* Profile Series. Ottawa: Canadian Centre for Justice Statistics.

———. (2002). Pilot Analysis of Recidivism Among Convicted Youth and Young Adults—1999/00. *Juristat, 22* (9). Ottawa: Canadian Centre for Justice Statistics.

———. (2003a). Crime Statistics in Canada, 2002. *Juristat, 23* (5). Ottawa: Canadian Centre for Justice Statistics.

———. (2003b). Custodial Remand in Canada, 1986/87 to 2000/01. *Juristat, 23* (7). Ottawa: Canadian Centre for Justice Statistics.

———. (2003c). Sexual Offences in Canada. *Juristat, 23* (6). Ottawa: Canadian Centre for Justice Statistics.

———. (2004a). Adult Court Statistics, 2003/04. *Juristat, 24* (12). Ottawa: Canadian Centre for Justice Statistics.

———. (2004b). Crime Statistics in Canada, 2003. *Juristat, 24* (6). Ottawa: Canadian Centre for Justice Statistics.

———. (2004c, September 16). Study: Neighbourhood Characteristics and the Distribution of Crime in Winnipeg. *The Daily* [Halifax].

———. (2004d). Youth Court Statistics, 2002/03. *Juristat, 24* (2). Ottawa: Canadian Centre for Justice Statistics.

———. (2004e). Youth Custody and Community Services in Canada, 2002/03. *Juristat, 24* (9). Ottawa: Canadian Centre for Justice Statistics.

———. (2005a). Children and Youth as Victims of Violent Crime. *Juristat, 25* (1). Ottawa: Canadian Centre for Justice Statistics.

———. (2005b). Crime Statistics in Canada, 2004. *Juristat, 25* (5). Ottawa: Canadian Centre for Justice Statistics.

————. (2005c). Criminal Victimization in Canada, 2004. *Juristat, 25* (7). Ottawa: Canadian Centre for Justice Statistics.

————. (2005d). Homicide in Canada, 2004. *Juristat, 25* (6). Ottawa: Canadian Centre for Justice Statistics.

————. (2005e). Youth Court Statistics, 2003/04. *Juristat, 25* (4). Ottawa: Canadian Centre for Justice Statistics.

Stevens, S. (1990). An Aboriginal View of the Canadian Justice System. *Legal Perspectives* (May), 10–12.

Stewart, J. (2005, September 27). Teen unnerved by late-night encounter with police officers. *The Chronicle Herald* [Halifax], A1.

Stewart, J. (2005, December 15). Teen killer unrepentant hearing told. *The Chronicle Herald* [Halifax], B3.

Stewart, J. (2005, December 16). McEvoy killer considered "significant threat." *The Chronicle Herald* [Halifax], B2.

Stinchcombe, A. (1964). *Rebellion in a High School.* Chicago: Quadrangle Books.

Strauss, M.A., & Gelles, R.J. (1990). *Physical Violence in American Families: Risk Factors and Adaptations to Violence in 8,145 Families.* New Brunswick, NJ: Transaction.

Strickland, R. (2002). Introduction: What's Left of Modernity? In R. Strickland, (Ed.), *Growing Up Postmodern: Neoliberalism and the War on the Young.* Oxford: Rowman & Littlefield Publishers, Inc.

Strickland, R. (Ed.). (2002). *Growing Up Postmodern: Neoliberalism and the War on the Young.* Oxford: Rowman & Littlefield Publishers, Inc.

Stuart, B. (1997). *Building Community Justice Partnerships: Community Peacemaking Circles.* Ottawa: Department of Justice, Aboriginal Justice Directorate.

Student gets life for chilling murders of parents. (2005, June 30). The Associated Press.

Sudworth, M., & deSouza, P. (2001). Youth Court Statistics, 1999–2000. *Juristat, 21* (3). Ottawa: Statistics Canada, Canadian Centre for Justice Statistics.

Sullivan, C., Grant, M., & Grant, J.D. (1957). The Development of Interpersonal Maturity: Applications to Delinquency. *Psychiatry, 20,* 373–385.

The Sunday Daily News [Halifax]. (2003, April 6). Act expected to staunch flow of public information on youth crime.

Sundeen, R. (1972). A Study of Factors Related to Police Diversion of Departmental Policies and Structures, Community Attachment and Professionalization of the Police. Ph.D. dissertation, University of Southern California.

"Suspended sentences" and dishonesty among minors in the city of Halifax. (1908, January 15). *Evening Mail* [Halifax], 5.

Sutherland, E. (1939). *Principles of Criminology* (3rd ed.). Philadelphia, PA: Lippincott.

Sutherland, E.H., & Cressey, D.R. (1974). *Criminology* (9th ed.). Philadelphia: Lippincott.

Sutherland, N. (1976). *Children in English-Canadian Society: Framing the Twentieth-Century Consensus.* Toronto: University of Toronto Press.

Suttles, G. (1972). *The Social Construction of Communities* Chicago: University of Chicago Press.

"Swarmers could be future killers," warns cousin of 15-year-old victim. (2005, March 28). The Canadian Press.

Schwendinger, J., & Schwendinger, H. (1983) *Rape and Inequality.* Newbury Park, CA: Sage.

Sykes, G., & Matza, D. (1957). Techniques of Neutralization: A Theory of Delinquency. *American Journal of Sociology, 22,* 664–670.

Sylvester, S. (1972). *The Heritage of Modern Criminology.* Cambridge, MA: Schenkman Publishing Company.

Szklarski, C. (2006, January 18). Grandparents' fate up to the judge—Couple accused of first-degree murder in starvation death of five-year-old. *The Chronicle Herald* [Halifax], A5.

Tannenbaum, F. (1938). *Crime and the Community.* Boston: Ginn.

Tanner, J. (1996). *Teenage Troubles: Youth and Deviance in Canada.* Scarborough, ON: ITP Nelson.

Tanner, J., & Wortley, S. (2002). *The Toronto Youth Leisure and Victimization Survey: Final Report.* Toronto: University of Toronto.

Taylor, C. (1993). *Girls, Gangs, Women and Drugs.* East Lansing, MI: Michigan State University Press.

Taylor, L. (1984). *Born to Crime: The Genetic Causes of Criminal Behavior.* Westport, CT: Greenwood.

Teen charged with assaulting officer. (2000, August 3). *The Chronicle Herald* [Halifax]. A6.

Teens who killed woman sent to penitentiary. (1997, July 10). *The Chronicle Herald* [Halifax], A18.

Teilmann, K., & Landry, P. (1981). Gender Bias in Juvenile Justice. *Journal of Research in Crime and Delinquency, 18,* 47–80.

Terry, R. (1967). Discrimination in the Handling of Juvenile Offenders by Social-Control Agencies. *Journal of Research in Crime and Delinquency, 4,* 218–230.

Thomas, J. (2005). Youth Court Statistics—2003/04. *Juristat, 25* (4). Ottawa: Statistics Canada, Canadian Centre for Justice Statistics.

Thomas, M. (2004). Adult Court Statistics—2003/04. *Juristat, 24* (12). Ottawa: Statistics Canada, Canadian Centre for Justice Statistics.

Thomas, M., Hurley, H., & Grimes, C. (2002). Pilot Analysis of Recidivism among Convicted Youth and Young Adults—1999/00. *Juristat, 22* (9). Ottawa: Statistics Canada, Canadian Centre for Justice Statistics.

Thomas, W. (1923). *The Unadjusted Girl.* New York: Harper & Row.

Thompson, A.H. (1988). Young Offender, Child Welfare, and Mental Health Caseload Communalities. *Canadian Journal of Criminology,* 135–144.

Thornberry, T. (1973). Race, Socioeconomic Status, and Sentencing in the Juvenile Justice System. *Journal of Criminal Law and Criminology, 64* (March), 90–98.

Thornberry, T. (1987). Towards an Interactional Theory of Delinquency. *Criminology, 25,* 863–891.

Thornberry, T., Huizinga, D., & Loeber, R. (1995). The Prevention of Serious Delinquency and Violence: Implications from the program of research on the causes and correlates of delinquency. In J.C. Howell, B. Krisberg, D. Hawkins, & J.J. Wilson, (Eds.), *Serious, Violent, & Chronic Juvenile Offenders: A Sourcebook* (pp. 213–237). Thousand Oaks, CA: Sage.

Thornberry, T., Lizotte, A., Krohm, M., Farnworth, M., & Jang, S. (1991). Testing Interactional Theory: An Examination of Reciprocal Causal Relationships among Family, School, and Delinquency. *Journal of Criminal Law and Criminology, 82* (1), 3–33.

Thrasher, F. (1927). *The Gang: A Study of 1,313 Gangs in Chicago.* Chicago: University of Chicago Press.

Time/CNN Teen Poll. (1999, 10 May). *Time.*

Tobin, A. (1987). Creating and Operating Community-Based Mediation Programs. In C. Griffiths, (Ed.), *Northern Youth in Crisis: A Challenge for Justice.* Joint publication of the Northern Conference and Simon Fraser University.

Toronto mom turns in son after finding AK-47 in his room. (2006, January 6). The Canadian Press.

Toronto Star. (2002, October 19). Singled out.

Toronto Star. (2002, October 20). Police target black drivers.

Totten, M. (2000). *Guys, Gangs & Girlfriend Abuse.* Peterborough, ON: Broadview Press.

Totten, M. (2000, March 14). *Community Reintegration Project Fact Sheet.* Youth Services Bureau of Ottawa-Carleton.

Totten, M. (2002). *The Special Needs of Females in Canada's Youth Justice System: An Account of Some Young Women's Experiences and Views.* Ottawa: Department of Justice, Canada.

Totten, M. (2004, May 4). Gender-responsive young offender services and the need for female staff. Ottawa: Youth Services Bureau.

Tremblay, R.E., McCord, J., Boileau, H., Charlebois, P., Gagnon, C., Le Blanc, M., & Larivee, S. (1991). Can Disruptive Boys Be Helped to Become Competent? *Psychiatry, 54,* 148–161.

Trépanier, J. (2004). What Did Quebec Not Want? Opposition to the Adoption of the Youth Criminal Justice Act in Quebec? *Canadian Journal of Criminology and Criminal Justice, 46* (3), 273–299.

Tribble, S. (1972). Socioeconomic Status and Self-Reported Juvenile Delinquency. *Canadian Journal of Criminology* and Corrections, *14,* 409–415.

Trichur, R. (2004, April 1). "What's up? Behind bars: Is locking kids up the solution to youth crime? *The Chronicle Herald* [Halifax], F3.

Turk, A.T. (1969). *Criminality and Legal Order.* Chicago: Rand McNally.

Two girls terrorize west end with crime spree. (2003, February 25). *The Daily News* [Halifax].

Tyler, T. (1995, December 24). Justice for youths can begin with a hug. *Toronto Star,* A21.

Umbreit, M.S. (1995). *Mediation of Criminal Conflict: An Assessment of Programs in Four Canadian Cities.* Ottawa: Department of Justice.

The Vancouver Sun. (2003, May 7). When justice means restoring the moral bond of community.

Van Ness, D. W., & Heetderks Strong, K. (2002). Restoring Justice (2nd ed.). Cincinnati, OH: Anderson.

Varma, K.N. (2002). Exploring "youth" in court: An analysis of decision-making in youth court bail hearings. *Canadian Journal of Criminology, 44* (2), 143–164.

Vedder, C., & Somerville, D. (1975). *The Delinquent Girl* (2nd ed.). Springfield, IL: Charles C. Thomas.

Vincent, I. (1995, September 23). Ruthless violence part of girl gang reality. *The Chronicle Herald* [Halifax], C2.

Vincent, I. (1998, January 22). Police arrest members of girl gang. *The Globe and Mail,* A3.

Visher, C. (1983). Gender, Police Arrest Decisions, and Notions of Chivalry. *Criminology, 21,* 5–28.

Vold, G., & Bernard, T. (1986). *Theoretical Criminology* (3rd ed.). New York: Oxford University Press.

Von Kintzel, C. (2005, October 14). Teenage killer gets maximum sentence: 3 years. *The Chronicle Herald* [Halifax], A1.

Voter's Guide to the Issues. (1993, October 1). *The Globe and Mail,* A5.

Wallace, A.M. (1997). The psychological and familial factors associated with female juvenile delinquency: Concomitants and contributors. *Dissertation Abstracts International: Section B: The Sciences & Engineering, 57* (7-B), 4731.

Wallace, M. (2003). Crime Statistics in Canada—2002. *Juristat, 23* (5). Ottawa: Statistics Canada, Canadian Centre for Justice Statistics.

Wallace, M. (2004). Crime Statistics in Canada—2003. *Juristat, 24* (6). Ottawa: Statistics Canada, Canadian Centre for Justice Statistics.

Wallerstein, J., & Blakeslee, S. (1989). *Second Chances.* New York: Ticknor and Fields.

Wallerstein, J., & Kelly, B.J. (1980). *Surviving the Breakup.* New York: Basic Books.

Ward, J. (2006, March 29). Fewer youths jailed under new act. *The Chronicle Herald* [Halifax], A3.

Warr, M. (1993). Parents, Peers, and Delinquency. *Social Forces, 72,* 247–264.

Warren, M.Q. (1970). The Case for Differential Treatment of Delinquents. In H.L. Voss, (Ed.), *Society, Delinquency and Delinquent Behavior.* Boston: Little, Brown.

Wattie, C. (1996, August 30). 11-year-old taunted cops. *The Chronicle Herald* [Halifax], A22.

Weagant, B., & Milne, C. (1992). *Using the Criminal Code to Punish Group Home Residents: What Are We Teaching Them?* Discussion paper presented at the National Youth in Care Conference, Victoria, British Columbia.

Webber, M. (1991). *Street Kids: The Tragedy of Canada's Runaways.* Toronto: University of Toronto Press.

Weber, B. (2005, December 26). Using hunting to reduce youth crime: Nunavut gambles on old ways. *The Chronicle Herald* [Halifax], A3.

Weinberg, M., Rubington, E., & Hammersmith, S. (1981). *The Solution of Social Problems.* New York: Oxford University Press.

Wells, E., & Rankin, J. (1991). Families and Delinquency: A Meta-Analysis of the Impact of Broken Homes. *Social Problems, 38,* 71–93.

Werthman, C., & Piliavin, I. (1967). Gang Members and the Police. In D.J. Bordua, (Ed.), *The Police.* New York: John Wiley.

West, D., & Farrington, D. (1977). *The Delinquent Way of Life.* London, UK: Heinemann.

West, G. (1984). *Young Offenders and the State: A Canadian Perspective on Delinquency.* Toronto: Butterworths.

West, G. (1991). Towards a More Socially Informed Understanding of Canadian Delinquency Legislation. In A. Leschied, P. Jaffe, & W. Willis, (Eds.), *The Young Offenders Act.* Toronto. University of Toronto Press.

Whitbeck, L.B., Hoyt, D.R., Yoder, K.A., Cauce, A.M., & Paradise, M. (2001). Deviant Behaviour and Homeless and Runaway Adolescents. *Journal of Interpersonal Violence, 16* (11), 1175–1204.

Wiatrowski, M., Hansell, S., Massey, C., & Wilson, D. (1982). Curriculum Tracking and Delinquency. *American Sociological Review, 47,* 151–160.

Widom, C., & Maxfield, M. (2001). *An Update on the "Cycle of Violence."* National Institute of Justice research brief. U.S. Department of Justice: Office of Justice Programs.

Wieckowski, E., Hartsoe, P., Mayer, A., & Shortz, J. (1998). Deviant Sexual Behavior in Children and Young Adolescents: Frequency and Patterns. *Journal of Research and Treatment, 10* (4), 293–303.

Wilbanks, W. (1975). *The Insertion/Diversion Decision at the Juvenile Police Level.* Ph.D. Dissertation, State University of New York at Albany.

Wilson, J., & Herrnstein, R. (1985). *Crime and Human Nature.* New York: Simon & Schuster.

Wilson, J.Q. (1968). *Varieties of Police Behavior.* Cambridge: Harvard University Press.

Wilson, L. (1982). *Juvenile Courts in Canada.* Toronto: Carswell.

Windspeaker. (2003, March). New youth justice act sends mixed messages.

Winslow, R.W. (1973). *Juvenile Delinquency in a Free Society* (2nd ed.). Encino, CA: Wadsworth.

Winterdyk, J.A. (1996). Trends and Patterns in Youth Crime. In J.A. Winterdyk, (Ed.), *Issues and Perspectives on Young Offenders in Canada.* Toronto: Harcourt Brace and Company.

Wonders, N.A. (1999). Postmodern feminist criminology and social justice. In B.A. Arrigo, (Ed.), *Social justice, criminal justice.* California: Wadsworth.

Wong, S.K. (1999). Acculturation, peer relations, and delinquent behavior of Chinese-Canadian youth. *Adolescence, 34* (133), 107–108.

Wooden, W. S., & Blazak, R. (2001). *Renegade Kids, Suburban Outlaws: From Youth Culture to Delinquency* (2nd ed.). Belmont, CA: Wadsworth Publishing Company.

Worrall, A. (2002). Rendering women punishable: The making of a penal crisis. In P. Carlen, (Ed.), *Women and Punishment: The struggle for justice.* Cullompton, UK: Willan Publishing.

Worrall, A. (2004). Twisted Sisters, Ladettes, and the New Penology: The Social Construction of "Violent Girls." In C. Alder & A. Worrall, (Eds.), *Girls' Violence: Myths and Realities.* Albany: State University of New York Press.

Yablonsky, L. (1959). The Delinquent Gang as a Near-Group. *Social Problems, 7,* 108–117.

Y.M.C.A. Making a Feature of the "Boy Problem." (1909, May 11). *Morning Chronicle,* 5.

York, G. (1990). *The Dispossessed: Life and Death in Native Canada.* London, UK: Vintage.

Yoshikawa, H. (1994). Prevention as Cumulative Protection: Effects of Early Family Support and Education on Chronic Delinquency and Its Risks. *Psychological Bulletin, 115,* 28–54.

Young, M. (1993). *The History of Vancouver Youth Gangs,* 1900–1985. Master's thesis, Simon Fraser University, School of Criminology.

Youth Criminal Justice Act: 2005 Annual Statement, Executive Summary. (2005, June 22). Ottawa: Department of Justice.

Youth Alternative Society. (1997). Information pamphlet on the Ally Project. Youth Alternative Society of Halifax, Nova Scotia.

Yumori, W.C., & Loos, G.B. (1985). The Perceived Service Needs of Pregnant and Parenting Teens and Adults on the Waianae Coast. Working paper. Hawaii: Kamehameha Schools/Bishop Estate.

Zatz, M. (1985). Los Cholos: Legal Processing of Chicano Gang Members. *Social Problems, 33* (1), 13–30.

Zatz, M. (1987). Chicago Youth Gangs and Crime: The Creation of a Moral Panic. *Contemporary Crisis, 11,* 129–158.

Zehr, H. (1990). Changing Lenses: A New Focus for Crime and Justice. Scottdale, PA: Herald Press.

Zehr, H. (2002) *The Little Book of Restorative Justice.* Intercourse, PA: Good Books.

Zhang, S. X. (1998). In Search of Hopeful Glimpses: A Critique of Research Strategies in Current Boot Camp Evaluations. *Crime and Delinquency, 44* (2), 314–334.

CASES CITED

Alberta v. K.B. and M.J. [2000]. Alberta Judgements No. 838 (Provincial Court) (QL), reversed [2000] Alberta Judgements No. 1570 (Court of Queen's Bench) (QL)

R. v. A.D. [2001] B.C.J. No. 2529 (QL)

R. v. A.J.S. [2002] A.J. No. 429 (QL)

R. v. D.L.C. [2003] N.J. No. 94 (QL)

Gault, 387 United States 1 (1967)

R. v. G. K. [1985], 21 C.C.C. (3D) 558 (Alta. C.A.)

R. v. Gladue [1999] 133 C.C.C. (3D) 385 (S.C.C.)

R. v. H.A.M. [2003] M.J. No. 147 (QL)

R. v. James Albert C. (T) [1991] O. J. Number 936 (Provincial Division) (QL)

R. v. J. J. M. [1993] C. S. J. 14

R. v. Jones [1979] 4 C.R. (3D)

R. v. L.B. [2001] M.J. No. 141 (QL)

R. v. L.M.F. [2003] A.J. No. 1171 (QL)

R. v. M. (B.) [2003a] C.N.L.R. 277 Sask. Prov. Ct. Turpel-Lafond

R. v. M. (J.J) [1993] 2 S.C.R. 421

R. v. M. T., April 15 [1993] Yukon Territorial Court

R. v. O. [1986], 27 C.C.C. (3D) 376 (Ont. C.A.)

R. v. Richard I. [1985], 17 C.C.C. (3D) 523, 44 C.R. (3D) 168 (Ont. C.A.)

R. v. R.L.R. [2001] B.C.J. No. 1812 (QL)]

R. v. Shelson, S. [1990] 2 S.C.R. 254

R. v. T.(V.) [1992], 71 C.C.C (3D) 32

INDEX

| CREDITS

p. 5, Policy Primer, Chronicle Herald January 21, 2005 A6; **p. 5**, Table 1.1: Policy Primer, Chronicle Herald January 21, 2006 A6; **p. 7**, Box 1.1: Street Kids' Perspectives from Homeless Youth in Perspective (1994: 12–21). Reprinted with permission from the Nova Soctia Public Interest Reserach Group; **p. 11**, Table 1.2: Juvenile Convictions for Indictable Offences, 1885–1899 adapted from Statistical Yearbook of Canada, 1899; **p. 14**, Text: Excerpted from Carrigan, O.D., Crime and Punishment in Canada: A History, Copyright © 1991 Oxford University Press; **p. 14**, Text: Excerpted from Carrigan, O.D., Crime and Punishment in Canada: A History, Copyright © 1991 Oxford University Press; **p. 15**, Text: Excerpted from Stansell, C., *City of Women: Sex and Class in new York 1789–1860*, Copyright © 1986 Alfred Knopf. Reprinted with permission; **p. 16**, Text: Excerpted from Carrigan, O.D., Crime and Punishment in Canada: A History, Copyright © 1991 Oxford University Press; **p. 18**, Kelso, J.J (1907a) Delinquent Children, Canadian Law review 6, 106–10; **p. 19**, Drucker, S., and M. Hexter (1923). *Children Astray.* Cambridge, MA; Harvard University Press; **p. 25**, Table 1.3: "Convictions of Juveniles for Major Offences, by Province, Years Ended September 30, 1922–1945", adapted from Statistics Canada publication "Canada Year Book", Catalogue 11-402, 1947, page 253; **p. 25**, Table 1.4: Juvenile Crime: Selected Offences, 1963–1983, adapted from the Statistics Canada publications, "Penetentiary Statistics", Catalogue 86-210, 1975, Juvenile Delinquents", Catalogue 85-202, 1925–1926, "Cnadaian Crime Statistics", Catalogue 85-205, various years; **p. 35**, Box 2.1: Some precursors to the Juvenile Delinquents Act, adapted from Leon, J.S., The Development of Canadian Juvenile Justice: A Background for Reform, *Osgoode Hall Law Journal* 15:75–59, 82–83, 88. Reprinted with permission; **p. 37**, Box 2.2: Legal Definitions of Neglect, adapted from Sutherland, NI, *Children in English-Canadian Society: Framing the 20th Century Consensus.* Copyright © University of Toronto Press, Reprinted with Permission; **p. 38**, Text: Excerpted from Leon, J.S., The Development of Canadian Juvenile Justice: A Background for Reform: *Osgoode Hall Law Journal* 15:96, 98, 100. Reprinted with permission; **p. 40**, Adapted from Reid and Reitsma-Street (1984), Reid-MacNevin (1991:28); Corrado (1192:4), Adapted from Juristat, Cat.No. 85-002, 15(12); Cat. No. 85-002, 23(5); Cat. No. 85-002 25(5); **p. 41**, Box 2.3: Scott, W.L (1908). The Juvenile Delinquent Act. Canadian Law Times and Review 28, 892-904; **p. 43**, Wilson, L. (1982), *Juvenile Courts in Canada.* Toronto. Carswell; **p. 44**, Box 2.4: Kelso J.J (1907b) Children's Courts. Canadian Law Times and Review 26, 163–66; **p. 44**, Box 2.5: The Right of Trial by Jury, adapted from Leon, J.S., The Development of Canadian Juvenile Justice: A Background for Reform, Osgoode Hall Law Journal 15:99. Reprinted by Permission of Jeffrey S. Leon, courtesy of Osgoode Hall Law Journal; **p. 59**, Text: Excerpt from *The Cycle of Juvenile Justice*, Bernard T.J (1992) "by Permission of Oxford University Press, Inc.; **p. 61**, Text: Excerpted from U.N Document A/44/736, Reprinted with permission of the United Nations; **p. 66**, Sandra Bell; **p. 68**, Statistics Canada, Canadian Crime Statistics, 1992. Adapted from Doob, Marinos and Varma (1995:7); **p. 70**, Table 3.3: "Youth Charged in Criminal Code Incidents, Canada, 1986–2004", adapted from the Statistics Canada publications, "Juristat", Catalogue 85-002, Vol 23, No 5, released July 24, 2003, and Vol. 25, No. 5, released July 21, 2005, (Population estimates from Statistics Canada Census and Demogrpahy Statistics, Demography Division); **p. 72**, Sandra Bell; **p. 72**, Figure 3.2: "Youth Crime Rates: 1984–2204", adapted from the Statistics Canada publicaiton "Juristat", Catalogue 85-002, Vol. 25, No. 5, released July 21, 2005, page 13; **p. 74**, Adapted from de Souza (1995); Statistics Canada (1998:xiii); 2001:4, 14; **p. 80**, Figure 3.4: "Age and Sex of Victims of Violent Crimes Committed by Youth, 1998" adapted from the Statistics Canada Publication "Juristat", Catalogue 85-002, Vol. 19, No. 13, released December 21, 1999; **p. 82**, Box 3.1: Typology of Adolescent Sex Offenders, adapted from O'Brien, M.J., and W.H. Bera, Adolescent Sexual Offenders: A Descriptive Typology

(1986), Preventing Sexual Abuse 1, 1–4. Reprinted by permission of Dr. Walter H. Bera; **p. 85**, Figure 3.5: Canadian Criminal Statistics (1994): Doob, Marinos, and Varma (1995), Fedorowycz (1999); Logan (2001); **p. 87**, Box 3.2, excerpted from Kaihla, Paul, Maclean's (8/15/1994:32–39). reprinted with permission; **p. 95**, Table 3.4: "Persons Charged by Age Status, Selected Incidents, 2002", adapted from the Statistics Canada publication "Juristat", Catalogue 85-002, Vol. 23, No. 5, released July 24, 2003, page 22; **p. 100**, Box 4.1: Joey; The Crime, adapted from MacDonald, Jo-Anne, 15 Years Old and Flush with Cash, *Sunday Daily News* (9/4/1994a:6); **p. 103**, Text: Excerpted from Ratner, R.S., in Cultural Limbo, *Adolescent Aboriginals in the Urban Life World.* Copyright © 1996; **p. 106**, CCJS, UCR Survey, Cat No. 85-205, 1991; 1991 Census of Canada; Adapted from Nova Scotia Youth Secretariat (1993); **p. 108**, Table 4.2: "Yputh Charged by Sex, Selected Incidents, 2003", adapted from the Statistics Canada publication "Juristat", Catalogue 85-002, Vol 24, No. 6, released July 28, 2004, page 25; **p. 109**, Adapted from Statitics Canada. Cat. No. 85-002, Vol. 19. No. 25(4); **p. 110**, Adapted from Statistics Canada. Table 252-0007 Youth Court Survey-3309; **p. 114**, Adapted from Reitsma-Street (1993b:441; 1999:343), Statistics Canada Cat. No. 85-002, 25(4); **p. 117**, Figure 4.3: "Average Rates if Homicide by Age Group of Victims, 1991–1994", adapted from the Statistics Canada publication "Juristat", Catalogue 85-002. Vl. 15, No. 15, released December 19, 1995, page 13; **p. 119**, Box 4.2: Fact Sheet: "Teenage Victims of Violent Crime: Facts to Consider", adapted from the Statistics Canada publication "Juristat", Catalogue 85-002, Vol. 12, No. 6, released March 23, 1992, and Vol. 25, No. 1, released April 20, 2005; **p. 121**, Text: Excerpted from Webber, M., The Growing Trade in Young Boys, *Street Kids: The Tragedy of Canada's Runaways.* Copyright © 1991 University of Toronto Press. Reprinted with permission; **p. 128**, "Republished with permission from The Halifax Herald Limited"; **p. 129**, Sandra Bell; **p. 134**, Defective Children Discussed at Annual Conference in Buffalo. (1909, June 8), *Morning Chronicle;* **p. 158**, "Reprinted by special permission of Northwestern University School of Law, *The Journal of Criminal Law and Criminology.*"; **p. 160, 161, 171**, Regoli, R., and J. Hewitt. (1994). Delinquency in Society: *A Child-Centered Approach.* New York: McGraw-Hill; **p. 165**, Lombroso, C. and W. Ferrero ([1895] 1959). *The Female Offender.* New York: Peter Owen; **p. 171, 172**, Text: Excerpted from Reitsma-Street, M. (1191b), Girls Learn to Care, Girls Policed to Care, In C. Baines, P. Evans, and S. Neysmith, eds., *Women's Caring,* Copyright ©1991 McClelland and Stewart, p. 111, 118, 119; **p. 184**, Box 7.1: *The Coast* Halifax (June 16–23,2005); *The Chronicle Herald* (Halifax) (February 21, 24, 2006), researched and written by Nicole Landry; **p. 185**, Statistics Canada, 1994 and 1996 National Longitudinal Survey of Children and Youth, Cycles 1 & 2, Children and Youth in Canada, Statistics Canada Cat No. 85F0033MIE, 2001 p. 14; **p. 187**, "Reprinted with permission of Northwestern University School of Law, *The Journal of Criminal Law and Criminology;* **p. 188**, Text: Excerpted from Leyton, E., *The Myth of Delinquency.* Copyright © 1979. Reprinted by permission of Oxford University Press Canada; **p. 190**, Text: Excerpted from Chesney-Lind, M., and R. Shelden, *Girls, Delinquency and Juvenile Justice.* Copyright © 1992 Wadsworth Publishing Co. reprinted with permison; **p. 196**, Adapted from Regoli and Hewitt (1994:263); **p. 203**, Figure 7.2: "Peer influence on risk-taking behaviour", from the Statistics Canada publication "Canadian Centre for Justice Statistics profile series", Children and Youth in Canada, 1999, Catalogue 85F0033M1E2001005, Released June 14, 2001, page 14; **p. 208**, Mark D. Totten, "On The Street: Developing Familial and Gender Ideologies," Copyright © 1935 by Nellie McClung, reprinted from *Nellie McClung: The Complete Autobiography: Clearing in the West & The Stream Runs Fast*, by Nellie McClung, ed.y Veronica Srtong0-Boag and Michelle Lynn Rosa, Ontario: Broadview Press, 2003, pp. 25–26, 145–147. Reprinted by permission of Broadview Press; **p. 209, 210**, Joe, K., and M. Chesney-Lind. (1993) Just Every Mother's Angel. Paper presented at meeting of the American Society of Criminology, Phoenix, AZ, October 1993; **p. 215**, Box 8.1: Joey:Police Apprehension, MacDonald, Jo-Anne, 15 years Old and Flush with Cash, *Halifax Daily News* (9/4/1994a). Excerpted with permission; **p. 220**, Text: Excerpted from Neugubauser-Visano, R., Kids, Cops and Colour: The Social Organization of Police Minority Youth Relations. In G. O'Bireck, ed., Not a Kid Anymore. Copyright © 1996 ITP Nelson. Reprinted with Permission;

p. 221, Melchers (2003); The Chronicle Herald (March 20, 2006); **p. 231**, Northwest Territoris Department of Justice, Community Justice Policies and Procedures Manual (2005), p. 4; John Howard Society and The Alberta Law Foundation, YCJA Handbook (2003), p. 12; **p. 232**, Box 8.6: Essay by a Young Offender Who Participated in a Diversionary Program, adapted from Youth Alternative Society Newsletter, Jan/Feb 1997. Reprinted with Permission; **p. 236**, R.v. Jones (1979) 4 C. R. (430); **p. 238**, Box 8.8: Diversionary Measures and Meditation, Tobin A., Creating and Operating Community-based Meditation Programs. In C. Griffiths, ed., *Northern Youth in Crisis: A Challenge for Justice* Joint Publication of Northern Conference and Simon Fraser University (1987) Reprinted by permission of Dr. Curt T. griffiths; **p. 245**, The Chronicle Herald Halifax (December 15, 2005; January 12, 26, 2006; Februrary 23, 2006); B. Hayes (February 8, 2006); D. Jeffrey (December 20, 2005); **p. 247**, Table 9.1: Number and Percentage of Cases in Youth Court, 2003–04, by Type of Offence and Pecentage Change from 1991–92", adapted from the Statistics Canada Publications "Juristat", Catalogue 85-002, Vol. 24, No. 2, released March 12, 2004, pages 15,16, and Vol. 25, No. 4, released June 24, 2005, page 14; **p. 258**, R.v G.J.M., 21 April 1992, unreported (Alta. Q.B.): T.P, 33; **p. 265**, Sandra Bell; **p. 265**, Box 9.8: Bell (1993); **p. 266**, Sandra Bell; **p. 271**, Box 9.10: Bell (1993); **p. 288**, Box 10.1: *The Chronicle Herald* (Halifax) (December 15b, 16a, 2005); D. Jeffrey (December 20, 2005). Researched and Written by Nicole Landry; **p. 290**, Box 10.2: A Young Person's Thoughts about Detention, From *Heroes and Villians*, an anthology of poems by young people in detention. Via Magenta, Adelaide, Australia, 1994; **p. 295**, Table 10.1: "Distribution of Custodial Admissions by Offence Type, 1998–1999, 2001–2002", adapted from the Statistics Canada publications, "Juristat", Catalogue 85-002, Vol. 24, No. 3, Released March 30, 2004, and Vol. 20, No. 8, released September 29, 2000; **p. 297**, Table 10.2: "Provincial Incarceration Rates per 10,000 Youth: 1994–95, 1998–99 and 2001–02", adapted from the Statistics Canada Publicaitons, "Youth Custody and Community Services Data Tables", 1998–1999, Catalogue 85-226, released September 29, 2000, pages 48–49, and from "Juristat", Catalogue 85-002, Vol. 24, No. 3, released March 30, 2004, page 13; **p. 301**, Dorey (1996); Trichur (2004); **p. 322**, Box 11.1: Different Views on Therapeutic Intervention, excerpted from Ross R., *Dancing with the Ghost: Exploring Indian Realty.* Copyright © 1992, Octopus Publishing Group, p. 32–34 Reprinted with permission; **p. 323**, Box 11.2: Different Views of Correctional Philosophy, excerpted from Ross R., *Dancing with the Ghost: Exploring Indian Reality.* Copyright © 1992, Octopus Publishing Group, p. 168–169. Reprinted with permission; **p. 324**, Box 11.3 Sharpe, S. (1998) Restorative Justice: A Vision of Healing and Change. Reprinted with permission from The Mediation and Restorative Justice Centre; **p. 326**, Latimer, J., and Casey Foss, L. A One-Day Snapshot of Aboriginal Youth in Custody Accross Canada: Phase II. Ottawa: Department of Justice Canada, 2004; **p. 329**, Criers, Liars and Manipulators: Probation Offficers' Views of Girls, Justice Quarterly Emily Gaarder et al, vol 21 no. 3 (2004), pp. 547–578, Taylor and Francis Ltd. http://www.tamdf.co.uk; **p. 331**, Box 11.6: A judge's Point of View on Girls in Detention, excerpted from McCully, S. Detention Reform from a Judge's Viewpoint, In I.M. Schwartz and W.H. Barton, eds., *Reforming Juvenile Detention: No More Hidden Closets.* Copyright © 1994, Ohio State University Press. Reprinted with permission; **p. 343**, The Chronicle Herald (Halifax) (December 15, 17, 2005, Februrary 7, 21, 22, 2006); B. Hayes (February 9, 2006. Researched and written by Nicole Landry; **p. 351**, Box 12.2: Latimer, J., C. Dowden, K.E. Morton-Bourgon, J. Edgar, and M. Bania. (2003). Treating Youth in Conflict with the Law: A New Meta-Analysis. Department of Justice Canada; **p. 353**, Box 12.3: Youth Reflections on the Consequences of Their Criminal Actions, excerpted from youth letters, Youth Alternative Society files, Halifax/Dartmouth, Nova Scotia. Reprinted with permission of the Youth Alternative Society; **p. 355**, Sandra Bell.